THE
DANGEROUS
CASE OF
DONALD
TRUMP

THE DANGEROUS CASE OF DONALD TRUMP

27 PSYCHIATRISTS AND MENTAL
HEALTH EXPERTS ASSESS A PRESIDENT

EDITED BY
BANDY X. LEE, M.D., M.DIV.

A THOMAS
DUNNE
BOOK

ST. MARTIN'S PRESS
NEW YORK

THOMAS DUNNE BOOKS.
An imprint of St. Martin's Press.

www.thomasdunnebooks.com
www.stmartins.com

Designed by Omar Chapa

Library of Congress Cataloging-in-Publication Data

Names: Lee, Bandy X., 1970– editor.
Title: The dangerous case of Donald Trump : 27 psychiatrists and mental health
experts assess a president / edited by Bandy X. Lee, M.D., M.Div.
Description: First edition. | New York : Thomas Dunne Books,
St. Martin's Press, 2017.
Identifiers: LCCN 2017028497 | ISBN 9781250179456 (hardcover) |
ISBN 9781250179463 (ebook)
Subjects: LCSH: Trump, Donald, 1946—Mental health. | Trump, Donald,
1946—Psychology. | United States—Politics and government—2017—Moral
and ethical aspects. | Despotism—Psychological aspects—Case studies. |
Heads of state—Mental health—Case studies. | Public administration—
Decision making—Psychological aspects—Case studies. | Political
leadership—Psychological aspects—Case studies. | Presidents—
United States—Psychology—Case studies.
Classification: LCC E913.3 .D36 2017 | DDC 973.933092 [B] —dc23
LC record available at https://lccn.loc.gov/2017028497

10 9 8 7 6 5 4 3

COPYRIGHT ACKNOWLEDGMENTS

This work is dedicated to my grandfather, Dr. Geun-Young Lee,
who believed medical practice always involves social responsibility,
and to my mother, Dr. Inmyung Lee, who continued the tradition.

CONTENTS

FOREWORD

Our Witness to Malignant Normality
ROBERT JAY LIFTON, M.D.

Our situation as American psychological professionals can be summed up in just two ideas—we can call them themes or even concepts: first, what I call *malignant normality*, which has to do with the social actuality with which we are presented as normal, all-encompassing, and unalterable; and second, our potential and crucial sense of ourselves as *witnessing professionals*.

Concerning malignant normality, we start with an assumption that all societies, at various levels of consciousness, put forward ways of viewing, thinking, and behaving that are considered desirable or "normal." Yet, these criteria for normality can be much affected by the political and military currents of a particular era. Such requirements may be fairly benign, but they can also be destructive to the point of evil.

I came to the idea of malignant normality in my study of Nazi doctors. Those assigned to Auschwitz, when taking charge of the selections and the overall killing process, were simply doing what was expected of them. True, some were upset, even horrified, at being given this task. Yet, with a certain amount of counseling—one can call it perverse psychotherapy—offered by more experienced hands, a process that included drinking heavily together and giving assurance of help and support, the great majority could overcome their anxiety sufficiently to carry through their murderous assignment. This was a process of *adaptation to evil* that is all too possible to initiate in such a situation. Above all, there was a *normalization of evil* that enhanced this adaptation and served to present participating doctors with the Auschwitz institution as the existing world to which one must make one's adjustments.

There is another form of malignant normality, closer to home and more recent. I have in mind the participation in torture by physicians (including psychiatrists), and by psychologists, and other medical and psychological personnel. This reached its most extreme manifestation when two psychologists were revealed to be among architects of the CIA's torture protocol. More than that, this malignant normality was essentially supported by the American Psychological Association in its defense of the participation of psychologists in the so-called "enhanced interrogation" techniques that spilled over into torture.

I am not equating this American behavior with the Nazi example but, rather, suggesting that malignant normality can take different forms. And nothing does more to sustain malignant normality than its support from a large organization of professionals.

There is still another kind of malignant normality, one brought about by President Trump and his administration. Judith Herman and I, in a letter to the *New York Times* in March 2017, stressed Trump's dangerous individual psychological patterns: his creation of his own reality and his inability to manage the inevitable crises that face an American president. He has also, in various ways, violated our American institutional requirements and threatened the viability of American democracy. Yet, because he is president and operates within the broad contours and interactions of the presidency, there is a tendency to view what he does as simply part of our democratic process—that is, as politically and even ethically normal. In this way, a dangerous president becomes normalized, and malignant normality comes to dominate our governing (or, one could say, our antigoverning) dynamic.

But that does not mean we are helpless. We remain a society with considerable openness, with institutions that can still be life-enhancing and serve truth. Unlike Nazi doctors, articulate psychological professionals could and did expose the behavior of corrupt colleagues and even a corrupt professional society. Investigative journalists and human rights groups also greatly contributed to that exposure.

As psychological professionals, we are capable of parallel action in confronting the malignant normality of Trump and his administration. To do so we need to combine our sense of outrage with a disciplined use of our professional knowledge and experience.

This brings me to my second theme: that of witnessing professionals, particularly activist witnessing professionals. Most professionals, most of the time, operate within the norms (that is, the criteria for normality) of their particular society. Indeed, professionals often go further, and in their practices may deepen the commitment of people they work with to that normality. This can give solace, but it has its perils.

It is not generally known that during the early Cold War period, a special governmental commission, chaired by a psychiatrist and containing physicians and social scientists, was set up to help the American people achieve the desired psychological capacity to support U.S. stockpiling of nuclear weapons, cope with an anticipated nuclear attack, and overcome the fear of nuclear annihilation. The commission had the task, in short, of helping Americans accept malignant nuclear normality. There have also been parallel examples in recent history of professionals who have promoted equally dangerous forms of normality in rejecting climate change.

But professionals don't have to serve these forms of malignant normality. We are capable of using our knowledge and technical skills to expose such normality, to bear witness to its malignance—to become witnessing professionals.

When I did my study of Hiroshima survivors back in 1962, I sought to uncover, in the most accurate and scientific way I could, the psychological and bodily experience of people exposed to the atomic bomb. Yet, I was not just a neutral observer. Over time, I came to understand myself as a witnessing professional, committed to making known what an atomic bomb could do to a city, to tell the world something of what had happened in Hiroshima and to its inhabitants. The Hiroshima story could be condensed to "one plane, one bomb, one city." I came to view this commitment to telling Hiroshima's story as a form of advocacy research. That meant combining a disciplined professional approach with the ethical requirements of committed witness, combining scholarship with activism.

I believe that some such approach is what we require now, in the Trump era. We need to avoid uncritical acceptance of this new version of malignant normality and, instead, bring our knowledge and experience to exposing it for what it is. This requires us to be disciplined about what we believe we know, while refraining from holding forth on what we do not know. It also requires us to recognize the urgency of the situation in which the most powerful man in the world is also the bearer of profound instability and untruth. As psychological professionals, we act with ethical passion in our efforts to reveal what is most dangerous and what, in contrast, might be life-affirming in the face of the malignant normality that surrounds us.

Finally, there is the issue of our ethical behavior. We talk a lot about our professional ethics having to do with our responsibility to patients and to the overall standards of our discipline. This concern with professional ethics matters a great deal.

But I am suggesting something more, a larger concept of professional ethics that we don't often discuss: including who we work for and with, and how our work either affirms or questions the directions of the larger society. And, in our present situation, how we deal with the malignant normality that faces us. This larger ethical model applies to members of other professions who may have their own "duty to warn."

I in no way minimize the significance of professional knowledge and technical skill. But our professions can become overly technicized, and we can be too much like hired guns bringing our firepower to any sponsor of the most egregious view of normality.

We can do better than that. We can take the larger ethical view of the activist witnessing professional. Bandy Lee took that perspective when organizing the Yale conference on professional responsibility,* and the participants affirmed it. This does not make us saviors of our threatened society, but it does help us bring our experience and knowledge to bear on what threatens us and what might renew us.

A line from the American poet Theodore Roethke brings eloquence to what I have been trying to say: "In a dark time, the eye begins to see."

Robert Jay Lifton, M.D., is Lecturer in Psychiatry at Columbia University and Distinguished Professor Emeritus of John Jay College and the Graduate Center of the City University of New York. A leading psychohistorian, he is renowned for his studies of the doctors who aided Nazi war crimes and from his work with survivors of the atomic bombing of Hiroshima. He was an outspoken critic of the American Psychological Association's aiding of government-sanctioned torture and is a vocal opponent of nuclear weapons. His research encompasses the psychological causes and effects of war and political violence and the theory of thought reform.

---

* Please see Appendix for the link to the Yale conference transcript.

PROLOGUE

Professions and Politics

JUDITH LEWIS HERMAN, M.D., AND BANDY X. LEE, M.D., M.DIV.

> Professions can create forms of ethical conversation that are impossible between a lonely individual and a distant government. If members of professions think of themselves as groups . . . with norms and rules that oblige them at all times, then they can gain . . . confidence, and indeed a certain kind of power.
>
> Timothy Snyder, *On Tyranny:*
> *Twenty Lessons from the Twentieth Century* (2017)

Soon after the presidential election of 2016, alarmed by the apparent mental instability of the president-elect, we both separately circulated letters among some of our professional colleagues, expressing our concern. Most of them declined to sign. A number of people admitted they were afraid of some undefined form of governmental retaliation, so quickly had a climate of fear taken hold. They asked us if we were not wary of being "targeted," and advised us to seek legal counsel. This was a lesson to us in how a climate of fear can induce people to censor themselves.

Others who declined to sign our letters of concern cited matters of principle. Psychiatry, we were warned, should stay out of politics; otherwise, the profession could end up being ethically compromised. The example most frequently cited was that of psychiatrists in the Soviet Union who collaborated with the secret police to diagnose dissidents as mentally ill and confine them to prisons that fronted as hospitals (Medvedev and Medvedev 1971).

This was a serious consideration. Indeed, we need not look beyond our own borders for examples of ethics violations committed by professionals who became entangled in politics. We have recently witnessed the disgrace of an entire professional organization, the American Psychological Association, some of whose leadership, in cooperation with officials from the U.S. military, the CIA, and the Bush White House, rewrote its ethical guidelines to give legal cover to a secret government program of coercive interrogation and to excuse military psychologists who designed and implemented methods of torture (Hoffman et al. 2015; Risen 2014).*

Among the many lessons that might be learned from this notorious example, one in particular stayed with us. It seemed clear that the government officials responsible for abusive treatment of prisoners went to some lengths to find medical and mental health professionals who would publicly condone their practices. We reasoned that if professional endorsement serves as important cover for human rights abuses, then professional condemnation must also carry weight.

In 2005 the Pentagon organized a trip to the Guantánamo Bay detention camp for a group of prominent ethicists, psychiatrists, and psychologists. Participants toured the facility and met with high-

---

* It should be noted that a majority of the American Psychological Association membership did not approve this revision of the Association's ethics code and tried to rescind it. They did not succeed, however, until the matter became a public scandal.

ranking military officers, including the commanding general. They were not allowed to meet or speak with any of the detainees.

Dr. Steven Sharfstein, then the president of the American Psychiatric Association, was one of the invited guests on this trip. Apparently, what he saw and heard failed to convince him that the treatment of detainees fell within the bounds of ethical conduct. "Our position is very direct," he stated on return. "Psychiatrists should not participate on these [interrogation] teams because it is inappropriate" (Lewis 2005). Under Dr. Sharfstein's leadership, the American Psychiatric Association took a strong stand against any form of participation in torture and in the "interrogation of persons held in custody by military or civilian investigative or law enforcement authorities, whether in the United States or elsewhere" (American Psychiatric Association 2006).

Contrast this principled stand with the sorry tale of the American Psychological Association. Its involvement in the torture scandal illustrates how important it is for leaders in the professions to stand firm against ethical violations, and to resist succumbing to the argument that exceptional political circumstances, such as "the war on terror," demand exceptions to basic ethical codes. When there is pressure from power is exactly when one must abide by the norms and rules of our ethics.*

Norms and Rules in the Political Sphere

Norms and rules guide professional conduct, set standards, and point to the essential principles of practice. For these reasons, physicians

---

* We hold no brief for the general moral superiority of the American Psychiatric Association, which has had its own ignominious history in the ways that its diagnostic code for many years reinforced institutional homophobia and misogyny. In the particular case that we are discussing, however, the APA was fortunate enough to have good leadership that resulted in a position of moral clarity.

have the *Declaration of Geneva* (World Medical Association 2006) and the American Medical Association *Principles of Medical Ethics* (2001), which guide the American Psychiatric Association's code for psychiatry (American Psychiatric Association 2013). The former confirms the physician's dedication to the humanitarian goals of medicine, while the latter defines honorable behavior for the physician. Paramount in both is the health, safety, and survival of the patient.

Psychiatrists' codes of ethics derive directly from these principles. In ordinary practice, the patient's right to confidentiality is the bedrock of mental health care dating back to the ethical standards of the Hippocratic Oath. However, even this sacrosanct rule is not absolute. No doubt, the physician's responsibility is first and foremost to the patient, but it extends "as well as to society" (American Psychiatric Association 2013, p. 2). It is part of professional expectation that the psychiatrist assess the possibility that the patient may harm himself or others. When the patient poses a danger, psychiatrists are not merely allowed but mandated to report, to incapacitate, and to take steps to protect.

If we are mindful of the dangers of politicizing the professions, then certainly we must heed the so-called "Goldwater rule," or Section 7.3 of the APA code of ethics (American Psychiatric Association 2013, p. 6), which states: "it is unethical for a psychiatrist to offer a professional opinion [on a public figure] unless he or she has conducted an examination and has been granted proper authorization for such a statement." This is not divergent from ordinary norms of practice: the clinical approaches that we use to evaluate patients require a full examination. Formulating a credible diagnosis will always be limited when applied to public figures observed outside this intimate frame; in fact, we would go so far as to assert that it is impossible.

The Goldwater rule highlights the boundaries of practice, helps to preserve professional integrity, and protects public figures from defamation. It safeguards the public's perception of the field of psychiatry as credible and trustworthy. It is reasonable to follow it. But even this respectable rule must be balanced against the other rules and principles of professional practice. A careful ethical evaluation might ask: Do our ordinary norms of practice stop at the office of president? If so, why? If the ethics of our practice stipulate that the health of our patient and the safety of the public be paramount, then we should not leave our norms at the door when entering the political sphere. Otherwise, a rule originally conceived to protect our profession from scandal might itself become a source of scandal. For this very reason, the "reaffirmation" of the Goldwater rule in a separate statement by the American Psychiatric Association (2017) barely two months into the new administration seems questionable to us. The American Psychiatric Association is not immune to the kind of politically pressured acquiescence we have seen with its psychological counterpart.

A psychiatrist who disregards the basic procedures of diagnosis and treatment and acts without discretion deserves reprimand. However, the public trust is also violated if the profession fails in its duty to alert the public when a person who holds the power of life and death over us all shows signs of clear, dangerous mental impairment. We should pause if professionals are asked to remain silent when they have seen enough evidence to sound an alarm in every other situation. When it comes to dangerousness, should not the president of a democracy, as First Citizen, be subject to the same standards of practice as the rest of the citizenry?

Assessing dangerousness is different from making a diagnosis: it is dependent on the situation, not the person. Signs of likely dangerousness due to mental disorder can become apparent without a full diagnostic interview and can be detected from a distance, and one is expected to err, if at all, on the side of safety when the risk of inaction is too great. States vary in their instructions. New York, for example, requires that two qualifying professionals agree in order to detain a person who may be in danger of hurting himself or others.

Florida and the District of Columbia require only one professional's opinion. Also, only one person need be in danger of harm by the individual, and the threshold is even lower if the individual has access to weapons (not to mention nuclear weapons).

The physician, to whom life-and-death situations are entrusted, is expected to know when it is appropriate to act, and to act responsibly when warranted. It is because of the weight of this responsibility that, rightfully, the physician should refrain from commenting on a public figure except in the rarest instance. Only in an emergency should a physician breach the trust of confidentiality and intervene without consent, and only in an emergency should a physician breach the Goldwater rule. We believe that such an emergency now exists.

Test for Proper Responsibility

When we circulated our letters of concern, we asked our fellow mental health professionals to get involved in politics not only as citizens (a right most of us still enjoy) but also, specifically, as professionals and as guardians of the special knowledge with which they have been entrusted. Why do we think this was permissible? It is all too easy to claim, as we did, that an emergency situation requires a departure from our usual practices in the private sphere. How can one judge whether political involvement is in fact justified?

We would argue that the key question is whether mental health professionals are engaging in political *collusion* with state abuses of power or acting in *resistance* to them. If we are asked to cooperate with state programs that violate human rights, then any involvement, regardless of the purported justification, can only corrupt, and the only appropriate ethical stance is to refuse participation of any sort. If, on the other hand, we perceive that state power is being abused by an executive who seems to be mentally unstable, then we may certainly speak out, not only as citizens but also, we would argue, as professionals who are privy to special information and have a responsibility to educate the public. For whatever our wisdom and expertise may be worth, surely we are obligated to share it.

It doesn't take a psychiatrist to notice that our president is mentally compromised. Members of the press have come up with their own diagnostic nomenclature, calling the president a "mad king" (Dowd 2017), a "nut job" (Collins 2017), and "emotionally unhinged" (Rubin 2017). Conservative columnist George Will (2017) writes that the president has a "disorderly mind." By speaking out as mental health professionals, we lend support and dignity to our fellow citizens who are justifiably alarmed by the president's furious tirades, conspiracy fantasies, aversion to facts, and attraction to violence. We can offer a hand in helping the public understand behaviors that are unusual and alarming but that can all too easily be rationalized and normalized.

An important and relevant question that the public has been asking is this: Is the man simply crazy, or is he crazy like a fox? Is he mentally compromised or simply vile? When he lies, does he know he is lying, or does he believe his own lies? When he makes wild accusations, is he truly paranoid, or is he consciously and cunningly trying to deflect attention from his misdeeds?

We believe that we can help answer these questions by emphasizing that the two propositions are not mutually exclusive. A man can be both evil and mentally compromised—which is a more frightening proposition. Power not only corrupts but also magnifies existing psychopathologies, even as it creates new ones. Fostered by the flattery of underlings and the chants of crowds, a political leader's grandiosity may morph into grotesque delusions of grandeur. Sociopathic traits may be amplified as the leader discovers that he can violate the norms of civil society and even commit crimes with impunity. And the leader who rules through fear, lies, and betrayal may become increasingly isolated and paranoid, as the loyalty of even his closest confidants must forever be suspect.

Some would argue that by paying attention to the president's mental state, we are colluding with him in deflecting attention from that by which he should ultimately be judged: his actions (Frances 2017). Certainly, mental disturbance is not an excuse for tyrannical behavior; nevertheless, it cannot be ignored. In a court of law, even the strongest insanity defense case cannot show that a person is insane all the time. We submit that by paying attention to the president's mental state *as well as* his actions, we are better informed to assess his dangerousness. Delusional levels of grandiosity, impulsivity, and the compulsions of mental impairment, when combined with an authoritarian cult of personality and contempt for the rule of law, are a toxic mix.

There are those who still hold out hope that this president can be prevailed upon to listen to reason and curb his erratic behavior. Our professional experience would suggest otherwise; witness the numerous submissions we have received for this volume while organizing a Yale conference in April 2017 entitled "Does Professional Responsibility Include a Duty to Warn?"* Collectively with our coauthors, we warn that anyone as mentally unstable as Mr. Trump simply should not be entrusted with the life-and-death powers of the presidency.

> *Judith Lewis Herman, M.D., is Professor of Psychiatry at Harvard Medical School. She is a renowned expert in the traumas of interpersonal violence and author of the now-classic* Trauma and Recovery. *She is a cofounder of the Victims of Violence Program in the Department of Psychiatry at Cambridge Health Alliance, a Distinguished Life Fellow of the American Psychiatric Association, and the recipient of numerous awards, including the Lifetime Achievement Award from the International Society for Traumatic Stress Studies.*

---

* Please see Appendix for the link to the Yale conference transcript.

Bandy X. Lee, M.D., M.Div., is Assistant Clinical Professor in Law and Psychiatry at Yale School of Medicine. She teaches at Yale Law School, cofounded Yale's Violence and Health Study Group, and leads a Violence Prevention Alliance collaborators project for the World Health Organization. She is the author of more than one hundred peer-reviewed articles, editor of eleven academic books, and author of the textbook Violence.

Acknowledgments

We thank Nanette Gartrell, Dee Mosbacher, Gloria Steinem, Robin Morgan, Jaine Darwin, Frank Putnam, and Grace Lee, for their helpful editorial comments and assistance in the preparation of this Prologue.

References

American Medical Association. 2001. *AMA Code of Medical Ethics: AMA Principles of Medical Ethics.* www.ama-assn.org/sites/default/files /media-browser/principles-of-medical-ethics.pdf.

American Psychiatric Association. 2006. *Position Statement on Psychiatric Participation in Interrogation of Detainees.* www.psychiatry.org/File%20 Library/About-APA/Organization-Documents-Policies/Policies /Position-2014-Interrogation-Detainees-Psychiatric-Participation.pdf.

———. 2013. *Principles of Medical Ethics with Annotations Especially Applicable to Psychiatry.* www.psychiatry.org/psychiatrists/practice/ethics.

———. 2017. "APA Remains Committed to Supporting Goldwater Rule." www.psychiatry.org/news-room/apa-blogs/apa-blog/2017/03/apa -remains-committed-to-supporting-goldwater-rule.

Collins, Gail. 2017. "Trump Stays Buggy." *New York Times*, March 17. www .nytimes.com/2017/03/17/opinion/trump-stays-buggy.html.

Dowd, Maureen. 2017. "Mad Trump, Happy W." *New York Times*, March 4. www.nytimes.com/2017/03/04/opinion/sunday/mad-trump-happy-w .html?_r=0.

Frances, Allen. 2017. "An Eminent Psychiatrist Demurs on Trump's Mental State." *New York Times*, February 14. www.nytimes.com/2017/02/14

/opinion/an-eminent-psychiatrist-demurs-on-trumps-mental-state
.html.

Hoffman, David H., Danielle J. Carter, Cara R. Viglucci Lopez, Heather L.
Benzmiller, Ava X. Guo, S. Yasir Latifi, and Daniel C. Craig. 2015.
*Report to the Special Committee of the Board of Directors of the American
Psychological Association: Independent Review Relating to APA Ethics
Guidelines, National Security Interrogations, and Torture* (revised). Chi-
cago: Sidley Austin LLP.

Lewis, Neil A. 2005. "Guantánamo Tour Focuses on Medical Ethics." *New
York Times*, Nov. 13. www.nytimes.com/2005/11/13/us/guantanamo
-tour-focuses-on-medical-ethics.html.

Medvedev, Zhores, and Roy Medvedev. 1971. *A Question of Madness:
Repression by Psychiatry in the Soviet Union.* New York: Vintage.

Risen, James. 2014. *Pay Any Price: Greed, Power, and Endless War.* New York:
Houghton Mifflin.

Rubin, Jennifer. 2017. "Will Comey's Request Push Trump over the Edge?"
Washington Post, March 6. www.washingtonpost.com/blogs/right-turn
/wp/2017/03/06/will-comeys-request-push-trump-over-the-edge
/?utm_term=.65aa62ca0657.

Snyder, Timothy. 2017. *On Tyranny: Twenty Lessons from the Twentieth
Century.* New York: Crown/Archetype.

Will, George F. 2017. "Trump Has a Dangerous Disability." *Washington Post*,
May 3. www.washingtonpost.com/opinions/trump-has-a-dangerous
-disability/2017/05/03/56ca6118-2f6b-11e7-9534-00e4656c22aa_story
.html?utm_term=.90f21a74dc93.

World Medical Association. 2006. *Declaration of Geneva.* www.wma.net
/policies-post/wma-declaration-of-geneva/.

INTRODUCTION

Our Duty to Warn

BANDY X. LEE, M.D., M.DIV.

Possibly the oddest experience in my career as a psychiatrist has been to find that the only people not allowed to speak about an issue are those who know the most about it. Hence, truth is suppressed. Yet, what if that truth, furthermore, harbored dangers of such magnitude that it could be the key to future human survival? How can I, as a medical and mental health professional, remain a bystander in the face of one of the greatest emergencies of our time, when I have been called to step in everywhere else? How can we, as trained professionals in this very area, be content to keep silent, against every other principle we practice by, because of a decree handed down from above?

I am not speaking of the long-standing "Goldwater rule," which is discussed in many places throughout this book and is a norm of ordinary practice I happen to agree with. I am rather speaking of its radical expansion, beyond the status we confer to any other rule, barely two months into the very presidency that has made it controversial. This occurred on March 16, 2017, when our professional organization essentially placed a gag order on all psychiatrists (American Psychiatric Association 2017), and by extension all mental health professionals. I am also speaking of its defect, whereby it does not have a countervailing rule, as does the rest of professional ethics, that directs what to do when the risk of harm from remaining silent outweighs the damage that could result from speaking about a public figure—which, in this case, could even be the greatest possible harm. Authors in this volume have been asked to respect the Goldwater rule and not to breach it unnecessarily, but I in turn respect their choices wherever their conscience has prompted them to take the professionally and socially radical step to help protect the public. Therefore, it would be accurate to state that, while we respect the rule, we deem it subordinate to the single most important principle that guides our professional conduct: that we hold our responsibility to human life and well-being as paramount.

My reasons for compiling this compendium are the same as my reasons for organizing the Yale conference by the title, "Does Professional Responsibility Include a Duty to Warn?": the issue merits discussion, not silence, and the public deserves education, not further darkness. Over the course of preparing the conference, the number of prominent voices in the field coming forth to speak out on the topic astonished me. Soon after the 2016 presidential election, Dr. Herman (coauthor of the Prologue), an old colleague and friend, had written a letter urging President Obama to require that Mr. Trump undergo a neuropsychiatric evaluation before assuming the office of the presidency. Her cosignatories, Drs. Gartrell and Mosbacher (authors of the essay "He's Got the World in His Hands and His Finger on the Trigger"), helped the letter's publication in *The Huffington Post* (Greene, 2016). I also reached out to Dr. Lifton (author of the Foreword), whose "Mass Violence" meetings at Harvard first acquainted me with Dr. Herman years ago; together, they had sent a letter to the *New York Times* (Herman and Lifton 2017). His ready consent to speak at my conference sparked all that was to follow.

I encountered others along the way: Dr. Dodes (author of "Sociopathy"), who published a letter in the *New York Times* with thirty-five signatures (Dodes and Schachter 2017); Ms. Jhueck (author of "A Clinical Case for the Dangerousness of Donald J. Trump"), who co-wrote and posted a letter to the head of New York City's Department of Health and Mental Hygiene with seventy signatures; Dr. Fisher (author of "The Loneliness of Fateful Decisions"), who also expressed concerns in a letter to the *New York Times* (Fisher 2017); and Dr. Gartner (author of "Donald Trump Is: [A] Bad, [B] Mad, [C] All of the Above"), the initiator of an online petition, now with fifty-five thousand signatures, who cofounded the national coalition, "Duty to Warn," of (as of this writing) seventeen hundred mental health professionals.

The Yale Conference

On April 20, 2017, Dr. Charles Dike of my division at Yale started the town hall–style meeting by reaffirming the relevance and reasons for the Goldwater rule. As assistant professor in law and psychiatry, former chair of the Ethics Committee of the American Academy of Psychiatry and the Law, chair of the Connecticut Psychiatric Society Ethics Committee, member of the Ethics Committee of the American Psychiatric Association, and Distinguished Fellow of the American Psychiatric Association, he was more than qualified to do so. It was important that we start with a firm ethical foundation: whatever our conclusion, it could not hold if we were not scrupulous about our ethical grounding. I invited as additional panelists Drs. Lifton, Herman, and Gilligan (the last the author of "The Issue Is Dangerousness, Not Mental Illness"), with the purpose of bringing together the finest minds of psychiatry I could to address the quandary. They are all colleagues I have known for at least fifteen years and highly esteem not only for their eminence in the field but also for their ethics. They were beacons during other dark times. They abided by the Goldwater rule in that they kept the discussion at the

level of dangerousness, without attempting to diagnose.* The transcript of the meeting can be found in an online appendix, the link to
which is at the end of this book.

The conference was initially meant to be a collaboration between
Yale School of Medicine, Yale School of Public Health, and Yale
School of Nursing, but when the other schools fell away as the date
approached, I released the School of Medicine for what I correctly
perceived would be "inevitable politicization." In case something
went wrong, I did not wish to imperil my alma mater and home
institution.

Our nation is now living, in extremes, a paradigm that splits
along partisan lines, and the quick conclusion will be that the speak-
ers or contributors of this volume "must be Democrats" if they are
casting a negative light on a Republican president.

However, there are other paradigms. For the mental health professional, the paradigm we practice by is one of health versus disease. We appeal to science, research, observed phenomena, and
clinical skill developed over years of practice in order to promote life
and to prevent death. These goals cannot be contained within the
purposes of a political party or the campaigns of a candidate. Rather,
we are constantly trained to bring medical neutrality—or, if we cannot, to recuse ourselves of the therapeutic situation. It is a glimpse of
this perspective that we hope to bring to the reader.

Our meeting gained national and international attention (Milligan 2017; Bulman 2017). While only two dozen physically attended

---

* Assessing dangerousness requires a different standard from diagnosing so as
to formulate a course of treatment. Dangerousness is about the situation, not
the individual; it is more about the effects and the degree of impairment than
on the specific cause of illness and it does not require a full examination but
takes into account whatever information is available. Also, it requires that the
qualified professional err on the side of safety, and it may entail breaking other,
ordinarily binding rules to favor urgent action.

the conference in an atmosphere of fear, about a hundred tuned in online, and hundreds more got in touch with me for recordings or in a show of support. It felt as if we had tapped into a groundswell of a movement among mental health professionals, and also an army of people who wanted to speak about the issue (DeVega 2017). What was intended as a publication of the proceedings led to this volume (initially so large that we had to reduce it by a third), and five top-tier publishers in the country vied for it.

Authors had to submit their manuscripts within three weeks of the meeting. It was a harrowing time, as the nation's mood changed from relief as Mr. Trump seemed to settle into his office after the first one hundred days, to a new onslaught of scandals, starting with his firing of FBI director James Comey on May 9, 2017.

Many of the contributors here do not need an introduction, and I am humbled to have the opportunity to present such an assembly of brilliant and principled professionals.

A Compendium of Expertise

This volume consists of three parts, the first being devoted to describing Mr. Trump, with an understanding that no definitive diagnoses will be possible. In "Unbridled and Extreme Present Hedonism," Zimbardo and Sword discuss how the Leader of the Free World has proven himself unfit for duty by his extreme ties to the present moment, without much thought for the consequences of his actions or for the future. In "Pathological Narcissism and Politics," Malkin explains that narcissism happens on a scale, and that pathological levels in a leader can spiral into psychosis and imperil the safety of his country through paranoia, impaired judgment, volatile decision making, and behavior called gaslighting. In "I Wrote *The Art of the Deal* with Trump," Schwartz reveals how what he observed during the year he spent with Trump to write that book could have predicted his presidency of "black hole-level" low self-worth, fact-free self-justification, and a compulsion to go to war with the world.

In "Trump's Trust Deficit Is the Core Problem," Sheehy high-lights the notion that beneath the grandiose behavior of every nar-cissist lies the pit of fragile self-esteem; more than anything, Trump lacks trust in himself, which may lead him to take drastic actions to prove himself to himself and to the world. In "Sociopathy," Dodes shows that someone who cons others, lies, cheats, and manipulates to get what he wants, and who doesn't care whom he hurts, may be not just repetitively immoral but also severely impaired, as socio-paths lack a central human characteristic, empathy. In "Donald Trump Is: (A) Bad, (B), Mad, (C) All of the Above," Gartner empha-sizes the complexity of Trump's presentation, in that he shows signs of being "bad" as well as "mad," but also with a hypomanic temper-ament that generates whirlwinds of activity and a constant need for stimulation.

In "Why 'Crazy Like a Fox' versus 'Crazy Like a Crazy' *Really* Matters," Tansey shows that Trump's nearly outrageous lies may be explained by delusional disorder, about which Tansey invites the reader to make the call; even more frightening are Trump's attraction to brutal tyrants and also the prospect of nuclear war. In "Cognitive Impairment, Dementia, and POTUS," Reiss writes that a current vulnerability in our political system is that it sets no intellectual or cognitive standards for being president, despite the job's inherently requiring cognitive clarity; this lack of clarity can be even more serious if combined with other psychiatric disorders. In "Donald J. Trump, Alleged Incapacitated Person," Herb explains how, as a guardianship attorney (in contrast to a mental health professional), he is required to come to a preliminary conclusion about mental incapacity *before* filing a petition, which he does in his essay, while reflecting on the Electoral College and the Twenty-Fifth Amend-ment to the U.S. Constitution.

The second part of the book addresses the dilemmas that mental health professionals face in observing what they do and speaking out when they feel they must. In "Should Psychiatrists Refrain from

Commenting on Trump's Psychology?" Glass argues against a technicality that would yield a simple yes-or-no answer to the Goldwater rule; instead, he advocates for a conscientious voicing of hazardous patterns, noting that the presence of mental illness is not as relevant as that of reliable functionality. In "On Seeing What You See and Saying What You Know," Friedman notes that technological advances that allow assessment and treatment from a distance, especially in underserved areas, have changed the clinician's comfort level with remote evaluations, even when detecting a totalitarian mind-set or a multidimensional threat to the world. In "The Issue Is Dangerousness, Not Mental Illness," Gilligan discusses the ethics of *not* diagnosing a public figure versus the duty to warn potential victims of danger; when invoking the latter, he emphasizes, what matters is not whether a person is mentally ill but whether he is dangerous, which is possible to assess from a distance.

In "A Clinical Case for the Dangerousness of Donald J. Trump," Jhueck notes that the United States legally confers mental health professionals and physicians considerable power to detain people against their will if they pose a danger due to likely mental illness—and Trump more than meets the requisite criteria. In "Health, Risk, and the Duty to Protect the Community," Covitz offers an ancient reference and two fables to illustrate just how unusual the mental health profession's response is to a dangerous president, as we do not to speak up in ways that would be unthinkable for our role with other members of society. In "New Opportunities for Therapy in the Age of Trump," Doherty claims that the Trump era has ruptured the boundary between the personal and the public, and while clients and therapists are equally distressed, integrating our roles as therapists and citizens might help us better help clients.

The book's third part speaks to the societal effects Mr. Trump has had, represents, and could cause in the future. In "Trauma, Time, Truth, and Trump," Teng points out the irony of seeing, as a trauma therapist, all the signs of traumatization and retraumatization from a peaceful election; she traces the sources of the president's sudden military actions, his generation of crises, his shaken notions of truth and facts, and his role in reminding patients of an aggressive abuser. In "Trump Anxiety Disorder," Panning describes a unique post-election anxiety syndrome that has emerged as a result of the Trump presidency and the task that many therapists face with helping clients manage the stress of trying to "normalize" behavior that they do not feel is normal for a president. In her essay "In Relationship with an Abusive President," West illustrates the dynamics of "other blaming" in individuals who have feelings of low self-worth and hence poor shame tolerance, which lead to vindictive anger, lack of accountability, dishonesty, lack of empathy, and attention-seeking, of which Trump is an extreme example.

In "Trump's Daddy Issues," Wruble draws on his own personal experiences, especially his relationship with his strong and successful father, to demonstrate what a therapist does routinely: uses self-knowledge as an instrument for evaluating and "knowing" the *other*, even in this case, where the other is the president and his followers. In "Birtherism and the Deployment of the Trumpian Mind-Set," Kessler portrays the broader background from which "birtherism" began and how, by entering into the political fray by championing this fringe sentiment, Trump amplifies and exacerbates a national "symptom" of bigotry and division in ways that are dangerous to the nation's core principles. In "Trump and the American Collective Psyche," Singer draws a connection between Trump's personal narcissism and the American group psyche, not through a political analysis but through group psychology—the joining of group self-identity with violent, hateful defenses is as much about us as about Trump.

In "Who Goes Trump?" Mika explains how tyrannies are "toxic triangles," as political scientists call them, necessitating that the tyrant, his supporters, and the society at large bind around narcissism; while the three factors animate for a while, the characteristic oppression, dehumanization, and violence inevitably bring on downfall. In "The Loneliness of Fateful Decisions," Fisher recounts the Cuban Missile Crisis and notes how, even though President Kennedy surrounded himself with the "best and the brightest," they disagreed greatly, leaving him alone to make the decisions—which illustrates how the future of our country and the world hang on a president's mental clarity. In "He's Got the World in His Hands and His Finger on the Trigger," Gartrell and Mosbacher note how, while military personnel must undergo rigorous evaluations to assess their mental and medical fitness for duty, there is no such requirement for their commander in chief; they propose a nonpartisan panel of neuropsychiatrists for annual screening.

A Disclaimer

In spite of its title, I would like to emphasize that the main point of this book is not about Mr. Trump. It is about the larger context that has given rise to his presidency, and the greater population that he affects by virtue of his position. The ascendancy of an individual with such impairments speaks to our general state of health and well-being as a nation, and to how we can respond: we can either improve it or further impair it. Mental disorder does not distinguish between political parties, and as professionals devoted to promoting mental health, including public mental health, our duty should be clear: to steer patients and the public on a path toward health so that genuine discussions of political choice, unimpeded by emotional compulsion or defense, can occur. Embracing our "duty to warn," as our professional training and ethics lead us to do at times of danger, therefore involves not only sounding an alarm but continually educating and engaging in dialogue our fellow human beings, as this compilation aspires to do.

I am grateful to all the authors who have generously contributed their insights without an expectation of personal reward. I especially thank Drs. Judith Herman and Grace Lee for their very helpful advice in editing this manuscript and for their help in organizing the Yale conference; Drs. Nanette Gartrell and Dee Mosbacher for their additional assistance; and Drs. Lance Dodes and John Gartner for their help in conceiving this publication in the first place. I would also like to express my appreciation for Dr. Robert Rohrbaugh, who as deputy chair for education made the conference possible; Dr. Howard Zonana, who as director of the Law and Psychiatry Division, and as a role model, supported me with legal advice along with Dr. Madelon Baranoski; and Dr. John Krystal, who, as department chair, bore the brunt of the controversies surrounding the conference. I thank Mr. Scott Mendel, the most intellectually astute literary agent one could ask for; and Mr. Stephen Power, the most enthusiastic editor one could have. I am grateful to Atty. Glen Feinberg, specialist of psychiatric law, and Atty. Max Stern, civil rights counsel, who have graciously donated hours of their time to what they deemed "a worthy cause"; as well as Atty. Ronald London, First-Amendment lawyer, and Atty. Henry Kaufman, the publisher's counsel. Finally, I would like to share my gratitude for my grandfather and physician, Dr. Geun-Young Lee, who is the inspiration for all my work in the world.

Bandy X. Lee, M.D., M.Div., is Assistant Clinical Professor in Law and Psychiatry at Yale School of Medicine. She earned her degrees at Yale, interned at Bellevue, was Chief Resident at Mass General, and was a Research Fellow at Harvard Medical School. She was also a Fellow of the National Institute of Mental Health. She worked in several maximum-security prisons, cofounded Yale's Violence and Health Study Group, and leads a violence prevention collaborators group for the World Health Organization. She's written more than one hundred peer-reviewed articles and chapters, edited eleven academic books, and is author of the textbook Violence.

References

American Psychiatric Association. 2017. "APA Remains Committed to Supporting Goldwater Rule." www.psychiatry.org/news-room/apa -blogs/apa-blog/2017/03/apa-remains-committed-to-supporting -goldwater-rule.

Bulman, May. 2017. "Donald Trump Has 'Dangerous Mental Illness,' Say Psychiatry Experts at Yale Conference." *Independent*, April 21. www .independent.co.uk/news/world/americas/donald-trump-dangerous -mental-illness-yale-psychiatrist-conference-us-president-unfit-james -gartner-a7694316.html.

DeVega, Chauncey. 2017. "Psychiatrist Bandy Lee: 'We Have an Obligation to Speak About Donald Trump's Mental Health Issues . . . Our Survival as a Species May Be at Stake.' " *Salon*, May 25. www.salon.com /2017/05/25/psychiatrist-bandy-lee-we-have-an-obligation-to-speak -about-donald-trumps-mental-health-issues-our-survival-as-a-species -may-be-at-stake/.

Dodes, Lance, and Joseph Schachter. 2017. "Mental Health Professionals Warn About Trump." *New York Times*, February 13. www.nytimes.com /2017/02/13/opinion/mental-health-professionals-warn-about-trump .html?mcubz=1.

Fisher, Edwin B. 2017. "Trump's Tweets Attacking Obama." *New York Times*, March 6. www.nytimes.com/2017/03/06/opinion/trumps-tweets -attacking-obama.html?mcubz=1.

Greene, Richard. 2016. "Is Donald Trump Mentally Ill? 3 Professors of Psychiatry Ask President Obama to Conduct 'A Full Medical and Neuropsychiatric Evaluation.' " *Huffington Post*, December 17. www .huffingtonpost.com/richard-greene/is-donald-trump-mentally_b _13693174.html.

Herman, Judith L., and Robert Jay Lifton. 2017. " 'Protect Us from This Dangerous President,' 2 Psychiatrists Say." *New York Times*, March 8. www.nytimes.com/2017/03/08/opinion/protect-us-from-this -dangerous-president-2-psychiatrists-say.html?mcubz=1&_r=0.

Milligan, Susan. 2017. "An Ethical Dilemma: Donald Trump's Presidency
    Has Some in the Mental Health Community Re-Evaluating Their
    Role." *U.S. News and World Report*, April 21. www.usnews.com/news
    /the-report/articles/2017-04-21/mental-health-professionals-debate
    -ethics-in-the-age-of-trump.

PART 1

THE TRUMP PHENOMENON

UNBRIDLED AND EXTREME PRESENT HEDONISM

How the Leader of the Free World Has Proven Time and Again He Is Unfit for Duty

PHILIP ZIMBARDO AND ROSEMARY SWORD

In the summer of 2015, we commenced what would become an ongoing discussion about Donald Trump. He had just thrown his hat in the ring as a Republican presidential candidate, and our initial conversation was brief: he was in it for the publicity. For us, as for many Americans, Donald Trump had been in the periphery of our consciousness for years, first as a well-publicized New York City businessman and later as a mediocre television personality. And like most, we didn't take him seriously. Why would we have? He had no political experience, and he failed to show any real interest in philanthropy, much less in helping the American people or non-Trump businesses. His products were made outside the United States, and multiple lawsuits indicated he didn't pay those small businesses that supplied him with goods and services. He had also created Trump University, for people who wanted to get certified in business administration, at a fee of $43,000 for one year. It was a scam—the same lessons were available online for free for anyone, and the mentors who were supposed to give students personal guidance were rarely available. Students who took Trump University to court won their lawsuits, and Trump U got dumped. Simply put, Donald Trump was a businessman interested primarily in personal gain, sometimes using unscrupulous methods.

We also knew that, for decades, Trump had flip-flopped, switching political parties—first a Democrat, then a member of the Reform Party, then a Republican, then a Democrat, and finally a Republican again. Surely, it seemed, "The Donald" was in the running merely to gain media coverage, to place himself in a better position to make even more big deals and to up-level his product line: Donald J. Trump.

Then, as the months progressed, we became increasingly concerned that, given his "straightforward" or "outsider" presentation and his charisma, he would appeal to people who were unaware of the dangers of narcissism in extremis, or of the offensive behaviors that can accompany it. While we are not trying to diagnose here (which would be close to impossible in any case), we would like to call the reader's attention to associated behaviors that include but are not limited to condescension, gross exaggeration (lying), bullying, jealousy, fragile self-esteem, lack of compassion, and viewing the world through an "us-vs.-them" lens. Having observed the schoolyard bully tactics Trump employed during the Republican debates, and his absurdly boastful presentation during interviews, we felt it was important to raise awareness about this set of behaviors. So, in January 2016, we published an online *Psychology Today* column about bullies and the hostile social environments they create in schools and businesses (Sword and Zimbardo 2016a).

As Trump's campaign, and his narcissism, gained momentum, so did our efforts to make people aware of the potential dangers he posed for our democracy. In March 2016 we published a column about the narcissistic personality (Sword and Zimbardo 2016b). In it, we shared clinically documented narcissistic behaviors, hoping it would be easy for readers to come to their own conclusions that Trump fit every example. We did not mention his numerous romantic dalliances, or the growing number of sexual harassment lawsuits he faced, or his three marriages, in which he traded up for younger, more beautiful women. Each of these, on its own, is not exceptional, but it doesn't take a mental health professional to determine that these behaviors, coupled with his ever-shifting political party affiliations (changes that could be viewed as having been made to bolster his image and ego), indicated that this person's main focus was self-interest, and were incongruent with one important character trait the American people have come to appreciate in their president—at least up until November 2016: stability.

Furthermore, through our observations, it was glaringly apparent, based on Zimbardo's time perspective theory (Zimbardo and Boyd 2009), later developed into time perspective therapy by Sword and Sword (Zimbardo, Sword, and Sword 2012), that Trump embodied a specific personality type: an *unbridled, or extreme, present hedonist*. As the words suggest, present hedonists live in the present moment, without much thought of any consequences of their actions or of the future. An extreme present hedonist will say whatever it takes to pump up his ego and to assuage his inherent low self-esteem, without any thought for past reality or for the potentially devastating future outcomes from off-the-cuff remarks or even major decisions. Trump's behavior indicates that his time perspectives are totally *unbalanced*. It's not necessary for him to take the Zimbardo Time Perspective Inventory (either the long or short forms) in order for us to come to this conclusion. Our assertion that Trump qualifies as among the most extreme present hedonists we have ever witnessed comes from the plethora of written and recorded material on him, including all his interviews, hundreds of hours of video, and his own tweets on his every personal feeling.

What follows is meant to help readers understand how we've come to the conclusion that Donald Trump displays the most threatening time perspective profile, that of an extreme present hedonist, and is therefore "unfit for duty."

Time Perspective Theory and Time Perspective Therapy (TPT)

We are all familiar with the three main time zones: the past, the present, and the future. In TPT, these time zones are divided into subsets: *past positive* and *past negative, present hedonism* and *present fatalism,* and *future positive* and *future negative.* When one of these time perspectives is weighed too heavily, we can lose out on what's really happening now and/or lose sight of what could happen in our future. This can cause us to be unsteady, unbalanced, or temporally biased.

Being out of balance in this way also shades the way we think, and negatively impacts our daily decision making. For instance, if you are stuck in a past negative experience, you might think that from now on everything that happens to you will be negative. Why even bother planning for your future? you might think. It's just going to continue to be same old bad stuff. Or, if you are an extreme present hedonist adrenaline junky intent on spiking your adrenal glands, then you might engage in risky behaviors that unintentionally endanger you or others because you are living in the moment and not thinking about the future consequences of today's actions. If you are out of balance in your future time perspective, constantly thinking and worrying about all the things you have on your endless to-do list, you might forget about or miss out on the everyday, wonderful things happening in your life and the lives of your loved ones in the here and now.

SIX MAIN TIME PERSPECTIVES IN TPT

1. **Past positive people** focus on the good things that have happened.
2. **Past negative people** focus on all the things that went wrong in the past.
3. **Present hedonistic people** live in the moment, seeking pleasure, novelty, and sensation, and avoiding pain.

4. **Present fatalistic people** feel that planning for future decisions is not necessary because predetermined fate plays the guiding role in one's life.
5. **Future positive people** plan for the future and trust that things will work out.
6. **Future negative people** feel the future is predetermined and apocalyptic, or they have no future orientation.

THREE MAIN TP BIASES

1. **Past bias:** Good and bad things happen to everyone. Some of us view the world through rose-colored glasses (past positive), whereas others see the world through a darker lens (past negative). We have found that people who focus primarily on the past value the old more than the new; the familiar over the novel; and the cautious, conservative approach over the daring, more liberal or riskier one.

2. **Present bias:** People who live in the present are far less, or not at all, influenced by either past experiences or future considerations. They focus only on the immediate present—what's happening *now* (present hedonism). Decisions are based on immediate stimulus: internal hormonal signals, feelings, smells, sounds, the attractive qualities of the object of desire, and what others are urging them to do. Present-biased people who are influenced by past negative experiences are likely to feel stuck in the mire of the *past now* (present fatalism).

3. **Future bias:** No one is born thinking about how to plan for the future. A number of conditions, including living in a temperate zone (where it's necessary to anticipate seasonal change), living in a stable family or stable economic/political society (where a person learns to trust promises made to him), and becoming

educated, can create future-positive-oriented people. In general, future-oriented people do very well in life. They are less aggressive, are less depressed, have more energy, take care of their health, have good impulse control, and have more self-esteem. Those stuck in the past, and locked into negative memories, feel fatalistic about the present and may have lost the ability even to conceive of a hopeful future (future negative).

Healthy Versus Unhealthy Time Perspectives

Through years of research, we have discovered that people who live healthy, productive, optimistic lives share the following traits—what we call an "ideal time perspective":

- High past positive/low past negative;
- Low present fatalism/moderate selected present hedonism; and
- Moderately high future-positive orientation.

Conversely, we have found that people with pessimistic time perspectives, usually due to trauma, depression, anxiety, stress, or posttraumatic stress, share the following time perspective profile:

- High past negative/low past positive;
- High present fatalism and/or high present hedonism; and
- Low future/no future orientation.

Having a dose of selected present hedonism in one's overall time perspective profile is important because enjoying oneself and having fun is a healthy part of life. Yet, too much of a good thing can cause numerous problems.

Present Hedonism and Arrested Emotional Development

As just mentioned, present hedonists live and act in the moment, frequently with little to no thought of the future, or the consequences of their actions. Most children and teenagers are present hedonists. Each day, they build on past experiences, but their concept of the future is still under development. People suffering from arrested emotional development, usually caused by a childhood trauma, are also present hedonists. Without therapy, the ability to mature emotionally beyond the age of trauma is difficult to impossible. When they reach adulthood, they may be able to hide their lack of emotional maturity for periods, but then, when in a stressful situation, they revert to behaving the emotional age they were when they were first traumatized. Depending on the degree to which the childhood trauma affected the person suffering from arrested emotional development, they may find that, over time, their present-hedonistic time perspective has morphed into extreme present hedonism.

Without proper individual assessment, we can only make a best guess as to whether Donald Trump suffers from arrested emotional development, which may or may not be a factor in his extreme present hedonism. Yet, with access to the extensive amount of print and video media exposing his bullying behavior, his immature remarks about sex, and his childlike need for constant attention, we can speculate that the traumatizing event was when he was sent away to military school at the age of thirteen. According to one of his biographers, Michael D'Antonio, Trump "was essentially banished from the family home. He hadn't known anything but living with his family in a luxurious setting, and all of a sudden he's sent away" (Schwartzman and Miller 2016). This would help explain his pubescent default setting when confronted by others.

Extreme Present Hedonism

An extreme present hedonist will say or do anything at any time for purposes of self-aggrandizement and to shield himself from previous (usually negatively perceived) activities, with *no* thought of the future or the effect of his actions. Coupled with a measure of paranoia, which is the norm, extreme present hedonism is the most unpredictable and perilous time perspective due to its "action" component. Here's how it works:

The extreme present hedonist's impulsive thought leads to an impulsive action that can cause him to dig in his heels when confronted with the consequences of that action. If the person is in a position of power, then others scramble either to deny or to find ways to back up the original impulsive action. In normal, day-to-day life, this impulsiveness leads to misunderstandings, lying, and toxic relationships. In the case of Donald Trump, an impulsive thought may unleash a stream of tweets or verbal remarks (the action), which then spur others to try to fulfill, or deny, his thoughtless action.

Case in point: Trump's impulsive tweet "How low has President Obama gone to tapp [sic] my phones during the very sacred election process. This is Nixon/Watergate. Bad (or sick) guy!" (Associated Press 2017) caused members of his staff to scramble to find evidence to make the false and slanderous claim "real." That one extreme present hedonistic tweet has led, ironically, to multiple investigations into the Trump campaign's possible Russian connections at the expense of taxpayers' hard-earned dollars.

Another concerning characteristic of extreme present hedonists is the often unwitting—we like to give some extreme present hedonists the benefit of the doubt—propensity to dehumanize others in order to feel superior. This lack of foresight and compassion is also a trait of narcissism and bullying, which we address later in this chapter.

Donald Trump's Extreme Present Hedonistic Quotes

It could be argued that almost anyone can be presented in a negative light when scrutinized or quoted out of context. However, when one runs for the highest office in the land, and then wins that prize, such scrutiny is expected. In the case of Donald Trump, a rich trove of recorded examples gives us a strong picture of the inner workings of his unbalanced psyche. The following well-known quotes, which we've organized into categories—some of them overlap multiple categories—compiled by Michael Kruse and Noah Weiland for *Politico Magazine* ("Donald Trump's Greatest Self Contradictions," May 5, 2016) illustrate his extreme present hedonistic penchant for off-roading from his script and/or saying or tweeting whatever pops into his mind, making things up, repeating fake news, or simply lying:

DEHUMANIZATION

- "Sometimes, part of making a deal is denigrating your competition" (*The Art of the Deal*, 1987).

- "When Mexico sends its people, they're not sending their best . . . They're sending people that have a lot of problems, and they're bringing those problems with us. They're bringing drugs. They're bringing crime. They're rapists. And some, I assume, are good people" (Republican rally speech, June 16, 2015).

- "Written by a nice reporter. Now the poor guy. You ought to see this guy" (remark made while contorting his face and moving his arms and hands around awkwardly, at a campaign rally in South Carolina, November 24, 2015, about journalist Serge Kovaleski, who has arthrogryposis, a congenital condition that can limit joint movement or lock limbs in place).

LYING

- "Made in America? @BarackObama called his 'birthplace' Hawaii 'here in Asia'" (Twitter, November 18, 2011).

- "I watched when the World Trade Center came tumbling down . . . And I watched in Jersey City, New Jersey, where thousands and thousands of people were cheering as that building was coming down. Thousands of people were cheering" (at a rally in Birmingham, Alabama, November 21, 2015). The next day, *This Week* host, George Stephanopoulos, pointed out that "the police say that didn't happen." Trump insisted otherwise: "It was on television. I saw it happen."

- "In addition to winning the Electoral College in a landslide, I won the popular vote if you deduct the millions of people who voted illegally" (Twitter, November 27, 2016).

MISOGYNY

- "You could see there was blood coming out of her eyes. Blood coming out of her—wherever" (remarks during CNN interview with regard to Megyn Kelly, following the previous night's Fox News debate co-moderated by Kelly in which Kelly asked Trump about his misogynistic treatment of women, August 7, 2015).

- "Look at that face! Would anybody vote for that? Can you imagine that, the face of our next president? . . . I mean, she's a woman, and I'm not supposed to say bad things, but really, folks, come on. Are we serious?" (remarks in *Rolling Stone* interview with regard to Republican presidential candidate Carly Fiorina, September 9, 2015).

- "When you're a star, they let you do it. You can do anything . . . Grab 'em by the pussy . . . You can do anything" (off-camera boast recorded over a hot mic by *Access Hollywood* in 2005 and published by the *Washington Post* in October 2016).

PARANOIA

- "The world is a vicious and brutal place. We think we're civilized. In truth, it's a cruel world and people are ruthless. They act nice to your face, but underneath they're out to kill you . . . Even your friends are out to get you: they want your job, they want your house, they want your money, they want your wife, and they even want your dog. Those are your friends; your enemies are even worse!" (*Think Big: Make It Happen in Business and Life*, 2007).

- "My motto is 'Hire the best people, and don't trust them' " (*Think Big: Make It Happen in Business and Life*, 2007).

- "If you have smart people working for you, they'll try to screw you if they think they can do better without you" (*Daily Mail*, October 30, 2010).

RACISM

- "You haven't been called, go back to Univision" (when dismissing Latino reporter Jorge Ramos at an Iowa rally, August 2015).

- "Donald J. Trump is calling for a total and complete shutdown of Muslims entering the United States" (at a rally in Charleston, South Carolina, December 2015).

- "Look at my African American over here. Look at him" (at a campaign appearance in California, June 2016).

SELF-AGGRANDIZEMENT

- "I'm, like, a really smart person" (during an interview in Phoenix, Arizona, July 11, 2015).

- "It's very hard for them to attack me on my looks, because I'm so good looking" (in an interview on NBC's *Meet the Press*, August 7, 2015).

- "I'm speaking with myself, number one, because I have a very good brain and I've said a lot of things. . . . My primary consultant is myself" (from MSNBC interview, March 16, 2016).

Trump also exhibits two generally known personality traits that, when combined with extreme present hedonism, amplify our concern: *narcissism* and *bullying behavior*. In order to help readers understand the complexities of narcissists and bullies, how these two characteristics dovetail with extreme present hedonism, and demonstrate how the president displays these predispositions, we've condensed years of study on these two subjects.

The Narcissistic Personality

I alone can fix it.

Donald Trump, Republican National Convention, July 2016

In the early 1900s, Sigmund Freud introduced narcissism as part of his psychoanalytic theory. Throughout the ensuing decades, it was refined and sometimes referred to as megalomania or severe egocentrism. By 1968, the condition had evolved into the diagnosable *narcissistic personality disorder*. Narcissistic people are out of balance in that they think very highly of themselves while simultaneously thinking very lowly of all those whom they consider their inferiors, which is mostly everybody. Narcissists are emotional, dramatic, and can lack compassion and empathy, as those traits are about feeling for others.

What follows are some of the symptoms of narcissistic personality disorder. (Note that because this is about narcissists, we use the term *you*.)

- **Believing that you're better than others:** This is across the board in your world; you look down your nose at other people.

- **Fantasizing about power, success, and attractiveness:** You are a superhero, among the most successful in your field; you could grace the cover of *GQ* or *Glamour* magazine, and you don't realize this is all in your mind.

- **Exaggerating your achievements or talents:** Your ninth-place showing in the golf tournament becomes first place to those who weren't there and, if you're brazen enough, even to those who were. Although you plunked poorly on a guitar in high school before you lost interest in the instrument, you tell others you took lessons from Carlos Santana.

- **Expecting constant praise and admiration:** You want others to acknowledge when you do anything and everything, even if it's taking out the garbage.

- **Believing that you're special and acting accordingly:** You believe you are God's gift to women/men/your field/the world, and that you deserve to be treated as such by everyone. They just don't know this.

- **Failing to recognize other people's emotions and feelings:** You don't understand why people get upset with you for telling it the way you think it is or what you think they did wrong.

- **Expecting others to go along with your ideas and plans:** There is only one way and that's your way, so you get upset when others share their thoughts or plans because surely theirs aren't as good as yours.

- **Taking advantage of others:** You take your parent's/friend's car/tools/credit card/clothing without asking, or cut in line in front of an elderly person, or expect something much more significant in return for doing a small favor. "What's the big deal?"

- **Expressing disdain for those whom you feel to be inferior:** "That homeless person isn't even wearing a coat or shoes in freezing weather. What an idiot!"

- **Being jealous of others:** You, and not so-and-so, deserved the award/trophy/praise and recognition. Also, if you think someone is more attractive/intelligent/clever or has a more prestigious car/significant other/house, you hate and curse him.

- **Believing that others are jealous of you:** You believe everybody wants to be you.

- **Having trouble keeping healthy relationships:** Your family and friends don't understand you, so you don't stay in touch with them anymore. You lose interest in your romantic relationships each time someone better comes along; you have recurring unsatisfying affairs.

- **Setting unrealistic goals:** You believe that one day you will be a CEO/president/great musician/artist/best-selling author, marry a movie star, or have Bill Gates's billions.

- **Being easily hurt and rejected:** You don't understand why people purposefully hurt your feelings, and either it takes a long time for you to get over it or you don't ever get over it.

- **Having a fragile self-esteem:** Underneath it all, you are just a delicate person, which makes you special, and you don't understand why people don't see this about you.

- **Appearing tough-minded or unemotional:** Read: You act like Mr. Spock.

While some of these symptoms may come across as simply elevated personal confidence or high self-esteem, they're different in people who have a healthy dose of confidence and self-esteem because whereas these people don't value themselves more than they value others, the narcissist looks down on others from his lofty pedestal. The narcissistic personality frequently appears to be a conceited, pompous braggart who dominates conversations and has a sense of entitlement. He wants the best of whatever is available, and when he doesn't get his way, he may become annoyed or angry. He becomes Mr. or Ms. Petulant in action.

Interestingly, what lies underneath this personality type is often very low self-esteem. Narcissists can't handle criticism of any kind, and will belittle others or become enraged or condescending to make themselves feel better when they perceive they are being criticized. It's not unusual for a narcissistic personality to be blind to his own behavior because it doesn't fit his view of his perfect and dominant self. But a narcissistic personality can spot one of his kind a mile away, and will either put down or generally avoid that other mindless competing narcissist.

Unfortunately, narcissistic people may find their relationships falling apart. After a while, folks don't want to be around them; all their relationships (personal, work, or school) become problems. Sometimes their finances are troublesome, too, because it's hard to keep up their image without expensive accoutrements.

The Bully Personality

I hope Corrupt Hillary Clinton chooses Goofy Elizabeth Warren as her running mate. I will defeat them both

Donald Trump, Twitter, May 6, 2016

Bullying is defined as systematically and chronically inflicting physical hurt and/or psychological distress on one or more people, whether they are students at school, peers in the workplace, or family members. Research indicates that some bullies may suffer from narcissistic personality disorder, while others may have difficulty interpreting or judging social situations and other people's actions—they interpret hostility from others when none was meant. For example, a person unintentionally bumps into a bully, who views this accident as an act of aggression; he therefore overreacts, which triggers the bully response of seeking revenge.

Bullying behavior is often learned at home from family members, such as parents or older siblings who display this form of aggression. Generally, bullying behavior is caused by stress in the bully's life. Bullies have often been abused or are driven by their insecurities. They typically want to control and manipulate others to feel superior. The anger they feel as a result of their hurt is directed toward others. Their targets are those whom they consider weaker than they and/or different.

A bully's actions are intentional: to cause emotional or physical injury to one or more people, usually on a repeated basis. Many readers might recall basic types of bully as portrayed in film or on television, such as Biff in *Back to the Future* or Eddie Haskell on the television show *Leave It to Beaver*. As the decades have unfolded and our technology has evolved, so have the numbers and types of bullies.

- **Physical bullying** occurs when people use physical actions to gain power and control over their targets. It's easiest to identify and most likely what people think of when they think of bullying.

- **Verbal bullying** involves using words, statements, and name-calling to gain power and control over a target. Typically, verbal bullies use relentless insults to belittle, demean, and hurt others.

- **Prejudicial bullying** is based on prejudices people have toward people of different races, religions, or sexual orientations. This type of bullying can encompass all the other types of bullying. When prejudicial bullying occurs, those who are somehow considered "different" are targeted and the door is opened to hate crimes.

- **Relational aggression**, frequently referred to as **emotional bullying**, is a sneaky, insidious type of bullying that manifests as social manipulation. The goal of the relational bully is to ostracize others to gain social standing and to control others.

- **Cyberbullying** refers to using the Internet, cell phones, or other technology to harass, threaten, embarrass, or target another person; cyberbullying usually involves a teen or tween. If an adult is involved in this harassment, it is called **cyber-harassment** or **cyberstalking**. This form of bullying has gained momentum, as there is much less risk of being caught.

- **Sexual bullying** consists of repeated, harmful, and humiliating actions (sexual name-calling, crude comments, vulgar gestures, uninvited touching or sexual propositioning) that target a person sexually. It can occur in a group and can be considered a show of bravado among the perpetrators; when done one on one, it can lead to sexual assault.

If you take into account the sexual harassment/assault lawsuits that have targeted Trump over the years, you will find that he has displayed every one of these bullying types. Bullying is not "normal" and is therefore unacceptable behavior—or, at least, it was unacceptable up until the 2016 presidential election. Culturally in the past, bullying was considered a normal rite of passage (while this line of thinking may never have been realistic); it is certainly not so today. With extreme bullying becoming increasingly pervasive, often with tragic results, we can no longer view it as simply a part of growing up, much less a part of being a grown-up.

The Trump Effect

> *I'm gonna bomb the shit out of them!*
>
> Donald Trump during campaign rally in Fort Dodge,
>
> Iowa, November 13, 2015

One person *can* affect an entire nation, and nowhere do we see this more clearly than with "the Trump Effect," which was originally defined as an increase in bullying in schools caused by the rhetoric used by Donald Trump during his campaign. This particular definition of the Trump Effect—not to be confused with definitions that refer, for example, to the stock market, to Trump's publicly skirting the truth, or to the uptick in populism in Europe—gained traction in the media as campaign season deepened and Donald Trump won the election.

In short order, the bullying crept beyond schools to include religious and racial bullying by adults. At least four mosques were burned to the ground. Jewish cemeteries across our nation have been desecrated. Two innocent Indian engineers were shot while having dinner, as was a white American who tried to intervene. One of the engineers died, but not before his killer yelled racial slurs at him that culminated in "Get out of my country!" More recently, articles about the Trump Effect have largely been replaced by continuing coverage of Trump's tweets, his odd behavior, and his campaign team's possibly illegal ties to Russia. However bizarre it may seem, the Trump Effect exists, and is a growing phenomenon.

A report from Maureen Costello of the Southern Poverty Law Center's (SPLC) Teaching Tolerance project, "The Trump Effect: The Impact of the 2016 Presidential Campaign on Our Nation's Schools," lays out in no uncertain terms the dire consequences of Donald Trump's behavior. It indicates that immigrant students, children of immigrants—close to one-third of pupils in American classrooms are the children of foreign-born parents—African Americans, and other students of color were fearful, while their friends worried for them and wanted to protect them.

Yet, many children were not afraid at all. Rather, some used the name "Trump" as a taunt or chant as they ganged up on others. Muslim children were called terrorists; those of Mexican descent were told that they or their parents would be deported; children of color were afraid they would be rounded up and put into camps. The bullying caused some of these children to have panic attacks and suicidal thoughts.

One consistent theme across grade levels emerged: the students understood that the behavior on display was not okay. Also, our research revealed that the great many people who witness such bullying do nothing, and many of these passive bystanders feel prolonged shame for their inaction against this injustice experienced by friends and classmates—another negative fallout of bullying, beyond its targeted victims.

While the long-term impact of these noxious experiences on children's well-being may be impossible to measure, the students were stressed and anxious in a way that threatened their health, their emotional state, and their schoolwork. It is common knowledge that stressed students have a more difficult time learning, and in fact, the report indicated that there were many instances in which anxiety was having an impact on grades and was affecting students' ability to concentrate. All students, though, regardless of whether they are members of a targeted group, are vulnerable to the stresses of the Trump Effect.

If we dive a little deeper, we realize that children are a reflection of their upbringing. More than likely, the angry acting-out of some students toward others in our schools is a reflection of what they observe in their homes. So, how has a small but active segment of our population been reacting to Donald Trump's presidency? Statistics show that they have become even more emboldened and, in recent months, have taken to engaging in hate crimes against Jews as well as Muslims and Mexicans; speculation about Trump's approval of white supremacist/anti-Semitic groups has emboldened them.

According to the SPLC, in the two-week period between Election Day and February 9, 2017, there were seventy anti-Jewish incidents and thirty-one anti-Muslim incidents, the majority being bomb threats. These figures are proportional to the respective populations of Jews and Muslims in the United States, which means Jews and Muslims have a roughly equal chance of being victimized.

The recent rash of desecrations of Jewish graveyards and places of worship, and the burning of mosques, should be extremely concerning to all of us as Americans, as we are a nation composed largely of immigrants. These insults against the identity of Jews and Muslims promote the dehumanization of our fellow human beings. Although the president was eventually forced to condemn the acts of anti-Semitism, in our research for this chapter, we could find little evidence of his condemnation of the attacks against American Muslims. This reluctance to serve and protect segments of his population is yet another sign for bullies that their behavior is acceptable to the man in charge.

A Scary Venn Diagram

In Donald Trump, we have a frightening Venn diagram consisting of three circles: the first is extreme present hedonism; the second, narcissism; and the third, bullying behavior. These three circles overlap in the middle to create an impulsive, immature, incompetent person who, when in the position of ultimate power, easily slides into the role of tyrant, complete with family members sitting at his proverbial "ruling table." Like a fledgling dictator, he plants psychological seeds of treachery in sections of our population that reinforce already negative attitudes. To drive home our point, here are what we consider to be two of Trump's most dangerous quotes:

- "If she gets to pick her judges, nothing you can do, folks. Although the Second Amendment people—maybe there is, I don't know" (remark made during a campaign rally in Wilmington, North Carolina, August 9, 2016); and

- "I could stand in the middle of Fifth Avenue, shoot somebody, and I wouldn't lose any voters" (remark made during a campaign appearance in Sioux City, Iowa, January 23, 2016).

Before Donald Trump, it was unfathomable for American citizens to consciously consider voting for, and then inaugurating, a person as unbalanced as this president. Admittedly, it's possible, as Guy Winch points out in his February 2, 2016, *Psychology Today* article, "Study: Half of All Presidents Suffered from Mental Illness." According to Winch, many of our previous presidents may have suffered from mental health issues, including depression (Abraham Lincoln), bipolar disorder (Lyndon Johnson), alcoholism (Ulysses S. Grant), Alzheimer's disease (Ronald Reagan), and transient bouts of extreme present hedonism (John F. Kennedy and Bill Clinton). We have also survived a president who blatantly lied to cover his criminal tracks before he was caught in those lies (Richard Nixon). In the past, Americans have pulled together and worked to overcome our differences. We moved forward collectively as one great country. Unfortunately, in more recent times, it appears we have become a bipolar nation, with Donald Trump at the helm as his followers cheer him on and others try to resist him.

The Results

In presenting our case that Donald Trump is mentally unfit to be president of the United States, we would be remiss if we did not consider one more factor: the possibility of a neurological disorder such as dementia or Alzheimer's disease, which the president's father, Fred Trump, suffered from. Again, we are not trying to speculate diagnoses from afar, but comparing video interviews of Trump from the 1980s, 1990s, and early 2000s to current video, we find that the differences (significant reduction in the use of essential words; an increase in the use of adjectives such as *very*, *huge*, and *tremendous*; and incomplete, run-on sentences that don't make sense and that could indicate a loss of train of thought or memory) are conspicuously apparent. Perhaps this is why Trump insists on being surrounded by family members who love and understand him rather than seasoned political advisers, who may note, and then leak, his alarming behavior.

Whether or not Donald Trump suffers from a neurological disorder—or narcissistic personality disorder, or any other mental health issue, for that matter—will, undeniably, remain conjecture unless he submits to tests, which is highly unlikely given his personality. However, the lack of such tests cannot erase the well-documented behaviors he has displayed for decades and the dangers they pose when embodied in the president of the United States.

In line with the principles of *Tarasoff v. Regents of the University of California* 17 Cal. 3d 425 (1976), known as the "Tarasoff doctrine," it is the responsibility of mental health professionals to warn the citizens of the United States and the people of the world of the potentially devastating effects of such an extreme present-hedonistic world leader, one with enormous power at his disposal. On the whole, mental health professionals have failed in their duty to warn, in a timely manner, not only the public but also government officials about the dangers of President Donald Trump. Articles and interviews intent on cautioning the masses prior to the election fell on deaf ears, perhaps in part because the media did not afford the concerned mental health professionals appropriate coverage, perhaps because some citizens discount the value of mental health and have thrown a thick blanket of stigma over the profession, or perhaps because we as mental health professionals did not stand united. Whatever the reason, it's not too late to follow through.

When an individual is psychologically unbalanced, *everything* can teeter and fall apart if change does not occur. We wonder how far-reaching, in our society over time, the effects of our unbalanced president's actions will be and how they will continue to affect us as individuals, communities, a nation, and a planet. We believe that Donald Trump is the most dangerous man in the world, a powerful leader of a powerful nation who can order missiles fired at another nation because of his (or a family member's) personal distress at seeing sad scenes of people having been gassed to death. We shudder to imagine what actions might be taken in broader lethal confrontations with his personal and political enemies.

We are gravely concerned about Trump's abrupt, capricious 180-degree shifts and how these displays of instability have the potential to be unconscionably dangerous to the point of causing catastrophe, and not only for the citizens of the United States. There are two particularly troubling examples: (1) his repeatedly lavishing praise on FBI director James Comey's handling of an investigation into Hillary Clinton's emails and then, in early May 2017, abruptly and abusively firing Comey for the very investigation that garnered such praise, but in this case actually because of Comey's investigation into the Trump campaign's ties to Russia; and (2) his stating during the campaign that NATO was obsolete and then, later, unexpectedly stating that NATO was necessary and acceptable. As is the case with extreme present hedonists, Trump is "chumming" for war, possibly for the most selfish of reasons: to deflect attention away from the Russia investigation. If another unbalanced world leader takes the bait, Trump will need the formerly "obsolete" and now-essential NATO to back him up.

We as individuals don't have to follow our nation's leader down a path headed in the wrong direction—off a cliff and into a pit of past mistakes. We can stand where we are at this moment in history and face forward, into a brighter future that *we* create. We can start by looking for the good in one another and for the common ground we share.

In the midst of the terrorist attacks on places of worship and cemeteries mentioned earlier, something wonderful emerged from the ashes: a spirit of overwhelming goodness in humanity. In the wake of the attacks, Jews and Muslims united: they held fundraisers to help each other repair and rebuild; they shared their places of worship so that those burned out of theirs could hold gatherings and services; and they offered loving support to those who'd faced hatred. By observing ordinary people engaging in acts of everyday heroism and compassion, we have been able to witness the best aspects of humanity. *That's* us! *That's* the United States of America!

A final suggestion for our governmental leaders: corporations and companies vet their prospective employees. This vetting process frequently includes psychological testing in the form of exams or quizzes to help the employer make more informed hiring decisions and determine if the prospective employee is honest and/or would be a good fit for the company. These tests are used for positions ranging from department store sales clerk to high-level executive. Isn't it time that the same be required for candidates for the most important job in the world?

Philip Zimbardo, Ph.D., Professor Emeritus at Stanford University, is a scholar, educator, and researcher. Zimbardo is perhaps best known for his landmark Stanford prison study. Among his more than five hundred publications are the best seller The Lucifer Effect *and such notable psychology textbooks as* Psychology: Core Concepts, *8th edition, and* Psychology and Life, *now in its 20th edition. He is founder and president of the Heroic Imagination Project (heroicimagination.org), a worldwide nonprofit teaching people of all ages how to take wise and effective action in challenging situations. He continues to research the effects of time perspectives and time perspective therapy.*

Rosemary Sword is codeveloper of Time Perspective Therapy and coauthor of The Time Cure: Overcoming PTSD with the New Psychology of Time Perspective Therapy *(in English, German, Polish, Chinese, and Russian);* The Time Cure Therapist Guidebook *(Wiley, 2013);* Time Perspective Therapy: Transforming Zimbardo's Temporal Theory into Clinical Practice *(Springer, 2015);* Time Perspective Theory *(Springer, 2015);* Living and Loving Better with Time Perspective Therapy *(McFarland, 2017); and* Time Perspective Therapy: An Evolutionary Therapy for PTSD *(McFarland, forthcoming). Sword and Zimbardo write a popular column for* PsychologyToday .com *and contribute both to* AppealPower, *a European Union online journal, and to* Psychology in Practice, *a new Polish psychological journal. Sword is also developer of Aetas: Mind Balancing Apps (www.discoveraetas.com).*

References

Associated Press. 2017. "President Trump's Claim That Obama Wiretapped Him Basically Died This Week." *Time*, March 24. http://amp.timeinc.net /time/4713187/donald-trump-obama-wiretap-fact-check/?source=dam.

Kruse, Michael, and Noah Weiland. 2016. "Donald Trump's Greatest Self Contradictions." *Politico Magazine*, May 5. www.politico.com/magazine /story/2016/05/donald-trump-2016-contradictions-213869.

"Mental Health Experts Say Donald Trump Is Unfit to Serve." 2017. *The Last Word with Lawrence O'Donnell*. MSNBC, February 21. www.msnbc.com /the-last-word/watch/mental-health-experts-say-trump-is-unfit-to -serve-882688067737.

Psychology Today Editorial Staff. 2017. "Shrinks Battle Over Diagnosing Donald Trump," January 31. www.psychologytoday.com/blog /brainstorm/201701/shrinks-battle-over-diagnosing-donald-trump.

Schwartzman, Paul, and Michael E. Miller. 2016. "Confident. Incorrigible. Bully: Little Donny Was a Lot Like Candidate Donald Trump."

Washington Post, June 22. www.washingtonpost.com/lifestyle/style /young-donald-trump-military-school/2016/06/22/f0b3b164-317c-11e6 -8758-d58e76e11b12_story.html?utm_term=.961fefcee834.

Stetka, Bret. 2017. "As Presidents Live Longer, Doctors Debate Whether to Test for Dementia." NPR, February 17. www.npr.org/sections/health -shots/2017/02/17/514583390/as-our-leaders-live-longer-calls-for -presidential-dementia-testing-grow-louder.

Sword, Rosemary, and Philip Zimbardo. 2016a. "Bullies." *PsychologyToday .com*, January 24. www.psychologytoday.com/blog/the-time-cure /201601/bullies.

———. 2016b. "The Narcissistic Personality: A Guide to Spotting Narcissists." *PsychologyToday.com*, March 29. www.psychologytoday.com/blog /the-time-cure/201603/the-narcissistic-personality.

Winch, Guy. 2016. "Study: Half of All Presidents Suffered from Mental Illness." *PsychologyToday.com*, February 2. www.psychologytoday.com /blog/the-squeaky-wheel/201602/study-half-all-presidents-suffered -mental-illness.

Zimbardo, Philip, and John Boyd. 2009. *The Time Paradox*. New York: Atria.

Zimbardo, Philip, Richard Sword, and Rosemary Sword. 2012. *The Time Cure*. San Francisco, CA: Wiley.

PATHOLOGICAL NARCISSISM AND POLITICS

A Lethal Mix

CRAIG MALKIN, PH.D.

My twitter has become so powerful that I can actually make my enemies tell the truth.

Donald J. Trump, tweet from October 17, 2012

In 1952, a young Richard Nixon, rising star in the Republican Party, had been handpicked as Eisenhower's running mate, and by all accounts, the Republicans made a sound choice. Nixon's great strength was the message he'd pounded like a drumbeat into voters' ears: Washington needed a major cleanup, a White House full of good moral upstanding people. The elites, like the previous administration under Harry Truman and Eisenhower's opponent, Adlai Stevenson—a brilliant orator and skilled lawyer—had ruined it for everyone with their corruption, communism, and cronyism ("pay for play," as we've come to call it).

America embraced the message for a time—the Ike-Nixon team held a substantial lead in the polls—but just as he and Eisenhower were gearing up to stump for votes on their "whistle stop" tours of the country—Nixon on his train, *the Nixon Express*, Eisenhower on his, the *Look Ahead, Neighbor*—Nixon became embroiled in a potentially career-ending controversy. Stories erupted of a secret slush fund of money from his supporters that he used to live the high life: a mink coat for his wife, Pat; lavish dinners for himself and his friends; and—worst of all—special favors for those who'd subsidized him. The story, courtesy of the *New York Post*'s Leo Katcher, spread like wildfire, fueled by an especially incendiary headline: *Secret Rich Men's Trust Fund Keeps Nixon in Style Far Beyond His Salary.*

Public outcry was loud and clear: Nixon should resign as Eisenhower's running mate. As late election season disasters go, this one was a juggernaut; behind the scenes, the entire team scrambled to rescue a troubled campaign. With no solution in sight, Nixon made a bold decision: he'd appeal directly to the American people by laying bare every financial detail of his life. His wife, Pat, was reportedly mortified at the thought of his sharing their economic history with the entire country, but Nixon remained undeterred.

On the evening of September 23, 1952, Nixon sat before a TV audience of 60 million, his alarmed wife beside him, mostly off screen, and went through each and every one of his accounts: what he owned and what he owed, line by line. Nixon reassured viewers that an independent audit had found no wrongdoing and that he hadn't used a penny of the money he'd been given for personal gain. But, he confessed, there was one gift that had brought personal benefit that he couldn't bear to return:

> It was a little cocker spaniel dog in a crate . . . sent all the way from Texas. Black and white spotted. And our little girl—Tricia, the six-year-old—named it Checkers. And you know, the kids, like all kids, love the dog and I just want to say this right now, that regardless of what they say about it, we're gonna keep it.

Though Nixon was unsure how successful he'd been, and political opinion was divided along party lines, the speech worked with the American public, earning him a place in people's hearts and securing his position on the Republican ticket. Eisenhower and Nixon trounced their opponents, and President Eisenhower assumed office as the thirty-fourth commander in chief.

To some, Nixon's comeback wasn't surprising. Despite his unassuming hangdog look, Nixon brought a blend of brutal ambition and relentless determination to politics that few had seen before. And he used that same drive to survive one defeat after another, including, later, his losses to John F. Kennedy in 1960 as president of the United States and Pat Davis, in 1962, as governor of California. The last defeat was supposed to be his curtain call in politics; famously, in his "final" press conference, he dourly announced, "Just think what you're going to be missing. You won't have Nixon to kick around anymore." But if Nixon worried about being kicked, he certainly didn't show it. He remained in politics, and continued to thrive, ultimately becoming president of the United States in 1968.

Everything finally seemed to be going Nixon's way, despite his trouble leaving behind his nickname from the 1950s, "Tricky Dick." He even enjoyed accolades for bringing U.S. troops back from Vietnam, opening diplomatic relations with Communist China, and kibitzing with Neil Armstrong and Buzz Aldrin after they walked on the moon. Even with the carnage of Vietnam looming in the background, he appeared to have a largely successful first term, and sailed to victory again in 1972, to serve his second term.

If the fund scandal ambushed Nixon, the next threat crept up on him like a thief in the night. After months of rumblings about Tricky Dick's dirty dealings, he finally came face-to-face with the scandal that brought him down once and for all: Watergate. As details of illegal wiretappings, blackmail, and burglaries trickled out, Nixon's dark side came fully into the light. Here, the public learned, was a self-serving suspicious man who secretly taped every Oval Office conversation, arranged the break-in at the Democratic National Committee (DNC) headquarters, and—when distressed—paced the White House halls, holding court with portraits. Here was a man who swore lividly about the Jews taking over, employed unsavory characters like former FBI agent-cum-mercenary, G. Gordon Liddy, and spent much of his time becoming belligerently drunk while Cambodia was carpet-bombed.

Strangely, this profanity-prone, paranoid tyrant both was—and wasn't—the man people thought they knew: a comeback king, resilient in defeat, humble in victory, but always, behind the scenes it seems, on the precipice of some self-made disaster. This was the paradox of Nixon.

Nixon's story, as fascinating as it is terrifying, tells us a great deal about the relationship between personality and politics. What's most surprising about Nixon is the fact that his apparently contradictory character appears to be rather *un*remarkable among presidents and politicians. That is, Nixon displayed a combination of intense ambition, authority, grandiosity, arrogance, entitlement, subterfuge, and self-importance that appears to have been common in the Oval Office throughout history. Nixon was a narcissist.

Narcissism: The Good, the Bad, and the Ugly

Despite what you may have read, *narcissist* isn't a diagnosis and it never has been. *Narcissism* isn't a diagnosis either. Narcissism, in fact, is best understood as a trait that occurs, to varying degrees, in all of us: *the drive to feel special, to stand out from the other 7 billion people on the planet, to feel exceptional or unique.*

Instead of thinking of narcissism as all or none, think of it along a spectrum, stretching from zero on the low end, signifying no drive to feel special, to moderate at 5, and finally, spiking to 10 at the extreme:

| 0 | 5 | 10 |

Moderate narcissism (around 4 to 6) is where we have the healthiest amount of the trait. Lower and higher on the scale present problems. If you imagine feeling special like a drug, moderate ("healthy") narcissism gives us a little boost when we need it, a way to press on when the world and sometimes common sense tell us our reach might exceed our grasp. According to 30 years of research, the vast majority of happy healthy people around the world feel a little special, even if privately. Healthy narcissism isn't simply self-confidence, self-care, or self-esteem. It's a *slightly* unrealistically positive self-image. Think of it as rose-colored glasses for the self—the glasses are strong enough to tint the world, but not so opaque they blind us to reality.

Healthy narcissism comes with a host of benefits. Moderately narcissistic teens are less anxious and depressed and have far better relationships than their low and high narcissism peers. Likewise, corporate leaders with moderate narcissism are rated by their employees as far more effective than those with too little or too much. And in our team's research, we're finding that people with healthy narcissism are happier, more optimistic, and more consistently self-confident than those at the low or high end of the spectrum.

When someone scores well above average in narcissistic traits (picture above 6 on the spectrum), they earn the label *narcissist*. There are many types of narcissists, though we're most familiar with the *extroverted* kind (a.k.a obvious, overt, or grandiose, in the research): ambitious, outgoing charismatic individuals, often drawn to the spotlight. Most politicians, actors, and celebrities exhibit this louder, chest-thumping brand of narcissism. Presidents seem to be especially likely to rank high in extroverted narcissism.

In fact, psychologist Ronald J. Deluga, of Bryant College, used biographical information to calculate a Narcissistic Personality Inventory score (a tool for measuring extroverted narcissism) for every commander in chief, from George Washington through Ronald Reagan. He found that high-ego presidents like Richard Nixon and Ronald Reagan ranked higher than more soft-spoken leaders like Jimmy Carter and Gerald Ford, but almost all presidents scored high enough to be considered "narcissists."

A more recent study led by psychologists Ashley L. Watts and Scott O. Lilienfeld of Emory University yielded similar results, but also revealed something that helps explain Nixon's dual nature: as the presidents' narcissism scores increased, so did their likelihood of facing impeachment proceedings, "abusing positions of power, tolerating unethical behavior in subordinates, stealing, bending or breaking rules, cheating on taxes, and having extramarital affairs." The authors' conclusion: narcissism is a double-edged sword, much as we've seen in Nixon's and Bill Clinton's case—and as we may be seeing in Donald Trump's case.

Donald Trump's brand of narcissism is clearly the obvious, loud kind, and it certainly comes with a downside. While he's extremely extroverted—he was, after all, the star of his own reality TV show—he also demonstrates many of the worst qualities we see in a narcissist. He brags: "I'll be the best jobs president God ever created." He boasts: "It's in my blood. I'm smart," he assured a crowd at a South Carolina rally. "Really smart." And he freely insults people, mocking their looks ("Rosie O'Donnell is a fat Pig"), their talent (Meryl Streep is "one of the most overrated actresses in Hollywood"), and—perhaps because they mattered most to him as a TV star—their ratings. He sparked a Twitter feud with Arnold Schwarzenegger, accusing him of killing Trump's beloved show, *The Celebrity Apprentice*.

> *Wow, the ratings are in and Arnold Schwarzenegger got "swamped" (or destroyed) by comparison to the ratings machine, DJT. So much for being a movie star—and that was season 1 compared to season 14. Now compare him to my season 1.*
>
> Donald J. Trump, Tweet from January 6, 2017

But perhaps the most startling display of Trump's numbers obsession took place when he had his press secretary, Sean Spicer, hold a briefing, the principal subject of which was the *size* of his inaugu-ration crowd. Many watched and listened in disbelief while report-ers pressed the question: why is this topic the central point of the administration's first press briefing?

A preoccupation with size is certainly laughably Freudian, but is it reason enough to question Trump's leadership capacity? When does the double-edged sword of narcissism—Trump's or any other president's—turn dangerous? That answer is more complicated than it seems, but it turns, in part, on whether or not their narcissism is high enough to count as an illness.

Pathological narcissism begins when people become so addicted to feeling special that, just like with any drug, they'll do anything to get their "high," including lie, steal, cheat, betray, and even *hurt* those closest to them. Imagine this starting around 9 on the spectrum and getting worse as we approach 10. At these points, you're in the realm of narcissistic personality disorder (NPD).

For a detailed description of NPD, see the latest edition of the *Diagnostic and Statistical Manual* (DSM-V), but for now, here's a simple explanation. People with NPD have a strong need, in every area of their life, to be treated as if they're special. To those with NPD, other people are simply mirrors, useful only insofar as they reflect back the special view of themselves they so desper-ately long to see. If that means making others look bad by comparison—say, by ruining their reputation at work—so be it. Because life is a constant competition, they're also usually riddled with envy over what other people seem to have. And they'll let you know it. At the heart of pathological narcissism, or NPD, is what I call *Triple E*:

- *Entitlement*, acting as if the world and other people owe them and should bend to their will
- *Exploitation*, using the people around them to make themselves feel special, no matter what the emotional or even physical cost to

others (battering away at their self-esteem or running them into the ground with late-night work projects)
- *Empathy-impairment*, neglecting and ignoring the needs and feelings of others, even of those closest to them, because their own need to feel special is all that matters

Exploitation and entitlement (or EE, in the research) are linked to just about every troubling behavior pathological narcissists demonstrate: aggression when their ego is threatened, infidelity, vindictiveness, extreme envy, boasting, name-dropping, denial of any problems or wrongdoing—even workplace sabotage.

As people become more addicted to feeling special, they grow ever more dangerous. Here's where pathological narcissism often blends with *psychopathy*, a pattern of remorseless lies and manipulation. Psychopaths may carry on affairs, embezzle funds, ruin your reputation, and still greet you with a smile, without feeling any guilt, shame, or sadness.

Unlike NPD, psychopathy is marked not by impaired or blocked empathy but a complete *absence* of it (apart from being able to parrot words that *sound* like empathy, known as "cognitive empathy"). In fact, some neuroimaging evidence suggests that psychopaths don't experience emotions the same way non-psychopaths do. The emotion centers of their brains simply fail to light up when they confess shameful events, say, cheating on a spouse or punching a friend, or when they see pictures of people in pain or suffering or anguish.

When NPD and psychopathy combine, they form a pattern of behavior called *malignant narcissism*. This isn't a diagnosis, but a term coined by psychoanalyst Erich Fromm and elaborated on by personality disorder expert, Otto Kernberg, to describe people so driven by feeling special that they essentially see other people as pawns in their game of kill or be killed, whether metaphorically or literally. Hitler, who murdered millions, Kim Jong-un, who's suspected of ordering his uncle's and brother-in-law's deaths, and Vladimir Putin, who jokes about "liquidating journalists"—no doubt all fall in the category of malignant narcissist (among possessing other pernicious traits, like sadism, or delight in hurting others).

The problem is not all malignant narcissists are as overtly dangerous as people like Hitler, Putin, or Kim Jong-un, especially in democracies like the U.S., where it's still presumably illegal to kill people who disagree with you—even if they do write articles you don't like. That means if we're trying to determine whether or not a pathologically narcissistic president poses a threat to our country or the world, we'll also have to look to subtler indicators than a penchant for murder. We need to examine whether or not they can perform their jobs, one of the most important of which is to preserve the safety of our country—and the world.

Mentally Ill Leaders: Are They Functional or Impaired?

The diagnosis of a mental illness—NPD or any other—is not by itself a judgment about whether a person is a capable leader. Steve Jobs, by all accounts, had NPD—yelling at staff, questioning their competence, calling them "shit"—but he also galvanized Apple's engineers into developing the iMac, the iPod, and the iPhone. No doubt more than a few shareholders would have objected to Job's re-removal (he'd already been ousted for his nasty attitude once) from the company. He may have had what mental health clinicians call "high functioning" NPD—he was narcissistic enough to show Triple E, but still able to be incredibly productive, maintain decent (enough) family relationships and friendships, and mostly keep his angry explosions from completely blowing up the workplace.

What mental health experts concern themselves with most when it comes to assessing the *dangers* of mental illness are "functional impairments." That is, how much do the symptoms of a person's mental illness interfere with their ability to hold down a job, maintain meaningful relationships, and—most importantly—manage their intense feelings, such as anger or sadness or fear, without becoming a danger to themselves or others? This is particularly important when it comes to positions as powerful as president of the United States. Steve Jobs calling another CEO "a piece of shit" has far less troubling implications than the leader of the free world telling a volatile dictator he's "very dumb."

In other words, in tackling the question of whether or not a leader's narcissism is dangerous, it's not enough to say they're mentally ill; I've helped many clients over the years with active psychotic illness, who have wonderful loving relationships and maintain steady jobs, even while anxiously worrying, for example, about devices being implanted in their teeth. Equating mental illness with incapacity merely stigmatizes the mentally ill.

When it comes to the question of whether or not someone who's mentally ill can function, *danger is the key—to self or other*s. This is where pathological narcissism and politics can indeed become a toxic, even lethal, mix. When peace at home and abroad are at stake—not just the feelings of coworkers, friends, or partners—pathological narcissism unchecked could lead to World War III.

The greatest danger, as we saw with Nixon, is that pathological narcissists can lose touch with reality in subtle ways that become extremely dangerous over time. When they can't let go of their need to be admired or recognized, they have to *bend* or *invent* a reality in which they remain special despite all messages to the contrary. In point of fact, they become *dangerously* psychotic. It's just not always obvious until it's too late.

Just like narcissism and most traits or conditions, psychosis lies on a spectrum. On the low end, people become "thought-disordered," that is, use tortured logic, deny embarrassing facts, and show horrendous judgment. On the upper end, they may have auditory and visual hallucinations and paranoid delusions. As their special status becomes threatened, people with NPD bend the truth to fit their story of who they are. If reality suggests they're not special, but flawed, fragile, and—even worse—mediocre, then they simply ignore or distort reality.

Did Nixon's psychotic deterioration, for example, lead to more carnage in Vietnam? One biographer claims he bombed the country, at least once, to impress his friends, and that Henry Kissinger, the secretary of state, kept Nixon's rashest decisions in check, making sure any escalation of conflict cleared a committee of military experts.

Did Nixon foment more unrest internally than the U.S. would have seen otherwise? Certainly, his "the press is the enemy" mantra, which dated back to his anger over the slush fund scandal, pitted the administration against the people. Paranoia is easy to catch when the POTUS suffers from it; everyone starts looking over their shoulders for danger when the free world's leader says it surrounds us. Turmoil, rage, and distrust swirled through the 1970s. Are we living through that again?

Did Nixon make decisions of state while drunk, drowning the pain of his persecution, imagined or real? Given the widespread reports of how much he drank, it's hard to imagine he didn't. Multiple biographers report his staff scrambling to contain his threatened actions, including IRS audits, against the people on his burgeoning "Enemies List."

Did Nixon ever draw counsel from the paintings he spoke to? Did he follow it?

These all constitute dangerous functional impairments for a leader. They're the foreign and domestic policy equivalent of leaping from a building, believing you can fly. And they're all part of the *psychotic spiral* that afflicts pathological narcissists confronted with the troubling truth that they're not as special as they think they are.

The Psychotic Spiral

If we wish to preserve the safety of our country and the world, we have to remain vigilant to the signs of the psychotic spiral in pathologically narcissistic leaders:

Increasing Paranoia

Increasing Paranoia: Pathological narcissists abhor admitting to vulnerability—feeling scared, insecure, unsure of themselves— because they don't trust people to support them when they're upset, a problem called *insecure attachment* in the research. They don't even like people knowing they're upset (except over feeling attacked). So they divide the world into good and bad, friend and enemy, in simple black-and-white terms, the advantage being that if they want to feel safe again, if they want to feel assured of their special status, all they need do is flee (or eliminate) their enemies and cozy up to their friends.

In other words, pathological narcissists in a psychotic spiral *project*, imagining the danger they feel inside themselves (anxiety, panic, confusion, doubts) is coming from *outside*, so that they can escape or destroy it. Unfortunately, because the sense of danger is internal (their insecurity), they have to step up their efforts to attack their enemies in order to feel safe.

Imagine this on a global scale, where enemies are Communists or Muslims or immigrants or any kind. Nixon was far happier complaining about Communist threats than recognizing his errors and correcting them. How often did that lead to additional violence in Vietnam? Could such "splitting" as it's called lead to unnecessary violence again?

Impaired Judgment

As pathological narcissists become increasingly thought-disordered, their vision becomes clouded. That's because if you see the world not as it is, but as you *wish* or *need* it to be in order to preserve the belief you're special, you lose touch with crucial information, brute facts, and harsh realities. On a global scale that means, as it did with Nixon, that if it feeds your ego, step up military action. The precariousness of the world or careful assessments of the dangers of a military assault don't matter at this point; displays of power and superiority are soothing when pathological narcissists feel like they're falling apart inside.

The resulting chaos can be hard to keep up with (and fruitless in the end) as we saw with Nixon's staff chasing after his drunken calls and egregious rants about the Jews working against him. In a startlingly parallel lapse of judgment, Trump reportedly boasted to the Russian ambassador about the impressiveness of his intelligence assessment, spilling secrets Israel shared (without their permission).

Volatile Decision Making

This sign of a psychotic spiral is particularly troubling. Impaired judgment naturally leads to reactivity and ill-conceived plans. If all that matters to a pathologically narcissistic leader is any action that preserves their special status (at least in their mind), then reality, circumstance, and facts cease to matter. Which means that what a leader says from day to day or even hour to hour may shift based on what feels best, not what's best for the country.

Right after his staff and appointees spread the message that Trump fired FBI director James Comey, who was investigating his campaign's and administration's ties to Russia, for incompetence and on the recommendation of the deputy attorney general, Rod Rosenstein, the president blithely contradicted the statement.

"I'd already decided to fire him," Trump proudly proclaimed, as though what mattered most was proving he could make his own decisions, not the appearance, at least, of neutrality or a separation of powers. Trump went on to call Comey "crazy, a nut job" and said that firing him relieved the "pressure" of the Russia investigation.

Whether or not this is a sign of thought disorder, at the very least, it shows a remarkable lack of self-preservation. Trump totally ignored that Nixon, too, fired those investigating him—and with fatal consequence.

Gaslighting

Often, people with NPD resort to an insidious strategy called *gaslighting*—a term drawn from the 1938 play about a man who persuaded his wife she was crazy by, among other means, dimming the gas-lights and claiming he'd never touched them. As people with NPD become increasingly psychotic, they're determined to convince others that they're the "crazy" ones who can't see reality for what it is. Gaslighting reassures pathological narcissists that their own grip on reality remains firm because they can't bear to acknowledge their sanity is slipping away. We might ask if we're seeing this now, as Trump and his closest advisers appear on TV claiming he didn't make statements that journalists often simply play back—or if it's a tweet, flash an image—to prove that he did indeed say what he said.

Lately, these incidents have become commonplace. Many in the press and public at large now refer to them as *alternative facts*, alluding to Trump spokesperson Kellyanne Conway's now infamous "expla-nation" for why Sean Spicer had berated the press for misreporting Trump's inauguration size: "this was the largest audience to ever witness an inauguration, period, both in person and around the globe," Spicer peevishly told a stunned press corps. This turned out to be patently false, though Conway defended the statement, saying Spicer had simply been providing "alternative facts."

Those who embrace Trump's reality, where the mainstream media lies and remains "the enemy," signify their support with red hats bearing the inscription MAGA (Make America Great Again). Those who *believe* what the news reports about Trump have donned the symbol of resistance—pink pussy hats, a reference to his now infamous hot mic comments about women, "I just grab 'em by the pussy . . ."

That the country is currently split—and our shared reality with it—seems without question at this point.

Spotting Lethal Leaders: How to Save the World

Currently, it's up to you to decide if the evidence cited points to func-tional impairments in Trump or any other politician. That's not something mental health professionals in the United States are allowed to do—not yet.

Nevertheless, we have in our midst people already trained to provide functional and risk assessments based *entirely* on observation—forensic psychiatrists and psychologists as well as "profilers" groomed by the CIA, the FBI, and various law enforcement agencies. They spend their whole lives learning to predict how people behave.

We could, if we wish, assemble a panel of politically independent specialists within government to provide these assessments. That means suspending the Goldwater rule—or at least allowing risk assessment (to the country, to the world) to take precedence over the sanctity of current ethics.

If pathological narcissists, in their reality-warping efforts to feed their addiction, bring themselves to the precipice of disaster, why should we, as nations, allow them to pull us into the abyss with them?

It's *this* urgent existential question that faces democracies throughout the world today.

Craig Malkin, Ph.D., is author of the internationally acclaimed Rethinking Narcissism, *a clinical psychologist, and Lecturer for Harvard Medical School with twenty-five years of experience helping individuals, couples, and families. His insights on relationships and narcissism have appeared in newspapers and magazines such as* Time, *the* New York Times, *the* Sunday Times, Psychology Today, Women's Health, *the* Huffington Post, *and* Happen Magazine. *He has also been featured multiple times on NPR, CBS Radio, and the Oprah Winfrey Network channel, among other stations and shows internationally. Dr. Malkin is president and director of the Cambridge, Massachusetts–based YM Psychotherapy and Consultation Inc., which provides psychotherapy and couples workshops.*

References

Ackerman, R. A., E. A. Witt, M. B. Donnellan, K. H. Trzesniewski, R. W. Robins, and D. A. Kashy. 2011. "What Does the Narcissistic Personality Inventory Really Measure?" *Assessment* 18 (1): 67–87.

Alicke, Mark D., and Constantine Sedikides. 2011. *Handbook of Self-Enhancement and Self-Protection.* New York: Guilford Press.

Baumeister, Roy F., and Kathleen D. Vohs. 2001. "Narcissism as Addiction to Esteem." *Psychological Inquiry* 12 (4): 206–10.

Brown, Jonathon D. 2010. "Across the (Not So) Great Divide: Cultural Similarities in Self-Evaluative Processes." *Social and Personality Psychology Compass* 4 (5): 318–30.

———. 2012. "Understanding the Better Than Average Effect: Motives (Still) Matter." *Personality and Social Psychology Bulletin* 38 (2): 209–19.

Deluga, Ronald J. 1997. "Relationship Among American Presidential Charismatic Leadership, Narcissism, and Rated Performance." *The Leadership Quarterly* 8 (1): 49–65.

Drew, Elizabeth. 2007. *Richard M. Nixon: The American Presidents Series: The 37th President, 1969–1974.* New York: Macmillan.

Farrell, John A. 2017. *Richard Nixon: The Life.* New York: Doubleday.

Grijalva, E., D. A. Newman, L. Tay, M. B. Donnellan, P. D. Harms, R. W. Robins, and T. Yan. 2014. "Gender Differences in Narcissism: A Meta-Analytic Review." *Psychological Bulletin* 141 (2): 261–310.

Grijalva, Emily, and Daniel A. Newman. 2014. "Narcissism and Counterproductive Work Behavior (CWB): Meta-Analysis and Consideration of Collectivist Culture, Big Five Personality, and Narcissism's Facet Structure." *Applied Psychology* 64 (1): 93–126.

Grijalva, Emily, Peter D. Harms, Daniel A. Newman, Blaine H. Gaddis, and R. Chris Fraley. 2014. "Narcissism and Leadership: A Meta-Analytic Review of Linear and Nonlinear Relationships." *Personnel Psychology* 68 (1): 1–47.

Hill, Patrick L., and Daniel K. Lapsley. 2011. "Adaptive and Maladaptive Narcissism in Adolescent Development." (2011): 89–105.

Hill, Robert W., and Gregory P. Yousey. 1998. "Adaptive and Maladaptive Narcissism Among University Faculty, Clergy, Politicians, and Librarians." *Current Psychology* 17 (2–3): 163–69.

Isaacson, Walter. 2011. *Steve Jobs*. New York: Simon and Schuster.

Jakobwitz, Sharon, and Vincent Egan. 2006. "The Dark Triad and Normal Personality Traits." *Personality and Individual Differences* 40 (2): 331–39.

Lapsley, D. K., and M. C. Aalsma. 2006. "An Empirical Typology of Narcissism and Mental Health in Late Adolescence." *Journal of Adolescence* 29 (1): 53–71.

Malkin, Craig. 2015. *Rethinking Narcissism: The Bad—and Surprising Good—About Feeling Special*. New York: HarperCollins.

Malkin, Craig, and Stuart Quirk. 2016. "Evidence for the Reliablity and Construct Validity of the Narcissism Spectrum Scale." *Research in progress*.

Pailing, Andrea, Julian Boon, and Vincent Egan. 2014. "Personality, the Dark Triad and Violence." *Personality and Individual Differences* 67: 81–86.

Penney, Lisa M., and Paul E. Spector. 2002. "Narcissism and Counterproductive Work Behavior: Do Bigger Egos Mean Bigger Problems?" *International Journal of Selection and Assessment* 10 (1–2): 126–34.

Raskin, Robert N., and Calvin S. Hall. 1979. "A Narcissistic Personality Inventory." *Psychological Reports* 45 (2): 590.

Reidy, Dennis E., Amos Zeichner, Joshua D. Foster, and Marc A. Martinez. 2008. "Effects of Narcissistic Entitlement and Exploitativeness on Human Physical Aggression." *Personality and Individual Differences* 44 (4): 865–75.

Ronningstam, Elsa. 1998. *Disorders of Narcissism: Diagnostic, Clinical, and Empirical Implications*. 1st ed., Washington, DC: American Psychiatric Press.

Sosik, John J., Jae Uk Chun, and Weichun Zhu. 2014. "Hang On to Your Ego: The Moderating Role of Leader Narcissism on Relationships Between Leader Charisma and Follower Psychological Empowerment and Moral Identity." *Journal of Business Ethics* 120 (1): 65–80.

Spain, Seth M., Peter Harms, and James M. LeBreton. 2014. "The Dark Side of Personality at Work." *Journal of Organizational Behavior* 35 (S1): S41–S60.

Summers, Anthony, and Robbyn Swan. 2000. *The Arrogance of Power: The Secret World of Richard Nixon.* New York: Viking.

Taylor, Shelley E., Jennifer S. Lerner, David K. Sherman, Rebecca M. Sage, and Nina K. McDowell. 2003. "Portrait of the Self-Enhancer: Well Adjusted and Well Liked or Maladjusted and Friendless?" *Journal of Personality and Social Psychology* 84 (1): 165.

Watts, Ashley L., Scott O. Lilienfeld, Sarah Francis Smith, Joshua D. Miller, W. Keith Campbell, Irwin D. Waldman, Steven J. Rubenzer, and Thomas J. Faschingbauer. 2013. "The Double-Edged Sword of Grandiose Narcissism." *Psychological Science* 24 (12): 2379–89. doi: 10.1177/09567976 13491970.

Wink, Paul. 1992. "Three Types of Narcissism in Women from College to Mid-Life." *Journal of Personality* 60 (1): 7–30.

Woodworth, Michael, and Stephen Porter. 2002. "In Cold Blood: Character-istics of Criminal Homicides as a Function of Psychopathy." *Journal of Abnormal Psychology* 111 (3): 436.

Young Mark S., and Drew Pinsky. 2006. "Narcissism and Celebrity." *Journal of Research in Personality* 40 (5): 463–71.

I WROTE *THE ART OF THE DEAL* WITH DONALD TRUMP

His Self-Sabotage Is Rooted in His Past

TONY SCHWARTZ

Why does President Trump behave in the dangerous and seemingly self-destructive ways he does?

Three decades ago, I spent nearly a year hanging around Trump to write his first book, *The Art of the Deal*, and got to know him very well. I spent hundreds of hours listening to him, watching him in action, and interviewing him about his life. To me, none of what he has said or done over the past four months as president comes as a surprise. The way he has behaved over the past two weeks—firing FBI director James B. Comey, undercutting his own aides as they tried to explain the decision, disclosing sensitive information to Russian officials, and railing about it all on Twitter—is also entirely predictable.

Early on, I recognized that Trump's sense of self-worth is forever at risk. When he feels aggrieved, he reacts impulsively and defensively, constructing a self-justifying story that doesn't depend on facts and always directs the blame to others.

The Trump I first met in 1985 had lived nearly all his life in survival mode. By his own description, his father, Fred, was relentlessly demanding, difficult, and driven. Here's how I phrased it in *The Art of the Deal*: "My father is a wonderful man, but he is also very much a business guy and strong and tough as hell." As Trump saw it, his older brother, Fred Jr., who became an alcoholic and died at age 42, was overwhelmed by his father. Or as I euphemized it in the book: "There were inevitably confrontations between the two of them. In most cases, Freddy came out on the short end."

Trump's worldview was profoundly and self-protectively shaped by his father. "I was drawn to business very early, and I was never intimidated by my father, the way most people were," is the way I wrote it in the book. "I stood up to him, and he respected that. We had a relationship that was almost businesslike."

To survive, I concluded from our conversations, Trump felt compelled to go to war with the world. It was a binary, zero-sum choice for him: You either dominated or you submitted. You either created and exploited fear, or you succumbed to it—as he thought his older brother had. This narrow, defensive outlook took hold at a very early age, and it never evolved. "When I look at myself in the first grade and I look at myself now," he told a recent biographer, "I'm basically the same." His development essentially ended in early childhood.

Instead, Trump grew up fighting for his life and taking no prisoners. In countless conversations, he made clear to me that he treated every encounter as a contest he had to win, because the only other option from his perspective was to lose, and that was the equivalent of obliteration. Many of the deals in *The Art of the Deal* were massive failures—among them the casinos he owned and the launch of a league to rival the National Football League—but Trump had me describe each of them as a huge success.

With evident pride, Trump explained to me that he was "an assertive, aggressive" kid from an early age, and that he had once punched a music teacher in the eye and was nearly expelled from elementary school for his behavior.

Like so much about Trump, who knows whether that story is

true? What's clear is that he has spent his life seeking to dominate others, whatever that requires and whatever collateral damage it creates along the way. In *The Art of the Deal*, he speaks with street-fighting relish about competing in the world of New York real estate: They are "some of the sharpest, toughest, and most vicious people in the world. I happen to love to go up against these guys, and I love to beat them." I never sensed from Trump any guilt or contrition about anything he'd done, and he certainly never shared any misgivings publicly. From his perspective, he operated in a jungle full of predators who were forever out to get him, and he did what he must to survive.

Trump was equally clear with me that he didn't value—nor even necessarily recognize—the qualities that tend to emerge as people grow more secure, such as empathy, generosity, reflectiveness, the capacity to delay gratification, or, above all, a conscience, an inner sense of right and wrong. Trump simply didn't traffic in emotions or interest in others. The life he lived was all transactional, all the time. Having never expanded his emotional, intellectual, or moral universe, he has his story down, and he's sticking to it.

A key part of that story is that facts are whatever Trump deems them to be on any given day. When he is challenged, he instinctively doubles down—even when what he has just said is demonstrably false. I saw that countless times, whether it was as trivial as exaggerating the number of floors at Trump Tower or as consequential as telling me that his casinos were performing well when they were actually going bankrupt. In the same way, Trump would see no contradiction at all in changing his story about why he fired Comey and thereby undermining the statements of his aides, or in any other lie he tells. His aim is never accuracy; it's domination.

The Trump I got to know had no deep ideological beliefs, nor any passionate feeling about anything but his immediate self-interest. He derives his sense of significance from conquests and accomplishments. "Can you believe it, Tony?" he would often say at the start of late-night conversations with me, going on to describe some new example of his brilliance. But the reassurance he got from even his biggest achievements was always ephemeral and unreliable—and that appears to include being elected president. Any addiction has a predictable pattern: the addict keeps chasing the high by upping the ante in an increasingly futile attempt to re-create the desired state. On the face of it, Trump has more opportunities now to feel significant and accomplished than almost any other human being on the planet. But that's like saying a heroin addict has his problem licked once he has free and continuous access to the drug. Trump also now has a far bigger and more public stage on which to fail and to feel unworthy.

From the very first time I interviewed him in his office in Trump Tower in 1985, the image I had of Trump was that of a black hole. Whatever goes in quickly disappears without a trace. Nothing sustains. It's forever uncertain when someone or something will throw Trump off his precarious perch—when his sense of equilibrium will be threatened and he'll feel an overwhelming compulsion to restore it. Beneath his bluff exterior, I always sensed a hurt, incredibly vulnerable little boy who just wanted to be loved.

What Trump craves most deeply is the adulation he has found so fleeting. This goes a long way toward explaining his need for control and why he simply couldn't abide Comey, who reportedly refused to accede to Trump's demand for loyalty and whose continuing investigation into Russian interference in the election campaign last year threatens to bring down his presidency. Trump's need for unquestioning praise and flattery also helps to explain his hostility to democracy and to a free press—both of which thrive on open dissent.

As we have seen countless times during the campaign and since the election, Trump can devolve into survival mode on a moment's notice. Look no further than the thousands of tweets he has written attacking his perceived enemies over the past year. In neurochemical terms, when he feels threatened or thwarted, Trump moves into a fight-or-flight state. His amygdala is triggered, his hypothalamic-pituitary-adrenal axis activates, and his prefrontal cortex—the part of the brain that makes us capable of rationality and reflection—shuts down. He reacts rather than reflects, and damn the consequences. This is what makes his access to the nuclear codes so dangerous and frightening.

Over the past week, in the face of criticism from nearly every quarter, Trump's distrust has almost palpably mushroomed. No importuning by his advisers stands a chance of constraining him when he is this deeply triggered. The more he feels at the mercy of forces he cannot control—and he is surely feeling that now—the more resentful, desperate, and impulsive he becomes.

Even 30 years later, I vividly remember the ominous feeling when Trump got angry about some perceived slight. Everyone around him knew that you were best off keeping your distance at those times, or, if that wasn't possible, that you should resist disagreeing with him in any way.

In the hundreds of Trump's phone calls I listened in on with his consent, and the dozens of meetings I attended with him, I can never remember anyone disagreeing with him about anything. The same climate of fear and paranoia appears to have taken root in his White House.

The most recent time I spoke to Trump—and the first such occasion in nearly three decades—was July 14, 2016, shortly before *The New Yorker* published an article by Jane Mayer about my experience writing *The Art of the Deal*. Trump was just about to win the Republican nomination for president. I was driving in my car when my cell phone rang. It was Trump. He had just gotten off a call with a fact-checker for *The New Yorker*, and he didn't mince words.

"I just want to tell you that I think you're very disloyal," he started in. Then he berated and threatened me for a few minutes. I pushed back, gently but firmly. And then, suddenly, as abruptly as he began the call, he ended it. "Have a nice life," he said, and hung up.

Tony Schwartz is the author of several books, including The Art of the Deal, *which he coauthored with Mr. Trump. He also wrote* The Power of Full Engagement: Managing Energy, Not Time *(with Jim Loehr) and* The Way We're Working Isn't Working, *a* New York Times *and* Wall Street Journal *bestseller. He is also CEO and founder of The Energy Project, a consulting firm that helps individuals and organizations solve intractable problems and add more value in the world by widening their worldview.*

TRUMP'S TRUST DEFICIT IS THE CORE PROBLEM

GAIL SHEEHY, PH.D.

The narcissism and paranoia are issues, but the biggest concern is that Donald Trump trusts no one. This will be his downfall—or maybe ours.

In a world spinning radically out of control, can we trust President Trump to rely on his famous "instincts" as he alienates U.S. allies and plays brinksmanship with our enemies? Writing from the perspective of his first one hundred days, and from a year and a half of reporting on the president-elect, I can't help worrying how much closer the day of reckoning has to come on charges of collusion with Russia before he needs a war to provide the ultimate distraction?

The fundamental bedrock of human development is the formation of a capacity to trust, absorbed by children between birth and eighteen months. Donald Trump has boasted of his total lack of trust: "People are too trusting. I'm a very untrusting guy" (1990). "Hire the best people, and don't trust them" (2007). "The world is a vicious and brutal place. Even your friends are out to get you: they want your job, your money, your wife" (2007).

His biographers have recorded his worldview as saturated with a sense of danger and his need to project total toughness. As we know, his father trained him to be a "killer," the only alternative to being a "loser." Trump has never forgotten the primary lesson he learned from his father and at the military school to which he was sent to be toughened up still further. In Trump's own words, "Man is the most vicious of all animals, and life is a series of battles ending in victory or defeat."

In the biography *Never Enough*, Trump describes to Michael D'Antonio his father's "dragging him" around tough neighborhoods in Brooklyn when he collected the rents for the apartments he owned. Fred Trump always told the boy to stand to one side of the door. Donald asked why. "Because sometimes they shoot right through the door," his father told him.

Today, this man lives mostly alone in the White House, without a wife or any friends in whom to confide, which he would never do anyway, because that would require admitting vulnerability.

Leon Panetta, former CIA director and defense chief under Clinton, stated on Fox Business channel in February 2017, "The coin of the realm for any president is trust—trust of the American people in the credibility of that president." In the nearly two years that Donald Trump has been in our face almost daily, he has sown mistrust in all his Republican rivals, alienated much of the conservative Republican bloc he needs in the House for legislative success, ignored congressional Democrats, and viciously insulted Democratic leaders, calling them liars, clowns, stupid, and incompetent, and condemning Barack Obama as "sick" and Hillary Clinton as "the devil." When he represents the American people abroad, his belligerent behavior and disrespect for leaders of our closest allies rips apart the comity and peace-keeping pledges built over decades. Yet, he never hesitates to congratulate despots, such as Turkey's Erdogan, Egypt's General Sisi, and, most lavishly of all, Russia's Putin.

As president, Trump is systematically shredding trust in the institutions he now commands. Having discredited the entire seventeen-agency intelligence community as acting like Nazis, he also dismissed the judiciary because of one judge's Hispanic background and another's opposition to his travel [née Muslim] ban. Even his Supreme Court justice, Neil Gorsuch, said it was "disheartening" and "demoralizing" to hear Trump disparage the judiciary. Not content to smear the media on a daily basis, Trump borrowed a phrase used by Lenin and Stalin to brand the American media as an "enemy of the people."

By his own words, Trump operates on the assumption that everyone is out to get him. The nonmedical definition of paranoia is the tendency toward excessive or irrational suspiciousness and distrustfulness of others. For a man who proclaims his distrust of everyone, it is not surprising that Trump drew closest to him two legendary conspiracy theorists: Stephen Bannon and Gen. Michael Flynn.

And even after he was forced to fire his choice for top national security adviser after Flynn blatantly lied, Trump's White House desperately stonewalled congressional investigators to keep them from getting their hands on documents that could prove Flynn's paid collusion with Russia on Trump's behalf. The closer that case comes to a criminal referral to the Justice Department, the closer Trump's survival instincts will propel him to a wag-the-dog war.

A leader who does not trust his subordinates cannot inspire trust. Though Trump boasts of fierce personal loyalty, he himself is loyal only until he isn't. Among his anxious aides, only Jared Kushner, it seems, may be safe, deputized as Trump's de facto secretary of state. Where Trump succeeds in inspiring trust is by giving his subordinates the license to lie. In fact, this virus of licentiousness has spread from the White House to congressional Republicans, to wit the stunt that exposed Rep. Devin Nunes as unfit to lead the House Intelligence Committee probe into Trump operatives' possible collusion with Russia. As the chaos of the White House rolled with a crisis-a-day fever into the month of May, a hide-and-seek commander in chief began sending out his most trusted national security advisers to defend him (Gen. James "Mad Dog" Mattis, Gen. H. R. McMaster, and the muted secretary of state, Rex Tillerson) and then cut the legs out from under them with his own blurted half-truths.

We hear repeatedly that Trump as a manager likes chaos. I asked a deputy White House counsel under Obama, a decorated former officer in Iraq and former White House counsel to President Obama, how such a management style impacts trust. "Trump explicitly or implicitly manages the situation so it's never possible for his advisers to know where they stand," he said. "It's the opposite of what you want in a high-functioning organization." Trump's anxious aides must know just how easy it is to fail his loyalty test, or to be the fall guy if a scapegoat is needed. While publicly they may defend him, it is clear to reporters that White House staffers are leaking information constantly. The leaks can only exacerbate Trump's mistrust, perpetuating a vicious circle.

His failure to trust or to inspire trust is even more dangerous on a global scale. He sees alliances such as NATO as suspect (until he changes his mind); he sees trade agreements such as NAFTA as ripping off America (until he changes his mind three or four times in the same week). "This is because Trump's worldview is that we live in a snake pit where everybody is out for themselves," observes the former White House counsel. He and his co-conspiracy theorist adviser Bannon take everything that the left-behind white working class hates about globalization and they turn it into personalized enemies: Muslims, Mexicans, and refugees whom they believe are taking away their jobs. "Those people aren't like us," is the alt-right message; "they're polluting our culture."

In the course of his first one hundred days, Trump appeared to be increasingly out of touch with the reality in which the majority of us live. His pathological propensity to lie is not the worst of it—his monomaniacal attachment to his lies is, such as the transparent one in his March 4 twitterstorm accusing President Obama of putting a tap on his phone. It raises the question: Is this president floating in his own alternate reality?

When I attended Dr. Bandy Lee's Yale town hall meeting to write about it for *The Daily Beast*, I cited insights delivered there by two of the authors in this book. Dr. Robert Jay Lifton, the eminent former professor of psychiatry at Yale University and today at Columbia University, elaborated in a follow-up interview, "Trump creates his own extreme manipulation of reality. He insists that his spokesmen defend his false reality as normal. He then expects the rest of society to accept it—despite the lack of any evidence." This leads to what Lifton calls "malignant normality"—in other words, the gradual acceptance by a public inundated with toxic untruths of those untruths until they pass for normal.

Dr. James F. Gilligan is a psychiatrist and author who has studied the motivations behind violent behavior over his twenty-five years of work in the American prison systems. "If we psychiatrists who have experience in assessing dangerousness, if we give passive permission to our president to proceed in his delusions, we are shirking our responsibility," Gilligan said. Today a senior clinical professor of psychiatry at NYU School of Medicine, Gilligan told Dr. Lee's town hall attendees, "I don't say Trump is Hitler or Mussolini, but he's no more normal than Hitler."

We don't have to rely on psychiatrists to see that this president is not consistent in his thinking or reliably attached to reality. We have had vastly more exposure to Donald Trump's observable behavior, his writing and speaking, than any psychiatrist would have after listening to him for years. It is therefore up to us, the American public, to call him on it. And some of the most experienced hands in and around the White House are doing so.

Presidential historian Douglas Brinkley believes that Donald Trump represents a very different subculture from any commander in chief. "He represents the New York building business—where you don't let your right hand know what your left hand is doing," says Brinkley. "In Trump's world, he must win at all costs. It's not about character or public service or looking out for your band of brothers."

The president to whom Trump is most often compared is Richard Nixon. John Dean, the famous White House counsel who testified against his fellow conservative Republican, compared Trump to that notably paranoid president. "Nixon was two personae—in public and with his top aides, he was trusted. But in private, his deeply paranoid and vengeful dark side came out."

Asked for the best example, Dean snapped, "He had zero empathy!" Just like Trump. "Nixon let twenty-two thousand more Americans die in Vietnam [after he sabotaged the 1968 Paris peace talks], plus who knows how many Cambodians and Laotians and Vietnamese, all to ensure his election." It took forty years before Nixon's worst crime was revealed: treason. That was when then-presidential candidate Nixon was heard on tape (from recordings ordered by President Johnson) scuttling the Vietnam peace talks to derail the reelection campaign of the Democratic candidate. Nixon sent a message to the South Vietnamese negotiators that they should withdraw from the peace talks and wait for him to be elected, at which point he would give them a much better deal.

Sound familiar? Fifty years later, Donald Trump's go-between with Russian officials, General Flynn, hinted to Putin's ambassador that Russia could get a much better deal if it didn't retaliate against Obama's sanctions and instead sat tight until Trump was elected. Also, Trump frequently tweeted about his eagerness to lift those sanctions—that is, until his fantasy bromance with Putin looked like it could arouse a federal investigation. Trump's appetite for vengeance is also matched by Nixon's with his long "Enemies List." No two modern presidents have had a more serious case of "political hemophilia," in the phrase of the latest Nixon biographer, John Farrell, by which he means: "Once wounded, these men never stop bleeding."

To the dismay of even conservative observers, Trump appears totally indifferent to the truth. *Time* magazine gave Trump an opportunity to clarify his refusal to correct his long string of falsehoods. What the March 23 interview produced instead was an astonishing revelation of his thinking: He states what he wants to be true. If his statement is proven false, he is unfazed, and confidently predicts that the facts will catch up with his belief: "I'm a very instinctual person, but my instinct turns out to be right." Even when the top sleuth in the country, FBI director James Comey, condemned Trump as a fabulist, Trump ignored the public rebuke and bragged about his ability to persuade millions of his paranoid version of Obama as "sick" and surreptitiously spying on him.

"Narcissistic people like Trump want more than anything to love themselves, but desperately want others to love them, too," wrote professor and chair of the Psychology Department at Northwestern University, Dan P. McAdams, in *The Atlantic*. "The fundamental goal in life for a narcissist is to promote the greatness of the self, for all to see."

Yet, what is an extreme narcissistic personality such as Trump to do when he fails to win glorification? "Trump, from his own writings, has shown massive hypersensitivity to shame or humiliation," says Dr. Gilligan. Yet, how does he dodge the humiliation when he is exposed as sacrificing the nation's security on the altar of his infantile need to impress Russian officials by giving away sensitive foreign intelligence?

Beneath the grandiose behavior of every narcissist lies the pit of fragile self-esteem. What if, deep down, the person whom Trump trusts least is himself? The humiliation of being widely exposed as a "loser," unable to bully through the actions he promised during the campaign, could drive him to prove he is, after all, a "killer." In only the first four months of his presidency, he teed up for starting a war in three places, Syria, Afghanistan, and North Korea. It is up to Congress, backed up by the public, to restrain him.

Gail Sheehy, Ph.D., as author, journalist, and popular lecturer, has changed the way millions of women and men around the world look at their life stages. In her fifty-year career, she has written seventeen books, including her revolutionary Passages, *named one of the ten most influential books of our times. As a literary journalist, she was one of the original contributors to* New York *magazine and, since 1984, has written for* Vanity Fair. *A winner of many awards, three honorary doctorates, a Lifetime Achievement Award in 2012 by Books for a Better Life, she has regularly commented on political figures, including in her acclaimed biography of Hillary Clinton,* Hillary's Choice.

SOCIOPATHY

LANCE DODES, M.D.

"Crazy like a fox or just crazy?" This question has surrounded Donald Trump since his campaign for president. The question is whether a person who is repetitively immoral—who cons others, lies, cheats, and manipulates to get what he wants, doesn't care whom he hurts just as long as he is gratifying himself—whether such a person's indifference to the feelings of others for personal gain is just being clever: crazy like a fox. Or are these actions a sign of something much more serious? Could they be expressions of significant mental derangement?

The answer to that question is emphatically, "Yes." To understand why, it's necessary to understand the psychological condition called "sociopathy," and why sociopathy is such a severe disturbance.

Caring for others and trying not to harm them is a fundamental quality of not just humans, but many mammals. Normal people, as well as normal wolves, dolphins, and elephants, appreciate when another of their species is in pain or danger and, unless fighting over territory or sexual partners, react to protect one another. Such caring and cooperation has major survival value for any species, and its clear evolutionary advantages have made these qualities basic across much of the animal kingdom. In humans, the ability to sense the feelings of one another, care about one another, and try to avoid harming one another even to the extent of placing ourselves at a disadvantage (think of animals that will stand all together to protect against a threat) is called empathy. It is a characteristic of all people no matter what individual emotional conflicts and issues they have. Unless they are sociopaths.

The failure of normal empathy is central to sociopathy, which is marked by an absence of guilt, intentional manipulation, and controlling or even sadistically harming others for personal power or gratification. People with sociopathic traits have a flaw in the basic nature of human beings. Far from being clever like a fox, they are lacking an essential part of being human. This is why sociopathy is among the most severe mental disturbances.

Yet, we are a culture that admires external success in wealth and power, regardless of how it is achieved. People with sociopathic qualities who are able to achieve high status and power precisely because of their manipulations and cheating are, therefore, sometimes seen as not only psychologically healthy, but superior. This contributes to the confusion: "How crazy can someone be who is so successful?" It has even been said that Mr. Trump couldn't possibly have serious mental problems because he got to be president.

Indeed, there are generally two life paths for people with severe sociopathy. Those who are unskilled at manipulating and hurting others, who are not careful in choosing their victims, who are unable to act charming well enough to fool people, have lives that often end in failure. They are identified as criminals or lose civil court battles to those they've cheated, or are unable to threaten their way back to positions of power. But those who are good at manipulation, at appearing charming and caring, at concealing their immoral or illegal behavior, and can bully their way to the top, do not end up as outcasts or in prison. There is a term for these people: "successful sociopaths." They are the ones who most fool others into thinking they are "crazy like a fox." Even their characteristic rages may appear almost normal. Instead of having a visible tantrum, they may simply fire people, or sue them. As their power increases, their ability to disguise their mental disturbance may also increase, concealed behind a wall of underlings who do the dirty work, or armies of lawyers who threaten those who are currently seen as the enemy. What is important to understand is that their success is on the outside. They are no different from those who are less skilled at concealing their lack of empathy, even if they require an expert to recognize them. They are still severely emotionally ill.

Diagnostic Labels

The word "sociopathy" is sometimes used interchangeably with "psychopathy," though some have defined the words a bit differently. Sociopathy is also a major aspect of the term, "malignant narcissism," and is roughly synonymous with the official (Diagnostic and Statistical Manual, or DSM) psychiatric diagnostic term, "antisocial personality disorder." All refer to a disturbance in an individual's entire emotional makeup (hence the term "personality" disorder in the DSM).

A label can never capture everything about a person, though. This may create diagnostic confusion if laypersons expect any individual to fit exactly into their conception of the problem. Cold-blooded murderers and cruel, sadistic rulers may treat their pets kindly, for instance. Consequently, it is the *traits* of sociopathy that are important to recognize in order to evaluate anyone or assess his fitness to hold a position of power. This is, in fact, the way the DSM does it. Each label has a set of observable behaviors that define it, and these groupings change often. We are now on the fifth version of the DSM, and there will be many more to come as knowledge, understanding, and even diagnostic fads change. Traits, however, are fixed. Therefore, in assessing whether a person is "sociopathic," what we really need to know is whether he has the observable, definitive traits that indicate the condition.

Without being concerned about a formal diagnostic label, it's useful to consider the traits of antisocial personality disorder as defined in the current DSM:

A pervasive pattern of disregard for and violation of the rights of others, occurring since age 15 years, as indicated by three (or more) of the following:

1. Failure to conform to social norms with respect to lawful behaviors;
2. Deceitfulness, as indicated by repeated lying . . . or conning others for personal profit or pleasure;
3. Impulsivity or failure to plan ahead;
4. Irritability and aggressiveness, as indicated by repeated physical fights or assaults;
5. Reckless disregard for safety of self or others;
6. Consistent irresponsibility, as indicated by repeated failure to sustain consistent work behavior or honor financial obligations;
7. Lack of remorse, as indicated by being indifferent to or rationalizing having hurt, mistreated, or stolen from another; and
8. Evidence of conduct disorder [impulsive, aggressive, callous, or deceitful behavior that is persistent and difficult to deter with threats or punishment] with onset before age 15 years.

Other systems of diagnosis use different words for the essential sociopathic traits: *sadistic*, unempathic, cruel, devaluing, immoral, primitive, callous, predatory, bullying, dehumanizing.

The term "primitive" as a descriptor of sociopathic traits de-

serves special attention. The word derives not from ancient historical times, but from ancient personal times: the early years of life. It
helps to explain why there is a multiplicity of defects in these people.

In early development, everything is happening at once. Major
emotional capacities are developing alongside major cognitive capacities. Children must develop ways to manage emotional distress:
anxiety, confusion, disappointment, loss, fear, all while they are
growing in their capacity to think, and sorting out what is real and
what is their imagination. We all develop systems to do this, to tolerate and control our emotions, understand and empathize with the
people around us, and tell the difference between reality and wishes
or fears.

But not people with the early, primitive emotional problems
seen in sociopathy. They do not tolerate disappointments; instead,
they fly into rages and claim that the upsetting reality isn't real. They
make up an alternative reality and insist that it is true. This is the
definition of a delusion. When it is told to others, it is basically a
lie. As described earlier, successful sociopaths may not look very
"crazy," but this capacity to lose touch with reality shows up when
they are stressed by criticism or disappointment. Later, when they
are less stressed, they explain their loss of reality with rationalizations or simply more lies.

The primitive nature of people with sociopathic traits can also
be seen through the findings of brain research. In early life, along
with its psychological developments, the brain is developing physically. It is notable that people with sociopathic traits have been found
to have abnormalities in the prefrontal cortex and the amygdala regions of their brains, areas closely associated with essential cognitive and emotional functions.

Psychological Mechanisms in Sociopathy

People with sociopathic traits employ specific abnormal emotional
mechanisms. Primary among these is "projective identification."

"Projection" by itself refers to a belief that others have feelings or thoughts which are actually in the mind of the individual doing the projecting. Commonly, these are aggressive and dangerous feelings, which are managed by being projected to others, who are then seen as aggressive and dangerous. When this process occurs regularly, it is simply called paranoia. "Projective identification" is the most serious version of paranoia. The "identification" part of the term refers to seeing others not just as having threatening characteristics, but as entirely dangerous people—people who have to be attacked or destroyed.

This psychological mechanism contributes to loss of reality, rage outbursts, and attacks on others. When it is combined with a lack of empathy and its corresponding lack of guilt for harming others, the danger from such people is enormous.

Projective identification is not the only defective psychological mechanism in sociopaths. Because of the incapacity to realistically appraise (or care for) people, others are alternately seen as evil or good, according to the projection in use at the moment. The sociopath may treat people as though they are great friends, charmingly complimenting them on how wonderful they are, then abruptly turn on them as the enemy. Loyalty is highly prized by sociopaths because it serves their personal ends, but there is no real relationship. Dividing the world into good and bad in an unstable, fluctuating way is called "splitting."

Although sociopathy always means a lack of empathy, there is one way in which severe sociopaths do have a certain, frightening type of empathy. It is the empathy of the predator. A tiger stalking his prey must have an ability to sense the prey's fear, or at least to be aware of the small signs of that fear (Malancharuvil 2012). The tiger is "empathic" with its prey, but not sympathetic or caring. Successful sociopaths are like that. They are closely attuned to their victim's emotional state. Does the victim buy what the sociopath is selling? Does he need false reassurance, a compliment on his intelligence or appearance, a lying promise, or a friendly gesture to keep him thinking the sociopath is honorable? The successful sociopath's predatory "empathy" reflects a definite perceptive acumen, making him a genius at manipulation. When this works, it produces a disastrous trust in him. Yet, like the tiger, he is unconcerned about the welfare of his target.

The pathological emotional problems in sociopathy make one another worse. An inability to have a consistent realistic view of the world, or to maintain emotionally genuine relationships, leads to more paranoia. The weakness in impulse control which arises from enraged reactions to imagined slights and produces reckless, destructive behavior, leads to a greater need to deny criticism with more lies to tell oneself and everyone else, and an increasing distance from reality. The more a sociopath needs to scapegoat others the more he genuinely hates them, making him even more aggressive and sadistic. Life is devoted to endless destruction in the service of an endless quest for power and admiration, unmitigated by basic empathy or guilt.

Donald Trump

Because Mr. Trump has been a very public figure for many years, and because we have been able to hear from many who have known him for a long time, we are in an excellent position to know his behaviors—his speech and actions—which are precisely the basis for making an assessment of his dangerousness, whether we assess him using the official DSM criteria for antisocial personality disorder (APD), as below, or whether we apply our knowledge of malignant narcissism, both of which include the signs and symptoms of sociopathy. Let us consider these in turn.

Lack of Empathy for Others; Lack of Remorse; Lying and Cheating

Mr. Trump's mocking the disability of a handicapped reporter, unconcern for the safety of protesters at a rally ("Get rid of them!"),

sexually assaulting women, threatening physical harm to his opponent in the election (alluding to gun owners eliminating her), repeatedly verbally attacking a family who lost their son fighting for
the country, personally degrading people who criticize him (calling
them insulting names, as he did in both the Republican primaries
and the general election), a history of cheating people he's hired by
not paying them what he owes, creating the now forced-to-disband
Trump University, targeting and terrifying minority groups, all
provide overwhelming evidence of profound sociopathic traits,
which are far more important than trying to assign any specific diagnostic label.

Loss of Reality

Mr. Trump's insistence on the truth of matters proven to be untrue
("alternative facts") is well-known. His insistence has occurred both
repeatedly and over a long time, even when such denial is not in his
interest and it would be better for him to acknowledge that he spoke
in error. He has falsely claimed that President Obama is not an
American and that he wiretapped Mr. Trump's building, that his
own loss in the vote total of the general election was caused by illegal aliens, that he had the largest inauguration crowd in history, etc.
Together, these show a persistent loss of reality.

Rage Reactions and Impulsivity

Mr. Trump's rages have been reported on multiple occasions in the
press, leading to sudden decisions and actions. He fired and subsequently threatened the director of the FBI after hearing him testify
in unwanted ways before Congress, launched more than 50 missiles
within 72 hours of seeing a disturbing image on the news—reversing
his stated Middle East policy, precipitously violated diplomatic
norms, creating international tensions (as with reports of threatening to invade Mexico, hanging up on the prime minister of Australia, antagonizing Germany, France, Greece, and others), issued illegal

executive orders, apparently without vetting them with knowledge-
able attorneys, and so on.

Conclusion

Donald Trump's speech and behavior show that he has severe sociopathic traits. The significance of this cannot be overstated. While
there have surely been American presidents who could be said to
be narcissistic, none have shown sociopathic qualities to the degree
seen in Mr. Trump. Correspondingly, none have been so definitively
and so obviously dangerous.

Democracy requires respect and protection for multiple points
of view, concepts that are incompatible with sociopathy. The need to
be seen as superior, when coupled with lack of empathy or remorse
for harming other people, are in fact the signature characteristics of
tyrants, who seek the control and destruction of all who oppose
them, as well as loyalty to themselves instead of to the country they
lead.

The paranoia of severe sociopathy creates a profound risk of
war, since heads of other nations will inevitably disagree with or
challenge the sociopathic leader, who will experience the disagreement as a personal attack, leading to rage reactions and impulsive
action to destroy this "enemy." A common historical example is the
creation, by sociopathic leaders, of an international incident to have an
excuse to seize more power (suspend constitutional rights, impose
martial law, and discriminate against minority groups). Because
such leaders will lie to others in government and to their citizens,
those who would check the sociopath's power find it difficult to
contradict his claims and actions with facts. Would-be tyrants also
typically devalue a free press, undermining journalists' ability to
inform and resist the move toward war and away from democracy.

Mr. Trump's sociopathic characteristics are undeniable. They
create a profound danger for America's democracy and safety. Over
time these characteristics will only become worse, either because

Mr. Trump will succeed in gaining more power and more grandiosity with less grasp on reality, or because he will engender more criticism producing more paranoia, more lies, and more enraged destruction.

Lance Dodes, M.D., is a Training and Supervising Analyst Emeritus at the Boston Psychoanalytic Society and Institute and retired Assistant Clinical Professor of Psychiatry at Harvard Medical School. He is the author of many academic articles and book chapters describing a new understanding of the nature and treatment of addiction, and three books: The Heart of Addiction; Breaking Addiction; *and* The Sober Truth. *He has been honored by the Division on Addictions at Harvard Medical School for "Distinguished Contribution" to the study and treatment of addictive behavior, and been elected a Distinguished Fellow of the American Academy of Addiction Psychiatry.*

References

Aragno, Anna. 2014. "The Roots of Evil: A Psychoanalytic Inquiry." *Psychoanalytic Review* 101 (2): 249–88.

Malancharuvil, Joseph M. 2012. "Empathy Deficit in Antisocial Personality Disorder: A Psychodynamic Formulation." *American Journal of Psychoanalysis* 72 (3): 242–50.

Watt, Douglas. 2007. "Toward a Neuroscience of Empathy: Integrating Affective and Cognitive Perspectives." *Neuropsychoanalysis* 9 (2): 119–40.

DONALD TRUMP IS:
A) BAD
B) MAD
C) ALL OF THE ABOVE

JOHN D. GARTNER, PH.D.

Donald Trump is so visibly psychologically impaired that it is obvious even to a layman that "something is wrong with him." Still, putting a name to that disturbance has been a challenge for two reasons. First, because of the Goldwater gag order, discussed extensively in Part 2 of this book, which has forced mental health professionals to censor themselves, despite how alarmed they might be; and second, Trump's is a genuinely complex case. Like the story of the blind men and the elephant, many writers have tried to analyze and diagnose Trump, and have gotten pieces of the elephant right. What is missing is the whole elephant. There are *a lot* of things wrong with him—and together, they are a scary witch's brew.

One of the most recurrent debates, and a genuine mystery, is to what extent is Trump just a really bad person and to what extent is he really crazy? Psychoanalyst Steven Reisner has written in *Slate*, "This is not madness. Impulsivity, threats, aggression, ridicule, denial of reality, and the mobilization of the mob that he used to get there [to the presidency] are not symptoms. It is time to call it out for what it is: evil" (Reisner 2017). According to this view, Donald Trump is "crazy like a fox." That is, his abnormal persona is an act, a diabolical plan to manipulate the public's worst instincts for fun, power, and profit.

When Trump tweeted about his imaginary inauguration crowd size and about Obama having tapped his phones, was there any part of him that believed this "denial of reality"? If so, then Michael Tansey ("Why 'Crazy Like a Fox' versus 'Crazy Like a Crazy' *Really* Matters"), who writes here about Trump having delusional disorder, may be right that Trump is not crazy like a fox but "crazy like a crazy."

My old boss Paul McHugh, longtime chairman of psychiatry at Johns Hopkins University School of Medicine, used to say that "a dog can have both ticks and fleas." I will argue that Trump can be both evil *and* crazy, and that unless we see how these two components work together, we will never truly understand him. Nor will we recognize how much danger we are in.

Bad: Malignant Narcissism

"The quintessence of evil" was how Erich Fromm (1964) described *malignant narcissism*, a term he introduced in the 1960s. Fromm, a refugee from Nazi Germany, developed the diagnosis to explain Hitler. While Fromm is most well known as one of the founders of humanistic psychology (whose basic premise, ironically, is that man's basic nature is good), the Holocaust survivor had a lifelong obsession with the psychology of evil. Malignant narcissism was, according to Fromm, "the most severe pathology. The root of the most vicious destructiveness and inhumanity."

The modern figure most associated with the study of malignant narcissism is my former teacher Otto Kernberg (1970), who defined the syndrome as having four components: (1) narcissistic personality disorder, (2) antisocial behavior, (3) paranoid traits, and (4) sadism. Kernberg told the *New York Times* that malignantly narcissistic leaders such as Hitler and Stalin are "able to take control because their inordinate narcissism is expressed in grandiosity, a confidence in themselves, and the assurance that they know what the world needs" (Goode 2003). At the same time, "they express their aggression in cruel and sadistic behavior against their enemies: whoever does not submit to them or love them." As Pollock (1978) wrote, "the malignant narcissist is pathologically grandiose, lacking in conscience and behavioral regulation[,] with characteristic demonstrations of joyful cruelty and sadism."

Much has been written in the press about Trump having narcissistic personality disorder. Yet, as critics have pointed out, merely being narcissistic is hardly disqualifying. However, normal narcissism and malignant narcissism have about as much in common as a benign and malignant tumor. The latter is far rarer, more pathological and dangerous, and, more often than not, terminal. It's the difference between life and death.

Narcissism

Narcissistic personality disorder is described in this book by Craig Malkin ("Pathological Narcissism and Politics: A Lethal Mix"). Trump finds himself to be uniquely superior ("Only I can fix it"), and appears to believe that he knows more than everyone about everything, despite his lack of experience, study, intellectual curiosity, or normal attention span. Since he took office, an amusing video montage has made its way through social media in which, in the course of three minutes, Trump brags about being the world's greatest expert in twenty different subject areas. "No one knows more about [fill in the blank] than me," he repeats over and over.

Antisocial Personality Disorder

In his piece in this book, Lance Dodes describes antisocial personality disorder, or "Sociopathy." Antisocials lie, exploit, and violate the rights of others, and they have neither remorse nor empathy for those they harm.

While we will not give a final diagnosis here, the fact-checking website PolitiFact estimated that 76 percent of Trump's statements were false or mostly false (Holan and Qui 2015), and *Politico* estimated that Trump told a lie every three minutes and fifteen seconds (Cheney et al. 2016).

We have ample evidence of Trump's pervasive pattern of exploiting and violating the rights of others. According to New York State attorney general Eric Schneiderman, Trump University was a "straight up fraud . . . a fraud from beginning to end" (Gass 2016). Also, dozens of lawsuits attest to Trump's pattern and practice of not paying his contractors. Finally, there is Trump's pattern of serial sexual assault, which he bragged about on tape even before a dozen women came forward, whom he then called liars.

Trump is allergic to apology and appears to feel no remorse of any kind. It is as if being Trump means never having to say you're sorry. When political consultant Frank Luntz asked Trump if he had ever asked God for forgiveness, Trump said, "I'm not sure I have . . . I don't think so" (Scott 2015). His unrepentance notwithstanding, he also boasted that he had "a great relationship with God."

And empathy? Even Trump's former mentor, the notorious Roy Cohn, lawyer for gangsters and Joseph McCarthy, said that when it came to his feelings for his fellow human beings, Trump "pisses ice water" (Lange 2016).

Paranoia

Paranoia is not a diagnosis but, rather, a trait that we see in some conditions. When Donald Trump was asked to document his false claim that "thousands and thousands" of New Jersey Muslims openly celebrated the attacks of 9/11, he cited a link to Infowars, the website of radio talk show host Alex Jones. Jones, nicknamed "the king of conspiracies," believes that the American government was behind the September 11 attacks, that FEMA is setting up concentration camps, and that the Sandy Hook school shooting was a hoax. Yet, according to Trump, Jones is one of the few media personalities he trusts. "Your reputation is amazing," Trump told Jones when he appeared as a guest on Jones's show on December 2, 2015. Trump vowed that if he were elected president, "you will find out who really knocked down the World Trade Center."

In the same week, both the *New York Times* (Haberman 2016) and the *Washington Post* (*Washington Post* Editorial Board 2016) ran front-page stories on Trump as a conspiracy theorist. Before the election, Right Wing Watch (Tashman 2016) accumulated a list of fifty-eight conspiracies that Trump had proclaimed or implied were true. Of course, that list has grown since then. Many are truly bizarre. For example, not only is Obama a Muslim born in Kenya but, according to Trump, he had a Hawaiian government bureaucrat murdered to cover up the truth about his birth certificate ("How amazing, the state health director who verified copies of Obama's birth certificate died in a plane crash today. All others lived," Trump said); Antonin Scalia was murdered ("[T]hey say they found a pillow on his face, which is a pretty unusual place to find a pillow"); later, fake news websites sponsored by the Russians laid this "murder" at Hillary's feet; and Ted Cruz's father aided the Kennedy assassination, the mother of all conspiracy theories ("What was he doing with Lee Harvey Oswald shortly before the death? Before the shooting? It's horrible").

And still the world was shocked when Trump accused Barack Obama of illegally wiretapping Trump Tower. Why were we surprised?

When you combine these three ingredients, narcissism, antisocial traits, and paranoia, you get a leader who feels omnipotent, omniscient, and entitled to total power; and who rages at being persecuted by imaginary enemies, including vulnerable minority groups who actually represent no threat whatsoever. With such a leader, all who are not part of the in-group or who fail to kiss the leader's ring are enemies who must be destroyed.

Sadism

Because he is a sadist, the malignant narcissist will take a bully's glee in persecuting, terrorizing, and even exterminating his "enemies" and scapegoats. When a protester was escorted out of a Trump rally, Trump famously said, "I'd like to punch him in the face," in a tone that suggested it would genuinely bring him great pleasure. Narcissists often hurt others in the pursuit of their selfish interests:

> A notable difference between normal narcissistic personality disorder and malignant narcissism is the feature of sadism, or the gratuitous enjoyment of the pain of others. A narcissist will deliberately damage other people in pursuit of their own selfish desires, but may regret and will in some circumstances show remorse for doing so, while a malignant narcissist will harm others and enjoy doing so, showing little empathy or regret for the damage they have caused.

We often see Trump "punch down," demeaning and humiliating people weaker than he. In fact, a substantial portion of the thirty-four thousand tweets he has sent since he joined Twitter can be described as cyberbullying. Sometimes he will send the same nasty tweet six times across a day's news cycle in order to maximally humiliate his victim.

Erich Fromm saw evil up close, thought about it throughout his life, and applied his genius to boil it down to its psychological essence. A malignant narcissist is a human monster. He may not be as bad as Hitler, but according to Fromm, he is cut from the same cloth. "The Egyptian Pharaohs, the Roman Caesars, the Borgias, Hitler, Stalin, Trujillo—they all show certain similar features," Fromm writes.

Malignant narcissism is a psychiatric disorder that makes you evil. What's scary is that's not even the worst of it.

Mad

Before the 2016 election, I wrote an article for the *Huffington Post* (Gartner 2016) warning about Trump. At that point, in June 2016, there was still a strong hope that Trump would "pivot" and become more presidential—a hope based on the assumption that while he might be a wicked opportunist and a con man, he was still a rational actor, and thus would change tack when it was in his own best interest. I wrote, "[T]he idea that Trump is going to settle down and become presidential when he achieves power is wishful thinking. Success emboldens malignant narcissists to become even more grandiose, reckless and aggressive. Sure enough, after winning the nomination, there has been no 'pivot' towards more reasonable behavior and ideas, just the opposite. He has become more shrill, combative, and openly racist." After riding his angry base to the White House, to alter his behavior to a saner presentation after the election would have been in Trump's best interest. As Rob Reiner put it on *Real Time with Bill Maher*, "People don't understand why Trump doesn't just stop acting mentally ill? Why can't he just stop being mentally ill?" Why? Because his illness is not a ruse. It can't just be turned off when it's convenient.

According to Fromm, "malignant narcissism is a madness that tends to grow in the life of the afflicted person." In *The Heart of Man*, Fromm argues that malignant narcissism "lies on the borderline between sanity and insanity." In more benign forms of narcissism, "being related to reality curbs the narcissism and keeps it within bounds," but the malignant narcissist recognizes no such boundaries. His grandiose fantasy trumps reality.

The thing that distinguishes the malignant narcissistic leader from a run-of-the-mill psychotic patient is his power to coerce and seduce others to share his grandiose and persecutory delusions.

"This Caesarian madness would be nothing but plain insanity," Fromm writes, "were it not for one factor: by his power Caesar has bent reality to his narcissistic fantasies. He has forced everyone to agree he is god, the most powerful and wisest of men—hence his megalomania seems to be a reasonable feeling."

According to Fromm's description of the disorder, Trump lives on the border of psychosis. Does he ever go over the border? Is it all for effect, to rile up his base, deflect blame, and distract from his shortcomings, or does Trump actually believe the crazy things he says? If you take Donald Trump's words literally, you would have to conclude that he is psychotic.

A delusion is technically defined as a "rigidly held, demonstrably false belief, which is impervious to any contradictory facts." Is he "crazy like a fox," asks Michael Tansey (2017b), or simply "crazy like a crazy?" With Trump, it's often genuinely difficult to know, but as Tansey makes frighteningly clear, this is not a trivial academic distinction. Literally, the fate of the entire world may depend on the answer:

> Surpassing the devastation of climate, health care, education, diplomacy, social services, freedom of speech, liberty, and justice for all, nothing is more incomprehensible than the now-plausible prospect of all-out nuclear war ... Because of this existential threat, it is absolutely urgent that we understand the differences between a president who is merely "crazy like a fox" (shrewd, calculating, the truth is only spoken when it happens to coincide with one's purposes) versus what I have termed "crazy like a crazy" (well-hidden-core grandiose and paranoid delusions that are disconnected from reality). (Tansey 2017b)

Insight into this question comes from, of all sources, Joe Scarborough, host of the popular MSNBC show *Morning Joe*. After Trump claimed that Trump Tower had been bugged by Barack Obama, Scarborough tweeted, "His tweets this weekend suggest the president is not crazy like a fox. Just crazy."

Some of Trump's false claims can be seen as giving him a perverse strategic advantage. For example, his claim that Obama was not born in the United States appealed to the racist portion of the electorate who were already inclined to see a black president as foreign and illegitimate. Other false statements of his seem more blatantly crazy, precisely because they offer him no discernible strategic advantage. Take his false claim that he had the biggest inaugural crowd in history. On the first day of his presidency, he lost credibility with the entire world with that demonstrably false claim—as Groucho Marx said, "Who are you going to believe, me or your lying eyes?"—when there was no longer any need to motivate his base, which was already ecstatically celebrating his inauguration. He needed to broaden his base and shore up his authority as president, but did the opposite.

On *Morning Joe* on April 3, Joe Scarborough and Donny Deutsch, both of whom had known Trump personally for over a decade, came to two conclusions: first, that Trump must suffer from a mental illness, because his behavior since ascending to the presidency had been so irrationally self-destructive; and second, that Trump had gotten dramatically worse since he was inaugurated.

> **Scarborough:** People, stop tweeting at me "How could you not have known?" We've known this guy for ten, eleven, twelve years. We had misgivings, but it's safe to say neither you [Donny Deutsch] nor I thought it would be this bad. We were concerned. Really, really concerned, but never thought this guy would be this much of a petulant brat. We didn't think he would wake up every day and hit his hand with a hammer.

Deutsch: I also think it's time. I know the psychiatric community has the Goldwater rule about not diagnosing from a distance. I just think he's not a well guy. Period.

Scarborough: During the campaign, he would do things that were offensive to us [that energized his base], but that's not like hitting your hand with a hammer. What he's doing now is *not* in his self-interest. Then you start saying how well is he [pointing to his own head] when he's doing things that any sane rational person would know would hurt him politically?

For these same reasons, Michael Tansey suggests that Trump may meet DSM-V criteria for delusional disorder, which require evidence of a delusion lasting longer than a month in the absence of a more serious psychotic disorder such as schizophrenia or bipolar disorder type 1, which would in themselves explain the presence of delusional thinking.

Trump doesn't show signs of being schizophrenic, but we should explore where he fits on the bipolar spectrum. He definitely has the hypomanic temperament I wrote about in my two books, *The Hypomanic Edge: The Link Between (a Little) Craziness and (a Lot) of Success in America* (2005) and *In Search of Bill Clinton: A Psychological Biography* (2008). Hypomanic temperament is genetically based, running in the families of people with bipolar relatives, but it represents a milder and more functional expression of the same traits as mania. Historically, hypomanic temperament has received little attention compared to bipolar disorder, but the founders of modern psychiatry, Eugen Bleuler, Emil Kraepelin, and Ernst Kretschmer, first described these personalities early in the twentieth century (Bleuler 1924; Kraepelin 1908, 1921; Kretschmer 1925). In an article in

The New Republic (Gartner 2005), I summarized the traits of hypomanic temperament as follows:

> Hypomanics are whirlwinds of activity who are filled with energy and need little sleep, less than 6 hours. They are restless, impatient and easily bored, needing constant stimulation and tend to dominate conversations. They are driven, ambitious and veritable forces of nature in pursuit of their goals. While these goals may appear grandiose to others, they are supremely confident of success—and no one can tell them otherwise. They can be exuberant, charming, witty, gregarious but also arrogant. They are impulsive in ways that show poor judgment, saying things off the top of their head, and acting on ideas and desires quickly, seemingly oblivious to potentially damaging consequences. They are risk takers who seem oblivious to how risky their behavior truly is. They have large libidos and often act out sexually. Indeed all of their appetites are heightened.

This description sounds an awful lot like Trump who reports, "I usually sleep only four hours a night" (1987), which by itself is usually a pretty reliable indicator of hypomania Indeed, he boasts about it: "How can you compete against people like me if I sleep only four hours?" He claims to work seven days a week and, in a typical eighteen-hour day, to make "over a hundred phone calls" and have "at least a dozen meetings." He also tweeted, "Without energy you have nothing!"—hence his taunt of Jeb Bush as "a low energy person," by contrast, a charge that proved quite effective. Like most hypomanics, Trump is easily distracted. We could add attention deficit disorder to the Trump differential, except attention deficit disorder almost always goes with the territory for hypomanics. "Most successful people have very short attention spans. It has a lot to do with imagination," Trump wrote with Meredith McIver in *Think Like a Billionaire* in 2004. He is correct. The same rapidity of thought that helps engender creativity makes it difficult for one to stay on one linear track of ideas without skipping to the next. Like most hypomanics, Trump trusts his own ideas and judgment over those of anyone and everyone else, and follows his "vision, no matter how crazy or idiotic other people think it is."

One of my dictums when working with hypomanic patients is that "nothing fails like success." If they succeed in achieving one of their wildly ambitious goals, there is often a noticeable uptick in their hypomania, sometimes even precipitating a full-blown hypomanic episode, which, unlike hypomanic temperament, is a diagnosable disorder. They become more aggressive, irritable, reckless, and impulsive. Now seemingly confirmed in their grandiosity, they drink their own Kool-Aid and feel even more invincible and brilliant. They pursue even bolder, riskier, and more ambitious goals, without listening to dissent, doing their due diligence, or considering contradictory facts. Their gut is always right. Once, Trump was asked whom he went to for advice. With a straight face, he said, "Myself." Trump is Trump's most trusted adviser. In the same vein, with the increase in grandiosity comes a corresponding increase in paranoia over the fools and rivals who might nay-say the hypomanic's insights, impede his progress, or destroy him out of jealousy or ignorance.

In fact, this is a pattern for Trump. In 1988, after the publication of his best-selling book *The Art of the Deal*, Trump's celebrity really took off. His response was an increase in his hypomania, according to *Politico* writer Michael Kruse (2016) in his article "1988: The Year Trump Lost His Mind":

> [H]is response to his surging celebrity was a series of manic, ill-advised ventures. He cheated on his wife, the mother of his first three children. In business, he was acquisitive to the point of recklessness. He bought and sold chunks of

stocks of companies he talked about taking over. He glitzed up his gaudy yacht, the yacht the banks would seize less than three years later. He used hundreds of millions of dollars of borrowed money to pay high prices for a hotel and an airline—and his lenders would take them, too. And he tussled for months with game-show magnate Merv Griffin for ownership of his third casino in Atlantic City, the most expensive, gargantuan one yet, the Trump Taj Mahal, which led quickly to the first of his four corporate bankruptcy filings.

During that period, Trump the storied dealmaker went on a buying binge, and made impulsive, ill-advised investments, often paying the asking price without negotiating at all. As Kruse wrote in his *Politico* piece:

> That spring, though, he purchased the Plaza Hotel because he openly coveted the Manhattan landmark, so much so that he paid more for it than anybody anywhere ever had spent on a hotel—$407.5 million—[for] a hotel that wasn't turning enough profit to service the debt to which Trump [was] committed.
>
> And in the fall, he agreed to buy the Eastern Airlines [*sic*] Shuttle, which he wanted to rename the Trump Shuttle, for a sum that analysts and even his own partners considered excessive—more than the airline itself thought the shuttle was worth. . . .
>
> "It was not a lengthy financial analysis," [said] Nobles [president of Trump Shuttle], describing it as "back-of-the-envelope" and "very quick. . . . Donald said, 'I really want to buy it.'"

Trump could be the poster child for the dictum that when it comes to hypomanics, nothing fails like success. Kruse continued:

If Trump's current campaign is the culmination of a lifelong effort to turn his name into a brand, his brand into money and all of it into power, 1988 was the first sustained look at what the man who is the shocking favorite to be the Republican Party's nominee does when he gets ahold of it. It was the year when Trump's insatiable appetites and boundless ego—this early, spectacular show of success—nearly did him in.

Fast-forward twenty-eight years, to 2016, when Trump once again achieved success beyond anyone's wildest imaginings. He became addicted to rallies, where he excited crowds with his hypomanic charisma, and where they in turn threw gasoline on the fire of his hypomanic grandiosity. This culminated in the Republican National Convention, at which Trump made a grandiose statement that encapsulates it all: "Only I can fix it."

David Brooks (2016) is not a mental health professional, but he astutely commented on what appeared to him to be Trump's increasing hypomania:

> He cannot be contained because he is psychologically off the chain. With each passing week, he displays the classic symptoms of medium-grade mania in more disturbing forms: inflated self-esteem, sleeplessness, impulsivity, aggression and a compulsion to offer advice on subjects he knows nothing about.
>
> His speech patterns are like something straight out of a psychiatric textbook. Manics display something called "flight of ideas." It's a formal thought disorder in which ideas tumble forth through a disordered chain of associations. One word sparks another, which sparks another, and they're off to the races. As one trained psychiatrist said to me, compare Donald Trump's speaking patterns to a Robin Williams monologue, but with insults instead of jokes.

Trump's first hypomanic crash resulted only in a few bankrupt-cies, but while he is president, the consequences could be on a scale so vast it's difficult even to contemplate.

Let's put these two moving parts together, bad and mad. Trump is a profoundly evil man exhibiting malignant narcissism. His wors-ening hypomania is making him increasingly more irrational, gran-diose, paranoid, aggressive, irritable, and impulsive. Trump is bad, mad, and getting worse. He evinces the most destructive and dangerous collection of psychiatric symptoms possible for a leader. The worst-case scenario is now our reality.

Often as therapists we are called on to help our patients see that their life circumstances are not as catastrophic as they might feel. In the case of Trump, however, our job is the opposite: to warn the public that the election of Donald Trump is a true emergency, and that the consequences most likely will be catastrophic.

It's a catastrophe that might have been avoided if we in the mental health community had told the public the truth, instead of allowing ourselves to be gagged by the Goldwater rule. "See some-thing, say nothing" appears to be the APA's motto when it comes to national security. History will not be kind to a profession that aided the rise of an American Hitler through its silence.

John D. Gartner, Ph.D., is a clinical psychologist. He taught in the Department of Psychiatry at Johns Hopkins University Medical School for twenty-eight years. He is the author of In Search of Bill Clinton: A Psychological Biography *and* The Hypomanic Edge: The Link Between (a Little) Craziness and (a Lot of) Success in America. *He practices in Baltimore and New York.*

References

Bleuler, Eugen. 1924. *Textbook of Psychiatry.* New York: Macmillan, p. 485.

Brooks, David. 2016. "Trump's Enablers Will Finally Have to Take a Stand." *New York Times*, August 5.

Cheney, Kyle, et al. 2016. "Donald Trump's Week of Misrepresentations, Exaggerations, and Half-Truths." *Politico*, September 25.

Fromm, Erich. 1964. *The Heart of Man*. New York: American Mental Health Foundation, p. 63.

Gartner, John. 2005. *The Hypomanic Edge: The Link Between (a Little) Craziness and (a Lot of) Success in America*. New York: Simon and Schuster.

———. 2008. *In Search of Bill Clinton: A Psychological Biography*. New York: St. Martin's Press.

———. 2015. "Donald Trump and Bill Clinton Have the Same Secret Weapon." *The New Republic*, August 25.

———. 2016. "What Is Trump's Psychological Problem?" *Huffington Post*, June 9.

Gass, Nick. 2016. "New York AG: Trump U 'Really a Fraud from Beginning to End.'" *Politico*, September 25.

Goode, Erica. 2003. "The World; Stalin to Saddam: So Much for the Madman Theory." *New York Times*, May 4.

Haberman, Maggie. 2016. "Even as He Rises, Donald Trump Entertains Conspiracy Theories." *New York Times*, February 29.

Holan, Angie, and Linda Qui. 2015. "2015 Lie of the Year: The Campaign Misstatements of Donald Trump." *PolitiFact*, December 21.

Kernberg, O. 1970. "Factors in the Psychoanalytic Treatment of Narcissistic Personalities." *Journal of the American Psychoanalytic Association* 18: 51–85.

Kraepelin, Emil. 1908. *Lectures on Clinical Psychiatry*. Bristol, UK: Thoemmes, pp. 129–30.

———. 1921. *Manic Depressive Insanity and Paranoia*. Edinburgh: Livingstone, pp. 125–31.

Kretschmer, Ernst. 1925. *Physique and Character*. New York: Harcourt and Brace, pp. 127–32.

Kruse, Michael. 2016. "1988: The Year Donald Lost His Mind." *Politico*, March 11.

Lange, Jeva. 2016. "Donald Trump Turned His Back on His Closest Friend When He Heard He Had AIDS." *The Week*, April 8.

Pollock, G. H. 1978. "Process and Affect." *International Journal of Psychoanalysis* 59: 255–76.

Reisner, Steven. 2017. "Stop Saying Donald Trump Is Mentally Ill." *Slate*, March 15.

Scott, Eugene. 2015. "Trump Believes in God, but Hasn't Sought Forgiveness." CNN.com, July 8.

Tansey, Michael. 2017a. "Part VIII. Delusional Disorder." *Huffington Post*, February 24.

———. 2017b. "Part X. Trump and the Codes: Why 'Crazy Like a Fox' vs. 'Crazy Like a Crazy' *Really* Matters." *Huffington Post*, March 19.

Tashman, Brian. 2016. "58 Conspiracy Theories (and Counting): The Definitive Trump Conspiracy Guide." *Right Wing Watch*, May 27.

Trump, Donald. 1987. *The Art of the Deal*. New York: Random House.

Washington Post Editorial Board. 2016. "Donald Trump's Campaign of Conspiracy Theories." *Washington Post*, February 19.

WHY "CRAZY LIKE A FOX" VERSUS "CRAZY LIKE A CRAZY" *REALLY* MATTERS

Delusional Disorder, Admiration of Brutal Dictators, the Nuclear Codes, and Trump

MICHAEL J. TANSEY, PH.D.

Since becoming president, Donald Trump has made increasingly staggering statements contradicted by irrefutable evidence to the contrary (videos, photos, tweets), such that we have no choice but to consider whether his psychological disturbance is far more severe than what has widely been proposed as *merely* narcissistic personality disorder, *merely* antisocial personality disorder, or *merely* pathological lying.

Delusional Disorder

I begin with a presentation of the exceedingly rare diagnosis of delusional disorder, which may help us understand why DT makes such jaw-dropping statements. I am intending not to diagnose but to educate the general public so that each person can make his or her own informed assessment. (The criteria from the *Diagnostic and Statistical Manual*, 5th ed., are easily observable, simple behavioral characteristics that even a fifth-grader could understand.) I will then examine the final five minutes of a meandering, free-flowing, fifteen-minute videotaped speech DT delivered to the CIA the morning after Trump's inauguration, to see if the diagnosis can provide a lens through which to make sense of three egregious, separate, and startling statements contained in a mere five minutes.

Delusional disorder is coded as 297.1 (F22) for the purpose of insurance coverage for treatment. Those with delusional disorder scoff at the notion that there is a problem in the first place, such that insurance coverage for treatment is irrelevant. This "stealth" disorder is exceptionally beguiling because such individuals can seem perfectly normal, logical, high functioning, and even charming so long as the delusion itself is not challenged. Delusional disorder is described as "one of the less common *psychotic* disorders in which patients have delusions that differ from classical symptoms of schizophrenia." Psychosis is defined as "a condition in which there is profound loss of contact with external reality." The schizophrenic person tends to display bizarre behavior, hallucinations, and overtly disordered thinking. Whereas in schizophrenia the disconnection tends to be highly visible and all-encompassing, the less serious delusional disorder is neither bizarre nor readily apparent to the outside observer:

- Delusions are beliefs that exist despite indisputable, factual evidence to the contrary.

- Delusions are held with absolute certainty, despite their falsity and impossibility.

- Delusions can have a variety of themes, including grandeur and persecution.

- Delusions are not of the bizarre variety ("I am being poisoned by the CIA") but, rather, seem like ordinary figures of speech except that *each word is meant literally*: e.g., "I alone am the chosen one, invincible, extraordinary beyond words, the very best of the best in every way."

- Delusional people tend to be extremely thin-skinned and humorless, especially regarding their delusions.

- Delusions are central to the person's existence, and questioning them elicits a jolting and visceral reaction.

- Delusional disorder is chronic, even lifelong, and tends to worsen in adulthood, middle age, and beyond.

- Words and actions are consistent and logical if the basic premise of the delusion is accepted as reality: "Because I am superior to all, it follows that I would never apologize because I am never wrong."

- General logical reasoning and behavior are unaffected unless they are very specifically related to the delusion.

- The person has a heightened sense of self-reference ("It's always all about me"), and trivial events assume outsize importance when they contradict ("You are a con man, not a great businessman") or, conversely, support the delusional belief ("These adoring crowds recognize that I am extraordinary beyond measure"), making trivial events, whether positive or negative, hard to let go of and move past ("Have I mentioned my greatest ever electoral landslide?").

Delusional disorder may help us make sense of the last five minutes of DT's CIA address (CNN videos 2017), which contain three staggering statements that lead us to think, "He can't possibly mean that." In the tenth minute, DT declared he was "a thousand percent behind" the CIA, and accused the Fake Media, "some of the most dishonest people on the planet . . . of making it sound like I had a feud" with the intelligence community, when the truth is the "exact opposite." Anyone in the audience with a cell phone who doubted his own memory could instantly have googled DT's innumerable tweets about the incompetence and dishonesty of the "so-called intelligence community," a position he has since reverted to. Did DT actually believe that the truth was defined by his words and not hard facts to the contrary? Why would he merely lie despite knowing that each and every person in attendance knew there was not an iota of truth to the claim? His stunning falsehood lacks the shrewdness of the typical pathological liar. If he had been hooked up to a reliable lie detector test and were in fact delusional, he would have passed with flying colors because he literally believes every word he says, despite irrefutable facts to the contrary. He takes it as a given that the world around him will conform to his own warped view of events, and that those who do not believe so are irrational enemies backed by the Fake Media.

A minute later in the speech, he described his disappointment that, as he began his inaugural address, it was raining, but then he claimed, with a finger to the sky, "God looked down and said, 'We're not going to let it rain on your speech.'" He then insisted that the rain stopped immediately and it became "really sunny" before it "poured right after I left." Again, anyone at the CIA that day with a cell phone could immediately have watched the video demonstrating clearly that the drizzle on Inauguration Day *started* as DT began to speak, and that it never got sunny. It never subsequently poured. Again, did he believe every word he was saying? If the answer is yes, this would be compelling evidence of underlying delusional disorder leaking through the veneer of normality.

The third statement, of course, was his insistence that the inaugural grounds were packed "all the way to Washington Monument."

Despite his badgering the National Park Service to come up with photo angles that might suggest a larger crowd, the aerial shots clearly showed that DT's audience was many hundreds of thousands fewer than Obama's in 2009. Again, DT claimed this was another example of Fake News, because the photos did not accord with his certainty of his personal reality. Again, his otherwise inexplicable insistence can be explained only by an understanding of grandiose, delusional detachment from reality.

These three incidents of demonstrably factually false statements made in the space of five minutes exemplify scores of other completely false claims: He has claimed to know more than all the generals. He has said he has the best temperament of anyone ever to be president. He still bellows (Sarlin 2016) that the black and brown teenagers wrongly convicted of raping and brutally beating a woman jogger in the 1989 "Central Park Five" case are guilty, this despite the fact that the actual rapist confessed nine years after the crime and knew intimate details of the scene, and despite the rapist's DNA matching a sample from the crime scene. DT insists he saw on TV thousands of Muslims in New Jersey celebrating the collapse of the World Trade Center towers on September 11, 2001. He insists that he was the very best high school baseball pro prospect in New York City (Maddow 2016). He has bragged that, "in a movement like the world has never seen," he won the presidency by the greatest electoral landslide since Reagan when, in fact, he trailed five of the previous seven electoral totals. And so on, and so on. The fact that he lost the popular vote by three million, because it does not comport with his grandiose delusions, he explains away by declaring that these votes were made by were fraudulent voters, despite study after bipartisan study demonstrating at most a few thousand illegal votes nationwide.

Though the term *solipsism* comes from philosophy, not psychology, it appears relevant to this discussion: "Solipsism is the belief that the person holding the belief is the only real thing in the uni-

verse. All other persons and things are merely ornaments or impediments to his happiness."

DT lies regularly and reflexively, telling the truth only when it
randomly suits his purposes. Yet, pathological lying does not nearly
seem to account for the staggering, self-aggrandizing statements I
have referred to. Does he actually believe what he is saying based
upon underlying delusions of grandeur? Had he been hooked up to
a lie detector test during his CIA speech, would he have passed without so much as a blip, as I believe?

You now have the simple diagnostic criteria. You make the call.

Why Does Trump Admire Brutal Dictators?

Thomas Jefferson insisted that an "informed citizenry" is the best
protection for democracy. It is therefore extremely disconcerting that a
staggering percentage of Americans cannot name our president
during the Civil War or the country from whom we won our independence. Even more worrisome is that DT himself did not understand that there are three branches of the federal government and
that judges cannot simply "sign bills into law." During a late campaign interview (Stephanopoulos 2016), he was unaware that Russia
had not only invaded but had been occupying Crimea for two years.
In his first global tour, he commented that he was happy to be in Israel after coming from the Middle East.

In keeping with Jefferson's warning, if in fact DT harbors an
underlying delusional disorder, from a clinical perspective, his delusions would likely be grandiose and paranoid in nature. This
would help us to answer once and for all the question of why, during the 2016 presidential campaign and beyond, DT has repeatedly
and openly expressed admiration for Kim Jong-un of North Korea,
Bashar al-Assad of Syria, Iraq's Saddam Hussein, and especially
Vladimir Putin. *There is considerable evidence to suggest that absolute
tyranny is DT's wet dream.* The unopposed dictator is the embodiment
of the ability to demand adulation on the one hand and to eradicate

all perceived enemies with the simple nod of the head on the other. With statues and thirty-foot portraits everywhere attesting to his godlike status, there would be no problem whatsoever with critical Fake Media, marching protesters, pesky appellate courts, or the slightest political opposition. Such is the awesome power of the despots whom DT so inexplicably reveres.

Here are statements (Keneally 2016) DT made about each during his campaign, followed by brief illustrations that barely scratch the surface of their hideous brutality:

- **Kim Jong-un:** "You gotta give him credit . . . when his father died, he goes in, he takes over these tough generals and he's the boss. It's incredible. He wiped out the uncle, wipes out this one, that one. It's incredible." Kim's uncle was ripped out of a large government meeting as an example and summarily executed by a machine-gun-toting firing squad, along with seven of his aides. Kim's aunt, his father's sister, was poisoned. All their remaining children and grandchildren were killed. He executed one general with a *firing squad of antiaircraft missiles at close range* and another, bound to a post, with a mortar round, while requiring multitudes to watch, including their families. His entire country is quite literally starving to death while he finances his nuclear ambitions.

- **Bashar al-Assad:** "I think in terms of leadership, he's getting an A and our president is not doing so well." In his struggle to stay in power, Assad has ruthlessly suppressed his countrymen, resulting in hundreds of thousands of deaths of civilian men, women, and children, many by gassing. If deposed, he will be charged with crimes against humanity.

- **Saddam Hussein:** "Okay, so he was a very bad guy. But you know what he did so well? He killed terrorists. He did that so good! He didn't read them their rights. They didn't talk. You were a terrorist, it's over!" Hussein is universally regarded as perhaps the most monstrous tyrant of the last several decades. Among his countless atrocities, in what has been described as "the worst chemical-weapons attack in human history," he gassed more than 100,000 of his Kurdish citizens, then hunted down tens of thousands of survivors, whom he buried alive, for a total of 180,000 murdered in this slaughter alone.

- **Vladimir Putin:** "If he says great things about me, I'm going to say great things about him. He's really very much of a leader . . . very strong control over his country . . . and look, he has an eighty-two-percent approval rating!" Stunning comments. DT states clearly that his radiant view of Putin required *only* that he be flattered by him. In fifteen years of Putin's tyranny, journalists who dissent are shot in the back of the head. Dissidents who flee the country are regularly stalked and murdered, with poison the favored method, KGB style. Others in asylum are in constant fear for their lives, including the former world chess champion and current chairman of the Human Rights Foundation, Garry Kasparov, and the Russian Olympic runner who blew the whistle on Russia's pervasive doping program, Yuliya Stepanova. Either DT is incomprehensibly naïve regarding Putin's popularity at home—the 82 percent rating was fabricated—or he was swooning from the compliment when Putin called him "bright" (*not* a "genius," as DT has bragged ever since).

In addition, during the campaign, DT spoke of "fighting for peaceful regime-change" if elected. (America is not ruled by a regime.) He bloviated that he would "blow out of the water" the seven small Iranian boats whose sailors had harrassed and given the finger to our "beautiful destroyers." He bragged that "Russia and I would get along really well." He suggested that maybe "the Second Amendment people" might be able to stop Hillary; that his supporters should patrol voting sites to ensure he was being treated fairly, and that he would love to "hit and hit and hit [his critics from the DNC] until their heads spin and they'll never recover."

He insisted that he will "bomb the shit out of ISIS" and order our soldiers to kill their presumed families. He repeatedly goaded supporters to rough up hecklers at his speeches and pontificated that NFL players who refuse to stand for the national anthem should find another country. He quoted Mussolini's "Better to live one day as a lion than a hundred years as a sheep," and he expressed genuine bewilderment about why we build nuclear weapons if we don't use them.

In the clinical assessment of such frightening characteristics, why would DT admire grotesque tyrants while never praising our own past presidents but boasting that he himself could be the greatest in history, "except maybe Abe Lincoln"? From childhood throughout life, we all look for role models to emulate, especially when trying to navigate new and unfamiliar life challenges and transitions. We select inspirational people, often from a different time or place, who guide us by their example of how to get it right. We search for what has been called an "ego ideal" who best personifies our own highest intentions.

Whether or not his admiration for despots derives from an underlying delusional disorder, grandiose and paranoid in nature, DT is drawn to leaders who already fit his fundamental personality makeup. While anticipating the presidency, he looked for role models for how to preside, what that would look like, which leaders performed in ways that were inspiring. For Obama, it was Kennedy, Reagan, Dr. King, and Mandela. Bill Clinton turned to JFK; and Hillary to Eleanor Roosevelt. George W. Bush modeled his leadership after Jesus and Winston Churchill. For DT, it was Hussein, Jong-un, Assad, and Putin. Those guys know how to run a tight ship!

Once elected, certainly DT, many argued, would moderate his words and actions in a so-called "soft pivot." When a person is character-disordered or worse—especially one who always blames others, never apologizes or displays accountability, and who never for an instant believes there is anything wrong with himself—the only possibility for change is for him to become worse, not better. In fact, all DT's despicable traits have been frighteningly exacerbated by his ascension to the presidency. *He has tried to become more of the tyrant he wants to be, not less.*

And since becoming president, what has DT's attitude been toward brutal dictators? He has congratulated President Rodrigo Duterte of the Philippines for dealing with his country's drug problems in the "right way," with the vigilante slaughter of nearly ten thousand people merely *suspected* of using or dealing drugs. In April, DT invited him to the White House, though Duterte has not yet come.

He has expressed support and approval to President Recep Erdogan of Turkey, another invitee to the White House, who has engaged in a harsh, systematic purge of all opposition over the past year while arrogating dictatorial powers to himself alone over what had previously been a democratically elected government. During his Washington visit, Erdogan unleashed his bodyguard thugs to savagely repel peaceful protesters in front of the Turkish embassy.

Despite their clashes and nuclear saber rattling, DT has referred to Kim Jong-un as a "smart cookie," one whom he continues to admire for the insanely harsh methods Kim has used to maintain control over North Korea since his father's death. Bizarrely, Kim, too, has been invited to the White House. Ditto President Abdel-Fattah al-Sissi, who has viciously ruled Egypt with an iron fist since taking office in 2013.

By contrast, shortly after his inauguration DT insulted Prime Minister Malcolm Turnbull of Australia in a phone call, reportedly slamming the phone down, and he childishly refused to shake the hand of German chancellor Angela Merkel, with live television cameras broadcasting the world over, during her April visit to the White House. Australia and Germany have long been among our closest allies. DT also stunningly shoved aside, while all the world watched, the prime minister of Montenegro, Dusko Marcovic, in his haste to get to the front row for a group photo op during a G20 conference.

Far beyond his staggering affinity for monstrous tyrants, Trump, since coming to office, has railed against a critical free press; vilified millions of marching protesters as paid professionals; denigrated our federal appeals courts for thwarting his Muslim travel ban as unconstitutional; abruptly fired forty-six state attorneys general; and, shockingly, fired FBI director James Comey for what DT brazenly admitted was Comey's ongoing investigation of potential collusion between Russia and the 2016 Trump campaign.

The day following Comey's abrupt departure, despite the mind-boggling optics, DT welcomed Russian ambassador Sergey Kislyak and Russian foreign minister Sergey Lavrov to the White House, and allowed Russian film crews into the meeting, while blocking American press and photographers.

Days later, reports circulated that DT had shared, without permission, highly classified information given to the United States by Israel, possibly leading to the deaths of embedded Israeli spies. DT reportedly did so in an impulsive and boastful way, seeming to try to impress the Russians. The event has rattled our allies, who now feel they cannot trust the United States with intelligence, and thus exposed and endangered the intelligence sources who provided the information. In addition, he reportedly bragged to the Russians about firing FBI director Comey, whom he called a "nut job," and expressed relief that the Russia-Trump campaign collusion investigation was over. (It is not.)

His honeymoon with Putin has already cooled, but what is DT capable of when the bromance ends? Given his mental instability, his thirst for adulation is rivaled only by his obsession for vengeance, even for the tiniest of slights. What happens when he discovers that Putin has been playing him like a fiddle or when Putin potentially humiliates him on the world stage? As Trump stated dozens of times during the primary, "As long as they're nice to me, I'll be nice to them. But if they get nasty and hit me, I'll hit back much, much harder."

Checks and balances? Hey, nobody writes checks anymore. And you can't see his balances until his IRS audit is completed!

The Constitution? Believe me, those are rules, and rules are meant to be broken. Besides, rules are for losers, and DT's a winner. He's a winner!

Like the despots he idolizes, DT intends to rule, not lead; to control, not compromise. The 2016 presidential election was not about traditional Republican-versus-Democratic views. Quite literally, it was about apocalypse, not politics.

This can't be happening? It can and it is. Jefferson's warning has never been more relevant.

Why "Crazy Like a Fox" versus "Crazy Like a Crazy" Really Matters

DT's penchant for brutality alone would be disconcerting. Yet, given the evidence of delusional disorder, we must ask why the distinction of "crazy like a fox" versus "crazy like a crazy" even matters. Although there are several areas in which DT's particular version of personality disorder is vital to understand, none is more compelling or terrifying than his control of the nuclear codes. Surpassing the devastation of climate, health care, education, diplomacy, social services, freedom of speech, and liberty and justice for all, nothing is more incomprehensible than the now-plausible prospect of all-out nuclear war. For all but the few remaining survivors who witnessed the atomic bombing of Japan and its aftermath, we simply have nothing in our own experiences to imagine instantaneous annihilation. Quite literally, we are here one second and vaporized the next, along with everyone and everything.

Because of this very real existential threat, it is absolutely urgent that we comprehend the titanic differences between a president who is merely "crazy like a fox" (shrewd, calculating, and convinced that the truth is spoken only when it happens to coincide with his purposes) versus what I have termed "crazy like a crazy" (possessing well-hidden, core grandiose and paranoid delusions that are disconnected from factual reality). To illustrate the differences, let's look at two actual episodes from recent American history and consider how DT might act faced with similar circumstances.

The 3:00 a.m. Call: President Carter

In 1979, near the end of Jimmy Carter's presidency, the nightmare phone call (Sagan 2012) came at 3:00 a.m., awakening Carter's national security adviser, Zbigniew Brzezinski, with the news that 250 Soviet nuclear missiles were bearing down on America. Knowing that he still had five or six minutes to act and that mistakes could cause false alarms, Brzezinski directed an aide to find further verification. The aide immediately called back, this time to report that 2,500 missiles were incoming. As Brzezinski prepared to call President Carter to advise a full-fledged counterattack, he elected not to wake his sleeping wife, reasoning that she would be dead in a matter of minutes. As he was reaching to phone the president, a third call came in announcing that the report of the incoming missiles was a false alarm caused by a computer glitch.

It is extremely disconcerting to note that false alarms and accidents are by no means a rare occurrence.

The Cuban Missile Crisis: President Kennedy

Unlike the nightmarish false alarm of 1979, lasting five minutes, which few were aware of, the Cuban Missile Crisis of October 1962 lasted thirteen white-knuckle days, played out before the entire world in a series of very real, terrifying actions and reactions between America and the USSR. At several junctures, the world was within an eyelash of all-out nuclear holocaust. The gist of the crisis entailed Russia's intention to place nuclear missiles in Cuba in response to the United States' having deployed nuclear sites close to Russia's borders in Turkey and Italy. The Joint Chiefs of Staff unanimously pressured President John F. Kennedy to preemptively attack

Cuban missile sites already in place, with the rationale that Russia would back down and not counterattack, especially given its much smaller nuclear capability. Fortunately, JFK had the equanimity to hold off and follow the advice of his civilian advisers, notably RFK and Secretary of Defense Robert McNamara.

Interviewed many years later, McNamara described leaving the White House late in the crisis. Marveling at a beautiful sunset, he thought that it might well be the last any of us would ever see. Government families in DC, as well as those from cities and towns everywhere, were fleeing to remote regions in the hope of surviving a nuclear attack.

The standoff climaxed when Russia agreed to remove the existing missile sites from Cuba and to build no new ones in exchange for the United States' public commitment never to invade Cuba. Saving face, JFK also secretly agreed to remove the missiles from Turkey and Italy. The world exhaled.

The "crazy like a fox" characterization of DT needs little explanation. The phrase describes someone who may appear "crazy" (e.g., erratic, irrational, impulsive) on the surface, but whose seemingly crazy external behavior is a cleverly designed strategy to mislead, distract, and deceive others into responding in precisely the manner that is secretly desired. This is indeed one aspect of DT's behavior. Someone who is "crazy like a fox," during that given moment, is actually the exact opposite of crazy.

When insisting that the Fake Media created the feud between him and the intelligence community, such a person would fail a reliable lie detector test because he would know he was lying.

The most jarring evidence yet of DT's "crazy like a crazy" delusional disorder came with his early morning tweets (subsequently deleted) in March that his Trump Tower phones had been wiretapped by a "bad (or sick!) Obama"; the tweets included insane comparisons to Watergate and McCarthyism. DT's actions immediately generated bipartisan criticism, and there was a complete lack of evidence from anyone, anywhere, that he had been targeted for surveillance. The suspicion that one is being wiretapped is an absolutely classic expression of paranoid delusions.

When insisting that the Fake Media created the feud between him and the intelligence community, DT would unequivocally have passed a lie detector test because he believed the delusion was actually true. "Crazy like a fox" defines a person whose apparent external irrationality masks underlying rational thinking. "Crazy like a crazy" characterizes a person whose apparent external rationality masks underlying irrational thinking.

Returning to our historical examples of nuclear emergencies, is there anyone who could possibly believe DT would have shown Brzezinski's grace under pressure had he himself received that 3:00 a.m. call? If, indeed, Trump harbors grandiose and paranoid delusions (for which there is mounting evidence), he would have launched missiles faster than he fires off paranoid tweets on a Saturday morning.

Given the thirteen days of excruciating tension during the very real nuclear threat of the Cuban Missile Crisis, is there anyone who possibly believes that DT could have demonstrated JFK's composure, wisdom, and judgment, especially in the face of unanimous pressure from his military advisers? If DT were indeed merely "crazy like a fox," it would still be a huge stretch—but, increasingly, that appears not to be the case.

Michael J. Tansey, Ph.D. (www.drmjtansey.com), is a Chicago-based clinical psychologist, author, and teacher. He is a graduate of Harvard University (A.B., 1972, in personality theory) and Northwestern University Feinberg School of Medicine (Ph.D., 1978, in clinical psychology). In addition to his full-time practice, he was an assistant professor teaching and supervising students, interns, residents, and postdoctoral fellows. He has been in private practice for more than thirty-five years, working with adults, adolescents, and couples. Along with a coauthored book on empathy and the therapeutic process, he has written numerous professional journal articles as well as twenty-five blogs for the Huffington Post.

References

Chang, Laurence; Kornbluh, Peter, eds. (1998). "Introduction." The Cuban Missile Crisis, 1962: A National Security Archive. http://nsarchive.gwu.edu/nsa/cuba_mis_cri/declass.htm.

CNN.com video. 2017. January 21. www.youtube.com/watch?v=4v-Ot25u7Hc.

Keneally, Meghan. 2016. "5 Controversial Dictators and Leaders Donald Trump Has Praised." ABC News.com, July 6.

Maddow, Rachel. 2016. *The Rachel Maddow Show.* MSNBC, October 27.

Sagan, Scott. 2012. The National Security Archive, George Washington University, Washington, DC, March 1.

Sarlin, Benjy. 2016. NBC News, October 7.

Stephanopoulos, George. 2016. *This Week with George Stephanopoulos.* ABC News, July 31.

Wright, David. 2015. TK. Union of Concerned Scientists. November 9, http://blog.vcsusa.org/david-wright/nuclear-false-alarm-950.

COGNITIVE IMPAIRMENT, DEMENTIA, AND POTUS

DAVID M. REISS, M.D.

Obviously, it is difficult to conceive of a more stressful, demanding job than being POTUS. Leaving aside all the serious, critical, and snarky questions we hear regarding presidential "vacations," golf outings, and so on, the office demands the ability to be emotionally and cognitively alert and intact, and fully "on duty" at a moment's notice, 24/7. Potentially, the lives and well-being of millions of people are at stake in any number of the presidential decisions required to be developed over time, with appropriate advice and counseling, or within minutes, without any prior notice regarding the specific details or options.

It goes without saying that the position of POTUS inherently requires an almost inhuman degree of cognitive clarity at all times, regardless of the personal situation or circumstances of the man or woman holding the office. It is not surprising that the idea of a "dual presidency," at least some division of tasks, has been considered at different times (Rediff.com n.d., Smith 2015) (including, briefly, during the last election cycle) (Lerer 2016), although implementation of the idea has never seemed practically or politically possible.

In general, the populace values exuberance, energy, and experience as essential qualities in a POTUS, some would say with each cycle which traits are considered of primary importance at different times. Historically, longings for an experienced leader and the seeking of a "paternal," even "grandfatherly," presidential persona and political presence have often yielded male candidates who are in their senior years, with Donald Trump being the oldest person to be sworn in as POTUS.

With age comes experience and, it is hoped, wisdom—but also, medically, concerns regarding cognitive decline. It is now recognized that while some neurological functioning has peak efficiency during earlier adult years (e.g., physical reaction time), in general, cognitive functioning remains remarkably intact until quite late in the life cycle (with minor deterioration during the seventies and a more measurable decline after age eighty, but such decline certainly is not universal) of the *healthy* older adult (Levin 2016, Ramer 2013). Thus, the key issue to be addressed is not age-related cognitive decline but *illness-related* cognitive decline and decline related to other non-age-dependent physiological factors (the use of prescribed medications, a history of past or present substance abuse, a history of injury to the head, etc.). In general, older persons are more likely to be using multiple prescribed medications than younger persons, and many medications may have a subtle negative impact upon cognition, but that is not an age-related issue in and of itself.

Therefore, concerns regarding the cognitive abilities of a POTUS can be divided into five general areas: (1) innate, baseline, intellectual/cognitive skills and ability; (2) impairment due to an ongoing neurological deterioration (Alzheimer's disease or other types of dementia); (3) impairment caused by acute illness (especially in older individuals; even a urinary tract infection can negatively impact cognition); (4) toxic effects of prescribed medications or use of illicit substances; and (5) cumulative effects of head trauma and/or use of

licit or illicit toxic agents (an issue that has received much more attention, clinically and publicly, vis-à-vis sports-related concussion
injury).

Baseline Intellectual and Cognitive Skills

The current political system sets no intellectual or cognitive standards (or physical/medical well-being standards) for someone to
become POTUS. Clearly, this is a vulnerability. Equally as clearly, the
question of where any "line should be drawn" regarding health or,
in particular, intellectual and cognitive prowess, as well as how and
by whom those parameters would be measured, in my opinion,
make it practically unlikely that any such standards will ever be implemented. In essence, we rely upon the candidates to voluntarily
divulge their medical history (which Trump did not do with any in-
dication of clinical validity), and we rely upon the voting populace
to determine if a candidate's intellectual abilities "measure up," an
inherently flawed system, as the populace has access only to pre-
packaged presentations and observations of a candidate in debates
and while he or she is giving speeches—hardly an adequate database for accurately gauging intellectual ability.

Based upon the limited information available, persons with professional training could provide public opinions regarding a candidate's intellect, but the database that even professionals can use
remains inadequate and incomplete, and differentiation between
objective and clinically "solid" opinions versus politically based
propaganda is an insurmountable problem.

At the current time, I view this as a problem without any solution in the near future.

Impairment Due to an Ongoing Neurological Deterioration

In the vernacular, the term *Alzheimer's* is often used nonspecifically
to refer to dementing illness, which is not clinically accurate, as deterioration of cognitive functioning can occur due to multiple differ-

ent degenerative neurological disease processes. However, with regard to the issue at hand, the important question is whether a degenerative process is present, not necessarily a specific diagnosis. Other than in certain relatively uncommon acute illnesses, cognitive decline due to degenerative neurological disorders is a relatively slow process that can begin insidiously. As just noted, but not commonly appreciated, absent other factors, "normal aging" is a very infrequent cause of significant cognitive impairment prior to true "old age" (i.e., above eighty years). It is not unusual for early indications of a degenerative process to be "excused" or minimized as age-related and not seen as particularly significant acutely (which they may not be) or recognized as implying a problematic prognosis.

This is an area in which sophisticated clinicians may notice, *even from public appearances and interactions,* that a person is exhibiting indications suggestive of an early stage of a dementing process. Without a full medical history and without formal testing, no diagnosis can be provided based upon such observation, but certainly a trained observer can identify cause for concern and *suggest the prudence of obtaining a formal evaluation.*

However, it is obviously problematic for many reasons to rely upon unsolicited opinions from practitioners whose level of expertise, objectivity, and ulterior motivations may be suspect (legitimately or defensively/manipulatively). This is, in fact, what has occurred regarding the candidacy and election of Donald Trump. Multiple experts have voiced concern, some referring to an inherent "duty to warn." Multiple differing opinions have been expressed, ranging from denial of any evidence necessitating concern; to suggestions of the need for a formal evaluation; to speculation about, provision of, and even rumor of specific diagnoses.

Objectively, I personally do not see how any informed clinician would not notice a significant difference between the cognitive performance of Trump in videos from fifteen years ago to his current presentation. Objectively, I personally do not see how any informed clinician cannot conclude that there is reason for concern and/or a formal evaluation.

Yet, at the same time, the videos from the past were produced under very different situations (vis-à-vis planning, scripting, stress, and in some cases, editing), and it has been my stance that the promulgation of anything beyond a general warning, along with education regarding the "differential diagnoses" (i.e., *possible* causes for the apparent change), is not clinically supported without additional data, as well as being ethically questionable.

Thus, in my opinion, it has been appropriate and, in fact, prudent for clinicians to speak out regarding their concerns of possible neurological deterioration, but the public discussion has been so muddied that serious and legitimate concerns voiced have had no practical impact.

Although the presidency of Donald Trump is still young and, in the view of many, including me, quite problematic, with very high and dangerous risks present, in essence we have probably already "dodged a bullet" at least once. During the first 1984 debate between Ronald Reagan and Walter Mondale, Reagan obviously experienced a moment of disorganization. A brief lapse can happen to anyone under stress and need not be assumed to indicate the presence of pathology (e.g., Rick Perry's forgetting "the third department" he wished to disband during the 2012 primary debate). In retrospect, Reagan's "becoming lost" appeared more significant. There were already public concerns regarding his medical status, and it was later reported that friends and family were well aware that a degenerative disease was progressing (Corn 2011). Yet, there was no significant expression of public concern by clinicians, and the issue was, out of (in my opinion, misplaced) "politeness," not seriously raised within the political discourse. Perhaps if clinicians had spoken up, there could have been a reasonable call for appropriate medical records or evaluation. It might have backfired, and the election could have been determined on the spot, but personally, I always wonder what might have happened if, in the second debate, in a sincere and diplomatic manner, Mondale had directly raised the question to Reagan: "Sir. The last time we met, you appeared to have a moment of significant confusion. What would the consequences be if that occurred during a national emergency?" It is conceivable that Reagan could have deftly deflected the question, and Mondale would have been pilloried, his campaign essentially ended. Yet, it is also conceivable that if Reagan had some awareness of his difficulties, the question could have led to his becoming acutely disturbed and discombobulated—perhaps revealing his vulnerability and swinging the election in the other direction. We will never know, and thankfully whatever neurological impairment Reagan suffered while in office did not (to anyone's knowledge) ever lead to any inappropriate action, behavior, or decision. Nonetheless, that is not a risk the country should look forward to taking again.

While neurological degenerative disease can occur even at relatively young ages, this is quite uncommon, and perhaps the wisest course would be for there to be a legal imperative for candidates above a certain age to undergo neuropsychological testing to rule out the process of a progressive illness. It would still be problematic to determine exactly what tests should be administered, who should administer them, and where a "cut-off" for eligibility/determination of "fitness to serve" should be set. It is conceivable that a bipartisan effort based upon clinical knowledge could at least set standards for disqualifying a candidate for whom there is objective medical evidence of a progressive disorder.

Short of such a procedure, in my opinion, qualified professionals should not hesitate to carefully, judiciously express any concerns they may have, providing as much educative information as possible—while appreciating that, practically, the situation will remain confusing and controversial to a large segment of the population and that pernicious manipulation by unscrupulous clinicians cannot be avoided.

Impairment Caused by Acute Illness and Toxic Effects of Prescribed Medications or Illicit Substances

Any number of medical conditions can negatively impact cognition in any person, regardless of age—although, in general, as age progresses, vulnerability to cognitive impairment increases. Similarly, many medications very legitimately and appropriately prescribed for medical purposes can result in side effects ranging from mild word-finding difficulties (not uncommon with anticholinergic agents) to more significant cognitive slippage or confusion and even overt delirium. It goes without saying that those risks are higher with use of specific psychotropic medications and, of course, illicit drugs or alcohol. Acute side effects are very often reversible, while some agents (definitely alcohol; other illicit drugs; controversially, some rather common medications generally considered benign) may result in irreversible cognitive problems.

However, practically, identifying these issues in a candidate does not appear to be nearly as problematic as addressing the question of a degenerative process. Simply by the release of objective and clinically sound medical records, including a toxicological screen and consideration of potential medication side effects (with formal neuro-psychological testing performed if indicated by the clinical history and findings), issues of acutely impaired cognitive functioning can be identified and often remedied. Or, at least such as in the possibility of illicit drug use, or mild, insignificant side effects (e.g., some simple word-finding difficulties due to use of anti-hypertensives) be made public. If any such findings cannot be remedied, then the situation would essentially fall into section (2) as described above.

Cumulative Effects of Head Trauma and/or Use of Licit or Illicit Toxic Agents

It is now recognized and generally accepted that a history of even "mild" head trauma, especially if there have been multiple events, as well as past use of licit or illicit psychoactive agents, can produce acute cognitive impairment that lasts longer than was previously thought and can trigger an ongoing cognitive deterioration (the specific mechanism of which is not yet well understood). Increasing evidence is being obtained from those who participated in contact sports (and even relatively non-contact sports that involve use of the head, e.g., soccer; as well as victims of domestic violence or abuse that involved blows to the head), can suffer from increasing cognitive difficulties as they age, even years after the injuries/exposure occurred and even if acute symptomatology did not seem particularly severe. While the medical details regarding CTE (Chronic Traumatic Encephalopathy) (Boston University CTE Center 2017) remain controversial and under investigation, it cannot be denied that many persons with a history of head trauma or substance abuse suffer from cognitive decline that is not related to Alzheimer's Syndrome or other "typical" degenerative neurological disorders. However, determining the presence and severity of any such decline (and establishing a prognosis) is somewhat more complicated than determining the presence or absence of a well-established disease process.

Thus, this is not an issue that is practically different than described in (2) above, but it is an area of a person's medical history that (to this day) often remains overlooked and deserves appropriate consideration and evaluation within any review of a candidate's medical history.

Summary

No reasonable person would want someone with compromised cognitive/intellectual functioning to serve as POTUS. However, to date, there is no process or procedure (beyond voluntary release of medical records) that provides the public with any reliable knowledge regarding whether a candidate for the office of POTUS suffers from cognitive impairment or is at high risk for cognitive degeneration.

Others have discussed the very problematic aspects of the candidacy of Donald Trump with regard to acute psychiatric illness and chronic characterological dysfunction/pathology. Especially in a person for whom questions of acute or chronic psychiatric issues come into play (issues that inherently impact cognition, judgment, decision making, etc.), additional or superimposed neurologically based cognitive impairment becomes even more critical. Yet, absent the specific circumstances of the Trump candidacy/election, the candidate selection and electoral processes do not in any manner take into account the medical and neurological knowledge gained since the time of the Founding Fathers—knowledge that continues to expand, and will continue to expand, with ever-increasing sophistication and understanding.

Nevertheless, applying clinical/medical knowledge to a political process is practically complex and daunting with regard to issues of objectivity, the setting of parameters (e.g., for qualification/disqualification), and the avoidance of ill-informed and/or malicious manipulation. The process of taking into account a candidate's cognitive abilities and status is fraught with danger. Those who speak out must do so carefully, not without risk, and to a populace that *should* be reasonably skeptical.

This is, indeed, a very "slippery slope." However, it is far wiser to attempt to maintain an appropriate balance upon that slope than to totally ignore its presence and remain in total denial regarding the potential risks to the country and the world.

David M. Reiss, M.D., attended Northwestern University (chemical/biomedical engineering; medical school) and has maintained a private psychiatric practice in California since 1982. Dr. Reiss has evaluated/treated more than twelve thousand people; has served as interim medical director of Providence Hospital (Massachusetts), and has recently been associated with the Brattleboro Retreat (Vermont). He is a California-qualified medical examiner and a member of professional organizations, including the Society for the Exploration of Psychotherapeutic Integration, the Sports Lawyers Associa-

tion, and the International Psychohistory Association. Dr. Reiss has appeared in all media formats addressing clinical issues and psychological aspects of social and political phenomena.

References

Corn, David. 2011. "How Close Did Lesley Stahl Come to Reporting Reagan Had Alzheimer's While in Office? Very Close." *Mother Jones*, January 20. www.motherjones.com/politics/2011/01/reagan-alzheimers-family-feud-lesley-stahl.

Rediff.com. n.d. "Dual Presidency Theory." Rediff.com. http://pages.rediff.com/dual-presidency-theory/731558.

Lerer, Lisa. 2016. "Hillary Clinton Brings Back Talk of Dual Presidency." *Boston Globe*, May 17. www.bostonglobe.com/news/nation/2016/05/16/hillary-clinton-brings-back-talk-dual-presidency/PHde6zkoaUOnD3bFWV7PgM/story.html.

Levin, Michael C. 2016. "Memory Loss." *Merck Manual Professional Version* (online). www.merckmanuals.com/professional/neurologic-disorders/symptoms-of-neurologic-disorders/memory-loss.

Ramer, Jessica. 2013. "How Does Aging Affect Reaction Time?" LiveStrong.com. www.livestrong.com/article/442800-how-does-aging-affect-reaction-time/.

Smith, Jeff. 2017. "David Orentlicher, Two Presidents Are Better Than One: The Case for a Bipartisan Executive Branch." *European Journal of American Studies* [online], Reviews 2015-4, document 10. http://ejas.revues.org/11162.

Boston University CTE Center. 2017. "What Is CTE?" Boston University CTE Center. www.bu.edu/cte/about/what-is-cte/.

DONALD J. TRUMP, ALLEGED INCAPACITATED PERSON

Mental Incapacity, the Electoral College, and the Twenty-Fifth Amendment

JAMES A. HERB, ESQ.

Donald J. Trump became an "alleged incapacitated person" on October 4, 2016, when I filed a petition to determine his mental incapacity in the Palm Beach County Circuit Court. I claim legal standing to commence such a proceeding as an adult and a resident of Florida, and based on the fact that Trump's apparent lack of mental capacity to function could impact me and possibly the whole world, in addition to him.

Before the Election

I have a B.A. and M.A. in political science, and have always been a political junkie of sorts. I followed the televised Watergate hearings leading up to President Nixon's resignation in 1974. I taught a course on the Constitution and politics after I received my law degree. I followed the impeachment proceedings of President Clinton. I lived through each day of *Bush v. Gore*, but nothing prepared me for Trump's presidential campaign, which started with a ride down an escalator. Perhaps the symbolism was prophetic: instead of ascending to the heights, he was descending to the depths, and taking us all with him. How low could an escalator go? I never imagined that Trump's style of campaigning could thrive in our society.

Like many, I assumed that Trump would not get the Republican nomination for president. Then, in July 2016, he did. I started to agonize over the possibility of a Trump presidency. It was true, of course, that two hurdles still stood between Trump's nomination and what I believed might be the Apocalypse. One was the general election, to take place on November 8, 2016. The second (should Trump win) was the voting of the Electoral College, to take place on December 19, 2016. Was there anything that I, a simple probate attorney, an ordinary citizen, could do?

I started to review the public record regarding things Trump had said and done. I compiled a list of two hundred items that I believed reflected his mental disability to discharge the duties of a president. The list could have been substantially larger, but I stopped at two hundred.

There was a lot of commentary on the Internet about Trump's mental state. There were also Internet petitions seeking a determination (by someone) that Trump lacked the mental capacity to be president. No one suggested a court proceeding. I reviewed the Goldwater rule (discussed in more detail in part 2 of this book) and its apparent prohibition of certain mental health professionals from diagnosing the mental health of a public official from afar. The irony of this is that I, not a mental health professional and perhaps less formally trained to make such a diagnosis, in no way come under the Goldwater rule prohibition. To the contrary, part of my job as a guardianship attorney is to come to a preliminary conclusion about the mental incapacity of a person *before* I file a petition to determine incapacity.

Once, when I tuned in to watch a Trump rally on TV, he was reciting lyrics from a song titled, "The Snake," about a tenderhearted woman who rescues a half-frozen snake, only to be fatally bitten by it once it has revived. The snake says, "You knew damn well I was a snake before you took me in." I thought Trump was speaking about himself, and the American people were the tenderhearted woman. It turned out he was speaking about immigrants as being vicious snakes.

This story is similar to other animal fables, perhaps best illustrated by the story of the scorpion and the frog, which is told in various forms. In one telling, a scorpion asks a frog to carry him on his back in a swim across a pond. The frog is reluctant, fearful of the scorpion's sting. The scorpion argues that he obviously won't sting the frog, because if he does, they will both drown. So, they start crossing the pond, and midway across, the scorpion stings the frog. Just before they sink below the surface of the water, the frog asks the scorpion why he has stung him. The scorpion replies, "I can't control my nature."

I was concerned that we might end up with a scorpion king in the White House, someone who was unable to control a dangerous part of his nature.

Having practiced guardianship law for almost forty years, I believed that it might be appropriate to start an "incapacity" proceeding in Palm Beach County (where Trump maintains a residence at Mar-a-Lago), and, ultimately, to have a three-person examining committee appointed to interview Trump and file reports as to whether he lacked the mental capacity to be president. While I have handled many incapacity proceedings, I would be dealing with someone who was clearly not a *normal* abnormal person.

If the court had proceeded and ultimately determined that Trump was incapacitated, it could not have prevented him from running—Trump met the age and other eligibility requirements to be president as set forth in the Constitution—but such a determination would have been an appropriate consideration for the electorate in going to the polls and deciding for whom to vote.

My petition was ready to go in mid-August 2016, but instead of filing it, I decided to speak to various people about it. These people were not part of any presidential campaign and were not political party officials. I spoke to lawyers, nonlawyers, and retired judges. I spoke to Republicans, Democrats, and Independents. To me, it wasn't an issue of partisan politics; it was an issue of the survival of our democracy. I also thought long and hard about proceeding. Did I wish to antagonize someone who might become president? Did I want to antagonize someone so vindictive, so litigious? Might I be sued for defamation? Might my life, as I knew it, end?

I decided that the issue was so extremely important to everyone in our country, and possibly to everyone in the world, that I felt compelled to file the petition to determine incapacity, as a patriotic duty.

I filed the petition a little more than a month before the November 8, 2016, election. It alleged that Trump was or might be incapacitated to seek or retain employment, based on the following factual information: (1) that his actions/statements appeared to support a diagnosis of histrionic personality disorder, DSM-V 301.50, meeting diagnostic criteria 1 through 8; and (2) that his actions/statements appeared to support a diagnosis of narcissistic personality disorder, DSM-V 301.81, meeting diagnostic criteria 1 through 9. I attached my list of two hundred supporting statements made by Trump during the course of his campaign.

The first judge assigned to the case recused herself. The second assigned judge ordered that I explain why my petition ought not be dismissed, and to address whether a state court could restrict Trump from seeking the presidency, given that Trump met the sole eligibility requirements to be president as set forth in Article II, Section 1, Clause 5 (at least thirty-five years old, a U.S. resident for fourteen years, and a natural born citizen), of the Constitution.

The day before the election, the court dismissed my incapacity proceeding.

After Election Day: The Electoral College

After Election Day (and before the date for the Electoral College to meet and vote), I asked that the court reconsider its decision, arguing that the issue of whether Trump was mentally incapacitated was not moot, given that the president is selected by members of the Electoral College, and not by a direct vote of the electorate. Perhaps the Electoral College could save us.

I argued that it was the *original intent* of the Framers of the Constitution, as explained in Alexander Hamilton's Federalist No. 68, March 12, 1788, that the electors were to provide wisdom and judgment (beyond that held by the general public) in making the selection of the president. The president is to be selected by the "sense of the people" operating through electors selected by the people for that particular purpose. The election of the president "should be made by men most capable of analyzing the qualities adapted to the station, and acting under circumstances favorable to deliberation and to a judicious combination of all the reasons and inducements, which were proper to govern their choice." Hamilton also wrote, "A small number of persons, selected by their fellow citizens from the general mass, will be most likely to possess the information and discernment requisite to so complicated an investigation." The process of election through electors "affords a moral certainty, that the office of president, will seldom fall to the lot of any man, who is not in an eminent degree endowed with the requisite qualifications."

I pointed out that Supreme Court Justice Robert H. Jackson (who was also the architect of the international war crimes trials of Nazi leaders as well as the lead American prosecutor at Nuremberg) said that the plan originally contemplated was "that electors would be free agents, to exercise an independent and nonpartisan judgment as to the men best qualified for the Nation's highest office." Justice Jackson went on: "This arrangement miscarried. Electors, although often personally eminent, independent, and respectable, officially became voluntary party lackeys and intellectual nonentities to whose memory we might justly paraphrase a tuneful satire:

> *They always voted at their Party's call*
> *And never thought of thinking for themselves at all.*

"As an institution, the Electoral College suffered atrophy almost indistinguishable from *rigor mortis*" (*Ray v. Blair*, 343 U.S. 214, 232 [1952], Justice Robert H. Jackson dissenting).

I added that the Framers intended electors to be persons of "superior discernment, virtue, and information," who would select the president "according to their own will" and without reference to the immediate wishes of the people (*Ray v. Blair*, 343 U.S. 214, 232 [1952], Justice Robert H. Jackson dissenting). That "Electors constitutionally remain free to cast their ballots for any person they wish and occasionally they have done so" (U.S. Senate 2013).

While a state court determination that Trump lacked "mental capacity" to be president would *not* automatically have disqualified him from serving, such a determination would have been vital information for members of the Electoral College to have. Having as much relevant information as possible is a prescription from the Founders to the members of the Electoral College, necessary for members to perform their function properly.

The court did not change its holding. Trump was selected by the Electoral College on December 19, 2016, and was inaugurated on January 20, 2017.

After Inauguration: The Twenty-Fifth Amendment

I saw no "presidential pivot" by Trump in his first ten days in office, so, on January 30, 2017, I filed a second petition to determine incapacity.

In those first ten days, Trump espoused at least two delusional beliefs. One was as to the size of the crowd at his inauguration; a second was that Secretary Clinton had won the popular vote in the presidential election only because between three million and five million illegal votes had been cast.

Also in those first ten days, Trump issued various executive orders that demonstrated his mental inability to comprehend the following: what is and is not legal (the immigration ban); what he can and cannot do without getting funding approval from Congress (building a border wall with Mexico); and what is and is not in the best interest of our country's security (Steve Bannon is in, and certain Cabinet-level officers are out). Trump alienated Mexico; alienated nations across the world with his immigration ban; displayed an inability to vet issues and actions with appropriate parts of the U.S. government before taking action; and displayed a total inability to anticipate (or even consider) the impact of his statements and actions.

My petition asserted that in order for him to continue as president, he needed to have the mental capacity to:

- separate fact from fiction;
- think through an issue or matter before speaking or taking action;
- be able and willing to learn about issues;
- apply coherent decision making to fact;
- communicate coherently;
- be consistent (without vacillating or "flip-flopping") with statements he makes;
- comprehend likely results from saying certain things or taking certain actions;
- differentiate between acceptable decisions and horrendous decisions;
- be willing to understand, protect, and defend the U.S. Constitution, including its provisions that relate to the functioning of the

executive branch and the rights of citizens under the Bill of Rights;

- keep himself from committing high crimes and misdemeanors as that term appears in the U.S. Constitution, Art. II, Sec. 4, regarding impeachment;
- make agreements and keep those agreements;
- learn about and conduct foreign policy on behalf of the United States;
- deal reasonably and effectively with other people;
- not be delusional;
- understand basic democratic principles, including: the importance of a free and fair election (and the importance of not claiming it is "rigged" before it has occurred); the undemocratic nature of intending to jail his election rival; and the danger of propounding multiple conspiracy theories against him; and
- be stable (i.e., not having mental instability) in his thoughts and speech.

I asserted that the statements of Trump support a determination that he suffers from *narcissistic personality disorder*, which would make him mentally incapable of continuing as president, and that he:

- has a grandiose sense of self-importance;
- is preoccupied with fantasies of unlimited success, power, or brilliance;
- believes that he is special and unique;
- requires excessive admiration;
- has a sense of entitlement (i.e., has unreasonable expectations of especially favorable treatment or automatic compliance with his expectations);
- is interpersonally exploitive (i.e., takes advantage of others to achieve his own ends);

- lacks empathy, being unwilling or unable to recognize or identify with the feelings and needs of others; and
- shows arrogant, haughty behaviors or attitudes.

I asserted that the statements of Trump support a determination that he suffers from *histrionic personality disorder*, which would make him mentally incapable of continuing as president, and that he:

- has had interactions with others that are often characterized by inappropriate sexually seductive or provocative behavior;
- displays rapidly shifting and shallow expressions of emotions;
- has a style of speech that is excessively impressionistic and lacking in detail;
- shows self-dramatization, theatricality, and exaggerated expression of emotion; and
- is suggestible (i.e., easily influenced by others or circumstances).

I asserted that Trump appears to suffer from delusional beliefs, which would make him incapable of continuing as president, citing various of the more than two hundred troubling statements made by him during the election campaign.

I asserted that the U.S. Constitution does have provisions that deal with the inability of a president (once in office) to discharge the powers and duties of that office, being Sections 3 and 4 of the Twenty-Fifth Amendment.*

---

* Sections 3 and 4 of the Twenty-Fifth Amendment state:

> Section 3. Whenever the President transmits to the President pro tempore of the Senate and the Speaker of the House of Representatives his written declaration that he is *unable* to discharge the powers and duties of his office, and until he transmits to them a written declaration to the contrary,

Section 3 provides for a voluntary (and possibly temporary) relinquishment of the powers and duties of the president to the vice president, who becomes acting president. The president transmits a written declaration to the president *pro tempore* of the Senate and the Speaker of the House that he is unable to discharge the powers and duties of his office. This relinquishment continues until the president transmits to them a written declaration to the contrary.

Section 3 has been invoked three times in our history—once in 1985, by Ronald Reagan (colon cancer surgery), for about eight hours; once in 2002, by George W. Bush (colonoscopy), for less than two

---

such powers and duties shall be discharged by the Vice President as Acting President.

Section 4. Whenever the Vice President and a majority of either the principal officers of the executive departments or of such other body as Congress may by law provide, transmit to the President pro tempore of the Senate and the Speaker of the House of Representatives their written declaration that the President is *unable* to discharge the powers and duties of his office, the Vice President shall immediately assume the powers and duties of the office as Acting President.

Thereafter, when the President transmits to the President pro tempore of the Senate and the Speaker of the House of Representatives his written declaration that no *inability* exists, he shall resume the powers and duties of his office unless the Vice President and a majority of either the principal officers of the executive department or of such other body as Congress may by law provide, transmit within four days to the President pro tempore of the Senate and the Speaker of the House of Representatives their written declaration that the President is *unable* to discharge the powers and duties of his office. Thereupon Congress shall decide the issue, assembling within forty-eight hours for that purpose if not in session. If the Congress, within twenty-one days after receipt of the latter written declaration, or, if Congress is not in session, within twenty-one days after Congress is required to assemble, determines by two-thirds vote of both Houses that the President is unable to discharge the powers and duties of his office, the Vice President shall continue to discharge the same as Acting President; otherwise, the President shall resume the powers and duties of his office [emphasis added].

hours; and once in 2007, by George W. Bush (colonoscopy), for less than two hours. We have accordingly had two acting presidents: George H. W. Bush and Richard B. Cheney. These relinquishments were (and were intended to be) temporary.

Section 4 provides for an involuntary relinquishment of the office. If the vice president and a majority of the Cabinet officers transmit to the president *pro tempore* of the Senate and the Speaker of the House their written declaration that the president is unable to discharge the powers and duties of his office, the vice president immediately becomes acting president.

However, it doesn't end there. If the president transmits to the president *pro tempore* of the Senate and the Speaker of the House his written declaration that no inability exists, he resumes his office— unless the vice president and a majority of the Cabinet officers transmit to the president *pro tempore* of the Senate and the Speaker of the House their written declaration that the president is unable to discharge his office. Congress then decides the issue. If Congress determines by a two-thirds' vote of both houses that the president is unable to serve, the vice president continues to serve as acting president; otherwise, the president resumes the powers and duties of his office.

I asserted that the Florida state court had the power to determine that Trump was mentally incapacitated to serve as president. While such a determination is not self-executing—that is, it does not automatically remove him from office—it could provide the basis on which a removal relinquishment could go forward under the Twenty-Fifth Amendment.

On February 21, 2017, the court dismissed my second petition, and I filed a notice of appeal of that decision to the Florida Fourth District Court of Appeal. The appeal is pending.

I filed my appellate brief on May 1, 2017. My "May Day/May-day" brief asks the appellate court to order the trial court to proceed with the incapacity proceeding against Trump, to the ultimate determination of whether he is mentally incapacitated to serve as president. If the appellate court agrees with me and grants my requested relief, this procedure will go forward.

Quo Vadis

Perhaps given a holding that he lacks mental capacity to be president, Trump will follow the voluntary proceeding set forth in Section 3 of the Twenty-Fifth Amendment, and declare himself to be unable to discharge the powers and duties of his office. Given the somewhat bizarre nature of our current *Alice in Wonderland* world, though, this may not be out of the question. If he does not choose a voluntary relinquishment under Section 3, then Section 4 of the Twenty-Fifth Amendment sets forth an involuntary procedure involving the vice president, the Cabinet, and the Congress. This section has never been invoked. Perhaps now is the time.

All are equal before the law. As far as Florida guardianship law is concerned, Trump has the right to be protected from himself—just like anyone else. But, for now, Trump is an alleged incapacitated person, and will remain so until there is a determination otherwise.

To be continued . . .

James A. Herb, M.A., Esq., has practiced law in Florida for forty years. He is a Florida Supreme Court–certified circuit court mediator, a certificated arbitrator, and a professional member of the National College of Probate Judges. He is author of four chapters in Florida law practice books and has chaired or spoken at more than fifty legal seminars.

Reference

U.S. Senate. 2013. *The Constitution of the United States of America, Analysis and Interpretation.* 112th Congress, 2nd Session, Senate Document No. 112-9.

PART 2

THE TRUMP DILEMMA

SHOULD PSYCHIATRISTS REFRAIN FROM COMMENTING ON TRUMP'S PSYCHOLOGY?

LEONARD L. GLASS, M.D., M.P.H.

You might think the answer is obvious, but it isn't.

Obviously "No"

There's a historical basis for objecting to mental health professionals injecting their opinions into political debate: the Goldwater rule (Friedman 2017). Psychiatrists' painful experience of suffering legal humiliation for offering their armchair diagnoses of Barry Goldwater in 1964 chastened the leaders of mental health organizations, who then acted to protect their professions' reputation by including in their code of ethics a prohibition against the diagnosis of public figures.

The central argument is that one can claim professional authority to comment on an individual's mental functioning only if one has followed the precepts of the profession for a bona fide evaluation: that is, a thorough vis-à-vis interview buttressed by a personal history derived from the patient and reliable family sources, a complete mental status examination, a physical exam, relevant lab studies, and so on. Otherwise, any opinion offered by a mental health professional, though it would be seen as valid by the public, would, some hold, lack the accepted foundation to be appropriately taken as such.

Recently, the American Psychiatric Association's Ethics Committee expanded its interpretation of the Goldwater rule to prohibit *any* comment by psychiatrists on a public figure that included reference to their professional status (American Psychiatric Association 2017).

Other "no" arguments opposed to such diagnoses are essentially variations on the theme of protecting the guild from disgrace: mental health professionals might speak in biased, uninformed, or merely disparate ways, and this could discredit the psychological professions, which are always vulnerable to critique and often not taken seriously, as seen in cartoons in *The New Yorker* and in other, less affectionate forms of ridicule.

But, Less Obviously, "Yes"

The Goldwater rule, especially in its expanded interpretation, makes an error in categorizing: it conflates a "professional opinion" (i.e., a clinical assessment that is the basis for the care of a patient) with "the opinion of a professional" commenting in a *nonclinical* role (i.e., as a mental health expert offering his perspective in the public square). There is *no patient* in the latter instance, and hence the standards for providing only a clinically derived assessment with the patient's authorization and with due regard for the patient's confidentiality are not applicable: again, here there *is no patient*. For example, you might be interested in "the opinion of a professional" when deciding on an investment or a catering menu, or when reading an op-ed in the *New York Times*.

By the same token, I question the literal application of the so-called Tarasoff duty to warn, so named after the landmark legal case from which it arose. The Tarasoff duty is relevant when, in a doctor-patient relationship, the professional becomes aware of a concrete threat to a third party. In those circumstances, the duty to warn overrides the patient's right to confidentiality. But where there is no doctor-patient relationship, the duty to warn is more metaphoric— that is, we professionals can "connect the dots" and alert the public to what appears to us to be a pattern of irrationality, impulsivity, and intolerance of divergent views that suggests a dangerous vulnerability in a man occupying the most powerful of positions. Our duty to warn is an expression of our concerns as *citizens* possessed of a particular expertise; not as *clinicians* who are responsible for preventing predictable violence from someone under our care.

The public could benefit from psychologically expert commentary on phenomena that are, on the face of it, confusing. Indeed, one of the explicit ethical principles guiding physicians is to make "relevant information available to . . . the general public" (American Psychiatric Association 2013). For instance, what to make of a person who characteristically proclaims his successes and never acknowledges his mistakes, who instead blames and vilifies others (e.g., the generals who planned the mission, the Fox News analyst whose opinion Trump proclaimed as fact, the press who exposed the problem, the leakers/whistleblowers who alerted the press). While it may seem obvious to some that such a person is driven to inflate himself out of insecurity, some not very psychologically sophisticated segments of the public may well take his boasts at face value. Thus, it is precisely the role of trained professionals to offer expert perspectives to the public at large.

While it's true that, in the case of Donald Trump, we professionals don't have the data we traditionally rely on in a clinical setting, it's also true that, thanks to Trump's facility in garnering public attention, the many years he has been in the news, and most especially the abundance of videotaped evidence of his behavioral reactions, there is an impressive quantity of Donald Trump's emotional responses and spoken ideation for us to draw on. While the prior understanding of the Goldwater rule sought to prevent speculation about the inner, unobservable workings of a public figure's mind, the newly propounded interpretation blocks psychiatrists from helping to explain widely available and readily observed behaviors.

As for the prohibition against identifying oneself as a psychiatrist when commenting on a public figure, consider the orthopedist interviewed on local television who is asked to assess the implications of the injury sustained by the local team's quarterback in today's game played on the opposite coast. Is she prohibited from offering her professional opinion because she hasn't examined the football star? Of course, her opinion is conditioned by her not having examined him or seen the X-rays, but this is so obvious and implicit that it often isn't stated. (It would be prudent to do so, lest there be any doubt about the certainty of her opinion.) Psychiatrists' being gagged by their professional association bespeaks that association's profound lack of respect for and confidence in the maturity and judgment of its members.

By attempting to preclude psychiatry as a profession from the public discussion, the American Psychiatric Association is, inescapably, devaluing the relevance and importance of the very profession it imagines it is protecting.

Now, it is undoubtedly true that mental health professionals are not exempt from bias and that some would speak without due reflection and circumspection. Though professionals are trained to bear in mind the potential confounding influence of their own attitudes and feelings, they're human and fallible. I think a more appropriate action by the American Psychiatric Association would be to urge members to recognize the need for discretion when speaking out, rather than compelling them to choose between submitting to a gag rule or risk being found in violation of its ethical code. Such a policy would recognize the dictates of the individual psychiatrist's conscience to engage with the public and not require that his or her moral prompting be subordinated to protect the psychiatric profession from appearing less than scientifically respectable because some members might speak out in an insufficiently considered way.

I do respect the difference between, on the one hand, making a diagnosis of a public person one hasn't examined and, on the other, offering a professionally informed perspective. Diagnosing is intrinsically more specific and requires a more substantial level of confidence rooted in the professional procedures and discipline in which a more definitive conclusion is grounded. Offering a definitive medical diagnosis without a thorough personal evaluation and the consent of the person being assessed can easily degenerate into speculation and name-calling, which discredits the clinician making the less than optimally founded diagnosis. Nonetheless, one can acknowledge the limitations of relying on publicly available evidence and the lack of certainty inherent in that foundation and still offer valuable professional perspectives on the apparent psychological impediments of a public figure.

In the End, It's a Matter of Opinion

I believe that either a "yes" or a "no" answer to the question of the legitimacy of a professional making a statement about a public figure's mental fitness without a personal examination can be made on firm moral ground. In withholding comment, one places a premium on the traditional methodology and restraint of the profession, but also privileges the public image of the profession over a psychiatrist's right to abide by the dictates of individual conscience. By offering an opinion conditioned on the publicly available data (but lacking the sources one relies on in clinical practice), one prioritizes the professional duty to engage with and educate the public and to identify hazards that are most starkly evident and comprehensible to the clinician's eye.

To demonize those conscientiously holding either view is, I feel, the only indefensible position.

Why I Choose to Speak Out

These are frightening times. The current occupant of the White House is widely perceived as erratic and vindictive (Chollet, Kahl, and Smith 2017; Remnick 2017; Shelbourne 2017; Tumulty 2017).* Yet, those very elements of his character may well have endeared him to his base. He speaks without hesitation or reflection, and repudiates "political correctness." That convinces some that he is authentic, saying things that they've felt but have feared to say out loud. He appears to be easily moved to anger and heedless retaliation. That, too, could be appealing to people who feel powerless and oppressed by an economic system and the societal changes that haven't preserved their status or allowed them to fulfill their dreams and potential. I can identify with those feelings—ironically, even better now, because I am experiencing a variation on the powerlessness I've just described. It would be comforting to believe I had a forceful advocate who possessed the authority and motivation to fix what worries me. Alas, the shoe is on the other foot. (Although, I have profound doubts about how sincerely motivated Mr. Trump is to pursue the interests of the truly powerless.)

Yet, I can feel a sense of community with those who share my apprehension by raising an alarm in the hope that others will be comforted by seeing that their concerns are shared. Still others may feel empowered with a heightened, psychiatrically informed understanding of the nature of the danger, and may be better equipped to respond effectively by virtue of what I and others write.

The Essentially Dangerous Nature of Donald Trump as Commander in Chief

What I and many others discern in Mr. Trump's behavior and speech is a pattern of *impulsivity* that leads to vengeful attacks on those who challenge him. He doesn't seem to pause to consider the validity of

---

* As discerned by videotaped exchanges and acknowledging the limitations of relying on such material as opposed to a traditional and in-person psychiatric evaluation.

facts and perspectives that are unfamiliar or displeasing to him. He presents himself as "knowing more than the generals" and having "great" plans that are sure to succeed: "You will be sick of winning," he has said. This combination of *overconfidence* and rash reactions may have been an asset in the world of real estate deals, where the stakes are financial, personal, and presumably recoverable. But "shooting from the hip" without feeling the need to obtain a genuine understanding of complex matters has much graver consequences when the safety of the nation and the global environment are on the line.

Viewed from a mental health perspective, a person who constantly extols his abilities and feels driven to diminish and ridicule others (and here I am not speaking of political campaigning, where promoting oneself vis-à-vis one's opponents is part of the game) often arises from *profound insecurity*, the very opposite of the supreme confidence that is being projected.

This may seem contradictory, that someone who has succeeded in one realm of life will keep insisting that he is masterful in unrelated areas, areas where he has, in fact, no demonstrated competence, but it soothes such a person's inner doubts and, simultaneously, may appeal mightily to those who crave an all-powerful ally.

This impulsivity, the need to support an insupportably inflated image of oneself, added to a profound inability to acknowledge what one doesn't know, all augur profound psychological interference with the rational and considered exercise of power. *We* need to understand this, all the more so because it is the very awareness that Mr. Trump himself and his acolytes feel they mustn't acknowledge to themselves and us, the people whose safety he is entrusted to protect. Our understanding that this is a recognizable personality style that predictably impedes reliable judgment and a sound, considered response to crises allows us to take appropriate action within the law to contain and limit the damage that we can clearly envision and, collectively, must try to prevent.

Is Donald Trump Mentally Ill?

In my opinion, this is decidedly *not* the question to be addressed, for two reasons: First, mental illness per se is not incompatible with reliably functioning at a high level, e.g., Abraham Lincoln (depression), Winston Churchill (bipolar disorder). Second, without a bona fide psychiatric examination, any speculation about a definitive diagnosis can be seen (and sometimes be) just that, speculation. To compound matters, it's counterproductive because of its irrelevance (see my first point) and because the uncertain conclusions facilitate the easy dismissal of genuine, observable, and profound impediments in Mr. Trump's capacity to deal thoughtfully and reliably with the complex and grave responsibilities of being a reliable president and commander in chief.

To put it another way, operationally and day to day, we don't know and can't tell if Mr. Trump knows that what he is saying is demonstrably not true. What we *do* know is that he can't be relied upon to recognize having been wrong; nor does he seem to able to learn from experience such that he could avoid repeating the same untruth or another the next day, possessed as he appears to be of the same absolute conviction that characterized his previous error.

Conclusion

Donald Trump's presidency confronts the psychiatric profession and, much more important, our country with the challenge of dealing with an elected leader whose psychological style (marked by impulsivity, insistence on his own infallibility, vengeful retaliation, and unwarranted certainty in uncertain circumstances) is a profound impediment to sound decision making and presages the erratic and ill-considered exercise of enormous power.

Leonard L. Glass, M.D., M.P.H. is a psychiatrist and psychoanalyst in Newton, Massachusetts. He is an associate professor of psychiatry (part time) at Harvard Medical School and a senior attending psychiatrist at McLean Hospital. Dr. Glass was president of the Boston Psychoanalytic Society and Institute and was a Distinguished Life Fellow of the American Psychiatric Association until he resigned in protest of the Goldwater rule in April 2017. He has written professionally about ethics, the psychology of men, psychiatric risks of large groups, and boundary issues in psychotherapy. He has also authored popular articles about road rage and spectator violence at sporting events.

ON SEEING WHAT YOU SEE AND SAYING WHAT YOU KNOW

A Psychiatrist's Responsibility

HENRY J. FRIEDMAN, M.D.

Can experienced psychiatrists well trained in both psychiatry and psychoanalysis and seasoned by decades of clinical work actually turn off their powers of observation? And if they could, why would they choose to do so? As important, why should the public be deprived of our expertise? These are relevant and necessary questions to ask before exploring the question of how to process the experience of being exposed to President Donald Trump in the media. Such a series of questions and concerns would be entirely unnecessary were it not for the position taken by the American Psychiatric Association that insists it is unethical for psychiatrists to comment on or diagnose a public figure such as President Trump unless you have seen him in your office. There is a certain irony in this position because if, as a psychiatrist, you examined him in person, you would be prohibited, by ethical standards of confidentiality, from revealing anything about his diagnosis without his permission to do so, even if you had concluded that he was in some way unfit for office.

The American Psychiatric Association came to the Goldwater rule after *Fact Magazine* had surveyed psychiatrists, asking them to diagnose Barry Goldwater, who was running for the presidency against Lyndon Johnson in 1964. A majority of those responding felt that Goldwater's endorsement of the use of nuclear weapons in the Cold War with the Soviet Union justified giving him a diagnosis of paranoia (even paranoid schizophrenia) in some form or another. This fact alone was felt to be sufficient for many to use this diagnosis in responding to the question asked by the magazine. Goldwater successfully sued the magazine for libel; the resulting panic and concern expressed in the APA's adoption of the Goldwater rule was understandable at the time but would certainly have been expected to be modified in response to the very different world that has evolved since the early 1970s. Changes in the world of media, such as the presence of cable news with its 24/7 cycle of reporting and broadcasting visual images of events and leaders, should have led, in my opinion, to the abandonment of the Goldwater rule. Instead, the Ethics Committee of the APA decided, without polling the members, to double down on the Goldwater rule by extending it beyond the realm of diagnosis to include any and all comments on the mental functioning of this or any president or prominent public figure.

In addition to changes in the availability of coverage on TV, there has been an evolving use of phone and Skype in the distant treatment of patients in both psychotherapy and psychoanalysis. Many contemporary psychiatrists no longer feel that their patient must be present in the consulting room with them. While clinicians vary in their comfort and experience with phone and Skype therapies, there is a definite trend toward these modalities as essential if one is to conduct a full-time practice and extend treatment into underserved areas. This shift in attitude toward "remote" treatment conducted through previously untried communication methods is relevant to why commenting on President Trump's mental function feels not only comfortable but necessary.

Because of the constant exposure to Donald Trump on TV news and his open expression of his thinking in rapidly expressed tweets and a multitude of other extemporaneous, unscripted remarks, a trained observer cannot avoid noting the style of his thinking and his reaction to the existence of frustrating realities that challenge his version of events. In this regard, observations about President Trump require some professional clarification concerning the concepts of paranoid thinking and character. The applicability of these concepts to the president can be considered by the nonclinical observer, thus facilitating a more enlightened, critical-thinking public better capable of acting in its interest.

Paranoid thinking, when persistent, is indicative of a paranoid character structure. This means that an individual with such a basic character will consistently produce ideas and responses that find exaggerated danger and malevolent intent in others and in the situations he encounters. The major totalitarian leaders of the twentieth century have all manifested paranoid thinking. Their destructive behavior has been an enactment of their disturbed ideation. Inevitably we have watched as such individuals have taken over entire countries, always acting to increase their power by suppressing freedom of the press and media, jailing or killing the political opposition, and militarizing their political power. Hence, the resemblance between Hitler and Stalin with regard to the senseless murder of millions of people for reasons of pure paranoid-based ruthlessness once they had entered the leader's mind as "enemies of the people."

When attention is called to the resemblance between Hitler and Trump, it tends to elicit a veritable storm of objection. Those who object so strongly are, in effect, calling attention to Hitler's actions in immediately taking over the press and arresting or killing his opposition. While it is true that the restraints operating in our country have prevented Trump from moving as swiftly as Hitler did, this can be attributed to the balance of powers and the greater strength of our democratic traditions rather than to any sense that Trump's patterns of emotional thinking are greatly different from those that motivated Hitler.

The totalitarian mind is remarkably reproducible because it depends upon paranoid ideation presented in a dramatic fashion designed to mobilize both fear and hate, particularly in the less well-educated citizens. Trump, like Hitler, began with his insistence on identifying the United States as in decline, a decline, in Trump's case, caused by our first African American president, who, according to Trump, had left our country in a mess, an "American carnage." This, despite the actual spectacular record of President Obama in saving the economy after the crash of 2008, preventing the worst recession from becoming another Great Depression, the extension of health care to the poor and middle class, and the general spreading of enlightened attitudes toward minorities and women.

The insistence that grave danger exists in reality because it exists in one's mind is the hallmark of the dictator. For Hitler, the Jews represented an existential threat; for Trump, it is illegal immigrants and Mexicans in particular. Also, the disregard for facts, the denial that "factualization" is a necessity before making an assertion of danger or insisting on the nefarious intent of a large group (i.e., the Jews for Hitler, the Muslims for Trump) is typical of paranoid characters who need an enemy against whom to focus group hate.

Many critics of Trump, particularly journalists but also those in the mental health field, have focused on his so-called narcissism, his need to be constantly approved of, the childlike nature of his character. In this they are minimizing the significance of his paranoid beliefs and, in so doing, are relegating his psychological dysfunction to a much higher level than is actually the case. This is also true of those who believe he is simply using his attack on illegal immigrants and Muslims to feed his base. In doing so, they are suggesting that he himself knows better, that he knows that he is merely using these ideas because they will appeal to the white working-class men who make up the bulk of his voters. Yet, this overlooks and minimizes the more ominous probability: that he actually is paranoid and that there is an overlap of his personal hatreds and those of his followers.

Together, they represent a desire to undo the impact of all that has changed since Franklin Delano Roosevelt, the New Deal, and the general liberalization of society and life in the United States.

Progress within our liberal democracy can hardly be said to have been rapid. Rather, it has been slow, coming in bursts of activity followed by the integration of the change, but that integration has always been opposed by those who found the particular change unacceptable. The civil rights movement established a new identity for African Americans, one in which they refused to accept a designation as inferior individuals expected to be treated as second-class or lesser citizens. Their ability to use passive resistance and marching to achieve recognition of their right to equal status was furthered by the registration of black voters against local resistance and the establishment of their votes as a powerful determinant in both state and national elections. The combined power of African American, women, and liberal voters resulted in the election of the first African American president, a result that led many liberals, including President Obama, to believe that the United States had at last arrived at a postracial position as a society. Unfortunately, this proved to be anything but the case. Instead of proving to be the sign of decreased racism, the very fact of a black man in the White House appeared to generate a degree of hatred and resistance to President Obama that was, if anything, a grim reminder of the legacy of slavery and the split in the United States between the North and the South that has never come close to actually healing or even scarring over.

In his successful campaign to capture the Republican Party nomination, candidate Trump used the racism of the white working class to engage their enthusiastic support by attacking each of the other Republican candidates in terms never seen before in such a competition. Mostly, however, he depended upon his populist appeal to his followers' discontent and disdain for the establishment. What tended to get lost even in the process of securing the nomination was his ability to make things up and, at the same time, to believe them himself. Trump managed a variation on Descartes's "I think, therefore I am": "I think it, therefore it is." This reckless relationship to reality on Trump's part has continued to represent a reliably occurring part of his character; no fact that he believes to be true, often after reading it on some alt-right website, is fact-checked or questioned. This form of grandiosity is part of the paranoia that clearly dominates Trump's thinking.

Am I making a diagnosis of President Trump? Well, yes and no—and even maybe—but whatever it is I am doing, there is one thing that I am refusing to do: to deny what I am hearing and seeing coming from Trump himself on the TV news and in the printed reliable press. The effort on the part of CNN, MSNBC, the *New York Times*, and the *Washington Post* to keep the public informed about Trump and his administration has undoubtedly been a crucial element in preventing him from doing more harm, from going the really radical route of Hitler. Hence, his attack on the press, accusing real reporting of facts as being "fake news," is an attenuated version of the more extreme takeover of the media that is usual in totalitarian governments. Trump hasn't been able or willing to seize the news media and close them down, but he has tried by insisting that those who question his campaign's involvement with the Russian interference with our election are refusing to accept that there is no basis for investigating this possibility. Some reporters, such as Thomas Friedman, Rachel Maddow, and Lawrence O'Donnell, have suggested that Trump is "crazy." Recently, in relationship to his firing of FBI director James Comey, many have made the observation that President Trump is "unhinged." These descriptions are made by intelligent nonpsychiatrists who are limited in using such terms to describe their impression of the man and his thinking. Donny Deutsch on *Morning Joe* actually spoke out against the Goldwater rule and asked when the psychiatrists were going to comment on what they see in watching President Trump. Deutsch emphasized the need to ignore the Goldwater rule in favor of supporting those who correctly doubt that Trump's mental state is compatible with the office he currently inhabits.

A paranoid, hypersensitive, grandiose, ill-informed leader such as Donald Trump, who has surrounded himself with a Cabinet and a set of advisers who either are unable to bring him out of his paranoid suspicions and insistences or, worse, identify with his positions, represents a multidimensional threat to our country and the world. The most common concern I hear from my patients is that Trump's impulsivity will result in a nuclear war with North Korea. The intensity of this concern tends to mask an awareness of what has already begun in the United States, namely, an erosion of the just and decent society that has been evolving since FDR's New Deal. That society reached the pinnacle of decency under the presidency of Barack Obama, a leader who personified what it means to be a stable leader of a great and powerful nation. Trump's need to destroy everything that Obama achieved derives from the paranoid character's hatred of goodness in others whose achievements he cannot attain, understand, or tolerate. This degree of destructiveness in any individual makes him a poor candidate for therapy of any sort. The goodness of any therapist, his or her competence, and his or her ability to provide needed responsiveness can and will be targeted for destruction. Treating such individuals is always arduous and rarely effective, and yet they often present when in trouble as motivated to receive help. Once they have managed to solve the problem that has brought them to therapy, they quickly reveal a lack of investment in the therapy or the therapist.

This brings us to the question of analyzing President Trump from a distance; is it possible, is it ethical, and who is to decide this issue? In particular, does the stance of the APA, with its newly minted version of the Goldwater rule, prevent a psychiatrist-psychoanalyst from attempting such an analysis? A classical psychoanalyst would scoff at the idea that any psychoanalysis could be done from a distance, whether by telephone or by Skype. For such an analyst, both analyst and analysand must be present in the consulting room, so that observations of the patient who is practicing free association can be made continuously. The unconscious is to be found and interpreted to the patient at the moment of interaction. Judged by the criteria of classical psychoanalysis, no analysis of candidate or President Trump is possible. But taken from the perspective of an interpersonal or relational psychoanalyst, it is possible to think psychoanalytically about him only from a distance. Because of the unlikely possibility that Trump could form a significant attachment to a therapist, we need to see him as a fit subject for descriptive reflection rather than treatment of any kind; we need to believe what we see in all that he reveals to us without hesitation or inhibition. As important, we need to emphasize that these revelations cannot be normalized; nor will they change. Trump challenges us with the question "Are you going to believe me, or are you going to believe your lying eyes?"

Whatever Trump thinks at the moment is translated into tweets or speech with no regard for linking his idea with any previously stated idea or with any context that should be obviously relevant to what he is now asserting. He may be beyond the scope of even the most broadly defined idea of applied psychoanalysis, but what he does gives us ample access to is his characteristic style of responding to others who oppose him. His critics often treat him as if he were childish—that is, were merely acting like a child rather than a mature adult—suggesting that, as a child, he can still "grow up." The problem with such an approach is that it is a manifestation of wishful thinking, and it is incorrect in that it grossly underestimates the importance of Trump's adult paranoid character with its belief in an apocalyptic vision of a weak, diminished United States that only he can save from the liberal Democrats who oppose his authority. Any attempt to "understand" Trump from the perspective of his childhood or of what he is reenacting from the past is, in all probability, a hopeless and unnecessary task. Character formation of the paranoid typology becomes so autonomous that, once it has solidified, it is practically meaningless to try to find an explanation for its existence in a particular individual.

Ultimately, the response to the Trump administration will have to come from the electorate. All the policies that he wants to promote may not in themselves be absolutely ruinous to our country. The poor and disenfranchised will undoubtedly suffer, but the real danger will be from the president's paranoid character, which will continue to be present and active for as long as he is in office. Perhaps the observations of this psychiatrist-psychoanalyst, and of others in the mental health field, will help clarify why the threat of President Trump exceeds the issue of his policies, and resides instead in his core paranoid personality. When, as a psychiatrist, I watch commentators and reporters struggling to understand or explain President Trump's latest irrational position—as when he lies about when and why he decided to fire James Comey or the claimed details of his exchanges with Comey before the firing occurred—I wish that I could help them understand his paranoid character and why there should be no surprise that Trump has behaved in this way. They should be prepared to witness many more situations in which Trump feels betrayed and turns on those who have previously served him. Paranoids are always finding betrayal in those surrounding them, and react with retaliatory anger—Hitler and Stalin, by murdering their newly minted enemies; and Trump, by firing them. Psychiatric knowledge and terminology will save reporters and the public from remaining confused and attempting to find explanations of behavior that could easily be understood if Trump's paranoid character were always kept in mind. This is the only way to ensure the preservation and viability of our democracy and our national security.

Henry J. Friedman, M.D., is an associate professor of psychiatry, Harvard Medical School (part time), on the editorial boards of Psychoanalytic Quarterly, *the* American Journal of Psychoanalysis, *and the* Journal of the American Psychoanalytic Association, *with main interests in the therapeutic action of psychoanalysis and analytic psychotherapy. Friedman is also chair of the "Meet the Author" at the biannual meetings of the American Psychoanalytic Association.*

THE ISSUE IS DANGEROUSNESS, NOT MENTAL ILLNESS

JAMES GILLIGAN, M.D.

Psychiatrists in America today have been told by two different official organizations that they have two diametrically opposite professional obligations, and that if they violate either one, they are behaving unethically. The first says they have an obligation to remain silent about their evaluation of anyone if that person has not given them permission to speak about it publicly. The second says they have an obligation to speak out and inform others if they believe that person may be dangerous to them, even if he has not given them permission to do so. The first standard is the Goldwater rule of 1973, which prohibits psychiatrists from offering a professional opinion in public about the mental health of anyone whom they have not personally examined. The second is the Tarasoff decision, which in 1976 ruled that psychiatrists have a positive obligation to speak out publicly when they have determined, or should have determined, that an individual is dangerous to another person or persons, in order both to warn the potential victim(s) of the danger they are in and to set in motion a set of procedures that will help protect the potential victim(s).

From both an ethical and a legal standpoint, the second of those two rulings trumps the first.

Insofar as psychiatrists function as clinicians, their primary duty is to their individual patients. Yet, psychiatry, like every other medical specialty, involves more than just clinical practice (that is, diagnosing and treating one patient at a time after those patients have already become ill). It is also a branch of public health and preventive medicine, and in that aspect of its functioning, we owe society a primary duty, for that is the level at which primary and secondary prevention can prevent individuals from becoming ill or violent in the first place, and injuring or killing others if either their illness or their behavior is contagious. In fact, this level of intervention can even prevent the whole society from becoming vulnerable to epidemics of illness, injury, and death. Clinical psychiatry, from a public health standpoint, is merely tertiary prevention, and it represents the least useful contribution we can make to the public health, compared to primary and secondary prevention (Gilligan 2001). From that standpoint, we have a positive obligation to warn the public when we have reason to believe, based on our research with the most dangerous people our society produces, that a public figure, by virtue of the actions he takes, represents a danger to the public health—whether or not he is mentally ill.

An intellectual precursor to the Goldwater rule was a comment that one of the most influential and brilliant German intellectuals made not long before the rise of Hitler. In his essay on "Science as a Vocation," Max Weber (1917) argued that intellectuals and scholars should not utter political opinions or say anything that could be regarded as "partisan." They could talk about politics in general, but they should not say anything that could be taken as support for or opposition to any particular party or politician.

I have always been troubled by that opinion, because it appears to me to have encouraged the intellectual and professional leaders of Germany to remain silent, even in the face of enormous and unprecedented danger. It does not seem to me that the German Psychiatric Association of the 1930s deserves any honor or credit for remaining silent during Hitler's rise to power. On the contrary, it appears from our perspective today to have been a passive enabler of the worst atrocities he committed—as were most German clergymen, professors, lawyers, judges, physicians, journalists, and other professionals and intellectuals who could have, but did not, speak out when they saw a blatantly obvious psychopath gaining the power to lead their country into the worst disaster in its history. Our current president does not have to be a literal reincarnation of Hitler—and I am not suggesting that he is—in order for the same principles to apply to us today.

The issue that we are raising is not whether Trump is mentally ill. It is whether he is dangerous. Dangerousness is not a psychiatric diagnosis. One does not have to be "mentally ill," as both law and psychiatry define it, in order to be dangerous. In fact, most mentally ill people do not commit serious violence, and most violence is committed by people who are not mentally ill. The association between violence and mental illness is very tenuous at best. Only about 1 percent of the perpetrators of homicide in this country are found to be "not guilty by reason of insanity." The rest are declared by our courts to be mentally healthy but evil, as those concepts are used in relevance to people's "criminal responsibility" for whatever violence they have committed.

President Trump may or may not meet the criteria for any of the diagnoses of mental disorders defined in the *Diagnostic and Statistical Manual* of the American Psychiatric Association, or for many of them, but that is not relevant to the issue we are raising here.

Also, the most reliable data for assessing dangerousness often do not require, and are often not attainable from, interviewing the individuals about whom we are forming an opinion. Such individuals often (though not always) deny, minimize, or attempt to conceal the very facts that identify them as being dangerous. The most reliable data may come from the person's family and friends and, just as important, from police reports; criminal histories; medical, prison, and judicial records; and other publicly available information from third parties. However, in Trump's case, we also have many public records, tape recordings, videotapes, and his own public speeches, interviews, and "tweets" of <u>his numerous threats of violence, incitements to violence, and boasts of violence that he himself</u> acknowledges having committed repeatedly and habitually.

<u>Sometimes a person's dangerousness is so obvious that one does not need professional training in either psychiatry or criminology to recognize it.</u> One does not need to have had fifty years of professional experience in assessing the dangerousness of violent criminals to recognize the dangerousness of a president who:

- **Asks what the point of having thermonuclear weapons is if we cannot use them.** For example, in an interview with Chris Matthews on an MSNBC town hall meeting, he said, "Somebody hits us within ISIS, you wouldn't fight back with a nuke?" When Matthews remarked that "the whole world [is] hearing a guy running for president of the United States talking of maybe using nuclear weapons. No one wants to hear that about an American president," Trump replied, "Then why are we making them?" Another MSNBC host, Joe Scarborough, reported that Trump had asked a foreign policy adviser three times, "If we have them, why can't we use them?" (Fisher 2016).

- **Urges our government to use torture or worse against our prisoners of war.** Throughout his presidential campaign, Trump repeatedly said that "torture works," and promised to bring back "waterboarding" and to introduce new methods "that go a lot further." After being reminded that there were by then laws prohibiting these practices, he responded by insisting that he would broaden the laws so that the United States would not have to play "by the rules," as ISIS did not do so (Haberman 2016).

- **Urged that five innocent African American youths be given the death penalty for a sexual assault even years after it had been**

proven beyond a reasonable doubt to have been committed by someone else. In 1989, Trump spent $85,000 placing ads in New York City's four daily papers calling for the return of the death penalty to New York State so that five African American youths who had been wrongfully convicted of raping a woman in Central Park could be executed, and he was still advocating the same penalty in 2016, fourteen years after DNA evidence and a detailed confession had proved that a serial rapist had actually committed the crime (Burns 2016).

- **Boasts about his ability to get away with sexually assaulting women because of his celebrity and power.** Trump was recorded saying, of his way of relating to women, that "I just start kissing them. It's like a magnet. . . . I don't even wait. And when you're a star they let you do it. You can do anything. Grab 'em by the pussy. You can do anything" ("Donald Trump's Lewd Comments About Women" 2016).

- **Urges his followers at political rallies to punch protesters in the face and beat them up so badly that they have to be taken out on stretchers.** In an editorial, the *New York Times* has quoted the following remarks by Trump at his rallies: "I'd like to punch him in the face, I'll tell you"; "In the good old days this doesn't happen, because they used to treat them very, very rough"; "I love the old days. You know what they used to do to guys like that when they were in a place like this? They'd be carried out on a stretcher, folks"; "If you see somebody getting ready to throw a tomato, knock the crap out of them, would ya? Seriously. Just knock the hell out of them. I will pay for the legal fees, I promise you." He even complained that his supporters were not being violent enough (even though many had assaulted protesters severely enough to be arrested and tried for assault and battery): "Part of the problem, and part of the reason it takes so long [to remove protesters], is because nobody wants to hurt each other anymore, right?" (*New York Times* Editorial Board 2016).

- **Suggests that his followers could always assassinate his political rival, Hillary Clinton, if she were elected president or, at the very least, throw her in prison.** He has led crowds in chants of "Lock her up! Lock her up!" In his words, "If she gets to pick her judges, nothing you can do, folks. Although the Second Amendment people—maybe there is, I don't know" (remark made during rally on August 9, 2016).

- **Believes he can always get away with whatever violence he does commit.** He said, "I could stand in the middle of Fifth Avenue and shoot somebody, and I wouldn't lose voters" (remark made at rally on January 23, 2016).

And so on and on and on—in an endless stream of threats of violence, boasts of violence, and incitements to violence.

While Trump has not yet succeeded in undoing the rule of law to such a degree as to become a dictator, it is clear that he speaks the language of dictatorship. Only dictators assassinate or imprison their personal political rivals and opponents.

Trump did not confess that he personally assaulted women himself; he boasted that he had. That is, he acknowledged having done so repeatedly, and gotten away with it, not as an expression of personal feelings of guilt and remorse for having violated women in this way but, rather, as a boast about the power his celebrity had given him to force women to submit to his violations of their dignity and autonomy.

As for inciting violence by his followers against his enemies, he sometimes used the same tactic that Henry II used to incite his followers to assassinate Thomas Becket, by implication rather than by an explicit order: "What miserable . . . traitors have I nourished and promoted in my household, who let their lord be treated with such shameful contempt by a low-born clerk!" Of course, his vassals got the point, and did what Henry had made clear he wanted done.

In this regard, however, Trump sometimes went further than his historical predecessors and explicitly, rather than implicitly, encouraged his followers to "punch protestors in the face," and "beat them up so badly that they'll have to be taken out on stretchers." Indeed, a number of his supporters did assault anti-Trump dissenters, and are now being tried for assault and battery. The defense of some has been that they were merely doing what Trump had asked them to do, though the courts may reject that defense on the grounds that Trump was indeed as indirect (notwithstanding that he was just as clear) as Henry II.

If psychiatrists with decades of experience doing research on violent offenders do not confirm the validity of the conclusion that many nonpsychiatrists have reached, that Trump is extremely dangerous—indeed, by far the most dangerous of any president in our lifetimes—then we are not behaving with appropriate professional restraint and discipline. Rather, we are being either incompetent or irresponsible, or both.

However, while all psychiatrists, by definition, have studied mental illness, most have not specialized in studying the causes, consequences, prediction, and prevention of violence, which is considered a problem in public health and preventive medicine. Nor have most studied the principles on which the assessment of current and future dangerousness is based, regardless of whether any particular individual is mentally ill, and regardless of what diagnosis or diagnoses, if any, he may merit according to the criteria outlined in DSM-V.

That is why it is so important and so appropriate for those few of us who have done so—whether by investigating the psychology of Nazi doctors and Japanese terrorists, as Robert Lifton has done; or by studying sexual violence (rape, incest, etc.), as Judith Herman has done; or by examining murderers and rapists (including those who have committed "war crimes") in prisons and jails throughout the world, as I did while working with the World Health Organization's Department of Violence and Injury Prevention on the epidemiology and prevention of violence—to warn the potential victims, in the interests of public health, when we recognize and identify signs and symptoms that indicate that someone is dangerous to the public health.

One implication of this is that we need to identify the potential causes of injury and illness before they have harmed any given population of potential victims as severely or extensively as they would if allowed to go unchecked. In other words, we need to recognize the earliest signs of danger before they have expanded into a full-scale epidemic of lethal or life-threatening injury. The analogy here is to the proverb about how to get a frog to become unaware that it is being boiled to death: place it in a pot of cold water and then heat the water up bit by bit. Something analogous to that is the danger with the Trump presidency.

The United States has been blessed with a little over two centuries of democracy. That is actually a rather short period in comparison with the millennia of monarchy. However, it is long enough to have made most of us complacent, and perhaps overconfident, with respect to the stability of our democracy. In fact, if we are prone to making a mistake in this regard, we are far more likely to underestimate the fragility of democracy than we are to become unnecessarily alarmist about it.

Here again, it is the behavioral scientists who have studied violence (including but not limited to psychiatrists) who owe it to the public to share what we have learned before we experience the epidemic of violence that would be unleashed by the collapse or undermining of the rule of law, the system of checks and balances, the freedom of the press, the independence and authority of the judiciary, the respect for facts, the unacceptability of deliberate lying, the prohibition on conflicts between a political leader's private interests and the public interest, and the even stronger prohibition on physically assaulting one's political rivals or opponents and threatening to imprison or even assassinate them—in other words, dictatorship—all of which have been characteristic of Donald Trump's public statements throughout his electoral campaign and presidency.

To wait until the water reaches boiling temperature, or our democracy collapses, before we begin saying anything about the fact that the water is warming already would mean that anything we said or did in the future would come too late to be of any help. Let us not make the same mistake that the German Psychiatric Association did in the 1930s.

There is an unfortunate and unnecessary taboo in the social and behavioral sciences generally against regarding politics and politicians as appropriate and legitimate subjects for discussion, inquiry, and conclusions. On the contrary, if a psychiatrist or psychologist, or any other behavioral scientist, expresses an opinion that is relevant to the political debates that occur in our country, he is likely to be accused of being "partisan" rather than "professional," or engaging in a discussion that is "just political" rather than "scientific."

I would argue that the opposite is true. At a time when more and more medical scientists are urging us to practice "evidence-based medicine," isn't it even more important that we learn to practice "evidence-based politics"? But of course we cannot do that unless we are willing to apply the methods and accumulated knowledge of all the social and behavioral sciences to this subject, and to publicize the conclusions we reach so that all our fellow citizens, which means all our fellow voters, can benefit from the knowledge we have gained through our clinical, experimental, and epidemiological research into the causes and prevention of violence—concerning which data from politics and economics certainly figure prominently (Gilligan 2011; Lee, Wexler, and Gilligan 2014).

If we are silent about the numerous ways in which Donald Trump has repeatedly threatened violence, incited violence, or boasted about his own violence, we are passively supporting and enabling the dangerous and naïve mistake of treating him as if he were a "normal" president or a "normal" political leader. He is not, and it is our duty to say so, and to say it publicly. He is unprecedentedly and abnormally dangerous.

This is not to inform the public of something it does not already know, for most people in the lay public already appear to know it. Most voters voted against Trump. As our most recent Nobel Prize winner in Literature, Bob Dylan, has put it, "You don't have to be a Weatherman to know which way the wind is blowing!"

In fact, Trump's dangerousness is so obvious that he might be said to have preempted the role other people might otherwise have to play in warning the public as to how dangerous he is. For, in his many public statements on that subject, he himself has warned us about how dangerous he is far more clearly and eloquently than we have been able to do, or need to do. Our role here is not so much to warn the public ourselves, but merely to heed the warnings Trump himself has already given us, and to remind the public about them.

In that regard, one final clarification is in order. Trump is now the most powerful head of state in the world, and one of the most impulsive, arrogant, ignorant, disorganized, chaotic, nihilistic, self-contradictory, self-important, and self-serving. He has his finger on the triggers of a thousand or more of the most powerful thermonuclear weapons in the world. That means he could kill more people in a few seconds than any dictator in past history has been able to kill during his entire years in power. Indeed, by virtue of his office, Trump has the power to reduce the unprecedentedly destructive world wars and genocides of the twentieth century to minor footnotes in the history of human violence. To say merely that he is "dangerous" is debatable only in the sense that it may be too much of an understatement. If he even took a step in this direction, we will not be able to say that he did not warn us—loudly, clearly, and repeatedly. In that case, the fault will not be his alone. It will also be ours.

James Gilligan, M.D., is Clinical Professor of Psychiatry and Adjunct Professor of Law at New York University. He is a renowned violence studies expert and author of the influential Violence: Our Deadly Epidemic and Its Causes, *as well as* Preventing

Violence *and* Why Some Politicians Are More Dangerous Than Others. *He has served as director of mental health services for the Massachusetts prisons and prison mental hospital, president of the International Association for Forensic Psychotherapy, and as a consultant to President Clinton, Tony Blair, Kofi Annan, the World Court, the World Health Organization, and the World Economic Forum.*

References

Burns, Sarah. 2016. "Why Trump Doubled Down on the Central Park Five." *New York Times*, October 17.

"Donald Trump's Lewd Comments About Women." 2016. Transcript and video. *New York Times*, October. 8.

Fisher, Max. 2016. "Donald Trump, Perhaps Unwittingly, Exposes Paradox of Nuclear Arms." *New York Times*, August 3.

Gilligan, James. 2001. *Preventing Violence: An Agenda for the Coming Century.* London and New York: Thames and Hudson.

———. 2011. *Why Some Politicians Are More Dangerous Than Others.* Cambridge, UK: Polity Press.

Haberman, Maggie. 2016. "Donald Trump Again Alters Course on Torture." *New York Times*, March 15.

Heilpern, Will. 2017. "Trump Campaign: 11 Outrageous Quotes." CNN.com, January 19. cnn.com/2015/12/31/politics/gallery/donald-trump-campaign-quotes/index.html.

Lee, Bandy X., Bruce E. Wexler, and James Gilligan. 2014. "Political Correlates of Violent Death Rates in the U.S., 1900–2010: Longitudinal and Cross-Sectional Analyses." *Aggression and Violent Behavior* 19: 721–28.

New York Times Editorial Board. 2016. "The Trump Campaign Gives License to Violence." *New York Times*, March 15. www.nytimes.com/2016/03/15/opinion/the-trump-campaign-gives-license-to-violence.html.

Weber, Max. 1917. "Science as a Vocation." In *From Max Weber*, tr. and ed. by H. H. Gerth and C. Wright Mills. Repr. New York: Free Press, 1946.

A CLINICAL CASE FOR THE DANGEROUSNESS OF DONALD J. TRUMP

DIANE JHUECK, L.M.H.C., D.M.H.P.

Mental illness in a U.S. president is not necessarily something that is dangerous for the citizenry he or she governs. A comprehensive study of all thirty-seven U.S. presidents up to 1974 determined that nearly half of them had a diagnosable mental illness, including depression, anxiety, and bipolar disorder (Davidson, Connor, and Swartz 2006). Notably, however, personality disorders were not included in this study, even though they can be just as debilitating. This addition would most certainly have increased the number of presidents with mental illness to something well past 50 percent. Yet, psychiatric illness alone in a president is not what causes grave concern. A second and crucial part of the equation is: Is the president dangerous by reason of mental illness?

Favoring civil liberties, U.S. law gives a lot of latitude for behavioral variation. When the law allows, even requires, that mental health professionals and physicians detain people against their will for psychiatric reasons, they must demonstrate that those people are a danger to themselves or others, or are gravely disabled. Initially, we need to look at what it means to be a danger to others due to mental illness. It is important to separate mental symptoms from things such as poor judgment or opinions and points of view that differ from one's own, which the law clearly permits. In the United States, it must be a disturbance of cognition, emotion regulation, or behavior, as described in the fifth edition of the *Diagnostic and Statistical Manual of Mental Disorder* (DSM-V), that is driving the patterns of dangerous behavior. Additionally, the magnitude of the perceived harm must be considered. Is it that feelings are being hurt? Or is there actual damage being perpetrated? Are there patterns of behavior and statements of intent that reasonably indicate that harm is imminent? Does the person carry weapons or any other instruments of harm?

People holding high political office inevitably cause some form of harm, whether they intend to or not. Leaders must often select what they think are the best options from a list of bad ones in areas as complex as military policy, the allocation of limited resources, or the line between safety nets and deregulation. When an individual in high office makes decisions, some people may be hurt in some way because of the sheer magnitude of that individual's power. A good leader will attempt, to the extent he or she can, to minimize that harm and to comfort those impacted, but damage is still unavoidable. This remains an unfortunate effect of governing large groups of people. This is also the very reason it is more, not less, important that the leader of the United States be mentally and emotionally stable. As president, Donald J. Trump has control over our executive branch and its agencies; is commander in chief of our military; has unilateral authority to fire nuclear weapons (which the secretary of defense authenticates but cannot veto). For the leader of the free world, inappropriate words alone may create a snowball effect that ultimately results in devastating harm to others.

The MacArthur Violence Risk Assessment Study has a number of indicators for whether an individual will commit future violence. Some examples include: a past history of violence, a criminal or substance-abusing father, personal chemical abuse, having a generally suspicious nature, and a high score on the Novaco Anger Scale. In regard to categories of mental health disorder, and perhaps counterintuitively, major illnesses (such as schizophrenia) have a lower rate of harm to others than personality disorders. "Psychopathy, [antisocial personality disorder] as measured by a screening version of the Hare Psychopathy Checklist, was more strongly associated with violence than any other risk factor we studied" (Monahan 2001). The twenty-item Hare checklist measures interpersonal and affective presentation, social deviance, impulsive lifestyle, and antisocial behavior (Hart, Cox, and Hare 1995).

The president, in a position of great power and making critical decisions, should theoretically meet higher standards of mental stability. Also, having access to a nuclear arsenal capable of destroying the world many times over, he should be of lower risk of violence than the average citizen. Despite these higher standards, our response is the opposite, for there is protection of public perception to consider: the president is supposed to be our protector, and he is unwell and harmful. The more unwell and unwilling to admit of any disturbance (in an extreme-case scenario), the more a mental health detention may need to be considered—and how would that appear to the public? Or, if we did not act, would we continue to deny until we were at a point of no return? Additionally, those who dare apply these mental health principles, such as those who dare apply justice to our First Citizen, may find themselves at risk of their jobs, their security, or even their personal safety—by the president or that segment of our society currently feeling empowered by the rise of the present regime, who would be driven around the emotional bend if these actions were successful. A complex web of factors requires consideration, which is why public education and collaboration with other professionals (e.g., politicians, lawyers, social psychologists) is highly important.

There is a preponderance of information in the public record regarding Donald J. Trump's aberrant behavior. The following list of incidents is neither all-inclusive nor deeply analytical. Each topic is a potential theme for an entire book in its own right. The intent here is to isolate enough indicators of record to reach a reasoned conclusion about whether President Trump's patterns of behavior indicates a clinically relevant "danger to others."

During a rally in Wilmington, North Carolina, Trump stated, "Hillary wants to abolish, essentially abolish the Second Amendment. . . . And by the way, if she gets to pick her judges, nothing you can do, folks. Although [for] the Second Amendment people, maybe there is, I don't know." A reporter covering this incident was moved to say, "While the remark was characteristically glib, it finds Trump again encouraging violence at his rallies. Worse, it marks a harrowing jump from threatening protestors to suggesting either an armed revolt or the assassination of a president" (Blistein 2016). It was not just journalists who heard Trump's statement in these terms: "The former head of the CIA, retired Gen. Michael Hayden, told CNN's Jake Tapper, 'If someone else had said that outside the hall, he'd be in the back of a police wagon now with the Secret Service questioning him'" (Diamond and Collinson 2016). It is true also for medical and mental health professionals: if a patient had said that, an emergency certificate would have been signed, and the person taken to the nearest emergency room for further questioning and evaluation.

Trump has said that he did not mean the statement the way it sounded. A common explanation by his defenders of aggressive and untoward remarks made by him in public settings is that what he said was a joke. This in no way discounts the dangerousness of his remark. In fact, his deeming the remark so lightly as to consider that it could be a joke would in itself be concerning. Moreover, his holding life-and-death matters themselves to be inconsequential may indicate serious pathology and risk—which cannot fully be ruled out without a detailed examination. This statement, in this context, exemplifies the "willingness to violate others" and the lack of empathy that characterize antisocial personality disorder (American Psychiatric Association 2016, pp. 659–60). In modern history, no other candidate for president of the United States has joked about his followers murdering his opponent.

In his response to the release by the *Washington Post* of the now-infamous "Grab 'em by the pussy" video, Trump the candidate stated that the audio was recorded more than ten years ago and did not represent who he is. The recording was made by *Access Hollywood*'s Billy Bush on September 16, 2005. It includes the following comments from the newly married Trump when he sees actress Arianne Zucker outside the bus where he is being recorded: "I better use some Tic Tacs, just in case I start kissing her." (Sound of Tic Tacs being dispensed). "You know I'm automatically attracted to beautiful—I just start kissing them. It's like a magnet. Just kiss. I don't even wait" (Fahrenthold 2016). During the course of the video, he is on record as saying even more disturbing and assaultive things regarding women.

After this video was aired, a significant number of Republican senators, representatives, governors, political appointees, and others stated publicly that they would not endorse Trump for office. Lisa Murkowski, Republican senator from Alaska, stated, "The video that surfaced yesterday further revealed his true character," she said. "He not only objectified women, he bragged about preying upon them. I cannot and will not support Donald Trump for President—he has forfeited the right to be our party's nominee. He must step aside" (2016). Brian Sandoval, Republican governor from Nevada, declared, "This video exposed not just words, but now an established pattern, which I find to be repulsive and unacceptable for a candidate for President of the United States" (Graham 2016). While senators and representatives have a more complicated relationship to Trump as president, governors and political appointees are more removed from him politically and warrant closer inspection. Of note, with less to lose politically, both these groups had a higher percentage of members state that they would not endorse Trump. Of the fifteen Republican governors who went on record, 53 percent stated that they would not endorse the nominee for president. Two of the seven who said they would endorse him now have jobs in his administration, as vice president and United Nations ambassador. Of the twenty-three Republican political appointees who made statements on record, an astounding 87 percent of them said they would not endorse or vote for Trump. Only three said they would (Graham 2016). Therapists of mental health across the country report having to expand their practices to include what is being called "election trauma." "What I'm seeing with my clients, particularly with women who experienced sexual abuse when younger, is that they are being re-wounded, re-traumatized," said Atlanta licensed professional counselor Susan Blank. "They can't escape it. It's all around them, written large on the national stage" (LaMotte 2016).

Among the many truly disturbing behaviors of this man now serving as the leader of the free world is his relationship to his daughter Ivanka. What follows are some of the more unsettling things Trump has said about her while knowingly being recorded:

- "You know who's one of the great beauties of the world, according to everybody? And I helped create her. Ivanka. My daughter Ivanka. She's 6 feet tall, she's got the best body" (King 2016).

- During an interview with Howard Stern when Ivanka was twenty-two years old (Cohen 2016): "I've said that, if Ivanka weren't my daughter, perhaps I'd be dating her" ("Donald Trump Nearly Casually Remarks . . ." 2006).

- And in another appearance on the Howard Stern radio show, in response to Stern's saying, "By the way, your daughter . . ." Trump responded, "She's beautiful." Stern added, "Can I say this? A piece of ass," to which Trump replied, "Yeah" (Kaczynski 2016).

- To a reporter about Ivanka: "Yeah, she's really something, and what a beauty, that one. If I weren't happily married and, ya know, her father..." (Solotaroff 2015).

- On Fox's *Wendy Williams Show*, in 2013: "Ivanka, what's the favorite thing you have in common with your father?" Williams asked. "Either real estate or golf," Ivanka replied. "Donald?" Williams asked Trump. "Well, I was going to say sex, but I can't relate that to . . ." Trump answers, gesturing to Ivanka (Feyerick 2016).

One of the first acts of mass citizen resistance against Trump's presidency occurred the day after his inauguration, when much of the country went to the streets in protest. The 2017 Women's March was the largest protest gathering in the history of the United States. Researchers Jeremy Pressman and Erica Chenowith (2017) estimate that more than four million people participated nationwide. They calculate that approximately three hundred thousand people marched in other countries, partly in response to an assaultive attitude and behavior against women unprecedented in a U.S. president.

A great danger to vulnerable groups and the potential for human rights abuses arise from the type of individuals Trump's psychopathy leads him to look to for affirmation and support. Unable to tolerate criticism and perceived threats to his ego, and with a documented obsessive need to be admired, he has notably selected as his advisers either family members or people who, in clinical jargon, "enable" his illness. This is one of the more significant ways in which he has become a danger to others as president. Members of vulnerable communities often write and speak about grave concerns regarding those whom he is choosing to guide him. Using his proposed federal budget as a lens, Jessica González-Rojas writes, "It outlines President Trump's spending priorities and program cuts that make clear his utter contempt for communities of color, and it edges this country and its moral compass closer to the nativist vision espoused by the likes of White House advisers Steve Bannon and Stephen Miller, and Attorney General Jeff Sessions" (González-Rojas 2017).

His mental health symptoms, including impulsive blame-shifting, claims of unearned superiority, and delusional levels of grandiosity, have been present in his words from his very first campaign speech: "They're bringing drugs. They're bringing crime. They're rapists, and some, I assume, are good people" (Elledge 2017). "I would build a Great Wall, and nobody builds walls better than me, believe me, and I'll build them very inexpensively. I will build a great, great wall on our southern border and I will have Mexico pay for that wall, mark my words" (Gamboa 2015). Regarding U.S. district judge Gonzalo Curiel, who was born in Indiana, Trump claimed it was a conflict of interest for the judge to hear a fraud case against Trump University, telling CNN, "He's a Mexican. We're building a wall between here and Mexico" (Finnegan 2016).

Trump's unhinged response to court decisions, driven as they appear to be by paranoia, delusion, and a sense of entitlement, are of grave concern. While president of the United States, he has on more than one occasion questioned the legitimacy of the court, as in this example: "We had a very smooth roll-out," he insisted, claiming that "the only problem with the [Muslim] ban was the 'bad court' that halted it" (Friedman, Sebastian, and Dibdin 2017). In February 2017, he tweeted, "The opinion of this so-called judge, which essentially takes law-enforcement away from our country, is ridiculous and will be overturned!" To which Representative Jerry Nadler responded, on February 8, 2017: "@realDonaldTrump's conduct—attacking judges+undermining independent judiciary—is inappropriate and dangerous." According to the Department of Homeland Security, at least 721 individuals and their families were denied the entry they had expected at U.S. borders under a ban soon deemed illegal by more than one court. At least 100,000 visas were revoked, according to a Justice Department lawyer (Brinlee 2017).

"We're hearing from really, really scared people," said Rachel Tiven, CEO of Lambda Legal, a nonprofit legal advocacy organization for LGBTQ rights. She adds, "We're seeing a fear of an atmosphere of intolerance that began with Trump's campaign." In the same article, Kris Hayashi, executive director of the Transgender

Law Center, states, "It was clear in 2016 that we saw an upswing in anti-trans legislation, more than we'd ever seen before . . . We anticipated that was not going to lessen but increase in 2017" (Grinberg 2016). "These are situations that put fear, not just into the individual who is targeted, but the entire community," said Heidi Beirich, director of the Southern Poverty Law Center's (SPLC) Intelligence Project, in a *Boston Globe* article about increased hate-based crimes at schools in Massachusetts. The SPLC reports that a record 16,720 complaints were filed nationwide with the Office for Civil Rights of the U.S. Department of Education in 2016, which they state is a 61 percent increase over the previous year (Guha 2017).

The American Association of University Professors' national council has approved the following resolution (2016): "Since the election of Donald J. Trump almost two weeks ago, the US has experienced an unprecedented spike in hate crimes, both physical and verbal, many of them on college and university campuses. . . . These have been directed against African Americans, immigrants, members of the LGBTQ community, religious minorities, women, and people with disabilities. In some instances, the perpetrators have invoked the president-elect in support of their heinous actions." Within the resolution, the council affirms the concept of free speech, stating, "No viewpoint or message may be deemed so hateful or disturbing that it may not be expressed. But threats and harassment differ from expressions of ideas that some or even most may find repulsive. They intimidate and silence."

Two social psychologists at the University of Kansas conducted a study on prejudice that involved surveying an even split of four hundred Trump and Clinton supporters. The scientists noted that "Trump's campaign over the preceding 18 months featured a procession of racist and ethnocentric rhetoric, with repeated insults, gross generalizations, and other derogatory speech hurled at Mexicans, Muslims, and women." So they asked one hundred of the Trump and one hundred of the Clinton supporters to rate their personal feelings toward a variety of social groups that the Trump campaign had disparaged at one time or another over the course of the race: Muslims, immigrants, Mexicans, fat people, and people with disabilities. All study participants were also polled on groups that Trump had not publicly maligned: alcoholics, adult film stars, rich people, members of the National Rifle Association, and Canadians. When the participants were surveyed again after the election, Crandall and White found that "Both personal and general prejudices remained unchanged for both sets of supporters with regard to the groups that Trump had not publicly targeted. But for the groups that Trump *had* disparaged, both Trump and Clinton supporters reported slightly lower levels of personal animus, and significantly higher levels of perceived acceptance for discriminatory speech. . . . In short: The perceived norm had shifted." Research suggests that individual expressions of prejudice and potential violence depend highly on perceived social norms; Trump surely had the effect of changing those norms (Crandall and White 2016).

Sometimes overlooked is the extent to which this president's mental health issues are harming our children. His impact is pervasive enough to have earned a label: "the Trump Effect." It has been used specifically to describe the trauma American children are experiencing because of Trump's candidacy and now presidency. "We have a bully in our midst, some therapists and school counselors say, traumatizing the most vulnerable of us. That bully is the 2016 presidential campaign, including the so-called 'Trump Effect.'" SPLC Teaching Tolerance director Maureen Costello has said, "I'm concerned children are coming to school every day terrified, anxious, disappointed, fearful. Feeling unwanted" (LaMotte 2016).

As the issue of Trump's mental illness was not of intense national concern until he ran for office and assumed the presidency, assessment by individuals with intimate understanding of what that job entails are useful for analyzing his dangerousness. It is instructive to remove the variable of political ideology from our determination and narrow our review to the perspective of Republicans only. In August 2016, a letter signed by fifty such individuals was published in the *New York Times*. While some of their concern centers on lack of experience, a portion of the letter made more direct reference to Trump's mental and emotional stability: "The undersigned individuals have all served in senior national security and/or foreign policy positions in Republican Administrations, from Richard Nixon to George W. Bush. We have worked directly on national security issues with these Republican Presidents and/or their principal advisers during wartime and other periods of crisis, through successes and failures. We know the personal qualities required of a President of the United States. None of us will vote for Donald Trump. From a foreign policy perspective, Donald Trump is not qualified to be President and Commander-in-Chief. Indeed, we are convinced that he would be a dangerous President and would put at risk our country's national security and well-being." A president, they continue, ". . . must be willing to listen to his advisers and department heads; must encourage consideration of conflicting views; and must acknowledge errors and learn from them . . . must be disciplined, control emotions, and act only after reflection and careful deliberation . . . must maintain cordial relationships with leaders of countries of different backgrounds and must have their respect and trust," and must be able and willing "to separate truth from falsehood" in order to aspire to be president and commander in chief, with command of the U.S. nuclear arsenal. They conclude: "We are convinced that in the Oval Office, he would be the most reckless President in American history."

Hillary Clinton's remark "A man you can bait with a tweet is not a man we can trust with nuclear weapons" was not just campaign hyperbole (Broad and Sanger 2016). The president of the United States has approximately 2,000 deployed nuclear warheads at his or her disposal and has the authority to order these weapons to be launched even if our country has not yet been attacked. Weapons fired against the United States from a submarine would take about twelve minutes to hit Washington, DC. Missiles fired from most continents would reach this country in around thirty minutes. The nightmare scenario of this unstable, impulsive, blame-shifting, and revenge-obsessed individual having mere minutes to make the kind of decision required in such a scenario is of the gravest concern possible in our era.

In an interview on Fox News, then–Vice President Dick Cheney stated, "He [the president] could launch a kind of devastating attack the world's never seen. He doesn't have to check with anybody. He doesn't have to call the Congress. He doesn't have to check with the courts. He has that authority because of the nature of the world we live in" (Rosenbaum 2011). The entire focus in the missile launch decision process is on whether the launch command is authentic, not whether it is reasonable. Ron Rosenbaum describes the case of Maj. Harold Hering, who, during the period when Nixon was displaying erratic behavior, was troubled by a question he was not allowed to ask. "Maj. Hering decided to ask his question anyway, regardless of consequences: How could he know that an order to launch his missiles was 'lawful'? That it came from a sane president, one who wasn't 'imbalance[d]' or 'berserk?' as Maj. Hering's lawyer eventually, colorfully put it." Hering was a career military officer and asked the question while attending a missile training class. He was discharged from the air force for asking it. To this day, Harold Hering's question remains unanswered.

If we who have come together to write this book are accurate in our assessments, one must ask why Donald J. Trump's dangerousness was not addressed earlier in his life? The extensive public record on him shows that he has been insulated by inherited wealth and that his father had similar mental health disturbances. As we are all witnessing now, with his politically inexperienced daughter and son-in-law taking key advisory positions at the White House, Trump has distanced himself from possible checks and balances while enabling his own disorder: a lack of insight and confirmation-seeking that make certain mental disorders particularly dangerous in a position of power.

A substantive change in the level of his dangerousness came with his assumption of the role of leader of the free world. Although an argument can be made that, by taking this office, he has shaken the global political structure to the extent that the U.S. presidency is rapidly losing that standing. His narcissistic traits (manifesting in blatant lying, impulsive and compulsive decision making against rational interests, and immature relational abilities) are creating a leadership gap that other political actors may well seek to fill. Yet, it is impossible for him, through the lens of his mental dysfunction, to evaluate his actual presentation and impact.

As the ultimate representative of our nation, Donald J. Trump is normalizing previously outrageous behaviors, negatively impacting everyone from leaders of other nations to our own children. From the outset of his presidency, although clearly absent a mandate from the population he now governs, he has repeatedly declared himself "the greatest," or "tremendous," or "knowing more than anyone," and other statements consistent with narcissistic personality disorder, with regard to an "expectation of being viewed as superior without commensurate achievements" (American Psychiatric Association 2013, p. 669). He exhibits extreme denial of any feedback that does not affirm his self-image and psychopathic tendencies, which affords him very limited ability to learn and effectively adjust to the requirements of the office of president. Rather, he consistently displays a revenge-oriented response to any such feedback. Holding this office at once feeds his grandiosity and claws at the fragile sense of self underneath it. His patterns of behavior while in the role of president of the United States have potentially dire impact on every individual living not only in this nation but across the entire globe. The earth itself is in peril, both from the urgent issues that are not being addressed while an unstable man sits in the Oval Office and by the new urgencies he creates. Mr. Trump is and has demonstrated himself to be a danger to others—not just one person or a few, but possibly to *all* others.

*Diane Jhueck, L.M.H.C., D.M.H.P., has operated a private ther-
apy practice for several decades. In addition, she performs mental
health evaluations and detentions on individuals presenting as a
danger to self or others. In a previous social justice career, she was
a women's specialist at the United Nations, in New York City. She
founded the Women's and Children's Free Restaurant, an empowerment project that has been in operation for thirty years. She
also founded the People's AIDS Project and was an assistant re-
gional manager for Feeding America. She has directed agencies
addressing food aid, domestic violence, apartheid, low-income
housing, and LGBTQ rights.*

Acknowledgments

I thank Bandy Lee, M.D., for her exceptional assistance in the preparation of this chapter.

References

American Association of University Professors (AAUP). 2016. "The Atmosphere on Campus in the Wake of the Elections." AAUP.org, November 22. www.aaup.org/news/atmosphere-campus-wake-elections#.WP
-oOMa1tPb.

American Psychiatric Association. 2013. *Diagnostic and Statistical Manual of
Mental Disorders*. 5th ed. Arlington, VA: American Psychiatric Association, pp. 659–60, 669.

Blistein, Jon. 2016. "Donald Trump Hints at Hillary Clinton Assassination."
Rolling Stone, August 9. www.rollingstone.com/politics/news/donald
-trump-hints-at-hillary-clinton-assassination-w433591.

Brinlee, Morgan. 2017. "27 Real Things Trump Has Actually Said Since
Becoming President." Bustle, February 13. www.bustle.com/p/27-real
-things-trump-has-actually-said-since-becoming-president-37189/amp.

Broad, William J., and David E. Sanger. 2016. "Debate Over Trump's Fitness
Raises Issue of Checks on Nuclear Power." *New York Times*, August 04.

www.nytimes.com/2016/08/05/science/donald-trump-nuclear-codes
.html.

Cohen, Claire. 2016. "Donald Trump Sexism Tracker: Every Offensive
Comment in One Place." *The Telegraph*, June 4. www.telegraph.co.uk
/women/politics/donald-trump-sexism-tracker-every-offensive
-comment-in-one-place/.

Crandall, Chris S., and Mark H. White II. 2016. "Donald Trump and the
Social Psychology of Prejudice." *Undark*, November 17. https://undark
.org/article/trump-social-psychology-prejudice-unleashed/.

Davidson, J. R., K. M. Connor, and M. Swartz. 2006. "Mental Illness in U.S.
Presidents Between 1776 and 1974: A Review of Biographical Sources."
The Journal of Nervous and Mental Disease, January 194 (1): 47–51. http://
journals.lww.com/jonmd/Abstract/2006/01000/Mental_Illness_In_U
_S__Presidents_Between_1776_and.9.aspx.

Diamond, Jeremy, and Stephen Collinson. 2016. "Trump: Gun Advocates
Could Deal with Clinton." CNN, August 10. www.cnn.com/2016/08/09
/politics/donald-trump-hillary-clinton-second-amendment/.

"Donald Trump Nearly Casually Remarks About Incest with Daughter
Ivanka." 2006. *The View*. Season 9. Episode 119. March 6. www.youtube
.com/watch?v=DP7yf8-Lk80.

Elledge, John. 2017. "Here Are 23 Terrifying Things That President Trump
Has Done in the Last Seven Days." January 26. www.newstatesman
.com/world/2017/01/here-are-23-terrifying-things-president-trump
-has-done-last-seven-days?amp.

Fahrenthold, David A. 2016. "Trump Recorded Having Extremely Lewd
Conversation About Women in 2005." *Washington Post*, October 8.
www.washingtonpost.com/politics/trump-recorded-having-extremely
-lewd-conversation-about-women-in-2005/2016/10/07/3b9ce776-8cb4
-11e6-bf8a-3d26847eeed4_story.html?utm_term=.8e1252766ffe.

Feyerick, Diane. 2016. "Donald Trump's Uncomfortable Comments About
His Daughter Ivanka." CNNuTube, October 12. Accessed April 9, 2017.
https://youtu.be/GcnBuE3ExWo.

Finnegan, Michael. " 'It's Going to Be a Big, Fat, Beautiful Wall!': Trump's
    Words Make His California Climb an Even Steeper Trek." *Los Angeles
    Times,* June 3, 2016. Accessed April 11, 2017. www.latimes.com/politics
    /la-na-pol-trump-california-campaign-20160602-snap-story.html.

Friedman, Megan, Michael Sebastian, and Emma Dibdin. "11 of the
    Craziest Things President Trump Said at His Latest Rollercoaster of a
    Press Conference." *Cosmopolitan,* February 16, 2017. www
    .cosmopolitan.com/politics/amp8943522/trump-press-conference
    -crazy-moments/.

Gamboa, Suzanne. "Donald Trump Announces Presidential Bid by Trash-
    ing Mexico, Mexicans." NBCNews.com. NBCUniversal News Group,
    June 16, 2015. Accessed April 11, 2017. www.nbcnews.com/news/latino
    /donald-trump-announces-presidential-bid-trashing-mexico-mexicans
    -n376521.

González-Rojas, Jessica. "Trump's First 100 Days: A Blueprint to Hurt
    People of Color." *Rewire,* April 24, 2017. Accessed April 27, 2017.
    https://rewire.news/article/2017/04/24/trumps-first-100-days
    -blueprint-hurt-people-color/.

Graham, David A. "Which Republicans Oppose Donald Trump? A Cheat
    Sheet." *The Atlantic,* November 06, 2016. Accessed April 7, 2017. www
    .theatlantic.com/politics/archive/2016/11/where-republicans-stand-on
    -donald-trump-a-cheat-sheet/481449/.

Grinberg, Emanuella. "What a Trump Presidency Could Mean for LGBT
    Americans." CNN, November 11, 2016. Accessed April 11, 2017. https://
    amp.cnn.com/cnn/2016/11/11/politics/trump-victory-lgbt-concerns
    /index.html.

Guha, Auditi. "Campuses Wrestle with Wave of Hate-Based Incidents Since
    Election." *Rewire,* April 24, 2017. Accessed April 27, 2017. https://rewire
    .news/article/2017/04/24/campuses-wrestle-wave-hate-based
    -incidents-since-election/.

Hart, S.D., D. N. Cox, and R. D. Hare. *Manual for the Psychopathy Checklist:
    Screening Version* (PCL:SV). 1995. Toronto, ON: Multi-Health Systems.

Kaczynski, Andrew. "Donald Trump to Howard Stern: It's Okay to Call My

Daughter a 'Piece of Ass.'" CNN, October 9, 2016. Accessed April 9, 2017. www.cnn.com/2016/10/08/politics/trump-on-howard-stern/.

King, Shaun. " Donald Trump Is a Pervert." New York *Daily News*, June 22, 2016. www.nydailynews.com/news/politics/king-donald-trump -pervert-article-1.2683705.

LaMotte, Sandee. "Is the 'Trump Effect' Damaging Our Psyches?" CNN, October 14, 2016. Accessed April 7, 2017. www.cnn.com/2016/10/14 /health/trump-effect-damaging-american-psyche/.

"A Letter from G.O.P. National Security Officials Opposing Donald Trump." 2006. *New York Times*, August 8. www.nytimes.com/interactive/2016 /08/08/us/politics/national-security-letter-trump.html.

Monahan, J. The MacArthur Violence Risk Assessment: Executive Summary. 2001. Accessed April 6, 2017. www.macarthur.virginia.edu/risk.html.

Murkowski, Lisa. "Full Statements on Donald Trump from Alaska Sens. Lisa Murkowski and Dan Sullivan." *Alaska Dispatch News*, December 12, 2016. Accessed April 7, 2017. www.adn.com/politics/2016/10/08 /full-statements-from-sens-lisa-murkowski-and-dan-sullivan-on -donald-trump/.

Pressman, Jeremy, and Erica Chenowith. "Crowd Estimates, 1.21.2017." Google, January 26, 2017. Accessed April 11, 2017. University of Connecticut and University of Denver. https://docs.google.com/spreadsheets /d/1xa0iLqYKz8x9Yc_rfhtmSOJQ2EGgeUVjvV4A8LsIaxY/htmlview?sle =true.

Rosenbaum, Ron. "How Cold War Maj. Harold Hering Asked a Forbidden Question That Cost Him His Career." *Slate Magazine*, February 28, 2011. Accessed April 11, 2017. www.slate.com/articles/life/the _spectator/2011/02/an_unsung_hero_of_the_nuclear_age.html.

Solotaroff, Paul. "Trump Seriously: On the Trail with the GOP's Tough Guy." *Rolling Stone*, September 9, 2015. Accessed April 9, 2017. www .rollingstone.com/politics/news/trump-seriously-20150909.

HEALTH, RISK, AND THE DUTY TO PROTECT THE COMMUNITY

HOWARD H. COVITZ, PH.D., A.B.P.P.

Don't go loose-lipped among your people (but)
Don't stand idly by either as your neighbor bleeds;
I am God.

Leviticus 19:16*

This collected volume of essays is about the investigation of a tension between two goods, a balancing act that is at least as old as the Bible. Leviticus (see epigraph) argues for a version of confidentiality that is almost unlimited: "Don't go loose-lipped among your people." Indeed, the psalmist would specify further:

Who is the man who desires life. . . .
Guard your tongue against speaking ill and
your lips against uttering gossip. (Psalms 34:12)

---

* My own translation from the Hebrew. A literal take on this passage might be "Go not rumoring among your people; Stand not on the blood of your neighbor: I am God."

Looking back to the Leviticus text, we see that an exception is immediately rendered, as there would be times when speaking up was necessary to protect another from harm. In traditional cantillation, the halfway melody mark of the sentence (*esnachtah*) is immediately before "I am God." The intent of the ancient writer seems to be: Oh, yes, there is a tension between Confidentiality and the Duty to Warn and recognizing this tension holds the essence of Godliness . . . or Goodness, as we might say today. And after two to three millennia, the mental health community is just beginning to recognize this dialectic. This, indeed, is *the* dialogue that developed within the community of practitioners during and after the 2016 U.S. presidential election. This tension is known as the one between the Goldwater rule, which protects a limited privacy for public figures, and the duty to warn those who may be at risk of serious harm from the very same public figures.

At least three complexities stand in the way of offering up a simple solution: Are mental health professionals duty-bound to speak their truth about a presidential candidate's fitness for duty, or should they, rather, be constrained by professional ethics from doing so? What are the measurements by which we evaluate the first? What are the injuries of its absence? Is it a matter of a personal decision, or a decision by the community in which one lives?

The second difficulty has to do with the following: When we investigate the wellness of an individual, are we focused on his freedom from disabling characteristics that compromise his own life or, rather, do we concern ourselves with whether he is a danger to himself or others? Finally, we will briefly turn to how we evaluate risk, whether publicly shared or not.

Two Types of Mental Illness

More than eighty years ago, in a polemic against religion and politically based theories, Freud asked, "Does psychoanalysis lead toward a particular *Weltanschauung*?" (Freud, Sprott, and Strachey, 1933,

p. 158). Answering this question in the negative, Freud chose empirical science over what he considered to be illusion and emotion. His
new psychotherapies would, if Freud had his way, rely on no assumptions whatever about the good life, but solely on scientific methodology and clear-minded examination of the observable. While this
may seem perfectly reasonable, let me point out that the sciences—
as is the case with the purest of them all, mathematics—depend not
only on the correctness of the investigators' logical moves but also on
the postulates or axioms we begin with.

Let me, then, state my own position: While in the natural sciences, it is assumed that researches and classification systems are
generally independent of values, in the psychological and social sciences, such theoretical neatness is a luxury. Psychological theories of
health are inextricably intertwined with the views of a healthy polity, with the need to protect the community, and with a vision of the
good life. When we apply knowledge from one group to another, we
speak of an error of *cultural bias*. Even science cannot be thoroughly
free of assumptions and values.

Whatever paradigms one selects for describing mental health
and mental illness, there will be questions of how the individual
processes feelings, thoughts, and actions. Consider, for instance,
anxiety. Humankind has developed anxiety as an adaptive signal
to the body to prepare for danger—danger from another person or
from a feral predator. However, if the anxiety expresses itself in
eating disorders or digestive failure or in facial tics, we see it as
maladaptive. Similar constructions can be offered for other responses,
such as depression, anger, guilt, and shame.

On the other side is the arguable value in examining mental
structures that foster civilized behavior and a capacity for nonde-
structive membership in *polities of mutual concern*. These, too, are
adaptive and promote wellness both in the individual and in groups.
These two perspectives are joined in a three-part definition of emotional health. The healthy person has:

- the capacity to recognize his own wishes and impulses and those of others with clarity;
- the ability to determine whether the actions that express these impulses are likely to cause avoidable damage to himself or others, and when such actions or speech are deemed safe; and
- the agency necessary to act upon those impulses without intrusive anger, anxiety, depression, guilt, prohibition, or shame.

Those who either are incapable of or disinterested in measuring the impact they may have on another or on others may well appear symptom-free, functional, and at times even quite successful in their work lives, but they are typically not so in their relationships. In very general terms, those who suffered internally were thought to be living with *symptomatic disturbances*, while the latter group was described as having character pathology, or *personality disorders*.

Here, too, our discussion gets more than a little messy. As noted earlier, what constitutes healthy interpersonal relationships varies from culture to culture; perhaps a recognition of this messiness contributed to the unwillingness of some mental health professionals to define what is meant by a healthy individual or a well community. And here, too, we cannot escape making certain postulates about the good life.

Freud focused on the puzzling development of conscience. He reasoned that the child begins life with a sense that all are present to serve him. A youngster eventually recognizes that others exist but not initially that they are complex beings with their own thoughts and relationships. Freud discovered that the child's life changes dramatically when he realizes that others are *subjects*, just as he is: *subjects in their own right* (Covitz 2016). Until that time, the child understands others more or less only in their capacities to satisfy his needs: as either good or bad, as satisfying his demands or not. When the child accepts the complexity of family relationships and is able to understand that Mom and Dad have an independent relationship, he has begun to embrace them as subjects (i.e., as doers) with their own thoughts, feelings, and relationships. He has, Freud would say, developed a conscience (an *uber-Ich*, or a "Guiding I"). Those who fail to accept others as *subjects in their own right* comprise the personality-disordered subgroup of humanity.

Let me be a little more specific as to the typical characteristics seen in personality-disordered individuals.

1. Such people are generally incapable of understanding and responding in an emotionally empathic way to how another feels. They may well, in an intellectual way, be able to know how others react or even what they might be thinking, but this has little bearing on how they treat others, who remain objects to them, like pieces on a chessboard to be moved about in order to win the game.

2. This black-and-white thinking effectively splits the world into friend or foe, into those who support him and all those others who are against him. Such a person may, indeed, grow to be incapable of bigotry—for, to be bigoted or racist or sexist, one must feel allegiance to a group. Still and all, they may have no qualms about using bigotries for their own purposes.

3. Lacking the need to evaluate how their actions may impact others, these people react more quickly, and with less skepticism about the correctness of their actions.

4. Such individuals have not yet developed respect for others' thinking, relationships, or efforts, which leads them to put little value in the accomplishments of others. As such, they tend not to recognize the necessity for maintaining extant organizations, government structures, conventional practices, and laws. They may appear civilized but are not safely socialized.

5. Due to the aforementioned (points 1–4), their thinking is focused but lacks nuance. They demonstrate no apparent ability to see

more than one not-unreasonable view: a monomania of sorts. These views, additionally, can flip to their opposite, since what makes any new attitude acceptable to them is under the control of a "my will be done" syndrome, no matter what that will is.

6. Finally (following on 1–5), they display a limited capacity to distinguish the real from the wished for or imagined, and demonstrate a ready willingness to distort the truth.

Two Fables

There are two distinct general types of emotional illness: those that precipitate symptoms in the individual and those that represent a risk to relationships and the communities in which the person lives. This leads directly into our second concern: Is the mental health of a powerful leader to be measured by the person's relationship to oneself or by one's ability to be safe and constructive in a *polity of mutual concern*?

I'll ask the reader to imagine two fables and some thought experiments.

Fable 1. The Policeman

I was driving down Old York Road in my police cruiser when I saw this driver, a funny-looking kind of old guy. He was driving his brand-new Bentley, so I assumed he was pretty safe, even though he was weaving just a little haphazardly. Y'know, a little erratic. He had his window open and was calling some immigrant-looking pedestrians pretty angry names. I pulled him over. He had a small arsenal of automatic weapons up front and what looked like an RPG launcher on the backseat. I asked him: "What's with all the weapons, sir?"

He says, "Officer, I've got a license and Montgomery County is Open Carry. I have every right to go where I want. Anyhow, it's a pretty dangerous world out there. You know, there are a lot of immigrants, and I think I saw Muslims dancing in Wall Park."

I go back to my cruiser and call the station house. "Sarge. Any report of dancing foreigners in the park?" Sarge asks me what I've been smoking; I understand his intent. So, I go back to the guy's car. "Sir, I cannot confirm any disturbance going on in Wall Park." "Officer, I saw it myself, and I should know because I have a lot of money." The man then goes on and on talking trash about people who are different, saying that everybody who disagrees with him is a liar and one of them might have killed a Kennedy and another one should be sent to the Women's Detention Center because she's the world's biggest crook. Then he tells me it's not raining and that it never rains when he's riding in his Bentley. Meanwhile, the water's pouring off my Stetson. He starts swearing about the township commissioners and accusing them of being stupid. In any case, I have choices, don't I? I think to myself, I could say any of the following:

1. "Sir. You be careful now, and have a blessed day."
2. "Sir. I just wanna say that your car is the tiger's roar. Be careful, now!"
3. "Sir. I think you might be batshit crazy, but I can't be sure, so, have a good day."
4. "Sir. Take me for a ride in your car, please, and gimme a good job, and we'll forget about all this silliness."

or

5. "Sir, would you step out of the car and we'll take a ride and see if we can't settle down those images in your head of Muslims dancing in the park? By the way: Were they barefoot?"

Fable 2. The Casual Customer and the Man in the Psychotherapist's Office

A person comes into my psychoanalytic office or, for that matter, sits down next to me at Starbucks carrying a small-caliber handgun. I ask the reader to imagine that, in listening to him, I recognize the six characteristics I've just described. In any case, imagine further that time is up on our meeting or that our coffee is finished. I've not administered any objective tests. The man shows no signs of anxiety; he has only expressed disdain for others, and assuredly no shame or guilt. He seems to be oriented in time and space. Still, I have a strong if tentative diagnostic impression that this man suffers from serious character disorders. What shall I do, and what is my ethical duty to do as a citizen, and/or as a citizen possessing special training?

But back to President Trump. I've gone back, in my mind, to Leviticus time after time since the election. It occurred to me more than once that the behaviors of candidate, President-elect, and now President Trump may have been—as is the case with the television persona Stephen Colbert presented for many years—an act.

As a psychologist and psychoanalyst with more than forty years of experience, I cannot say with certainty, for instance, whether Trump's sexist comments and claims of sexual acting out, his unempathic responses to the Khans (who'd lost their soldier son overseas) or to a handicapped man at his rally, or his calls for violence at those rallies were no more than performance art. Perhaps, in his heart of hearts, I thought, Mr. Trump has an empathic soul, does not split the world into with-him and against-him groups, and is a careful and nuanced thinker. Perhaps, even, Mr. Trump knows the difference between alternate reality and reality, and perhaps he simply uses alternate reality as a strategic ploy. I did consider this and concluded, nonetheless, that his actions still showed severe gaps. After all, and briefly, the damage to the Khans was done, the lies were believed by tens of millions of Trump's followers, violent rhetoric at his meetings produced real harm, and Mr. Trump has irresponsibly alienated (so far) five of our closest trading partners.

The Simple Arithmetic of Risk Management

Since the attack on the Twin Towers and the Pentagon of September 11, 2001, the leaders in the United States and other nation states have communicated to their citizens the need to be vigilant. George W. Bush advocated repeatedly our need to go on living our lives, walking about freely, and carrying out the tasks of living, working, and shopping that preceded the many terrorist attacks the world has come to know as, more or less, weekly events. In addition, however, President Bush and others have advocated that we all remain vigilant. We are told that if we see a suspect package on a bus or airplane or at the Boston Marathon, or if we notice a suitcase left alone at an airport, we should immediately leave the area, warn others, and contact the police. Schools have since developed zero-tolerance rules requiring that if a student is heard speaking of violence toward himself or others, he must immediately be removed from the school and not reinstated until an expert deems him safe to return.

Mathematicians use an intuitive construction that combines the probability of a negative outcome multiplied by the result of that negative outcome. For example, if the probability of losing a certain wager is 1 percent and would result in their losing $10, most people would feel comfortable taking that risk. The risk in mathematical terms? One percent x $10 or 10 cents. However, if the probability is the same and the loss would result in losing a $200,000 home, it's time to buy insurance! There, the risk is 1 percent x $200,000 or $2,000, which is more than the cost of an insurance policy to recoup such losses, making it, so to speak, a reasonable expenditure to buy the insurance. Having said that, I feel that our risk calculation involves considerably more than whether it is a reasonable expenditure to buy the insurance; the loss of a home for most people would be devastating.

Conclusion

Donald Trump has displayed, frequently, all six of the characteristics that I and many other mental health professionals associate with severe character pathology. I cannot say with certainty what diagnostic box, if any, he fits—not, indeed, before and without careful examination and testing, as those who support the Goldwater rule avow. Some of my colleagues, citing the duty to warn others of possibly imminent danger, are comfortable assigning Mr. Trump in this category or some other condition from the American Psychiatric Association's *Diagnostic and Statistical Manual* (DSM-V); I am not comfortable doing so. Still, I strongly agree with the likelihood that these fit the preponderance of people who behave as President Trump does. This doubt is equally present when I'm reporting to the appropriate social service agency my sense that there is a likelihood that a certain child is being molested or that one of my patients may be planning to shoot his wife's lover. I needn't be certain if the outcome is potentially dire. When the outcome is possibly devastating, even if the probability that it will occur is relatively small, the clinician and perhaps every citizen is *duty-bound to warn*.

In becoming president and commander in chief of the most powerful armed forces on earth, Trump is armed to the teeth and has openly spoken about the wonder he experiences, though we simultaneously maintain this nuclear firepower, that we have a reluctance to use it. He displays all the signs of a seriously personality-disordered person and has repeatedly spoken of using violence. And the outcome? The outcome, if he is indeed as ill as some sizable portion of the mental health professional community suspects, could well be potentially devastating to a significant percentage of humanity.

Back to me: I believe that my ethical duty to warn is unquestionable, as is my ethical responsibility to work within the confines of the law to have Mr. Trump psychologically and psychiatrically examined—or, in the absence of his willingness to do so, to have him removed from office.

Indeed, I am in good company. The policeman who meets a driver armed and talking crazy is ethically bound to disarm that driver. The shopper or passenger on a city bus or marathon route who sees an unattended package lying about is responsible for taking action. The coffee-drinking Starbucks customer, as well as the psychotherapist in her office, who is confronted by a gun-toting, crazy-talking person has the citizen's responsibility either to disarm that person or to arrange to have it done. How much less can I or any other mental health professional be ethically bound by a duty to warn and by the biblical proscription not to stand idly by as others are placed in potential danger (Leviticus 19:16)? This assuredly applies to a possibly unfit-to-serve president who is in possession of the U.S. nuclear codes.

Howard H. Covitz, Ph.D., A.B.P.P., has combined the practice of psychoanalysis in the suburbs of Philadelphia with a variety of other interests. He has taught university-level mathematics, psychology, and biblical characterology (1968–2011), was a training analyst at the Institute for Psychoanalytic Studies and the Institute for Psychoanalytic Psychotherapies, and its director (1986–98). He also ran a school for disturbed inner-city adolescents in the 1970s. His Oedipal Paradigms in Collision *(1998, reissued in 2016) was nominated for the Gradiva Book of the Year Award. His connectedness to his wife, grown children, and grandchildren motivates his writing and thinking.*

References

American Psychiatric Association. 2013. *Diagnostic and Statistical Manual of Mental Disorders.* 5th ed. Arlington, VA: American Psychiatric Association.

Covitz, Howard. 2016. *Oedipal Paradigms in Collision: A Centennial Emendation of a Piece of Freudian Canon (1897–1997).* 1988. Repr. New York: Object Relations Institute Press.

Freud, Sigmund, Walter John Herbert Sprott, and James Strachey. 1933. *New Introductory Lectures on Psycho-Analysis.* Vol. 22. New York: Norton.

Freud, Sigmund. 1955. *The Standard Edition of the Complete Psychological Works of Sigmund Freud,* vol. 24. London: Hogarth.

NEW OPPORTUNITIES FOR THERAPY IN THE AGE OF TRUMP*

WILLIAM J. DOHERTY, PH.D.

The boundary between the personal and public has ruptured in the age of Trump. A fixed, hard boundary was of course a fiction—we are always influenced by what's going on in society, and our personal actions affect the whole. Yet, before Trump, we therapists who felt comfortable in the mainstream of a democratic society could assume that our therapist "hat" and our citizen "hat" were separate. In our therapist role, we told ourselves, we were professional healers; as citizens, we followed public issues, supported candidates, and cast votes. The main crossover was our advocacy for better mental health policies and reimbursement.

Feminist, ethnic minority, and LGBT therapists have argued for decades against this personal/political split in the therapy world—witness the big literature on therapy and social justice. But that perspective was relegated to the sidelines of the therapy world, confined

---

* Portions of this essay were adapted with permission from his article "Therapy in the Age of Trump," in *The Psychotherapy Networker* (May–June 2017): 34–35.

to situations in which the clients were part of an oppressed minority. For the most part, psychotherapy marched along with its traditional focus on the intrapsychic and interpersonal realms—in part, I think, because many of us assumed that we and our clients had personal lives adequately buffered from public turmoil and stress. Yes, occasionally an event such as 9/11 burst that bubble, but it soon re-formed.

After the election of Donald Trump in November 2016, however, the bubble did not return. Many of our clients across social classes and racial groups are distressed by what's happening to the country and are living with current anxiety, worries for the future, and the reactivation of past fears. This is occurring both for people immediately at risk, such as immigrants, and for those less personally vulnerable who are watching the rise of hate, the disregard for the truth, and the flouting of core democratic values such as a free press and respect for the rule of law. What's more, we have a president whose public behavior represents the triumph of the antitherapeutic—a lionizing of the unexamined life where personal insecurities are boldly projected onto the world and where self-serving beliefs become public facts.

In the face of these challenges, a number of professions are facing a paradigm crisis: How do they go forward with business as usual when the democratic foundations of their work are being threatened? As an example, consider the soul-searching among journalists now: they are having to call out systematic lying, not just reporting the shading of the truth or one take on the facts versus another.

For psychotherapists, the challenge is to integrate our roles as therapists and citizens so that we can help our clients do the same. This has to begin with the "self of the therapist"—how do our personal lives intersect with our professional practice? Nearly every therapist I know is feeling personal stress and is dealing with clients whose reactions range from reliving experiences of being bullied to fears of deportation to a sense that the arc of the moral universe no longer seems to bend inevitably toward justice. We're seeing families and friendships fracture along political lines. I do know some therapists who are glad that Trump ascended to the presidency, but they, too, are concerned with the polarization in the country and the tearing of the social fabric.

This is bigger than Trump and the November 2016 election. It's the culmination of at least two decades of increasing divisiveness in our culture and in politics, where those who differ are seen as dangerous enemies, not just misguided opponents. So how do we respond as therapists and citizens to the impact of Trump in the context of these broader trends? How do we handle our personal reactivity to these events? The starting point is to acknowledge that we need new ways to think about ourselves and our clients as members of the broader public (i.e., citizens), and not just as providers and consumers of services.

Expanding the Frame of Psychotherapy in the Age of Trump and Beyond

Clearly, we have to help our clients deal with the Trump Effect in their lives. Yet, the challenges are bigger, just as Trump represents larger trends. If our approach to therapy is to go beyond helping clients deal with the impact of this one president, we need new conceptual categories for what we address in our work. I'd like to introduce two: public stress and political stress. I define them in this way:

- *Public stress* refers to challenges for personal and relational well-being stemming from forces in neighborhood, the community, and local institutions (such as schools and the police), as well as forces in the larger political, economic, cultural, and historical environment.

- *Political stress* (a type of public stress) refers to how the words, actions, and policies of government bodies, elected officials, and candidates for public office create challenges for personal and re-lational well-being.

Using the language of public and political stress allows thera-pists to expand beyond our traditional intrapsychic and microsocial frames while still paying attention to the personal: how our clients are thinking, feeling, and acting in the face of stress.

This broader thinking about our clients' lives can be reflected in the questions we ask at intake. Every profession communicates its area of interest in its intake forms. For example, medicine is domi-nated by biological disease–based questions. Mental health profes-sionals ask mainly about psychological symptoms and interpersonal functioning. I've developed two intake questions to signal my inter-est in the public lives of my clients. The first asks about public stress and the second about clients' engagement in their world.

1. Sometimes people in counseling feel stress from events and forces in their community, the nation, or the world. If that's true for you, I encourage you to briefly let me know. (Otherwise, just skip this section.) Here's what is causing me stress:_____.

2. Sometimes people in counseling have commitments to groups or causes outside their family and close social world. If that's true for you, could you briefly write down what those commitments are for you? (Otherwise, just leave this section blank).

I've found that these intake questions provide door openers to conversations about the public realm in clients' lives—both how they are affected and how they engage as citizens. And then there are other door openers at the outset of sessions. One is to inquire whether clients are following what's going on in the political world right now, and if so, how it's affecting them. The result is that many clients open up about Trump-related anxieties and relationship strains they hadn't previously shared, probably because they had thought the therapy room was supposed to be a politics-free zone—as we ourselves may have believed.

Another way to signal openness to discussing public/political stress is an open letter placed in the waiting room. Here's an example of such a letter:

Dear Clients,

We're living in troubled times. I feel it, and most people I know feel it. I'm writing this note to let you know that I'm open to talking about something not always brought up in therapy: how what's going on in the public and political world is affecting you and your relationships, and how you're coping.

- *After a divisive presidential election, a lot of people are upset and feeling discouraged by the political infighting in this country.*
- *There's great uncertainty about what the upcoming years will look like. Some people are feeling alarmed, insecure, and threatened, while others feel hopeful that necessary change will happen. And those two kinds of people are often at odds with one another.*
- *I see both liberal and conservative members of our community feeling as if their values are no longer acceptable in the public arena—or to some of their friends and family.*

The list could go on. For now, consider yourself invited to bring your concerns about the public world into our conversations in therapy. No expectation or requirement that you do so, of course—just if you think it might be helpful.

I'm here to listen, support you, and help you figure out how to manage today's stresses while living a life that's in keeping with your personal and community values.

Once clients open up, we can help them cope with political stress just as we do any other kind of stress: through buffering methods such as reducing exposure to the 24/7 news cycle, refusing to be baited by people who just want to goad them, and self-care efforts. The other kind of coping, active coping, is about helping clients enact their civic values in the world via action steps such as getting better informed through reputable sources, donating to causes they support, volunteering to help others, getting politically active, or (as one client decided) being kinder in public to society's "others." And when clients are having powerful, dysregulated emotional responses to the political situation, we can help them unpack how it connects to their personal journeys.

I see our job as helping clients avoid the twin dangers of being either numb/reactive or agitated/reactive in the face of political stress. The middle is where we're aiming, for ourselves and our clients: being grounded/responsive, where we're in touch with our feelings and can act thoughtfully according to our values. Therapy like this can be an incubator for an empowered citizenry in a democracy in which we're neither victims nor flamethrowers.

The Citizen Therapist in the Larger World

Donald Trump has done me the favor of helping me better see the connection between psychotherapy and democracy. In fact, there is a close connection between the personal agency focus of psychotherapy and the work of democracy understood not just as an electoral system but as a collective agency for building a shared life in community: We the (responsible) People. In our offices, we promote the kind of personal agency that's necessary for a self-governing, democratic people, a people whose worlds are public as well as private. In other words, we are growing citizens of democracies. And therapy needs the larger system of democracy in order to thrive. (I've trained non-American therapists who went home to dictatorial systems that greatly inhibited what they could encourage their clients to say and do in their social world.)

Still, to truly fulfill the potential of our professional role in a democracy, we have to be active outside our offices. I feel passionately that we're healers with something important to offer our neighbors and communities. Here's a short definition of the concept of the citizen therapist: A citizen therapist works with people in the office and the community on coping productively with public stress and becoming active agents of their personal and civic lives. Citizen-therapist work is not separate from the traditional practice of psychological and interpersonal healing—it's integrated with it.

As an example of citizen-therapist work in today's toxic public environment, I've been doing depolarization workshops with "Red" and "Blue" Americans. One stands out in particular: thirteen hours over a December weekend in rural Ohio with eleven Hillary supporters and ten Trump supporters. The goal was to learn if people could better understand their differences (beyond stereotypes) to see if there were common values, and to share, if possible, something hopeful with their community and the larger world. For me, it was like couples' therapy with twenty-one people—intense, painful, illuminating, and ultimately gratifying. After a second, equally successful weekend in southern Ohio, a new action-for-depolarization group was formed of Red and Blue citizens, a chapter of a national organization called Better Angels. I've also developed a series of different kinds of workshops and trainings, offered through Better Angels, that therapists can learn to conduct in their local communities.

The age of Trump calls therapists beyond the personal/public split, a blind spot that has kept us from engaging in comprehensive care for people who bring to us their whole selves, private and public, intimate and civic. It's an invitation to expand and enrich the work we do for our clients and communities.

William J. Doherty, Ph.D., is a professor of family social science and director of the Minnesota Couples on the Brink project and the Citizen Professional Center at the University of Minnesota. In May 2016, he authored the Citizen Therapist Manifesto Against Trumpism, *which was signed by more than 3,800 therapists. After the election, he founded Citizen Therapists for Democracy (www.citizentherapists.com). He is a senior fellow with Better Angels, an organization devoted to depolarizing America at the grassroots level. He helped pioneer the area of medical family therapy, and in 2017 he received the American Family Therapy Academy Lifetime Achievement Award.*

PART 3

THE TRUMP EFFECT

TRAUMA, TIME, TRUTH, AND TRUMP

How a President Freezes Healing and Promotes Crisis

BETTY P. TENG, M.F.A., L.M.S.W.

In the days following the November 8, 2016, election of Donald Trump as president of the United States—the most powerful leadership position in the world—many individuals, particularly those targeted by Trump's rageful expressions of xenophobia, racism, sexism, and Islamophobia, experienced the event as traumatic, without quite knowing why. "I feel like I did after 9/11," said one colleague. "I am in shock," reported a patient. "I don't know what to think."

Throughout the next weeks, patients and colleagues alike told me that the very idea of a President Trump left them feeling exposed, vulnerable, and helpless. "I have four out of six identity markers Trump will target: Arab, gay, immigrant, and woman," commented one patient. "I don't feel safe walking around anymore." One woman who was conflicted about whether to report her rape decided she would not. "How could it matter anymore?" she asked. "No one would believe me now." Another survivor was more blunt: "We elected a rapist to the presidency," referring to the accusations of sexual assault (Crockett and Nelson 2017) that several women brought against him, to no consequence. A colleague who treated New

Yorkers in the months following the 9/11 terrorist attacks on the World Trade Center said the reactions he has seen in his patients to Trump's election and presidency are far worse. "The difference is, the attacks of 9/11 were finite and enacted by an outside source," he observed. "Trump was elected by those among us, and his aggression feels incessant and never ending."

These reactions were also my own. I, too, was in shock; sitting with patients, I struggled to focus. I was prone to spontaneous tears. When asked, I found it difficult to summon the words to explain my distress. I recognized these responses as symptoms of traumatic shock, the possible harbingers of PTSD—posttraumatic stress disorder—which is commonly experienced by traumatized patients.

I am a psychotherapist—specifically, a trauma therapist who treats at a major hospital in New York City adult survivors of sexual assault, domestic violence, and childhood sexual abuse. My job is to have some clinical understanding of trauma and how it impacts individuals and knowing how to treat its subjugating effects. Yet, I was baffled. How could a nonviolent event such as the peaceful election of a president generate a trauma response? Whatever one's political leanings, one could not equate Trump's win with an actual physical attack or a natural catastrophe.

Or could one?

The American Psychological Association defines *trauma* as "an emotional response to a terrible event like an accident, rape, or natural disaster." And for many people—especially, but not confined to, those in groups that Trump targeted during his campaign—his election and now his presidency are truly terrible, even disastrous, events.

Indeed, in the months since November, psychotherapists nationwide have reported an unprecedented focus on politics in their sessions, and a surge in new patients (Gold 2017) seeking help with the high anxiety and stress they feel in reaction to Trump's steady stream of extreme tweets and impulsive actions. Indeed, from the confusion and worry caused by his disastrous immigration travel ban; his irrational accusations that President Obama wiretapped Trump Tower; and his sudden military actions against Syria and North Korea, President Trump appears more concerned with drawing attention to his power through creating crises rather than resolving them.

It is inevitable that such destabilizing behavior in one who holds the most powerful leadership position in the world will heighten anxiety and fear in not only the previously traumatized, but the untraumatized as well. Media pundits and clinicians have coined terms such as *post-election stress disorder* (Gold 2017), *post-Trump stress disorder* (Pierre 2016), and *headline stress disorder* (Stosny 2017) to draw parallels between the anxiety reactions suffered by increasing numbers of concerned Americans and the symptoms of PTSD. If what we read about is true—and I will return to this, as Trump and his top advisers have also shaken our notions of truth and fact—PTSD-like symptoms of insomnia, lack of focus, hypervigilance, irritability, and volatility now afflict not only combat veterans, first responders, and survivors of rape, violent crime, natural disaster, torture, and abuse, but many of the rest of us as well.

Again, as a trauma therapist, I puzzle over this correlation of symptoms in greater numbers of the general American populace to PTSD, where the source of trauma is not a physical attack or a natural catastrophe, but the incessant barrage of aggressive words and daily reports of the erratic conduct of a powerful, narcissistic, and attention-seeking world leader. There is much debate over whether post-Trump stress disorder is "real" or just another example of how "snowflake liberals," goaded on by a "hysterical" left-leaning media, overinflate their suffering. There are questions about whether this trivializes the suffering of "true" trauma survivors, who have experienced "real" attacks and harm.

From a clinical perspective, however, such debates at best distract and at worst shame us away from a more thorough consideration of the root causes of this unique phenomenon: how the election and actions of a president such as Donald Trump could cause a large swath of American citizens to feel traumatized or retraumatized. It is important to remember that Trump's ascendance to the White House is unprecedented and incongruous. We are in uncharted territory. How a New York City real estate magnate and reality television celebrity who had no previous legal, legislative, government, or foreign policy experience could become president of the United States is a circumstance many still find difficult to comprehend. If we agree that the skills of a U.S. president are as crucial as that of a heart surgeon—whose professional judgment and expertise can mean life or death for his patients—then it is terrifying to see that the American body politic has, in Donald Trump, a cardiac surgeon who has never set foot inside an operating room. He is a doctor who has no knowledge of, and arguably no interest in, the inner workings of the American government's heart. It therefore makes sense that his lack of qualifications and his insensitivity to the complexities and impact of his role would inspire great anxiety, if not even panic, in those of us whose lives depend on his care—regardless of political affiliation or trauma history.

For those previously traumatized, however, Trump is even more triggering. Such individuals may experience his volatile, retaliatory, and unilateral behavior as mirroring that of the abusive parent, the wanton bully, the authoritarian teacher, or the sexually aggressive boss who subjugated them in the past. Because a trauma survivor's brain often exists in a heightened state of hyperarousal, Trump's daily outrages deliver unnecessary neurobiological overstimulation, narrowing a survivor's "window of tolerance," or cognitive space for calm, linear thinking. Such individuals are thus more likely to feel more anxious or even to fall out of their "window of tolerance" into panic attacks, flashbacks, and dissociation. And when we consider who is particularly vulnerable to such heightened anxiety, the numbers of Americans who hold one form of trauma or another are greater than we may think. According to Harvard trauma expert Dr. Bessel van der Kolk (2014):

Research by the Centers for Disease Control and Prevention has shown that one in five Americans was sexually molested as a child; one in four was beat by a parent to the point of a mark being left on their body; and one in three couples engages in physical violence. A quarter of us grew up with alcoholic relatives, and one out of eight witnessed their mother being beaten or hit.

When we consider how many Americans experience, personally or intergenerationally, the traumas of slavery, immigration, war, natural disaster, and genocide, we start to understand on another level how it is that Donald Trump, a wholly unqualified president who neglects history, highlights divisions, and makes impulsive decisions, would foment unrest in us all.

Trauma, Time, Truth, and Trump

Thus, President Trump is a destabilizing force that stirs some of us to the point where we experience him as a psycho-socio-political tornado. In fact, the debate over whether post-Trump stress disorder is "real," and if it is as serious as PTSD, is itself a kind of trauma response. Queries voiced among Americans in response to Trump's election and after his first one hundred days in office—"Is this real?"; "This is not serious, or is it?"; and "I don't know what happened, but I can't move on"—mirror those asked by many of my patients after they begin treatment. They grapple with experiences that are paradoxically too upsetting to consider and too overwhelming to deny. When a U.S. president inspires such internal confusion among the citizens he has been elected to serve, this bears serious consideration. Is Donald Trump causing a trauma epidemic?

From my perspective as a trauma therapist, I highlight two key components of trauma (time and truth) to illuminate how Trump impacts so many of us in a traumatogenic way. In so doing, I aim not only to validate the trauma responses many have had to this president, but also to point out how we can minimize Trump's effect on us. If we know how trauma is constructed, we can do something with its component parts to lessen its effect. In this way, we can prevent ourselves from becoming overwhelmed and immobilized by anger or anxiety in the face of Trump's erratic and vindictive behavior.

Time and Trauma

Media ecologist and cultural studies professor Jade E. Davis (2014) considers how online digital media reflects and shapes our perceptions of historical or current events. In her breakdown of the phenomenon, Davis states that "trauma can exist only in the post-tense," after survivors have been able to find words to describe the horrific event. This is to say, our ability to consider trauma is always contingent on time.

Davis's assertion that trauma is "located in the narrative and accessible through testimony and witnessing" reflects a cornerstone of our work in trauma therapy. A main objective of treatment is to provide the traumatized individual with a sense of safety so she can relate her story, trusting in the fact that her therapist has the tolerance and compassion to bear witness to the survivor's pain, fear, and shame. This relieves the deep isolation that plagues the traumatized. Van der Kolk (2014) agrees:

> This is one of the most profound experiences we can have, and such resonance, in which hitherto unspoken words can be discovered, uttered, and received, is fundamental to healing the isolation of trauma. Communicating fully is the opposite of being traumatized.

In trauma therapy as in daily life, "communicating fully," be it with oneself or another, takes skill, care, and time. Mental reflection relies on our having the space and time to take an experience in and to sift through its various parts, in order to engage in dialogue with oneself and others. This is how we orient ourselves to our experiences, our opinions, and our values; this is how we verify our realities. This is how we *think*.

When we are traumatized, our capacity to think and communicate can become so compromised that we need extra support. Neurobiologically, traumatic experiences silence the speech centers of the brain (van der Kolk 2014), rendering us literally speechless. When a survivor has no time or ability to find the words to tell her side of the story in a traumatic situation, Davis defines this as *crisis*. She describes crisis as a closed and sealed circle representing a situation inaccessible to time and witnessing—that is, a circumstance that lacks space for perspective, one that is subsequently isolated from exchange, change, and growth (Davis 2014).

The following diagram (Davis 2014) illustrates the difference between trauma and crisis:

SOCIETY AT LARGE

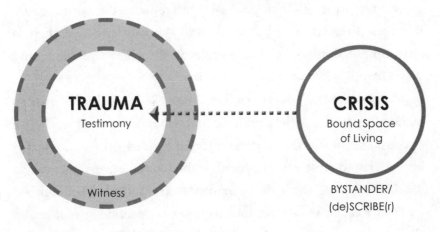

Illustration courtesy of Jade E. Davis

Trauma refers to a response to a disastrous event that exists in language and time. In Davis's illustration, it has a porous, dashed-line boundary because a traumatic narrative is a testimony that allows others to bear witness and enter the experience of the traumatized. It is open, not closed. By listening, a witness helps contain the trauma,

as represented by the outer dashed-line circle. In the exchange between a traumatized patient and her witness, shifts in the traumatic
narrative naturally occur, and growth results. This narrative eventually moves to a fully mourned space, freeing the patient from
being controlled by heightened anxiety and triggers that prompt
flashbacks and panic attacks.

By contrast, "Crises are histories that exist in closed circles . . .
there are no testimonies and no witnesses . . . People in crisis become
bounded, out of place and out of time" (Davis 2014). In Davis's diagram, crisis is illustrated by a sealed circle. It shows that within its
nonporous boundary, events are cut off from time and language, and
therefore inaccessible. Without the crucial perspective that time and
language afford, a disastrous experience can neither be thought
about nor shared, nor mourned. Possible witnesses can only be helpless bystanders, unable to hear or respond to those imprisoned
within. Individuals in crisis remain stuck in place; there can be no
growth or letting go. Their internal chaos remains the same because
there are no words to make sense of it. Without language, there is
only mindless action and reaction, a cycle driven by fear, panic, and
dissociation.

This is the state that President Trump keeps us in. He does so
by flooding media outlets, both old and new, with myriad vindictive
tweets, defensive press conferences, and sudden firings. Context is
key; if Trump were not president of the United States, his ravings
would simply be those of an arrogant, unmindful, loudmouthed
reality TV celebrity who compulsively seeks attention by cultivating
shock and outrage on both ends of the political spectrum. The "no
press is bad press" boorishness of his actions would find traction
only on reality TV and in tabloid and gossip pages that, before the
2015–2016 election cycle, were the main sites trafficking in Trump's
baldly self-promotional broadcasts. While it is beyond the scope of this
essay to delve into the social, economic, political, and demographic
circumstances that allowed Trump to morph from entertainment

persona to leader of the free world, it is important to note aspects of our current technological climate, which combine with Trump's now-central role as U.S. president and his narcissistically compulsive personality, to keep the American public fixated on his toxic behavior and stuck in a state of chaotic, meaningless crisis.

Our ever-increasing use of the Internet demands that we process new information at the speed of the supercomputers that drive it. As Brown University digital media scholar Wendy Chun (2016) observes, "[T]here is an unrelenting stream of updates that demand response, from ever-updating Twitter.com feeds to exploding inboxes. The lack of time to respond, brought about by the inhumanly clocked time of our computers that renders the new old, coupled with the demand for response, makes the Internet compelling."

"I think, therefore I am," Descartes's Enlightenment-era definition of human existence, has become, in the twenty-first century, "I *post*, therefore I am." Compelling as this is, there is a falseness to this promise. This is marked by the exhaustion we experience when we spend too much time online. For the insomnia-stricken among my trauma patients, I recommend removal of screen time at least an hour before bedtime; Web-surfing scatters attention and overstimulates the brain. Moreover, backlit screens have been proven to block the brain's production of melatonin, a natural sleep-promoting hormone. For the traumatized, whose neurobiological systems are already in a state of hyperarousal, heightened anxiety and sleep disturbance narrow their "windows of tolerance." This makes finding calm even more challenging and hinders healing significantly.

We are not machines; feeding our quest for knowledge and defining our existences online delivers a synthetic fulfillment that is fleeting and unsustainable. Seeking such satisfaction via the Internet is like trying to quench thirst by sipping water from a fire hose. By drinking from the Internet's fire hose, we not only end up still thirsty, but we may get seriously hurt in the process. Because this onslaught of information disallows us from taking the time to truly consider any of it, we open ourselves to believing dangerous and unchecked falsehoods. Both Chun and Stanford University election law scholar Nathaniel Persily (2017) warn of the alarming political consequences of our collective inability to think or verify the truth of what is broadcast online. As Chun (2016) observes, "The Internet . . . has been formulated as the exact opposite of Barlow's dream (of an unregulated space for a free marketplace of ideas): a nationalist machine that spreads rumors and lies."

While Chun points to the Internet's potential for fostering the seeds of nationalist propaganda, Persily asks, "Can Democracy survive the Internet?" in the very title of his recent paper. By analyzing the 2016 digital campaign for U.S. president, he orients us to what today's Internet amplifies: social media retweets, false news shares, bot-driven articles, and troll-inspired critiques that reflect and stir reactivity rather than disseminate the truth: "What the Internet uniquely privileges above all else is the type of campaign message that appeals to outrage or otherwise grabs attention. The politics of never-ending spectacles cannot be healthy for a democracy. Nor can a porousness to outside influences that undercuts the sovereignty of a nation's elections. Democracy depends on both the ability and the will of voters to base their political judgments on facts."

Persily highlights the maladaptive match between Trump, a spectacle-driven reality TV persona, and our current technological age. The pairing of online media sites that rely on page views to maximize advertising dollars with Trump's factually thin but impossible-to-ignore shock effect ravings has resulted in his effortlessly infecting media outlets primed to spread his viral-ready broadcasts. His success at capitalizing on the mass market use and influence of social media is something that social and political scientists, digital media scholars, campaign experts, journalists, and government officials are scrambling to understand. As Persily observes, "For Trump, his assets included his fame, following, and skill in navigating the new media landscape. He also figured out that incendiary language could command media attention or shift the narrative. These combined strategies allowed him to garner roughly $2 billion worth of free media during the primaries, and probably a comparable amount during the general-election campaign."

Trump's immense talent for grabbing attention and turning it into material wealth and power, makes him, first and foremost, a master of marketing. What Chun and Persily point out is that in the Internet era, the filterless, open, and interactive nature of online media channels promotes the spread of rumors and spectacle because information traffics too quickly to favor the nuances and subtleties of truth. In a climate where the "new" becomes "old" (Chun 2016) in a matter of moments, where the mobile devices of dissemination are literally in our hands at all times, it is too easy and compelling to immediately spread what feels alarming or outrageous to our audiences of social media "friends," who are just a click away.

Trauma and Truth

Looking through the lens of trauma treatment, it is of particular concern that we find ourselves in a perfect storm where we have, as our U.S. president, a narcissist fixed on broadcasting his own unilateral and inconsistent versions of reality in a climate driven by Internet media channels that produce information so quickly that they privilege falsehoods over truth. It is a tenet of trauma therapy to validate our patients' truths—that is, their experiences of their subjugation. Without it, the work of healing cannot progress. Being believed and not having one's experience denied are crucial to anyone who has seen unspeakable horrors or who has been subjugated by another through torture, rape, or physical or sexual abuse. Such events turn one's world upside down, and a cornerstone of our work is to help a patient stabilize herself by affirming the truth of what her experience was. Only then can we build, with words, a narrative of the event so that the patient can make sense of and communicate to herself and others what happened. She is thus able to move out of her isolation and shame to recruit witnesses to help her bear such a painful burden. This allows the patient to move her experience from crisis, or wordless reactivity; to trauma, a narrative of pain; to history, a story about the past. With time to validate truths and make meaning out of chaos, a patient can reduce her panic attacks, flashbacks, and dissociation. Rather than being caught in a cycle of meaningless crisis, she can regain stability, increase her sense of calm, and move on with her life. Again, as trauma expert van der Kolk (2014) put it, "Communicating fully is the opposite of being traumatized."

Thus, it is traumatizing to have, in the White House, a president and an administration intent on confounding "full communication" by manipulating the truth to serve their own ends. As Columbia University psychoanalyst Joel Whitebook points out (2017), according to Trump and his team, there is only one reality—Donald Trump's:

> Armed with the weaponized resources of social media, Trump has radicalized this strategy in a way that aims to subvert our relation to reality in general. To assert that there are "alternative facts," as his adviser Kellyanne Conway did, is to assert that there is an alternative, delusional, reality in which those "facts" and opinions most convenient in supporting Trump's policies and worldview hold sway. Whether we accept the reality that Trump and his supporters seek to impose on us, or reject it, it is an important and ever-present source of the specific confusion and anxiety that Trumpism evokes.

When a world leader as powerful as the president of the United States insists on there being "alternative facts" derived from a reality only he knows, this is alarming and destabilizing for us all. Democracy and the rule of law are threatened without an agreement between government and its citizens on the objectivity of truth and reality. A breakdown in this agreement puts the definition of truth and reality into the hands of those with the most social, political, and/or economic power. In history, this has supported the severe wrongdoings of institutions intent more on preserving their power than on protecting individual rights. The sexual molestation of children by priests in the Catholic Church represents a stark and long-standing example of an institution that insisted on its own truth and reality rather than those of abused innocents. To hold on to power, Catholic Church leaders permitted the ongoing sexual abuse of society's most vulnerable, the very individuals they had a holy mandate to protect.

In trauma therapy, we see the corrosive long-term effects upon the human spirit when an individual's truth and reality are denied, particularly when those individuals grapple with traumas that take away their sense of subjectivity and self-efficacy. In his constant attempts to redefine the truth against the wrongdoings he has enacted, Donald Trump behaves like an aggressive perpetrator who fundamentally has no respect for the rights and subjectivities of those in American society who disagree with him. He shows this through his insistence on overpowering and shaming individuals who will not bend to his opinion or his will. From my stance as a trauma therapist, it is heartbreaking to see the damage Donald Trump is wreaking upon American society. It is a perpetration, creating deep wounds from which, I fear, it will already take us years to heal.

Conclusion

When the U.S. presidency, a position that already occupies the focus of global attention, is held by an extreme individual such as Donald Trump, his dramatic and inconsistent behavior captures all media attention. This constant coverage becomes a compulsive fixation for us all. For those of us who have been previously subjugated, this kind of exposure is particularly overstimulating and blocks us from recruiting the tools so necessary for healing from trauma. We are prevented from taking time to use language to validate truths and create meaning through narratives of those experiences. Without adequate time to process what shocks or destabilizes us, we cannot make sense of what happened; nor can we communicate our horrors to others. This robs all of the opportunity to humanize the subjugating effects of terror, abuse, and attack or to lift the isolation and shame that accompany them.

Moreover, the unfortunate symbiosis of our president's narcissistic, attention-hungry outrageousness with our Internet era's insatiable appetite for spectacle has resulted in a flood of incendiary news and information that none of us, whether previously traumatized or not, has the time or mental space to process. Yet, we gorge ourselves on such toxic infotainment with a niggling sense of impending doom. As *New Yorker* editor in chief David Remnick said of White House press secretary Sean Spicer's unusually high ratings for press briefings: "Undoubtedly, some people watch Spicer to be entertained. But there's another reason his ratings are high: we watch because we're worried" (Remnick 2017).

Indeed, we are worried. Due to Trump and his administration's constant and volatile shifts in mood, communication, and representations of basic truths, far more Americans now possess narrower "windows of tolerance" in managing stress. As president, Trump has created an epidemic of heightened anxiety. By denying us access to time and calling our perceptions of truth into question, he shuts down our ability to reflect, causes us to doubt reality, and thus encourages reactivity and stress, keeping us in a difficult-to-sustain state of crisis.

It is hard to predict how tenable this is for us, as individuals or as a society. Uncertain times call for collective strength and stability, and such disempowerment is detrimental to our individual and national mental health. We can, however, use this deeper understanding of trauma, and of its elements of time and truth, to promote measured thought instead of reactive freezing, panic, or avoidance. We can be aware of the propensity for new media outlets to privilege emotionally stimulating falsehoods over measured and nu-anced facts. We can unplug ourselves and take time simply to enjoy the act of thinking freely. It is a privilege we still enjoy in the United States, and it will be the skill we need to prevent us from careening toward crisis, as it seems Donald Trump would have us do.

Betty P. Teng, M.F.A., L.M.S.W., is a trauma therapist in the Of-fice of Victims Services of a major hospital in Lower Manhattan. A graduate of Yale College; UCLA's School of Theater, Film, and Television; and NYU's Silver School of Social Work, Ms. Teng is in psychoanalytic training and practices at the Institute for Con-temporary Psychotherapy. She is also an award-winning screen-writer and editor whose credits include films by Ang Lee, Robert Altman, and Mike Nichols.

References

Chun, Wendy. 2016. *Updating to Remain the Same: Habitual New Media.* Cambridge, MA: MIT Press.

Crockett, Emily, and Libby Nelson. 2017. "Sexual Assault Allegations Against Donald Trump: 15 Women Say He Groped, Kissed, or Assaulted Them." *Vox.* www.vox.com/2016/10/12/13265206/trump-accusations -sexual-assault.

Davis, Jade E. 2014. "The Catholic Schoolgirl and the Wet Nurse: On the Ecology of Oppression, Trauma and Crisis." *Decolonization: Indigeneity, Education, and Society* 3 (1): 143–58.

Gold, Jenny. 2017. " 'Post-Election Stress Disorder' Strikes on Both Sides." CNN, February 20. www.cnn.com/2017/02/20/health/post-election -stress-partner/index.html.

Persily, Nathaniel. 2017. "Can Democracy Survive the Internet?" *Journal of Democracy* 28 (2): 63–76.

Pierre, Joe. 2016. "Understanding Post-Trump Stress Disorder" *Psychology Today,* November 10. www.psychologytoday.com/blog/psych-unseen /201611/understanding-post-trump-stress-disorder.

Remnick, David. 2017. "The Presidency and the Press." *The New Yorker* weekly e-mail newsletter, May 14.

Stosny, Steven. 2017. "He Once Called It 'Election Stress Disorder.' Now the Therapist Says We're Suffering from This." *Washington Post*, February 6. www.washingtonpost.com/news/inspired-life/wp/2017/02/06 /suffering-from-headline-stress-disorder-since-trumps-win-youre -definitely-not-alone/.

Van der Kolk, Bessel A. 2014. *The Body Keeps the Score.* New York: Penguin Books.

Whitebook, Joel. 2017. "Trump's Method, Our Madness." *New York Times*, March 20. www.nytimes.com/2017/03/20/opinion/trumps-method -our-madness.html.

TRUMP ANXIETY DISORDER

The Trump Effect on the Mental Health of Half the
Nation and Special Populations

JENNIFER CONTARINO PANNING, PSY.D.

Two thousand sixteen marked a period of intense uncertainty and upheaval leading up to the contentious American presidential election on November 8, 2016, between Donald J. Trump and Hillary R. Clinton. Despite the vast majority of polls (Silver 2016) indicating that Hillary Clinton's odds of winning the election were 70–95 percent, and many individuals believing that Trump's candidacy was a farce, Trump won the presidency (although he lost the popular vote by more than 3 million votes).

This stunning result led to an unprecedented level of post-election shock, grief, and anxiety in about half the American population, many being progressive by political persuasion, but not always (American Psychological Association 2017).

This chapter will detail the pre- and post-election anxiety (dubbed "Trump anxiety disorder") widespread in the general public. However, unlike generalized anxiety symptoms, these symptoms were specific to the election of Trump and the resultant unpredictable sociopolitical climate. The role of the media, with a focus on biased and fake news reporting, is another factor in the development of these symptoms. This chapter will conclude with the author illustrating examples of this disorder from her clinical work with psychotherapy clients—most of whom are from an upper-middle-class background, intelligent, and educated.

Many of Trump's bombastic, grandiose attitudes and campaign untruths created an environment of uncertainty, with Americans feeling threatened in their personal safety; these ideologies created the perfect environmental factors for Trump's nonsupporters' anxieties to develop (Sheehy 2016). According to the "Stress in America" report, half of Americans (49 percent) endorsed that the 2016 election had been a significant stressor in their lives (American Psychological Association 2017). Many therapists were faced with the task of helping their clients manage this stress as well as the frustration of trying to "normalize" behavior that they did not feel was normal for an American president (Sheehy 2016).

It is important to differentiate generalized anxiety disorder and Trump anxiety disorder. The *Diagnostic and Statistical Manual of Mental Disorders*, 5th ed. (commonly referred to as DSM-V), is widely used among mental health professionals (American Psychiatric Association 2013). It describes generalized anxiety disorder (GAD) as characterized by excessive, uncontrollable, and often irrational worry—that is, apprehensive expectation about events or activities. This excessive worry often interferes with daily functioning, as individuals with GAD typically anticipate disaster and are overly concerned about everyday matters such as health issues, money, death, family problems, friendship problems, interpersonal relationship problems, or work difficulties. Individuals often exhibit a variety of physical symptoms, including fatigue, fidgeting, headaches, nausea, numbness in hands and feet, muscle tension, muscle aches, difficulty swallowing, excessive stomach acid buildup, stomach pain, vomiting, diarrhea, bouts of breathing difficulty, difficulty concentrating, trembling, twitching, irritability, agitation, sweating, restlessness, insomnia, hot flashes, rashes, and an inability to fully control the anxiety. These symptoms must be consistent and ongoing, persisting at least six months, for a formal diagnosis of GAD (American Psychiatric Association 2013). Generalized anxiety disorder is one of the more prevalent mood disorders in Americans; according to the National Institute of Mental Health, 3.1 percent of American adults struggle with GAD within a year, or over 7 million.

Symptoms associated with Trump anxiety disorder include: feeling a loss of control; helplessness; ruminations/worries, especially about the uncertain sociopolitical climate while Trump is in office; and a tendency toward excessive social media consumption. In fact, the polarization that this has created has caused a deep divide between families and friends of differing political beliefs. Trump's specific personality characteristics, and his use of psychological manipulation tools such as gaslighting, lying, and blaming, are described as contributing factors to Trump anxiety disorder.

Trump anxiety disorder, albeit not a formal diagnosis, differs from GAD in regard to several measures. One difference is in the duration of time for the symptoms to develop. The volatile events leading up to the 2016 election (i.e., false news reports, Comey's report questioning Clinton's ethics) were challenging in themselves, but many Americans were reassured by multiple polls (e.g., Silver 2016) predicting that Hillary Clinton would win the election in a landslide. This led to a sense of shock and disbelief after Trump was announced as president of the United States.

An additional symptom of Trump anxiety disorder is that symptoms are directly related to the uncertain sociopolitical climate. An elevated stress level when reading articles about numerous topics— the Muslim ban, the threat/promise of disbanding the Affordable Care Act, tensions between the United States and North Korea, the possibility of Russia's having interfered in the 2016 election and Russia's financial connection to Trump, the U.S./Mexican wall, immigration issues, the defunding of environmental groups such as the

National Park Service and the Environmental Protection Agency, and the defunding of medical research—is strong. An individual impacted by Trump anxiety disorder may be directly impacted by one of these singular issues, have multiple concerns, or worry about the future democratic state in America given these issues. Therefore, the ruminative worry associated with an anxiety disorder is specific to these events (Clarridge 2017).

Social media have changed the way Americans are exposed to news. Internet news sites (CNN, *Huffington Post*, etc.) and social media such as Facebook and Twitter provide immediate access to news as well as to comments from other readers with differing viewpoints. Many Americans impacted by Trump anxiety disorder have admitted to an unhealthy obsession with checking news websites much more often than they previously did, and the amount of news involving Trump and his new administration has been constant, chaotic, confusing, and often overwhelming. When struggling with anxiety, many individuals, in an attempt to maintain control, will falsely assume that the more they know, the more they can be prepared. However, this tends to give them a false sense of control and, paradoxically, may increase anxiety symptoms once they realize their grip on control is not solid.

Other symptoms endorsed by many Americans post-election have included: feelings of helplessness and paralysis, an inability to focus on work or family obligations, and difficulty sleeping. Maladaptive coping strategies have included stress eating, drinking, smoking, and other ways to avoid feeling anxious.

Gaslighting, a term popularized in psychological literature over the past ten to fifteen years, describes unhealthy dynamics in a power relationship (Stern 2007). A gaslighter is "someone who desperately needs to be right in order to bolster his own sense of self and hold onto his own sense of power" (Stern 2007). Our gaslighter in chief has created anxiety for many Americans. During Trump's campaign, there were many examples of his lies, untruths, and other information that served to create doubt and to manipulate. However, gaslighting also serves to deceive someone into doubting her own perception of reality (Gibson 2017).

A February 2017 survey by the American Psychological Association (2017), "Stress in America: Coping with Change," indicated that two-thirds of Americans say they are stressed about the future of our nation. Although 76 percent of Democrats have reported stress about the future of our nation, 59 percent of Republicans have also endorsed the same stress level.

This also related to the therapists themselves. While mental health professionals were helping their clients deal with the stress of the post-election period, they were also struggling to handle and process their own feelings, which often were very similar to those of their clients.

One Psychologist's Work with Clients with Trump Anxiety Disorder

I am a licensed clinical psychologist and owner of a small group practice in Evanston, Illinois, a suburban, liberal, higher-socioeconomic-status, and educated suburb just north of the Chicago city limits. Evanston is a college town, home to Northwestern University, with much of its sixty-five thousand residents comprising professionals who work at Northwestern or at other white-collar, professional jobs. The majority of my clients are Northwestern University undergraduate and graduate students diagnosed with disorders as straightforward as adjusting to college life and struggling with identity development as well as more serious diagnoses such as major depressive disorder, bipolar disorder, eating disorders, stress, and other mood disorders (primarily anxiety-related). I should note that given the very progressive area in which I practice, I had zero Trump supporters among my caseload of clients during this time.

After the 2016 election, and most especially the week after it, the vast majority of my clients discussed and processed their feelings about the election. In fact, it was unusual when a client did *not* mention the election during this period. Most clients struggled with similar feelings of shock, sadness, worry, panic, uncertainty for the future, and anger. Some were still in shock, and many endorsed feeling as if the election results were a nightmare that they hadn't yet woken up from.

Most notably, the clients who came in the day after the election were still in disbelief. As their therapist, I concentrated on validating, normalizing, and maintaining a safe place for them to discuss their troubled feelings. We also discussed basic self-care, such as getting enough sleep, eating healthy meals, connecting with friends and family, and limiting consumption of election news stories. Certain clients were satisfied with discussing this for a short period of time and then resuming discussing their personal issues, while others struggled with daily functioning during the days and weeks after the election.

I (along with many other mental health professionals) have struggled to help clients while struggling myself with similar feelings of shock, anger, disbelief, frustration, and fear. The majority of mental health professionals tend to be liberal in their leanings (Norton 2016), which is unsurprising, given our profession's focus on social justice, health care rights, and other progressive causes. Therefore, many therapists were saddled with both helping their clients deal with their anxieties while also struggling with their own symptoms. Some of this work was comforting. Being able to help clients gave us welcome relief from the constant barrage of news stories. It also helped me not feel as helpless; being "in the trenches" with clients was a way to feel productive.

I found that clients with a loved one (usually a parent or a partner) with a personality disorder (most notably narcissistic personality disorder) were more impacted than others. Much of the work done with these individuals helps them to acknowledge the gaslighting involved in their relationship with their loved one; to identify that they are not crazy and do have sound and intact judgment regarding their impaired loved one; to acknowledge the limitations of their loved one; and to develop healthy coping strategies to cope with their loved one's erratic mood changes, blaming, and lying.

One woman, "Claire" (all names in clinical situations have been changed and placed in quotation marks where they first appear), a mother of a young child with special needs and a husband with narcissistic traits, had been referred to me by her husband because he felt that she was "going crazy" and needed professional help. Part of our work together was to help her understand the legitimacy of her husband's assessment; continue to work on her anxiety, which had been triggered by this dynamic; and to set healthier boundaries with her husband. Claire was very educated, politically liberal, and struggled with the impact of Trump's being elected. Her anxiety symptoms were exacerbated during the post-election and post-inauguration period. Her treatment focused on normalizing her feelings and encouraging her to establish control by making a difference in the ways she could. For her, this entailed volunteering, expressing appreciation to her child's teachers and other related professionals, and by calling her local congressional representatives.

Another woman, "Ida," was in her early twenties and an undergraduate student in her junior year. Ida was gifted and also extremely sensitive and inquisitive. She had struggled in therapy to make sense of her relationship with her father, who had narcissistic traits. I remember her stating after the election, "I feel like we are all in an emotionally abusive relationship with our president." She struggled with increased anxiety as well, and our work was to help ground her in what she could and could not control. She participated in several protest marches, which helped her feel less helpless. However, she struggled with minimizing her social media consumption and would often come into sessions feeling overwhelmed by the latest news.

Working in a very progressive area without one Trump supporter as a client enabled me to be honest with my clients that I was experiencing similar feelings, and that many of these feelings were universal to progressives post-election. I like to think that my clients appreciated my honesty and my ability to see a very human side to their therapist. However, many times the role of the therapist involves helping clients feel more hopeful and confident in their lives. This task proved to be quite difficult, as we therapists were left with similar feelings of helplessness and, perhaps due to our professional training, more concern given the characterological issues we saw in Trump's behavior and personality.

> *Jennifer Contarino Panning, Psy.D., is a licensed clinical psychologist and owner of Mindful Psychology Associates, a small group practice in Evanston Illinois. She received her doctorate in clinical psychology from the Chicago School of Professional Psychology in 2003, and completed training at Northern Illinois University and Northwestern University. Panning opened her private practice in 2004, and now has three psychologists and a postdoctoral fellow on staff. She specializes in the treatment of mood disorders, eating disorders, college student mental health, stress, and trauma using an integrative approach of cognitive behavioral therapy, mindfulness, and dialectical behavioral therapy, and is also trained in clinical hypnosis.*

References

American Psychiatric Association. 2013. *Diagnostic and Statistical Manual of Mental Disorders*. 5th ed. Arlington, VA: American Psychiatric Association.

American Psychological Association. 2017. "Many Americans Stressed About Future of Our Nation, New APA Stress in American Survey Reveals." APA.org, February 15. www.apa.org/news/press/releases /2017/02/stressed-nation.aspx.

Clarridge, Christine. 2017. "Mental Health Therapists See Uptick in Patients

Struggling with Postelection Anxiety." March 29. www.chicagotribune
.com/lifestyles/health/ct-mental-health-postelection-anxiety-20170329
-story.html.

Gibson, Caitlin. 2017. "What We Talk About When We Talk About Donald
Trump' and 'Gaslighting.'" January 27. www.washingtonpost.com
/lifestyle/style/what-we-talk-about-when-we-talk-about-donald-trump
-and-gaslighting/2017/01/27/b02e6de4-e330-11e6-ba11-63c4b4fb5a63
_story.html.

Glinton, Sonari. 2016. "Survey Says Americans Are Getting Stressed by the
Elections." October 15. www.npr.org/sections/the two-way/2016/10/15
/498033747/survey-says-Americans-are-getting-stressed-by-the-
elections.

National Institute of Mental Health. "Any Anxiety Disorder Among
Adults." www.nimh.nih.gov/health/statistics/prevalence/any-anxiety
-disorder-among-adults.shtml.

Norton, Aaron. 2016. "The Political Beliefs of Mental Health Counselors." *In
Thought* (blog), May 9. www.aaronlmhc.blogspot.com/2016/05/political
-beliefs-of-mental-health-counselors.html.

Sheehy, Gail. 2016. "America's Therapists Are Worried About Trump's Effect
on Your Mental Health." October 16. www.politico.com/magazine
/story/2016/10/donald-trump-2016-therapists-214333.

Silver, Nate. 2016. "Election Update: Clinton Gains, and the Polls Magically
Converge." November 7. https://fivethirtyeight.com/features/election
-update-clinton-gains-and-the-polls-magically-converge/.

Stern, Robin. 2007. *The Gaslight Effect*. New York: Morgan Road Books.

IN RELATIONSHIP WITH AN ABUSIVE PRESIDENT

HARPER WEST, M.A., L.L.P.

As "Amelia"* describes her husband's behavior in my therapy office, it immediately strikes me as emotionally abusive, although she acts as if his behavior were completely normal.

"Justin" can be harshly critical, calling her a "fat loser" and her home-cooked meals "a disaster." If she asks even reasonable questions, he lashes out at her: "You're always so negative and critical." If she states a fact he disagrees with, he accuses her of making up "fake" stories. Despite Justin's family and financial security, he is joyless and scowls much of the time.

Amelia is mystified how the most minor disagreements seem to escalate into major arguments. I ask if Justin can apologize or admit fault. "Oh, never," she says. "He's very stubborn. It's always my fault. I call him 'Justifying Justin.'"

Their most recent argument began when she asked if he had paid a bill. He became enraged and said he had paid it. She later

---

* This is a fictional couple.

learned that he had not paid the bill, but he refused to apologize for the lie, the ensuing argument, or his excessive anger.

Justin has lied so frequently that Amelia has become concerned she is "losing her mind" or has a poor memory, a belief aided by the fact that Justin accuses her of these faults. He insists that she forget his mistakes, but he brings up her mistakes repeatedly during arguments.

She describes Justin as being successful at business, very decisive, and a strong leader. She hesitates to confront him because she has learned that it leads to arguments escalating, with no resolution. She is always the one to compromise.

Amelia reports high levels of anxiety, and fears Justin's unpredictable reactions.

This couple is a composite of many cases where the pattern of abuse ranges from subtle to glaring. Not coincidentally, this couple is an analogy for the current relationship between America and a psychologically unstable, emotionally abusive president.

Domestic abusers and President Donald Trump share common personality traits because they share common human drives, emotions, and reactions. These characteristics negatively impact relationships, whether interpersonal or with an entire country, and they must be addressed for the health of those being harmed.

Renaming Narcissists

Some mental health professionals have associated Trump with a variety of diagnoses, such as narcissistic personality disorder, antisocial personality disorder, paranoid personality disorder, delusional disorder, malignant narcissist, and some form of dementia (Lenzer 2017).

Some of these labels come from the *Diagnostic and Statistical Manual* (American Psychiatric Association 2013), which numerous authors have identified as an unscientific, arbitrary categorization system that overcomplicates and falsely medicalizes emotional and behavioral problems ("DSM: A Fatal Diagnosis?" 2013; Caplan 1995; Deacon and McKay 2015; Kinderman 2014; Miller 2010; Whitaker and Cosgrove 2015).

To avoid this categorization system and to simplify and focus on the character flaw that is at the core of these personalities, I will call these types of people Other-blamers.

The cause of their behaviors is low self-worth, which leads them to have poor shame tolerance. They learned in childhood to manage feelings of inadequacy by adopting unhealthy coping mechanisms to forestall or avoid shaming experiences.

Poor shame tolerance causes behaviors associated with the just-mentioned DSM disorders, including vindictive anger, lack of insight and accountability, dishonesty, impulsivity, entitlement, paranoia, lack of remorse and empathy, self-importance, and attention-seeking. Trump is an extreme example, but "subclinical" versions of this behavior exist in millions of people, including domestic abusers.

It may be difficult to discern the low self-worth of Other-blamers because they often adopt an aggressive, dominating persona to achieve emotional self-protection. They rarely admit feelings of in-adequacy because they believe this would make them vulnerable to the same abuse and control they are perpetrating.

As a psychotherapist, I see the victims of Other-blamers in my office every day. Less-severe Other-blamers cause high-conflict or estranged relationships. More-severe cases can engage in emotional and physical abuse of partners and children, criminal behavior, and addictive behaviors. I have often said we should not be diagnosing those who come into therapy but, rather, those who *caused* them to come to therapy.

Despite their toxic behavior, Other-blamers rarely voluntarily agree to therapy because of their aversion to the shaming experience of self-awareness and accountability. Yet, they are quite often the subject of the therapy of others.

Certainly, Other-blamers are aided to some degree by the deferential behaviors of individuals who employ two other types of shame management strategies: self-blaming and blame avoidance (West 2016).

Other-blamers instinctively seek out those willing to be controlled, manipulated, or intimidated. This sets up relationships with submissive people who will not challenge, correct, or blame them. Dictators throughout history have surrounded themselves with a coterie of family members and sycophants who avoid questioning the leader for fear of his angry retribution.

(For the sake of clarity, this article will refer to abusers as males, but both genders can be Other-blamers and abusers.)

Causes of Other-blamer Behavior

As children, Other-blamers were likely exposed to developmental or attachment trauma, such as abusive, shaming, rejecting, or neglectful parenting. Parents who are substance abusers or psychologically troubled often underfocus on a child's needs. Parents may have exhibited narcissistic or Other-blaming behaviors that the child models. Another possible cause is parents who were permissive or conflict avoiding and did not hold the child accountable. Parents who overfocus on achievement or behavioral compliance can also encourage a fear of failure that may bring on Other-blaming tendencies.

These experiences can cause children to feel unloved, unprotected, and inadequate. They may struggle to experience empathy for others and may develop an unhealthy hypersensitivity and overreaction to shaming experiences. While Other-blaming as a shame-management strategy may be adaptive in childhood, it causes difficulties for adult relationships at all levels, from presidential to personal.

Emotional Reactivity with Fear, Shame, and Anger

In all humans, survival fear overwhelms the deliberative, logical functioning of the cognitive brain (Pasquali 2006). Children exposed to trauma continually rehearse "fight-or-flight" reactions so that their brains become habituated to and easily hijacked by survival emotions (Anda et al. 2006). Chronic exposure to the fear response leads to anxiety-based behaviors, such as impulsivity, hyperactivity, irrationality, volatility, impetuousness, poor frustration tolerance, and poor concentration—all of which Trump exhibits on a daily basis. Trump's incoherent gibberish may be a sign of his fearful, reactive emotional state; he cannot calm his brain enough even to form a complete sentence. One must be calm to be mindful of one's thoughts, feelings, and experiences and to gain self-awareness.

Although they are adept at hiding it, Other-blamers know a lot about fear. They spend their lives in an emotional survival panic, in terror of being judged and found unworthy. They are in a mad scramble to find some way to feel better about themselves or at least to protect themselves from feeling additional shame. That shame can lead to protective anger, as recognized in the aphorism "Anger is shame's bodyguard."

For extreme Other-blamers, elevated "fight-or-flight" reactivity can lead to shame-driven rage and abusive violence. Domestic violence incidents are usually triggered when the abuser feels challenged, demeaned, or rejected by the partner. Abusers failed to learn to tolerate shame in healthy ways, so even minor or perceived slights to their weak self-worth, such as dinner not being served on time, may throw them into an uncontrollable rage.

Trump's first wife, Ivana, accused him of raping her in sworn deposition testimony, an accusation she later softened, as a part of a lucrative divorce settlement, but did not completely retract. This alleged violence fits with the personality of someone fearful of rejection and living with elevated anxiety who might be triggered into violent rage. Abusers can escalate to murder/suicide when a relationship is ending and they must face the humiliation of undeniable rejection. That some abusers will kill others or even themselves to avoid experiencing this emotion shows the power of shame.

This pattern of escalating instability is concerning when considering Trump. As the pressures of governing and of the investigations such as that of alleged collusion with Russia increase, he may be overwhelmed by fear, which will further limit his cognitive and prosocial capabilities. His behaviors may become increasingly volatile and unpredictable.

Healthy relationships require partners who are calm, thoughtful, and deliberate, not fearful and reactive. Fear-driven behaviors and a lack of insight are exactly the opposite of what we should expect of a safe, dependable partner or a leader.

Lack of Accountability

With shame and fear as the primary emotions driving Other-blamers, a lack of accountability becomes their most obvious and destructive character flaw.

They have difficulty being introspective and acknowledging the effect of their behavior. This would involve gaining insight, admitting fault, and demonstrating remorse—actions that Other-blamers find devastatingly humiliating. In therapy, I get the sense that an Other-blamer wants to put his hands to his ears and sing "la-la-la" in an attempt to avoid hearing the truth. Other-blamers do not like to be held accountable because they do not hold themselves accountable.

In general, Other-blamers do not believe they must play by the same societal or relational norms as others, which can be disorienting to partners. Trump's refusal to release his tax returns or comply with ethics regulations is clear evidence of this thought process.

Lack of accountability causes escalating arguments in couples because Other-blamers stubbornly refuse to admit fault, even if the facts are staring them squarely in the face. Or they admit fault reluctantly, but only after much lying and excuse-making. The betrayals of trust mount up, driving a wedge into the relationship.

During arguments, Other-blamers frantically attempt to manage shame by shifting blame, making excuses, or denying behavior. One wife said about her emotionally abusive husband, "During conversations, he is not really listening, because he is trying to figure out how to make it not his problem."

Domestic abusers are notorious for their lack of accountability. They can go to extremes of rationalization. One abuser noted that while he had locked his wife in the closet for hours, thrown her to the floor repeatedly, and pointed a gun at her head, he had not punched her—as if this arbitrary demarcation excused his inexcusable crimes. The Other-blamer routinely blames the victim, as if a late dinner were worth a slap in the face.

Unlike Harry Truman, who placed a sign on his Oval Office desk stating, "The Buck Stops Here," Trump appears to be completely lacking in accountability. He regularly shifts blame to others and never seems to apologize for any of his lies or mistakes. Trump's blame shifting is so predictable that he can barely make one statement without a deflection (Millbank 2017). His assertion, although false, that he does not settle lawsuits is an example of his distaste for being held responsible. Trump's tendency to ridicule facts or the opinions of others is another way of avoiding dealing with a situation honestly.

Because of their lack of accountability and resulting lack of insight, Other-blamers are highly resistant to change, leaving their partners with limited power to affect the relationship. In an interpersonal relationship, the partner can leave. Yet, as a country, we have little recourse other than faith that our democratic institutions will keep Trump in check.

Unfortunately, abusers and authoritarians such as Trump do not like laws, which are ultimately about holding people accountable. This worldview is a danger to a democracy founded on the rule of law.

In contrast, emotionally mature people can accept the boundaries others establish. When they violate expectations, they can apologize promptly and gracefully, which resolves arguments and repairs relationships. Healthy relationships require awareness of one's faults;

care for one's impact on others; and an ability to handle mistakes, defeats, and criticism with equanimity.

Lack of Prosocial Emotions

An Other-blamer's inability to apologize clearly signals to others a lack of conscience and empathy. Compassion, kindness, and altruism are prosocial traits and moral behaviors that are largely innate (Martin and Clark 1982). Yet, those described as sociopaths and narcissists (American Psychiatric Association 2013) are often noted for their lack of remorse, guilt, or empathy.

Other-blamers lack these emotional traits for several reasons. Some did not experience warm interactions in early attachment relationships with caregivers. Perhaps they learned to be hurtful toward others through experiencing or witnessing abuse. Being raised in an environment of trauma increases one's reliance on the survival responses of "fight-or-flight" and decreases access to "tend-and-befriend" responses, making one less inclined to aid others or even be aware of the needs of others.

When in distress or cornered, people often lash out, especially if they have a model of relationships that may not include safety, comfort, or love. An abuser's violent rage is an extreme version of a fear-based deficit in prosocial sentiment. An abuser may say he loves his partner and claim he would never hurt her, but his emotionally reactive behaviors speak the truth: that, when dysregulated by fear and shame, he can care only about himself.

For Other-blamers, it is their emotional struggle to protect their fragile self-image from shame that makes them lack consideration. Other-blamers become overwhelmed by their own emotional pain, so they prefer offloading it onto another, even if that means harming that person or the relationship.

Even those with less-severe Other-blaming traits end up damaging relationships because they lack an ability to attend or respond to their partner's emotions with kindness and caring. The resulting lack of emotional connection is a major reason relationships fail. In couples' therapy, it is difficult to get an Other-blamer to pay attention to his effect on his partner. Even if his wife is crying, the Other-blaming husband may sit there unmoved or, worse yet, argumentative and defensive. He is so busy protecting himself from experiencing shame and blame that he has little capacity to be warmly responsive. Certainly, abusers are harming the relationship every time they react violently.

Other-blamers often have difficulty attuning to the emotional status of others because, as one Other-blamer admitted in a rare moment of self-awareness, "I care more about being right than doing the right thing for the relationship."

And this is exactly what is happening in Trump's relationship with America. He cares far more about sheltering his fragile psyche than doing what is right for the country. Trump's lack of empathy has been on display for decades, with well-documented bigotry, greed, name-calling, intimidation, and vindictiveness.

Because he is in emotional survival mode, Trump fails to notice that his ranting press conferences or bullying tweets are destabilizing. His goal is merely to lash out so he can feel better about himself in that moment. Trump has no concern that his divisive hate speech leads many to fear for their safety and liberty. He is unconcerned about the long-term effect on the country. He is too busy being right at any cost to notice that his lies and accusations are damaging his relationship with the citizens he is leading.

Trump has no apparent moral urge to care for others or serve his constituents. He may cite "America First" slogans, but he has no real understanding of the selfless giving in true patriotism. Trump got five deferments during the Vietnam War, yet he has repeatedly verbally attacked war heroes. His policies emphasize cruelty toward the less fortunate and an abdication of caring stewardship of the earth's resources.

As is the case with most Other-blamers, the country is learning quite clearly that Trump is in it only for himself. The pervasive sense that an Other-blamer does not care about you is a betrayal and leads, rightfully, to distrust and disconnection. This type of behavior violates our primal need for mutuality and trust in relationships and is why relationships with narcissists are toxic and usually end poorly.

Depersonalizing the Victim

A lack of emotional attunement and prosocial responsiveness leads to an objectification or depersonalization of others. This distancing is an adaptive mechanism that allows Other-blamers to experience less guilt when they harm their partners.

"An abusive man has to bury his compassion in a deep hole in order to escape the profound inherent aversion that human beings have to seeing others suffer. He has to adhere tightly to his excuses and rationalizations, develop a disturbing ability to insulate himself from the pain he is causing, and learn to enjoy power and control over his female partners" (Bancroft 2002).

Trump, for decades, has made demeaning comments about women's looks and has bragged on videotape about sexually assaulting women. During the campaign, he mocked a disabled reporter.

When most pundits said Trump's behavior might improve in the White House, I predicted that his behavior would get worse. His extreme depersonalization of others will worsen as his entitlement increases with the power of his position.

"Objectification is a critical reason why an abuser tends to get worse over time. As his conscience adapts to one level of cruelty—or violence—he builds to the next. By depersonalizing his partner, the abuser protects himself from the natural human emotions of guilt and empathy, so that he can sleep at night with a clear conscience. He distances himself so far from her humanity that her feelings no longer count, or simply cease to exist" (Bancroft 2002).

It is frightening to consider that we have a president who may have lost the ability to care about the human lives he is charged with protecting.

Entitlement

Other-blamers exhibit entitlement, which is closely linked to depersonalization and a lack of accountability. Trump seems to believe he is above reproach, once stating that he could shoot someone on Fifth Avenue and not lose any voters (Johnson 2016).

Most abusers try to hide socially unacceptable traits; they are often polite to others but abusive to a partner. Sadly, Trump makes no effort to mask his verbal abuse. He feels entitled to publicly shame and demean. Name-calling with comments of "loser" and "lock her up" were a staple of his campaign. He appears unrestrained by any sense of moral propriety, which indicates a very dangerous, extreme abuser who does not even attempt to plaster over his ill will with a sociopath's charm. He cannot even pretend to be good-natured, despite all his popularity, wealth, and power.

Deception

Other-blamers lie to exaggerate achievements in an attempt to seek approval, deflect blame, and avoid accountability. They become adept at outright deception, lies of omission, twisted responses, denial, and subject changing.

Lying to others is second nature to Other-blamers because they lie to themselves constantly. To routinely shift blame to others is a massive, lifelong effort at self-deception. Other-blamers lie by rationalizing, convincing themselves that their behavior is appropriate, with the goal of avoiding hearing the truth and experiencing shame.

Author Tony Schwartz has said about Trump that "Lying is second nature to him . . . More than anyone else I have ever met, Trump has the ability to convince himself that whatever he is saying at any given moment is true, or sort of true, or at least ought to be true" (Meyer 2016).

Other-blamers and abusers lie so frequently that their partners often do not know what to believe. How can a relationship of any kind withstand the betrayal of a constant barrage of deception, excuses, and denials?

Humans have a survival-oriented need for trust in relationships: "Can I really count on you when it matters? Do you have my back?" With repeated lies, interpersonal partners (and national allies) will learn that the answer is no.

This is exactly what is causing distress for many Americans since Trump's election. They sense, correctly, that he will impulsively betray us to achieve his aims, even if it is not in the best interest of the country.

Rep. Adam Schiff, a Democrat from California, noted that Trump's constant lies may lead to a loss of trust in a leader's words that may have major international implications. "When a president of the U.S. makes claims that are proved baseless, it weakens the presidency and undermines our security and standing in the world. Presidential credibility once squandered may never be fully regained. If the president may one day assert that North Korea has placed a nuclear weapon on a ballistic missile and action is necessary, it will be an enormous problem if untrue. If true, it may be an even bigger problem if the president has lost the capacity to persuade our allies of the facts, let alone the American people" (Schiff 2017).

Other characteristics of abusive Other-blamers include:

- **Placing high value on personal loyalty, surrounding themselves with "yes men."** Trump relies almost exclusively on family members as advisers, even though none has government experience.

- **Isolating their partners and often convincing their victims that others do not have their best interests at heart.** Throughout the campaign, Trump created an "us-versus-them" mentality in his followers, belittling anyone who might weaken his hold on those followers' hearts and minds.

- **Being attracted to power and tending to misuse it.** They use an authoritarian style of speaking that gets others to doubt reality. Trump boldly repeats lies so that the truth has little opportunity to flourish.

- **Promoting an image of success.** Trump's gold-plated lifestyle and obsession with crowd sizes and vote counts provide ample evidence that protecting his delicate ego takes precedence.

Driven to Distraction: Trump's Effect on Our Psychological Health

A fundamental problem with a Trump presidency is not merely that his poorly thought-out policies may harm us. It is that his character defects will normalize immoral Other-blaming behaviors and encourage their full expression among those who may have previously been held in check by expectations of socially acceptable behavior. If the recent uptick in racial violence is an indicator, Trump has given his followers a green light to act out.

Just as the trauma of witnessing domestic violence damages children, an emotionally immature president can affect the future of our nation regarding moral behavior, cultural stability, and psychological wellness.

Other-blamers can be restrained only by prompt, calm boundary setting and an enforcement of moral and social norms. Without these influences, Other-blamers grow in boldness and their presumption of power. Other-blamers will take as much ground as they can get.

We must resist, not only to contain Trump's behaviors, but also to signal to his followers that abusive behavior is not appropriate. Unfortunately, now that millions of Other-blamers have been encouraged by Trump to misbehave, it may be impossible to get that genie back in the bottle.

In therapy, it is common to see families where a narcissist or sociopath has not been held in check—sometimes multiple generations of them—and the resulting dysfunction creates ripples of psychological trauma, including insecure attachment patterns in children, addictions, estrangement, and conflict.

Because the Other-blamer refuses to compromise or engage in fair play, it becomes "every man for himself." Family members resent having to always give so the Other-blamer can take. They resent the Other-blamer lying and refusing to agree on facts. They resent always being blamed while the Other-blamer can never admit fault. Abuse victims often experience frustration because when they try to get through to the abuser, the rules of fair play do not apply.

As a country, we are attempting to apply democratic rule of law to Trump. If Trump refuses to play by the rules, and the courts and Congress do not hold him accountable, we citizens have little recourse, which will cause us to have the sense of helpless desperation of an abused spouse.

Compromise and reciprocity are key parts of politics and healthy relationships. Other-blamers are inclined to adopt an attitude of "my way or the highway," as Trump did with his ham-handed rushing through of a replacement for the Affordable Care Act without debate. If Trump has to be right and win at all costs, and if he views discussion and compromise as losing, this offers little hope for the future of the country's relationship with him.

It is common for a jealous spouse to angrily text his wife thirty times a day, call repeatedly, and argue for hours. The effort it takes to manage the abuser causes the partner to have less time and energy for parenting, career, or self-care. In narcissistic relationships, one has little left over after the arguments. Abused partners tend to overfocus on the relationship, rather than address their own self-improvement, until the relationship is ended.

In the same way, since the 2016 election, much of the world has been in a panic, overfocused on Trump and unable to deal with much else but his foibles and follies. The world is scrambling to respond to chaos, which leaves little energy to address legitimate issues. When the Japanese prime minister visited, the discussion about Trump's bizarrely aggressive handshaking style overtook talk of trade deals or North Korea. Antarctic ice shelf breaking off? Wars, refugees, the European Union in turmoil? These issues receive inadequate attention because the world is trying to make sense of the attention-seeking distraction in the White House. This is potentially tragic for those people and issues ignored as a result of the dysfunctional relationship we have with this president.

I am experiencing this personally, as I spend much more time reading news articles, organizing rallies, writing letters, and making phone calls. This is time and energy I could be spending championing worthy causes. In fact, here I am writing about Trump's mental health when, with a different person in office, I could be working to improve the mental health care system.

This narcissistic president is doing what all narcissists do: sucking the air out of the room. When in relationship with an Other-blamer, one must spend one's time and energy arguing about the arguing, rather than living peacefully and productively. Trump will continue to have a toxic effect at the individual and global level, not just through his harmful, ill-considered policy decisions, but through increased anxiety and the diversion of attention from other issues.

A true leader or a caring spouse manages his or her behaviors and emotions in a mature, temperate way. The country will have less ability to focus on solutions to complex problems until we get rid of the Other-blamer in chief we are in relationship with. The coarsening of society and the loss of civility and empathy will likely be irreparable in the near term. We can only hope that we break up with this abusive president before he breaks up the country.

Harper West (www.HarperWest.co), M.A., L.L.P., is a licensed psychotherapist in Clarkston, Michigan. She graduated from Michigan State University with a degree in journalism and worked in corporate communications, later earning a master's degree in clinical psychology from the Michigan School of Professional Psychology. Ms. West is the developer of self-acceptance psychology, which challenges the biological model of mental disorders and offers a new paradigm that reframes emotional problems as adaptive responses to fear, trauma, shame, and lack of secure attachment. Her self-help book Pack Leader Psychology *won an Independent Book Publishers Association Ben Franklin Award for Psychology.*

References

American Psychiatric Association. 2013. *Diagnostic and Statistical Manual of Mental Disorders.* 5th ed. Arlington, VA: American Psychiatric Association.

Anda, Robert F., Vincent J. Felitti, J. Douglas Bremner, John D. Walker, Charles Whitfield, Bruce D. Perry, Shanta R. Dube, and Wayne H. Giles. 2006. "The Enduring Effects of Abuse and Related Adverse Experiences in Childhood." *European Archives of Psychiatry and Clinical Neuroscience* 256: 174–86. doi: 10.1007/s00406-005-0624-4.

Bancroft, Lundy. 2002. *Why Does He Do That? Inside the Minds of Angry and Controlling Men.* New York: Berkley Books.

Caplan, P. J. 1995. *They Say You're Crazy: How the World's Most Powerful Psychiatrists Decide Who's Normal.* Boston: Da Capo Press.

Deacon, Brett, and Dean McKay. 2015. *The Behavior Therapist, Special Issue: The Biomedical Model of Psychological Problems* 38: 7.

"DSM-5: A Fatal Diagnosis?" 2013. [Editorial.] *British Medical Journal* 346, f3256.

Johnson, Jenna. 2016. "Donald Trump: They Say I Could 'Shoot Somebody' and Still Have Support." *Washington Post.* www.washingtonpost.com /news/post-politics/wp/2016/01/23/donald-trump-i-could-shoot -somebody-and-still-have-support/?utm_term=.31d27df01dc5.

Kinderman, Peter. 2014. *A Prescription for Psychiatry: Why We Need a Whole New Approach to Mental Health and Wellbeing.* London: Palgrave Macmillan.

Lenzer, Jeanne. 2017. "Do Doctors Have a 'Duty to Warn' If They Believe a Leader Is Dangerously Mentally Ill?" *The BMJ* 356 (March 9): j1087. https://doi.org/10.1136/bmj.j1087.

Martin, Grace B., and Russell D. Clark. 1982. "Distress Crying in Neonates: Species and Peer Specificity." *Developmental Psychology* 18: 3–9. doi:10.1037/0012-1649.18.1.3.

Meyer, Jane. 2016. "Donald Trump's Ghostwriter Tells All." *The New Yorker*, July 25. www.newyorker.com/magazine/2016/07/25/donald-trumps -ghostwriter-tells-all.

Millbank, Dana. 2017. "Personal Irresponsibility: A Concise History of Trump's Buck-Passing." *New York Times*, April 5. www.nytimes.com.

Miller, Gregory A. 2010. "Mistreating Psychology in the Decades of the Brain." *Perspectives on Psychological Science* 5: 716. doi: 10.1177/17456916 10388774.

Pasquali, Renato. 2006. "The Biological Balance Between Psychological Well-Being and Distress: A Clinician's Point of View." *Psychotherapy and Psychosomatics* 75 (2): 69–71.

Schiff, Adam. 2017. "Rep. Schiff Delivers Democratic Weekly Address on Need for an Independent Commission." March 25. www.youtube.com /watch?v=IsB5n_qVdvE.

West, Harper. 2016. *Self-Acceptance Psychology.* Rochester Hills, MI.: WingPath Media.

Whitaker, Robert, and Lisa Cosgrove. 2015. *Psychiatry Under the Influence: Institutional Corruption, Social Injury, and Prescriptions for Reform.* New York: Palgrave Macmillan.

BIRTHERISM AND THE DEPLOYMENT OF THE TRUMPIAN MIND-SET

LUBA KESSLER, M.D.

Donald Trump straddles the country's divide between those who cheer his ascendance to the presidency and those who are greatly disturbed by it. This intensely felt division points to the highly emotional effect he has on the nation. What is it? People have cited a variety of factors. This chapter offers a singular look at Trump's method of political insinuation through an examination of his embrace and loud propagation of the "birtherism" conspiracy. His use of it as a jumping-off platform to launch his presidential candidacy showed from the start the unmistakable signs of an unabashed bending of reality and a deployment of demagoguery to achieve his political aims.

What is birtherism? Since 2011, Donald Trump was the loudest and most persistent spokesperson for the conspiracy theory that Barack Obama was not a native U.S. citizen. In denying that Obama was a naturally born American, Trump joined the "birtherism" argument espoused by the national far-right political fringe.

It was Trump's first visible political falsehood, initiating a perversion of the political discourse that ultimately led to his election.

√ A false covenant with the public followed, spawning a multitude of other "alternative" realities.

This brings up disturbing questions. Why did this falsehood take root? And what are the ramifications of a presidency based on it? This chapter attempts to consider this question in light of recent history.

The first decade of the country's political history in the twenty-first century saw two profoundly transformative national events. America suffered the first and only foreign attack on its mainland since the War of 1812, on September 11, 2001. And in 2008, it elected a black man as its president, and reelected him for a second term in 2012. One event came from the outside; the other, from developments inside the country. Is there something about this convergence between the shock of the one and the internal ripples of the other? Let us examine.

The 9/11 terrorist attacks shook the country's sense of invincibility. Ever since then, the United States has been at war in foreign lands, in an effort to recover its sense of security and prowess. Our nation has always been proud of its sovereignty, its expansive Manifest Destiny at home and its voice of authority abroad. The adjustment of its post-9/11 self-image on the national and international stage has been painful. We entered the new millennium with a great deal of self-questioning. American millennials came face-to-face with ethnic and religious Otherness with an urgency unknown to previous generations. On the one hand, it widened their horizons, fueling greater interest in and openness to the world. Yet, on the other hand, life became more unsettled; the breakdown in the social and family sense of security made their entrance into this new world more susceptible to feelings of mistrust and fearfulness. The impulse to "circle the wagons" and turn inward encouraged suspicion of Others: xenophobia.

The election of Barack Obama as the U.S. president also represented a great shift in the nation's life and psychology, though of a different nature. Blacks have historically carried connotations of Otherness in America, by the difference of their skin color and the circumstances of their arrival on the continent, compared to the majority population, which has led to persistent racism. Certainly, the election of an African American man to the highest office in the land represented a dramatic civic achievement in the country's history. It gave cause to consider the possibility that the United States may have reached a postracial consciousness.

Yet, the production of the "birtherism" movement, in this historical context, tells a different story. How so?

The questioning of the authenticity of Barack Obama's native birth is without precedent in the history of the American presidency. No other president, all of whom were white, was ever subjected to the deep offense of such a cruel falsehood. It was as if such an arrogant affront to the dignity of the president, or any man, was permissible because he was black. With such calumny, Donald Trump signaled thinly veiled bigotry. While not expressing directly an outright racist slur, his embrace of birtherism was a "dog whistle," an unmistakable call to delegitimize a black American citizen as the Other because he aspired to the presidency of the nation.

The American public takes great pride in the fact that any of its native born could become president. It has always been the aspirational ideal of this country's self-image as a place of freedom and opportunity for all. Both Barack Obama, an African American professor of constitutional law with a record of community service and the audacity of hope, and Donald Trump, a brash real estate developer with no political experience, could succeed in the quest for the highest office in the land on the strength of their appeal to the citizenry.

The bigotry of birtherism set a limit on this national aspiration. It signaled that a black person could not be truly American. Just as the election of Barack Obama thrilled the nation, imbuing us with civic pride in the seeming achievement of a postracial society, birtherism signaled that it was permissible for America, deep in its soul, to continue harboring and nursing the historic racial prejudice. It said that a black president could not be legitimate, and so the factual reality of his very birth on American soil had to be denied. In this willful distortion of fact, Donald Trump showed the essential quality of his personality: the perversion of his relationship to truth. It showed that he could and would distort and deform the truth in his quest to secure any deal he was after. Truth and reality were commodities just like any other—a matter for a transactional sale of a desired acquisition. This appears to be the hallmark of the Trumpian mind-set. Birtherism was its opening political bid.

We are living in a time of great demographic, economic, social, and political transformation at home and abroad. What it means is that the pressures from outside the national realm resonate with those within it. America's unrivaled democratic diversity, as seen in its immigrant descendants continues to evolve, just as its standing in the global transformation is adjusting anew to evolving realities, global terrorism among them. This stretches the psychological resources of the nation, and its resilience. The American citizenry meets its moment of truth under conditions of shaken security and changing identity. It becomes a matter of paramount importance to the well-being of the country, therefore, that it withstand and manage these pressures with a calm resolve based on a moral sense of decency and reason.

At such times, the nation looks to its leader to uphold its vital interests and values. It is for this reason that we celebrate those presidents who showed the capacity to meet the challenging realities of their moment in history with dignity, and appeal to what Abraham Lincoln called the "better angels of our nature." This is the reason that Lincoln stands in the American presidential pantheon with George Washington and Franklin Delano Roosevelt. Each of these men lifted the nation not with partisan transaction but with vision and moral purpose.

Donald Trump's appeal has just the opposite effect. It debases civic discourse and corrodes national unity.

Birtherism shows the essential characteristics of Donald Trump's mind-set: A self-professed ultimate dealmaker first and foremost, he pursued the presidency in an entirely transactional manner. He did not hesitate to make up falsehoods or wink at bigotry to win. In a manner similar to exploiting every available tax loophole; every feasible advantage over his debtors, contractors, and workers; every opportunity to have "special" relationships advance his deal-making aims, he made an unerring political calculation to seize the transitional moment of national insecurity. His business acumen worked brilliantly, against all odds. But his transactional win represents a profound danger to the nation because it sells out the most essential qualities of democratic values, of moral integrity, and of true inventiveness. What binds us together is the shared reality of our country's history and its present: *E pluribus unum.* "Out of many, one." The country's cherished motto cannot hold when truth is open to transactional competition from "alternative facts."

We are left with the question about what made the American public receptive to Donald Trump's promissory bid despite his falsehoods. Yes, our country is ever open to enterprising inventiveness and grand boldness. But it is not naïve. There has been too much toil, hardship, and strong civic pride in building this nation for its citizenry to surrender the habits of common sense and clearheaded pragmatism. However, this does not make America immune to the lingering effects of its own historical legacy of slavery and racism. Without a full reconciliation between that legacy and the nation's founding ideals, the significant fault line between the two will open up in times of increased strain. The startling fabrication of the birtherism movement offers a window into just such a fault line.

It does not require particular professional schooling to recognize that birtherism was a telltale sign of a preoccupation with Otherness. It is easy to grasp the sense of threat from the foreign Other in the age of terrorism and massive global migration. It is more difficult to acknowledge the persistent fear and lingering mistrust of the black Other at home in America.

We want to believe in our postracial integration and equality. We are proud of the progress we have made. The election of Barack Obama is its rightful proof. It is a lot more difficult to recognize the prejudices of an inborn and ingrown kind of stereotyping. The fact that Donald Trump could successfully use the myth of birtherism as an under-the-radar deployment of bigotry attests to its subterranean persistence.

This is not an indictment of American society. It is a call for recognition of America's historical conditions. We associate the settling of the country with white colonists. We grow up with those lessons of our history and culture. Although the labor of the Blacks was indispensable to the fledgling American economy, slavery denied them the recognition and rights of equal participation. The result was persistent discrimination, which further disenfranchised them from full civic participation, with each perpetuating the other. White and black cultural traditions came to develop their own idioms, furthering the racial divide.

It is beyond the scope of this chapter to consider the myriad ways in which racism continues to plague our national realities. It remains our challenge to right the political, civic, and interpersonal relations needed for the mutual benefit of the present and future American generations: white, black, and any Other. In order to rise to the challenge, we need the courage of truth and awareness. We need to question rationalized public policies that maintain segregation and inequality, be it at the voting booth or in judicial or police protection. We need to tune into and question habits of prejudice and bigotry. We need to probe better the stereotypes of our culture and of ourselves. Such an examination will inoculate our civic consciousness against the lies masquerading as truth. We will choose worthy leaders aware of their responsibility to represent the integrity of the nation's essential values. Birtherism shows Donald Trump not only as unworthy but as dangerous to the nation's central tenet: *E pluribus unum*. It is not negotiable.

> *Luba Kessler, M.D., is a psychiatrist and psychoanalyst in private practice. Born in the post-Holocaust displacement in the Ural Mountains, she has lived and received her education in the Soviet Union, Poland, Italy, and the United States. That journey included essential lessons in history, geography, culture, art, and politics. Postgraduate training and faculty appointments followed, in psychiatry at Hillside Hospital on Long Island, and in psychoanalysis at NYU Psychoanalytic Institute (now the Institute for Psychoanalytic Education, affiliated with NYU Medical School). She is editor of* Issues in Education *for* The American Psychoanalyst *of the American Psychoanalytic Association.*

TRUMP'S DADDY ISSUES:

A Toxic Mix for America

STEVE WRUBLE, M.D.

As a psychiatrist, I am interested in why people are the way they are. Ultimately, the more I understand others, and my relationship to them, the better I understand myself. I am intrigued by the factors that have guided Donald Trump into the Oval Office and into the hearts, minds, and clenched fists of so many Americans. I'm especially frustrated by his having captured the attention and respect of the man I have always craved a closer relationship with—my father.

Fathers and sons have a storied history of playing off each other as they grapple with their evolving separate and shared identities. We tumble through time doing our best to make sense of all that we witness and experience. I, like Donald Trump, grew up watching and interacting with a strong, proud, and successful father. We both looked up to our fathers for guidance, but at the same time we also felt a certain competitiveness with them as we fought for our innate need for separation and individuation. The spectrum of how sons interact with their fathers is vast. The early beliefs that each has about himself will determine the path chosen to act out their drama. As much as I am disturbed by Trump's behavior, I can't help but wonder what of him is in me and vice versa. Who is this man who has captivated so much of the American electorate, and for that matter, the whole world? As a son locked into a drama with a father, can I shed light on that question?

Politically, many people in America are single-issue voters. Whether it be abortion, the economy, or foreign policy, it's that one main issue that holds sway over their vote. In my family's case, that one issue is Israel. I come from a family of Modern Orthodox Jews, and Orthodox Jewry as a group has thrown its support behind President Trump because it feels Israel will be safer under his watch. Of course, other issues are also important to Orthodox Jews, but these are usually overshadowed by concern for Israel.

About ten years ago, I made the difficult decision to let my family know that I had stopped following the many dictates that an Orthodox Jew is expected to follow. This new choice was quite freeing for me, since I had already been living this way secretly for a few years. At the same time, it was upsetting to my parents and especially my father, because Judaism is a major part of his identity. He said he was worried that this would create chaos in our family and wished, for my children's sake, that I would keep my secret to myself. On a deeper level, it felt as if he perceived it as a threat to his leadership in the family.

My decision to leave Orthodox Judaism feels connected to the evolution of my political views toward a more liberal agenda. This, at first, was uncomfortable because it was frowned upon in my community to question anything that supported the State of Israel. Donald Trump's behavior was clear and disturbing to me and overshadowed his support for Israel. However, my misgivings were not echoed in my community. My attempts to be understood by family and friends were surprisingly difficult.

Many Republicans seem to be locked in a dysfunctional relationship with Trump as a strong father figure who appears to have far less to offer than they're pining for. Yet, like myself, they are looking to their "father" in the hope that he will deliver them from what feels broken within them and the lives they are leading.

Before addressing the difficulties in my family around what it's like to see the political world so differently and yet to continue to share family events and happy occasions, I'd like to take a short drive through Donald Trump's life to show you some things that help make sense of what we're all witnessing.

There are several details that seem to shine a light on how Trump's relationship with his father, Fred Trump, may have impacted his development. Donald is the fourth of five children. His oldest sister is a circuit court judge and his oldest brother, Freddie Jr., died at the age of forty-three from complications due to alcoholism. According to a *New York Times* article (Horowitz 2016), it was apparent to those who watched Fred Trump with his children that his intensity was too much for Freddie Jr. to tolerate. As Donald watched the tragedy unfold, he stepped up and became his father's protégé in his building empire. I can only imagine that following a brother who drank himself to death didn't leave Donald much room to do anything but try and fill the void where his older brother had failed. Obviously, he was successful at this endeavor in his father's world of real estate, and the two spent many years working together until Donald moved on to captain his own company. Fred Trump could never understand why Donald wanted to take the financial risk of building in Manhattan. The elder Trump felt that the ease they enjoyed being successful in Brooklyn and Queens should have been intoxicating enough for his son. However, Donald appeared to be attracted to the bright lights of the big city and the challenge of being more successful than his father.

From the same *New York Times* article, "Trump's childhood friends have said they see in him his father's intensity, but also a constant and often palpable need to please and impress the patriarch who ruled his family with a firm hand. Even today, Donald Trump seems to bathe in his father's approval. A framed photo of Fred Trump faces him on his cluttered desk." Donald said he learned his father's values, and his killer sense of competition, by following him to building sites and watching him squeeze the most out of every dollar. In a speech to the National Association of Home Builders, Trump said, "My father would go and pick up the extra nails and scraps, and he'd use whatever he could and recycle it in some form or sell it."

According to an article in *The Guardian* (Dean 2016), when Fred Trump died in 1999, Donald Trump gave a cheerful quote for his father's *New York Times* obituary, focusing on the way his dad had never wanted to expand into Manhattan. "It was good for me," he said. "You know, being the son of somebody, it could have been competition to me. This way, I got Manhattan all to myself!" At his father's wake, Donald stepped forward to address family, friends, and the society power brokers in the crowd. One attendee recalled Mr. Trump's unorthodox eulogy to his father, "My father taught me everything I know. And he would understand what I'm about to say," Mr. Trump announced to the room. "I'm developing a great building on Riverside Boulevard called Trump Place. It's a wonderful project." Not the warmest send-off, but it highlighted the language and sentiment that the two men shared. It was the point of their connection. When Donald's father, Fred Trump, was fifteen, he started in the building business alongside his mother due to the fact that his father died just three years earlier. At the age of fifty-three, Donald, with the death of *his* own father, was wasting no time on tears; he was moving forward in the familial quest for financial success.

Donald witnessed his father's tough negotiating style, even at home. One time, some of Donald's friends were confused as to why his wealthy father would not buy him a new baseball glove. Trump said it was because his father suspected him, correctly, of playing dumb about the high price of the glove he wanted, and of trying to get the salesman to go along with this ruse. It appears Donald learned early on that his father's frugality would leave him wanting. It also may have taught him that he needed to be sneaky at times to get what he desired.

When I was about the same age, I remember my father telling me how surprised and impressed he was that I was able to convince a salesman to refund our money and take back an expensive board game that we had already opened but didn't like. I could see in my father's face that he was enamored of my moxie. The power of a father's attention to our behavior forms a strong lock and key for that behavior to become something we depend upon in order hopefully to receive that same coveted attention again and again. Of course, I've learned the hard way that behaviors I picked up from pleasing my father don't always translate to the healthiest way to relate to others. Those habits take time and experience to break.

Fred Trump's housing projects made him wealthy and powerful. Some tenants appreciated him for his solid, well-priced apartments; others loathed him for his suspected exclusion of blacks from his properties. The famous folk singer Woody Guthrie, who wrote "This Land Is Your Land," was a tenant of Mr. Trump's Beach Haven apartments for two years. In the early 1950s, he composed two songs that address his disgust with the racist practices of Fred Trump that he witnessed. Here are some of his lyrics from the songs he wrote: "I suppose Old Man Trump knows just how much Racial Hate he stirred up in the blood-pot of human hearts when he drawed that color line here at his Eighteen hundred family project. . . . Beach Haven looks like heaven where no black ones come to roam! No, no, no! Old Man Trump! Old Beach Haven ain't my home!"

Unlike Trump, I was fortunate to watch my father come home daily from saving lives as a physician. I can only imagine how ashamed I would have felt if my father had been accused of being racist by anyone, much less a famous composer. That being said, Donald may not have given it a second thought.

The human brain can protect us from seeing and feeling what it believes may be too uncomfortable for us to tolerate. It can lead us to deny, defend, minimize, or rationalize away something that doesn't fit our worldview. Actually, as I observe President Trump's behavior, I imagine that there is a good chance he identifies with his father's aggressive business style and parenting, and is now employing that orientation to his role as president. In psychology, this is called *identification with the aggressor*. At first, it may appear counter-intuitive to identify with an aggressor who has abused his position of power to take advantage. However, our brains often use this early relationship as a template to shape our future behavior. We are attracted to the power we witness from our powerless position. We can be hungry for the same power that we originally resented or even fought against. Taking all this into consideration, President Trump's aggressive behavior seems to illuminate the part of his father that still lives on within him.

Individuals with such a history often exhibit insecurities that can lead to all kinds of compensatory behaviors. However, no matter how successful a person is at alleviating the associated anxiety, fear usually still exists unconsciously and can be uncovered at times of stress. Trump's sensitivity to being seen as weak or vulnerable along with his need to exaggerate and distort the truth are signs of his deep-seated insecurity. His confabulation protects his fragile ego. Meanwhile, his blustering becomes fodder for comedians and the media. Watching reporters try to address the "alternative facts" and Trump's impulsive tweets with his press secretary staff is comically surreal.

In simplified fashion, in order for Trump to avoid feeling the effects of his insecurities, and to feed his narcissistic needs, he appears to compensate by trying to be seen as powerful and special with the hope that he will indeed *feel* powerful and special. Only he knows the truth about how successful he is at this. The human brain has a unique ability to work in the background, using past beliefs as if we were living in the times when those beliefs are birthed. From a survivalist standpoint, our brains work off the assumption that we are safer to believe that situations will most likely repeat themselves. We don't challenge those beliefs unless something drastic occurs that overwhelms our defenses. We have learned through research on trauma survivors that early events that stimulate our fight-or-flight response have long-lasting effects. It usually directs us to create a negative belief about ourselves, which in turn leads to the counterbalancing behaviors that try to minimize the deleterious effects of those negative beliefs. Therefore, President Trump will most likely change his way of being only if reality throws him a large enough curveball to which he is unable to respond using the signature defensive measures he has grown accustomed to.

The beliefs and compensatory mechanisms that young Donald created to help steward him through the turbulent waters of his childhood are probably still in effect today. They were reinforced during his years working with his father, and later as a successful businessman. As the owner of his own company, he was able to exact control and demand loyalty in ways that he cannot as president. Transferring his strategies and expectations to the culture of government has been frustrating for him, and his responses to that frustration have been eye-opening. He doesn't appear to have the flexibility to switch gears in order to deal with the function of his job as president. His handling of FBI director James Comey is a good example. Conversations about loyalty appear to have contributed to his firing. Trump's befuddlement regarding all the fireworks that ensued makes it appear that he is either limited in understanding the impact of his behavior or insensitive to it. Either way, his leadership leaves a large segment of the population feeling insecure and fearful about what to expect next.

Fred Trump's competitiveness was quite apparent near the end of his life, when he was quoted as saying that his thrice-divorced son would never beat him in the "marital department," since he had been married to the same woman for sixty years. In addition, when Donald Trump was asked in 2016 while he was running for office what his father would have said about him running for president, he said, "He would have absolutely allowed me to have done it." Allowed?? Despite being seventy years old, Trump answered as if he were an adolescent in an oedipal battle with his father who had died seventeen years earlier.

In August of 2016, I was speaking with my father on the phone about the presidential election, and he was addressing his confusion as to why Trump was acting so erratically. This was at a time when there were several articles being written out about how Trump's advisers were having difficulty getting him to stop tweeting his aggressive thoughts and feelings. I was surprised when my father asked me what my understanding as a psychiatrist was regarding Trump's behavior. Usually, my father has his own ideas about why things are the way they are and enjoys teaching me what he feels the truth is. Although I had strong feelings and ideas about why Trump was acting the way he was, my father's inquiry felt like an easy path to receiving some of the attention and respect that I continue to look for. It felt powerful and invigorating to be asked by my father what my thoughts were.

As I proceeded to describe my hypothesis of what was happening with Trump, I confidently and proudly told my father that I believed that Trump was unconsciously sabotaging his chances of winning the election because a part of him probably recognized he wasn't worthy and/or capable of being successful in that position. I went on to say that Trump appeared to be more comfortable complaining about, and fighting against, the system that he believed was conspiring against his bid to be elected. In response, my father said, "Well, whatever's going on, I wish he would just shut up because if Hillary wins, it'll be horrible for Israel." Despite giving my father what I felt was my intellectual gold, he only commented on what was important to him.

Since Trump has taken office, I have tried to engage my father, and others within my family and in the Orthodox Jewish community, about my concerns with Trump's exaggerations and lying, along with his xenophobia, all of which appear to be playing on the fears and insecurities of his support base. Almost invariably I hear, "Yeah, he's a little crazy, but he'll be better than Obama ever was," or something like, "Don't be such a bad sport. You guys lost; deal with it!" And when people were protesting peacefully around the country, I would hear, "When Obama won, we never acted this way." When I explained that it's a wonderful thing that we live in a place where we have the right to protest, my words usually fell on deaf ears. I couldn't believe that Trump's behavior was being down-played. By questioning it, I was automatically labeled by some as having drunk the liberal Kool-Aid. Some inferred that I must be-lieve that Israel wasn't without sin in its fight to live in peace with the Palestinians. Others accused me of wanting a socialist state. It became clear that, in parts of my family and within the wider com-munity of Orthodox Jews, there was an "us-versus-them" mentality. It's frustrating to be told that my thoughts and clinical ideas about unfolding events are really just politically motivated.

It is especially difficult for me to be thrown into a category where family and friends wrongly assume that I must not care about Israel enough, or that I am more sympathetic to the plight of Syrian refugees than to the safety of Israelis and Americans. I try to explain that my love for Israel is separate from my feelings for anybody who is being trampled on by Trump's process. No lives should be dis-missed as unimportant. All this feels surreal as I try to emphasize that any end, even Israel's security, that follows an inappropriate pro-cess is dangerously fragile and not worth depending on.

The online environment of Facebook has taken center stage as the arena of choice for many Jews to fight about politics in general and about Trump specifically. I had a "friend" on Facebook say that in continuing to attack Trump's behavior, I was forgetting the Holocaust. I was told that Trump's policies were protecting Americans by keeping "dangerous" people outside our borders. The fact that innocent people were being harmed, they said, was an unfortunate but necessary side effect. Conversely, a few Jewish patients I treat who are children of Holocaust survivors fear that another Holocaust is more likely because of Trump's policies and his association with the likes of Steve Bannon. They are afraid that those in bed with white nationalists send a message to anti-Semitic people that it is safe to act out their racist and prejudiced agendas.

I recently spent the Jewish holiday of Passover with my family at a resort where a conservative political writer had been hired to speak. My family and I attended the talk, which I assumed would be pro-Trump. I sat with my father while the speaker made clear that he was not happy with Trump and, furthermore, he felt that Trump's leadership style was dangerous. I almost laughed out loud as I watched my father's mouth drop open. During the question-and-answer session, I asked about the impact on Orthodox Jews voting for a man who has such a flawed process of leading, yet who strongly supports the State of Israel. The speaker validated my concerns by responding that the ends do not justify the means, stating emphatically, "President Trump needs to shut up and just let those he has selected for his Cabinet do their jobs and push their conservative agenda forward." Afterward, my father minimized what he had heard as if acknowledging the speaker's full message would leave him too vulnerable. In the end, I felt as if I had won a battle. Perhaps, more importantly, this situation illustrates the dance my father and I often fall into when we unknowingly work out where we stand in relationship to each other.

My father and I, like Donald and his father, are men with unique flavors of insecurity. Unwittingly, we use each other to make a case for the verdict we already believe about ourselves. Donald and I are expert at putting our fathers on pedestals while at the same time trying to knock them off in order to make room for us to have our time being seen as special. A part of us believes this will lead to feeling special, but it's fleeting. It only lasts long enough to make us keep wishing for it again and again. Unfortunately, since it's a cover for our true negative beliefs about ourselves, we often sabotage and cut short our stay on this shaky pedestal. It's a precarious perch for us. A lonely view from a place we actually don't feel we fully deserve.

On the night that Donald Trump won the election, he couldn't be found for a number of hours for comment on his momentous victory. In Leslie Stahl's *60 Minutes* interview aired three days later, he was asked where he had been during those hours. He soberly responded, "I realized this is a whole different life for me." It was as if the president-elect had never imagined actually winning. He seemed stunned that he had knocked out his formidable opponent and now would be expected to put his angry fighter persona on the shelf and go to work as the next president. Is that what he really wanted? One wonders if he even had a victory speech prepared at all.

As with all adults, Donald Trump's early development created who we are witnessing. Children need to receive love and attention in order to feel secure, but they receive only the love and attention that their parents are capable of providing. Indeed, his father's intensity left its mark on the entire family. Donald's oldest brother essentially killed himself under his father's rule. This tragedy must have played a prominent role in the formation of Donald's identity and left minimal room to rebel against his father's authority, except through competition in the realm of business success. Despite their appreciation for each other, the tension between father and son caused Donald psychological wounds that still fester. To compensate, Donald Trump puffs himself up to project a macho image that appeals to many of his followers. But it's empty, a defense against his fear of seeming weak and ineffectual like his brother. Before being elected, Trump could treat people as he wished, using his wealth and status as a means to achieve his goals. As the president of the United

States, he is expected to handle issues more delicately and follow the checks and balances that make up our democratic society. Unfortunately for him and possibly the nation, his strengths that got him elected president don't ensure success in that position.

Trump's base of support saw in him the strength to be powerful in ways they didn't see in themselves and/or in past leadership. What they may not be aware of is that President Trump appears to question his own ability to deliver what they are seeking. Evidence of this can be seen in his use of lying, distortion, marginalization, and the firing of those he fears are disloyal. Our fathers did the best they could with the resources they had, and our unique connection with them helps fill the gaps where we feel deficient. Despite the moments of contention, and maybe even because of them, I feel fortunate to have a relationship with a father who continues to do his part to help our relationship become closer. I'm also grateful for the insight I've received through psychotherapy to address those parts of myself that are either stuck or confused by my past. It's unfortunate that our president has not figured out how to heal himself or at least learn how to do his job without being defensive and aggressive with those that disagree with him. I feel for the young parts of the president that are trying desperately to help him swim through rough waters despite fear of drowning. What most concerns me is whether we Americans can tread water long enough to come together and avoid being pulled under.

Steve Wruble, M.D., is an accomplished singer-songwriter and storyteller. He has won the Moth StorySLAM, for which he uses a pseudonym in SLAM competitions. Dr. Wruble is also a board-certified child and adult psychiatrist in private practice in Manhattan and Ridgewood, New Jersey, at the Venn Center. He specializes in anxiety disorders, trauma, and attention-deficit hyperactivity disorders. He attended medical school in his hometown of Memphis,

Tennessee, and did his general psychiatry residency at North-western University. He did his child psychiatry fellowship at the Institute for Juvenile Research at the University of Illinois at Chicago, where he was chief fellow.

References

Dean, Michelle. 2016. "Making the Man: To Understand Trump, Look at His Relationship with his Dad." *The Guardian,* March 26. www.theguardian.com/us-news/2016/mar/26/donald-trump-fred-trump-father-relationship-business-real-estate-art-of-deal.

Horowitz, Jason. 2016. "Fred Trump Taught His Son the Essentials of Show-Boating Self-Promotion." *New York Times,* August 12. www.nytimes.com/2016/08/13/us/politics/fred-donald-trump-father.html?_r=0.

TRUMP AND THE AMERICAN COLLECTIVE PSYCHE*

THOMAS SINGER, M.D.

While I join those who believe that we need to question Donald Trump's psychological fitness to be president, my focus is less on individual psychopathology than on the interface between Trump and the American collective psyche. There are ways in which Trump mirrors, even amplifies, our collective attention deficit disorder, our sociopathy, and our narcissism. Therefore, this is less about diagnosing a public figure than about recognizing our own pathology.

Trump has mesmerized our national psyche like no other public figure in recent memory. There is no doubt that his appeal (his wealth, power, celebrity status, and his brash willingness to shoot from the hip) resonates powerfully with the collective psyche of many Americans, while these same qualities are repulsive to many others. The more vulgar, bullying, impulsive, and self-congratulatory

---

* This chapter has been adapted from an earlier essay, "Trump and the American Selfie," in *A Clear and Present Danger: Narcissism in the Era of Donald Trump*, coedited by Steven Buser and Leonard Cruz, and from the article, "If Donald Trump Had a Selfie Stick, We'd All Be in the Picture" (billmoyers.com /story/donald-trump-selfie-americas-worst-side/).

Trump's behavior and rhetoric, the more some people worship him, while others fervently denounce him as a grave danger to our republic. To probe the profound collective disturbance that Trump activates and symbolizes, I draw on my experience as a psychiatrist and Jungian psychoanalyst.

A Psychological Theory About Trump's Appeal: A Marriage of the Shadow, Archetypal Defenses, and the Self at the Group Level of the Psyche to Form a Cultural Complex

You don't need to be a psychologist or psychiatrist to see that Donald Trump has a problem of narcissism. Ted Cruz announced on May 3, 2016, the day of the Indiana Republican presidential primary, that Trump was "a pathological liar, utterly amoral, a narcissist at a level I don't think this country's ever seen and a serial philanderer" (Wright, Kopan, and Winchester 2016). In a series of papers and books written over the past decade, I have developed a working model of the theory of cultural complexes that may be useful for understanding Trumpism. I will be talking about the psyche of the *group*—what lives inside each of us as individual carriers of the group psyche and what lives between us in our shared group psyche. The group psyche engages with themes and conflicts that are not the same as our more personal psychological struggles.

I hypothesize a direct link between Trump's personal narcissism and the collective psyche of those American citizens who embrace his perception of America and who feel that he understands and speaks to them. This is not a political analysis. It is a psychological analysis of what we can think of as the *group psyche*, which contributes enormously to and fuels political processes. This analysis is based on the notion that there are certain psychological energies, even structures, at the level of the cultural or group psyche that are activated at times of heightened threats to the core identity of the group—what we might think of as the group Self. Three of these most important energies/structures are (1) the shadow, (2) archetypal defenses of the group Self, and (3) the group Self itself. These energies/structures take shape around social, political, economic, geographic, and religious themes that are alive in specific contexts and with particular contents. This same type of analysis may currently apply in the Brexit crisis in Great Britain, or in the Palestinian-Israeli conflict, with very different contexts and contents in which various groups can be seen as protecting their threatened or wounded Self from being further injured by pursuing a defensive, aggressive attack against imagined or real, dangerous enemies.

What is it about Trump that acts as an irresistible magnet with ferocious attraction or repulsion? Is Trump the end product of our culture of narcissism? Is he what we get and deserve because he epitomizes the god or gods we currently worship in our mindless, consumerist, hyperindulged cult of continuous stimulation and entertainment? Here is how Christopher Hedges states it in *Empire of Illusion: The End of Literacy and the Triumph of Spectacle*:

> An image-based culture communicates through narratives, pictures, and pseudo-drama. Scandalous affairs, hurricanes, untimely deaths, train wrecks—these events play well on computer screens and television. International diplomacy, labor union negotiations, and convoluted bailout packages do not yield exciting personal narratives or stimulating images . . . Reality is complicated. Reality is boring. We are incapable or unwilling to handle its confusion . . . We become trapped in the linguistic prison of incessant repetition. We are fed words and phrases like *war on terror* or *pro-life* or *change*, and within these narrow parameters, all complex thought, ambiguity, and self-criticism vanish. (Hedges 2009)

In addition to our collective inability to sort out illusion from reality, our culture gets further hopelessly entangled with our cult of celebrity. Hedges does not spare us the dire consequences of our intoxication with celebrity, which both fuels the split between illusion and reality while simultaneously filling the gap between the two.

> Celebrity culture plunges us into a moral void. No one has any worth beyond his or her appearance, usefulness, or ability to *succeed*. The highest achievements in a celebrity culture are wealth, sexual conquest, and fame. It does not matter how these are obtained . . . We have a right, in the cult of the self, to get whatever we desire. We can do anything, even belittle and destroy those around us, including our friends, to make money, to be happy, and to become famous. Once fame and wealth are archived, they become their own justification, their own morality. (Hedges 2009)

It seems clear that Trump's narcissism and his attacks on political correctness dovetail with deep needs in a significant portion of the American population to enhance their dwindling sense of place in America and of America's place in the world. Trump's narcissism can be seen as a perfect compensatory mirror for the narcissistic needs and injuries of those who support him—or, stated another way, there is a good "fit."

With this general formulation in mind, I analyze how Trump's presidency speaks to three highly intertwined parts of the American group psyche: (1) a woundedness at the core of the American group Self; (2) the defenses mobilized in the groups that feel wounded, who wish to protect against further injury to the shared group Self; and (3) the promise or hope of a cure for the wound.

1. A Wound to the American Group Self

There is a wound at the core of the American group Self/spirit that is deeply felt by many, especially by those who have not participated in our nation's prosperity and by others who are relatively well off but are keenly aware that our system of government and our way of life are threatened at the core of our collective being. Here is a working definition of the group Self or spirit that I put forth in an earlier paper:

> The *group spirit* is the ineffable core beliefs or sense of identity that binds people together . . . that [is] known to its members through a sense of belonging, shared essential beliefs, core historical experiences of loss and revelation, deepest yearnings and ideals . . . One can begin to circle around the nature of a group's spirit by asking questions such as:
>
> What is most sacred to the group?
>
> What binds the group's members together?
>
> (Singer 2006b)

Many in our country, on the left, right, and in the center, feel that this stage in our history is less secure than earlier stages. This nervousness about our essential well-being is deeply felt by the progressive left, by the conservative right, and by all those who feel alienated and angered by the current leaders of all branches of government, whom they see as destroying the country, whether the archenemy be Donald Trump of the Republicans or Hillary Clinton of the Democrats. On the right, the threat of terrorism (Muslims), immigrants (Mexicans), the global economy (China and international trade agreements), or progressives are seen as leading us to the brink. On the left, the threats to a sense of well-being and security in our national group Self come as the result of the growing disparity in the distribution of wealth and income; the mistreatment of vulnerable minorities of different races, colors, ethnicities, sexual identities, or genders; our power relationships to other countries around the world; and of course the maltreatment of the environment.

I postulate that these threats are amplified on all sides by an even deeper, less conscious threat that I call *extinction anxiety*. Extinction anxiety exists both in the personal and group psyche and is based on the fear of the loss of supremacy by white Americans of the United States, the loss of America's place in the world as we have known it, and ultimately the destruction of the environment and the world itself. One might think of extinction anxiety as the cultural psyche's equivalent of *death anxiety* in the individual. For instance, climate change deniers on the right may be seen as denying the very real possibility of the planet's destruction as a way of defending themselves against the fear of extinction. Aligning himself with this attitude, Trump offers to dispel *extinction anxiety* by denying it is real and appointing a well-known climate change denier as head of the EPA. Denial, whether at the individual or group level, is the most primitive defense the mind employs to protect itself from psychic pain.

Here is how Joseph Epstein (2016) has described the injury to the group Self/spirit of those attracted to Trump:

> Something deeper, I believe, is rumbling behind the astounding support for Mr. Trump, a man who, apart from his large but less than pure business success, appears otherwise entirely without qualification for the presidency. I had a hint of what might be behind the support for him a few weeks ago when, on one of the major network news shows, I watched a reporter ask a woman at a Trump rally why she was supporting him. A thoroughly respectable-seeming middle-class woman, she replied without hesitation: *"I want my country back"* . . .
>
> I don't believe that this woman is a racist, or that she yearns for immigrants, gays and other minorities to be suppressed, or even that she truly expects to turn back the clock on social change in the U.S. What she wants is precisely

what she says: her country back . . . [S]he couldn't any longer bear to watch the United States on the descent, hostage
to progressivist ideas that bring neither contentment nor
satisfaction but instead foster a state of perpetual protest
and agitation, anger and tumult. So great is the frustration
of Americans who do not believe in these progressivist
ideas, who see them as ultimately tearing the country apart,
that they are ready to turn, in their near hopelessness, to a
man of Donald Trump's patently low quality. (Epstein 2016)

obvious

The Self or group spirit of America is built on more than three
hundred years of progress, success, achievement, resourcefulness,
and ingenuity, accompanied by almost endless opportunity and
good fortune. We love and believe in our heroic potential; our freedom and independence; our worship of height and speed, youth,
newness, technology; our optimism and eternal innocence. We have
enjoyed the profound resilience of the American spirit, which has
shown itself repeatedly through very difficult historical trials, including our Civil War, World War I, the Great Depression, World
War II, the Vietnam War, the 9/11 attacks, the Iraq War, the financial
collapse in 2008, and other major crises, including the one we may
be in now. As a country, we have been blessed in our capacity to
transcend loss, failure, and the threat of defeat in the face of crisis
time and again, and this has contributed to a positive vision of ourselves that has been fundamentally solid at the core for a long time.
Of course, that Self-image is subject to inflation, arrogance, and a
morphing into *hubris*, in which we believe in our own exceptional-
ism and are blind to our causing grave injury to peoples at home and
abroad. It is quite possible that Trump's personal inflation, arrogance,
and hubris represent a compensatory antidote in our group psyche
that is beginning to suffer severe self-doubt about our ability to navigate a highly uncertain future—the nostalgic longing of which is
perfectly articulated in the phrase "I want my country back."

2. Archetypal Defenses of the Group Self

A significant number of people in our society feel cut off from what they believe to be their inherited, natural birthright as American citizens. Although they would not use this language, they are suffering a wound and threat at the level of the group Self, even as they are also suffering individually. We can think of this as a narcissistic injury at the group level. I suggest that Trump has somehow intuited that injury and is playing to it, both as a self-proclaimed carrier of the group renewal and as a defender against those who would do further harm to it—be they terrorists, immigrants, Washington political insiders, the established Republican Party, Barack Obama, Hillary Clinton, James Comey, or anyone else who gets in Trump's way.

Trump's Embrace of the Shadow of Political Correctness

Trump's particular political genius in the 2016 presidential election cycle was to launch his campaign with an attack on political correctness. With incredible manipulative skill, Trump's call to arms, "Get 'em outta here!" made its first appearance at his rallies, when he urged the faithful in his crowds to get rid of protesters. "Get 'em outta here!" also seems to be his pledge to rid the country of Mexicans, Muslims, and other groups that are being portrayed as dangerous threats to the American Way of Life.

Trump's strategy has been shrewd. He sensed that *political correctness* could be the trigger word and target for unleashing potent levels of shadow energies that have been accumulating in the cultural unconscious of the group psyche. He rode a huge wave of pent-up resentment, racism, and hatred long enough to crush all opponents and become the president of the United States. The notion of a trigger word activating a complex goes back to Jung's early word-association tests, in which certain words detonated powerful emotions contained within personal complexes—such as the mother or father complex. Skillful politicians can trigger cultural or group complexes by a collective word association process that then takes on a life of its own.

Trump is at his best when he is at his most awful: his willingness to be politically incorrect became a sign, to many, of his "truth-telling." Amid a most dangerous battle between the "alternative facts" of the alt-right and "fake news" came an outpouring of the paranoia and hostility embedded in the cultural complex of those who loathe "the deep state." Collective emotion is the only truth that matters. A group caught up in a cultural complex has highly selective memory—if any historical memory at all—and chooses only those historical and contemporary *facts* that validate their preexisting opinion. Evidence of this is that no matter what Trump does or how many lies he tells, his base remains steadfast in its support of him, as the polls tell us.

This kind of shadow energy is available for exploitation if a group that previously saw itself as having a solid place in American society (such as white middle-class Americans in the Rust Belt or coal miners in West Virginia) finds itself marginalized and drifting downward, both socially and economically. How easy it is for such a group to see recent immigrants to this country as stealing the American dream from them.

Here is how George Orwell, in *1984*, imagined the exploitation of those most subject to intoxication with an authoritarian leader like Trump:

> In a way, the world-view of the Party imposed itself most successfully on people incapable of understanding it. They could be made to accept the most flagrant violations of reality, because they never fully grasped the enormity of what was demanded of them . . . They simply swallowed everything.

Donald Trump uncovered a huge sinkhole of dark, raw emotions in the national psyche for all of us to see. Rage, hatred, envy, and fear surfaced in a forgotten, despairing, growing white underclass who had little reason to believe that the future would hold the promise of a brighter, life-affirming purpose. Trump tapped into the negative feelings that many Americans have about all the things we are supposed to be compassionate about—ethnic, racial, gender, and religious differences. *What a relief,* so many must have thought, to hear a politician speak their unspoken resentments and express their rage. Trump tapped into the dirty little secret of their loathing of various minorities, even though we may all be minorities now. Trump's formula for repairing these deep wounds had him chanting around the country the hopeful mantra of making better "deals." Once the complex takes over the narrative or the narrative gives voice to the complex's core, facts simply become irrelevant. Inevitably, this leads to the kind of terrifying *1984* scenario in which

> The Ministry of Peace concerns itself with war, the Ministry of Truth with lies, the Ministry of Love with torture, and the Ministry of Plenty with starvation. These contradictions are not accidental, nor do they result from ordinary hypocrisy: they are deliberate exercises in doublethink . . . If human equality is to be forever averted—if the High, as we have called them, are to keep their places permanently—then the prevailing mental condition must be controlled insanity.

Trump's cabinet appointments strongly suggest that this is what is happening in our own country. The job of each new Cabinet leader is to reverse or dismantle the very reason for which his or her department exists.

Unholy Marriage of Shadow, Archetypal Defenses of the Group Self, and the Group Self

What makes Trump's unleashing of the shadow in the American psyche even more dangerous is that these energies become linked or even identical with what I call *archetypal defenses* of the group spirit:

> When this part of the collective psyche is activated, the most primitive psychological forces come alive for the purpose of defending the group and its collective spirit or Self. I capitalize *Self* because I want to make it clear that it is not just the persona or ego identity of the group that is under attack but something at an even deeper level of the collective psyche which one might think of as the spiritual home or *god* of the group. The tribal spirit of the clan or of the nation often lies dormant or in the background, but when it is threatened, the defenses mobilized to protect it are ferocious and impersonal. The mobilization of such potent, archaic defenses is fueled by raw collective emotion and rather simplistic, formulaic ideas and/or beliefs [that] dictate how the group will think, feel, react, and behave. (Singer 2006b)

These activated archetypal defenses of the group spirit find concrete expression in forms as varied as the unrest of divided populations over the legal status of foreign immigrants in countries around the world; the threatened development of nuclear weapons by nation-states such as Iran or North Korea; the deployment of suicide bombers by terrorist groups; or the launching of massive military expeditions by world powers. And these same kinds of archetypal defenses come alive in all sorts of skirmishes between diverse groups of people who perceive their most sacred values in jeopardy—the LBGTQ community, blacks, Latinos, white men, women, the Christian right in the United States, Jews around the world, the Muslim

Brotherhood throughout the Middle East. The list of groups threatened at the core of their being or at the level of the group Self seems
endless (Singer 2006b). What makes Trump's narcissism so dangerous in its mix of shadow (his attacks on all sorts of groups of people)
and Self elements (his self-aggrandizing, inflated sense of himself
and those for whom he pretends to speak) is that it plays to the un-
holy marriage of Self and the aggressive, hateful, and violent elements in the collective psyche.

Trump's example gives permission for shadowy thoughts, feelings, and actions on behalf of the Self. This underlying group dynamic
explains the comparison of Trump to Hitler. Evoking an archaic image of the German Self, Hitler mobilized the most shadowy forces
in modern history in the so-called service of that Self-image, which
centered on the supremacy of the Aryan race—first the Brownshirts,
then the Gestapo, SS, and other forces of the Third Reich, including
its highly efficient bureaucracy. Trump seems to be toying with the
collective shadow, encouraging its acting out in the name of the Self.
It is hard to imagine Trump leading the United States in the same
direction that Hitler led Germany—I certainly hope I don't live to
regret writing these words!—but the dynamic is still terrifying.
From a Jungian perspective, when the shadowy defenses of the group
spirit and the group Self closely align, there is great danger of violence, tyranny, and absolutism—especially with an authoritarian
leader and a citizenry responsive to authoritarianism.

3. Curing the Wounded Self of America: Trump's "Selfie" and America's "Selfie"

The third and final component of this intertwined triad of forces
in the group psyche is Trump's implicit promise of providing a cure
for the wound at the level of the group Self. This is where his narcissism is most prominent and most dangerous. The unconscious equation can be stated as follows: "I am the Greatness to which America
may once again aspire. By identifying with how great I am, you

can rekindle your wounded American dream and make yourself and America great again." Or even more bluntly: "I have achieved the American dream; I am the American dream; I am the incarnation of the Self that the country aspires to." This, of course, is a massive inflation. Trump's identification of his personal being with the Self of America is his source of demagogic appeal. He is encouraging those who have lost a foothold in the American dream to place their trust in him as a mirror of their own potential—a potential that he has already achieved. Trump's book *The Art of the Deal* characterizes his magnetic appeal:

> I play to people's fantasies. People may not always think big themselves, but they can still get very excited by those who do. That's why a little hyperbole never hurts. People want to believe that something is the biggest and the greatest and the most spectacular. I call it truthful hyperbole. (Fisher and Hobson 2016; Trump with Schwartz 1987)

Trump has managed to cultivate and catch the projection of a powerful and successful person who, by virtue of his alleged business acumen and ability to negotiate, is able to make things happen for his own betterment—though rarely for the betterment of others, despite his false claims of giving generously to charities and creating untold jobs. "You, too, can be like me: aggressive, successful, big, powerful," he is saying. This is the narcissism of Trump joining with the injured narcissism of those Americans who have seen their chances for well-being and security rapidly slip away. Trump celebrates the materialistic, power version of the American dream—of the big man who has made himself rich and powerful through the strength of his personality. He is free to speak his own mind and to pursue, without limits, his own self-aggrandizing goals that he equates with those of America.

The negative aspects of Trump's narcissism strike those who are repelled by him both at home and abroad as a symbolic mirror of everything negative about a culture of narcissism. For many, he has become the very embodiment of everything bad about America: a self-promoting brand; an arrogant bully bursting with hubris; gross insensitivity to others' needs; possession by consumerism and greed; and entitlement in good fortune, which we have come to believe is our natural due. These are core characteristics of an American cultural complex that betrays that best Self or spirit on which the nation and its constitution were founded. Trump's narcissism is a perfect mirror of our national and even personal narcissism.

Ultimately, I believe that the Trump phenomenon is less about Trump than about us—about who we are as a people: the elephant in the room turns out to be "We the People of the United States." How terrifying to think that our politics and our lives today have gotten horribly confused with reality TV, social media, computer and cell phone technology, and their infinite capacity to turn reality into illusion, Self into narcissism.

Conclusion: Groping the American Psyche and Psychic Contagion

There are so many potentially destructive consequences of the emerging Trump presidency—on the climate, on minorities, on immigrants, on women's rights, on the integrity of the Constitution, and on our relationships with China, Russia, Syria, Iran, North Korea, and even our own allies. But one of the most disturbing thoughts about the Trump presidency is that he has taken up residence not just in the White House but in the psyches of each and every one of us. We are going to have to live with him rattling around inside us, all of us at the mercy of his impulsive and bullying whims, as he lashes out at whatever gets under his skin in the moment with uninformed, inflammatory barbs. The way a president lives inside each of us can feel like a very personal and intimate affair. Those who identify with Trump and love the way he needles the "elites" whom they fear, envy, and despise may relish the fact that he lives inside us as a tormentor. Trump is well versed in brutally toying with his enemies, who include women, professionals, the media, the educated classes, and minorities—to mention just a few.

What most frightens me about Trump is his masterful skill at invading and groping the national psyche. Many tired of the Clintons' taking up permanent residence in our national psyche. Trump will soon put the Clintons to shame in his capacity to dwell in and stink up our collective inner space, like the proverbial houseguest who overstays his welcome. And many of us never invited Trump into our psychic houses in the first place. That is perhaps why the image that has stayed with me the most from the national disgrace that was our election process in 2016 is that of the woman who came forward to tell her story of allegedly being sexually harassed by Trump (Legaspi 2016).

Some years ago, she was given an upgrade to first class on a plane and found herself sitting next to "the Donald." In no time at all, she says, he was literally groping her all over—breasts and below. She describes the physicality of the assault as akin to being entangled in the tentacles of an octopus, and she was barely able to free herself and retreat to economy class.

It now feels as though we have all been groped by the tentacles of Trump's octopus-like psyche, which has invaded our own and threatens to tighten its squeeze for several years. To put it as vulgarly as Trump himself might: Trump has grabbed the American psyche by the "pussy."

As we slowly collect ourselves after the devastating and unexpected tsunami of Trump winning the presidency and the rollercoaster ride of his early days as president, many are finding renewed energy and commitment to challenge his shadowy agenda in new and creative ways. I hope that in a deep resurgence of activism to reclaim our most cherished and threatened American values, we will resist our tendency to cocoon ourselves in a self-righteous, arrogant bubble of narcissistic ideals, even in the name of being "progressive."

> *Thomas Singer, M.D., is a psychiatrist and Jungian psychoanalyst practicing in San Francisco. In addition to private practice, he has served on Social Security's Hearing and Appeals Mental Impairment Disability team. His interests include studying the relationships among myth, politics, and psyche in* The Vision Thing *and the* Ancient Greece, Modern Psyche *series. He is the editor of a series of books exploring cultural complexes, including* Placing Psyche, Listening to Latin America, Europe's Many Souls, The Cultural Complex, *and a book in preparation on Asia. He is the current president of National ARAS, an archive of symbolic imagery that has created* The Book of Symbols.

References

Epstein, Joseph. 2016. "Why Trumpkins Want Their Country Back." *Wall Street Journal*, June 10. www.wsj.com/articles/why-trumpkins-want-their-country-back-1465596987.

Fisher, Marc, and Will Hobson. 2016. "Donald Trump Masqueraded as Publicist to Brag About Himself." *Washington Post*, May 13. www.washingtonpost.com/politics/donald-trump-alter-ego-barron/2016/05/12/02ac99ec-16fe-11e6-aa55-670cabef46e0_story.html?hpid=hp_rhp-top-table-main_no-name%3Ahomepage%2Fstory.

Hedges, Chris. 2009. *Empire of Illusion: The End of Literacy and the Triumph of Spectacle.* New York: Nation Books.

Legaspi, Althea. 2016. "Woman Says Trump Groped Her on Plane: 'It Was an Assault.'" *Rolling Stone*, October 13. www.rollingstone.com/politics/news/woman-says-she-was-groped-by-trump-on-plane-it-was-an-assault-w444700.

MacWilliams, Matthew. 2016. "The One Weird Trait That Predicts Whether You're a Trump Supporter." *Politico*, January 17. www.politico.com/magazine/story/2016/01/donald-trump-2016-authoritarian-213533.

Orwell, George. 1949. *1984*. Repr. New York: Houghton Mifflin Harcourt, 1983.

Singer, Thomas. 2006a. "The Cultural Complex: A Statement of the Theory and Its Application." *Psychotherapy and Politics International* 4 (3): 197–212. doi: 10.1002/ppi.110.

———. 2006b. "Unconscious Forces Shaping International Conflicts: Archetypal Defenses of the Group Spirit from Revolutionary America to Confrontation in the Middle East." *The San Francisco Jung Institute Library Journal* 25 (4): 6–28.

Trump, Donald, with Tony Schwartz. 1987. *The Art of the Deal*. New York: Random House.

Wright, David, Tal Kopan, and Julia Winchester. 2016. "Cruz Unloads with Epic Takedown of 'Pathological Liar,' 'Narcissist' Donald Trump." CNN Politics, May 3. www.cnn.com/2016/05/03/politics/donald -trump-rafael-cruz-indiana/.

WHO GOES TRUMP?

Tyranny as a Triumph of Narcissism

ELIZABETH MIKA, M.A., L.C.P.C.

Tyrannies are three-legged beasts. They encroach upon our world in a steady creep more often than overcome it in a violent takeover, which may be one reason they are not always easy to spot before it is too late to do much about them. Their necessary components, those three wobbly legs, are: the tyrant, his supporters (the people), and the society at large that provides a ripe ground for the collusion between them. Political scientists call it "the toxic triangle" (Hughes 2017).

The force binding all three is narcissism. It animates the beast while, paradoxically and not, eating it alive, bringing its downfall in due time. This force and its influences, which knit the beast into such a powerful and destructive entity, remain invisible to us for reasons that are clearly hinted at but somehow continue to evade our individual and collective comprehension. They make sure we don't recognize the tyranny's marching boots, which can be heard from miles away and months away, until they show up on our doorstep, and that's despite the fact that this very same process has repeated itself countless times in history.

We have known who tyrants are and how tyrannies form since

antiquity, and this knowledge has been supported by the ever-growing tragic evidence of the tyrannies' effects on humanity. Yet, despite making promises to ourselves and one another to "Never forget," we seem not to remember or not to know, always with devastating consequences. Our forgetting stems partly from miseducation (Giroux 2014) and partly from denial. It gives us clues to the kind of work (psychological, social, political, and economic) that we must do if we are to avoid the self-destruction promised by tyrannies today.

Let's take a look at tyranny's components and their interactions.

The Tyrant

Tyrants come in different shapes and sizes, and depending on perspective, various writers stress similarities or differences among them (Newell 2016). This paper will not delve into those classifications but, rather, attempt to simplify and maybe even illuminate their most salient common features.

Although the terms *dictator* and *tyrant* are used interchangeably, it makes sense perhaps to stress that not all dictators are tyrants. Tyrants are dictators gone bad. A leader may start as a seemingly benevolent dictator but turn into a tyrant as his reign progresses, becoming ruthlessly destructive with time, something we have seen repeatedly in history.

All tyrants share several essential features: they are predominantly men with a specific character defect, narcissistic psychopathy (a.k.a. malignant narcissism). This defect manifests in a severely impaired or absent conscience and an insatiable drive for power and adulation that masks the conscience deficits. It forms the core of attraction between him and his followers, the essence of what is seen as his "charisma." In his seminal paper on "Antisocial Personality Disorder and Pathological Narcissism in Prolonged Conflicts and Wars of the 21st Century" (2015), Frederick Burkle observes that narcissism augments and intensifies the pathological features of a psychopathic character structure, making those endowed with it especially dangerous, not in the least because of their ability to use manipulative charm and a pretense of human ideals to pursue their distinctly primitive goals. We talk about the chief feature of narcissistic psychopathy, the impairment of conscience, and its destructive consequences in "The Unbearable Lightness of Being a Narcissist" (Mika and Burkle 2016).

Impulsive, sensation-seeking, and incapable of experiencing empathy or guilt, a narcissistic psychopath treats other people as objects of need fulfillment and wish fulfillment. This makes it easy for him to use and abuse them, in his personal relationships and in large-scale actions, without compunction. His lack of conscience renders him blind to higher human values, which allows him to disregard them entirely or treat them instrumentally as means to his ends, the same way he treats people.

This dangerous character defect, however, serves him well in the pursuit of power, money, and adulation. Not having the inhibitions and scruples imposed by empathy and conscience, he can easily lie, cheat, manipulate, destroy, and kill if he wants to—or, when powerful enough, order others to do it for him.

The characteristics indicative of narcissistic psychopathy are observable already in childhood. Biographies of tyrants (Fromm 1973; Miller 1990; Newell 2016) note the early manifestations of vanity, sensation-seeking, and impulsivity often accompanied by poor self-control, aggression and callousness, manipulativeness, and a strong competitive drive and desire to dominate coexistent with a lack of empathy and conscience. Plato remarked on the "spirited" character of a future tyrant showing the above-mentioned symptoms already in his youth.

Another common, but not universal, biographical finding is a history of childhood abuse. Here, however, accounts vary; for example, while some, like Miller (1990), stress Hitler's purported severe abuse at the hands of his stepfather, others (Fromm 1973; Newell

2016) note that his childhood was uneventful in this respect. Biographies can be incomplete or tendentious, intentionally and not, and so it is not always possible to verify the truth. It is impossible to rule out narcissistic upbringing as being involved in raising a future tyrant—creating a narcissistic injury that shapes the child's life and sets him on a path of "repairing" it through a ruthless and often sadistic pursuit of power and adulation—even when there is no evidence of overt abuse and/or neglect in his biographical data.

While the exact causes of this character defect are a matter of speculation, their possible origins offer intriguing possibilities explaining their clinical manifestations. For example, a narcissistic injury in the first years of a child's life could possibly impair development of the object constancy capacity. This results in an inability to grasp and adhere to the solidity of facts and, consequently, in a disregard for the truth and other human values, the understanding of which comprises a large part of our conscience. The narcissistic psychopath's propensity to lie, whether on purpose to achieve a specific result or, seemingly effortlessly, to invent a universe of "alternative facts" that just happen to affirm his grandiose and guiltless image of himself, could be a result of that impaired object constancy capacity.

His lack of empathy, whether resulting from an inborn cause or narcissistic/authoritarian upbringing, would further (or separately) limit development of his conscience and influence not only the child's socioemotional development but also his cognitive capacities, resulting in what Burkle (2016) calls being smart but not bright. Dąbrowski (1996) termed this as one-sided development, where intelligence and certain cognitive skills develop more or less normally but one's emotional growth remains stunted. The capacity for emotional development is crucial, as this is the only kind of growth possible throughout our lifespan: expanding and deepening our conscience, and spurring us to learning and meaningful change.

Whether the developmental arrest typical for this form of

pathology is inborn, acquired, or a combination of both nature and nurture, it results in the narrow and inflexible character structure, with intelligence subsumed under primitive drives (for power, sex, and adulation).

As Dąbrowski (1986, trans. E. Mika) writes:

> A psychopath is emotionally rigid and narrow. He has strong ambitions and significant talents, but they remain narrow and under the influence of primitive drives. He does not experience inner conflicts, but instead he creates external ones. He is not capable of empathy, and so he strives to gain control over others, or, before he can gain dominance, he submits to the control of others. He is usually deaf and blind to the problems of others, to their development and developmental difficulties. He relentlessly realizes his own goals. A psychopath exists on the level of *primary integration* and is emotionally stunted.
>
> We can distinguish "small" and "big" psychopaths. We find the big ones among the most notorious world criminals, and among aggressive tyrants and dictators (e.g., Nero, Hitler) who do not hesitate to sacrifice others for their own goals. For a big psychopath, a person and a social group do not have any moral value. To him, rules of justice do not exist. Genocide or concentration camps are not a moral problem for him, but a means to an end.
>
> Small psychopaths are miniatures of the big ones. In general, they submit to big psychopaths in the right circumstances. A small psychopath looks for opportunities to realize his own interests and to satisfy his desire to wreak havoc in society. A psychopath thinks that laws are to be broken and that they do not apply to him. He uses any circumstances to secure his position, money, and fortune, regardless of the consequences for others, without any

consideration for ethical norms. Psychopaths do not know how to emotionally compare themselves with others, they cannot emotionally understand others, and they lack an empathic attitude.

The individual distinctions between "small" and "big" psychopaths, a.k.a. tyrants, appear to lie predominantly in the level of their narcissism, observed by Burkle (2015), but also in the presence of some socially approved skills, an ability to modulate and/or mask their aggressive impulses and deeds, as well as life opportunities and luck. A narcissistic psychopath without sufficiently developed self-control or advantageous life opportunities may turn into a mass killer whose crimes will land him in prison before his grandiose dreams of power and domination come to fruition.

Narcissistic psychopaths turned tyrants possess the right combination of manipulativeness, self-control, and intelligence to convince others to support them long enough to put their grandiose ideas to work on a large scale. They also appear to possess skills that are seen as charisma, the most frequent of which is the ability to deliver public speeches that inspire others to follow them. More often than not, however, this "charisma" is simply their ability to tell others what they want to hear (i.e., to lie), to make them go along with whatever scheme they've concocted for the moment. Their glibness is something that easily fools normal people, who do not understand the kind of pathology that results from a missing conscience.

Once in positions of power, tyrants can fully unleash their sadism under the cloak of perverted ideals, which they peddle as a cover for their primitive drives. Instead of turning into common criminals condemned by society, they become oppressors and/or murderers of thousands or millions, with their atrocities always justified in their own minds and those of their supporters. This is why Pol Pot could say without hesitation: "[Y]ou can look at me. Am I a savage person? My conscience is clear" (Mydans 1997), even though he was directly responsible for the deaths of millions of his compatriots.

Tyrants identify with other tyrants and find inspiration in their successes, while remaining oblivious to their failures. They recognize and respect power as much as they are envious of and despise its wielders. The greater and more ruthless the living or historical tyrant, the bigger an inspiration he is for aspiring ones. His disdain for morality and law and his unbridled aggression in pursuit of power appeal to the tyrant in the making and form a template for his behavior, showing him what is possible.

On the eve of invading Poland in 1939, Hitler, after issuing orders to "mercilessly and without pity" annihilate "every man, woman, and child of Polish ethnicity and language," spoke admiringly of one such role model: "Genghis Khan had sent millions of women and children to their deaths, and did so consciously and with a happy heart. History sees in him only the great founder of states." Then he exhorted his subordinates in Poland to "be hard, spare nothing, act faster, and more brutally than the others"—and they eagerly obliged (Gellately 2007).

The upcoming tyrant dreams of becoming as great as and preferably greater than his favorite tyrannical role models; and if those role models are alive, the tyrant-in-the making can be expected to curry favor with the existing ones while plotting their demise and besting them in the tyrants' world rankings. To accomplish this, though, he must obtain a position of ultimate power within his own nation first.

This brings us to the second leg of the tyrannical beast . . .

The Tyrant's Supporters

The process through which the tyrant gains popularity and power usually baffles the outside observers and historians looking at it from the perspective of time, as its main ingredient, narcissism, somehow remains invisible to both participants and observers.

The tyrant's narcissism is the main attractor of his followers, who project their hopes and dreams onto him. The more grandiose his sense of his own self and his promises to his fans, the greater their attraction and the stronger their support. As Plato wrote in *The Republic*, "The people have always some champion whom they set over them and nurse into greatness."

Through the process of identification, the tyrant's followers absorb his omnipotence and glory and imagine themselves as powerful as he is, the winners in the game of life. This identification heals the followers' narcissistic wounds, but also tends to shut down their reason and conscience, allowing them to engage in immoral and criminal behaviors with a sense of impunity engendered by this identification. Without the support of his narcissistic followers, who see in the tyrant a reflection and vindication of their long-nursed dreams of glory, the tyrant would remain a middling nobody.

The interplay of grandiose hopes and expectations between the tyrant-in-the-making and his supporters that suffuses him with power and helps propel him to a position of political authority is an example of narcissistic collusion: a meshing of mutually compatible narcissistic needs. The people see in him their long-awaited savior and a father substitute, hinting at the narcissistic abuse implicated in the authoritarian upbringing that demands obedience and worship of the all-powerful parental figure. In their faith and unquestioning admiration, he in turn receives a ready line of narcissistic supply, thousands of mirrors reflecting his greatness.

Describing the narcissistic collusion between the tyrant and his supporters, Erich Fromm (1980) stressed the elements of submission to and identification with the strongman:

> The highly narcissistic group is eager to have a leader with whom it can identify itself. The leader is then admired by the group which projects its narcissism onto him. In the very act of submission to the powerful leader, which is in

depth an act of symbiosis and identification, the narcissism of the individual is transferred onto the leader. The greater the leader, the greater the follower. Personalities who as individuals are particularly narcissistic are the most qualified to fulfill this function. The narcissism of the leader who is convinced of his greatness, and who has no doubts, is precisely what attracts the narcissism of those who submit to him. The half-insane leader is often the most successful one until his lack of objective judgment, his rage reaction in consequence to any setback, his need to keep up the image of omnipotence may provoke him to make mistakes which lead to his destruction. But there are always gifted half-psychotics at hand to satisfy the demands of a narcissistic mass.

Jerrold Post (2015) underscored the authoritarian parenting aspect of that identification when discussing Hitler Youth:

> Especially for the Hitler Youth Movement, which was at the forefront of Hitler's support, Hitler's externalizing hate-mongering rhetoric was a comforting and inspiring message, and Hitler provided the strong inspiring father figure that these children could not find within their own families. But, in rebelling against their own families, they submitted uncritically to Hitler's authoritarian leadership. Importantly, Adolf Hitler's unleashing of the demons of war was turning the passive humiliation of defeat [in World War I] into the active experience of redemptive action.

The narcissistic mixture of elevated expectations, resentments, and desire for revenge on specific targets and/or society in general for not meeting those expectations is what sociologist Michael Kimmel (2013) called aggrieved entitlement. Although Kimmel talked specifically about white American men in the twenty-first century, some form of aggrieved entitlement has been driving tyrants and their supporters, as well as organized and "lone wolf" terrorists, the world over since time immemorial.

The tyrant makes many good-sounding—but also openly unrealistic, bordering on delusional—promises to his supporters, and usually has no intention or ability to fulfill most of them (if any). He holds his supporters in contempt, as he does "weaker" human beings in general, and uses them only as props in his domination- and adulation-oriented schemes.

The narcissistic collusion between the tyrant and his supporters is also driven by the latter's need for revenge, for the tyrant is always chosen to perform this psychically restorative function: to avenge the humiliations (narcissistic wounds) of his followers and punish those who inflicted them.

However, as the wounds often date to the supporters' personal ancient past and more often than not are perceived rather than real, the choice of the object of this vengeful punishment is not based on reality. Rather, it is based on the displacement and projection characteristic of the scapegoating process that becomes an inextricable part of the narcissistic collusion between the tyrant and his followers.

The scapegoating designates the Others as an object upon which the narcissistic revenge will be inflicted. The Others always represent the split-off, devalued, and repressed parts of the narcissistic individual's own psyche, which are projected onto them. These projections are shared and augmented through a narcissism of small differences (Freud 1991), which allows us to focus on and enlarge insignificant differences between ourselves and the Others in order to solidify our negative projections and justify our contempt and aggression toward them.

The tyrant and his followers typically choose as vessels for their negative projections and aggression the members of society who are not just different but weaker. The tyrant fuels that aggression in order to solidify his power but also to deflect it from himself, shield his own narcissism, and repair his own narcissistic injuries dating to his childhood. The figure of the narcissistic parental abuser/tyrant is protected through the scapegoating and the return to the authoritarian, order- and obedience-based mode of social functioning promised by the tyrant, as he himself assumes the mantle of father-protector and directs his own and his supporters' aggression onto the Others, who have nothing to do with those supporters' real and perceived wounds.

The tyrant's own narcissism hints at the level of woundedness in his supporters. The greater their narcissistic injury, the more grandiose the leader required to repair it. While his grandiosity appears grotesque to non-narcissistic people who do not share his agenda, to his followers he represents all their denied and thwarted greatness, which now, under his rule, will finally flourish. Hitler's bizarre dream of a Thousand-Year Reich spread upon the world did not seem at all preposterous or dangerous to so many Germans suffering from the pain, humiliation, and privations inflicted upon them by the fiasco of World War I, just as Stalin's vision of communism as dictatorship of the working class taking over the world did not appear strange or dangerous to his beleaguered followers. Narcissism is blind to itself.

The natural consequence of scapegoating that stems from the projections of the narcissist's devalued parts of himself is dehumanization of the Others, which then justifies all kinds of atrocities perpetrated on them. The ease with which this attitude spreads in narcissistic groups is frightening, and indicative of a narcissistic rage that fuels it, a rage focused on purging, psychically and physically, all that is weak and undesirable from the narcissists' inner and external worlds.

That rage, along with dreams of glory, is what makes the bond between the tyrant and his followers so strong that it remains impervious to reality. It also makes the tyrant's rule easier, as he does not have to exert himself much to infect his followers with contempt for the dehumanized Others and incite aggression against them. In fact, the tyrant's permission for such aggression appears to be a large part of his appeal to his blood- and revenge-thirsty followers.

The tyrant's and his followers' projections always reveal much about their own pathology. In his private notes about Jews in Nazi-occupied Poland, Hitler's propaganda minister, Joseph Goebbels, wrote that they were "not people anymore" but "beasts of prey equipped with a cold intellect" (Gellately 2007), the latter description obviously more applicable to Goebbels and the Nazis themselves than their victims (who, it must be stressed, were observed by Goebbels in captivity, under dehumanizing conditions of ghetto life).

Once we dehumanize the Others and imbue them with a murderous motivation directed at us, we can easily rationalize any act of violence we perpetrate upon them as self-defense. And so, removing en masse and without mercy those "beasts of prey" became one of the main goals of the Nazis, who believed that Jews, Poles, Gypsies, and other non-Aryans threatened their existence. The fear, whether genuine or faked, stemming from this false belief was used as a sufficient justification for mass murder on a scale unseen previously in the modern world.

It must be noted that the tyrant's supporters and especially sycophants within his closest circle tend to share his character defect. The sycophantic echo chamber around the tyrant magnifies but also hides his pathology. His surrogates usually serve as ego substitutes to his rampaging id, and are responsible for introducing and implementing his destructive plans in ways that would seem rational and acceptable to the public.

Their role becomes more important with time, as he psychologically decompensates, which inevitably happens to narcissistic psychopaths in positions of ultimate power. As his paranoia, grandiosity, and impulsivity grow, his aides, family members, and surrogates, fearful for their positions and often their lives, scramble to preserve an image of his "normalcy" and greatness for public consumption to the very end. Their loyalty can be fierce and undying, unlike that of the tyrant himself.

The Society

Tyrants do not arise in a vacuum, just as tyranny does not spring on the world unannounced. It takes years of cultivation of special conditions in a society for a tyranny to take over. Those conditions invariably include a growing and unbearably oppressive economic and social inequality ignored by the elites who benefit from it, at least for a time; fear, moral confusion, and chaos that come from that deepening inequality; a breakdown of social norms; and growing disregard for the humanity of a large portion of the population and for higher values. In effect, we could see that the pre-tyrannical societies, whether nominally democratic or based on other forms of political organization, exhibit signs of a narcissistic pathology writ large. Those involve the inevitable split into their grandiose and devalued parts, including those of the society's self-image, and a denial of their shadow, which is projected outward onto Others.

Oppressive, dehumanizing (narcissistic) systems, like narcissists themselves, cultivate their delusions of superiority on the basis of that internal, unseen, and unspoken split between the grandiose blameless I/Us and the devalued, inferior Others. The Others become repositories of the narcissists' repressed vices, just as the tyrant is the vessel for their grandiose beliefs about themselves.

Another narcissistic aspect of such societies is the growing and ruthless competition, jealousy, and aggression within its borders, but also directed externally toward other nations in a scapegoating mechanism that is meant to prevent an internal breakdown of a society by redirecting its narcissistic rage onto external objects. Oftentimes, these vulnerable societies reel from some form of a narcissistic injury, such as the humiliation of a lost war, international sanctions, or treaties perceived as unfair, as Germany did after the Treaty of Versailles after World War I.

None of these processes is openly acknowledged or even noticed by the members of the society, save by a few typically ignored Cassandras. Just as individual narcissists are incapable of experiencing guilt, taking responsibility for their vices, or making genuine efforts to set things right in their lives, narcissistic societies also persist in their self-destructive blindness. While the chaos and discord brew in the underclasses, the elites, ensconced in their narcissistic bubbles, remain oblivious to the suffering of their fellow citizens and the fate it portends for the nation.

Fritz Stern (2005) has said that "German moderates and German elites underestimated Hitler, assuming that most people would not succumb to his Manichean unreason; they did not think that his hatred and mendacity could be taken seriously." Hitler was seen by many as a bombastic but harmless buffoon, while many others, including members of clergy, intellectual elites, and the wealthy were nevertheless mesmerized by his grand visions of Germany's future glory, and eagerly supported his agenda.

Narcissism of the elites makes them as well blind to the encroaching tyranny. It is a convenient—and yes, narcissistic—myth that only the dispossessed and uninformed would support the tyrant. It is not the economic or educational status that determines such susceptibility, but one's narcissism, and that cuts across socioeconomic strata. Dorothy Thompson describes it brilliantly in her 1941 essay, "Who Goes Nazi?," in which she identifies those threads of frustrated grandiosity, resentments, and hatreds in the well-heeled individuals' characters that make them fall for tyrannical ideologies and movements. She also observes those who would naturally resist the toxic pull of Nazism, noting their humility and depth.

Stern (2005) quotes a letter from philosopher and Nobel Prize–winning physicist Carl Friedrich von Weizsäcker, who confessed to him "that he had never believed in Nazi ideology but that he had been tempted by the movement, which seemed to him then like 'the outpouring of the Holy Spirit.' On reflection, he thought that National Socialism had been part of a process that the National Socialists themselves had not understood. He may well have been right. The Nazis did not realize that they were part of a historic process in which resentment against a disenchanted secular world found deliverance in the ecstatic escape of unreason."

Note that the process that the Nazis themselves had not understood is the very narcissistic collusion, a near-psychotic infection with this virus of grandiosity and rage on a mass scale. It is rarely grasped, not even from the perspective of time, as our blindness makes it impossible to acknowledge it, which renders our narcissism the last taboo in a world that has dispensed with taboos. Our denial and social amnesia further entrench our incomprehension and ensure that history repeats itself.

Part of our forgetting involves distortions of historical and psychological facts. Safely removed, time- and distance-wise, from the latest tyranny-caused mayhem, we tend to imagine tyrants as instantly recognizable evil beings and tyrannies as something exotic enough never to happen to us. But as history and experience demonstrate, power-hungry narcissistic psychopaths do not look different from normal people; and if they stand out, it is often for socially approved reasons: their resolve, charisma, decisiveness, and ability to inspire others.

No tyrant comes to power on the platform of genocidal tyranny, even though such ideas may be brewing already in the recesses of his mind. Each and every one of them promises to bring back law and order, create better economic conditions for the people, and restore the nation's glory.

These empty promises—for the tyrant has little desire and even less ability to fulfill them—are always tied together with the thread of scapegoating Others, a necessary component that channels the narcissistic rage outward and increases the society's cohesion. But the tyrant sows discord and division among his own peoples as well. He cannot help it: pitting people against one another satisfies his irrepressible sadistic urge and makes it easier for him to dominate and control them.

The tyrant shows up in a society that is already weakened by disorder, blind to it, and unable and/or unwilling to take corrective measures that would prevent a tyrannical takeover. Once he and his sycophantic cabal assume power, they deepen and widen the disorder, dismantling and changing the society's norms, institutions, and laws to fully reflect their own pathology.

Andrew Łobaczewski (2007) discusses at length the formation and progression of *pathocracies*, political and other systems run by characterologically impaired individuals, predominantly psychopaths and narcissists. He describes how pathocracies change the society by the introduction of *paralogisms*, ways of distorting reality and truth; and *paramoralisms*, methods of perverting moral values. Under tyranny, paralogisms and paramoralisms are unleashed on a large scale through various propagandist means that include repetition of flat-out lies, accompanied by denials and obfuscations served through the increasingly centralized and controlled media. Fortified by magical thinking and contempt for reason, these distortions lead to the creation of the kind of absurdist unreality well known to people raised in authoritarian regimes, where up is down and black is white, and where what one knows to be true may have nothing to do with the officially sanctioned version of the truth.

We can see the tyrant's own pathology influencing every area of a society's functioning, from politics through culture and social mores to science and technology. What is being seen, said, and studied, and what's ignored and silenced, depends on the tyrant's whims, and soon enough the society itself and its ideology are structured in ways that meet his pathological needs for power and adulation. The implementation of this ideology is usually a gradual process, one that is eventually reinforced by the use of violence against persistent objectors.

As freedom of speech, the press, and assembly disappears and the tyrant's destructive "reforms" take hold, an ethos of the New Man, an ideal of a human being compatible with the disordered ideology, is forced upon the populace.

This New Man is a dehumanized caricature of a human person, usually exemplifying the tyrant's distorted views and thus meeting his pathological needs, mainly for dominance and adulation. He—we will use the male pronoun, but there is of course a compatible version of the New Woman to go with the New Man—is wholly devoted to the Cause and the Leader (which, in tyrannies, are often one and the same, an ultimate expression of the tyrant's narcissism) and acts in prescribed ways meant to demonstrate this devotion in his life. Hero worship and utmost loyalty become parts of the New Man's prescribed behavior, reinforced by new laws and norms, but also by individuals who eagerly cooperate with the authoritarian rules by spying on and denouncing their fellow citizens' ideologically improper behavior.

Our human propensity to submit to inhumane rules established by pathological authority cannot be overestimated. We have plenty of historical and contemporary evidence for it, as well as experimental data (Milgram 1974). An approving nod from an authority figure, no matter how insignificant or even real, can easily absolve us of responsibility in our minds and override any scruples imposed by our conscience, proving its perplexing malleability.

The ease with which many so-called normal people shut down their conscience makes them not very different from functional psychopaths. This disturbing fact of human life is something the tyrant counts on when he establishes his reign. He knows that he can expect loyalty from his followers and successfully demand it from the majority of society. And those unwilling to follow his dictates and/ or actively opposing them will be eliminated.

The New Man's thoughts must of course change, too, to better aid his transformation. Thus, the criteria of mental normalcy and pathology also are redefined, and psychology and psychiatry, like other branches of social science, are coopted to serve the regime. What's considered normal, both in the sense of statistical norm and mental health, is in fact pathological, and mental health, defined as the capacity for multilevel and multidimensional development, is pathologized.

The ease with which the tyrannical ideology spreads is always greater than we want to imagine. Our narcissistic blindness makes it impossible for us to believe that it could happen here and that we, too, could be as susceptible to it as any other human beings in history.

Tyranny feeds on the irrationality of narcissistic myths and magical thinking, even though its ideology may be disguised as hyperrationalism, as was the case with communism. In this, it very much resembles the narcissistically psychopathic character of the tyrant himself: solipsistic, withdrawn from reality, and full of grandiose and paranoid beliefs impervious to the corrective influences of objective facts.

These pathological factors ensure that eventually the tyrant's reign collapses. The inherent and violent irrationality, bereft of internal brakes that stem from a conscience, and unchecked by external forces, is the main reason tyrants and their regimes are doomed to fail (Glad 2002). Their growing malignancy (corruption, aggression, and oppression) provokes opposition, which eventually brings the tyranny down, but not until its pillaging and violent reign create much human suffering. The reset of a society's mores that follows the tragic aftermath of a tyrannical rule usually leads to a greater appreciation for the importance of universal human values (equality, justice, truth, and compassion), but if care is not taken to implement these values in consistent practice, our narcissistic tendencies creep in and lead to social disorder, making us susceptible to tyranny again. Given our growing potential for self-destruction, the stakes go up with every tyrannical turn.

Conclusion

Narcissism is as much a character problem as it is an error in our thinking. Seeing oneself as "above" is the general attitude of a narcissist toward the world, and the error of the tyrant and his followers. This error appears to grip many so-called civilized human societies, and is especially pronounced in those where inequality grows despite any official sloganeering to the contrary. Our narcissism is what gives rise to inequality, and inequality fuels our narcissism. The resultant suffering and despair, along with a desire for revenge, are among the necessary conditions for the emergence of tyranny.

As Burkle (2015) observes, we are seeing a resurgence of tyrannical leaders around the globe, even in nations that supposedly have learned the lessons of tyrannies past in the most painful ways. It is a sign of our pressing need to reckon with our collective shadow.

If we as a species are to flourish and prosper, we need to understand that our urgent and necessary task is to transcend and dismantle our narcissism, both individual and collective.

Elizabeth Mika, M.A., L.C.P.C., of Gifted Resources in Northern Illinois (in the Chicago area), received her degree in clinical psychology from Adam Mickiewicz University in Poznan, Poland. She specializes in assessment and counseling of gifted children and adults. Her professional interests include creativity and mental health, learning differences and learning styles, multiple exceptionalities, and emotional and moral development.

References

Burkle, Frederick M. 2015. "Antisocial Personality Disorder and Pathological Narcissism in Prolonged Conflicts and Wars of the 21st Century." *Disaster Medicine and Public Health Preparedness* 1 (October): 1–11.

Burkle, Frederick M., and Dan Hanfling. 2016. "When Being Smart Is Not Enough: Narcissism in U.S. Polity." March 2. http://hir.harvard.edu /article/?a=12701.

Dąbrowski, Kazimierz. 1986. *Trud istnienia.* Warszawa: Wiedza Powszechna.

———. 1996. *W poszukiwaniu zdrowia psychicznego.* Warszawa: Wydawnictwo Naukowe PWN.

Dąbrowski, Kazimierz, Andrew Kawczak, and Janina Sochanska. 1973. *The Dynamics of Concepts.* London: Gryf Publications.

Freud, Sigmund. 1991. *Civilization, Society, and Religion.* Canada: Penguin Freud Library, p. 12.

Fromm, Erich. 1973. *The Anatomy of Human Destructiveness.* New York: Holt, Rinehart and Winston.

———. 1980. *The Heart of Man.* New York, Evanston, and London: Harper and Row.

Gellately, Robert. 2007. *Lenin, Stalin and Hitler: The Age of Social Catastrophe.* New York: Alfred A. Knopf.

Giroux, Henry A. 2014. *The Violence of Organized Forgetting: Thinking Beyond America's Disimagination Machine.* San Francisco, CA: City Lights Publishers.

Glad, Betty. 2002. "Why Tyrants Go Too Far: Malignant Narcissism and Absolute Power." *Political Psychology* 23, no. 1 (March): 1–37.

Hughes, Ian. 2017. "The Solution to Democracy's Crisis Is More Democracy." DisorderedWorld.com. https://disorderedworld.com/2017/05/04/the -solution-to-democracys-crisis-is-more-democracy/.

Kimmel, Michael. 2013. *Angry White Men: American Masculinity at the End of an Era.* New York: Nation Books.

Łobaczewski, Andrew M. 2007. *Political Ponerology: A Science on the Nature of Evil Adjusted for Political Purposes.* Grande Prairie, AB, Canada: Red Pill Press.

Mika, Elizabeth, and Frederick M. Burkle. 2016. "The Unbearable Lightness of Being a Narcissist." *Medium*, May 13. https://medium.com/@ Elamika/the-unbearable-lightness-of-being-a-narcissist-251ec901dae7.

Milgram, Stanley. 1974. *Obedience to Authority: An Experimental View*. New York: Harper and Row.

Miller, Alice. 1990. *For Your Own Good: Hidden Cruelty in Child-Rearing and the Roots of Violence*. New York: Noonday Press.

Mydans, Seth. 1997. "In an Interview, Pol Pot Declares His Conscience Is Clear." *New York Times*, October 23. www.nytimes.com/1997/10/23 /world/in-an-interview-pol-pot-declares-his-conscience-is-clear.html.

Newell, Waller R. 2016. *Tyrants: A History of Power, Injustice and Terror*. New York: Cambridge University Press.

Plato, Grube, G. M. A., and C. D. C. Reeve, eds. 1992. *Republic*. Indianapolis, IN: Hackett Pub. Co.

Post, Jerrold. 2015. *Narcissism and Politics*. New York: Cambridge University Press.

Stern, Fritz. 2005. "Reflection: Lessons from German History." *Foreign Affairs* (May–June). www.foreignaffairs.com/articles/europe/2005-05 -01/reflection-lessons-german-history.

Thompson, Dorothy. 1941. "Who Goes Nazi?" *Harper's Magazine*, August. https://harpers.org/archive/1941/08/who-goes-nazi/.

THE LONELINESS OF FATEFUL DECISIONS

Social Contexts and Psychological Vulnerability

EDWIN B. FISHER, PH.D.

At nine o'clock, Tuesday morning, October 16, 1962, the special assistant for national security entered the living quarters of the White House with startling news: "Mr. President, there is now hard photographic evidence that the Russians have offensive missiles in Cuba" (Neustadt and Allison 1971). During the next thirteen days of the Cuban Missile Crisis,* the world faced a horrible threat. Fewer than one in five U.S. citizens alive today is old enough to remember well the experience of those events, but the sense of possible doom was profound. Sitting in Mr. Capasso's eleventh-grade History class, I thought that we all might not be there in a day or two. Spy satellite photos showed that the Soviet Union was within weeks or perhaps days of finishing the installation of missiles in Cuba capable of reaching major U.S. East Coast cities. As this is being written, many are calling the possibility of North Korea possessing operational

---

* This name for the crisis will be used for ease of communication, although it has been rightly criticized as reflecting a U.S.-centric view of the world.

nuclear-armed rockets capable of reaching U.S. West Coast cities within several years the greatest threat we face. Imagine if we were in the same position as in 1962: "Our military experts advised that these missiles could be in operation within a week" (Kennedy 1971).*

In reacting to the threat, President Kennedy brought together the "best and the brightest," to borrow David Halberstam's term for the Kennedy Cabinet and advisers (Halberstam 1972). They included the secretaries of state and defense, the UN ambassador, other senior policy advisers, the Joint Chiefs of Staff, and the president's highly trusted brother Robert, the attorney general. They debated daily over the period, considering varied alternatives. There was only one problem with this "best" and "brightest" advice. They disagreed. Indeed, they disagreed sharply. President Kennedy was left to make the decision. As President George W. Bush put it, President Kennedy was "the decider."

That the most powerful person in the world can be isolated and lonely in making fateful decisions dramatizes the importance of classic questions. How does the individual shape her/his world, and how does that world shape the individual? Research makes clear, for example, the fundamental value of social connections, that their absence is as lethal as smoking cigarettes (Holt-Lunstad, Smith, and Layton 2010; House, Landis, and Umberson 1988). So, too, the varied group of individuals who advised President Kennedy clearly influenced his perspectives and choices. On the other hand, President Kennedy shaped the variety of perspectives of that group of advisers.

This chapter examines two major themes. First, it examines the interplay among social contexts and individual characteristics as they were apparent in and around President Kennedy in 1962. The

---

* Much of the history of the October 1962 crisis has been drawn from Robert Kennedy's 1971 memoir of those events, *Thirteen Days: A Memoir of the Cuban Missile Crisis* (New York: W. W. Norton, 1971). Unless otherwise noted, quotations are from that source.

strategies, personal characteristics, and social settings that surrounded the president during those thirteen days pose important questions for our current evaluation of President Trump. The second theme is an emphasis on the patterns of behavior that result from that interplay of person and context. Emerging through that interplay, it is those behavior patterns themselves, not speculations about either their interpersonal or personal sources, that provide us confidence in a leader's ability to make fateful, lonely decisions.

The 1962 Crisis

Many of the Joint Chiefs of Staff felt that air strikes and an invasion were clearly necessary. In arguments that sound very current in 2017, they argued that the incursion of Soviet missiles into our hemisphere could not be allowed to stand, that a line needed to be drawn, and that clear and decisive action was required. Others argued that there was little reason to respond aggressively. Secretary of Defense McNamara articulated one of the strongest arguments for a modest response, pointing out that nuclear warheads would kill just as many people whether they came from Cuba or somewhere else. Others encouraged diplomacy and working with the Soviets. Complicating this strategy was the fact that the Soviet foreign minister had clearly lied to President Kennedy in denying the existence of the missiles after the president already had the satellite photos showing their installation.

In the end, President Kennedy chose a firm response, but one that did not include a direct attack in Cuba. He established a naval quarantine that would not allow any ships carrying munitions to enter waters around Cuba. Soviet ships were on their way and not turning back. What would happen if they challenged the quarantine? In written exchanges, two messages were received from the Soviets. One clearly reflected the hard-liners in the Kremlin. A second, apparently written by Premier Khrushchev himself, was far more conciliatory. In an important model of wise negotiation, President Kennedy ignored the belligerent message and responded to the conciliatory one. At almost the literal eleventh hour, 10:25 a.m. on Wednesday, October 24, a message came from the field: "Mr. President, we have a preliminary report which seems to indicate that some of the Russian ships have stopped dead in the water . . . or have turned back toward the Soviet Union." The world breathed.

President Kennedy's Strategies

Especially striking in his brother Robert's recounting of those thirteen days (Kennedy 1971), President Kennedy was determined to consider the position of the antagonists, Premier Khrushchev and the other Soviet leaders. Recognizing strong militarist forces in Moscow, Kennedy realized that "We don't want to push him to a precipitous action . . . I don't want to put him in a corner from which he cannot escape." From their previous communications, he recognized that Khrushchev also did not want war and agreed that a nuclear war would doom the planet. In a letter reflecting a remarkably personal dimension of their relationship, Khrushchev wrote to Kennedy during the height of the tensions:

> I have participated in two wars and know that war ends when it has rolled through cities and villages, everywhere sowing death and destruction . . . Armaments bring only disasters . . . they are an enforced loss of human energy, and what is more are for the destruction of man himself. If people do not show wisdom, then in the final analysis they will come to a clash, like blind moles, and then reciprocal extermination will begin . . .
> . . . Mr. President, we and you ought not to pull on the ends of the rope in which you have tied the knot of war, because the more the two of us pull, the tighter the knot will be tied. And a moment may come when that knot will be tied so tight that even he who tied it will not have the strength to

untie it . . . Consequently, if there is no intention to tighten that knot, and thereby to doom the world to the catastrophe of thermonuclear war, then let us not only relax the forces pulling on the ends of the rope, let us take measures to untie that knot. We are ready for this.

President Kennedy's understanding of the other person's point of view extended to his own advisers as well as international adversaries. In his memoir, Robert Kennedy noted that after the Russians agreed on Sunday, October 28, to withdraw their missiles from Cuba, "it was suggested by one high military adviser that we attack Monday in any case. Another felt that we had in some way been betrayed." He goes on: "President Kennedy was disturbed by this inability to look beyond the limited military field. When we talked about this later, he said we had to remember that they were trained to fight and to wage war—that was their life."

President Kennedy also cultivated allies. He recognized that a stand-off with the Soviet Union without allies would put the United States in a very weak position. He worked with the Organization of American States to gain endorsement of the U.S. position and was successful in its turning out to be unanimous. He cultivated European allies and gained a strong endorsement—"It is exactly what I would have done"—from President Charles de Gaulle, the assertively nationalist leader of France and its greatest World War II hero.

In cultivating his allies, President Kennedy was highly aware of the importance of his and the United States' credibility. He was careful throughout the crisis to communicate honestly, with neither hyperbole nor minimization, about the facts on the ground and the U.S. response.

Finally, President Kennedy was a cagy negotiator. In the course of negotiations, Premier Khrushchev raised a counterdemand that the United States remove its own Jupiter rockets from Turkey. This was especially frustrating because President Kennedy had previously recognized their obsolescence and very modest strategic value and so, sometime before the Cuban Missile Crisis, had directed that they be removed. Now he was clearly willing to meet this demand of the Soviets, but not publicly and not at the same time as the removal of the rockets from Cuba. So, he promised their removal in the months ahead and, fortunately for us all, had cultivated enough good faith with Premier Khrushchev that this unsecured promise was accepted.

Illustrative of his broad reading, President Kennedy had found much of this negotiating stance in a book he had reviewed in 1960, *Deterrent or Defense*, by the British military analyst Basil Liddell Hart: "Keep strong, if possible. In any case, keep cool. Have unlimited patience. Never corner an opponent and always assist him to save his face. Put yourself in his shoes—so as to see things through his eyes. Avoid self-righteousness like the devil—nothing is so self-blinding." Kennedy's habits of mind, organization, administration, and leadership have been accorded substantial responsibility for the avoidance of catastrophe in 1962.

Taking advantage perhaps of a time of more common bipartisanship, Kennedy sought counsel from a wide group, including Republicans such as John McCloy, a former U.S. ambassador to the United Nations, and Dean Acheson, secretary of state under President Truman and a highly opinionated authority in foreign affairs. His own secretary of defense, Robert McNamara, had been a Republican and a CEO of the Ford Motor Company. Even though he was secretary of the treasury, President Kennedy included Douglas Dillon, for whose wisdom he had great respect. Dillon had also been President Eisenhower's undersecretary of state. In addition to the highly respected "old hands" of McCloy, Acheson, and Secretary of State Dean Rusk, he included much younger individuals as well. McGeorge Bundy, a former Republican, had already been dean of the Harvard faculty when, at forty-one, he became special assistant for national security in 1961. Clearly, Robert Kennedy was a close, most trusted and apparently constant confidant, but beyond his brother, President Kennedy cultivated a broad and varied group of advisers, not an inner circle of three or four. President Kennedy was thoughtful not only in assembling these divergent views but also in cultivating them, such as by having his advisers meet without him so that his presence would not tilt opinions in his direction or stifle free exchange.

Actions such as those of President Kennedy are often attributed to the "great man," to the remarkable or praiseworthy characteristics of the individual. President Kennedy's actions in the Cuban Missile Crisis reflect his wisdom and skills but also the social relationships that surrounded him. That he took a hand in constructing and managing these relationships points to an important dialectic between the individual and the social, but diminishes neither.

Social Networks and Support

Many studies document the impacts of social relationships. One of the most provocative found that social connections with spouse, parents, family members, coworkers, groups or organizations protect against the "common cold" (Cohen et al. 1997). What was most important about this finding, however, was that it was not just the *number* of social connections that protected against symptoms such as a runny nose, but also their *variety*. Having many versus fewer friends was not protective, but having a variety of types of relationships with family, friends, etc. resulted in fewer symptoms following exposure to a cold virus. Similarly, the *variety* of social connections predicted death among older adults in a more recent study (Steptoe et al. 2013).

Why should the variety of social connections matter? One answer comes from work many years ago by the anthropologist Erving Goffman, in his study of "asylums" such as prisons and mental hospitals. Goffman observed that inmates or patients in such institutions have but one social role. The patient hospitalized in a psychiatric facility is seen by all (professionals and staff, family members, former acquaintances, and even other patients) as a patient with a mental illness, not as a spouse, child, friend, or coworker (Goffman 1961). Being stuck in one role limits our ability to buffer the stressors of daily life. This is because we often cope with stressors in one setting by complaining, getting advice, or simply seeking solace in another. We complain about our coworkers to our spouses and complain about our spouses, children, and/or in-laws with our coworkers or close friends. For the hospitalized schizophrenic patient, however, this is not possible. As all come to see her/him as schizophrenic, all complaints to or about family, friends, hospital staff, doctors, etc. are taken as expressions of schizophrenia, and thereby invalidated. The individual is isolated in only one role from which she or he cannot escape.

The importance of not being locked in one role, even as the all-powerful president, is reflected in a current book on the office of White House chief of staff (Whipple 2017). A recurrent theme is the importance of the chief of staff being the one person who can tell the president he cannot do something. President Carter's initial decision not to have a chief of staff and then appointing one who was not an effective manager is suggested as a major cause for problems in his administration. Turning to President Trump, doubts about his trust in his chief of staff are frequently cited as key to problems in the execution of his plans during the early days of his administration.

Applying Goffman's observations to the president of the United States is ironic. Goffman developed these ideas in observing and trying to understand the challenges of those stripped not only of their multiple roles but also of their independence and freedom. But the observation may also apply to those who become isolated in a single social role amid privilege. A concern one might raise about President Trump is his apparent choice always to be "the Donald." Consider, for example, his making Mar-a-Lago an extension of the White

House. Rather than preserving it as a place to which he can get away and separate himself at least somewhat from his role as president, he chose to go there weekly during the first months of his administration and to "bring his work home with him," including his official visitors, such as President Xi Jinping of China.

A final important feature of social connections points also to the importance of varied perspectives. In examining how groups adopt innovations, sociologist and communication theorist Everett Rogers noted the importance of tight-knit, cohesive networks in quickly and effectively acting to implement a good idea (Rogers and Kincaid 1981). But where do the good ideas come from? One source of good ideas was observed to be "weak ties." One member of a tightly knit group might have a connection to someone in another village, a sister-in-law who is a lawyer, or a job that takes him periodically to the "big city." Such weak ties, not intimate or especially important in day-to-day activities, nevertheless provide exposure to innovations. The combination of new ideas plus a cohesive network to implement them provides the idea for and the execution of innovation.

The variety, provision of multiple roles, and availability of weak ties in social networks seem to fit well the social setting in which President Kennedy worked through the Cuban Missile Crisis. The variety of connections was clear. An important feature of his network was Kennedy's preserving of his relationship with his brother, through which he could complain about his group of advisers, perhaps, but also seek an outside perspective in making sense of the advice he was getting. He also read widely and drew on that reading in his thinking. Barbara Tuchman's *The Guns of August*, detailing how European leaders miscalculated and slid into World War I, was much in Kennedy's mind. As noted, President Kennedy maintained "weak ties" with those with varied viewpoints through his wide reading, intellectual curiosity, and openness to a wide range of views.

Turning to President Trump's social connections, an April 2017 article in the *New York Times* noted a "group of advisers—from family, real estate, media, finance and politics, and all outside the White House gates—many of whom he consults at least once a week" (Haberman and Thrush 2017). They include nine millionaires or billionaires (Thomas Barrack, Carl Icahn, Robert Kraft, Richard Le-Frak, Rupert Murdoch, David Perlmutter, Steven Roth, Phil Ruffin, and Steve Schwarzman); the conservative television cable news host Sean Hannity; the conservative political strategists Corey Lewandowski and Roger Stone; Republican politicians Chris Christie, Newt Gingrich, and Paul Ryan; a financial lawyer, Sheri Dillon; President Trump's sons; and his wife. Although the article says that President Trump "needs to test ideas with a wide range of people," those in whom he confides are described as "mostly white, male and older" and were chosen based "on two crucial measures: personal success and loyalty to him."

A somewhat more critical characterization of President Trump's circle of relationships emerges through a recent article in *The New Yorker*, by Evan Osnos: "He inhabits a closed world that one adviser recently described to me as 'Fortress Trump.' Rarely venturing beyond the White House and Mar-a-Lago, he measures his fortunes through reports from friends, staff, and a feast of television coverage of himself."

Quoting Jerry Taylor, "the president of the Niskanen Center, a libertarian think tank," Osnos describes how "he is governing as if he is the President of a Third World country: power is held by family and incompetent loyalists whose main calling card is the fact that Donald Trump can trust them, not whether they have any expertise."

As the noted constitutional lawyer Lawrence Tribe (2017) has put it, "He only wants loyalists." Later, Osnos notes that:

> it's not clear how fully Trump apprehends the threats to his presidency. Unlike previous Republican Administrations, Fortress Trump contains no party elder with the stature to check the President's decisions. "There is no one around

him who has the ability to restrain any of his impulses, on any issue ever, for any reason," Steve Schmidt, a veteran Republican consultant said.

Of greatest concern, Osnos (2017) reports that

Trump's insulation from unwelcome information appears · to be growing as his challenges mount. His longtime friend Christopher Ruddy, the C.E.O. of Newsmax Media . . . noticed that some of Trump's associates are unwilling to give him news that will upset him . . . Ruddy went on. "I already sense that a lot of people don't want to give him bad news about things. I've already been approached by several people that say, "He's got to hear this. Could you tell him?"

Psychopathology

Although no firm conclusions should be ventured or considered possible without detailed, firsthand knowledge or examination of President Trump, categorizations of him that have been suggested have included narcissism, psychopathic deviance, and attention deficit/ hyperactivity disorder (ADHD). Despite the impossibility of a conclusion, discussion of which one of these may best fit the president has been lively. The assumption that there should be one best diagnosis, however, is at odds with important trends in how we view psychopathology in general. In fact, 50 percent of those qualifying for one diagnosis meet criteria for an additional diagnosis (Kessler et al. 2011). Thus, the inability to reach agreement among speculative diagnoses of the president's mental status may well reflect that *several* diagnoses may be pertinent. What is important is not a specific diagnosis but, rather, understanding the behavior patterns that raise concerns about mental status and that affect policy decisions and public welfare.

In addition to overlap among the categories, there is increasing recognition that the diagnostic categories of the DSM-V, the *Diagnostic and Statistical Manual* of the American Psychiatric Association (American Psychiatric Association 2013), are themselves flawed. For example, a diagnosis of major depressive disorder requires (a) either dysphoria or anhedonia (diminished ability to feel pleasure); (b) four of seven symptoms, such as insomnia, fatigue, decreased concentration/indecisiveness; and (c) the presence of these most of the day and nearly every day for at least two weeks (Ritschel et al. 2013). That means that one person with dysphoria and symptoms one through four and another with anhedonia and symptoms four through seven both meet criteria for the same disorder, even though they have only one feature in common. Similar problems exist with other diagnostic categories, each judged by the presence or absence of sufficient numbers of symptoms or characteristics from a longer list of possible symptoms or features.

A recent approach to categorizing psychopathology that has been promoted by the National Institute of Mental Health focuses on individuals' strengths or deficits in more discrete categories of psychological function rather than the broad categories of DSM-V. Among these, for example, are acute threat or fear, potential threat or anxiety, sustained threat (such as in PTSD), loss, working memory, cognitive control, affiliation/attachment, social communication, perception/understanding of self and understanding of others, arousal, and biological rhythms (Kozak and Cuthbert 2016). The theme of this approach is that individual functions or groups of functions might account for patterns of aberrant behavior. In the case of President Trump, acute threat, cognitive control, affiliation/attachment, social communication, perception/understanding of both self and others, arousal, and biological rhythms are all functions that may be pertinent to a number of the concerns that have been raised about his behavior. From such a perspective, the issue is not which of such a group of psychological functions might be primary, but how they interact to lead to troublesome patterns of behavior that, in the case of the president, have substantial societal implications. So, an inability to identify "whether it's basically perceptions of self or perceptions of others" is of little concern. Rather, recognizing the confluence of deficits in these functions as they build an alarming pattern of behavior becomes the basis for sounding an alarm.

If we are to focus on more specific behavior patterns that raise concerns about the mental fitness of President Trump, we still have an outstanding question. How do we judge that a particular characteristic is abnormal, pathological, or indicative of compromised mental fitness? The field of psychopathology and abnormal psychology has long wrestled with this question. When does a quirk or a distinctive personal style become the object of clinical concern and the basis for encouraging the individual to recognize her/himself as having a problem or, even, qualifying for loss of rights or enforced hospital commitment? Among the criteria that have often been proposed for identifying pathology are: resistance to change or to normal social pressure; an almost automatic repetitiveness; disregard for consequences or an inability to adjust behavior according to consequences; harmfulness to self or others; negative impacts on relationships, work, or key interests; and distortions of reality that are frequent, disruptive, and go beyond normal variation in judgments and perceptions. The criteria for identifying psychopathology might be applied to judging the fitness of the president to exercise his power.

For example, what is striking is the persistence of some of his behavior in spite of strong disconfirmation, such as in his arguments about why Hillary Clinton won the popular vote, the size of his inaugural crowd, or the assertion that President Obama had wiretapped him and his colleagues during the election campaign. So, too, he seems not to notice the harmfulness of his behavior, such as in his contradictory and self-indicting comments about the firing of former FBI director James Comey. He also appears to deny or ignore the aggressiveness of his behavior, as in his admonition to "beat the crap out of him" (referring to a protester being removed from a campaign rally) or in the Twitter threat to Comey about the possible existence of recordings of their conversations. Remarkably, these patterns persist despite their negative characteristics receiving broad attention and even though they may place President Trump in jeopardy of criminal charges or impeachment.

Another approach to making the judgment that behavior is a problem lies in the criminal law for judging innocence by virtue of insanity. In most jurisdictions, the criteria for innocence are an inability to appreciate the criminality of one's actions and to conform one's behavior to the requirements of the law. Whether this is by virtue of schizophrenia or depression or personality disorder or some other posited diagnosis is not critical. What is determinative is the inability to follow the law and understand how it applies to one's own behavior. Clearly, many of the instances observed and widely remarked upon with regard to President Trump would suggest an inability on his part to recognize how his behavior is at odds with applicable laws, including the U.S. Constitution. In his disparaging comments about judicial decisions, and in his ad hominem attacks on a judge who presides over one of the cases in which he is a defendant, and in the comments indicating that he asked Comey about investigations of him during a conversation about Comey's tenure as FBI director, President Trump manifests an apparent lack of recognition of how his behavior is at odds with law, the Constitution, and important precedents for the conduct of his office.

The judgment of "innocent by virtue of insanity" is a legal decision, a finding of innocence, not a finding of psychopathology. Expert opinion about possible pathology may be pertinent to the finding but is not determinative. This suggests considering the judgment of fitness for office as not a medical or psychiatric or psychological question but as a legal and political judgment. As James Gilligan noted at the Yale conference, "It's not whether [President Trump] is mentally ill or not. It's whether he's dangerous or not"

(Milligan 2017; Osnos 2017; and Gilligan's essay in this book, "The Issue Is Dangerousness, Not Mental Illness"). Research and clinical knowledge about mental health may be helpful in making the judgment of dangerousness, but they do not themselves determine the decision. Abraham Lincoln apparently suffered serious depression, but few would say it compromised his ability to serve. Yet, the observations of experts in mental health and psychopathology suggest real liabilities in President Trump's behavior. The question remains, however: does it matter?

One answer to that final question has recently been posed by strong voices on the conservative side of the political spectrum. Under the title "Trump Has a Dangerous Disability," George Will wrote in the *Washington Post*, on May 3, 2017:

> It is urgent for Americans to think and speak clearly about President Trump's inability to do either [i.e., think and speak clearly]. This seems to be not a mere disinclination but a disability. It is not merely the result of intellectual sloth but of an untrained mind bereft of information and married to stratospheric self-confidence . . .
>
> His fathomless lack of interest in America's path to the present and his limitless gullibility leave him susceptible to being blown about by gusts of factoids that cling like lint to a disorderly mind.
>
> Americans have placed vast military power at the discretion of this mind, a presidential discretion that is largely immune to restraint by the Madisonian system of institutional checks and balances.

Writing two days later, on May 5, 2017, also in the *Washington Post*, Charles Krauthammer articulated further the psychological dimensions of President Trump's fitness to serve:

And this is not to deny the insanity, incoherence and sheer weirdness emanating daily from the White House . . .

Loud and bombastic. A charlatan. Nothing behind the screen—other than the institutional chaos that defines his White House and the psychic chaos that governs his ever-changing mind . . .

Krauthammer goes on to describe what he considers to be a blunder of threatening to make South Korea pay for a defensive missile system and to renegotiate trade agreements. He asserts that this blunder forces

lingering fears about Trump. Especially because it was an unforced error. What happens in an externally caused crisis? Then, there is no hiding, no cushioning, no guardrail. It's the wisdom and understanding of one man versus whatever the world has thrown up against us. However normalized this presidency may be day to day, in such a moment all bets are off.

What happens when the red phone rings at 3 in the morning?

The Social, the Personal, and the President

Our culture tends to put the social and the personal in opposition. Echoing the tradition of the "self-made man," or Governor Romney's campaigning about "job creators," President Trump himself has bristled at suggestions that his business accomplishments are not wholly of his own doing. Consider, too, the scorn of many for Hillary Clinton's book title *It Takes a Village*, and contrast that title with Nancy Reagan's admonition to "Just say 'no.'" But a major trend in social and behavioral science of the past decades is toward an integration of the development and behavior of the individual with the contexts of culture, community, family, neighborhood (e.g., Fisher 2008).

Among numerous examples, living in a neighborhood with only fast-food outlets and no supermarkets raises one's chances of being obese far more than living in a neighborhood with only supermarkets, even after controlling for important factors such as education, ethnicity, and income (Morland, Diez Roux, and Wing 2006). Similarly, after controlling for other characteristics, community violence is associated with numbers of individuals with asthma and with the frequency of their problems with the disease (Wright et al. 2004; Sternthal et al. 2010). Thus, our social and community contexts have real impacts on our behavior and health. Key, however, to this perspective is recognition of the reciprocal nature of influence; just as the community may influence the family, so the family may influence the community, and the individual may influence both.

The interaction of the personal and the contextual can be seen in President Trump's often-alleged narcissism and heightened sensitivity to personal insult. A common effect of these is an erosion of social connections as slights lead to aggressive responses that drive others away. The contrast with President Kennedy's assembly of advisers during the Cuban Missile Crisis is not between one who is socially well connected and one who is socially isolated. President Trump clearly has a number of friends and social contacts. How his personal characteristics may limit the nature and variety of the advice he receives, however, may be a major difference. According to Robert Kennedy's memoir, if President Kennedy became aware that some with alternative views had been excluded from meetings, he would often "enlarge the meetings to include other options . . . President Kennedy wanted people who raised questions, who criticized, on whose judgment he could rely, who presented an intelligent point of view regardless of their rank or viewpoint."

The apparent extent of President Trump's narcissism has drawn increasing attention. In varied meetings and interviews, his preoccupation with and exaggeration of the size of his Electoral College victory, his claims that voter fraud accounted for Secretary Clinton's popular vote margin of over 3 million, and his claims about the size of the crowd at his inauguration have been remarkable. Central to narcissism is the self-referential defense. In response to strong condemnation of his sharing highly classified intelligence information with Russian foreign minister Lavrov and Russian ambassador Kislyak, his first tweet read, "As President I wanted to share with Russia . . . which I have the absolute right to do, facts pertaining . . ." Noteworthy is the primacy in the tweet of his role "as President" and his "absolute right." Closely related, too, is the attention to power. Commenting on the choices to disclose top-secret information to the Russians, to be the first to congratulate President Erdogan for a disputed election victory that shrank democratic processes in Turkey, and to praise and invite to the White House President Duterte, widely blamed for thousands of extrajudicial killings in the Philippines, political commentator and journalist Eugene Robinson (2017) summarized it well: "He conflates power with virtue."

Reflecting the interplay of personal and social, narcissistic concerns for self and a preoccupation with power may initially shape and limit those invited to the narcissistic leader's social network. Sensitivity to slights and angry reactions to them may further erode it. Those left tend to be indulgent of the individual and to persist for other gains. Either way, the advice and counsel they provide are liable to be guided by their motives for persisting. Also, those who remain are likely to be constrained lest ill-considered words create a rift that distances them and compromises the gains they anticipate. A disturbing feature of this kind of dynamic is that it tends to feed on itself. The more the individual selects those who flatter him and avoid confrontation, and the more those who have affronted and been castigated fall away, the narrower and more homogenous his network becomes, further flattering the individual but eventually becoming a thin precipice. President Nixon, drunk and reportedly conversing with the pictures on the walls, and praying with Henry Kissinger during his last nights in office, comes to mind.

The shrinking of the network to those most loyal in spite of affronts and exploitative treatment applies to the relationships of the office of the president with national and international allies. A number of commentators have suggested that Republicans in the House of Representatives who voted for a new health care bill in early May 2017 would have given President Trump an opportunity to claim an accomplishment around the end of his first one hundred days in office, while giving themselves major problems in their reelection campaigns in 2018. So, too, much has been written about the international importance of trust in the president's words. Especially as his own and his advisers' descriptions of the firing of FBI director Comey have collided, and after his sharing of highly classified intelligence information with the Russian foreign minister and ambassador to the United States, writers have questioned the ability of President Trump to draw allies together in a major crisis if they are untrusting of his assurances or his characterizations of events. Writing in 1967, Robert Kennedy anticipated much of this concern:

> [H]ow important it was to be respected around the world, how vital it was to have allies and friends. Now, five years later, I discern a feeling of isolationism in Congress and through the country, a feeling that we are too involved with other nations, a resentment of the fact that we do not have greater support in Vietnam, an impression that our AID program is useless and our alliances dangerous. I think it would be well to think back to those days in October, 1962.

Kennedy goes on to recount the importance of the support from the Organization of American States, the NATO allies, and critical countries in Africa (Guinea and Senegal), from which Russian planes might have delivered arms to Cuba, circumventing the quarantine.

The trust and affirmation of all of these "changed our position from that of an outlaw acting in violation of international law into a country acting in accordance with . . . allies."

The narcissism that is central to the shrinking networks of those who seek blind loyalty and flattery in their relationships leads also to a preoccupation with the credit and praise received. President Trump's preoccupation with his election or the size of his inaugural crowd contrasts sharply with President Kennedy's stance at the end of the thirteen days:

> After it was finished, he made no statement attempting to take credit for himself or for the Administration for what had occurred. He instructed all members of the Ex Comm and government that no interview should be given, no statement made, which would claim any kind of victory. He respected Khrushchev for properly determining what was in his own country's interest and what was in the interest of mankind. If it was a triumph, it was a triumph for the next generation and not for any particular government or people.

A fitting end to this chapter draws on the concluding words of Robert Kennedy's *Thirteen Days*: "At the outbreak of the First World War the ex-Chancellor of Germany, Prince von Bülow, said to his successor, 'How did it all happen?' 'Ah, if only we knew,' was the reply." Delicate are the dynamics and nuanced are the judgments that may keep the world safe or plunge it into the abyss. We are currently led by a man broadly flawed in his own person and supported by a truncated set of advisers. As the breadth and "vigor"—to use a word JFK favored—of advice sought by Kennedy in 1962 contrasts with that reported to surround President Trump, so the personal characteristics of President Trump leave us alarmed over the prospect of his narrowing further his network of advisers, leaving him few on whom to rely. The impulsive, ill-considered, narcissistic, reckless, and apparently intentional lies, threats, and bravado not only damage the country but may leave the president even more isolated. That President Trump might ever occupy the loneliness of deciding about a potentially catastrophic course of action is rightly our most urgent and greatest fear.

Coda

Apart from the contrasts drawn here, several similarities in their backgrounds and personal characteristics almost make Presidents Kennedy and Trump something of a natural experiment. Both of their fathers were highly successful in business, men who sometimes worked on both sides of the border of legality. Both were born to privilege. Both went to "the best schools." Both, apparently, were "womanizers," but also apparently cared much for their families. These similarities, along with the many contrasts in their behavior, point to the uncertainty in our understanding of all these matters. That uncertainty, however, leads us back to the wisdom of focusing on the actual behavior in question. Wisdom from the fields of psychology and medicine can illuminate our understanding of these problems, their social and personal sources, and the likelihood that they may change or be tempered by events, but judgment of them rests with us all.

Edwin B. Fisher, Ph.D., is a clinical psychologist and a professor in the Department of Health Behavior in the Gillings School of Global Public Health at the University of North Carolina at Chapel Hill. He is a past president of the Society of Behavioral Medicine and editor of Principles and Concepts of Behavioral Medicine: A Global Handbook *(Springer, 2017). In addition to community and peer support in health and health care, asthma, cancer, diabetes, smoking cessation, and weight management, he has written on concepts of psychopathology, including depression and schizophrenia, and on the relationships between mental illness and physical disease.*

Acknowledgments

Thanks to Rebecka Rutledge Fisher, Ruth Salvaggio, Kathryn Skol, Barbara and Richard Vanecko, and to the editor, Bandy Lee, for their helpful comments on a preliminary draft.

References

American Psychiatric Association. 2013. *Diagnostic and Statistical Manual of Mental Disorders.* 5th ed. Arlington, VA: American Psychiatric Association.

Cohen, S., W. J. Doyle, D. P. Skoner, B. S. Rabin, and J. M. Gwaltney. 1997. "Social Ties and Susceptibility to the Common Cold." *Journal of the American Medical Association* 277 (24): 1940–44.

Fisher, E. B. 2008. "The Importance of Context in Understanding Behavior and Promoting Health." *Annals of Behavioral Medicine* 35 (1): 3–18.

Goffman, E. 1961. *Asylums.* New York: Doubleday.

Haberman, M., and G. Thrush. 2017. "Trump Reaches Beyond West Wing for Counsel." *New York Times*, April 22.

Halberstam, D. 1972. *The Best and the Brightest.* New York: Random House.

Holt-Lunstad, J., T. B. Smith, and J. B. Layton. 2010. "Social Relationships and Mortality Risk: A Meta-Analytic Review." *PLOS Medicine* 7 (7): e1000316. doi: 10.1371/journal.pmed.1000316.

House, J. S., K. R. Landis, and D. Umberson. 1988. "Social Relationships and Health." *Science* 241: 540–44.

Kennedy, R. F. 1971. *Thirteen Days: A Memoir of the Cuban Missile Crisis.* New York: W. W. Norton.

Kessler, R. C., J. Ormel, M. Petukhova, K. A. McLaughlin, J. G. Green, L. J. Russo, D. J. Stein, A. M. Zaslavsky, S. Aguilar-Gaxiola, J. Alonso, L. Andrade, C. Benjet, G. de Girolamo, R. de Graaf, K. Demyttenaere, J.

Fayyad, J. M. Haro, Cy Hu, A. Karam, S. Lee, J. P. Lepine, H. Matchs-
inger, C. Mihaescu-Pintia, J. Posada-Villa, R. Sagar, and T. B. Ustun.
2011. "Development of Lifetime Comorbidity in the World Health
Organization World Mental Health Surveys." *Archives of General
Psychiatry* 68 (1): 90–100. doi: 10.1001/archgenpsychiatry.2010.180.

Kozak, M. J., and B. N. Cuthbert. 2016. "The NIMH Research Domain
Criteria Initiative: Background, Issues, and Pragmatics." *Psychophysiol-
ogy* 53 (3): 286–97. doi: 10.1111/psyp.12518.

Milligan, S. 2017. "An Ethical Dilemma. Donald Trump's Presidency Has
Some in the Mental Health Community Re-evaluating Their Role." *US
News & World Report*, April 21.

Morland, K., A. V. Diez Roux, and S. Wing. 2006. "Supermarkets, Other
Food Stores, and Obesity: The Atherosclerosis Risk in Communities
Study." *American Journal of Preventive Medicine* 30 (4): 333–39.

Neustadt, R. E., and G. T. Allison. 1971. "Afterword." In Robert F. Kennedy, *Thirteen Days: A Memoir of the Cuban Missile Crisis*. New York:
W. W. Norton.

Osnos, E. 2017. "Endgames: What Would It Take to Cut Short Trump's
Presidency?" *The New Yorker*, May 8, pp. 34–45.

Ritschel, L. A., C. F. Gillespie, E. O. Arnarson, and W. E. Craighead. 2013.
"Major Depressive Disorder." *Psychopathology: History, Diagnosis, and
Empirical Foundations.* Ed. by W. E. Craighead, D. J. Miklowitz, and
L. W. Craighead. Hoboken, NJ: Wiley, pp. 285–333.

Robinson, E. 2017. *Morning Joe.* MSNBC, May 16.

Rogers, E. M., and D. L. Kincaid. 1981. *Communication Networks: Toward a
New Paradigm for Research.* New York: Free Press.

Steptoe, A., A. Shankar, P. Demakakos, and J. Wardle. 2013. "Social Isolation,
Loneliness, and All-Cause Mortality in Older Men and Women."
Proceedings of the National Academy of Sciences USA 110 (15): 5797–801. doi:
10.1073/pnas.1219686110.

Sternthal, M. J., H. J. Jun, F. Earls, and R. J. Wright. 2010. "Community Violence
and Urban Childhood Asthma: A Multilevel Analysis." *European Respi-
ratory Journal* 36 (6): 1400–9. doi: 10.1183/09031936.00003010.

Tribe, Lawrence. 2017. On *Last Word with Lawrence O'Donnell*. MSNBC,
    May 11.

Whipple, Chris. 2017. *The Gatekeepers*. New York: Penguin Random House.

Wright, R. J., H. Mitchell, C. M. Visness, S. Cohen, J. Stout, R. Evans, and
    D. R. Gold. 2004. "Community Violence and Asthma Morbidity: The
    Inner-City Asthma Study." *American Journal of Public Health* 94 (4):
    625–32.

HE'S GOT THE WORLD IN HIS HANDS AND HIS FINGER ON THE TRIGGER

The Twenty-Fifth Amendment Solution

NANETTE GARTRELL, M.D., AND DEE MOSBACHER, M.D., PH.D.

In 1994, President Jimmy Carter lamented the fact that we have no way of ensuring that the person entrusted with the nuclear arsenal is mentally and physically capable of fulfilling that responsibility (Carter 1994). Throughout U.S. history, presidents have suffered from serious psychiatric or medical conditions, most of which were unknown to the public. A review of U.S. presidential office holders from 1776 to 1974 revealed that 49 percent of the thirty-seven presidents met criteria that suggested psychiatric disorders (Davidson, Connor, and Swartz 2006). For example, Presidents Pierce and Lincoln had symptoms of depression (Davidson, Connor, and Swartz 2006); Nixon and Johnson, paranoia (Glaister 2008; Goodwin 1988), and Reagan, dementia (Berisha et al. 2015). President Wilson experienced a massive stroke that resulted in severely impaired cognitive functioning (Weinstein 1981). Although military personnel who are responsible for relaying nuclear orders must undergo rigorous mental health and medical evaluations that assess psychological, financial, and medical fitness for duty (Osnos 2017; Colón-Francia and Fortner 2014), there is no such requirement for their commander in chief.

Over the course of the U.S. 2016 presidential campaign, it became increasingly apparent that Donald Trump's inability or unwillingness to distinguish fact from fiction (Barbaro 2016), wanton disregard for the rule of law (Kendall 2016), intolerance of perspectives different from his own (DelReal and Gearan 2016), rageful responses to criticism (Sebastian 2016), lack of impulse control ("Transcript" 2016), and sweeping condemnations of entire populations (Reilly 2016) rendered him temperamentally unsuitable to be in command of the nuclear arsenal. When Mr. Trump became the president-elect, we, as psychiatrists, had grave concerns about his mental stability and fitness for office. Despite the claim by gastroenterologist Dr. Harold Bornstein that Mr. Trump "will be the healthiest individual ever elected to the presidency" (Schecter, Francescani, and Connor 2016), there is no evidence that Mr. Trump has ever received psychological testing or a neuropsychiatric examination. In fact, there is no evidence that any prior president completed such an evaluation before assuming the duties of office.

On November 10, 2016, we received a call from our psychiatrist friend and colleague Judith Herman, M.D., who shared our concerns about Mr. Trump's grandiose, belligerent, and unpredictable behavior. She proposed that we send a private letter to President Obama outlining our observations, and recommending an impartial psychiatric evaluation of the president-elect. We agreed that such an assessment was warranted as a matter of national security. Dr. Herman offered to draft the letter. Each of us took responsibility for contacting colleagues who might be interested in cosigning.

The three of us have been allies since the early 1980s. As members of the Harvard Medical School faculty, Dr. Herman collaborated with Dr. Gartrell on national studies of sexually abusive physicians, and on mental health projects for the American Psychiatric Association. We knew that we could count on one another to be efficient and ethical.

At the end of November, the letter was sent to President Obama, stating that Mr. Trump's "widely reported symptoms of mental instability—including grandiosity, impulsivity, hypersensitivity to slights or criticism, and an apparent inability to distinguish fantasy from reality—lead us to question his fitness for the immense responsibilities of the office" (Greene 2016). We also strongly recommended that the president-elect receive a "full medical and neuropsychiatric evaluation by an impartial team of investigators."

We heard nothing from the White House. On December 16, Drs. Gartrell and Mosbacher were contacted by a journalist asking if we knew of any mental health professionals who would be willing to comment on Mr. Trump's psychiatric conditions. The three of us decided that we were willing to take the step of sharing our letter, in the interest of placing our recommendation in the public discourse. The journalist asked our permission to circulate the letter, and the next thing we knew, it was published in the *Huffington Post* (Greene 2016). It went viral (Pasha-Robinson 2016). The coverage seemed to reflect a sense of foreboding that Mr. Trump's erratic behavior represented a danger to the world order (Pasha-Robinson 2016; "Grave Concerns" 2016). We declined all requests for further comment, since most journalists wanted us to specify psychiatric diagnoses for the president-elect, even though we had not personally evaluated him.

Gloria Steinem posted the *Huffington Post* article on her Facebook page, and contacted JH to brainstorm about who in the government could implement our recommendation. Robin Morgan suggested that we convey our letter to Gen. Joseph Dunford, chairman of the Joint Chiefs of Staff, and reminded us of the series of events that transpired during the final days of the Nixon administration. Because President Nixon was drinking heavily and threatening war (Davidson, Connor, and Swartz 2006), the secretary of defense, James Schlesinger, instructed the military not to act on orders from the White House to deploy nuclear weapons unless authorized by Schlesinger or the secretary of state, Henry Kissinger (McFadden 2014). Robin Morgan thought that it would be useful for Chairman Dunford and the Joint Chiefs to be apprised of this history, because of Mr. Trump's imminent access to the nuclear arsenal. Drs. Gartrell and Mosbacher contacted colleagues to obtain Chairman Dunford's official e-mail address. On January 3, we sent our letter to Chairman Dunford, with the subject line: "An urgent matter of national security."

A week later, Dr. Gartrell met a woman who worked in government intelligence. Dr. Gartrell inquired if she would be willing to convey our recommendation to other professionals at the agency. The woman agreed to distribute our letter among key individuals who shared our views about Mr. Trump's mental instability.

As Inauguration Day grew closer, Dr. Gartrell, Dr. Mosbacher, Dr. Herman, Gloria Steinem, and Robin Morgan decided to send our letter to members of Congress whom we know personally or to whom we had access. We also agreed to publicize our recommendation whenever there was an opportunity. Dr. Mosbacher called House Minority Leader Nancy Pelosi and sent our letter to her. Gloria Steinem conveyed our letter to Senator Chuck Schumer, and Dr. Mosbacher discussed our recommendation with Senator Elizabeth Warren. At the Women's March on Washington, Gloria Steinem quoted our recommendation during her speech ("Voices of the Women's March" 2017). Robin Morgan read our letter during her Women's Media Center Live radio show (Morgan 2017a), and quoted it in her blog (Morgan 2017b).

Since being sworn in, Mr. Trump's impulsive, belligerent, careless, and irresponsible behavior has become even more apparent:

- He has angry outbursts when facts conflict with his fantasies (Wagner 2017). The day after the inauguration, he lashed out at the media for contradicting his claim that there were "a million, a million and a half people" on the Mall listening to his speech (Zaru 2017).

- His opposition to the press borders on paranoia (Page 2017). He screams at the television when his ties to Russia are mentioned (Pasha-Robinson 2017). He calls the media "the enemy of the people" (Siddiqui 2017).

- He deflects the blame for failed operations, such as the air strike he authorized in Yemen that killed thirty civilians and a U.S. Navy SEAL (Schmitt and Sanger 2017; Ware 2017).

- He makes false and unsubstantiated claims that are easily disputed, asserting, for instance, that the Yemen action yielded significant intelligence (McFadden et al. 2017), and accusing President Obama of spying on Trump Tower (Stefansky 2017).

- He discredits other branches of the government. After issuing an executive order banning immigration from seven Muslim-majority countries, Mr. Trump sought to delegitimize the decisions of federal courts that imposed a halt to the ban, and used demeaning language to dishonor the judiciary (e.g., referring to James Robart as a "so-called judge") (Forster and Dearden 2017).

- He praises authoritarian leaders of other countries. Mr. Trump admires despots Vladimir Putin, Kim Jong-un, and Rodrigo Duterte (*New York Times* Editorial Board 2017; Pengelly 2017), and invited Abdel Fatah al-Sissi and Recep Tayyip Erdogan to the White House (Nakamura 2017; DeYoung 2017).

- He deflects attention from Russia's interference in the 2016 election. After firing the director of the FBI during its criminal investigation into collaboration between Russian intelligence and the Trump campaign, Mr. Trump met with Putin's senior diplomat and revealed highly classified intelligence (Miller and Jaffe 2017).

- He is indifferent to the limits of presidential powers and fails to understand the duties of the office. He could not answer the simple question "What are the top three functions of the United States government?" (Brown 2016).

- He provokes North Korea with casual references to impending military actions. Mr. Trump claimed that an "armada" was steaming toward North Korea as a "show of force," resulting in a defensive response from Kim Jong-un, whose state news agency called Mr. Trump's bluff "a reckless act of aggression to aggravate tension in the region" (Sampathkumar 2017).

All in all, Mr. Trump's hostile, impulsive, provocative, suspicious, and erratic conduct poses a grave threat to our national security.

The Twenty-Fifth Amendment to the U.S. Constitution addresses presidential disability and succession (Cornell University Law School, 2017). Section 4 of this amendment has never been invoked to evaluate whether a standing president is fit to serve. We (Drs. Gartrell and Mosbacher) call on Congress to act now within these provisions to create an independent, impartial panel of investigators to evaluate Mr. Trump's fitness to fulfill the duties of the presidency. We urge Congress to pass legislation to ensure that future presidential and vice-presidential candidates are evaluated by this professional panel before the general election, and that the sitting president and vice president be assessed on an annual basis. We also recommend that panel members receive all medical and mental health reports on the president and vice president, with the authorization to request any additional evaluations that the panel deems necessary.

Our specific recommendations are as follows:

- Under Section 4 of the Twenty-Fifth Amendment to the U.S. Constitution, Congress should immediately constitute an independent, nonpartisan panel of mental health and medical experts to evaluate Mr. Trump's capability to fulfill the responsibilities of the presidency.

- The panel should consist of three neuropsychiatrists (one clinical, one academic, and one military), one clinical psychologist, one neurologist, and two internists.

- Panel members should be nominated by the nonpartisan, non-governmental National Academy of Medicine (Abrams 1999).

- The experts should serve six-year terms, with a provision that one member per year be rotated off and replaced (Abrams 1999).

- Congress should enact legislation to authorize this panel to perform comprehensive mental health and medical evaluations of the president and vice president on an annual basis. This legislation should require the panel to evaluate all future presidential and vice-presidential candidates. The panel should also be empowered to conduct emergency evaluations should there be an acute change in the mental or physical health of the president or vice president.

- The evaluations should be strictly confidential unless the panel determines that the mental health or medical condition of the president or vice president renders her/him incapable of fulfilling the duties of office.

Congress must act immediately. The nuclear arsenal rests in the hands of a president who shows symptoms of serious mental instability. This is an urgent matter of national security. We call on our elected officials to heed the warnings of thousands of mental health professionals who have requested an independent, impartial neuropsychiatric evaluation of Mr. Trump. The world as we know it could cease to exist with a 3:00 a.m. nuclear tweet.

Nanette Gartrell, M.D., is a psychiatrist, researcher, and writer who was formerly on the faculties of Harvard Medical School and the University of California, San Francisco. Her forty-seven years of scientific investigations have focused primarily on sexual minority parent families. In the 1980s and '90s, Dr. Gartrell was the principal investigator of groundbreaking investigations into sexual misconduct by physicians that led to a clean-up of professional ethics codes and the criminalization of boundary violations. The Nanette K. Gartrell Papers are archived at the Sophia Smith Collection, Smith College.

Dee Mosbacher, M.D., Ph.D., is a psychiatrist and Academy Award–nominated documentary filmmaker who was formerly on the faculty of the University of California, San Francisco. As a public-sector psychiatrist, Dr. Mosbacher specialized in the treatment of patients with severe mental illness. She served as San Mateo County's medical director for mental health and was senior psychiatrist at San Francisco's Progress Foundation. The Diane (Dee) Mosbacher and Woman Vision Papers are archived at the Sophia Smith Collection, Smith College. Dr. Mosbacher's films are also contained within the Smithsonian National Museum of American History collection.

Acknowledgments

We thank Esther D. Rothblum, Ph.D.; Madelyn Kahn, M.D.; Judith Herman, M.D.; Robin Morgan; Gloria Steinem; Mary Eichbauer, Ph.D.; Nate Gartrell; Marny Hall, Ph.D.; Kathryn Lee, M.D; and Patricia Speier, M.D., for their assistance in the preparation of this chapter.

References

Abrams, Herbert L. 1999. "Can the Twenty-Fifth Amendment Deal with a Disabled President? Preventing Future White House Cover-Ups." *Presidential Studies Quarterly* 29: 115–33.

Barbaro, Michael. 2016. "Donald Trump Clung to 'Birther' Lie for Years, and Still Isn't Apologetic." *New York Times*, September 16. www.nytimes .com/2016/09/17/us/politics/donald-trump-obama-birther.html?_r=1.

Berisha, Visar, Shuai Wang, Amy LaCross, and Julie Liss. 2015. "Tracking Discourse Complexity Preceding Alzheimer's Disease Diagnosis: A Case Study Comparing the Press Conferences of Presidents Ronald Reagan and George Herbert Walker Bush." *Journal of Alzheimer's Disease* 45: 959–63.

Brown, Lara. 2016. "Government Stumps Trump." *U.S. News & World Report*, March 31. www.usnews.com/opinion/blogs/opinion-blog/articles /2016-03-31/donald-trump-doesnt-understand-the-us-political-system -or-government.

Carter, Jimmy. 1994. "Presidential Disability and the Twenty-Fifth Amendment: A President's Perspective." *JAMA* 272: 1698.

Colón-Francia, Angelita, and Joel Fortner. 2014. "Air Force Improves Its Personnel Reliability Program." *U.S. Air Force News*, February 27. www .af.mil/News/Article-Display/Article/473435/af-improves-its-personnel -reliability-program/.

Cornell University Law School. 2017. "U.S. Constitution 25th Amendment." www.law.cornell.edu/constitution/amendmentxxv.

Davidson, Jonathan R. T., Kathryn M. Connor, and Marvin Swartz. 2006. "Mental Illness in U.S. Presidents Between 1776 and 1974: A Review of Biographical Sources." *Journal of Nervous and Mental Disease* 194: 47–51.

DelReal, Joseph A., and Anne Gearan. 2016. "Trump Stirs Outrage After He Lashes Out at the Muslim Parents of a Dead U.S. Soldier." *Washington Post*, July 30. www.washingtonpost.com/politics/backlash-for-trump -after-he-lashes-out-at-the-muslim-parents-of-a-dead-us-soldier/2016 /07/30/34b0aad4-5671-11e6-88eb-7dda4e2f2aec_story.html?utm_term= .b5ffdee05a40.

DeYoung, Karen. 2017. "U.S.-Turkish Relations Deeply Strained Ahead of Erdogan's Visit to White House." *Washington Post*, May 14. www .washingtonpost.com/world/national-security/us-turkish-relations -deeply-strained-ahead-of-erdogans-visit-to-white-house/2017/05/14 /40797a5c-3736-11e7-b412-62beef8121f7_story.html?utm_term= .58cb9d1f490f.

Forster, Katie, and Lizzie Dearden. 2017. "Donald Trump Calls Judge's Suspension of Immigration Ban 'Ridiculous' and Says It Will Be Overturned." *Independent*, February 4. www.independent.co.uk/news /world/americas/donald-trump-muslim-ban-judge-suspended-reacts -big-trouble-tweet-immigration-bob-ferguson-a7562671.html.

Glaister, Dan. 2008. "Recordings Reveal Richard Nixon's Paranoia." *Guardian*, December 3. www.theguardian.com/world/2008/dec/03/richard -nixon-tapes.

Goodwin, Richard N. 1988. "President Lyndon Johnson: The War Within." *New York Times*, August 21. www.nytimes.com/1988/08/21/magazine /president-lyndon-johnson-the-war-within.html?pagewanted=all.

" 'Grave Concerns' About Trump's Mental Stability: Top U.S. Professors." 2016. *Times of India*, December 20. http://timesofindia.indiatimes.com /world/us/grave-concerns-about-trumps-mental-stability-top-us -professors/articleshow/56076603.cms.

Greene, Richard. 2016. "Is Donald Trump Mentally Ill? 3 Professors of Psychiatry Ask President Obama to Conduct 'A Full Medical and Neuropsychiatric Evaluation.' " *Huffington Post*, December 17. www .huffingtonpost.com/richard-greene/is-donald-trump-mentally_b _13693174.html.

Kendall, Brent. 2016. "Trump Says Judge's Mexican Heritage Presents 'Absolute Conflict.' " *Wall Street Journal*, June 3. www.wsj.com/articles /donald-trump-keeps-up-attacks-on-judge-gonzalo-curiel-1464911442.

McFadden, Cynthia, William M. Arkin, Ken Dilanian, and Robert Windrem. 2017. "Yemen SEAL Raid Has Yielded No Significant Intelligence: Officials." NBC News, February 28. www.nbcnews.com/news

/investigations/yemen-seal-raid-yielded-no-significant-intelligence
-say-officials-n726451.

McFadden, Robert D. 2014. "James R. Schlesinger, Willful Aide to Three
Presidents, Is Dead at 85." *New York Times*, March 27. www.nytimes
.com/2014/03/28/us/politics/james-r-schlesinger-cold-war-hard-liner
-dies-at-85.html.

Miller, Greg, and Greg Jaffe. 2017. "Trump Revealed Highly Classified
Information to Russian Foreign Minister and Ambassador." *Washington Post*, May 15. www.washingtonpost.com/world/national-security
/trump-revealed-highly-classified-information-to-russian-foreign
-minister-and-ambassador/2017/05/15/530c172a-3960-11e7-9e48
-c4f199710b69_story.html?utm_term=.495bc0f95d9d.

Morgan, Robin. 2017a. "Women's Media Center Live with Robin Morgan."
WMC Live #197: Farai Chideya." February 19. http://wmclive.com
/wmc-live-197-farai-chideya-original-airdate-2192017.

———. 2017b. "20 Feb: The Real Story." *Robin Morgan* (blog). February 20.
www.robinmorgan.net/blog/the-real-story/.

Nakamura, David. 2017. "Trump Welcomes Egypt's Sissi to White House in
Reversal of U.S. Policy." *Washington Post*, April 3. www.washingtonpost
.com/politics/trump-welcomes-egypts-sissi-to-white-house-in-reversal
-of-us-policy/2017/04/03/36b5e312-188b-11e7-bcc2-7d1a0973e7b2_story
.html?utm_term=.8edadf26503f.

New York Times Editorial Board. 2017. "Donald Trump Embraces Another
Despot." *New York Times*, May 1. www.nytimes.com/2017/05/01/opinion
/donald-trump-embraces-rodrigo-duterte.html?_r=0.

Osnos, Evan. 2017. "How Trump Could Get Fired." *The New Yorker*, May 8.
www.newyorker.com/magazine/2017/05/08/how-trump-could-get
-fired.

Page, Clarence. 2017. "What's Next for Trump's War Against the Free Press?"
Chicago Tribune, February 21. www.chicagotribune.com/news/opinion
/page/ct-trump-media-war-fake-news-perspec-0222-20170221-column
.html.

Pasha-Robinson, Lucy. 2016. "Harvard Professor Says There Are 'Grave Concerns' About Donald Trump's Mental Stability." *Independent*, December 18. www.independent.co.uk/news/world/americas/us-elections /harvard-professors-us-president-barack-obama-grave-concern-donald -trump-mental-stability-a7482586.html.

———. 2017. "Donald Trump 'Has Been Screaming at the Television About Russia Links Investigation,' Says White House Adviser." *Independent*, May 10. www.independent.co.uk/news/world/americas/donald -trump-russia-links-scream-television-james-comey-fired-fbi-director -investigation-white-house-a7727516.html.

Pengelly, Martin. 2017. "North Korea: Trump Keeps Options Open Against 'Smart Cookie' Kim Jong-un." *Guardian*, April 30. www.theguardian .com/us-news/2017/apr/30/trump-vague-possible-us-strike-north-korea -chess-game.

Reilly, Katie. 2016. "Here Are All the Times Donald Trump Insulted Mexico." *Time*, August 31. http://time.com/4473972/donald-trump-mexico -meeting-insult/.

Sampathkumar, Mythili. 2017. " 'Armada' Trump Claimed Was Deployed to North Korea Actually Heading to Australia." *Independent*, April 19. www.independent.co.uk/news/world/americas/us-politics/donald -trump-north-korea-aircraft-carrier-sailing-opposite-direction -warning-a7689961.html.

Schecter, Anna R., Chris Francescani, and Tracy Connor. 2016. "Trump Doctor Who Wrote Whole Health Letter in Just 5 Minutes as Limo Waited." NBC News, August 26. www.nbcnews.com/news/us-news /trump-doctor-wrote-health-letter-just-5-minutes-limo-waited-n638526.

Schmitt, Eric, and David E. Sanger. 2017. "Raid in Yemen: Risky from the Start and Costly in the End." *New York Times*, February 1. www .nytimes.com/2017/02/01/world/middleeast/donald-trump-yemen -commando-raid-questions.html.

Sebastian, Michael. 2016. "Here's How Presidents and Candidates Who Aren't Donald Trump Respond to Protesters." *Esquire*, March 15. www

.esquire.com/news-politics/news/a43020/heres-how-presidents-and
-candidates-who-arent-donald-trump-respond-to-protesters/.

Siddiqui, Sabrina. 2017. "Trump Press Ban: BBC, CNN and Guardian
Denied Access to Briefing." *Guardian*, February 25. www.theguardian
.com/us-news/2017/feb/24/media-blocked-white-house-briefing-sean
-spicer.

Stefansky, Emma. 2017. "Trump Refuses to Apologize, Drags Germany into
Absurd Wiretapping Lie." *Vanity Fair*, March 18. Accessed May 11, 2017.
www.vanityfair.com/news/2017/03/trump-refuses-to-apologize-drags
-germany-into-wiretapping-lie.

"Transcript: Donald Trump's Taped Comments About Women." 2016. *New
York Times*, October 8. www.nytimes.com/2016/10/08/us/donald
-trump-tape-transcript.html?_r=0.

"Voices of the Women's March: Angela Davis, Gloria Steinem, Madonna,
Alicia Keys, Janet Mock, and More." 2017. *Democracy Now*, January 23.
www.democracynow.org/2017/1/23/voices_of_the_womens_march
_angela.

Wagner, Alex. 2017. "Trump vs. the Very Fake News Media." *The Atlantic*,
February 17. www.theatlantic.com/politics/archive/2017/02/trump-vs
-the-very-fake-news-media/516561/.

Ware, Doug G. 2017. "Trump Deflects Blame for Yemen Raid That Killed U.S.
Navy SEAL." UPI, February 28. www.upi.com/Top_News/US/2017/02
/28/Trump-deflects-blame-for-Yemen-raid-that-killed-US-Navy-SEAL
/3241488319168/.

Weinstein, Edwin A. 1981. *Woodrow Wilson: A Medical and Psychological
Biography.* Princeton, NJ: Princeton University Press.

Zaru, Deena. 2017. "It Took FOIA for Park Service to Release Photos of Obama,
Trump Inauguration Crowd Sizes." CNN Politics, March 7. www.cnn
.com/2017/03/07/politics/national-park-service-inauguration-crowd
-size-photos/.

EPILOGUE

Reaching Across Professions

NOAM CHOMSKY, PH.D., WITH BANDY X. LEE, M.D., M.DIV.

The expertise that gives weight to professional opinion can also be its limitation. The benefits of knowing one area well can also blind one to the need for other perspectives. For this reason, professionals should not only speak out but speak to one another, across disciplines. I thus reached out to linguist and philosopher-historian Dr. Noam Chomsky, because of the following: He has arrived at similar conclusions about the seriousness of the risks outlined in this book, through different methods, which can be a powerful confirmation. He has criticized Democrats as well as Republicans. As socially engaged as he has been, his contributions as a cognitive scientist have been prominent and continuous over several decades, and he remains first and foremost a scholar and a teacher. Therefore, while we do not count him among the twenty-seven mental health experts who have contributed to the opinions of this volume, we respect him as another professional with whom we can begin a conversation. In response, he offered to edit excerpts of some of his past interviews in service of this epilogue.

Bandy Lee

It is pretty clear what is responsible for the rise of the support for Trump, and there is general agreement about it. If you take a simple look at economic statistics, much of the support for Trump is coming from mostly white, working-class people who have been cast by the wayside during the neoliberal period. They have lived through a generation of stagnation or decline—real male wages are about where they were in the 1960s. There has also been a decline in a functioning democracy, overwhelming evidence that their own elected officials barely reflect their interests and concerns. Contempt for institutions, especially Congress, has just skyrocketed. Meanwhile, there has of course been wealth created. It has gone into very few hands: mostly into a fraction of the top one percent, so there is enormous opulence.

There are two huge dangers that the human species face. We are in a situation where we need to decide whether the species survives in any decent form. One is the rising danger of nuclear war, which is quite serious, and the other is environmental catastrophe. Trump wants to virtually eliminate the Environmental Protection Agency, Richard Nixon's legacy, to cut back regulations, and race toward the precipice as quickly as possible. On militarism, he wants to raise the military budget, already over half of discretionary spending, leading right now to confrontations which could be extremely hazardous (Newman 2016).

The Bulletin of Atomic Scientists regularly brings together a group of scientists, political analysts, other serious people, to try to give some kind of estimate of what the situation of the world is. The question is: How close are we to termination of the species? And they have a clock, the Doomsday Clock. When it hits midnight, we are finished. End of the human species and much else. And the question every year is: How far is the minute hand from midnight?

At the beginning, in 1947, the beginning of the nuclear age, it was placed at seven minutes to midnight. It has been moving up and back ever since. The closest it has come to midnight was 1953. In

1953, the United States and Russia both exploded hydrogen bombs, which are an extremely serious threat to survival. Intercontinental ballistic missiles were all being developed. This, in fact, was the first serious threat to the security of the United States. Then, it came to two minutes to midnight. And it has been moving up and back since.

In 2014, the analysts took into account for the first time something that had been ignored: the fact that the nuclear age—the beginning of the nuclear age—coincided with the beginning of a new geological epoch, the so-called Anthropocene. There has been some debate about the epoch in which human activity is drastically affecting the general environment; there has been debate about its inception. But the World Geological Organization is settling on the conclusion that it is about the same time as the beginning of the nuclear age. So, we are in these two eras in which the possibility of human survival is very much at stake, and, with us, everything else, too, of course, all living—most living things, which are already under very severe threat. Well, a couple of years ago, the *Bulletin* began to take that into account and moved the minute hand up to three minutes to midnight, where it remained last year.

About a week into Trump's term, the clock was moved again, to two-and-a-half minutes to midnight. That is the closest it has been since 1953. And that means extermination of the species is very much an open question. I do not want to say it is solely the impact of the Republican Party—obviously, that is false—but they certainly are in the lead in openly advocating and working for destruction of the human species. I agree that is a very outrageous statement (Goodman and González 2017), but extreme dynamics are behind it, and we are all responsible.

Sooner or later the white working-class constituency will recognize, and in fact, much of the rural population will come to recognize, that the promises are built on sand. There is nothing there.

And then what happens becomes significant. In order to maintain his popularity, the Trump administration will have to try to find some means of rallying the support and changing the discourse from the policies that they are carrying out, which are basically a wrecking ball, to something else. Maybe scapegoating, saying, "Well, I'm sorry, I can't bring your jobs back because these bad people are preventing it." And the typical scapegoating goes to vulnerable people: immigrants, "terrorists," Muslims, and elitists, whoever it may be. And that can turn out to be very ugly.

I think that we should not put aside the possibility that there would be some kind of staged or alleged terrorist act, which can change the country instantly (Frel 2017).

In the United States, power is overwhelmingly and increasingly in the hands of a very narrow sector of corporate wealth, private wealth, and power—and they have counterparts elsewhere, who agree with them and interact with them partly. There is another dimension of "who rules the world." The public can have, sometimes does have, enormous power. We can go back to David Hume's first major modern work on political philosophy: *On the First Principles of Government*. He pointed out that force is on the side of the governed. Those who are governed have the force if they are willing to and eager to recognize the possibility to exercise it. Sometimes they do (Newman 2016).

Perhaps the movements we have been witnessing, starting with the Women's March on the day after the inauguration, represent the force within humankind that resists annihilation and gropes toward health and survival. Like Dr. Chomsky, who has worked tirelessly to inform and engage the public, we as mental health professionals and healers should welcome and assist any action in this direction, regardless of political attribution.

Bandy Lee

Noam Chomsky, Ph.D., is Professor Emeritus at the Massachusetts Institute of Technology, which he joined in 1955. Dr. Chomsky has written and lectured widely on linguistics, philosophy, intellectual history, contemporary issues, international affairs, and U.S. foreign policy, and is the recipient of numerous honorary degrees and awards. Among his more recent books are The Essential Chomsky; How the World Works; 9-11: Was There an Alternative?; On Western Terrorism: From Hiroshima to Drone Warfare *(with Andre Vltchek);* What Kind of Creatures Are We?; Why Only Us: Language and Evolution *(with Robert C. Berwick);* Who Rules the World?; *and* Requiem for the American Dream.

References

Frel, Jan. 2017. "Noam Chomsky: If Trump Falters with Supporters, Don't Put 'Aside the Possibility' of a 'Staged or Alleged Terrorist Attack.'" *Alternet*, March 27. www.alternet.org/right-wing/noam-chomsky-it -fair-worry-about-trump-staging-false-flag-terrorist-attack.

Goodman, Amy, and Juan González. 2017. "Full Interview: Noam Chomsky on Trump's First 75 Days & Much More." *Democracy Now*, April 4. www.democracynow.org/2017/4/4/full_interview_noam_chomsky_on _democracy.

Newman, Cathy. 2016. "Noam Chomsky Full Length Interview: Who Rules the World Now?" *Channel 4 News*, May 14. www.youtube.com/watch?v =P2lsEVlqts0&list=PLuXactkt8wQg9av3Wtu_xhZaAcTi4lF1M.

APPENDIX:

TRANSCRIPT OF THE YALE CONFERENCE

https://us.macmillan.com/static/duty-to-warn-conference-transcript.pdf

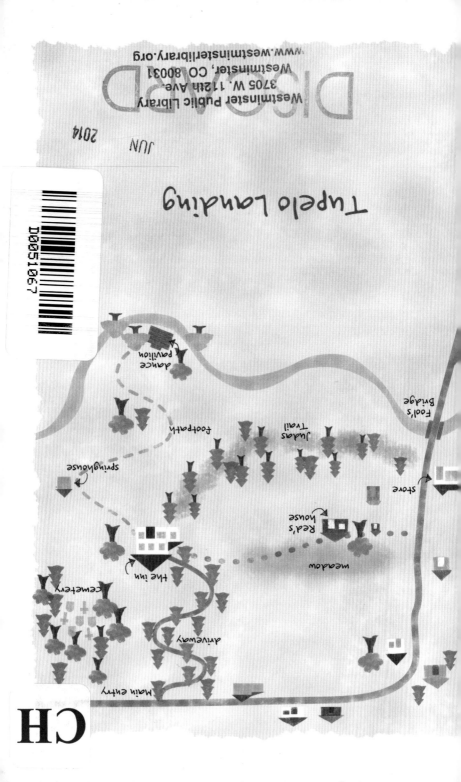

The Ghosts of Tupelo Landing

by Sheila Turnage

KATHY DAWSON BOOKS

an imprint of Penguin Group (USA) LLC

KATHY DAWSON BOOKS
Published by the Penguin Group
Penguin Group (USA) LLC
375 Hudson Street
New York, New York 10014

USA/Canada/UK/Ireland/Australia/New Zealand/India/South Africa/China

penguin.com

A Penguin Random House Company

Text copyright © 2014 by Sheila Turnage
Map copyright © 2014 by Eileen LaGreca

Library of Congress Cataloging-in-Publication Data
Turnage, Sheila.
The ghosts of Tupelo Landing / by Sheila Turnage.
pages   cm
Summary: "When Miss Lana accidentally buys a haunted inn at the
Tupelo Landing town auction, Desperado Detectives—aka Mo LoBeau and her
best friend Dale—opens up a paranormal division to solve the ghost's identity before
the town's big 250th anniversary bash"—Provided by publisher.
ISBN 978-0-8037-3671-9 (hardcover)
[1. Mystery and detective stories. 2. Hotels—Fiction.
3. Haunted places—Fiction. 4. Ghosts—Fiction. 5. Community life—
North Carolina—Fiction. 6. Identity—Fiction. 7. Foundlings—Fiction.
8. North Carolina—Fiction.] I. Title.
PZ7.T8488Gho 2014
[Fic]—dc23   2013019376

Printed in the United States of America

1 3 5 7 9 10 8 6 4 2

Designed by Jasmin Rubero
Text set in Carre Noir Std

For Rodney

Contents

The Ghosts of
Tupelo Landing

Chapter 1
A Master of Disguise

Desperado Detective Agency's second big case snuck up on Dale and me at the end of summer, dressed in the happy-go-lucky colors and excitement of an auction.

"Mystery is a master of disguise," Miss Lana always says, and this one proved her point. It pitched a red-and-white striped tent in a meadow by the ancient Tupelo Inn, on the edge of town, and plastered the countryside with notices of its arrival:

AUCTION, WEDNESDAY AUGUST 24—
THE OLD TUPELO INN!!
1880 inn & medicinal springs
Closed October 22, 1938
READ ALL FINE PRINT
Buddha Jackson, Auctioneer

The mystery Dale and I came face-to-face with there would wake up ghosts and shake up history.

Not that I—Miss Moses LoBeau, rising sixth grader and cofounder of Desperado Detective Agency—was thinking Mystery that Wednesday morning as I shov-

eled crushed ice into the café's water glasses. I scanned the breakfast crowd and the 7UP clock on the wall. 6:45 a.m.

Where on earth was Dale? He should have been here a half hour ago.

Dale Earnhardt Johnson III, my best friend and co-sleuth, lives just outside town. Ever since his daddy went back to jail, he's been sleeping ragged and long. So has his dog, Queen Elizabeth II.

"Order up!" the Colonel called over the café hubbub.

"Got it," Miss Lana cried, spinning past in her pale yellow 1950s sundress and glossy Ava Gardner wig. Miss Lana, a former rising star of the Charleston community theater, adores Old Hollywood and has the wigs to prove it. "Tuck your shirttail in, sugar," she murmured to me. "With the auction crowd blasting toward us, we'll be standing room only within the hour. We want to look our best center stage." She whirled away, her white sandals whispering against the tiles.

Miss Lana and the Colonel are my family of choice and I am theirs. We operate the café together. They like me to look good in a crowd.

I tucked in my shirt and grabbed some silverware for my friend Sally Amanda Jones, a fellow rising sixth grader. Salamander pushed her red Piggly Wiggly sunglasses up on top of her head. Sal's daddy stocks shelves

at the Pig and her mama sews. They aren't money, but there's not a sharper dresser in Tupelo Landing. "Pancakes, please. And . . . is Dale here?" she asked, her gray eyes hopeful as she peered toward the kitchen.

Sal loves Dale like midnight loves stars. So far, he hasn't noticed.

I broke the news easy: "Dale's in pre-arrival mode, but I'll check his ETA for you," I told her, and sped away.

"Batter Up on table four," I called as I passed the kitchen door.

The Colonel peeked out at me. He keeps his gray hair military short, but his brown eyes glow warm and friendly.

"Pancakes, sir," I explained. "New code."

He winked and the door swished shut behind him.

I grabbed the café phone and dialed. Dale picked up on the third ring. "H'llo," he mumbled. "Why is it?"

Why is it?

Unlike me, Dale doesn't wake up good. "Because," I replied. "They're auctioning the Tupelo Inn today and if you don't get over here, you'll miss our ride."

"Mo," he replied, and hung up. Dale's not an inline thinker.

I gave Sal a thumbs-up as a white minivan wheeled into our gravel parking lot. The Azalea Women, aka the Uptown Garden Club, tumbled out and scattered like

pigeons. They chatted their way to the café door, and threaded through the crowd.

"I'll be glad to see that old inn go," one said as they bumped two red Formica tables together near the jukebox.

"I hear murder closed it down," another added.

The café went quiet.

Murder?

Grandmother Miss Lacy Thornton, who sat at the counter serenely nibbling her toast, whipped around to stare at the Azalea Women. The toes of her navy pumps just grazed the floor. Grandmother Miss Lacy's short, like me. We aren't related by blood; she took me as her honorary granddaughter in first grade. She's the oldest *nice* person in Tupelo Landing. Also the richest.

"Rumor-mongering," she murmured. "How sad."

"Yes ma'am, it's tragic," I said, and waved at the Azalea Women. "Have a seat. I'll be right with you," I called, slipping a clue pad into my pocket.

Few people know it, but waitressing is like deep cover—with tips.

I ferried a tray of ice water to their table. "Did you mention a murder?" I asked, dealing the glasses around. "Because Desperado Detective Agency is now accepting new clients. Misdemeanors and felonies are our pleasure. Murder's our specialty. How may we help?"

It was borderline true.

Dale and me opened Desperado Detective Agency at the beginning of the summer and solved our first murder in June. Since then we'd had just two cases, both of a Lost Pet nature. First Hannah Greene's dog Mort, who we found running with a bad crowd at the trailer park. Then Sal's goldfish Big Frank, who'd gone dust-to-dust behind Sal's aquarium. Dale broke the news: "It looks like suicide," he'd told her, his voice grim.

A second high-profile murder would be good for business.

The Azalea Women looked away from Grandmother Miss Lacy's icy stare and studied their silverware.

I tried a different tack. "Today's low-carb iced beverage comes to you compliments of me," I said. I draped a paper napkin over my arm. "My name is Mo LoBeau, with the accent on the end. I'll be taking care of you ladies today."

"You don't need to introduce yourself, Mo," one of them said. "We've known you since the day you washed into town."

"True," I replied. "But I like to keep things professional to encourage tips—which, by the way, I'm saving for college. A possible orphan has to plan ahead. Today," I continued, "we got a breakfast menagerie, which is French for sausage and egg casserole with cheese. This

comes with hot biscuits au molasses for five dollars. For anyone trying to skinny down, I can substitute you a wheat toast with sugar free. What can I start you with?"

"Coffee and skinny," they chorused.

"An excellent choice. And your murder selection?"

This time the lead Azalea Woman stared straight at Grandmother Miss Lacy. "I won't go into details," she sniffed, "but I hear Red Baker's involved."

Crud. Another Red Baker rumor. Grandmother Miss Lacy shook her head.

"Believe you me," the Azalea Woman continued, her voice going stiletto, "whatever happened out at that old inn—if anything did—is Red Baker's fault. Or his people's before him."

I slapped my clue pad closed. A total dead end.

Red Baker, who lives outside town, mostly keeps to himself. The Colonel says he's second generation moonshine and 100 percent trouble. Mr. Red, who visits the café once in a blue moon, has never been mean to me. But it's a town rule that if anything goes wrong, he's behind it. Him or else Dale's daddy, Mr. Macon, if he's out on bail—which, at the moment, he ain't.

"Mark my words," the Azalea Woman said, her eyeglasses swinging on their chain, "Red Baker's people have always been bad news. And the apple doesn't fall far from the tree."

"Mine did," I reminded her. "I been searching for my family tree since the day I was born. All I know so far is it's somewhere Upstream." I headed for the kitchen. "I'll get your order in right away."

Minutes later, the café was hopping. "Let's chill things down, sugar," Miss Lana said, sashaying toward the air conditioner. Miss Lana's built tall and slender. I'm built more like a roller derby queen, but that could change at any minute.

Puberty happens.

While Miss Lana cranked the temp down, I turned the overhead fan to a quicker swipe. The auction notice on the bulletin board fluttered in the breeze. "Miss Lana," I said, "are we catering the auction? Because tips should be good once everybody gets whipped into a mindless frenzy, which the Colonel says is inevitable."

She smiled. Her Hollywood-style makeup gave her eyes a smoky, mysterious look. "Catering is a lovely idea. But no, you and I will travel incognito as part of the general public today. We'll leave after the breakfast rush," she added. "Miss Thornton's offered us a ride."

Miss Lana doesn't drive as a public courtesy.

"Batter Up," the Colonel barked, coming in from the kitchen. I grabbed Sal's pancakes as the café door swung open.

"Greetings, fellow citizens," Mayor Little sang, letting the door bang shut behind him. He smoothed his ice-blue tie over his round belly and took in Miss Lana's dark wig, sundress, and white sandals. "Ava Gardner, 1958," he guessed. He cocked his head. "Oh my, and Frank Sinatra on the jukebox. How romantic."

His tasseled loafers tick-tick-ticked across the tile floor. "Beautiful day for an auction," he said, slipping onto his regular stool. "Buddha gave me the VIP tour yesterday. The entire property is deliciously dilapidated, thoroughly antiquish. Nothing's changed since the day the inn closed. You can't put a price on that kind of charm, my friends. Not until the bidding starts, anyway," he added. He winked at the Azalea Women, who ignored him.

The Colonel splashed coffee in the mayor's cup. "What idiot would buy that dump?" the Colonel growled.

"Not me," Tinks Williams said, slapping his John Deere cap against his leg as he strolled in. "Roof leaks like a sieve last I heard."

The mayor tucked his napkin in his collar. "I'm picturing condos, golf courses . . . My friends, Fate smiles on Tupelo Landing today."

The Colonel snorted, did a quick about-face, and marched into the kitchen.

"Was it something I said?" Mayor Little asked, his neat eyebrows drifting up.

"Not exactly," I said, stepping onto the Pepsi crate I keep behind the counter for extra height. "It's just that the Colonel says Fate is bipolar and ought to be on medications. May I take your order?"

"The special," he said as Dale rocketed into view on his faded red bike, his mongrel dog Queen Elizabeth II loping behind. He performed a flying dismount at the edge of the parking lot and slung his bike into a patch of shade.

"Hey," he said, blasting through the door. His sandals squeaked to a halt and he ran his fingers through his blond hair. The men in Dale's family have scandalous good hair.

Sal knocked her pancake syrup over.

"Morning, Dale," Mayor Little said. "Solved any murders today?"

"No, sir," he replied, waving at Sal and me. "But it's early."

Like I say, Dale and me solved Mr. Jesse's murder at the beginning of the summer. We went famous for about a week until the gravity of habit pulled our lives back into regular orbit. Small towns have rules. One is, you got to stay who you are no matter how many mur-

ders you solve. That's why I'm back to being regular Mo LoBeau—the girl Luck washed into town the day she was born. And why Dale's back to being just plain Dale, the son of level-headed Miss Rose and the recently incarcerated Macon Johnson.

"Specials, you two?" Miss Lana offered, swishing by.

Dale vaulted onto a stool. Dale is athletic. I ain't. "Thanks, Miss Lana," he said. "Mama says will you please put it on her tab." Miss Lana smiled and slid us a basket of biscuits. Her and Miss Rose are best friends. There ain't no tab between them.

Fifteen minutes later, the café was standing room only— just as Miss Lana had predicted. Dale and me, who'd barely had time to brush the crumbs off our chins, flew around the café, carrying waters and taking orders. Miss Lana floated between phone, customers, and cash register, graceful as a dandelion seed on the wind.

I'd just cleared a table when Priscilla Retzyl, my teacher, swept in. A coffee cup shattered on the other side of the café. "No! My new shorts!" Dale cried. Even a whisper of teacher rattles him. Dale grabbed one of Miss Lana's aprons, and hustled to take another order.

As I turned, Anna Celeste Simpson—blond hair, brown eyes, perfect smile—stiff-armed me to grab a window table.

I am to Anna Celeste as Sherlock Holmes is to Moriarty: Enemies for life.

"Hey, *Attila*," I said.

"Mo-*ron*," she murmured. "Mother and I will have the Garden Omelets and tomato juice. Good morning, Miss Retzyl," she simpered, cutting her eyes toward our teacher. "I can't *wait* for school to start tomorrow."

School. Tomorrow.

The words thudded into my heart like dull wooden stakes.

"Make our omelets to go," Attila's sour-faced mother said, skinnying into the chair across from Attila. "I'm eager to scout the inn's antiques." She squinted at Attila. "Elbows, dear."

Attila took her elbows off the table.

I sighed. Take-out mostly means no tips. For me, tips matter. I currently got $7.26 to my name, plus a Canada dime somebody dumped in the tip jar.

"You look tired, Mo," Attila said, smiling to flaunt new braces. "Did your family vacation this summer? Mother and I loved Montreal."

Montreal? In *Canada?* I reached in my pocket, to my Canada dime.

I hate Anna Celeste Simpson.

"You want me to put an Official Rush on this order?

It only costs a dollar more per plate and that includes your tip," I offered.

"No," Attila said, flouncing her hair.

I scribbled her order: *2 Gardens. Take your time.*

As I worked my way back to the counter, Dale stuffed a biscuit in his apron pocket and headed for Queen Elizabeth II, who lay snuffling beneath a shrub. Queen Elizabeth's allergic to Miss Lana's rosemary plant. Also the big-haired twins.

I slid a special to Mayor Little, who smiled at Grandmother Miss Lacy. "Miss Thornton, do you remember the old inn's medicinal springs?"

"The springs? Goodness yes," Grandmother Miss Lacy said. "Those springs cured hundreds of people. Not everyone who came, of course. Which reminds me: Will the old cemetery be auctioned with the inn?"

The hair on the back of my neck stood up. *The old cemetery?*

The café clattered to silence.

"*Cemetery* is such an unwelcoming word," the mayor chided. "I prefer to think of it as a gated community for the dearly departed. Landscaping, ironwork, statuary . . ."

The screech of tires on pavement gobbled up the rest of his words.

The café whipped toward the window as a bright red

sports car skidded across the parking lot, spewing an arc of sand.

"Hey," Dale shouted, stepping in front of Queen Elizabeth. "Watch it!"

The car doors flew open. A dark-haired man and a blond woman jumped out, the woman shouting and the man jabbing his finger toward her face.

"Oh my," Miss Lana murmured as a boy—a younger, thinner version of the man—unfolded himself from the car. He wiped his palms on his shiny black slacks, looked from the man to the woman, and then at Dale.

Dale's flowered apron fluttered in the breeze.

The boy grabbed the man's arm and pointed. The trio turned to Dale like a pack of jackals. Dale's hand twitched toward the apron, but I knew he'd die before he took it off now. The man's laugh cracked like a whip.

Bullies.

My temper sprang straight to my mouth. "Hey you," I yelled, charging into the sunshine. "Crawl back in that clown car and get out of here."

Dale gasped.

"Not real clowns," I whispered. Dale has a terror of clowns. Also of ghosts.

The café door opened behind me, and the Colonel's hand fell gently on my shoulder. The man studied the Colonel and whispered in the woman's ear. The couple

jumped in the car and fishtailed across the parking lot.

"Wait!" the boy shouted. He chased the car for a few awkward steps. "Stop!" His arms fell to his sides as the car disappeared around the curve.

"Despicable," the Colonel muttered. "Never leave a comrade on the battlefield, Soldier."

"No sir," I said. "I won't."

"Me either," Dale said.

The Colonel glanced at Dale. "You're out of uniform, son."

Dale ripped the apron off and held it behind his back. "New shorts," he explained. That's what Dale bought with his summer job money: school clothes. That and a pawnshop guitar. Dale is musical. I ain't.

The boy from the car turned and walked toward us, barely whistling.

From a distance, I didn't like him. Up close, I liked him less. Black hair, thin face, mole under his left eye. Scuffed black shoes, cheap clothes put together to look like money. He walked up lanky as a coyote, his thin shoulders sloping a modicum to the left.

"At ease, you two," the Colonel said as the boy scuffled to a halt.

The boy's eyes drifted from the Colonel, to me, to Dale. "Crenshaw," he said, trying to make his voice low. "Harm Crenshaw." Like he was Bond, James Bond.

Give me a break.

"The Third," Dale replied. "Dale Earnhardt Johnson the Third. And this is LoBeau, Mo LoBeau. And . . ."

"The Colonel," I said before Dale could get tangled up.

Crenshaw, Harm Crenshaw nodded, not quite meeting our eyes. "I need a ride to the auction," he said, shoving his hands deep in his pockets. "Anybody going that way?"

Chapter 2
Crenshaw, Harm Crenshaw

An hour later Dale and me settled in the backseat of Grandmother Miss Lacy's old Buick. "I don't see why *he* has to ride with us," Dale said, watching Harm Crenshaw swagger across the parking lot.

"Grandmother Miss Lacy's generous about giving rides," I said. "It cuts both ways." The dark-haired boy opened Dale's door and peered in. "Queen Elizabeth gets queasy without a window seat," I told him. "You sit in the middle."

Harm Crenshaw crawled over Queen Elizabeth and Dale and collapsed into the space between us, reeking of cheap aftershave. I rolled my window down. "You aren't old enough to shave," I said. He stared straight ahead, his knobby knees nearly bumping his chin.

Grandmother Miss Lacy slipped behind the wheel and adjusted the rearview mirror. "You look familiar, Harm," she said as Miss Lana clambered into the front seat with her white parasol. "Have we met?"

"Nope. I'm here for the auction and then back to Greensboro fast as I can go."

"Don't 'nope' her," Dale said, pulling Queen Elizabeth into his lap. "It ain't polite."

Harm shifted, his pants legs rising to reveal pale, bony ankles and no socks. "Somebody told me the inn they're selling is haunted," he said. "It's got to be a lie. Who'd want to spend eternity *here?*"

I glared at him, but Dale gulped. "Haunted?"

"Don't be ridiculous," Grandmother Miss Lacy said. "I've lived here eighty years. If there were a ghost story connected to that inn, I assure you I'd know it."

We rode in silence past the Piggly Wiggly, past the old brick school, to the sign at town's edge: Tupelo Landing, population 148. Someone had scrawled a 7 over the 8. Harm Crenshaw raised an eyebrow. "Murder," I explained. "Dale and me solved it."

"Sure you did," he muttered.

"Press kit," Dale whispered.

I reached into my olive drab messenger bag and rummaged through the clue pads and hand-lettered business cards for our laminated newspaper clip. I passed it to him.

LOCAL KIDS HELP SOLVE MURDER

Miss Mo LoBeau and Dale Earnhardt Johnson III, ris-

ing sixth graders, have helped solve a murder, authorities say. In the process they also helped put Dale's father behind bars and jump-started the memory of Mo's guardian, the Colonel—a café owner who's had total amnesia for over a decade.

"To make a long story short, I remembered I'm an attorney and that I used to be engaged to Lana," the Colonel told this reporter. "Realizing I'm an attorney has been a blow, but Mo and Dale did a great job with their first case and I'm proud of them. Now order something or get out."

Mo and Dale, who founded Desperado Detective Agency in June, are accepting new cases. Call the café for details.

Harm Crenshaw handed it back without a word. *Jerk.*

"What are you buying today, Miss Lana?" I asked, to break the silence.

"An umbrella stand," she said. "A bit of Tupelo history."

"Boring," Harm Crenshaw said beneath his breath.

I elbowed him—hard.

"And I'm only here for the excitement," Grandmother Miss Lacy said.

We crept across Fool's Bridge, past the old store with its ancient bubble-headed gas pumps, through acres of

spent tobacco and drying corn. "Here's my old short-cut," Grandmother Miss Lacy said, easing the Buick onto a faint path. "Father used to come this way in the Duesenberg."

Dale jumped like Queen Elizabeth spotting a squirrel. "A *Duesenberg*?" He looked over at me. "Duesenbergs were super-expensive roadsters made in Germany," he said. Dale's people know cars.

"Made in Indiana, actually," Harm said as we bounced into a clearing. "Jeez," he gasped before Dale could reply. "Who lives *there*?"

The unpainted farm house listed on brick piers like a squared-off old woman rising on a bad knee. Queen Elizabeth jumped up, her tail wagging as she peered at a pack of bone-thin beagles in a rickety pen. "I believe that's Red Baker's place," Miss Lana said as the Buick eased forward. "Why?"

Harm shouldered Queen Elizabeth aside to stare out the window. "*Whose* place? Does he even have electricity?" Good question. There wasn't an electric line in sight.

"Red Baker," I said. "The moonshiner. The Azalea Women say—"

"Mo LoBeau," Grandmother Miss Lacy said, "I will not have you spreading rumors." She slammed on brakes, sending Queen Elizabeth tumbling to the floor,

and whipped around to stare at Harm. "Do you know Red Baker, young man?"

"Me? How would I know somebody like that?" The wind shifted and he grimaced. "Doesn't he ever clean out that dog pen? It stinks."

She gave him an inscrutable old-person stare as Dale hoisted a kicking Queen Elizabeth back in his lap. "Will wonders never cease," she murmured to Miss Lana, and turned back to her driving.

"Old people," Dale whispered. "Go figure."

Miss Lacy eased the Buick through Red Baker's dirt yard, into a grassy meadow of cars and trucks. Dale pointed to a red sports car as we tumbled from the Buick. "Over there," he said.

Harm stalked off without even a good-bye.

This time I said it out loud: "Jerk."

I did my Upstream Mother scan of the crowd—a check for possible relatives.

"See anybody that looks like you?" Dale asked.

I squinted. The grounds swarmed with strangers and townsfolk. The Azalea Women trooped toward the red-and-white auction tent. Sal, in her red sunglasses, sailed behind them. Miss Retzyl sat beneath the tent while Attila, who'd perched beside her, was chatting her so-called heart out.

I shook my head. "But there's Lavender!" I cried, and my morning went golden.

Dale's big brother, Lavender, stood in the shade of a maple, his tanned arms crossed, talking to one of the big-haired twins—either Crissy or Missy, I couldn't tell which. Have I mentioned I will one day marry Lavender? Lavender, who's nineteen, laughs whenever I ask him—which is not the same as saying no.

"Lavender," I bellowed, rocking up on my toes and waving. A grin split his face as I sprinted toward him. "Hey," I said, skidding to a sophisticated halt. "I see you run aground on a twin."

"Crissy," he said, "you remember Mo LoBeau and my little brother Dale, don't you?"

"Sure, I remember," she said, sipping a Diet 7UP. "I met them at the Speedway the night you wrecked your racecar. Met him too." She nodded toward a nearby picnic table. "He was driving the car that spun you into the wall."

"*He* did that?" I said, zeroing in on the driver of the red sports car.

"Flick Crenshaw," Lavender said. "He drives the 45 car." Flick looked about Lavender's age. Beyond that, they were alike as yes and no.

Lavender has eyes blue as October's sky and hair like

just-mown wheat. He's wiry and tall, and flows like a lullaby. Dark-haired Flick Crenshaw looked coiled and compact, an explosion set to happen. Flick smirked at us, scooped the blond woman close, and whispered in her ear. She barked out a laugh.

"Ignore them," Lavender said. "Cars bump, Mo. It's part of racing."

"Almost killing somebody ain't."

He shrugged. "Flick's one of those guys you pass in life. You steer around him if you can. If you can't, you don't let him slow you down more than you have to."

"Right," I said, making a mental note to hate Flick for eternity.

Crissy narrowed her eyes. "Wonder what Flick's doing here," she said. "You think he's buying the inn?"

"Nah," Lavender said. "If he has money he's driving it or wearing it. But I hear Red Baker's interested. His property backs up against this one. And he has money."

"He got most of Daddy's," Dale said. "That's what Mama says."

"Let's go talk to people," Crissy said, like Dale and me weren't people. She slipped her hand into Lavender's, but he didn't budge. I followed his gaze to Harm, who elbowed through the crowd with three drinks. Flick grabbed two, handed one to the blond, and punched Harm's shoulder. Harm swiveled with the blow, hiding a wince.

"That's Flick's little brother," Lavender said, glancing at Dale. "I'd stay away from him if I was you. He'll be trouble soon as he figures out how." Dale nodded.

"I'd love to stay and chat with you, Crissy," I said, "but I and Dale are here on detective business. Come on, Dale," I said. "Let's check out the inn."

"Now?" Dale gulped. "After what Harm said about a ghost?"

Lavender gave him a wink. "Go on, little brother. There's no such thing as ghosts," he said as Crissy tugged him away from us.

"Bye, Lavender," I called. "Good luck with those head lice." Crissy dropped his hand. Lavender grinned at me and followed her into the crowd.

I peered at the tent where auctioneer Buddha Jackson warmed up the crowd. "Everybody got a number?" Buddha asked, whipping the microphone cord behind him like a rock star. "Bidding's easiest with a number. We'll auction a little furniture, then the inn with whatever's left inside."

"I only want an umbrella stand," Miss Lana shouted. She'd slipped into her 1960s sunglasses—the round ones with the white rims—and closed her parasol.

Buddha pointed at her. "Yes ma'am, Miss Lana. I'll be looking for you. Now let's talk about what conveys. That means what goes with the inn itself. Those of you

bidding on the inn, listen up. I think you'll find this amusing." He continued as Miss Lana and Grandmother Miss Lacy Thornton meandered toward the refreshment wagon.

I turned to Dale. "As Tupelo Landing's most successful detectives, we really ought to scope out the inn. Investigating means bragging rights in sixth grade. And Lavender says it's safe," I reminded him.

To Dale, Lavender's word is gospel. He gave a faint nod.

"Race you," I said before he could change his mind. We sprinted for the wooded path leading to the inn, Queen Elizabeth at our heels.

"There it is," I said as the path opened onto a ragged lawn. The ancient two-story inn may have been a beauty in her day. But today, with her windows boarded up and her front porch sagging, she looked forlorn and helpless on her knee-deep carpet of weeds. The steps listed. Rust streaked the tin roof. Shaggy cedars crowded the drive.

"Okay, we've seen it," Dale said, stepping over a No Trespassing sign someone had pried from its post. "Let's go."

"Don't be a baby," I told him as a quick *pop-pop-pop* rolled from the thicket. My heart jumped. "Who's there?" I demanded.

The thicket rustled. A white-haired man with a sharp fox face peered between the branches. Queen Elizabeth growled, her hackles rising, and Dale grabbed her collar.

Red Baker stepped onto the path.

Most days, Mr. Red looks like a bundle of throw-away clothes. Today he wore shoes fresh from the box, creased chinos, a blinding white shirt, and a red bow tie. "Hey," I said, and his pale eyes flickered over me like lizard eyes over a fly.

Mr. Red looked Dale up and down. "You're Macon Johnson's boy," he said, his voice splintery as just-sawn pine. "I hear he's doing time in Raleigh for a murder he didn't commit."

"You almost heard right," Dale said, very smooth. Dale's family's jail prone. To him, jail time is as normal as clean socks. "Daddy's over in county lock-up on reduced charges. We're hoping for a plea bargain or a smart attorney."

That "we" would be Dale and Queen Elizabeth—not Dale's mama, Miss Rose, who hocked her diamond in June. Miss Rose ain't studying Dale's daddy. Neither am I. Not after the things he's done.

"You bidding today, Mr. Red?" I asked. "I hear you want to buy the inn."

"You're nosy," he said. He didn't say it mean; he said it straight out.

"Occupational hazard," I said. "Detective," I added, in case he hadn't heard. He cracked his knuckles. That explained the popping sound. Nervous joints.

He licked his thin lips. "You headed for the inn? There's nothing in there but run-down, wore out, and fell through. And it's haunted thicker than the devil's parlor. I'd turn around if I was you."

"Haunted? Thicker than the . . . the devil's parlor?" Dale stammered. "I didn't know he had one." He turned to me, his blue eyes worried. "Have you ever heard of that?" he whispered. "A parlor at . . . the bad place?" Dale is Baptist. He doesn't worry about much in life, but he worries about the devil afterwards.

Mr. Red stared at him. "You two best head for folks that make footprints." He peered up the path and cracked his knuckles again. "Who's that?"

A boy strolled around the bend, barely whistling.

"Harm Crenshaw," Dale said. "From Greensboro. You want to meet him? I've been working on my social skills. I can introduce you." He cupped his hands around his mouth. "Hey Harm, come meet Mr. Red Baker," he called.

Harm froze. He and Mr. Red stared at each other like wild animals. Harm spun and marched the other way as Mr. Red faded back into the forest.

"Weird," Dale murmured.

"True. But we got enough weird in our lives without worrying about theirs. Come on. We haven't got much time," I said, and plowed through the weeds to the inn's creaky steps. The wind blew, setting three splintery old rocking chairs rocking.

"And what did Mr. Red mean when he said we should head for folks that make footprints?" Dale asked as we crossed the front porch.

"He meant to scare you."

"Right," he said. "I'm pretty sure it worked."

I pushed the heavy front door and it moaned open, scraping an arc across the dusty floor. I followed Queen Elizabeth into the gloom, and waited for my eyes to adjust. A tin ceiling soared high above us. A snaggle-toothed mahogany staircase climbed along one cracked plaster wall. To our right, the huge dining room stood a-jumble in crippled tables and upturned chairs. Its chandelier wore a bride's veil of spiderwebs and dust.

Queen Elizabeth darted away, her nose zigzagging across a carpet worn so thin, I could see the plank skeleton underneath. "This way," I whispered, heading into a parlor of sheet-covered settees and chairs.

"Hey! A piano," Dale said, relaxing. Like I said, Dale's musical. He strained to open the keyboard. The hinges'

rusty squeal echoed around the room. Dale spread his hands over the uneven, yellowed keys and the piano's tinny voice plinked through the dusty silence.

The front door banged against the wall behind us and we jumped.

"For heaven's sake," a woman said, "I don't care what that hideous old man says, that is *not* a ghost playing the piano." A pin-skinny woman minced into the room trailed by a pudgy man. She surveyed us like we came with the furniture. "See? Just kids."

I surveyed her right back: thin face, spiky black hair, jittery eyes. Sleeveless black sweater, skinny pants, black stilettos. She crossed her bone-thin arms and jutted her hip forward like a high-fashion wharf rat. "She ain't from around here," Dale whispered.

Dale has a flair for the obvious.

The woman squinted at the pressed tin ceiling, clacked to a window, and peered between the boards. "At least it's waterfront. I'll pay two hundred ten thousand. Not a penny more. Let's register," she told the pudgy man. "You kids stay away from that piano. It's mine," she added, and headed out the door.

"Rat Face," I muttered. I would have said more, but Miss Lana don't allow cursing. She does allow the creative use of animal names.

"*She's* buying this place? Because she'd be a terrible

neighbor," Dale said, looking nervous. "Unless she sings alto, which Mama says if you can sing alto, that means a lot to people." Dale's mama directs the church choir.

"Don't worry," I said, "she'd only buy this place to tear it down. But she *would* make a rotten neighbor. Miss Lana would hate her. Grandmother Miss Lacy would too."

Upstairs, glass crashed to the floor. Queen Elizabeth yelped and darted behind me. "Who's there?" I shouted, trying to rub the goose bumps off my arms. I caught a whiff of rosemary, and Queen Elizabeth sneezed.

A laugh floated down the stairway, secret and low. My heart jumped. So did Dale. "Steady, Dale," I said, my voice shaking. "Don't leap to conclusions. A good detective starts with the obvious and works toward the strange."

"You're making that up," he whispered.

"It could still be true," I said. "Somebody's messing with us," I added, walking to the bottom of the stairs: two solid stairs, three missing steps, eight solid stairs. "Hello?" The dust on the stairs lay thick and untouched.

Someone skipped along the upstairs hall. "That's a definite girl," Dale whispered. "A boy would rather die than skip like that." He whipped around to stare at me, his blue eyes wide. "Did I say die? That's just a figure of speech. I didn't mean anything."

A laugh floated down the stairs.

"Run," Dale said.

I grabbed his arm, spinning him in a circle. "Hold your ground. If we run, it will be all over school. It's probably Attila, trying to show us up."

"I don't think so," he said, pointing to the open door. Outside, Attila sailed across the inn's lawn, making a beeline for the auction tent.

Another laugh floated down the stairs. Queen Elizabeth threw back her head and howled wild as a wolf in moonlight. I looked down at Queen Elizabeth. She looked up at me.

We both looked at the open door.

Dale was halfway across the yard, elbows and knees pumping like the devil's hounds were nipping at his heels.

Chapter 3
Going, Going, Gone

Moments later Dale and I skidded into our seats beneath the auction tent. "I was *not* scared," Dale said again. "I just hate being late is all."

"Stop panting and look professional," I said, wincing at the catch in my side. Onstage, Buddha Jackson wiggled out of his shiny suit jacket and pointed to a battered desk and chair. "Lot number six," he shouted, and launched into a wild chant. "Who will give me two hundred dollars, two two two two, who will give me two hundred dollars?" Silence. "A hundred and fifty? One fifty one fifty one fifty?" We stared at him blank as stones. "All right, Tupelo Landing. Make me an offer."

"Twenty-five dollars," Attila's mother said. Attila sat beside her, calm as pond scum. It sure wasn't her in the inn. Then who?

"I have twenty-five, who will give me thirty? There," Buddha said, pointing to the Azalea Women. "I have thirty over here, who will give me fifty?" The flow of the

chant, the pulse of the bid. The auction swept over me like a dizzy tide.

"Hey," Dale said, breaking the spell. "There's Thes." I looked across the crowd. Red-headed Thessalonians and his dad, Reverend Thompson, had miraculously found seats behind the Azalea Women. "Thes!" Dale hissed, waving. "Over here!"

"I got fifty dollars over here!" Buddha shouted, pointing at Dale.

"No!" Dale clamped his hands over his mouth and his blue eyes filled with tears. "I was just saying hey," he wailed between his fingers.

"Who will give me a hundred?" Buddha boomed.

"Please," Dale whispered. "Somebody bid. I'll sing in church every Sunday 'til Judgment Day." He grabbed my arm. "Mo," he said. "Bid."

I jerked my arm free.

"Going once," Buddha cried, pointing in our direction.

"Hide," I said, and threaded my way to the Azalea Women, who sat neat as a choir on the third row. "That's an out-of-towner bidding against you," I said. "She says keep your money for azaleas because yours are the tackiest she's ever seen." The Azalea Women gasped. Three hands shot into the air.

"A hundred in the third row!" Buddha crowed as I raced for the exit.

"Come on, Dale," I said, dragging him toward sunlight.

Dale had turned a throw-up shade of green. He leaned forward, putting his hands on his knees. "I ain't never going into an auction tent again, not even if somebody's life depends on it," he panted. "Well, maybe if Mama's life depended on it, I would," he said. "Or Lavender's." He looked up at me. "They're family. Of course, we're best friends. That's almost family."

"Take deep breaths," I told him.

I looked up. Harm Crenshaw slouched against a tree, a crooked smirk on his pale face. Of course. It must have been him in the inn. He had opportunity: We'd seen him on the path. And motive: He's a proven jerk.

"Dale, can you stand up?" I asked. "People are staring." Harm cradled his arms like he was rocking a baby, and kissed the air. "Come on, Dale," I said, glaring at Harm. "Let's get something to drink."

Two Pepsis later, Dale's color found his face. Buddha's voice wafted from the tent to the refreshment cart. "Sold to number 72—Miss Lana, you got your umbrella stand!"

Miss Lana exited the tent, lugging her trophy.

We ran to her as Rat Face scuttled by. "If you ask me, they should sell all this junk in one lot," Rat Face told Miss Lana. "But, when you go to a hick auction, this is what you get. Hicks."

Miss Lana's eyebrows rose unnaturally high on her forehead. Dale and me took a big step back.

"And what's that auctioneer's name?" Rat Face continued. "*Buddha* Jackson? Can you believe it?"

"If I'm not mistaken, Buddha's a family name," Miss Lana said in a voice shaved from ice. It was quasi-true. *Bubba* is a family name. Buddha's mama is dyslexic.

Rat Face narrowed her eyes. "Nice spot for condos, though. I'll wait," she said, and scurried away.

"Dreadful woman," Miss Lana said, watching her burrow back into the crowd. "Mo, would you and Dale put our umbrella stand in the Buick? Hurry, sugar. We have what we came for, but you don't want to miss the main event."

We made it back just in time. As we edged to the front of the tent, Dale took off his belt and handed it to me. "If I bid, strangle me," he whispered. "Mama will understand."

"Here we go," Buddha Jackson said, rubbing his hands together. "The inn with the furniture that's left, plus the medicinal springs, the pavilion, and all the fine print. Who will give me a half-million dollars?" Nobody breathed. "Four hundred thousand?" We sat still as tombstones. "Make me an offer," he said.

Mr. Red Baker scratched his sandpaper face. "Twenty thousand dollars," he rasped as Flick Crenshaw stepped up beside him.

"Forty thousand," Rat Face replied, studying her fingernails.

"Who will give me fifty?" Buddha sang. Mr. Red cracked his knuckles and nodded. "Fifty thousand says Mr. Red," Buddha said. "Now who will give me—"

"Sixty," Rat Face said, her voice like a steel trap.

"Seventy."

"A hundred thousand."

The crowd murmured like pines in a breeze. "A hundred twenty," Mr. Red said.

"One hundred fifty thousand," Rat Face called.

"Mr. Baker?" Buddha said. "It's up to you." Mr. Red shook his head. "Going once," Buddha said, pointing to Rat Face. "Going twice."

"A hundred and sixty thousand dollars," a familiar voice sang out from the back of the tent. The crowd swiveled. A white parasol popped open.

"No!" I tore across the tent. "Miss Lana," I cried, grabbing her parasol and popping it closed. "We don't have that kind of money!"

"I will *not* have that horrible woman for a neighbor," she said.

"And we won't have her replacing our history with condos," Grandmother Miss Lacy said, seething.

"One hundred eighty thousand dollars," Rat Face said, crisp as a poisoned apple.

Dale lurched to a stop beside me. "Stop, Miss Lana. That inn's haunted sure as I'm breathing."

"Pish," she replied. She looked at Grandmother Miss Lacy, who nodded. "Don't worry, my dears, we'll re-sell the inn to somebody nice," she said. The worry melted from Dale's face, just like that. "Two hundred thousand dollars," Miss Lana cried.

Rat Face jumped up, her thin face twitching. "Two hundred ten."

"Miss Lana, that's her top bid," Dale said. "We heard her say so in the inn." He reached in his pocket. "I got a five. It's yours if you want it. And Mo has a life savings of seven dollars and twenty-six cents," he said. "Plus a Canada dime."

"My little hero," she said, patting his face.

"We bid twelve dollars and twenty-six cents more than she does," Miss Lana screeched, pointing at Rat Face. "Plus a Canada dime."

"Sold to number 72," Buddha Jackson shouted. "Miss Lana, you just bought yourself a historic inn—with a bona fide ghost in the fine print!"

Chapter 4
Ghost in the Fine Print

"What?" Miss Lana cried as the crowd burst into applause.

She bowed gracefully, twice, and then rushed Buddha's stage.

"Congrats, ladies," Buddha said, rolling a speaker to the edge of the stage as the crowd jostled away, talking and laughing. "You got a real bargain."

"Yes," she said, twirling her parasol. "But for a moment I thought you said we have an actual *ghost* in the fine print. Imagine!"

Buddha nodded toward a stack of papers. "That's right," he said, and her smile wilted. "The law says you got to list ghosts strong enough to affect the property value. Same as a leaky roof, which you also got. This place has changed hands several times over the years, and your ghost got listed along the way. As you may recall, I talked about the fine print—including the ghost—before we got started. Sign here."

Miss Lana shot a look at Rat Face, who now stood chatting with Flick Crenshaw. *"Strong enough to affect*

the property value? But as soon as she's gone, we intend to re-sell the inn to someone *nice.*"

"There's no such thing as ghosts," Grandmother Miss Lacy said firmly, handing Buddha her pen. "Here you are, dear. Just X that bit out."

"Sorry," he said, winding a cord. "I could lose my license."

Miss Lana snapped her parasol closed and slammed it against a speaker. A bad sign. "For heaven's sake," she said through clenched teeth, "who in her right mind would buy a ghost?"

I clamped my hand over Dale's mouth. "Rhetorical," I whispered. Dale's a sucker for rhetorical questions, especially Miss Lana's.

I slipped a clue pad from my pocket. "The name of the alleged ghost?"

Buddha shrugged. "Fine print doesn't say. Maybe you can figure it out." He nudged the papers toward Miss Lana. "No refunds."

I slapped my clue pad closed. "Dale and I will be in our mobile crime unit if you need us," I said, very professional. Dale's blue eyes flew open. "The Buick," I whispered. I marched into the crowd, chin up and eyes straight ahead the way the Colonel taught me.

Sal, in her red Piggly Wiggly sunglasses, waved at Dale. He gave her an absent smile as Attila ambushed

us by her mama's Cadillac. "Interesting buy, Mo-ron," she said. "But I suppose a ghost friend would be nice for you. Someone like your long-lost mother—not quite here, not quite there."

"Leave my Upstream Mother out of this, Attila."

She looked across the crowd and did a double take. "Who's that?" she asked, her voice shifting gears.

I followed her gaze. Harm Crenshaw skulked by the refreshment wagon. "Anna," Attila's mother said, mincing up. "We don't mingle with the unsavory. Hurry, dear. You'll be late for Voice."

Attila's the only kid in rising sixth grade who takes Voice. It doesn't help her all that much. She hopped in the car, her eyes still on Harm Crenshaw. The Cadillac oozed through the crowd.

"Did she just call us unsavory?" Dale asked, his voice sharp. "Because that's rude." He lowered his voice. "What does it mean, exactly?"

"It means we reek. Look," I said. Flick Crenshaw had cornered Harm against a picnic table. As Flick talked, Harm's face went thunderous as an August storm. "Looks interesting," I said, darting through the crowd. We rocked to a halt behind a large, sweet-smelling woman in a flowered dress. I peeped around her sausage-like arm as Flick thumped his finger against Harm's chest.

"You'll do what I say," Flick growled.

"But *why?*" Harm demanded, his voice cracking. "It's not fair."

"Because I said so. Because I make the money. Because you're cramping my style."

"What style?" Harm muttered as Flick turned and pushed through the crowd. He climbed in his red sports car and roared away. Harm's eyes met mine and he blushed. "What are you gawking at, Ghost Girl?"

Ghost Girl. Great.

"Not much," I said, looking him up and down.

With that, I stalked through the crowd and climbed into the Buick. Dale helped Queen Elizabeth onto the seat between us as Miss Lana stormed up. She swung into the passenger's seat, breathing ragged as torn construction paper, and slammed the door. "As God is my witness, I never meant to buy a ghost," she said.

Grandmother Miss Lacy slipped behind the wheel. "We didn't buy a ghost, we bought an *inn*," she corrected. "That ridiculous ghost story doesn't make a whit of difference except that we planned to re-sell the inn and now we possibly . . . can't."

Miss Lana adjusted her wig. "Everyone breathe," she gasped. "We simply need a Plan B." Miss Lana thrives on Plan Bs. So do I. In fact, my entire life is one big fat Plan B.

"The inn's still a lovely purchase. The fact that there's a pedigreed poltergeist dwelling within is, well . . ."

I pictured myself walking into sixth grade the next day. "A paranormal disaster," I said.

Dale shot me a Sympathy Look and rummaged in his snack pocket. "Accidental ghost purchase. Your social life is certified roadkill," he said. "Peanuts, anyone?"

Miss Lana held out her hand.

"Very well," she said as he shook peanuts into her palm. "We've hit uncharted rapids on the river of life. Don't panic, don't stand up in the boat. And not a word of this to the Colonel until our Plan B is in place."

The Colonel!

I grinned. "Miss Lana," I said, "I know the Colonel hates to admit it, but he *is* an attorney. If anybody can get you out of fine print, it's him."

"Of course," she said, her face brightening. "How could I have forgotten?"

"Rhetorical?" Dale whispered, and I nodded.

"The Colonel will straighten this out in a jiffy," she said. "We just need to broach the subject artfully."

"And quickly," Grandmother Miss Lacy said, cranking the Buick. "The entire town will head to the café to see how he takes our news." We fishtailed across the meadow and headed for town.

⋆₊ ⋆ ₊⋆

Moments later Dale held the door as we filed into the empty café like a lineup of nervous suspects. Like Lavender, Dale has manners. This is thanks to Miss Rose—not his daddy. "Hey, Colonel," I said.

He peeked up from the coffeemaker. "Hello, Soldier. Your report?"

"The auction was exciting," I said. Which was true.

Miss Lana smiled. "Auctions are so electrifying."

Suspicion shot across his rugged face. "What did you buy?"

Dale jumped like somebody bit him, and Grandmother Miss Lacy peeled away to pour a glass of water. "An umbrella stand," Miss Lana replied. "It's in the Buick."

The Colonel relaxed. "Good. I thought we might offer tuna salad sandwiches for lunch today, with your Practically Organic Soup."

"Perfect," she said, sailing toward the kitchen. "I'll get the blue plates. They're so soothing. And while I'm thinking about it, I bought the inn. Would you like the sandwiches on white or whole wheat?"

"What?" the Colonel asked, wheeling to face her.

Poor Colonel. "She said white or whole wheat," I said.

"Lana? You bought that ramshackle hotel? Have you lost your mind? It's over a hundred years old. The roof leaks, the windows are busted, the wiring's shot. And

who would stay there? Nobody comes to Tupelo Landing. Not on purpose, anyway."

She shrugged. "Life takes unexpected turns, *mon cher*." Miss Lana likes to pretend she's French. She says it helps her metabolize stress.

"How much?" the Colonel demanded, his brown eyes wide.

"Two hundred ten thousand dollars. And change."

"A bargain, since she has a partner," Grandmother Miss Lacy added. "Me."

The Colonel sank into a chair, the vein on his forehead bulging. He took three deep breaths and I knew he was counting to twenty, which is what he tells me to do when counting to ten won't cover it.

The café door flew open. Mayor Little and the Azalea Women strolled in laughing.

"You people are a gold-plated hoot," Mayor Little said, beaming at us. "Congratulations. Historic inn, springhouse, pavilion. I can't wait to see what you do with the ghost!"

"*Ghost?*" the Colonel barked.

"The Colonel doesn't believe in ghosts," I said. "Neither do Miss Lana and Grandmother Miss Lacy."

The Azalea Women turned to the Colonel, their eyes glinting. He studied the parking lot as four cars and a pickup pulled in, spilling auction-goers toward our door.

Then he picked up a cloth and attacked a nonexistent spot on the counter. His lips weren't moving, but I knew he was still counting.

"I'll admit a historic inn is a risk," he finally said, giving the mayor a gray-lipped smile. To me, Miss Lana looked worried. "But Lana and Miss Thornton are astute businesswomen. I trust their instinct. As for the ghost story . . ." He swallowed hard. "We're regarding it as a public relations boon."

Miss Lana smiled. "That's right," she said. "People will come from the ends of the earth to visit our faux ghost. I'll handle the PR myself." As she drifted toward the kitchen, I slipped my arm around the Colonel's thin waist.

The Colonel is a genius. He's also a sure bet in a fight.

That night, I settled into bed and plucked *The Piggly Wiggly Chronicles,* Volume 6 off my bedside table. I started *The Chronicles* in kindergarten. Volume 1 features drawings of Attila Celeste covered in mud. Later volumes hold the clues to my life story and letters to the Upstream Mother who lost me in a flood the day I was born.

I used to think she would find me. Now I know she won't. I write anyway, mostly to focus my thoughts.

Dear Upstream Mother,

How are you?

Today, Miss Lana accidentally bought a haunted inn.

After our lunch rush, Miss Lana, the Colonel, and Grandmother Miss Lacy drove over to scout the place. The Colonel came home pale. Miss Lana and Grandmother Miss Lacy returned stiff and fake-cheerful, like plastic daisies at Christmastime.

We all hoped the Colonel could get Miss Lana out of the contract, but he can't. He says Buddha Jackson may appear to have the brains of a rutabaga, but his contract has less wiggle room than a straitjacket.

Tomorrow's the first day of school. The ghost news is all over town. My life can't get no worse than this.

Mo

Chapter 5
My Life Gets Worse

"Welcome to sixth grade," Miss Retzyl said the next morning, the sun from the windows gleaming off her neat white blouse and blue skirt.

"Thank you," I said very regal as ghost murmurs rippled across the room.

I bypassed the empty seat in the first row and slung myself into my usual desk next to Dale's. There were nineteen of us if you count the Exum boys, who I hoped were only visiting. "Who's the empty seat for?" I asked. "Because we're all here, plus some."

The Exums, on the back row, sat straight and still, one with brown hair and one with blond. They both wore pit bull faces, plaid shirts, jeans, and no necks. The Exums go to Creekside Baptist, with Dale. I know them from Bible school, where they've been voted Most Likely to Go to Hell three years running.

"Miss Retzyl, most of us been together since first grade," I said. "There's no point in adding Exums."

Dark-haired Jake Exum raised his hand. "I'm Jake

Exum," he said. "This is my brother Jimmy. Until now we been homeschooled."

"Mama expelled us," Jimmy added.

Miss Retzyl twitched like a squirrel but recovered fast. "Welcome, boys," she said, tucking a strand of auburn hair behind her ear. "In fact, welcome to all of you. We're going to have a wonderful time this year." That would be in comparison to last year, when we had her for fifth grade thanks to the Curse of the Combined Grades. "This year we're studying fractions, history, analogies, sentence construction, science . . . Anna, would you pass out the science books?" Attila jumped like a puppet possessed. "Any announcements before we get started?" Miss Retzyl asked.

"Miss Lana bought a ghost," Atilla said, gathering an armload of books.

The class snickered. I went for a diversionary tactic, which the Colonel says makes a good defense. "Thank you for that intro, Anna," I said, very smooth. "And let me be the first to congratulate you on those braces. Miss Retzyl, Dale and me got an announcement: We got our names in the newspaper this summer for solving a murder."

"We were in the paper in a good way," Dale added. "Not under *Recent Arrests*." Like I say, Dale's family's jail prone. *Recent Arrests* is practically his family newsletter.

Attila pulled a ragged science book from the bottom

of the stack and plunked it on my desk. "Actually, Miss Lana bought a *certified* ghost. Which is worse," she said.

"I also got a *What I Did on My Summer Vacation* paper in here somewhere," I lied, rummaging through my messenger bag. "It highlights the details of our recent cases. If you feel like extra crediting me, go ahead. I'll get it to you at the end of class."

Dale grabbed pencil and paper, and went into a quick scrawl:

WHAT I DID ON MY SUMMER VACATION
By Dale
What mo said.

He folded the paper and raised his hand. "I got that too," he said.

"Wonderful. I'll read them at home," she said. "Other announcements? No? Well, I have good news."

Good news from a teacher. Dale and I exchanged looks. Danger. We slid low in our desks.

"We have an unusual opportunity to do something important for our community, and we have an important guest to introduce that opportunity. Class, please help me welcome Mayor Little."

Our door swung open and Mayor Little bustled in, waving and beaming. "Good morning, future voters," he said, tossing his hat on Miss Retzyl's desk. "Thanks for inviting me here today."

Dale raised his hand. "We didn't invite you," he said.

"Thanks, Dale," the mayor said, smoothing his tie. "You have a wonderful way with the truth. The whole town appreciates what you and Mo did for us last summer."

Attila dropped the last book on Jake Exum's desk. "I don't," she said. "I also don't appreciate Miss Lana buying a ghost, which makes the entire town look stupid."

He rubbed his chubby hands together. "Thanks for that thought, Anna. Now, who knows what year it is?"

I raised my hand.

"Wonderful," he said. "Mo?"

"Miss Lana's not here to defend herself, so let's leave her out of this," I said, glaring at Attila.

Mayor Little looked uncertainly at Miss Retzyl, who stepped up beside him. "Class, let's hold our thoughts until the end of the mayor's presentation."

He shot her a grateful look. "All right," he said. "This is an important year for Tupelo Landing. Why?"

Thes raised his hand, but the mayor looked the other way.

"Because," the mayor continued, "this year marks our community's 250th anniversary. A milestone. And I am delighted to have led us to this dramatic moment in time. And where do you fit in?"

"Rhetorical," I whispered, and Dale nodded.

"I'm pleased to announce that you, the sixth grade, will have the honor of writing a history of our community based on your interviews with our town elders."

Dale folded forward, his forehead thumping against his desk. "Old people," he moaned. "There's nothing harder than old people."

"I share your excitement," the mayor replied. "I understand there's extra credit for the student interviewing the oldest person. And best of all, we'll make your papers into a book as part of our celebration. Miss Retzyl will handle the details."

Attila raised her hand. "How long do the papers have to be?"

"Three pages," Miss Retzyl said. "We'll start choosing subjects today."

Attila raised her hand again.

Miss Retzyl closed her eyes. "Before anyone asks, the papers will be half your history grade for first semester."

Attila lowered her hand.

"Your family is a good resource."

Dale stopped breathing. Dale and me both run short on elders. Mine live somewhere Upstream. His are mostly Up the River.

"We'll take Grandmother Miss Lacy," I whispered, and he exhaled.

Attila raised her hand. "Dibs on Miss Lacy Thornton."

"Hey!" I shouted. "She's *my* grandmother! I'm taking her!"

"Oh, she is not your grandmother," she sniped. "You only call her that because you don't know who your family is, plus she's richer than God."

"Take that back," I said.

"I asked her at the auction, and she said yes."

At the auction? She gave Mayor Little a smile that would put a bee in a sugar coma. "No fair, the mayor tipped her off," I said as Mayor Little grabbed his hat.

"Well, I'm glad this went so well," he said. "Ta-ta for now, future voters. And by the way, I'm sure Mother would give someone an interview. She's a real pip."

"Thank you, Mayor Little," Miss Retzyl said. "Class, please let me know by the end of the day who you'll ask for an interview."

That afternoon I sat watching the clock's hands jerk toward the final bell. Dale, who was practicing his ninja invisibility skills, sat so still, it was hard to be sure he was breathing. Miss Retzyl started taking names for interview subjects.

"Thes?" she asked.

"I got Great-Uncle Leroy," Thes said, his voice dull. "He served in a war."

"Wonderful," she said, marking her book. "A war hero.

Anna Celeste?" Attila sits in front of Dale. Dale stopped breathing altogether. His lips turned blue.

Atilla flounced her hair. "Like I said, I'm interviewing Miss Lacy Thornton, the oldest nice person in town. Automatic extra credit."

"Thief," I whispered.

"Thank you, Anna Celeste," Miss Retzyl said. "Mo? Did you say something?"

"Three minutes," Dale whispered, staring at the clock. "Stall."

I nodded. "Yes, ma'am. It's about you and Detective Joe Starr, which on behalf of the entire class I'd like to congratulate you on your rumored upcoming nuptials, which we're hoping you've set a date." The Exums applauded. "I also want to mention Dale does a killer 'Have-a-Maria,' which goes over good at weddings."

"That's '*Ave* Maria,'" she said.

"Exactly. Naturally, I'm available for emergency bridesmaid if needed," I added.

In truth, she could do better than Detective Joe Starr—Desperado Detective Agency's main competition. But Starr, who's from Winston-Salem, has somehow charmed Miss Retzyl and hangs around now much of the time.

Jimmy Exum raised his hand. "I got a suit. I can tote

rings," he said. The class gasped. The Exum boys are like crows when it comes to glittery objects.

"We can talk rings later," I said. "The main thing is, right now we'd all like to get your date down so we don't miss the Big Event."

Sal beamed and opened her weekly planner.

Miss Retzyl, who secretly likes me, narrowed her brown eyes. "Detective Starr and I haven't set a date, Mo. Let's get back to the interviews. I'd like to know—"

The classroom door swung open. A lanky boy slouched against the door frame: thin face, tan shirt, black pants, scuffed shoes.

Crenshaw, Harm Crenshaw. What is he doing here?

Miss Retzyl smiled. "You must be Harmond. I have a desk right here for you," she said, pointing to the front row.

He sauntered into the room. "It's Harm. Harm Crenshaw. Brother of racecar driver Flick Crenshaw. I'll be here a couple weeks and then I'm getting back to my real life in Greensboro." He swung into the empty seat and turned to smirk at me. "Hey Ghost Girl. Seen any haints?"

Attila tittered, and his eyes flashed over her.

"Harm, Mo was just telling us about her interview for her history paper."

"Dale and me are working together," I said, willing the bell to ring.

"That's fine," she said. "You'll need six pages rather than three."

Attila smiled at Harm, pointed at me, and rolled her eyes.

Heat walked up the back of my neck. "Dale and me are interviewing somebody older than Grandmother Miss Lacy," I said.

"Dale and *I*," Miss Retzyl said. "Mayor Little's mother is the oldest person in town."

I shivered. Mayor Little's mother is black-cat mean.

"No," Dale whispered. "Not her."

"It would mean extra credit," Miss Retzyl reminded me.

"Yes," Dale whispered. "Take her."

Extra credit looms large with Dale, who specializes in the Recess Arts. On the other hand, Mrs. Little curdles milk by smiling at it. "Thank you, Miss Retzyl, but Dale and me got somebody even older," I said, trying to think of someone.

Attila flashed her braces. "There isn't anyone older, Mo-ron."

Harm Crenshaw corkscrewed in his seat, his dark eyes laughing. "Mo-ron," he mouthed.

My temper popped like bacon on a hot skillet. "There

is too somebody older." I glared at him. "Dale and me are interviewing a ghost."

The problem with having a temper is you find out what you're going to say at the exact same minute everybody else does.

The class gasped.

"No," Dale moaned.

Like the Colonel says, sometimes the only way out is forward. "A ghost means extra credit," I said as the bell rang. "There ain't nobody older than dead."

Chapter 6
Pre-Flunked

"I am not interviewing a ghost. I want out," Dale said, hopping off his bike and dropping it by his mama's front steps. "Hey Liz," he murmured as Queen Elizabeth trotted over to greet him.

I leaned my bike against the porch. A scarecrow in a blue-plaid bathrobe watched over Miss Rose's sprawling fall garden: pumpkins, collards, cabbage, gourds. "Isn't that the robe you gave your daddy last Christmas?" I asked, squinting across the garden. Dale has a way with scarecrows.

"Don't use the Colonel's diversion tactics on me," he said. "This is sixth grade, Mo. We got to get *real* interviews. With quotes and footnotes. It's on the handout."

There was a handout? And Dale took one?

"And I'm scared of ghosts," he said. He picked up a stick and hurled it across the yard. Queen Elizabeth tilted her head, her pink tongue spilling out the side of her mouth. "Get it, girl," he said. "Fetch!" Queen Elizabeth sat. She's a self-starter unless she sees a squirrel,

in which case she can't be held responsible. "A ghost," Dale said, his voice bitter. "I just hope Miss Retzyl hasn't called Mama to pre-flunk us."

Pre-flunk us? My blood ran cold. "You're making that up."

"It's like being preapproved for a credit card you ain't never gonna get," he said. "Get on the pre-flunk list and you never get off." Dale's people ain't good with credit cards. Neither are mine, but that's because the Colonel doesn't allow them, not because they don't allow us.

Dale took the steps two at a time. "Mama," he called, letting the front door slam behind us. "I'm home. I brought Mo."

Miss Rose stuck her head out of the kitchen. "Hey, you two. How did it go?"

Dale slung his backpack on the settee and headed toward her. "That depends," he said. "Did Miss Retzyl call?"

"No," she said, looking puzzled.

"I guess it went okay then," he said. "Do we have orange juice?" Miss Rose nodded toward the refrigerator—an old, round-shouldered Frigidaire.

"Hey Miss Rose," I said. "You're looking nice." It was true. She wore faded blue corduroys and a blouse with the soft stripes washed near off of it. She held a tape measure. A yellow pencil jutted from behind her ear.

Miss Rose used to be smack-down gorgeous before Dale's daddy latched on to her. That's what people say. She's still pretty, but a tired shade of pretty: green eyes, bold chin, a sway that's almost like dancing. She's got music in her bones, Miss Lana says. Same as Dale.

Dale kicked the Frigidaire's door closed. "I might as well tell you, Mama," he said, pouring the juice and handing me a glass. "Sixth grade looks hard. I may be a repeat attender."

"Don't tell me your new ninja skills aren't paying off," she said, and I caught a hint of her dimples. "What's that paper you've been studying?"

"Breathwork and Focus—Go Invisible the Ninja Way," he said. "Sal and Skeeter found it on the Internet for me." Skeeter—a seventh-grade legal whiz—got high-speed in July. High-speed's rare in Tupelo Landing unless you live on First Street, which has cable. "My ninja skills are maybe working some," he continued. "I didn't disappear today, but I didn't get called on, either."

"Then what makes you think you'll repeat sixth grade?"

Dale tells Miss Rose everything sooner or later. My Detective's Instinct cried out for later. "Dale and me got assigned a history paper," I said. "Dale's antsy, is all.

"I hate to be nosy," I added, bending the conversation in a safer direction, "but why are you holding Lavender's tape measure?"

She laughed. "How do you know it's Lavender's?"

"I'm practically his assistant," I explained. "I know Lavender's tools by heart."

She stretched the tape across her faded countertop. "Lavender's installing a dishwasher for me," she said. "I'm deciding how I'd like my kitchen to flow." Miss Rose is one of the last in Greater Tupelo Landing to get a dishwasher. Dale's daddy used to say if he had a dishwasher, he wouldn't need a wife. That's before Miss Rose kicked him out.

"Good. A dishwasher beats Dale's daddy any day," I said. The words went rancid the instant they hit the air.

Miss Rose didn't look up from her tape measure, but a shadow darted across her face. "Macon is my ex-husband," she said, smoothing the sharp from her voice. "Not Dale's ex-father."

"Sorry," I mumbled, and Dale nodded.

She smiled at Dale. "That reminds me, Lavender says he'll take you over there Sunday if you want to visit your daddy." *Over there* means the county jail.

"Lavender's driving? I'll go," I offered.

"Maybe later," Dale muttered.

Dale's always claimed two speeds for forgiving: fast or never. Lately I suspect he's developing a new gear just for his daddy. One that grinds slow. Real slow.

"So what's this I hear about history?" Miss Rose asked, turning to her measuring.

"Ghost," Dale blurted. I winced.

She stopped scribbling. "What?"

"Mo volunteered us to interview a ghost for history. I'm going to fail sixth grade. I hope you aren't disappointed." Silence settled over us like plaster dust. Miss Rose tilted her chin and let her glasses slide down the bridge of her nose.

I gave her my best smile. "A ghost means extra credit, plus Miss Lana can use our interview for her public relations campaign, for the inn. It's win-win."

She blinked at me rapid-fire, like an alien brain-mapping a new life form. "There's no such thing as ghosts, Mo," she said. "I'm sure Miss Retzyl will let you choose a new subject."

"It's too late," I told her.

She picked up her tape. "It's never too late to make a better decision, Mo. Dale, why don't you show Mo what you've learned on your guitar?"

"Come on, Mo," he said. "I can already play a song."

"That went better than expected," he said, sinking into his beanbag chair.

I walked over to his terrarium, where his newt, Sir Isaac Newton, stirred beneath a leaf. By Newton's ter-

rarium sat a paperback, *Manners Girls Like*. Lately, Dale thinks about dates. I will never go out on a date until I am old enough to go with Lavender, which gives me seven years to plan my wardrobe.

"Social skills," Dale explained, watching me thumb through the book. "I need some in case a girl ever likes me." In case? If Sal likes Dale one degree more, she'll evaporate. "We got to think of somebody else to interview, Mo."

I walked to his bookshelf, playing for time. I scanned the titles: *I'm Okay, You're a Dog. Hound: A Spirit Journey. Get Rich with an Earthworm Ranch!* "You're missing the beauty of my plan," I said. "If we interview a ghost, we'll go famous." I let the word *famous* sit like bait on still water. I jiggled the line: "You enjoy famous."

He slipped me a sideways look. "Some," he admitted.

"If we *don't* land an interview with a ghost," I continued, "we'll fake one in ghostly voices. Easy A."

He shook his head. "Mama doesn't like me to cheat." He picked up his guitar and strummed. "I wish Miss Lacy Thornton would dump Attila so we could interview her. *That* would be an easy A." He snorted. "Attila probably didn't even ask her. She was probably bluffing."

Bluffing? I hadn't thought of that.

The Colonel says great leaders compromise. "How about this: If Attila's bluffing and Grandmother Miss

Lacy says yes to our interview, we'll grab her. If she says no, we'll stick with the ghost—if you don't mind risking fame."

"Deal," he said, laying his guitar aside. "Let's roll."

A few minutes later we dropped our bikes in a spatter of red dogwood leaves by Grandmother Miss Lacy's steps. "Who's that?" Dale asked as a silver BMW roared away from the curb.

"Rat Face, from the auction," I murmured. "What's she doing here?"

"Hello, dears," Grandmother Miss Lacy called. She sat in her porch swing, picking out pecans calm as Sunday. Grandmother Miss Lacy lives in the grandest house in town: two stories, with a wide front porch. Its clapboards wear dark green paint and its tall shutters wear black. Grandmother Miss Lacy keeps it decked out in flowers.

"What was Rat Face doing over here?" I asked.

"Don't worry, it's nothing a phone call won't fix. What are you two up to?"

Dale perched on the rail. "We're practicing our social skills," he said. He opened his pack, pulled out *Manners Girls Like,* and shyly tilted it toward her. "After my Anna Celeste disaster, I decided to brush up."

Groundwork for our interview request. Brilliant. "You may not realize it," I said, "but Anna Celeste liked Dale

for a few days this summer and then dumped him like a truckload of bad meat. She about broke his heart."

He nodded. "That's why I've taken up the guitar."

"A wonderful channel for heartbreak," she said. "How's sixth grade?"

I studied her powdered face. "That depends," I said. "On you." I took a deep breath. "Grandmother Miss Lacy, we want to interview you for history, only Anna Celeste claims she already asked. I hate to say anything bad about her but we feel like she's Devil Spawn and we're pretty sure she's lying. We dropped by to ask, may we please have the honor of an interview?"

She gave the swing a little push. "Oh, dear. She asked me at the auction. I'm sorry, dears, but I didn't realize I'd be such a popular commodity." She cracked a pecan. "I believe Myrt Little might be available, though."

"The mayor's mother? But she's mean as a snake," Dale said. "Unless she's your best friend," he added, very smooth. "In which case she could be secretly nice."

"Oh, I doubt that," she said. "Come in. I have some cookies for you. And don't worry, you'll stumble across a suitable old person somewhere."

As she disappeared down the paneled hall, Dale and I wandered into her parlor. "Wow," he said. "I didn't know she lived in a museum." I followed him across the flowery wine-colored carpet, past the settee, to a round

marble-top table. He picked up a photo in a silver frame. In it a slim, dark-haired woman leaned against a long pale car.

"That's the Duesenberg." He wandered to the fireplace, where black-and-white photos lined the mantelpiece. "Nice," he said as Grandmother Miss Lacy breezed in.

"Thank you, Dale." She put a plate of chocolate chip cookies on the marble-top table. "I find black-and-white film captures emotion so much better than color. The only exception would be school photos," she added, glancing at her Mo LoBeau Collection.

Dale perched on her settee and gulped cookies like a seal gulps fish. I nibbled, like Grandmother Miss Lacy. Miss Lana says that's how you learn manners. By watching people who've got them and doing what they do. She says that way you move like a bird in a flock, banking across the sky, adjusting so smooth, nobody notices you.

The Colonel says that's a good way to get shot.

"You know, dear," Grandmother Miss Lacy said, "since Dale's taking up the guitar, you might want an art form too." She went to her bookshelf, took down a small black box, and handed it to me. Its stippled sides felt cool in my hands.

Dale leaned forward. "What is it?"

"My old camera," she said.

I turned it in my hands. Two silver-rimmed portholes stared at me. I ran my finger across a series of levers and knobs on the front and top of the camera. "Where do the batteries go?"

"No batteries, dear." She flipped up a little window on the top of the box. "You look in here, focus here, and press the shutter," she said. "Light does the rest."

"It's solar," Dale breathed. "Cool."

"I thought you might document the inn's changes. They'll be dramatic. Historic."

"Historic?" Dale said, perking up.

"We could display the photos in the inn's lobby," she said.

"Sounds like extra credit," Dale said, looking at me.

I grinned. "Maybe I can even photograph the ghost."

Grandmother Miss Lacy laughed. "There's no such thing, Mo, but do give it your best shot. That's photography humor—best shot. And please tell Lana I'll see her at supper," she said, rising. "I'll bring the camera over and give you a few pointers."

"Yes, ma'am."

We ran down the steps and grabbed our bikes. "That went great," I said, picturing my photos on the inn's wall.

Dale swung onto his bike. "Not really. We're still stuck interviewing a ghost."

Chapter 7
Deadlines

The next afternoon—Friday—Miss Retzyl took out her grade book. "Let's nail down your interview subjects," she said, and scanned her book. "I'll need a potential interview subject from everyone today; otherwise you drop a grade. Mo? I encourage you and Dale to rethink your selection. I'm requiring taped interviews."

Sal raised her hand. "Plus they could lose their souls."

Dale went pale.

"Thank you, Miss Retzyl, but Dale and me plan to interview our ghost on a full moon to be arranged. We'll need the project deadlines as soon as possible, in case we need to consult outside experts," I added, very professional. "I understand they teach ghost hunting at the community college."

"Did she say *dead*lines?" Harm asked, and Attila tittered like a wind-up toy.

"Harm, that's enough," Miss Retzyl said. "Dale?"

Dale sighed. "I'm with Mo," he said, his voice limp as

an old sock. "We'll get modern historic photos. Maybe of the ghost too."

I nodded. Brilliant. All it would take is a sheet in a window.

"Grandmother Miss Lacy's loaning us her solar camera," I explained. "An automatic footnote. I had my first photography lesson last night."

The class buzzed.

"Photographs? A wonderful idea," Miss Retzyl said. "And of course you know I'll recognize your voices if you try to fake an interview with a ghost."

My stomach swallowed itself alive. "Fake an interview? We'd never dream of it."

Dale put his head on his desk.

"I'll also expect background interviews," she said. "With the living. Last chance, you two. Change your minds?" Harm and Attila smirked.

"We never back out on a case," I said. "Desperado Detective Agency's Paranormal Division is open for business."

She marked her book. "Very well. Sal? What do you have in mind?" Sal's the smallest girl in rising sixth grade—a full half inch shorter than Dale. She fluffed the Strategic Ruffles camouflaging her lipstick-shaped physique. "I'll interview Grandmama Betty, Retro Fash-

ionista. Her mother specialized in semi-tailoring deluxe Sears garments—which were the bee's knees in the '30s." She smiled at Dale, her eyes bright. He didn't even try to lift his head.

"Excellent. Harmond," Miss Retzyl said, "whom will you interview?"

Whom. She said it like it made sense.

Harm shifted his lean body. "Skip me. I won't be in the boondocks that long."

Miss Retzyl's pen clattered against her book.

The class gulped.

"I mean, I won't be in Tupelo Landing that long, Miss Retzyl," he finally said. "Besides, I don't know anybody here. I can't get an interview."

Attila raised her hand. "You have to know *somebody*. Where do you live?" she asked. "Not that I care," she added. "It's just that some of us wonder."

"Yeah," I said. "Guess whom." I smiled at Miss Retzyl, hoping for a compliment on *whom*. Nothing.

"Where I live is my business," Harm said, his voice cracking. He took a breath, packing calm around his anger the way Miss Lana packs tissue paper around her mother's crystal. "I'll give you an answer next week, Miss Retzyl," he said as the bell rang.

Our stampede for the door muffled her reply.

Dale and I walked across the playground, to our

bikes. The afternoon heat lay against the earth, swollen and still. "Why doesn't Harm want anybody to know where he lives?" I asked.

He shrugged. "Maybe he's in the witness protection program. Or maybe he doesn't want Attila zipping after him like a bloodhound. You want to come over and watch me practice my guitar?"

The school door banged opened and Harm swaggered out. Attila loitered near the edge of the playground, cradling her books in a sophisticated high school way. She zinged him her best smile. He looked her way, swung onto his bike, and headed toward Fool's Bridge and the inn.

I smiled at her and waved.

"Come on," Dale said. "I'll let you feed Newton."

Newton eats dead bugs. "I'd love to, but Newton's gaining weight and I'd hate to put too much strain on his knees. Miss Lana says added pounds mean added sorrow later in life." I watched Harm pedal away. "Where's he going? He headed the other way yesterday—toward the Piggly Wiggly."

"Who cares?" Dale yawned.

"Okay, I'll feed Newton, but let's swing by the inn first," I said. "We need *before* photos."

He grinned. "You want to follow Harm Crenshaw," he said, hopping on his bike. "I'm curious too."

Five minutes later, Dale skidded to a stop on the black-top. We stared up and down the empty highway. "Harm Crenshaw doesn't have invisibility skills, does he?"

The sweat trickled down my spine and wicked along the waistband of my shorts. "No. Just long legs and a fast bike. Maybe he hid," I said, scanning the drying corn-fields along the road. "Come on," I said, heading for the inn's drive. "Let's get some photos."

We stopped in the last curve of the cedar-lined drive. I held the old camera against my belly and lined up my first shot of the inn. *Click.* Dale pointed to an upstairs window. "Who's that?"

"Where?"

"In the corner room. Somebody's watching us."

The wavy old window glass glinted as a gust of wind shook the cedars, and the clouds shifted overhead. "The sun, maybe," I told him, but even in the afternoon heat a shiver tiptoed up my spine.

"Maybe it's the girl from auction day. I hate to say ghost," he whispered.

"Auction day? That was Harm Crenshaw."

"You're guessing," he said as we crept toward the inn.

"I'm deducing," I said. "Clue number one: We'd already caught him following us once—on the path with Mr. Red. Number two: Harm wasn't in the auction

tent when we got back. Clue three: Lavender said it himself—Harm's trouble."

I peered at the upstairs window. "In fact," I said, heading for the steps, "if anybody's in that window now, I'm betting it's Harm Crenshaw."

A gust of wind sent a swirl of leaves tumbling down the porch. An old rocking chair creaked. *Click.* I pushed the front door open, strolled to the foot of the staircase, and lined up a photo: two stairs, three steps missing, eight good stairs to the top. "Thirteen steps," Dale muttered. "That's bad."

"Detectives ain't superstitious," I told him. *Click.* "Hello?" I called, aiming my camera at the top of the stairs. "Harm?"

Nothing.

"Be careful, Dale," I said, starting up the stairs. "Keep to the edges." When I reached the missing steps, I balanced on the runners. "Hello?" Still nothing. I looked down the long hall. "Which room, Dale?"

He pointed to a closed door.

"If it's Harm, we got him cornered," I whispered.

"If it's a ghost, it's got *us* cornered," he said, his voice bleak.

I tiptoed to the door and turned the knob. The door squeaked open on a room lined with bookshelves. "A

library," I said. I walked to the window and pushed back a rotting curtain. "An old one," I added as dusty light flooded the room. *Click.*

Dale rounded an ancient leather sofa. He brushed a shelf, sending a book tumbling to the ragged carpet. I scooped it up and blew the dust off. "Geometry," I murmured, opening it. Faded brown ink flowed across the end paper.

"Cursive," Dale whispered, and I nodded. Miss Retzyl's a fan of cursive writing. I tilted the book to the window's light.

I hate math. N.B.—August 28, 1937.

Inky fingerprints stained the bottom of the page.

Dale ambled to the window. "I must have been seeing things," he said, peering behind the curtain. "There's nobody up here but us." He padded to a cabinet with double doors at its base. "What's in here?" he asked, squatting down.

He tugged. The doors didn't budge. He shifted his weight, and yanked hard. Harder. The doors flew open. Dale rolled backward, a ragged wave of mice scurrying across the rug. "Rats!" he screamed, swatting at his feet.

I grabbed the back of his shirt and dragged him toward the door. "Run!" We thundered down the stairs, hurling ourselves over the missing steps and landing at the bottom of the staircase, panting.

"Mice," Dale said, looking sheepish. "Maybe babies."

I tried to catch my breath. "Miss Lana says everything's relative," I told him, shoving the geometry book into my messenger bag. "They looked relatively huge to me," I lied. Dale scuffed to the old piano and opened the keyboard. Music settles Dale the way rain settles dust.

"'Heart and Soul'?" he invited, scooting the piano bench out. "Heart and Soul" is the only performance piece I got. Miss Rose tried to show me more, but when it comes to music, I'm a good listener. I put the camera on top of the piano, slipped onto the bench, and placed my fingers in the go position.

He sang as we played. "Heart and soul . . ."

Upstairs, a door slammed. Footsteps pounded to the top of the stairs.

"That's not mice!" Dale said, jumping up and spinning to face the stairs.

"Harm Crenshaw?" I bellowed. "Cut it out!"

A girl laughed and a wave of cold fell over us like a curtain of ice. "That ain't Harm," Dale whispered. Footsteps flew down the empty staircase like a ragged drumroll, hitting every step dead center—all thirteen of them.

They turned and clattered straight for us.

"Run," I cried, grabbing my camera. We scrambled to the door and yanked it open. I spun to the piano. *Click.*

The keyboard slammed closed, sending an unearthly collision of sound rolling through the inn as Dale pounded across the porch.

"I'm Mo and that's Dale and we need an interview!" I screamed, tossing our business card on the floor.

And I ran for my life.

Chapter 8
Blueprints and Party Plans

At the top of the driveway's curve, Dale skidded his bike to a halt. "That was *not* Harm Crenshaw," he said. "That ghost is real as we are. Maybe realer."

"Right." I looked up at the gray cloudbanks rushing overhead. "We better get home. It's going to storm."

"Mo," Dale whispered, clutching my arm. "Over there." A flash of silver melted into the trees as thunder rumbled across the sky.

Harm Crenshaw? *Again?* It couldn't have been, not this time.

I looked over my shoulder, at the inn—at a girl in the window—and my heart sputtered. I blinked and the window stared back empty. My mouth went desert dry. "Race you to the café," I said as raindrops pattered across the drive. "The Colonel and Miss Lana will know what to do."

Moments later we dropped our bikes in the café parking lot by a white minivan: Azalea Women. "Don't breathe a word of this until we get the Colonel and Miss

Lana alone," I warned. "Ghost news will zip through town lightning-fast. Maybe faster."

"Right," he panted as I opened the café door. "Not a word."

We stepped inside. "Ghost," he said.

Miss Lana and Grandmother Miss Lacy looked up from giant blueprints they'd spread over a corner table. Two Azalea Women by the window stopped drinking tea in mid-sip. Violin music wafted from the jukebox. The air smelled warm and yeasty.

"Sorry," he whispered. Sometimes I could kill Dale.

"He means ghost in the fine print," I said, very quick. "Old news," I added for the Azalea Women. "Don't bother telling it. It's all over town."

The Azalea Women slipped back into conversation.

The Colonel says loose lips sink ships. Dale's could sink a fleet.

"Buon giorno," Miss Lana said, smiling.

"Back at you," Dale said, and leaned toward me. "French?" he whispered.

"Italian," I replied, pointing to the Leaning Tower of Pisa salt and pepper shakers center stage of the red-and-white checked tablecloths.

The Colonel runs the café like a military operation—all polish and precision. Miss Lana prefers a theme. You know who's in charge the instant you walk through the

door. "Come in," Miss Lana said, smiling. "We're creating a new spinach lasagna tonight. We'd love to have your opinion, Dale. You're such a connoisseur."

"Connoisseur," I whispered. "French for know-it-all."

He headed for the phone, his sandals slapping against the floor. It was a comforting, real-world sound. "I'll ask Mama if I can stay," he said, grabbing the phone. "She'll probably want me to, with a storm rolling in." He stepped over something behind the counter. "Hey Lavender. What you doing under there?"

Lavender? Here?

I darted through the tables and slid to a halt, my plaid sneakers squeaking against the tiles. "Good afternoon," I said, hooking my elbow on the counter, very sophisticated. "What a pleasant surprise."

He looked up, flat on his back, his shoes braced against the baseboard. "Hey yourself, Mo LoBeau," he said. He tugged hard at something under the counter, straining until his arm muscles bulged and his face went red.

Even beet red, Lavender's fly-apart gorgeous.

"That should do it, Miss Lana." He stood up and dropped a pipe wrench in his battered red tool box. "If that fitting gives you more trouble, just call."

When Miss Lana wants something fixed, she mostly calls Lavender. She says it's less trouble than strangling

the Colonel. Plus she likes to contribute to Lavender's car fund. "Tell Mama hey for me," he told Dale.

As Dale dialed, the door swung open. Sal and twelve-year-old Skeeter MacMillan, Tupelo Landing's attorney-in-training, blasted in on a gust of wind. "Afternoon," Miss Lana said, heading for the milkshake machine. "The usual?"

"Yes please." Sal pushed her red sunglasses on top of her head and led the way to a table as Miss Lana scooped ice cream into a metal cup.

Skeeter ticked opened her briefcase. "Is the Colonel in? I'd like his opinion on a legal matter."

Miss Lana popped the metal cup in place. "He's in the kitchen. But if it's a legal matter, I hope you'll wait," she said as the Azalea Women looked up.

Miss Lana hit the milkshake machine's *whir* button.

"The Colonel would rather eat maggots than talk law," I told Skeeter, using the machine's whir for cover. "His amnesia only lifted a few weeks ago. He's still sensitive."

Skeeter closed her briefcase as the whir died and Dale hung up the phone. In the silence, I could just hear Grandmother Miss Lacy humming a familiar song.

The hair on my arms rose up like ghosts as I recognized the tune. "Heart and Soul"—the song Dale and me just played at the inn.

Dale leaned close to me, his eyes glued to Grand-

mother Miss Lacy. "That song," he whispered. He gulped. "I hope she ain't been repossessed."

Her melody morphed into another tune. "You mean possessed," I whispered. "Let's investigate."

He shook his head. "I want to talk to Salamander."

Right. I headed for Grandmother Miss Lacy. "Hey, I never heard you hum to yourself," I said, settling beside her. "How do you pick your tunes?"

"Oh! Was I humming?" she asked, running her finger over the blueprints. "Forgive me, dear; when you live alone, you find unusual comforts. Take a look at these blueprints, Mo. They're fascinating." At the window table, the Azalea Women gathered their rain gear and headed for the cash register, leaving a twenty-five-cent tip.

I leaned over the blueprints. Salt shakers at each corner kept them from curling like scrolls. "Where'd you get them?" I asked as Lavender sauntered over.

"Found them in the courthouse," he said. "Allow me. Here's the inn, and the main drive. Here's the shortcut by Red Baker's place. But look at this," he said. "A path from the inn to the old store—a path I've never seen before."

"That's the old Judas Trail," she said. "Nobody's used it since the inn closed. I doubt you can even find it anymore."

Dale gulped. "The *Judas* Trail? No wonder nobody

uses it, with a name like that." He smiled at Miss Lana as she passed the shakes around. "Mama says thanks for inviting me to supper and may I please spend the night. Her headache's back."

Miss Rose gets headaches ever since Dale's daddy went to jail again. Not because he's in jail, but because she's divorcing his sorry self. Miss Lana says even good changes can be stressful. "Of course you can stay," she said.

Excellent, I thought. We'll deliver our ghost news after supper.

"Hey Dale," Sal said, taking a package from her satchel. "Your order's in."

Skeeter and Sal started their new business—Skeeter-Bay—the day Skeeter went high-speed. They'll order anything that's legal if you pay cash up front plus twenty percent.

Sal blushed as Dale sat beside her. "*Instant Guitar: Three Chords to Fame and Fortune* with a bonus section: *Songwriting 101*. It looks like a great book, Dale." She tilted her head, her gray eyes soft. "I just know you're going to be a star."

"Thanks," he said modestly. Dale kills me.

Lavender pulled up a chair by mine—a gold-star moment in a so-far hideous day. "Where's the medicinal springs?" I asked, studying the blueprints. Lavender,

who's between cars, usually smells like motor oil. Today he smelled faintly of sawdust and pine.

"In the old springhouse," he said, pointing to a drawing of a small building with numbers clustered on the floor. "Each spring cured a different ill—or not," he added, tapping a prickle of tiny crosses in the woods.

"The old cemetery," Grandmother Miss Lacy said, and a chill skated across my skin. "It's on a pretty little rise, as I recall. Thousands came here hoping to be healed by the springs. But you're right: Some of them do rest in that cemetery."

And maybe some of them don't rest at all, I thought.

"Check out the date," Lavender said. "Norton Blake renovated the inn in 1938," he said, "which means the wiring's too old to be safe. We'll have to rewire it."

"Sounds expensive," Miss Lana said, her voice tight. She'd already bled her bank account dry to buy her half of the inn. "With the cost of the painting . . ."

"Don't worry," Grandmother Miss Lacy told her. "We'll be fine."

Like I say, Grandmother Miss Lacy's the richest person in town.

"There's good news too," Lavender continued. "The floors are heart pine, and the windows antique glass. The inn needs a lot of elbow grease and paint, but she'll be a work of art when she's done."

The Colonel marched in from the kitchen with a box of cups. "Lavender's agreed to supervise the day-to-day construction on the inn if I head the project," he told Miss Lana and Grandmother Miss Lacy. "We can start hiring tomorrow—if it suits you."

Lavender? At the inn? Every day?

"Suits me," I said. "Dale and me got a ton of research to do out there. And I'll immortalize you in film."

At the next table, Sal stripped the paper off her straw. "I'm glad you stuck with your ghost research, Dale. That's brave. I just hope you don't go zombie," she added, holding her arms out and rocking back and forth in her seat.

"Zombie?" Dale said, his voice quaking. "Can that happen?"

"We ain't worried," I told Sal, and Lavender grinned. Lavender's grin makes me feel like I can do anything except maybe fractions. "Dale and me already presented our card to the disembodied in question."

Dale choked on his milkshake. "We did?"

"Impressive," Sal murmured.

The café door swung open. Queen Elizabeth shot between the mayor's tasseled loafers, scuttled across the floor, and sprawled at Dale's feet, panting. "Darnedest thing I've ever seen, the way that dog can find you," Lavender said as Sal reached down to smooth Liz's ears.

"She's psycho," Dale explained, and Sal snatched her hand back.

"He means psychic," I told her.

Mayor Little smoothed his tie over his round belly. "Happy Friday afternoon, fellow citizens," he said. He sniffed and took in the tablecloths. "Rome?"

"Sì," I replied as the Colonel measured fresh coffee into the coffeemaker. "The spinach lasagna ain't ready but I can make you a PB&J Italiano. It comes hand-squished flat on the plate or fluffy, with a sprig of parsley on the side."

He tossed his rain hat on the counter. "Gratci Mo, but I'm here on business." He beamed at us. "Have I mentioned the town's 250th anniversary party?"

Miss Lana lit up like neon. She loves parties like Lavender loves the scream of tires. "We'll host it here, won't we, Colonel?"

The Colonel sighed. "Probably."

"Thanks, you two," the mayor said, "but I'm thinking full-blown gala. Music, food, out-of-towners. Maybe even the governor. I was wondering about the inn. We have a little jingle in the town coffers . . ."

"Jingle?" Sal said, looking up from her milkshake. Sal possesses a warp-speed calculator for a brain. She slipped a pencil sharpener from her book bag.

"Not a fortune," the mayor warned. "More like a little

mad money in my sock drawer. I'm thinking November first-ish."

"The inn closed October 22, 1938," I told him. "It's on the auction flyer."

"Perfect." He beamed. "October 22 it is."

"Of *this* year?" Lavender said. "Impossible. We have to rewire, patch, paint. There's no way we can be ready in time."

"Production bonus," Sal said. "If Lavender finishes on time, he gets cash for his car fund." She fluffed a ruffle. "A tight schedule means extra stress and possible therapy costs. And overtime means extra taxes. Lavender needs a thousand dollars and no penalty in the unlikely event that he fails."

Lavender blinked. His blue chambray shirt makes his eyes look even bluer—something he pretends not to know. "A thousand dollars? Are you serious?"

"Done," the mayor sighed.

"I'll draw up the agreement after I finish my homework," Skeeter said. She flashed the Colonel a look. "Unless you want to, sir."

The Colonel hesitated. For a split second, I thought he would say yes. "Thank you, Skeeter, but no. Carry on." He headed for the kitchen.

Sal smiled at Lavender. "We didn't discuss our fee, but we have a hair dryer smoking up our office space."

Skeeter's law office is in the storage room of her mama's hair salon. Sal's accounting firm occupies a corner desk. "If you could fix it . . ."

Lavender nodded. "Done again."

"We'll need entertainment," Miss Lana said.

"I'm developing DJ skills to defray future law school expenses," Skeeter said. "I'll *pro bono* you as a public service. I think my expenses are tax deductible?" she asked Sal, who nodded. Nobody knows for sure if Sal actually files taxes. Dale and me suspect she fills out the forms for fun, same as Miss Lana does Sudoku.

"Wonderful. I hope you'll spin some beach music classics," the mayor added, slithering his loafers across the floor and shaking his hips.

"Shoot me," Dale muttered.

The mayor twirled, his jacket flying open. "What was that, Dale?"

"I said I'll sing," Dale said. "And play my guitar if I learn it good enough. If anybody wants me to."

"I do," Sal said.

"Then it's settled," Miss Lana said. "This is just what we need to help us focus."

"She's right," Dale told his brother. "Stress focuses you right up until it sucks your brain dry. Standardized testing taught me that."

Mayor Little paused at the door. The wind grabbed

the sycamore, sending autumn's first golden leaves to the parking lot. "No pressure, Lavender," he said. "But the whole town's counting on you."

"Right," Lavender groused as the door banged shut. "We've got to replace windows, patch the roof, redo the kitchen . . ."

"And evict a ghost," I said.

Everybody laughed except Dale and me.

Chapter 9
A Plan of Attack

"We'll tell the Colonel and Miss Lana about the ghost straight out and professional," I told Dale that evening. Me, Dale, and Queen Elizabeth had kicked back in my flat, which some folks mistake for a closed-in side porch with a bathroom stuck on the end. Miss Lana and the Colonel had settled in the living room.

Our home, which takes up the back half of the café building, overlooks Miss Lana's gardens and the creek. The café, in the front half of the building, overlooks the parking lot and highway. Like me, the Colonel and Miss Lana each have their own living spaces. Miss Lana's suite lies across the living room from my flat. The Colonel keeps his quarters, near the kitchen, spit and polish neat.

I crossed to my Salvation Army desk and opened my top drawer. It sticks.

"Ghost news is like Band-Aid removal," I said. I jammed my hand all the way to the back and grabbed a

crumpled clue pad, just in case. "It's best to do it quick." I peeked into the living room. Miss Lana sat in her rocker, reading *Historic Hollywood* magazine. The Colonel sat at a card table, leafing through a law book.

"Are they kissing?" Dale whispered. "Because I don't want to see that."

"No," I said. "And they never will."

I hated to admit it, but since the return of the Colonel's memory, the possibility of romance had occurred to me too. And maybe to him. Last week he brought Miss Lana a scraggly handful of goldenrod, a pale root dangling from the stem. "Sorry," he'd said, "I'm rusty." She'd looked like Skeeter's little sister just bit her. Then she'd laughed and put it in a pale blue Mason jar, root and all.

I mentioned it to her that night, in her suite, as she brushed out her Jean Harlow wig. "I don't mean to sound negative, but the Colonel bringing you flowers gives me the dry heaves. Can you make him stop?"

"He's just remembering our long-ago engagement, sugar," she said. "It's history, but as his amnesia lifts, his truth expands. That shifts my truth a little. And yours too, apparently."

Sometimes Miss Lana talks like a fog bank. I do the best I can.

"This new truth doesn't suit me," I'd said.

She shook Jean Harlow. "The truth is like spandex, sugar. It may not look like a good fit at first, but if you ease into it and wiggle around, it winds up fitting like your skin. Hand me that comb," she'd said. "Jean's snarled."

Now I looked at Dale. "If they can handle spandex, I'm pretty sure they can handle a ghost. Remember," I told him. "Act professional."

We slipped into the living room, Queen Elizabeth ticking along behind, and settled on Miss Lana's old curlicue settee.

She looked up from her magazine. "Paws," she said. Queen Elizabeth hopped off the settee and stretched out at Dale's feet.

"Good evening," I said, very professional. The Colonel looked up from his law book. "Nice weather if you're a duck," I continued, "but Thes says the rain will clear out by morning."

"Excellent," he said, and smiled.

Miss Lana turned a page in her magazine. "Homework all done?"

"It's Friday," I reminded her. "We prefer our homework to age over the weekend, making it tender. We're here on business. It's about the inn."

She closed her magazine. "Wonderful. I've been considering your interview. A brilliant idea! Such creative children. Ghost stories can be very lucrative." The lamplight made her hair glow coppery. "We'll need a sweet ghost. A poster ghost, really, something amusing for guests. Have you composed your interview questions?"

"The questions aren't due for weeks," I said. "The thing is, Miss Lana . . ."

"I'd gladly give them a look-see when you're ready," she said, and winked. "Or help you get started." The Colonel cleared his throat. "Not that we'd cheat," she added. "But since I'll build my PR campaign on your interview, we want a good foundation. We might even bring in a ghost investigator. My treat."

The Colonel snorted.

"Thanks," I said. "I'm glad you're excited, because we got a Situation."

"Snacks?" Dale asked, jumping up. Dale is a stress eater.

The Colonel turned a page. "Pantry," he said without looking over. "Second shelf." Dale padded past Miss Lana's suite, into the kitchen.

"Dale and me bumped into the entity in question this afternoon," I continued. "She comes across kind of . . . cold. More like the Anti–Poster Ghost."

Dale ambled back with a bag of coconut macaroons and settled beside me.

Miss Lana blinked slowly. "What could I possibly do with a cold ghost?"

"Rhetorical," I whispered to Dale. Too late.

"You could try a catch and release, but you'd need a live trap," he said.

A *live* trap?

The Colonel looked up from his book.

"That's what Lavender does when possums come after Mama's chickens at night," Dale continued. "Of course," he added, "we'd have to consider bait."

A hush fell over the room.

The Colonel closed his book. "You actually believe there's a ghost in the inn? Why? Did you see something?"

"Not exactly," I said. "Unless you count the piano slamming shut on its own."

"I'd count that," Dale said. "And I *did* see a girl in a window, but she'd evaporated by the time we got there. Unless she was a shadow."

"But we *heard* her," I added, keeping my eyes on the Colonel. "She ran down the stairs—including the ones that aren't there. And she laughed."

"Alternative explanations?" he said. The Colonel's big

on alternative explanations. It's one of the things I like about him.

"The first time we heard her, I thought it might've been Harm Crenshaw," I said. "But today it couldn't have been."

"Well," Dale said, helping himself to another cookie, "we did see a silver flash at the edge of the meadow. And Harm's bike *is* silver."

"It couldn't have been him," I said again. "The footsteps ran straight at us. And those footsteps were empty. And it got cold—a funny cold, one without edges."

"Like a bite without teeth," Dale added.

Miss Lana and the Colonel exchanged looks. The Colonel tapped his long fingers against his law book. "I'll look into it first thing in the morning, Soldier. You have my word. Thank you for your report."

I relaxed. The Colonel's word is gold.

"Maybe Dale and me can look with you, sir," I said, and Dale choked, sending a soft spray of crumbs across the settee. "Tomorrow's Saturday, and this *is* our case," I said, staring at Dale. "And half our history grade."

"I guess so," he mumbled.

"We just need a good plan of attack."

The Colonel nodded. "I'd appreciate the reinforcements. Why don't you two come over after you help

with the breakfast rush?" He rose. "Cot or couch, son?"

"Couch," Dale said, heading for the linen closet. Dale stays here so much lately, Miss Lana gave him his own sheets.

I snatched Miss Lana's Rainbow Row pillows from the couch and tossed them into a chair. Ghost Patrol with the Colonel.

We'd have our ghost sorted out in no time.

Chapter 10
Ghost Patrol
with the Colonel

The next morning, Dale and me pedaled for the inn. "Let's take the shortcut by Red Baker's," I said, coasting across Fool's Bridge and into the countryside.

"No," he said, looking at Queen Elizabeth, who loped behind us.

Before he could explain, the cornfield beside me exploded in a flash of silver. I slammed on brakes, skidding sideways as Dale slid to a halt alongside.

"Looking for me?" Harm asked, balancing his bike with his toes. "I know you been following me. Thought I'd help you out."

"We have not been following you," I lied.

"Well, we did try," Dale admitted. Dale will go truthful faster than anybody I know. I like that about him, but it can cripple an investigation. He looked at Harm's bike. "Fast ride."

"Smart rider," Harm replied, smiling. He wasn't entirely

bad when he smiled. "Where you headed? Tell me and I'll go slow so you can keep up."

"To the inn," Dale said. "The Colonel's put us on—"

"On photography duty," I said before Dale could say *Ghost Patrol*.

"Right. I hear he's hiring," Harm said. "Him and Lavender. It's all over town."

"Maybe," I said. "What you doing in Red Baker's cornfield?"

"Waiting for you. I'm hoping you'll put in a good word for me with the Colonel," he said. "I can build most anything. I took shop in Greensboro."

Me? Put in a good word for *him?*

Dale whistled between his teeth. "Shop. Nice. I do a good scarecrow, but that's about it," he said. "I made one for Mama and I got a freelance one not too far from here. I'm self-taught. We don't have shop until high school."

"Right," Harm said, not even bothering to smile. "Think about it, Ghoul Girl," he said. "You'd be doing the Colonel a good turn." He shoved off, heading for town.

Dale leaned down to scratch Liz's ears. "He's got some nerve, asking you to do him a favor and calling you names in the same breath."

"Race you," I replied, and blasted off down the road.

As we rocketed up to the inn, Lavender's mechanic, Sam, stood on the porch talking to Tinks Williams. "Morning, sunshine," Sam said, giving me a lopsided grin. "The Colonel's inside. Me and Tinks just signed on."

"Great." I grabbed my camera and lined them up. *Click.* "Hey Dale, stand over there," I said. "I'll immortalize you."

Dale bounced up on the porch and leaned against a fancy post, Liz by his side. "Give me a second, this ain't automatic," I reminded him. I held the camera against my belly and peered into the window on top.

Dale grinned.

"Don't smile," I told him. "Think DVD cover. And hold still."

He crossed his arms and leaned against the post, setting off a shower of paint flakes. "Attitude, Liz," he said. She slouched as Dale blazed a look into the camera.

"Perfect." *Click.*

"Hey, there's Mama," Dale said as Miss Rose rumbled across the yard in a pickup, a horse trailer bouncing behind. Dale rushed to open the trailer. His ill-tempered mule, Cleopatra, stomped out braying and rolling her eyes. "Isn't she a beauty?" he said.

Miss Lana says beauty's in the eye of the beholder. Cleo proves it. Long soot-black ears, sullen black-

rimmed eyes in a maple-colored face, legs too stubby for her body. Miss Rose grabbed Cleo's bridle. *Click.*

"The Colonel invited Cleo to eat this grass down," Dale said, "which is lucky for us. Our pasture needs a rest." I nodded, but if I knew the Colonel, luck didn't write that invitation.

The inn's front door creaked open. Lavender in a tool belt. *Click.*

"Hey Mama," Lavender said. "Come in, I'll show you around. Mo, there's some shots in here that will blow you away." Lavender in a tool belt had already blown me away. Now I just needed the Colonel to handle our ghost.

The Colonel had his battle plan. We searched the downstairs room by room. First the vestibule, with its check-in desk. Then the dining room, small back rooms, and dungeon of a kitchen. "All clear," the Colonel sang.

Finally the parlor, with its piano.

Dale hadn't looked square at the piano since we got there. "We were playing 'Heart and Soul' last time, sir," I said. "Maybe we should play it again."

He nodded and grabbed a picnic basket. "Carry on. I'll set up Lana's picnic."

"Miss Lana's picnic and not his," Dale whispered. "That's good." It was true. Miss Lana packs a picnic like

it could be your last meal. The Colonel leans toward beef jerky and water.

"Come on, Dale," I said. He slipped onto the bench and opened the keyboard. "You might want to move away from the stairs," I told the Colonel. "She's fast."

"Ten-four, Soldier." He carried the basket to the desk, and lifted out a white tablecloth and a silver candlestick.

Dale rolled an easy river of sound through the inn and I placed my hands in the go position. "Now," he whispered. He sang as I plinked out the melody. "Heart and soul . . ."

I looked over my shoulder, at the staircase. "Keep singing," I whispered. We played the song top to bottom three times. Nothing, nothing, nothing.

Being stood up by a ghost hurts, mostly because there's no way to get even.

"Perhaps your ghost is upstairs. We'll check after lunch," the Colonel said. He shook open his cloth napkin. "Lana's picnic is served."

A half hour later he polished off the last of Miss Lana's chicken salad, licked his fingertips, and smiled. "Ready, Desperados?" he asked, looking at the stairs.

"I'd better go check on Cleo," Dale replied, grabbing a handful of Oreos.

"Cleo's fine," I told him, putting the lid on Miss Lana's

Practically Organic Bread-and-Butter Pickles. "We're ready, sir."

The Colonel stacked our plates in the basket and blew out the candles. Dale looked at the stairs. "I got a question before we go up, sir. In case I don't make it back down."

"We'll make it down," the Colonel replied. "But shoot."

"It's about Daddy."

I grabbed the tablecloth and bunched it up to hold in the crumbs.

I knew Dale would ask about Mr. Macon sooner or later. On one hand, it made perfect sense: Mr. Macon and the Colonel used to be friends, so you'd think the Colonel, who's turned out to be an attorney, might help Mr. Macon now. On the other hand, it didn't make a lick of sense, as Mr. Macon was in jail for helping kidnap the Colonel and Miss Lana, and for giving Miss Rose a black eye.

If you ask me, jail suits him fine. Nobody hurts my people and walks free—not if I can help it.

"Daddy needs a good lawyer," Dale said. "I know most people say you're crazy, but I figure you're still better than most."

"Thank you," the Colonel replied, and dropped his napkin in the picnic basket. "Dale, I can't represent

Macon, if that's what you're thinking." Dale bobbed his head, same as he does when he learns he flunked a test. "In fact," the Colonel said, "I'll probably be called as a witness against him." His brown eyes searched Dale's face. "You and Mo might be called too."

Us? Testify? I'd never thought of that.

"We're ready, sir," I said, and Dale twisted his napkin.

"I'm not," Dale said.

The Colonel studied him. "Macon's in jail because of what he did, Dale. Not because of what you did."

"That's what Mama says," Dale told him, twisting his napkin tighter. The Colonel took it from his hands and tossed it into the basket. "I just figured you ain't all that reliable as a witness because of your amnesia. So maybe they'd let you be an attorney instead." He gazed into the Colonel's eyes.

The Colonel grinned. "Good point. One that's sure to come up at trial. I can't defend Macon," he added. "But I'll make sure he gets a good attorney."

Dale smiled and offered his hand. "Thank you."

The Colonel shook his hand and clapped his shoulder. "I believe Lavender's put boards over those missing steps," he said. "Let's track your ghost."

I grabbed my camera and looked at the stairs. My chicken salad sandwich flapped its wings. "Age before beauty, sir," I said.

"Thank you, my dear," he replied, and headed up the steps.

The wide upstairs hallway, with its faintly stained wainscot and faded wallpaper, split two sets of rooms. An old steamer trunk stood halfway down the hall. I lined up a shot of its worn leather handle. *Click.*

The Colonel tried guestroom #1. Saggy brass bed, a rocking chair, a tilted washbasin. *Click.* "Nobody here," he said, peering in an open chifforobe.

We headed down the hall, opening door after door. #2, #3, #4. Nobody, nobody, nobody. #5, #6, #7. *Click, click, click.* "Last room," he announced.

The library door creaked open. A mouse scurried from the cabinet, and Queen Elizabeth bounded after it. "No, Liz," Dale shouted. "Spit it out!"

"Lana will love this room," the Colonel said, and plucked a ragged book from the shelf. He leaned against the window frame, opened the book, and held it flat on his palm. *Click.* A paper slipped from his book and swooped to the floor.

"A photo!" I said, picking it up.

Two girls in old-timey dresses peered at us from the photo. A blur of a boy reached for a third girl. The camera had caught only her heel and ragged skirt-tail as she ran away. "Who's this?" I asked, turning the photo over, hoping for a footnote. Nothing.

"Miss Thornton might know," the Colonel said, and Queen Elizabeth sneezed. "We're out of rooms," he added, his patient brown eyes watching mine.

"Colonel, I know I heard somebody run down those stairs," I said, pocketing the photo. "And the keyboard slammed shut and the place chilled meat-locker cold."

"I know it too," Dale said.

The Colonel crossed his arms over his thin chest. "Whatever you saw is no longer in evidence," he said. "I'm not sure what else we can do."

Downstairs, the front door opened and closed. Lavender called up to us. "Colonel? The mayor's here."

The Colonel scowled. "I'd rather go toe-to-toe with your ghost," he muttered. "I haven't had time to explore the grounds," he said. "Could you two investigate?" He reached in his pocket. "You're welcome to my compass."

The Colonel never leaves home without his compass.

"Thank you, sir," I said. "But we'll stick to the paths."

Downstairs, the Colonel headed for the mayor and I made a beeline for Lavender, who was sanding the old reservation desk.

"No key," he said, tugging at a small drawer. "I'd hate to call a locksmith." He smiled. "How'd Ghost Patrol go?"

"Bad," I admitted. "Just like our surveillance of Harm Crenshaw."

The door swung open. "Speak of the devil," Dale said.

"That's some hello." Harm walked over to Lavender and stuck out his hand. "Crenshaw," he said. "Harm Crenshaw. Mo tells me you're hiring."

I glared at him. "I did not."

"I'm good with tools. I'm strong. And I'm not afraid of ghosts. How about it?"

Lavender smiled, but the friendly didn't make it to his eyes. "Lavender Johnson," he said, giving Harm's hand a quick shake.

"You know my brother, Flick," Harm said—like that would be a good thing. "I'm only in this two-bit town until Flick gets me set up in Greensboro, but I'll work hard while I'm here. How about it? You could use a good man."

Lavender picked up his paint scraper. *Click.* "Thanks, but Miss Retzyl would pin my ears back if I kept you out of school," he said. "We have laws, even in this 'two-bit town.'"

I clicked the shutter again just as Harm shifted to one side. Crud. A photo of Harm.

"Didn't mean anything by it," Harm told Lavender. "Some people like two-bit towns." He shoved his hands in his pockets. He might have looked cool if his fists hadn't strained against the fabric. "As for Miss Retzyl, I'm not worried about that backwoods nag."

Backwoods nag? Miss Retzyl?

"Take that back!" I shouted. "You ain't known her long enough to call her names."

"Sorry," Harm said, keeping his eyes on Lavender. "An after-school job? How about it? Minimum wage won't hurt my feelings."

"No thanks," Lavender said, his voice firm.

He shrugged. "Suit yourself," he said, heading for the door. "See you around, Ghost Girl."

Click. Just in case I ever need a photo for evidence, I thought.

"That kid's too much like his brother," Lavender said, watching him mount his bike. Harm zipped past the window and headed for the meadow.

I smiled at Lavender. "We'd love to stay and chat, but the Colonel has entrusted us with a critical task of an outdoor nature."

"We got to look around," Dale added, peeling off his sweatshirt.

Lavender picked up his sandpaper. "Watch out for snakes if you go down to the water."

Snakes. Great.

We crossed the front yard and headed for the trail leading to the creek.

"I don't understand ghosts any more than I understand girls," Dale said, kicking a pinecone ahead for Queen Elizabeth. "Why didn't she come? We even played her song."

"Maybe the Colonel makes her nervous," I answered.

The path twisted down the hill to a small brick build-ing. Its sunken steps led to a door wearing a heavy chain and padlock.

"The springhouse," Dale said, circling the building. A ramble of kudzu draped the back wall; red bricks peeked between large, deep-green leaves. "Used to have a back door," he added. "Somebody filled it in with stacks of orange bricks. In a hurry too," he said, poking at a crooked brick. "Weird."

"Why would anybody do that?" I murmured. *Click.*

He looked toward the creek. "And there's the old pavilion where my granddaddy first danced with the girl he would marry." He gave me a shy smile. "My grand-mother," he said, like I couldn't figure it out.

We picked our way down the steep, washed-out path to a large riverside platform riddled by water and time. A snake slithered into the still water and zigzagged away. Dale didn't even blink. "The band played at that end," he said, pointing to a pile of boards. "Mama says they hung lanterns between these poles so light skipped across the water, and they kept the floor polished so the ladies could glide."

I looked at the broad cypress-lined creek and won-dered if my Upstream Grandmothers once danced—if they had more grace than me. *Click.*

A trace of rosemary drifted by. Queen Elizabeth sneezed and the hedge behind her moved against the breeze—just a glimmer of a form, a shimmer in the air, a rustle where a rustle shouldn't be.

Fear skated across my skin like heat lightning. "Dale," I whispered.

"I saw her," he said. And he took a step closer to me.

That night I settled into bed with the *Piggly Wiggly Chronicles*, Volume 6.

> Dear Upstream Mother,
>
> Today we saw the ghost.
>
> She followed Dale and me to the pavilion and stood behind a privet hedge, eavesdropping. Or watching. Seeing her froze me solid. I didn't even shoot her photo, which would have been proof positive. Also a certain A.
>
> It's hard when you got a ghost and nobody believes you. Not the Colonel, who searched. Not Miss Lana, who wants a Poster Ghost. Not even Lavender.
>
> Would you believe me? I think maybe you would.
>
> Mo

Chapter 11
The Alchemy of Light

On Monday, interview refusals flocked in from elders with second thoughts. Maybe the weekend had something to do with it, maybe the promise of autumn brought it on. Either way, Hannah Greene got shot down by travel.

"Grandmother went to Wrightsville Beach and decided to stay," she explained. "My great-aunt Tildy's subbing for me. She was at the Greensboro sit-ins." She smiled in Harm's direction. "You're from Greensboro. Maybe you've heard of them."

He didn't even look her way.

I opened my notebook to the empty section, the one marked math. *Harm = jerk.*

The Exums raised their hands. "Uncle Lewis remembered he can't stand us. He says we should get lost, maybe forever."

Miss Retzyl squeezed off a Pity Look. "I'm sure he didn't mean it."

Attila raised her hand. "I think he did."

"We're switching to Miss Delilah Exum," Jake replied. "She runs the best candy counter in the county."

"She has to like us," Jimmy added. "We're customers."

Thes raised his hand. "My uncle backed out too." He twisted in his desk, gazing hopefully at Attila. "Anybody want a partner?" Attila pretended to clean out her desk. "Fine," Thes sighed. "I'll take Mayor Little's mother."

The class gasped. Thes? And the meanest woman in town?

"I know," he said. "But she goes to our church and Daddy says I have to."

"She's a donut," Dale explained.

"Donor," Thes said. "She's a donor."

"I'm sure she'll be delighted," Miss Retzyl said. She looked at Harm, who sat with his eyes closed. "Harmond?" His snore zigzagged through the silence, soft and ragged as cotton. "Harmond Crenshaw!" she said, and he jumped like she'd Tasered him. "Whom will you interview? I need to know. Now."

"Interview?" Harm mumbled, his voice thick. "I'm working with Anna Celeste. She's got old what's-her-name."

Attila sat up. "Really?" she said. "I'm game if you are."

Thes gaped, his freckled face startled. "I thought you didn't want a partner."

"She doesn't want a partner with orange hair and

freckles," I explained. "Miss Retzyl, I object. I don't like Harm snooping around Grandmother Miss Lacy."

Miss Retzyl ignored me. "Harmond, you've already dropped a grade for taking so long to name an interview subject. The best you can make at this point is a B."

Anna's mouth fell open. "Does that apply to his partner too?"

"Oh no, not a B," Dale said, his voice quivering like a slap of lunchroom Jell-O.

"And how's *your* project coming?" Miss Retzyl asked, her stare ricocheting off me to hit Dale right between the eyes.

"Mo's got updates," he said, and stopped breathing.

"Thank you, Dale," I said. "Everything's going very smooth for Dale and me. We've introduced ourselves to our Entity, who prefers to remain anonymous for now, and presented our card. We've shot five rolls of film and we're working in the darkroom with Miss Lacy Thornton this afternoon."

"*I'm* interviewing Miss Thornton after school," Attila said. "She's not available for lesser endeavors until later."

Lesser endeavors? I hate Attila Celeste.

Miss Retzyl clapped her book shut. "Don't forget your science chapter tonight. Harmond, a word please," she said as the bell rang.

Yes. Detention for sleepy-headed Harm Crenshaw.

* * * * *

An hour later, I settled into Dale's beanbag chair. I pulled a clue pad from my bag and scrawled a title across the page: *Harm Crenshaw Investigation.*

"What do we know about the subject in question?" I asked.

Dale sat cross-legged on the floor, cradling his guitar. He twisted a key on the guitar's neck, sending the string's tone higher. He closed his eyes, listening. "If you're talking about science, I'm lost."

"I'm talking about Harm Crenshaw, our surveillance subject, who may be infiltrating Grandmother Miss Lacy's house as we speak."

He opened his music book and studied a diagram. "It's amazing how many songs you can play with just three chords. If you can sing, I mean. And I don't think Harm's infiltrating, Mo. I think he's just desperate not to fail history, same as us. Why else would he work with Attila?"

"What do we know about him, really?"

Dale looked up. "Okay, here's what I know: If Harm was any faster on that bicycle, we'd hear a sonic boom."

"First-class getaway vehicle. Check."

"He wears the same black pants and scuffed shoes every day, and has just three shirts. So he's poor. Which," he said, "poor happens."

Poor? I hadn't noticed, maybe because of the fancy bike.

He strummed his guitar. "That was a minor chord," he announced, strumming again. "Minor chords sound like Spanish moss." He was right. The sound felt lonely, like Spanish moss on a cloudy day. He played a cheerier chord. "Major chords sound like oak trees with their roots solid in the ground." He rested his arm against his guitar. "And Harm doesn't have a mother, same as you."

No mother? The words kicked me in the chest.

"What makes you say that?" I asked, my voice going tight as his guitar string.

"He eats a square meal every day," he said. "Orange four-cornered Nabs. Square, get it? He brings them from home the poor way instead of getting them out of a vending machine the flashy way. What mother gives you nothing but Nabs for lunch?" He strummed. Queen Elizabeth pawed at her ear. "That can't be right," he muttered.

He looked at me, his blue eyes serious. "Why do you care about Harm?"

"It's like Lavender says: Harm's trouble. I don't want him honing his evil skills on Grandmother Miss Lacy."

He shrugged. "Miss Thornton's smart. She can take care of herself."

I glanced at the clock. "Speaking of Grandmother Miss Lacy, she's expecting us at five o'clock to develop our photos. And I've shot enough photos of her and Miss Lana to paper the inn's lobby. With any luck I also got a portrait of our ghost. Academic jackpot. Feel free to applaud."

Instead of clapping, Dale squinted at Sir Isaac Newton. Newton stood on a piece of driftwood, staring at a fly. Even for an introvert, he looked moody. "I would go with you," Dale said, "but I promised Newton I'd write him a song." He lowered his voice. "He's going through an awkward stage and I'm the only friend he's got."

What? I'm being dumped for a newt?

"So far my entire life's an awkward stage, but you don't see me staring at flies," I said. "You're just afraid to see a possible ghost photo." I stood up, very dignified. "And since when can you write a song?"

"Since in about fifteen minutes from now."

Dale has an unusual grasp of time.

"Fine," I said. I closed the door behind me.

"Come in, dear," Grandmother Miss Lacy said, her carved oak door squeaking open. I peeped into the parlor. Attila perched on a velvet chair, a digital recorder at her side. "Anna Celeste is just finishing her interview," Grandmother Miss Lacy said loudly. She leaned close

to my ear. "Thank heavens you're here. That child has interviewed me half to death."

I swept into the parlor. No Harm. "Hey Attila. Did you dump your partner?"

"*Dump* is an unattractive term, Moses."

Sometimes I could kill the Colonel for naming me Moses. I know I washed into town, but give me a break.

"Harmond and I agreed it's to our mutual advantage to work alone." A car horn tooted outside. "There's Mother. Thank you, Miss Thornton. I may have follow-up questions."

"Good glory," Grandmother Miss Lacy said, closing the door behind Attila. "I didn't know one girl could be so pushy." She smiled at me, her eyes twinkling. "Now you," she said. "I've been looking forward to this all day. I can't wait to introduce you to this form of . . . well, magic," she said, heading down the hall. "The alchemy of light."

She opened a door and I followed her into her tiny darkroom. She plucked two heavy rubber aprons from a hook. She put on hers, and handed me the other. Metal pans spanned the countertops, an old-fashioned machine crouched in the corner like a giant praying mantis. The air smelled mysterious and sharp.

"What *is* this stuff?" I asked, slipping the apron over my head. I wrapped the sash around, like the Colonel

does with his cooking apron, and tied a half bow in front.

She closed the door, turned off the regular light, and flipped a red one on. "My darkroom," she said. I blinked in the eerie red glow. "Here's the film you've shot," she said, pointing to five strips of reddish brown negatives dangling from a line. "Some of your images mystify me, but I'd say you have a good eye, Mo. A very good eye.

"Now, let's see how things develop," she said, opening a pack of paper. She smiled like a schoolgirl. "Develop. Photography humor," she explained. "I haven't had this much fun in years. What expectations do you have, dear?"

"The Colonel says expectations are Fate's ambush," I said. "But I hope I've photographed a ghost."

I hadn't.

Two hours later my first batch of photos dangled from the wire, drying. "I don't get it," I said. "No ghost. And I've got all these nice crisp photos of Lavender, Dale, Miss Lana, the Colonel, the inn. But all my photos of you look like they're sprinkled with light. I don't have a single good photo of you in the inn, and you're half owner!"

"Perhaps I'm not photogenic," she said in the easy way of people who know they photograph good. I looked at my photos of Harm.

"Harm's came out just like yours," I said. "Like globs of light stuck to him."

"Maybe we splashed some chemicals," she murmured.

"Just on your photos and Harm's? If they were all on one roll that might make sense. And every time I photograph the piano, I get nothing but a blur."

"An exposure issue, I imagine. That piano's stood in that dark corner forever."

I grabbed a pair of tongs and swirled my last shot in its rinse. "Dale and me played 'Heart and Soul' on that piano the other day," I said, remembering her humming in the café. Her elbow clattered against the enlarger. "You know it?"

"Every child who's ever graced a piano bench knows that old song. I've played it many times, with many friends." She squinted at my library shots. "We'll reshoot the library too. It's as blurry as the piano. Don't worry, dear, I have beau-coodles of film."

"That reminds me, I got an old photo to show you," I said. "From the inn's library."

She hung her rubber apron on the door. I followed her to the kitchen, where she poured two glasses of milk. I hesitated, wanting to tell her about the glimmer at the pavilion, and the footsteps in the inn. I eased up to the subject, not sure she'd believe me.

"I'd hoped to photograph our ghost to prove things

to . . . people." She arranged our cookies on a plate. "You don't believe in ghosts," I said, sitting at her breakfast table. "I mean, I know you don't out loud, in the café. But just between you and me. When it's quiet. Do you?"

She shook her head. "There's all kinds of ghosts in this world, Mo, but the kind you mean? No, I don't believe. Oh, I'd like to," she added. "An unexplained breeze brushes my face or a sound turns my head, and I always hope to see someone I miss. So far, no one's come for me."

I scooted to the edge of my seat. "But you believe in other kinds?"

"In a way, I suppose," she said, putting the cookies on the table. "At my age, I sit down to breakfast with memories more often than with people I can touch," she said, and reached over to squeeze my hand.

"Memories aren't ghosts," I told her.

She smiled. "Perhaps not. I'm sure you'll sort it all out, dear. Eternity is no match for the Desperados. Here," she added, "try these cookies. They're my favorites."

I reached for a cookie. "They're homemade, I'm sure," I said, very polite.

"Mercy, no," she said. "When you're my age you don't waste time making cookies." We settled into a comfort-

able silence. "I wonder what a picture of a ghost would look like," she finally said. "Don't you?"

Actually, I'd given it zero thought. Or if negative numbers can hook up to that idea, less than zero thought. "Yes ma'am," I said, reaching for my milk. "Now that you mention it, I do. Speaking of photographs . . ."

I opened my messenger bag and lifted out the photo from the library: two girls looking into the camera, a skirt-tail, a blur of a boy. "We found this in the library," I said. "I hoped you might know who they are."

She grasped the photo in both hands and tilted it toward the lamp. "Will you look at that," she said. "Of course. That's me," she said, pointing to the thin, smiling girl. "The sourpuss is Myrt Little, the mayor's mother." She stared at the blurry figure. "The skirt's a mystery, but that's Red Baker," she said, tapping the boy's image. "Always moving, whirling, never could stand still. I probably photographed him twenty times, and didn't get more than two good photos for my trouble."

"Red Baker?" I said. "Why would you photograph *him*?"

She laughed. "We were children together—and friends." She propped her chin on her hand. "Don't look so surprised. Red was a very nice boy. Besides, I like to

live a little on the edge. And Red Baker was certainly edgy—in an old-fashioned way."

Grandmother Miss Lacy and Red Baker, friends? Had the earth reversed its poles? "Red Baker used to be nice? What happened to him?"

"Anger, I suppose. Anger can corrode most anything if it sits still long enough."

Someone rapped at the door and she bustled down the hall. "Dale," she said, opening the door. "What a lovely surprise. And Queen Elizabeth. Do come in."

"We can't," Dale said. "Our paws are muddy. Excuse us, Miss Thornton, but is Mo here? Because I left my sweatshirt at the inn and Mama's gonna skin me alive if we don't get it back."

We? He wants me to go in a haunted inn at dusk for a *sweatshirt*?

"Mama's murderous careful about new clothes. And Mo *is* my best friend," he added. True. Being a best friend has its price.

I grabbed my messenger bag and headed for the door. The sun slanted low across Grandmother Miss Lacy's lawn, outlining her old garage in soft, golden light. "Thank you for the darkroom lesson," I said. "I loved it."

"So did I. You two be careful," she called as we crossed the porch. "It'll be dark before you know it."

I shivered. "She's right, Desperado," I said. "Let's fly."

Chapter 12
A Secret Uncovered

We pedaled frantic as bats on a rising moon. "Hurry," Dale panted as we swerved onto the inn's drive and bounced down the path, Queen Elizabeth galloping behind us. We jumped off our bikes and landed on our feet running across the lawn as the bikes spiraled to the earth behind us.

The inn's windows stared at us blank and empty. "At least nobody's looking at us this time," Dale said, glancing at the upstairs windows.

"Stop looking. She'll feel it and know we're here," I said.

"Right," he said, squinting up at the window.

"I said don't look!" I told him. "Where'd you leave your sweatshirt?"

"On the piano."

The one slammed shut by ghost hands?

"You know Dale, I've never actually taken something from a ghost. I'm not sure how they feel about that—as

a people, I mean." He frowned. "Maybe you should let her have it," I said. "It *does* get cold when she's around. It could be a good deed."

He shook his head. "I promised Mama I'd bring it back."

Dale's a Mama's Boy through and through. Of course, with the daddy he's got, what choice does he have?

He pushed the front door open. "Hello? Anybody home?" He peeked inside. "There it is," he whispered. "I hope she hasn't been wearing it." He looked around the room. "Not that there's anything wrong with you having nice things," he said, louder. He turned to me. "I'll sneak in and grab it. You wait out here with Queen Elizabeth. But if I scream, come get me."

Wait out here? Joy surged through me.

"If anything happens, I'll save you," I said, hoping I wouldn't run the other way instead. He flexed his knees like he stood on the free-throw line. Then he tiptoed in, every muscle set to run. "Don't look at the stairs," I whispered. "Or touch the piano keys. And don't . . ."

He snagged the sweatshirt, wheeled, and sprinted toward me. "Did you see her?" I demanded, slamming the door behind him.

"No," he said. "But I feel her staring at us. Let's go."

I grabbed my bike. If we went the long way, it would

be pitch dark before we made the café. "The shortcut," I said, looking at Red Baker's path.

He gulped. "Stay close," he told Queen Elizabeth. "No trash-talking to Red's dogs. You ain't as big as you think."

We barreled across the meadow and onto the path, our tires crunching across a carpet of leaves. Near Red Baker's place, Dale hopped off his bike and waved toward the ground in the universally recognized signal for Dismount and Slink.

He swore softly as he peered across the yard. "Mr. Red's outside," he whispered. "Somebody's with him."

A man's harsh voice shoved through the silence. "They'll never make it," he said. A man stepped into the light. Flick Crenshaw! Flick spit in the grass. "That inn will bleed them dry. That wing nut and the old biddy . . ."

Mr. Red scowled. "Watch your mouth. I've known Lacy Thornton all my life."

Flick shrugged. "Have it your way." He got in his red sports car. It roared to life and sped toward us. "The bikes!" We yanked them into the bushes as Flick tore past, headed for the inn's driveway. The engine's sound faded away.

"Let's get out of here," Dale whispered. He stepped back, and a twig snapped.

Red Baker wheeled to face us. "Who's over there?" he

demanded, picking up a swing blade. We froze. "Detective Joe Starr? Come out where I can see you."

He took a step toward us. "I know you're there. Show yourself."

His front door scricked open. "Stew's ready, Gramps," a familiar voice said. "Is Flick staying? I made enough for all of us."

"Hush." Mr. Red's gaze patrolled the edge of his yard.

Behind us, a fox squirrel scampered along a tree limb and sprang to the ground. Dale grabbed Liz and clamped his hand over her muzzle.

Red stared at the squirrel, his face relaxing, and then turned toward the house. "Keep your shirt on, boy, I'm coming. You nag me worse than your mama ever did," he said, and headed for the house.

I bent the sassafras branch down. A dark-haired boy slouched tall and lanky in the doorway. Mr. Red clomped up the crooked cinderblock steps and across the porch. The boy at the door turned into the light.

"Crenshaw, Harm Crenshaw," I whispered. "He's Red Baker's grandson."

Chapter 13
Preemptive Strike

The next morning, we dropped our bikes and headed for the schoolhouse door. "Desperados," a voice called. "Wait up."

We turned to see Harm Crenshaw pedaling hard across the grounds. He hopped off his bike, chained it to the bicycle rack, and swaggered over to us. "Hey," he said.

"Hey," Dale replied, giving him a gunslinger look.

"I checked out your scarecrow," Harm said.

"Who cares?" I demanded.

"Good work," he told Dale. "The lederhosen are a nice touch."

"Of course it's nice work," I said. "Miss Lana says Dale's an artist. Like van Gogh, only with both ears."

He frowned and glanced at Dale's ears. "Right," he said. "Look, I'm sorry things didn't work out with Lavender. He seems like a nice guy. I'd like to help him and . . ." He hesitated and changed course. "Okay, I'll level with

you. I could use the money. If either of you could put in a word for me. With Lavender or the Colonel . . ."

He stared at me, making his eyes soft and pleading.

"Puppy eyes," Dale warned, his voice scornful.

Harm Crenshaw was trying to play me! I swung my messenger bag over my shoulder. "If you need money, maybe your granddaddy can help you out," I said, heading toward the school.

Harm's puppy eyes disappeared. "Don't know what you're talking about."

"Red Baker dresses poor but people say he carries a roll of moonshine cash that would choke a mule." I looked at Dale.

"I know. Figure of speech," he said, beating me to it.

Harm hooked his thumb in his pocket and tried to smirk, but he moved jerky and off rhythm. "What's that got to do with me?"

"Red Baker," I said, heading up the steps. "He's your grandpa. Right?"

The door flew open. Attila stood with her hands on her hips, studying Harm with the gleam she usually reserves for research frogs. "You're Red Baker's grandson?"

"What if I am?" he asked, blushing. For a half second I felt sorry for him. I hate a blush. It's like a traitor riding beneath your skin.

"You eavesdropping, Attila?" I said. "Because where I come from, that's rude."

"Yes," she said. "And where *do* you come from?" She eyed Harm up and down. "That explains why you didn't want us to know where you live. I'd be ashamed too."

"Who says I'm ashamed?" Harm shot back.

"Actions speak louder than words," Attila retorted. "Excuse me, I'd hate to miss morning announcements. Wouldn't you, Harmond?" The door hissed closed behind her.

"What did you do to *her*?" Dale asked.

Harm shrugged. "She dumped me as her history partner, so I called her queen of the backwater brown-nosers."

Dale whistled. "She'll be gunning for you," he said as the three of us headed down the hall and settled into our desks.

Miss Retzyl claimed her place at the front of the room looking pretty in a regular pink dress and her own hair. She doesn't own a wig—I've asked. Dressing normal's a way of life for her—something I appreciate after a lifetime with Miss Lana. "Good morning," she sang.

Attila raised her hand. "I have an announcement. Normally I wouldn't say this, but I feel full disclosure's best in a small town. I'm sure we'd all agree."

Full disclosure? Has she lost her mind?

"She's ratting him out," Dale whispered, and I nodded.

I looked at Harm, who clenched his fist and took a deep breath. He wasn't going down without a fight. The Colonel says my enemy's enemy is my friend. I raised my hand, buying Harm some time. "I hear the Exums got in trouble last night," I said. "I thought I'd mention it in the interest of full disclosure."

"We did not!" Jake cried. "We don't even own any paint!"

Paint? What was that about?

Miss Retzyl clapped her hands. "Anna Celeste, you have the floor," she said.

Harm's voice boomed out. "Miss Retzyl, I've decided on my history paper. I'm interviewing my grandfather Mr. Red Baker, well-known moonshine consultant." The class gasped. Attila looked like a first grader who'd swallowed her ice cream money.

"Preemptive strike," Dale murmured. "Good."

"Your *grandfather*?" Sal said, studying him. "So that's who you are."

"You're interviewing Red Baker?" Hannah said, her voice tinted with admiration. "He's even meaner than Mayor Little's mother."

Harm's eyes never left Miss Retzyl's face. "I know I can only make a B at this point, but it's taken me this long to confirm my interview. Red's temperamental. I

appreciate your patience and hope my paper's worth your wait."

The class swiveled to Miss Retzyl. "Thank you, Harmond," she said, her voice bland as vanilla pudding. "I look forward to your report."

He gave Attila a smile. "Sorry I interrupted you, Anna," he said. "What were you saying?"

Attila slammed her book report onto her desk. "Never mind."

I grinned. Anna Celeste Simpson had met her match.

Chapter 14
Somebody Screamed.
Maybe Me.

Labor Day—with Miss Lana's famous Farewell to Summer Parking Lot Cookout—came and went, clearing the way for the first quick breath of autumn. The next day—Tuesday—Dale and me dropped by the inn after school. We found Lavender fuming on the front porch.

"I've never seen anything like it," he said, grabbing an armload of tools and taking them to his truck. "Everybody we hire runs away. Even Sam and Tinks quit. I'm never going to get this place ready in time for the party." He raked his fingers through his hair. "What are you two doing out here, anyway?" he asked, slapping his cap against his knee. "I'm in such a bad mood, I forgot to ask."

Lavender's bad moods fall rare as snow and melt just as quick.

"We got to reshoot some photos," I said.

"Come in, then. Tell me what you think," he said, slamming the tailgate shut and heading up the steps.

He pushed the door open and we stepped inside. Without their skins of cobwebs and dust, the rooms stood sleek and elegant. The heart pine floorboards stretched on like rivers of honey, the windows flooded the rooms with afternoon light. We walked across the lobby, our steps echoing. "It's big as Kansas in here," Dale said as Queen Elizabeth sniffed the baseboards.

"Five rooms cleaned, seven to go. But without Sam and Tinks . . ." He slapped his cap against his leg again. "I might as well tell you. I don't believe in ghosts, but it looks like everybody else in the county does."

Including us, I thought.

"Ghosts?" Dale said, looking worried. "Plural?"

"They swear ghosts move their tools. They hear foot-steps and voices. A girl's voice, men's voices . . ." I heard myself swallow. "Window glass that shouldn't break does break. It's ridiculous," he said. "I'm in and out of this place all the time and I haven't heard a thing. But I still have to hire again. *Because of ghosts.*"

"Are you sure they hear *voices*?" Dale asked, darting an anxious peek at the stairs. "Because there's only one ghost in Miss Lana's contract." He looked at me, his face grave. "We could have squatters from the other side."

Lavender snorted. "There's no ghost, little brother," he said. "Those guys are scaring themselves out of here.

Which means telling the ladies we got to post another ad. Are they at the café?"

"Miss Lana is," I said. "Grandmother Miss Lacy's gone to see her accountant."

"Again?"

"It's a full-time job being rich," I said. "That's what Miss Lana says."

He stuffed his shirttail in his jeans. "I wouldn't know about that, but I'd like to find out."

"You will, soon as you win Daytona," I told him.

"I do admire your confidence, Mo," he said. "You all want a ride to the café? I can put your bikes in the back of the truck."

Riding in the GMC with Lavender. Tempting. But I didn't want to see Miss Lana's face when he told her their workers had flaked like crescent rolls. "Thanks," I said, "but Attila's burning a DVD of Grandmother Miss Lacy and we got to get top-grade photos or risk Comparative Flunking. Skeeter can give us PowerPoint for a fee—if we get the photos in time."

"PowerPoint? Good name for a bird dog." He grinned. "Dale?"

"I'll stay," Dale said, his voice dull. "If I don't come out, tell Mama I love her."

"I think she's noticed," Lavender said. "Let me get this

over with." He hates giving Miss Lana bad news. Even his hair lost its luster.

I made my voice easy, the way Miss Lana does when I head for school shy a book report. "Lavender, even if you fail and ruin the biggest party in history and even if the entire town turns against you, Dale and me won't feel let down."

"I might," Dale said, putting his hands in his pockets. "A little."

Outside, the wind set the porch chairs rocking. Lavender stared at me a moment, possibly overwhelmed by my compassion.

"Thanks, Mo," he said. "I appreciate your support. Close the door on your way out," he added, and strolled out whistling.

"I'll be quick, Dale," I promised. I shot three fast ones of the piano, and headed for the dining room. The chandelier looked great against the high, pressed-tin ceiling. I focused on a tear-shaped prism. *Click.* "Let's get the library," I called, backtracking.

"No," Dale said. "I'm not going up there. Neither is Queen Elizabeth."

As I started toward him, a low voice rumbled through the room. My sneakers squeaked to a halt. The dining room stood empty and still. "Lavender?"

Dale called, turning to the door. "Did you forget something?"

Thank goodness. Lavender. A voice shivered through the silence: *"Get . . . out."*

My heart stuttered. That wasn't Lavender.

"Mo?" Dale called, his voice off pitch.

"Get . . . out . . . of . . . my . . . inn." Every nerve in my body jumped. My fingers went numb. The voice floated out of nowhere, louder, whispery rough. *"Get . . . out . . . now . . ."*

Somebody screamed. Maybe me.

"Run!" Dale shouted, pounding toward the door. He jerked it open as a second voice shot down the stairs. *"Help,"* a high-pitched voice called. *"Help!"* I twirled on the dining room threshold as the chandelier started swinging. *Click.*

"Wait for me, Dale!" I shouted. I bolted across the porch and jumped the steps. Dale wobbled down the drive, steering his bike with one arm. Liz dangled wildly beneath the other, all four paws trying to run.

Chapter 15
Not for Sale

The next afternoon, Dale sat in the café nursing a milk-shake and poring over my photos. "What do you mean, what would a photo of a ghost look like?"

"Interesting question," Lavender said from the counter. He'd dropped by to pick up a couple checks for supplies. He'd lured Sam and Tinks back with the promise of a spin around the racetrack, once he's racing again.

"I see why you want to reshoot," Dale said. "We got blurry piano and library pictures, and Miss Lacy Thornton and Harm look like they got light blobs stuck to them." He smiled at Lavender. "At least she got some good shots of you," he said, thumbing through the stack. "This one's nice," he added, studying a photo of the Colonel and Lavender, side by side.

"It's yours," I said, and he slipped it into his pocket.

Miss Lana smiled. "Cousin Gideon might have some ideas about your photos, sugar," she said. "He dabbles in unusual things. Why don't you write to him? He loves letters, which he claims are a lost art."

The Colonel backed in from the kitchen carrying a tray of coffee cups. "With Gideon, working's a lost art," he said. "He should get a job."

Miss Lana ignored him. "And if Gideon can't answer your questions," she continued, signing the last check with a flourish, "he may know someone who can. He attracts interesting people."

"He attracts flakes," the Colonel said.

I nodded. I'd get Skeeter to email my note. It only cost a quarter, and it would save time.

Lavender slipped the checks in his pocket. "Thanks, Miss Lana," he said. "Ready, Colonel? We got a meeting with the building inspector in half an hour."

The Colonel sighed. "Roger." He headed for the Underbird.

Poor Colonel. Before his memory found him, he spent days plotting courses through wild forests and nights sleeping beneath the stars. Now he has mayors and building inspectors to deal with.

When you're not used to normal, it pinches like new shoes.

No sooner had Lavender and the Colonel rounded the curve than Red Baker's rattletrap truck wheeled into the parking lot. Mr. Red stepped out in his auction clothes: white shirt, red tie, pressed chinos, black shoes polished to a high sheen.

Now what?

"Good afternoon," Miss Lana said as he scuffed across the tiles to the counter. She patted her Marilyn Monroe wig into place. "How can we help you today?"

"You can't. I came to do you a favor." Miss Lana smiled so quick, I almost missed the suspicion in her eyes. I walked over beside her and stepped up on my Pepsi crate. Red Baker's eyes flickered over me. "Nobody wants to work for you," he told Miss Lana. "That inn's haunted, whether you got the eyes to see it or not."

"There's nothing wrong with Miss Lana's eyes," I told him.

"Didn't say there is." He ran a hand across his whiskers. "You got ghosts. People talk. You'll run out of money soon enough, and then what?"

He popped his knuckles. "I hate seeing Lacy Thornton struggle," he said. "If Lacy goes down, others go down. Lacy's a silent partner with his mama," he said, nodding at Dale. "And others besides."

Miss Lana's face went calm as porcelain. "How can I help you?" she asked. Miss Lana says when dealing with a person of Unknown Intentions, you should be double polite—once for them, once for you. The Colonel says you should look for a weapon. "Pear pie, perhaps?" she offered, removing the pie cover and picking up a knife.

"I'll take a piece if it will help," Dale offered, vaulting onto a stool.

"I didn't come for pie," Red Baker said. "I came to buy the inn."

She hesitated, the knife hovering over the crust. She cut a careful wedge and slipped it onto a saucer. Red Baker grinned like a snake smiling at a mouse. A shiver crept up the back of my neck. "Even if you fix that inn up, nobody will stay there," he said. "It's too haunted. I've seen them myself. I'll take the place off your hands, and pay you to boot."

"How much?" I asked.

"Uppity kid," he said without looking at me.

Miss Lana summoned a paper-thin smile. "Mo enjoys a certain *joi de vivre*. She also asks good questions."

"Twenty thousand dollars, cash on the barrelhead," he said. "Say the word."

"Twenty thousand dollars?" I said. "We paid ten times that."

"Good math," Dale whispered.

Miss Lana slid the pie to Dale. "Mr. Baker, if that inn's a bad investment, why would you buy it, even for that piddling amount?"

Another good question. *Pop-pop-pop.* "My pig operation bumps up against your property. I want to expand it."

Pig operation? What pig operation?

I looked at Dale as he shoved a forkful of pie into his mouth. "Ah nebba sthmel ana piiihs," he said, reaching for his milk.

"I never smelled any pigs either," I said.

"You won't." Mr. Red tugged a roll of dirt-streaked cash out of his pocket. "Here's my down payment. Take it or leave it."

This time, Miss Lana's smile was an out-and-out lie. "The inn's not for sale."

He shrugged. "Lacy Thornton can't keep you afloat forever," he said, stuffing his cash in his pocket. "She ain't as rich as people think."

"Grandmother Miss Lacy's plenty rich," I said.

"Really? Lacy Thornton's father drove a rich man's car," he said. "Lacy drives a Buick old as you are. You call yourself a detective. You figure it out."

He clomped to the door, leaving a trail of black shoeprints.

Chapter 16
Footnotes from Charleston

Friday evening, as I sat in my room contemplating the evils of fractions in general and common denominators in particular, my vintage bedside phone jangled. "Mo's flat, Mo speaking," I said. I possess killer telephone skills.

"Is this Mo LoBeau of Desperado Detective Agency?" a man asked.

"That's right. Your life disaster is our pleasure. How can we help?"

"This is Cousin Gideon, Esquire."

I laughed. "Cousin Gideon! How are you?"

"Fine, sugar. I hope you are. I just got your Skee-mail. Sounds like big goings-on in little Tupelo Landing."

"Huge," I agreed. "Dale and me hope to bring you on board as a footnote for our ghost case."

He laughed liquid and slow. "I am scared to death of ghosts, sugar," he drawled, "but I have an absolutely intrepid friend who investigates haunted places for a living. I showed her your questions and I have her answers here. Got a pencil handy?"

"Shoot," I said, turning a page in my notebook.

"First, my friend prefers film cameras to digital ones. Ghosts generally show up like orbs of light."

My heart skipped.

"She also suggests setting up a voice-activated recorder in the inn at night. I know Lana has one because I gave her one for Christmas years ago. It's so old, it uses tapes, but it should work just fine."

I shivered. "Ghosts talk to each other at night?"

"Well, I'm no expert, but I don't see any reason to stop chatting just because you're dead. Do you?" Cousin Gideon's a notorious chatter.

"I saw that tape recorder in Miss Lana's doodad drawer the other day," I told him. "Did your friend mention seeing ghosts? Because Mr. Red says he's seen them and Lavender's workers claim ghosts move their tools. And Dale and me have heard things and seen a possible glimmer."

"Hmmm." Tap tap tap. Cousin Gideon taps his pen against his teeth when he's thinking. A bad habit. "Well, she says some people see ghosts and others can't. Others hear them, or smell them. She didn't mention moving things specifically, but I suppose they can. I mean, they have a reputation for that kind of mischief, don't they?"

"Right. Thanks, Cousin Gideon," I said, jotting a few notes. "This makes dynamite background." I made an

executive decision. "In fact, I'm awarding you full foot-note status. Congratulations."

Miss Lana says people can hear you smile into the phone. She's right. I could hear Cousin Gideon beaming. "Appreciate it, darling," he said, and then hesitated. "You be careful with this stuff, Mo. You know what they say: Fools rush in where angels fear to tread. And you're no fool, Mo LoBeau."

"I ain't much of an angel either," I said, and he laughed.

"Come see me, sugar. Now, if Lana's nearby I'd love to hear her voice."

An hour later I pushed open the inn's door and tugged Miss Lana's tape recorder from my pocket. I crept across the lobby, Dale following so close, his toes snigged at my heels. "If Mama learns I snuck out, she'll kill me. Don't look at the chandelier. Or at the stairs," he whispered, putting his hand on my shoulder. *"Or the piano."*

I stopped and he slammed into me. "Open your eyes, Dale," I snapped. "I ain't a seeing eye friend." I tiptoed behind the reservation desk, clicked the recorder on, and put it under Lavender's dust mask. "We'll come back in the morning to see who we caught chatting."

I took Dale's cold, clammy hand and led him to the door.

⋆⋆⋆⋆⋆

The next morning, I called Dale the instant I opened my eyes. "Wake up," I said.

"Saturday morning. Ghost tape," he replied, and hung up.

The tape recorder sat right where we'd left it. Only one thing had changed: "It's nearly full," Dale said.

Ghost voices. On tape. Proof. Automatic A. The skin on the back of my neck crawled. "Let's hear it," I said.

He backed up, shoving his hands behind his back. "I don't touch ghost things. It's a rule."

"Fine." I hit rewind. Then play. We leaned toward the recorder, straining to hear. First, scrabbling. "Ghost fingers," Dale whispered. "Or mice." Then footsteps. My mouth went dry. "Ghost shoes," he whispered.

A man's voice jumped out at us: *"Will you look at this."*

"Ghost!" Dale cried, grabbing my arm. I yanked free. The voice sputtered, and I heard something heavy slide across the floor. Then: *"Where's that hammer?"*

"Ghost with hammer," Dale breathed. "Bad."

"Looks like they replaced that window glass again. Idiots."

"Hold on, Dale," I said, frowning. "I know that voice." *Pop-pop-pop.*

"That's Red Baker popping his knuckles like always, and that's his hateful old voice."

"No," Dale whispered.

I leaned closer to the recorder. "He's dragging something," I said. I looked around the inn, at a faint double track across the heart pine floor. "A stepladder," I said, glancing at the ladder propped against the wall. On the tape, faint footsteps scuffed up the ladder's steps. Then a sharp whack.

I looked at the parlor window. A crack zigzagged across its face.

A wave of anger nearly swept me off my feet. I jabbed the recorder, turning it off, and stared at Dale. "You know what this means, don't you?"

"Yes," Dale whispered. He collapsed onto the stairs and rested his forehead against his palms. He drew a jagged breath.

Poor Dale. He'd known Red Baker all his life. Now this.

I sat beside him. "Are you okay?" I asked, trying to sound sensitive.

He looked up at me, his blue eyes glistening. "I think so. It's just shocking is all. I mean, Red Baker." He shook his head. "He looks so . . . lifelike."

Lifelike?

Sometimes I wonder what it would be like to live in Dale's world. Other times I think I wouldn't last five minutes in there. "He *is* lifelike, Desperado. He's alive."

"Right," he said, sagging with relief. "I think so too."

I hopped up and paced, my hands behind my back. "We ain't got ghosts, Dale. We got Red Baker tricking us. And you know what that means, don't you?"

"We're failing history. Again."

"It means we're on the verge of solving a major crime," I said. "We need backup."

Detective Joe Starr blasted through the café door a half hour later. He's dark and handsome in a plainclothes cop way, but I still think Miss Retzyl could do better. "What's wrong?" he demanded, looking around the empty café.

Miss Lana looked up from her recipe book. "Well, I'm thinking of going vegetarian on Tuesdays, which I suppose some people could see as wrong. What do you think? You're more of a meat-and-potatoes man, I believe."

True. Joe Starr's a carnivore, tooth and nail. "Pris said you have an emergency," he said. He zeroed in on me, and his hands went to his hips. "You," he said.

"Good afternoon Detective," I replied, very professional. "Allow me to compliment you on your response time." He waited, his sleet-gray eyes unsmiling. "The Desperados have solved another major crime and we'd like you to make an arrest. Lavender's waiting for us at the inn. There's just one more person we need to notify."

"And without him we're pretty much dead," Dale added.

True. I dialed. Fortunately, Mr. Red picked up. "This is Mo LoBeau of Desperado Detective Agency. Miss Lana's selling the inn," I said. "Meet us there in a half hour." I hung up before he could get a word out.

Twenty minutes later Red Baker ambled through the inn door and froze. Detective Starr simmered by the window, his arms crossed. Miss Lana perched on a sawhorse, filing her nails. Lavender leaned against the desk, looking good in corduroy.

"Thanks for dropping by," I said.

He edged back toward the door, bumping into Harm. "I didn't drop by. I came because you said Lana's selling the inn. Why's Starr here?"

I pulled the tape recorder from my pocket. "First Dale and me got something we'd like you to hear." I pressed play. His gravelly voice flooded the room. *"Left their tape measures out again. Idiots."* Pop-pop-pop.

Miss Lana stood up. "Sabotage," she said, her voice drizzling scorn over the word.

I turned off the tape. "There's more," I said. "Moving tools, breaking that window." I gave Starr a detective-to-detective smile. "We'll turn our evidence over to you and prepare a press release including the correct spelling of our names."

Starr slipped the recorder into his pocket. "If you have an explanation, Mr. Baker, this would be a good time," he said.

Mr. Red shrugged. "Don't know what you're talking about."

"That's your voice and your popping knuckles," Lavender said. "We know it, and a jury will know it." He glared at Harm. "And what's your role in this?" he demanded. "No wonder you wanted a job. Talk about easy access to your crime scene." Harm's mouth fell open. I'd seen him fake surprise in class, but this looked real.

Mr. Red stepped in front of Harm. "I'll pay for your darned window," he said. "Leave Harm out of this."

"Who are you talking to on that tape?" Starr demanded.

"Myself," Mr. Red growled. "I'm an old man."

Interesting. Maybe Red Baker does care about Harm, I thought. He shoved Harm toward the door. On the other hand, I thought, maybe he doesn't.

"What about the rest of it?" I asked. "What about the footsteps upstairs?"

"Don't know what you're talking about," Mr. Red said, heading for the door.

Starr reached for his handcuffs. "I take it you'll press charges, Lana? Take your pick: malicious mischief, breaking and entering, harassment, trespassing. Mr. Baker, this way to the patrol car."

Harm swallowed so hard, I could hear him from across the room. Miss Lana's eyes went softer. "I'd like to talk to Lacy Thornton first, if you don't mind. She's home today, a little under the weather."

"Let's go see her then," Starr said, glancing at Harm. "Stay where I can find you," he said. "If Mr. Baker goes to jail, we'll make arrangements for you."

"Arrangements," Dale mumbled under his breath. "Bad."

Starr walked Mr. Red to the Impala, Lavender and Miss Lana trailing behind. That left me, Dale, and Queen Elizabeth. Plus Harm, and an accusing silence.

The Impala pulled away. "You getting left on your own is an Unforeseen Consequence of our good detective work," I said. "It wasn't part of our plan."

"Same as Daddy staying in jail so long," Dale said.

Harm shrugged, walked to the piano, and opened the keyboard. "It's not the first time I been left. I always land on my feet."

"Just between us, how did Mr. Red do the rest of the haunting?" I asked.

Harm stretched his hands across the piano keys and a soft chord rippled through the silence. Cold flooded the room. He spun to face us. "What the . . ."

"Like, how did he rig *that*?" Dale asked, snuggling into his sweatshirt.

Harm looked around the room. "How did he deep-freeze this dump?" he said, crossing his arms and shivering. "He didn't. How *could* he?"

"And what about her?" Dale asked, pointing to the staircase. "How does Mr. Red make *her* happen?"

"Who?" Harm and I asked together, turning.

My heart jumped like a racer out of the blocks as a swirl of pale pink light wandered down the stairs, to the piano. It hovered, and then sailed straight for Harm.

Harm's thin face went gray as a raw plaster wall. He backed, backed, backed away as the pink moved closer, closer, and churned to a halt inches from his face.

Red Baker didn't concoct *that*. I grabbed my camera and pointed it with shaking hands.

"She's . . . gone," Dale said, looking around the room as the mist faded and the temperature rose.

"What was *that*?" Harm demanded.

"Our history interview," Dale said. "She acted like she knew you."

"Knew me? That's crazy."

Dale looked Harm up and down. "Ghost bait," he said, his voice thoughtful. He looked at me. "I told you we'd need some."

And Harm sat down on the floor. Hard.

Chapter 17
Spitting Image

Harm stood waiting for us Monday morning at the bicycle rack—a definite surprise. "Hey Ghoul Girl," he said. Not a surprise. I nudged my bike into the rack.

"Hey yourself, Ghost Bait. What's up?"

"Shhh," he said, his gaze lingering on Attila and Hannah, who leaned against an oak tree, chatting. "Don't call me that," he said. "And nothing's up. I mean, nobody pressed charges, which was . . . nice. I appreciate it."

Thes blasted past. "Going to storm tonight," he said. "Eighty percent chance. And a cold front drifting down, but no snow. It's way too early for snow."

"Thanks, Thes," I said, and he trotted away. I looked at Harm. "Thes is weather-obsessed. There's no way to stop him, so Miss Lana says to thank him."

Dale jammed his bike in the rack. "Hey Harm, you want to talk ghosts? Because ours likes you, and as Ghost Bait for our interview, you got a right to ask."

Harm crossed his arms. "You want me to help with

your paper?" he asked, and we nodded. "Sure, I'll do it. Cost you a hundred dollars," he said.

"A hundred dollars?" I said. "We don't have that kind of money."

"Your call. You can get back to me," he said, slipping back into his smirk, just like that. "You got your interview questions?" he asked. "After what I saw Saturday, I'm thinking they'd better be darned good ones."

"We got them," I said. "You first."

To my surprise, he opened his notebook. "Questions for Red Baker. One: What's your earliest memory of your father, Mr. Truman Baker? Two: What did Truman's distillery smell like and how did it work? Three: How did Truman's business affect local culture and commerce?"

"Fancy words and good questions," Dale said. "Miss Retzyl will like those."

Harm closed his notebook and stuffed it in his pack. "They're only good questions if Red answers them. And since he hasn't actually agreed to an interview, I see an F in my future."

Dale shook his head. "He won't want a grandson to flunk." He tilted his head like a curious owl. "Funny, I never knew Mr. Red had a grandson. And I been knowing him all my life."

"Well, you got me beat," Harm said. "I only met him at the auction."

My stomach fluttered like I'd stepped in an elevator going down too fast. *He just met him?* What if I met Upstream Mother and she turned out to be like Red Baker?

"So *that's* why Mr. Red dressed up for the auction," Dale said, his voice going soft. "To meet you. That was nice of him."

"Charming," Harm said. "What about you, Ghost Girl? You got questions?"

I knew them by heart. "One: What's your name? Two: What happened to you? Three: How much allowance do you get in the next world?"

"Allowance," Dale said, pulling a crumpled paper out of his pocket. "Good." He smoothed his paper against his leg and read out his questions.

"One: Why are you still here? Two: Do you get lonely? Three: Do you dream about people you used to know?"

Sometimes it surprises me, the things Dale thinks about.

"Pathetic," Attila said, brushing by. "Maybe you should try these. One: Who do I think I'm kidding? Two: Am I lying through my teeth? Three: How many times will I repeat sixth grade?"

She shot us a withering glare. "*My* paper's done. I only need to print it."

"Like we care, Metal Mouth," Harm said. He looked sheepish as she stomped away. "I guess I'd have braces

too if I could afford them," he said. "Flick says a good smile's worth thousands of dollars later in life. Listen," he said, "what are you two doing this afternoon? Because I actually would like to talk about . . . things."

"We're going to Grandmother Miss Lacy's with our latest batch of film."

"*I'm* not," Dale said, backing away. "Not if you're carrying ghost film."

"You're just scared to look a ghost in the eye," I said. "But you are too going. If Miss Retzyl asks you about developing film, you got to answer. Besides, Grandmother Miss Lacy's not feeling good. It would be a good social skill to pay her a call."

For a split second I thought Harm would ask to come along. Then: "Thank her for me," he said. "For not pressing charges against Red. Thank Miss Lana too."

"Thank them yourself," I said, and headed up the steps.

That afternoon, Dale and I stood on Grandmother Miss Lacy's porch, shivering in a chill wind. Thes had nailed it: cold front. I knocked on the carved front door.

Dale stared at Queen Elizabeth hard enough to bend spoons. "Sit," he said. To my shock, she plopped down by the door. "Good girl. I can't believe you came to school," he told her, ruffling her ears. "She's never done that before, Mo."

"She's brilliant," I lied, and knocked again.

"Miss Thornton's yellow pansies look good," he said, peering at the wide-faced little flowers. "Mama says they're tougher than they look."

The door creaked open. "I thought I heard voices," Miss Lana said. "Miss Thornton's in the parlor. The doctor told her to rest and avoid stress. She's bored out of her mind. She'll be glad to see you." She kissed my face. "Don't get her too excited though, sugar," she said, and hurried toward the café.

"Too excited?" Dale echoed. "What does that mean, exactly?"

"No darkroom," I said, and he smiled like I'd yanked him out of detention.

"You go on in," he said. "I'll be there after Liz settles in."

I found Grandmother Miss Lacy thumbing through a photo album. She sat with a green shawl draped over her thin shoulders, her blue hair glinting in the glow of the fireplace. I knocked on the door casing. "Mo! Thank heavens. I'm bored within an inch of my life. Sit down and talk to me."

I filled her in on school faster than Lavender at the racetrack: word problems, analogies, book reports. "Plus I shot more film for history," I told her. "But it can wait."

Finally we turned to Red Baker and his fake ghost.

"I've known Red Baker all my life, and he has *never*

made me so furious," she fumed as Dale tiptoed by cradling something in his arms. "What did he hope to accomplish by scaring our workers away? He doesn't need land for his pigs."

"You're right," I said. "He's up to something."

"Red's been up to something since birth," she said, and then laughed like water breaking through a dam. She reached for her album and thumbed through the pages. "I have a photo I'd like you to see." I peeped at the pages. "Here I am with Father's Duesenberg," she said, showing me a black-and-white of a short, birdlike girl and a long, pale car. She turned the page. "And this blur in knickers is Red Baker."

She flipped the page. "Here's a rare image of him standing still." I peered at the photo as Dale walked into the room holding a clear bowl of suspiciously familiar yellow pansies.

"I hope you feel better soon," he said, trying not to slosh water on the floor.

Grandmother Miss Lacy blinked at her own pansies. "Thank you, dear," she said. "They'd look best on the marble-topped table, perhaps."

I turned back to the old photo of Mr. Red as a boy. Black hair, thin face. He wore a long-sleeve shirt and tie, knickers and argyles. He held a cap in his hand and stood lanky as a coyote, his thin shoulders sloping a modicum

to the left. "*That's* Red Baker?" I asked. "He's a dead ringer for Harm Crenshaw."

"Or the other way around," Dale said, peering at the photo.

She laughed. "It took me a while to place Harm the day we drove to the auction. But you're right. Harm's the spitting image of his grandfather."

People say that like it's nothing—being the spitting image of somebody else.

"Can I borrow this?" I asked.

"I suppose," she said, sliding it out and handing it to me. "I'll want it back, though," she added as the phone jangled. "Could you get that, dear? It's probably another Azalea Woman calling to see if I'm dying and if so, who's in the will. Take a message," she called as I trotted down the hall. "I'll return calls tomorrow."

I swept into the kitchen. The supper plate Miss Lana brought over rested on the counter, covered with a neat white napkin. I grabbed the phone, the antique kind that clings to the wall. "Grandmother Miss Lacy's residence, honorary granddaughter Mo LoBeau speaking," I said.

"Who?" a woman said.

"Mo LoBeau, cofounder of Desperado Detective Agency. Who's this?"

"Miss Filch, manager at State Bank, calling for Lacy Thornton."

I frowned. The old "I got a title and you don't" trick. I'd used it before, mostly on third graders.

"Greetings, Filch," I replied. "Miss Thornton is resting. I am Miss LoBeau, her ambassador. May I help you?"

"I need *her,* sweetie. Call her to the phone."

I smiled so wide my lips hurt, in case Miss Lana was right and smiling might put Filch in a better mood. "I can take a message. She'll call you."

She huffed like she could blow my house down. "Tell her Miss Filch called. *Again.* Tell her we have *still* not received payment. Tell her she needs to call me by ten o'clock tomorrow morning or I'll start the paperwork. Understand?"

I gasped. "Paperwork? What's going on?"

The phone went dead in my hand.

Chapter 18
A Paying Customer, Sort Of

"Paperwork?" Dale said that evening as thunder galloped across the sky. We sat in my flat—me on the bed and Dale at my desk—schoolbooks scattered around us. "Paperwork's bad," he said. "Paperwork happens just before they take your car. Not that anybody would want Miss Thornton's old Buick. And what payment? And how come it's late? Miss Thornton's got more gold than Fort Knox."

"I don't know," I said, trying to dis-remember Red Baker's warnings.

"Did you ask her?"

"Not exactly. I told her State Bank called and I'd left the message in the kitchen. She said 'that terrible Filch woman again.' Then she said not to worry, she'd handle it."

"Well then," he said, swiveling back and forth on my desk chair. "We might as well not worry."

Dale kills me. He's got a worry switch he flips just

like that. It's something he got from his daddy, not from Miss Rose. "I hate English," he said. "Why do we have to study a foreign language anyway?"

"English ain't a foreign language," I told him.

"Are *you* English?" he demanded. "Because I'm not." I could see his point, which made me uncomfortable. "What's an analogy again?" he asked.

"A double-barreled comparison. Miss Retzyl's crazy about them. Here, try another one: Chicken is to feather as mink is to blank."

"Coat?" he guessed.

"Fur," I said, drawing a picture of a fluffy chicken and a slender mink. I turned my notebook toward him. "See?"

He frowned. "What's that supposed to be? Dwarves? Because you can't make fun of people, Mo. It isn't right."

I took a moment. Only the intrepid study with Dale.

"Forget the pictures," I said. "Chickens have feathers and minks have fur. Chicken is to feather as mink is to fur. You got to give it both barrels. Our test is tomorrow, Dale. Try again: Dark is to night as light is to . . ." Dale sucked his lip in and squeezed his eyebrows together. If I waited any longer, he might swallow his face. *"Day,"* I said, exasperated. "Dark is to night as light is to day."

I sighed. I needed a hot chocolate. Maybe a double.

Dale jumped. "What was that?"

"The storm," I said as a gust of wind hit the house and rain pounded the roof. "You want some hot chocolate?"

Footsteps clomped across the porch. "Mo, somebody's out there."

"Probably the Colonel. Who's there?" I called. "Colonel?"

The footsteps stopped at my door. "It's Harm. Let me in."

Crenshaw, Harm Crenshaw? Here?

I opened the door on a night wild with bluster and rain. "What are you doing out on a night like this?"

Harm shrugged out of his soggy jacket, stepped inside, and shook his head like a dog, splattering storm across my wall. "I need a detective, and I've got cash."

Cash?

I went into my bathroom and grabbed a towel. "Here," I said, tossing it to him. "Park your shoes by the door."

He kicked his shoes off, revealing bare feet. "Have a seat," I told him, nodding to my rocking chair. "Dale and me were just wrapping up some paperwork. We'll listen to your story. I can't promise the Desperados will take your case, but anything you say to us is confidential."

Dale nodded, and settled back.

Harm sank into the rocker, leaned forward, and tossed the towel over his head. He emerged tousled and a little drier, his dark hair curling around his pale face.

He should wear his hair curly more often, I thought.

Not that I care.

"What's this about?" Dale asked.

"It's about Red. And Joe Starr."

Dale leaned forward. "You call your granddaddy by his first name," he said. "Lavender calls Daddy by *his* first name too: Macon. Daddy can be hard to live with."

"I know the feeling," Harm muttered as I picked up my pen and clue pad. "Anyway, Detective Starr's watching Red. Watching him close."

I tapped my pen against my pad. "Starr's a law man. Mr. Red's a moonshiner."

"Mr. Red is to Joe Starr as a bone is to Queen Elizabeth," Dale announced. "Analogy," he added in the silence that followed. I gave him a thumbs-up.

"Plus Starr's probably professionally ticked by that stunt Mr. Red pulled at the inn. You can't tell by looking at him, but Starr likes us."

Harm settled back and crossed his legs. "I've been watching Red. I think he's got a still somewhere—but he swears he doesn't. He doesn't have a job, but every couple weeks he disappears at night. He leaves broke and comes home flush. I can't find his still, but I'm worried Joe Starr will."

"Probably," Dale said. "But moonshining's a federal

charge, and a federal pen's like a Hotel 6 with a good weight room. Mr. Red can do that time standing on his head."

Harm's voice cracked out like a shot: "No. I don't want him to do any time."

Could Harm actually care about Red Baker? Interesting.

"You can't undo time once you're down for it," Dale said. "If you could, Daddy would be out by now." Like I've said, if things were up to me, Mr. Macon would stay put. Nobody hits Dale and Miss Rose and walks free if I can help it.

"We've worked with Starr before," I told Harm. "He's smart. And stubborn. And Dale's right: If he's decided to take Mr. Red down, he's going down."

"Not if you find the still first," Harm said. "We could destroy it before Starr throws Red in jail."

"Even if we do destroy it, he'll go right back at it," Dale said. "Dogs don't change their spots."

"Leopards," Harm said, frowning. "*Leopards* don't change their spots."

"The animal of the saying can be changed," Dale said, very cool. "The spots cannot."

I studied Harm as silence settled around us. The night had washed the smirk off of him. Without it, he looked tender and thin, like bamboo growing too fast for its

roots. "Why don't you want him doing time?" I asked.

"He can't," he said. "He's too old."

My stare pinned him to the chair the way Miss Lana's pins me when she waits for the truth. He did what I do: looked at my rug, my Elvis calendar, my NC wall map marking the many places I know my Upstream Mother ain't. Finally he looked at me.

"If Red goes to jail, I got nothing. And nowhere."

His words landed true as rain.

He reached into his pocket and pulled out a roll of dirt-streaked cash. "I've tried following him, but he's always watching me. Now you guys . . ." He drummed up a smile. "Don't ask me why, but he thinks you're idiots. You could watch him twenty-four/seven without him even caring."

"Automatic cover," I said.

"Excellent," Dale replied. "We'd need to come to your house," he added as Harm began counting the bills: $20, $30, $40. "A hundred dollars," Harm offered.

A hundred dollars? Dale's mouth fell open.

I narrowed my eyes. "That's what you wanted to charge *us* for being ghost bait."

"Really?" Harm said, grinning. "What a coincidence. If you still need my help with your interview, I'll put my money away and call it even."

Dale looked at me and I nodded. "Deal," Dale said.

"Done," Harm said, stuffing the cash in his pocket. "What's your ghost plan?"

"Stakeout," Dale replied faster than I could blink.

Dale's ideas often surprise me. Fortunately, this one made sense. "Dale's right," I said. "We'll treat the ghostly suspect like any other. We're going for proof of identification admissible in a court of law. Plus motive if we can find it."

"Motive?" Harm asked, looking puzzled.

"Motive for post-mortem loitering," I said. "I'll let you know when and where. Meanwhile, call us next time Mr. Red acts suspicious."

Harm slipped his feet into his shoes. "Come over Saturday if you want," he said. "You can check our place for clues. I'll be around all day."

As he headed into a blustery night, Dale looked at me. "Did he just do us a favor or did we do a favor for him?" he asked.

"Good question," I said. "Sometimes you got to wait and see."

Chapter 19
Mr. Red's Secret

After Saturday morning's breakfast rush, Dale and I climbed the crooked cinderblock steps to Red Baker's front door. "Stay sharp," I whispered as the door squeaked open.

"Hey," Harm said. "Come on in."

I stepped inside and blinked, waiting for my eyes to adjust to the dim light. The small, stuffy room smelled faintly of broccoli. Or worse. A gas heater sat in one corner. A fake leather couch the color of tired baloney hunkered against one wall, and a broke-down La-Z-Boy slumped beside it.

"Nice place," Dale lied.

"Not really, but have a seat anyway," Harm said, nodding to the sofa. I pushed a jacket out of the way and sat, ignoring the duct tape on the arm. Dale settled beside me. Harm slung himself into the La-Z-Boy, turned sideways, and draped his long legs over the arm. "I forgot to ask you if you wanted something to drink," he said, looking startled.

Dale grinned.

"What's so funny?"

"You're working on social skills." He raised one eyebrow. "Girls?" he guessed.

Harm shrugged. "Flick says they like manners. I got iced tea. I'd offer you something to eat, but . . ."

"Four-cornered Nabs would look nice on a plate," Dale suggested.

A few minutes later I brushed orange Nab crumbs off my shirt front. "We brought something," I said, opening my messenger bag. I handed him the photo from the library. "We found this in the inn."

"Who is it?"

"Sparrow-girl is Grandmother Miss Lacy," I said.

"She's pretty, in a birdy way," he said.

"And the scowling one's Myrt Little, the mayor's mom."

Harm barked out a laugh. "Thes's interview? She looks even meaner than Red."

Dale nodded happily. "Thes is doomed."

Harm squinted at the photo. "Who's the guy?"

"That's what we wanted to show you," I said. I waited for him to look at me—a trick Miss Lana taught me. "That's Red Baker."

"Get out of here." He turned a tiny knob on the lamp and clicked a switch. The lamp flared on as he shoved a

pile of clutter off the table—old newspapers, a compass, a set of keys. He held the photo to the light.

"If you like that photo, try this," I said. I handed him Grandmother Miss Lacy's photo of Mr. Red standing still. Harm's mouth fell open.

"Spittin' image," Dale said, leaning back and lacing his fingers behind his head.

Harm snorted. "If I ever had any doubt . . ."

"Doubt about what?" Red Baker demanded, clomping in from the hall. He stopped dead as his eyes settled on me. "What the Sam Hill are you doing in my house?"

"I invited them," Harm said, jumping up. "Look." He held out the photo. "We could be twins out of time."

Mr. Red rubbed his whiskery face. "If that's so, you haven't got much to look forward to in your old age."

A joke? From Mr. Red?

"Here's another one," Harm said, handing him the library photo. Mr. Red tilted it toward the light.

"Where'd you get this?"

"The inn," I said. "Grandmother Miss Lacy says it's her and Myrt Little and you. And somebody running out of the photo—she didn't know who."

"That's the old Duesenberg in the background," Dale said.

Red Baker swiped the side of his face. "Lacy's daddy must have taken this photo. He stuck that car in every

photo he took. Loved it like a baby." He handed the photo back. "How much longer you going to be?" he asked, staring at me. "Harm's got things to do."

"They just got here," Harm said. "We're doing homework. Which reminds me, I was hoping I could interview you about our family history. For school. It's half my history grade. It would mean a lot to me."

Mr. Red plucked his keys from the table. "My history's none of your business."

"Well . . . it's my history too," Harm said. "There's the evidence right there," he said, pointing to the photo and smiling. Mr. Red glared, and Harm's smile slipped.

"Don't fritter away the day," Mr. Red said, and stomped out the door.

"That went well," Harm muttered as the door slapped shut.

I slipped the photos into my pack and squinted at the lamp. "That lamp hasn't got an electric cord," I said, and looked around the room. "Nothing does. Is it all battery?"

"The house runs on methane," he said. "Red ran a gas line from the pig house."

Dale sat forward. "Pig house? That's a famous moonshiner's trick—putting your still in a pig house so nobody smells it. Have you looked in there?"

Harm nodded, and pushed his hair from his eyes. "It's

state-of-the-art, I'll say that for him. He treats the waste so it doesn't stink. But no still. I can show you."

An invitation to a pig parlor? My life has come to this?

"Another time maybe," I replied as Mr. Red slammed his truck door. I looked out the window. "How long before he comes back?"

Harm shrugged. "Your guess is as good as mine."

I looked at Dale. "We should come back when Mr. Red's not in and out."

"But we haven't seen Harm's room yet," Dale said. He lowered his voice. "You're supposed to show first-time visitors around," he told Harm. "It's a social skill."

Harm shot me a shifty look. "It's not exactly girl-ready."

"That's not a girl," Dale said. "That's Mo."

It grated, but a good detective can use anything for cover, even an annoyance of this magnitude. I drew myself to full height. "I have no interest in Harm's arm-pit of a room," I said. "But you go ahead, Dale. I'll wait."

Harm unfolded himself from the crippled La-Z-Boy. "Come on, then. Make yourself at home, Mo. Look around if you want to."

As Harm's door closed behind them, Mr. Red cranked his truck and rattled away. I'll never get a better chance, I thought. I wandered down the hall and pushed open a half-closed door. Mr. Red's room.

An uneven curtain hung across the window, the bed gaped half-made. A ladder-back chair faced a desk cluttered with pliers, wire, dirty socks. Gross. As I turned to leave, something in the corner caught my eye: blueprints. I carried them to the desk and unrolled them. The 1938 drawing of the Tupelo Inn.

But what were those?

Penciled-in numbers spidered across the blueprint: 14/238, 5/119, 12/142/, 4/84 . . . Some had been crossed out. "Fractions?" I murmured.

Laughter burst from Harm's room. I tucked the blueprints under my arm and headed down the hall, stopping to peek in a bathroom half the size of mine with a floor twice as slanty. The bare-pipe sink wore a faded yellow gingham skirt and the tub a rust-colored ring.

I wandered past Harm's room to the kitchen, past a sink piled with dishes, onto a screened-in back porch. An ancient washing machine stood at the far end of the porch, a shelf of dirty quart jars stretching above it. "Right," I heard Dale say, tromping down the hall. "What happened to Mo?"

I whirled to face them. "What's going on?" Harm asked.

"Just making myself at home, like you said." I spread the old blueprints over the top of the washer. "Any idea what these mean?"

Harm and Dale crowded close. I pointed out the numbers.

"Fractions, maybe?" Harm guessed. "But what do fractions have to do with the Tupelo Inn?"

"And why are some crossed out?" Dale asked, standing on his tiptoes to scan the farthest numbers.

"I found these by Mr. Red's bureau," I said, looking at Harm. "Keep an eye on them if you can. If he marks out more numbers, let us know which ones and when."

He nodded. "I'll put them back for you," he said.

I gazed across the backyard, past the sagging wash line, past the shovels and swing blade leaning against the shed. "Nice chickens," I told him, nodding toward the reds scratching up the yard. "How many you got?"

"About ten too many," he said. But he smiled when he said it. And his smile wasn't half bad.

Chapter 20
Ghost Stakeout

We set our stakeout for the next afternoon—Sunday. Dale and I pedaled down the inn's drive after church to find Harm rocking on the porch. "Nice truck," he said, nodding at Lavender's 1955 GMC pickup.

The GMC's a work of art, a mix of swooping lines, smooth blue paint, and salvaged parts. I toed my kickstand down. "Lavender's down at the pavilion putting in some overtime," I said. "That means we have complete access to the scene of the . . ."

Of the what?

"The encounter," Dale finished.

"Right. The scene of the encounter." I took my camera from my basket as Queen Elizabeth galloped up the steps and flopped down in the shade, her sides rising and falling like bellows. "We'll set up on the reservation desk," I said, and opened the door. "Hello? Anybody home?"

Nothing. I double-checked my camera.

Harm stepped gingerly through the door. "What's

the plan?" he asked, looking skittish. "Because I've been thinking. The other day was probably a fluke. The way the ghost acted, I mean."

"Denial," Dale whispered. "Show him the photos."

I spread my photos across the desk. "These are of you. These are Grandmother Miss Lacy."

Queen Elizabeth sneezed.

Dale leaned down to scritch her ears. "Liz is sneezing an awful lot lately," he said. "I hope she's not getting a cold."

I ignored him. So did Harm.

"These are ghost photos," I said, pointing to the speckles of light.

"*Ghost* photos?"

"According to Cousin Gideon, a footnoted source, ghosts show up like orbs of light. The ghost is all over you, every time."

Harm gulped.

"You and Miss Thornton," Dale said, fanning my photos out. He gave Harm a thoughtful look. "I'm thinking you two are our common denominators. Like in fractions," he said. "You're the bridge between us and the ghost."

Only Dale could turn ghosts into math.

Harm studied the black-and-whites, raked them into a stack, and tapped them against the desk. He's neat, I

thought. How can he stand living with Mr. Red? "I still don't know why a ghost would be interested in me," he said, handing them back.

"Maybe we'll find out," I said. "Today I'm hoping to get a sharp ghost photo, and learn her name. Then we can start figuring out what happened."

Harm jammed his hands in his pockets. "What if she, you know—touches me?"

"A ghost touch?" Dale said, his eyebrows rising. "Speaking as a professional? I'd scream like a first grader and run for my life."

"Sounds good," he muttered.

"All right," I said, looking around the room. "Last time she dropped by . . ."

"I'd just played a chord on the piano," Harm said.

Now that he mentioned it, almost every time she visited, someone had just played the piano. "Exactly," I said. "We'll re-create the scene. If you're not scared."

Harm squared his shoulders. "Me? Nah."

"I am," Dale said. "But I'm more afraid of telling Mama I'm flunking history." He looked at me. "We could play 'Heart and Soul' again."

Harm stepped up to the piano. "You want the treble or the bass?"

"Bass," Dale said, looking surprised as Harm

scooted the bench out of the way. They stood side by side, their backs to me, Harm a head taller than Dale. Dale's bass chords rolled through the air smooth as sunset and Harm moved easily into the lilting melody. "Heart and soul," Harm sang in a strong, clear voice.

Dale chimed in, their voices swirling together like molasses and butter on a hot biscuit. "Mo," Dale whispered, looking over his shoulder. "The stairs."

Queen Elizabeth sneezed.

I stepped back as an eddy of mist drifted down the steps. The temperature dropped. I picked up my camera. The mist floated toward Harm. Closer, closer, backing Harm across the room until his back touched the wall.

The mist hovered inches from his face. "Who . . ." he rasped. He closed his eyes. If the ghost got any closer to Harm, he'd inhale her. That couldn't be good even if it *did* get us an A. *Click.*

"Mo, do something," Dale whispered.

What?

I stepped forward. "How do you do," I said. "I am Miss Moses LoBeau of Desperado Detective Agency. These are my associates, Dale Earnhardt Johnson III by the piano and Harm Crenshaw, who you got pinned against the wall."

Dale bowed. Queen Elizabeth sneezed.

"We're pleased to meet you," I said, and hesitated. Ghost etiquette is an intuitive art. "I don't believe we caught your name," I added.

The mist backed away from Harm. It floated across the room, through a closed window, and across the porch onto the lawn. As we ran to the window, the mist bobbed across the lawn, down the path leading to the springhouse.

"Follow her," I said.

We rushed the door, jumped off the porch, and sprinted across the yard, stopping to catch our breath at the head of the path, Queen Elizabeth at our heels.

"Where's she going?" Harm murmured.

"To the river, maybe, where Lavender is," Dale said, sounding hopeful. I heard the distant sound of a hammer against wood as I lined up a shot. *Click.*

"Maybe," I said. But I doubted it.

We trailed her until, near the springhouse, she veered into the forest. "I don't know," Dale said, rocking to a stop. "It looks dark in there."

Harm peered into the woods. "Aren't you curious?"

"Only about twenty percent," Dale said. "The other half of me is scared stiff."

Harm looked at me. "Ghost Girl?"

I peered into the dense woods, catching a quick glim-

mer of pink against the forest green. My heart pounded. I stepped off the path and into the woods.

"Watch that briar, Harm," Dale said, plowing in behind me.

We crept into the woods, the tree canopy swallowing the day. I followed the faint glow. Twice, I thought we lost her. Both times she came back, hovering just ahead. Finally she headed up a slight rise. Dead ahead a shaft of light sliced the forest. "What's that?" Dale whispered.

A wrought iron fence marked off a small clearing. "I think I know," I said, remembering the blueprint's prickle of crosses. We slipped closer and the hair on the back of my neck stood up. Sunlight glinted off a crooked gray army of stones. "The old cemetery," I whispered.

We crept across damp leaves, their perfume rising round and sweet. "Looks like somebody keeps this place up," Dale said, stepping gingerly through the gate. He knelt to look at the stubble. "Somebody with a swing blade," he added, his voice shaking.

To our right the tree limbs rustled, sending a shower of twigs and leaves to the ground. Queen Elizabeth took off like a rocket, ears back, yelping as she shot across the graveyard and zipped into the woods. "Squirrel," Dale explained, his voice too high. "Liz!" he called. "Liz. Come here."

Her yelps faded into the forest.

I looked around the graveyard. "Over there," I said, pointing to a pale white stone towering above the rest. I ran my fingers across its chiseled letters: BLAKE.

"Here she comes," Dale whispered. The mist flowed through the gate and wound among the grave markers, settling at last over a small, sad stone. We crept closer.

"Nellie Blake," I read. "Beloved daughter and friend. 1927–1938."

Click.

"Hey Nellie," I said. "Nice to finally meet you."

Dear Upstream Mother,
   Tonight we got our first big break on our Ghost Case and met Nellie Blake, 1927-1938. Meeting her felt like electricity racing up and down my skin.
   After we said hello, Nellie faded away. We stood around trying to look calm and then stampeded like wild horses. Formally meeting your first ghost can get on your nerves. So can swing blade stubble in a graveyard. If Tupelo Landing ever needs an Olympic sprint team, we already qualified.

When I got home I called Grandmother Miss Lacy to see if she remembered Nellie Blake. "Yes, I believe so," she said. "But old memories blur, Mo. I'm afraid I can't help." Then she asked to speak to Miss Lana and I lost control of the phone.

Despite this small strikeout, all we need is background on Nellie, and a break on Harm's case. That's our deal: Harm would be Ghost Bait for us and we'd hunt Red's still for him.

Miss Lana says life is full of checks and balances. I think our deal with Harm balances out pretty good.

Mo

Chapter 21
AhhoooOOOoooo-Gah

We got the break we needed on Harm's case at quarter past dark the next Friday night.

My phone jangled. "Mo LoBeau, Detective on Call," I said. "Felonies and misdemeanors are our pleasure. How may we assist you?"

"Red's getting ready to make his move," Harm whispered.

"How long have we got?"

"An hour, max. He waits until I start my homework, and slips out. Hurry."

Harm does homework on Friday night? Weird.

I hung up and dialed Dale's number. Busy. I tied my sneakers, found my jacket, and dialed again. Busy. I crammed a flashlight and clue pad in my bag. Still busy.

I rushed to the café, stuffed a take-out bag with scraps, and headed for Dale's.

"Come in, Mo," Miss Rose called, placing her phone in its cradle. That explained the busy signal. Miss Rose can talk a post deaf when she's lonely, which Miss Lana

says is most of the time now that the idea of Mr. Macon is gone.

"Hey Miss Rose, you talking to your sister again? I hope her tomatoes are still producing and that you're not too lonely. Miss Lana says letting go of even a trace of somebody is hard."

She laughed. "I wasn't talking with my sister, the tomatoes are rolling in even this late in the season, I'm not *too* lonely, and Lana's right," she said. "It's hard. If you're looking for Dale, he's in his room."

The sound of Dale's guitar wandered through the house like smoke across still water. I tiptoed to his open door and found him sitting by Sir Isaac Newton's terrarium, his back to the door. He strummed the "lullaby and good night" Miss Lana sings to me when I dream wrong. But when he started singing, the words came out pure Dale—a terrifying mix of science and love.

> *Lullaby little newt,*
> *You are warty and look cute*
> *You're amphib-i-an, I'm not,*
> *You're cold-blood-ed, I'm hot.*
>
> *Born with gills you now breathe air*
> *I got thumbs and good hair*
> *Darwin says that we're still kin*
> *Glad I ain't got your chin.*

Dale laid his guitar down. "Sweet dreams, Newton," he whispered, and turned out the terrarium light.

It's hard to know what to say when your best friend serenades an amphibian. On one hand, Miss Lana likes me to be sensitive. On the other hand, the Colonel says most situations don't require my input. "Grab your flashlight, Dale," I said. "Mr. Red's on the prowl."

We blasted past Miss Rose with a promise not to miss Dale's curfew. A little later we ditched our bikes and crept across Mr. Red's barnyard. An owl hoo-hooed above us and flapped heavy and awkward as a flying encyclopedia to a nearby tree. "I don't see why we have to come over here *now*," Dale whispered. "Why don't we wait until Mr. Red checks his still in the daytime?"

"He's a *moon*shiner, not a sunshiner," I said. "He works nights. Besides, we're in school in the daytime."

"School," he muttered. "Why don't they have it when it's too dark for anything else?"

We froze as something—or someone—rustled behind us. I held my breath as it rustled closer, nearer . . . Queen Elizabeth jammed her nose between us and wedged her way in headfirst. "I told you to stay with Mama," Dale scolded.

"Shhhhh," I said, peering at the house. "You'll wake Mr. Red's dogs." Too late. Three rib-skinny dogs stared

through the tall fence. A fourth slunk from a dense thicket in the center of their pen. The pen's sharp odor rose into the night.

"Nice dogs," Dale whispered. "Good dogs. Sit." They growled.

I looked at the house. Two figures moved around the kitchen, silhouetted in the lamplight. "They're finishing supper," I whispered.

"Wish I was," Dale said. He sniffed the air. "What's in that take-out bag? I'm starving."

Dale's like a newborn. He likes to eat every three hours.

"Table scraps," I said.

Harm left the kitchen and the light came on in his room. The back door swung open. Mr. Red walked to the shed, grabbed a shovel, and reached in his pocket. Keys! "The truck," I told Dale. "Hurry," I whispered, flinging the take-out bag over the fence.

The dogs hurled themselves on the food and we darted to the driveway. "Brilliant," Dale murmured, grabbing Queen Elizabeth and scrambling into the back of the truck. I rolled across the open tailgate and snagged the corner of a tarp. "Liz!" Dale hissed, grabbing for her as she squirted out of his arms. She shot into the shadows as Red Baker ambled toward us, a shovel over his shoulder.

"Let her go!" I whispered, shoving Dale under the old tarp and diving in beside him. Mr. Red swung the shovel into the truck bed beside us. He slammed the cab door, and the old truck shuddered to life.

"Good," I whispered. "Surveillance is going according to plan."

"Stop it," he said, his voice accusing. "We're under a smelly old tarp in the back of a truck going who-knows-where with a mean old man and Queen Elizabeth is AWOL. You ain't got a plan and I know it."

Undercover work can make Dale irritable.

We bounced down a rutted path in silence. The truck swerved, and brambles scraped their sharp green fingers down the sides of the truck. "We should be on the blacktop by now," Dale whispered as the truck swerved, slamming us against the cabin.

"We must be going the other way. Toward the inn."

"Nellie's house," Dale said, covering his head with his arm. "Great."

The truck hit a hole, throwing us into the air and jolting us down hard. Again, brambles squeaked along the truck's panels. Finally the brakes squealed, and we lurched to a halt. "Shhh," I whispered. The truck door slammed, and Mr. Red crunched to the side of the truck. I held my breath as he fumbled with the tarp.

The shovel!

I nudged it toward him with my foot. He brushed my shoe as he grabbed it. His footsteps faded away. "Come on," I whispered.

We eased out from under the tarp, and slipped off the tailgate smooth as water over a dam. "He's over there," I said, pointing.

Mr. Red held the shovel by his side. He looked right and left, the way the Colonel does when he's lining up on something. I looked behind me. Through the trees, I could just make out the glint of moonlight tiptoeing the inn's roofline. Mr. Red peered over his shoulder, tugged something out of his pocket, and studied it a moment. He started through the forest, stepping long and careful and mumbling under his breath.

"What's he doing?" Dale whispered.

"Counting," I guessed. Mr. Red stopped, made a neat turn, and took off again. We crept through the moonlight-silvered trees and settled behind a black-berry thicket.

"Where are we?" Dale asked, looking around.

Good question.

"Somewhere between the springhouse and town. Maybe. The inn's behind us. The cemetery would be over there," I said, pointing.

Dale yanked my hand down. "Don't point," he said. "It bothers . . . people."

Mr. Red tipped the shovel into the ground and jumped on it, driving it into the earth.

"What's he doing?" I whispered.

"Digging. With a shovel."

Why do I even ask?

Mr. Red grunted softly as he worked, lifting shovel after shovel of soil and heaving it to one side. Finally, the rough shriek of metal against metal. He knelt and reached into the earth. "Flashlights. Now," I whispered, and we clicked on our lights.

Mr. Red looked up like an animal snared. "Who's there?" he asked, scrambling to his feet, a dirty Mason jar in his hands.

"Desperado Detective Agency. Mo and Dale at your service."

He shielded his eyes. "Turn those blasted things off. You're blinding me."

Dale clicked his light off and I tilted mine to the ground. "Hey Mr. Red," Dale said. "Nice night for digging. What did you find?"

"None of your business," he said.

"Moonshine, maybe?" I guessed.

"I wish you'd tell us," Dale said. "Because this doesn't look good, you digging up things on somebody else's land."

"I take care of my own. That's all you need to know," he said, settling the jar in the crook of his arm. "Get lost."

"We already are," Dale said, very even. A tree frog chirped.

"This land ain't yours," I added. "What's in that jar?"

Dale grabbed my arm. "Mo," he whispered.

"Not now," I told him. "I'm questioning a suspect."

"Mo," Dale said, pointing through the forest. "Look."

"What?" I peered through the trees. In the distance, a set of headlights charged toward us. "Is there a path through here?" I asked, looking at Mr. Red. "Maybe I'm turned around."

"Path? There's no path, not anymore," Red Baker said, staring at the lights. "That's . . . No . . . It can't be."

"Those are headlights," Dale said.

The hair on my arms stood up and my fingers tingled. "That car's driving right *through* those trees," I said. The headlights zoomed toward us like the trees didn't exist. The car roared closer, lights and engine blaring brighter and brighter, louder and louder.

"Move!" Dale cried.

Red Baker dropped his shovel and ran. My feet felt rooted as pines.

"AhhoooOOOoooo-Gah."

"MOVE!" Dale shouted, shoving me hard.

I slammed onto the forest floor and rolled, briars

ripping at my skin. Dale somersaulted past. The car thundered so near, I smelled its exhaust.

Dale jumped up. "That's a Model T!" he said, staring at the taillights.

Another horn blared as a second car zoomed by. "And an old Duesenberg." He looked at me. "Ghost cars."

"Ghost cars?"

"I just hope they don't turn around."

My heart pounded. We stood close, watching the lights disappear. The engine's roar faded away, swallowed by the uneven song of tree frogs. I peered into the dark. "Mr. Red? Are you okay?"

No answer.

"Mr. Baker?"

"I hope he ain't run over by ghosts," Dale whispered, slapping at a mosquito. "That would be hard to explain at the emergency room."

"Mr. Red?"

A truck door slammed somewhere distant. "Son of a gun," Dale said as Mr. Red's headlights flared and his truck choked to life. "He's leaving us."

His truck roared away, and we stood alone in the forest.

Chapter 22
The Judas Trail

I trained my light along the ghost cars' mysterious path—a path thick with trees and brambles—and then tilted my beam to the treetops. "These trees stand shorter than the others."

"The old Judas Trail from the inn to the store at the edge of town," Dale said. "The path they let grow up when the inn closed. It has to be."

A raw scream jolted the night, bouncing off trees, zinging my nerves. I hit the ground and looked over at Dale's feet.

"Screech owl," Dale whispered. "Get up."

Crud.

I jumped up and dusted myself off. "I knew that," I said, zipping my light along the forest floor. Something glinted: Mr. Red's jar. "It doesn't slosh," Dale said, picking it up. He tried the lid. "Rusted shut."

"We'll open it later. Turn your flashlight off," I whispered. "Somebody might come hunting us."

Mr. Red lay in wait behind us, probably at the inn, blocking two ways out—the inn's drive and his own path. The ghost cars had barreled toward the inn too. I made an executive decision. "We'll take the Judas Trail. I just hope we can find it in the dark."

As my words died, a mist gathered in the distance. "It's Nellie," I whispered.

Dale gulped. "That would be sweeter if she had a pulse." Nellie crept closer. "Don't crowd me," he called. "I'm ghost-shy." She faded back. "She has social skills," he whispered. "That's good." We began the slow trek following Nellie back to town.

"Cash," the Colonel said an hour later, wiping earth from the jar.

"Of course," Miss Lana said, pouring two glasses of milk and sliding them to Dale and me. "Moonshine is a cash-only business." She laughed. "No wonder Red wants the inn. It's his bank account."

I looked around the deserted café. The 7UP clock on the wall said five to nine. We hadn't mentioned Nellie or the ghost cars. Not yet. Talking solids seemed easier: We had the jar as proof.

The Colonel shook two dirt-streaked rolls of cash onto the table, each held tight by a rubber band. He

counted slowly, peeling each bill from the roll. "Three thousand dollars." He drummed his long fingers against the counter. "It was on your property," he said, glancing at Miss Lana. "It's yours."

Miss Lana adjusted her *Gone with the Wind* bed jacket on her shoulders. The Colonel and me gave it to her for Christmas last year. It looks good. "Technically it's ours, but Red put it there. I'll talk to Miss Thornton in the morning, and we'll decide what to do."

"There's something else," I said.

How to describe ghost cars to people who don't believe in ghosts?

"That's right," Dale said, looking dapper in a milk mustache. "I can't believe we didn't already say it."

Good. I'd let Dale take the lead.

He took a deep breath. "Queen Elizabeth got lost and she's not outdoorsy. We got to find her."

Queen Elizabeth, who can find Dale no matter where he is? Can't she find her own way home?

"Actually," I said, "I meant . . ."

The phone jangled and the Colonel scooped it up. "This is the Colonel. We're closed. Don't beg." He squinted. "I see." He lowered the phone. "It's Red Baker. He's taken Queen Elizabeth into custody."

Dale went six shades of pale.

The Colonel turned back to the phone. "Where was she when the alleged offense . . . I see. The charges?" He winced. "No, Mo and Dale are here. In fact, they have something you dropped. We can talk about it tomorrow morning when we pick up Queen Elizabeth. And Red," he said, making his voice level as moonlight, "we expect to find her in good health and good spirits when we get there."

He hung up. "Red says Queen Elizabeth killed a chicken. He's penned her for the night."

"He's a liar!" Dale shouted. "She's never killed a chicken in her life."

Miss Lana, who says never say never, raised her eyebrows.

I tried to think ahead. "Dale's right—unless maybe Queen Elizabeth yawned and a hen impaled herself," I added. Just in case.

"Red claims he has proof," the Colonel replied.

He put his hand on Dale's shoulder. "There's no point going over there when Red's angry. Let him cool off until morning. He'll keep her safe—he has to."

"Don't worry," Miss Lana said. "We'll get her back. Call Rose and tell her you're staying here tonight."

Dale dragged himself to the phone. I slipped my arm around the Colonel's waist. He's sinewy as an old oak,

the Colonel, with a heart just as true. He'd have Queen Elizabeth sprung by lunchtime.

Next to Lavender, he's the best father Dale's got.

That night, I couldn't sleep. Could have been the ghost cars, could have been Queen Elizabeth's capture, could have been the Colonel's snores rattling the house.

I clicked on my light. Miss Lana says insomnia is life's invitation to overachieve.

I grabbed Volume 6 and my homework list. In a diabolical display of teacher cunning, Miss Retzyl had combined our language arts and history assignments: *Write a polite business letter setting up a time for your history interview. Use good style.* I picked up my pencil.

DESPERADO DETECTIVE AGENCY
Paranormal Division
Mo and Dale, Chief Investigators

Miss Nellie Blake, Ghost
The Tupelo Inn
Tupelo Landing, NC

Dear Nellie,
Dale and me (or I, whichever is correct)

cordially invite you to meet with us on the evening of the next full moon. At that time we hope to immortalize you with a history interview and a few photos.

We look forward to hearing from you in a non-terrifying way.

Sincerely,

Mo LoBeau, Esquire

PS: We'll invite Harm too. I think he likes you.

I turned the page and licked the tip of my pencil.

DESPERADO DETECTIVE AGENCY
Paranormal Division
Mo and Dale, Chief Investigators

Mr. Red Baker, Moonshiner
Tupelo Landing, NC

Dear Mr. Red Baker,

Dale and me found your stupid jar and counted what you'd hid inside. Miss Lana or Grandmother Miss Lacy will be in touch soon.

I figured out what those little numbers are on your map, but I haven't mentioned it to anyone, not even Detective Joe Starr.

Not yet.

Harm needs a history interview and Dale and me do too. I hope you feel like helping us right away.

Mo

I turned the page one more time.

Dear Upstream Mother,

Today I wrote my first blackmail note. Tomorrow I will leave it in Mr. Red's truck. They say blackmail's wrong, but to me it felt good. Is persuasion in our blood? Please let me know.

Yours truly,

Mo

Chapter 23
Freedom!

"It's Liz!" Dale shouted the next morning, slamming a bowl of grits au red-eye on the café counter and bolting for the door. "She's free!"

I looked up from the toaster and my half loaf of Wonder Bread. Harm strolled across the parking lot, Queen Elizabeth trotting by his side. I slapped two slices of cold bread on a saucer and slid it to Tinks. "Today's special: Toast Tartare. Enjoy."

I ran across the parking lot as Dale dropped to his knees to hug Queen Elizabeth. He looked up at Harm. "Thanks. I owe you. And the . . . late chicken?" he asked, his voice tiptoeing up to the words.

Harm shrugged. "A weasel got that hen. Red knows that. For some reason, he came home in a bad mood last night."

A bad mood? Good, I thought. "I'd like to take a look at Mr. Red's blueprints again. Can you set it up?" He shook his head.

"He locked them in his dresser drawer last night.

Maybe he got antsy, with you all coming over." He scanned the packed parking lot. "Speaking of Red, any updates?"

Across the lot a car door opened, and an Azalea Woman popped out. "Yes, but we're not yet prepared to discuss the details," I whispered as she sashayed toward us.

"A jar full of money," Dale added. "And two ghost cars."

"Money and ghost cars?" Harm said, looking like Liz when she smells a squirrel.

Dale stood and dusted his knees. "We'll fill you in later. Breakfast is on me, to thank you for taking care of Liz. The special today's Miss Lana's Georgia toast and bacon."

"We've reserved a table overlooking the jukebox," I added. "We recommend reservations Saturday mornings. The place fills up fast."

He shoved his hands in his pockets and grinned. "Best offer I've had all day."

Harm had just settled in when Thes bellied up to the counter, his smile crinkling his freckled nose. "Better take your plants in, Miss Lana, I'm predicting frost."

"Frost?" an Azalea Woman chirped. "Already?"

"A light one," Thes said. "Don't worry, we'll be back in the seventies day after tomorrow. You know what they

say: If you don't like the weather in North Carolina, just wait a few minutes." He studied the Specials Board. "Georgia toast, please. And okra."

I tried not to retch. "Coming up," I said, scribbling on my order pad.

"I'll have the same," his father called from the other side of the room. Nobody works a room like Reverend Thompson. He'd already shaken a half-dozen hands and cornered the Exums by the jukebox.

"What did the Exums do this time?" Dale asked, pouring Thes a water.

Thes lowered his voice. "Spray painted a bad word on the church pump house." He glanced at me. "One I can't repeat in front of girls."

I studied the Exums. Jimmy's shoulders quivered. Jake hung his head. "What makes your daddy think they did it?"

"They signed it," Thes said.

Dale snickered and headed for Harm's table as I turned toward the kitchen. "Wait, Mo," Thes said. "I got to interview Mrs. Little and I'm hoping you Desperados might go with me. Like bodyguards."

"Mayor Little's mother?" I looked down the counter.

Mayor Little had spun backward on his stool. He leaned against the counter, his elbows back. "Mother simply dotes on the thorny plant family," he was tell-

ing the Azalea Women. "She calls them nature's barbed wire." He laughed. "Mother's such a hoot."

"Sorry Thes, but I ain't inspired for it. An excellent interview requires virtuoso-level questioning, plus Dale and me got a couple other cases under way. Don't worry. Your daddy can pray you out of there."

He cast a worried look at his father, who shook a finger in Jake Exum's face. "You're supposed to have a buddy in a dangerous situation," Thes said.

"That's when swimming over your head."

"I *am* in over my head," he said, his green eyes pleading. "Daddy set my interview up for this afternoon. All I got's three questions and a throw-up feeling."

I grabbed a Biscuit Carnivore for table six. "Sorry," I said, "but we already got all the *pro bono* work we can handle."

Skeeter looked up from her law book, one stool over. "That means for free."

Thes frowned. "Who said anything about free? I got seventeen dollars saved up. Cash. Bodyguard me this afternoon and it's yours."

Seventeen dollars? Why didn't he say so?

"You're on. I'll even throw in a photo."

Chapter 24
Murdered Sure as Sin

That afternoon, Dale and I headed for the neat cottage Mayor Little shares with his mother, Myrt. Queen Elizabeth pranced at our side.

A chilly wind whipped along the street. I buttoned my sweater and put my hands in my pockets. "I wrote to Nellie Blake requesting a full-moon interview, but I don't know how to mail it," I told Dale.

He took a hank of yellow yarn from his pocket and tied Liz to the fence post. "Maybe you could leave it on the piano." He nibbled his lower lip. "But a full-moon interview," he said, his voice doubtful. "I don't know."

"Don't worry, I got a plan."

"Am I in it?"

"Of course you're in it."

"Then I'm worried," he said as Thes wandered up.

"Thanks for coming," Thes said, handing me a wad of crumpled dollar bills. "We might as well get this over with." We trailed him up the walk. The door opened as he raised his fist to knock.

"Good afternoon, Thes and Desperados," Mayor Little said, smoothing his tie. "Welcome. Mother will receive you in the drawing room."

"Thanks," I said, unbuttoning my sweater. I smiled. "We're hoping you'll sit in on the interview since we assume she likes you."

"Well, for a few minutes," he said, ushering us to a hot, crowded room that smelled faintly of mothballs and cat. "Mother, your guests have arrived."

She looked up from her rocking chair.

As a member of Tupelo Landing's First Family, Mrs. Little naturally dresses good. Shiny dress with a ruffle at the collar, neat stockings, polished shoes. But above the collar floated a lemony face and yellow-gray hair pulled into a bitter bun.

We perched on her flowery sofa, me in the middle. "Good afternoon," I said. She stared at me with hooded eyes. "I think you know us, but in case Old Age ironed the wrinkles out of your brain, allow me. I'm Mo LoBeau of Desperado Detective Agency. To my left you got my partner Dale, and to my right, Thes. You know us from church."

I looked at Thes. Silence.

"On behalf of Thes, I'd like to say you look lovely," I added.

She rapped on her chair arm. "Get on with it."

The mayor chuckled. "I'm sure Mother meant to offer refreshments. Let me see what I can rummage up," he said, scurrying away. "Mother's been looking forward to this for days."

Thes smiled. "Thank you for talking to me today," he said, sounding like a robot. He placed a recorder on the coffee table. "It's for history."

Silence. His smile slid off his face.

"I got a few questions. First, how old are you? Extra credit's at stake."

"None of your business."

"Okay. Thanks for that," he said, marking an X on his paper. "What's your first memory of Tupelo Landing?"

"Pigs. We fenced in the town to keep them out."

Thes looked at his paper. "What's the most important thing you learned in life?"

"Drink water."

Mayor Little tipped in with a tray of soft drinks. We settled into a silence prickly as the cactus on the windowsill. The glasses sweated. So did Thes. "That's all the questions I got," he told me, looking worried. I opened my camera. Mrs. Little stared at Thes like a vulture eying carrion. *Click.*

"I got something," I said. I reached into my pocket and pulled out the old photo from the library. "Do you recognize these kids?"

Her face came to life. "Heavens yes," she said, her gnarled hand going to her throat. "That's Goody Two-Shoes Lacy Thornton grinning into the camera like a little gargoyle. I'm the pretty one standing next to her. The blurry boy's Red Baker, and the skirt-tail and shoe at the edge of the photo . . . Why, that's Nellie Blake."

I sloshed my Coke onto my pants. "Nellie Blake? Are you sure?"

"Of course I'm sure. See how that skirt's torn? Looks like a kite tail flapping behind her. Nellie had the prettiest clothes in town. Never did take care of them. She probably tore that climbing a tree or chasing her dog. Besides, where Lacy went, Nellie followed. They were practically joined at the hip."

Really? Grandmother Miss Lacy made it seem like she hardly knew Nellie.

"Nellie's folks owned the inn," she continued. "Nouveau riche. Not old money like Lacy Thornton's family. But nice enough."

"Nouveau riche?" Thes repeated.

"New money. Flashy money. Nellie was smart as a whip, but troublesome. Quick tempered. A pain in the sit bone." She jabbed a crooked finger at me. "Reminds me of you."

I counted to ten. "Thank you," I said. "Was she a good

reader? I mean, could she read invitations left on a piano for instance?"

"Of course she was a good reader," she said. "We all were." She laughed sudden as a swift flying up a chimney. "Nellie made Lacy drink that spring water like it was going out of style. Lacy's strung tighter than a warped fiddle, you know. Spring water calmed her down, I always thought."

She looked at Mayor Little. "Where's that musty old paper I found the other day?"

Mayor Little jumped up and rushed to the desk. "Here we go," he said, handing a time-yellowed pamphlet to me. "An old ad for the inn." I gave it a quick scan.

TUPELO SPRINGS CURE YOUR ILLS

SPRING 1. Cools fevers.

SPRING 2. Cures depression and illusions.

SPRING 3. Quickens faint hearts.

SPRING 4. Eases breathing.

SPRING 5. Invigorates the liver.

SPRING 6. Calms indigestion.

SPRING 7. Steadies the nerves.

"A footnote," Dale said. He smiled at her. "Thank you."

She leaned forward. "Nellie was murdered, you know."

Murdered? Is that why Nellie's still here? To solve her own murder?

"Mother! How unpleasant!" Mayor Little cried, jumping to his feet. "Well, this has been nice," he told us. "But I'm sure you need to run."

"No," Dale said, "we're good."

She ignored them. "Most people called it an automobile accident. Not me. I say someone sabotaged her car. Nellie was murdered sure as sin."

I gulped. "Why would somebody murder Nellie Blake?"

She looked at me, her eyes sharp. "Maybe they didn't want to. Maybe Nellie died in someone else's place. Maybe there's a Judas in our town," she said, and my heart pumped ice.

"Ask Red Baker. He was the first one there." She looked at her son. "I'm tired," she said. "Show these children to the door."

Chapter 25
Blackmail

Whoever says blackmail doesn't pay hasn't tried it. To everyone's surprise but my own, Red Baker agreed to see us the very next afternoon—Sunday.

"We'll pump Mr. Red for information on Nellie's murder and the ghost cars, plus his still," I told Dale as we walked across Mr. Red's front yard. "I just hope he's in a halfway decent mood."

He wasn't.

"I don't know what's got into him," Harm said as Dale and I tossed our jackets on an old footstool and settled on the duct-tape couch. "All I know is Red slammed his truck door this morning and stomped in here crumpling a piece of notebook paper. He said, 'Call those blasted friends of yours and tell them I'll do their dad-blamed interviews at four o'clock this afternoon. Yours too. You got twenty minutes. But that's the last I want to hear about it. Ever.'"

"That was real thoughtful," I said, slipping my tape

recorder out of my bag. Dale pulled a tape out of his pocket, blew off the lint, and popped it in.

"Gives me a chance to pass history," Harm said. "It's a long shot, but . . ."

"Life's a long shot," Red Baker growled from the hallway door. He stomped into the room, sank into the crippled La-Z-Boy and glared at me. "Twenty minutes. Go."

I turned Miss Lana's old tape recorder on and hit the record key. "Mo and Dale interview with Mr. Red Baker, Harm Crenshaw assisting. Take one.

"Thanks for inviting us," I said. "I'm glad Miss Lana and Grandmother Miss Lacy decided to let you have the money we found even if the Colonel says it's theirs."

"I see it different," Mr. Red snapped.

"There's a lot of 'seeing different' going around lately," I said, giving him a faux smile. "For instance, seeing ghost cars is different for Dale and me."

"Way different," Dale said, leaning forward. "You seen them before, Mr. Red?"

The same question had been pacing my mind, followed by others: Who'd drive dead cars down a forgotten path? Where were they going? Were they running away from or flying to?

Red Baker looked at us, his eyes like steel. "What cars?" he said.

Harm frowned. "You know what they're talking about."

"The ghost cars that ran us down," Dale said. "The ones you ran away from."

Red Baker crossed his arms. "Don't know what you're talking about."

"Really?" I said. "Because I figure you been in those woods plenty of times digging for treasure."

"You're crazy," he said, and pointed to the recorder. "You got fifteen minutes."

"Fine," I said, thrusting the word like a bayonet.

Harm wiped his palms on the legs of his pants. "Here's the deal. We need interviews," he said, looking at his grandfather. "All of us do. I'm writing about you, and our family's distillery. And they're writing about a girl you used to know."

Mr. Red slouched sideways. The sunshine cut a dusty beam through the window and across his grizzled face. "Dale and me are writing about Nellie Blake. Mayor Little's mom thought you could help us with some details."

Dale took out his clue pad. "We need thoughts from Nellie's friends because Nellie's . . . well, I hate to say dead exactly, but . . ."

"I know what she is," he said, his voice sharp. "You leave her alone."

I pictured the cemetery, every blade of grass just so.

Then I pictured the swing blade leaning against the shed. The room wobbled.

It's one thing knowing a ghost. It's another thing when an adult knows her too—even if that adult's Red Baker.

"Mrs. Little says you were first on the scene the night Nellie died," I said. "That makes you an eyewitness to history."

"Yes," he said, his voice going dull. "I was that."

"She also says somebody tampered with Nellie's car," I added. "That Nellie died in someone else's place."

He shrugged. "People say all kinds of things."

Dead end. I went another way.

"Your daddy and Nellie's daddy worked together. Yours owned the distillery," I prompted.

He nodded. "That's right. Blake supplied the spring water and the tavern inside the inn; Papa supplied the recipe and the know-how. We were as legit as they come—until Congress outlawed distilleries back in the 1920s and '30s.

"Old Man Blake threw us out like trash and tore the distillery down. It was on his land. We couldn't do a thing to stop him."

Dale whistled. "So Nellie's daddy ended up nouveau riche and yours . . ."

". . . Didn't. So what? You saying we tampered with

Nellie's car?" he said, his voice rising. "That we killed her? Over money? You wouldn't be the first to say it."

"Gramps," Harm said, reaching for his arm. "Calm down."

He snatched his arm away. "It's a bald-faced lie," he said, glaring at Dale.

Dale scooted to the edge of the settee. A ready-to-run move. "We're not saying anything mean, Mr. Red," Dale said. "We're just trying to pass history. Right Mo?"

"Right."

Mr. Red simmered like the Colonel's sauce pot. I changed tack. "What kind of car did Nellie's father drive?"

"Don't know. A Chevy, maybe. Why?"

He didn't know? *That* was a bald-faced lie. If people accuse you of tampering with a car and killing somebody, you remember.

"How about your daddy?" I asked, very easy. "What did he drive?"

"We drive Fords. Family tradition. He drove a Model A."

"Like in the woods," Dale said, his voice soft.

Mr. Red flushed. "Stop bringing up those woods, confound you."

Dale stood up. "We better go. Thanks Mr. Red, but I can see we're barking in the wrong direction on this."

"Barking up the wrong tree," Harm and me said at the same time.

Red Baker sprang to his feet. "Why did you follow me into those woods?" he shouted. I snatched up the recorder. "You couldn't have known I'd be there unless . . ."

He wheezed like somebody'd punched him in the gut and looked at Harm. His old face sagged. "You," he said, his voice going gray. "A traitor under my own roof."

"A traitor? No! I'm not," Harm said, rising uncertainly to his feet.

"Get out," Mr. Red said. "Get *out*!" he snarled, grabbing Harm's shirt and twisting it in his fist. He shoved him. Harm staggered toward us like an out-of-kilter scarecrow, his long legs scrambling. Red lunged forward and snatched the tape recorder from my hand.

"Go," he yelled.

He shoved all three of us out and slammed the door behind us.

We stood on the porch, stunned by sudden light. Harm stared out across the yard, blinking fast. The chickens clucked and scratched by the shed.

I straightened my messenger bag on my shoulder. "That didn't go quite as good as I hoped it would," I said.

"No," Dale sighed. "Probably not."

I looked at the closed door. Bully. "Hey!" I shouted, pounding the door with both fists. "Give us our jackets and Miss Lana's tape recorder. Don't, I'm calling the law." Silence. "You want Joe Starr over here? I'll have him here before sundown."

Mr. Red yanked the door open and hurled a pile of jackets to the porch. Miss Lana's tape recorder sailed by, landing on top. "Leave that fancy bike I paid for right where it is or *I'm* calling the law, you ungrateful whelp." He slammed the door and clicked the dead bolt into place.

I picked up the recorder. He'd kept the tape.

"Old people," Dale said, handing out the jackets.

Mr. Red jerked the window shade down.

"Let's go to the café," I said. "The special tonight's Goulash-a-Go-Go. Miss Lana's wearing her white go-go boots and a tie-dye outfit. Probably can't hold a candle to whatever you're planning," I told Harm, "but you might enjoy it. You too, Dale."

Dale shook his head. "I promised Mama I'd be home before dark." He gave Harm a shy smile. "I've been hoping you'd come see my room. You could meet Mama and Newton. It would be nice if you could spend the night."

Harm shrugged into his slate-gray jacket, not meeting our eyes.

"You'd be doing Dale a favor," I added. "His social

skills need work. And you could do your homework together."

I didn't mention it, but Harm's books were inside and when it comes to homework, the only excuse Miss Retzyl takes is Precise Death—death that happens to the Precise Student and not to a relative. If they have known relatives.

Harm zipped his thin jacket to his chin. He stood for a minute, scanning the bramble-and-trash dog pen, the old shed, the chicken house.

"I hate this place," he said, and tromped down the steps.

Chapter 26
Bad News or Worse?

Next morning, Miss Rose dropped Harm and Dale off at school, her ancient Pinto belching smoke as she turned toward the Piggly Wiggly. "Talk about ghost cars. I didn't know Pintos still roamed the earth," Harm said as they joined me by my bike.

Dale grinned. "Lavender's brought that old car back from the dead so many times, he named it Lazarus."

Harm went blank as sand.

"Sunday school joke," I explained, slinging my messenger bag over my shoulder.

"Right." He gave me a sleepy smile and headed for the door. He veered around Attila, who sat in the sun preening like a pigeon.

"Where's he going?" I asked.

"To ask Miss Retzyl for new books. Mr. Red might never take him back."

It could be true, I thought. The Colonel says Red Baker holds a grudge better than anybody in Tupelo Landing, including me. "How'd it go last night?"

"Good," he said, combing his fingers through his hair. "I like company." Nights wear thin at Dale's house, where Miss Rose keeps the TV dark to fend off brain rot.

Dale yawned. "Of course, Mr. Red kicking Harm out might be a sheep in wolf's clothing," he said. My brain did an unexpected backbend as I tried to follow. "You know, when something good is dressed up bad," he explained, heading inside and down the hall. "Maybe Harm's lucky to escape. Just too bad Mr. Red kept his stuff."

I looked across the classroom at Harm, who wore yesterday's rumpled clothes. "Good stuff's hard to come by," Dale said as we slid into our desks. "Especially if you're poor. And honest."

Miss Retzyl, dressed in a normal brown skirt and a blouse the colors of autumn, walked to the center of the room. She smiled like an angel. "Pop test—word problems," she said. An Exum retched. "Take out a clean sheet of paper."

When the lunch bell finally jangled, I cut Dale from the stampede and edged him toward the hall. I didn't ask about the test. Dale is to word problems as ship is to the Bermuda Triangle.

"Come on, Desperado," I said. "Skeeter's on office duty today and I got to make a call. Walk like you're innocent."

"I *am* innocent," he said.

"Pass, please," Skeeter said, looking up from her desk. I flashed a hall pass with Miss Retzyl's name on the bottom. Her signature's the only cursive the Exums know, but they know it perfect.

"Nice," she said, holding the forgery to the light. "You got a story for the log?"

I clutched my belly. "I may have caught something during math. I got to call Miss Lana for medical advice."

"She's been burping," Dale added, stepping away from me.

"Potential barf event. Check," Skeeter said, making a note. She tapped her pen against the log book. "Real reason? Anything you say to me is confidential."

"Property dispute," I said. "We got to make a call on our client's behalf."

"Bike-napping case," Dale added.

Skeeter studied her fingernails. "Have we discussed my fee? I can't recall."

I'd prepared a proposal during science. "Miss Lana's contemplating an online order: Her outfit for The Bash *and* the Colonel's." And mine, I thought, if I'm not careful. "She's planning on visiting a library, where the Internet's free," I said.

Skeeter frowned.

"But I can try to turn her business your way. Miss Lana's word-of-mouth is unstoppable."

She raised an eyebrow. "Deal. You have two minutes. I'll stand watch," she added, and we shot to the phone. Red Baker picked up on the fourth ring. I heard him slurp something. Maybe soup.

"Thanks for the half-interview," I said. The slurping stopped. "Give Harm his stuff, and we're even."

Red Baker slammed the phone down.

That afternoon when we left school, Harm's silver bike sat in the rack, a note duct taped to the handlebar. "It's from Red," Harm said, peeling it off. He read it and shoved it into his pocket. "Bad news and worse. Which you want first?"

"The bad news," Dale said.

He looked at Dale. "Looks like you're stuck with me," he said. "Until Gramps calms down, anyway, which could be never."

"That's not bad news," Dale told him. "You can take Lavender's room."

Lavender's room? That's like taking in boarders at Graceland.

"What's the worse news?" Dale asked.

"Gramps dropped off my stuff," he said, nodding to a

backpack propped at the end of the rack. "Including my books. No excuse not to do our homework."

I grabbed my bike. "Let's hit the café," I said. "I'm suffering from an ice cream deficiency."

Dale shook his head. "We told Mama we'd help in the garden." Miss Rose grows the vegetables for the café. That and her Tobacco Culture Tours keep her and Dale afloat. "You want to come?" Dale asked. "We could make notes for our Nellie Blake interview."

I nodded as Harm swung a long leg over his bike's narrow seat. "Hop on," he told Dale. Dale sprang like a cricket onto Harm's handlebars, and we took off.

That evening, Miss Lana cornered me behind the café counter. "Mo, we need to discuss costumes for The Bash," she said.

My universe screamed into slow motion, like a bad bicycle crash at the top of a steep hill. Outfits From The Past flashed before my eyes. My Heidi outfit from Oktoberfest two years back: blue dress, flowered apron, white anklets. Dale in his yodel-boy outfit: clunky shirt, knee socks, lederhosen.

The inside of my arms broke out in hives.

"Miss Lana, I thought I might go as a regular sixth grader. Maybe Miss Retzyl can point me in the right direction."

"Order up!" the Colonel barked.

"We'll talk, sugar," she said, and winked. She stacked three steaming plates along her arm and swayed to Skeeter's family, at a window table. Skeeter's little sister, Gray, a proven biter, slouched in a high chair like a sabertooth troll.

"How's the inn coming?" Skeeter asked as Miss Lana dealt the plates around.

"Don't worry," Miss Lana said. "We'll be ready."

"Excellent," Skeeter replied. "Let me know when you're ready to talk outfits. Skeeter-Bay is at your service."

Crud.

I draped a napkin over my arm and tried to smile at Tinks Williams. "Welcome," I said, my heart flat as a failed soufflé. "Tonight we're offering two specials. The Vegan Crunch—a delicate veggie pileup with a side of apple jerky—for seven dollars. Our Omnivore Odyssey features an epic chicken and broccoli stir-fry on a sea of rice for nine. What can I start you with?"

"Omnivore with sweet tea," he said, tossing his John Deere cap on the counter. "Anna Celeste tells me you're ghost hunting on the next full moon," he said. "You be careful, Mo, things aren't right in that inn. I'm used to you. I don't want to break in somebody new."

"Thanks," I said, giving him a smile. "I'm used to you too."

"Order up," the Colonel sang, and I whirled away.

⁺₊ * ₊ *

That night, I grabbed the interview notes we'd made in Miss Rose's cabbage row and scanned our assignment. *"Outline your history interview. Answer these questions: Who? What? When? Where? Why? Tell me when your interview will take place."*

I picked up my pencil.

> Outline. Interview with A Ghost. By Mo and Dale
>
> Who's the Ghost of Tupelo Landing? (Photo of Nellie Blake's tombstone PLUS proof admissible in a court of law. Maybe.)
>
> What happened? (Interviews with Nellie's mortal friends: Grandmother Miss Lacy Thornton, Mrs. Myrt Little, and Red Baker.)
>
> When and where did Nellie go ghostly? (Sad story. I'll tell you later.)
>
> Why is she still here? (To Be Discovered.)
>
> Desperado Detective Agency plans to interview Nellie Blake on the next full moon, with Harm Crenshaw as Ghost Bait. Extra credit welcome.

I walked over to my Elvis calendar and circled the next full moon—a little over two weeks away.

Chapter 27
Wrong. Dead Wrong.

I thought organizing our interview would be easy with Harm and Dale living in the same house. I was wrong. Dead wrong.

"Dale and Harm hide out after school like outlaws," I fumed a week later as Sal and I crossed the playground.

"Boy stuff," she said, very worldly. Her soft curls glistened in the autumn light. "Mama says they outgrow it in fifty years, give or take a decade."

"*Fifty years?* But our interview's on . . ."

"The full moon," she said. "Next week, Mo. It's all over school. The Exums are offering ten to one odds that you flake. Poor Dale."

Poor Dale? What about me?

She slipped her red Piggly Wiggly sunglasses to the top of her head. "Maybe you can spend time with Miss Lana while Dale's doing boy stuff," she suggested. "Mama says Miss Lana's worried about you."

"She's worried about outfits." I shot her a look. "For The Bash."

Dale trotted up, his backpack slung over his shoulder like a bandolier. "Hey, Salamander," he said. "Nice glasses." He leaned close, examining the tiny white pig faces along the rims. "I never saw them up close. Good art." Sal dropped her books. Dale scooped them up and handed them back.

"Dale, have you asked anyone to The Bash?" she asked. "Because I'd hate for you to be lonely."

"Lonely?" he said, frowning. "How could I be lonely? The whole town's going."

Sal pulled her sunglasses back over her eyes. "I'll get back to you," she said, and hurried away.

Dale tilted his head, watching her go. "I like Sal," he said, "but she thinks funny." He turned toward the school and cupped his hands around his mouth. "Harm, come on," he shouted. "I got to show Mama my math paper."

"Math paper?" I said, my heart diving. "Does Miss Rose have to sign it again? We should have studied. Fractions are tricky, and when you start trying to multiply . . ."

He grinned rakish as Lavender after a good race. "I got a B. Same as we got on our history outline. I'm doing good."

My world tilted. Dale got a B in math? "That's . . ." Actually, it practically ranked as a miracle, but it didn't seem right to say it. "Congratulations."

"Harm helped me," he said, rocking back on his heels. "He's a natural teacher."

A natural teacher? And what am I?

I counted to ten.

"Dale, the full moon's next week. We got to get ready."

He scuffed his sneakers. "Right." He looked across the playground, at Harm. "You want to come over after supper? You can see Mama's new dishwasher and we can talk to Ghost Bait about the interview."

What? Miss Rose had a dishwasher installation and didn't invite me?

I held my head high as I stalked away.

"Mo!" Miss Rose cried, looking up from her desk. "Come in!"

"Hey Miss Rose," I said. I crossed her neat living room to give her a hug. "I hear you had a dishwasher installation. I'm sorry I didn't immortalize you with an Appliance Portrait, but I'll stage one at no charge on my way out. A major appliance is a milestone."

She blinked her eyes, which are emerald. "An appliance portrait?"

"You may want to comb your hair," I replied. "Is Dale home?"

"He's in his room." She slid her glasses down her nose and studied me. Miss Rose reads me like yesterday's news. "I'm sorry I didn't call about the dishwasher, Mo.

I know you like to help Lavender. I've been so busy getting next year's tours lined up, it slipped my mind. We're starting the tours with planting next spring and heading straight through to harvest. I may even fire up that old barn and go into autumn, if we have enough interest. With any luck, I'll be able to keep Lana's inn full half the year."

Like me, Miss Rose has a head for business. The Colonel says her tours will make her rich once she picks up steam.

"I'm glad it's just business distracting you," I said, businesswoman to businesswoman. "I'd hate to see you fall into a crippling emotional spiral on account of divorcing Mr. Macon, which I feel like I speak for the entire town when I say you're better off without him."

Her smile went flat as a nailed tire.

I took a framed photo from her piano—an old one taken on a good day. In it, Mr. Macon looks near handsome as Lavender. Miss Rose leans against him, beaming. Dale, who's pre-first-grade, looks big-headed and scrawny as a kitten.

"Nice photo," I said. "I can burn Mr. Macon out of there if you want me to. I got darkroom skills."

Silence fell over us like a cloak of nettles.

"Or," I said, putting it back on the piano, "I could leave it alone."

"Thank you, Mo. Lavender's dropping by in a little while to take a look at my dishwasher," she said, turning back to her desk. "Something's squeaking . . . Perhaps you could take a mother-son-appliance portrait?"

Lavender? Here?

"You're on," I said. I trotted to Dale's room, pausing with my hand on the doorknob.

I could hear him through the door: "Take it from the top." The music leaped from his guitar strong and clear. His voice followed easy as swinging on the porch:

"Nothing could be finer than to be in Carolina in the morn-ing."

A second voice piped up:

"Nothing could be sweeter than my sweetie when I meet her in the morn-ing."

They both chimed in:

"If I had Aladdin's lamp for only a day
I'd make a wish and here's what I'd say
Nothing could be finer than to be in Carolina in the morn-ing."

I opened the door. Dale and Harm looked around like I'd caught them stealing hubcaps. "Hey. I need that blue T-shirt you borrowed last week," I said, for cover.

Queen Elizabeth wagged over and I scratched her head. "Was that you singing?" It was a stupid question, but Miss Lana says even stupid questions start conversations.

"Guilty," Harm said.

"We don't say that in this house," Dale told him.

"You sound good," I said. "*Real* good."

"See?" Dale said, beaming at Harm. "Told you so." He grabbed my T-shirt off his chair and tossed it to me. It smelled like Queen Elizabeth's shampoo. "I'm sorry we've been scarce, but we been practicing. We wanted to surprise you."

A surprise? For me?

"Actually, we want to surprise everybody at The Bash," he said. "If we can get good enough. We've been working up to letting you hear us face-to-face. Harm never sang in front of anybody before."

"You sang in the inn the other day," I told Harm. "You sounded good."

"Yeah," he said. "But I had my back to you. That's different."

Interesting. Harm has a shy spot. I sprinkled a bug buffet in Newton's terrarium.

"And Mo," Dale added, "we need a manager."

"Somebody used to dealing with the public," Harm said.

Dale nodded. "Somebody that can spell and make posters."

Manager Mo LoBeau? I smiled at Newton, who blinked. "I don't know," I lied. "I'd need to hear your material before I could commit."

"Right," Harm mumbled, and shoved his shaking hands deep in his pockets.

"Take it from the top," I said. "And impress me."

They did.

> Dear Upstream Mother,
>
> Tonight after Lavender fixed Miss Rose's dishwasher (guitar pick in the spin-around), I shot my first Mother-Son-Appliance Portrait. Lavender stood with one arm across Miss Rose's shoulders. I never noticed before, but he has Miss Rose's smile.
>
> Lavender invited me to meet him at the inn tomorrow afternoon—but don't get your hopes up. He also invited Dale and Harm. Harm said no but Dale and me said yes. Then Harm changed his mind, and shook Lavender's hand.
>
> We'll ride over with Grandmother Miss Lacy and Miss Lana. I hope to ask Grandmother Miss Lacy about Nellie while we're there, but Miss Lana says we can't wear her out. Rebuilding an old inn is more stressful than you'd think, and Dale says my questions can get on your nerves.
>
> I wonder if you and me share the same smile.
>
> Mo

Chapter 28
Return of the Rat

"Hey," Lavender said the next afternoon, opening the inn's door. "Come on in."

Grandmother Miss Lacy and Miss Lana breezed in. Harm, Dale, Queen Elizabeth, and me followed. The late-afternoon sun slanted through the tall windows, casting the floors in red and gold. "The Colonel should be here in a minute," he said.

"You've worked miracles in here," Grandmother Miss Lacy said, admiring the dining room's chandelier.

"The electricity's not hooked up yet," Lavender said, "but she'll sparkle like diamonds when it is." He nudged Harm. "I found out how Red made that old light fixture swing," he added. "Remote control."

"Cool," Dale murmured. Miss Lana frowned. "But bad," he added. "Very bad."

Harm shoved his hands in his pockets. "Yeah. I'm sorry Red—"

Miss Lana popped his arm with her fan. "Red's like the weather. There's no point in apologizing for it."

Lavender led us across the room. "Glad you like the dining room," he said, opening a small door. "Because the kitchen's a different story."

"Oh my," Miss Lana said, stepping through the door. "I'd forgotten."

If the dining room sang, the kitchen cried. The dining room stood high-ceilinged and open; the kitchen fought for breath beneath a ceiling so low, Harm could almost touch it. A rickety counter ran along the front wall, and a sloping, tin-lined sink drained toward the corner of the building.

"I didn't remember it being quite this bad," Grandmother Miss Lacy said.

I lifted my camera and focused on the grimy windows over the sink. *Click.* Dingy cupboards lined one wall. An ancient wood stove crouched at the far end of the room, its oven door hanging open, a rack spewing out like a crooked tongue. *Click.*

Dale gingerly opened a cabinet door. "Brown paint used to be cheap."

"Ugly is always on sale," Miss Lana said.

Lavender dusted off a chair for Grandmother Miss Lacy. "My goodness," she said, sitting. "Can you fix this?"

Lavender crossed his arms and leaned against the counter. "The building inspector says we have to tear it out and start over."

Miss Lana's face went the color of mashed potatoes. "Start over? How much?"

"Fifty thousand dollars," the Colonel said from the door. Even Grandmother Miss Lacy gasped. "We need special ovens, freezers, sinks, plumbing . . ."

Dale wheeled to me. "Fifty thousand dollars? How many pizzas is that?"

When it comes to math, Dale thinks in pictures. He needs numbers he can see. "This room full, give or take," I said.

"Where will we get fifty thousand dollars?" Miss Lana wailed. "Even with Rose booking her tours here, we can't . . ." Her eyes filled with tears. "Why did I buy this place?"

"We," Grandmother Miss Lacy said, sounding far away. "We bought this place. And . . . I might as well tell you. It seems I've made some . . . unfortunate investments."

Miss Lana gasped. "How unfortunate?"

"Very unfortunate, I'm afraid."

Dale slipped close to her. "Are you . . . nouveau broke?"

She bit her lip. "Not quite, dear," she said. "But I don't have another fifty thousand to put into this project. In fact, I've had to borrow to do what I've done. And that's becoming . . . problematic."

Problematic? My Detective's Instinct told me her

problematic drove a silver BMW. "Filch at State Bank," I guessed.

Her eyes swelled with tears. "The Colonel's doing what he can. But I can't imagine where the money for this kitchen's coming from. Or how we'll pay off the inn."

Not pay off the inn?

"You'll rebound," the Colonel said. He used the same tone he used to use on me when I'd receive time off from school, for fighting. "You need time to get your bearings in the new economy," he told her.

"Time? She's out of time," an ugly voice said behind us.

"Anita Filch," I said, wheeling to find Rat Face standing in the door.

She looked over her shoulder at someone behind her, and barked, "For heaven's sakes, hurry!"

Flick Crenshaw stepped through the door, and my stomach flopped. "Nice work, Lavender," he said. "We'll enjoy owning the place."

He smirked at his little brother. "Red told me you were running with a new crowd, Harm," he said, looking us up and down. "Can't say much for your taste."

Harm flushed dark as a summer storm.

"This would be a good time to say something nice about us," Dale whispered.

Harm nodded and took a breath. "Flick, these are my friends, and—"

"Meet your future sister-in-law," Flick interrupted. "Anita Filch." Harm gulped.

Miss Lana says love is blind. She never mentioned it being stupid.

Rat Face simpered and held out a limp hand. "Pleasure," she said. A shivery silence settled over the room.

Flick punched Harm's shoulder. "Say hello to my fiancée."

Harm shoved his hair back. "But I thought you were with that blond woman—old what's-her-name," he said, his voice low. "What happened?"

"Say hello, kid. You're embarrassing me."

Harm stuck out his hand. She grazed it like he had poison ivy and stalked across the kitchen, her stiletto heels clicking against the floor. "Lacy, you haven't returned my calls, so I thought I'd drop by," she said, running a finger along the old counter. "We've been discussing your situation at the bank. Yours too, Lana."

Miss Lana watched her the way she watches a garden snake.

The Colonel cleared his throat. "Miss Filch, I believe Miss Thornton's accountant and I have put something together that will satisfy your bank and—"

"Too late," she snarled. "We're calling the note. Pay off the inn in full by November first, or my bank takes it. If my bank takes it, the deed will be in my pocket

before sundown. Bet on it." Upstairs, a door slammed.

Nellie! Dale and Harm looked at me, their eyes wide.

Rat Face tapped her foot. "Are we clear, neighbors?" She said *neighbors* like a curse. Which the Colonel says maybe it is.

"November first?" Miss Lana cried as Nellie padded along the upstairs hall. "That's just weeks away. We can't possibly . . ."

"Pay up or get out," Rat Face snapped. Stealthy footsteps headed down the stairs. The Colonel looked toward the sound, curiosity playing like flame across his face.

"Hold it," Harm said, grabbing his brother's arm. "You're talking about my friends, Flick. You'll ruin them," he said. "And Red too. Red has—"

"I know what he has. Keep your mouth shut."

Harm looked like Flick had slapped him.

So that's it, I thought, remembering Flick and Rat Face chatting at the auction. They want Red Baker's money. And they'll take the inn to get it.

Nellie crept down the stairs and paused at the foot of the staircase. Dale gulped as Queen Elizabeth sneezed.

"Miss Filch," the Colonel said, basting his voice with calm the way he bastes a turkey, "Lacy Thornton's been a customer at your bank all her life. Surely . . ."

Rat Face put her hands on her hips. "We're calling the note," she said. A smile twitched at her lips. "There's

nothing you can do. But I do think it's nice for an attorney of your caliber to have the skills of a fry cook to fall back on."

"A *fry* cook," Miss Lana said, putting *her* hands on *her* hips.

"Uh-oh," Dale said, stepping back.

"The Colonel is a chef, Rat Face," I shouted. "With the skills of an *attorney* to fall back on."

"Thank you, Soldier," the Colonel said.

Rat Face's beady eyes flickered over him. "*Rat Face?* You let your foundling call people names?"

Foundling?

The Colonel sprang toward her, his hands balled into fists, the planes of his face white with rage. "*What* did you say?"

Rat Face backed up. The Colonel stepped forward and lowered his face to her level. "You get your skinny little streak of mean out of here. Now. And don't come back unless you have the deed in your hand. *Rat Face.*"

She scurried to the door—which creaked open for her. "November first," she shouted.

She stomped out. A wind tumbled leaves across the porch and across the dining room floor as Flick backed away from the Colonel. He stopped to glare at Lavender. "If you know what's good for you . . ."

"I do know. Get out," Lavender said, his voice like a razor blade.

Flick marched across the dining room and out the door. It slammed hard enough to rattle the windows.

Lavender frowned at Miss Lana. "The wind?" he guessed as Rat Face's silver BMW flashed by the window, her headlights playing against the cedars.

Grandmother Miss Lacy teetered to the window, panting like she'd run a relay. "What a terrible woman . . ." Her voice trailed away and her knees buckled.

"Catch her!" I shouted. Lavender got there just in time.

"Miss Thornton?" he said as a tide of frigid air swept across the room.

"The hospital," the Colonel ordered. "Now."

Grandmother Miss Lacy's shoe clattered to the floor as Lavender rushed across the dining room. Overhead, the chandelier hissed and sputtered like an angry cat. "Stop it, Nellie," Dale yelled, running behind the Colonel. "You'll set the place on fire!"

Miss Lana and Dale bolted for the car. Harm and I skidded to a halt at the door, our breath clouding in the inn's freezing air.

"It's okay, Nellie," I shouted. "We'll help her."

"We promise," Harm said.

The chandelier crackled and one by one, every door in the inn slammed shut.

It took forever for the ER doctor to come out. "She'll be fine," she said, and a million tight-wound springs inside me gave way.

"Thank you and amen," Dale whispered.

The doctor looked at Miss Lana. "Are you Lacy Thornton's daughter?"

Miss Lana didn't bat an eye. "I am."

"We'll keep her overnight for a few tests," the doctor said, leading her down the hall. "I need you to sign . . ."

Lavender stretched like a big cat. "Told you she'd be okay," he said, but he'd looked as scared as the rest of us on that putrid green plastic couch. "Excuse me, Desperados. I owe the Colonel and Harm a call. Mama too." He headed for the phone.

"Come on, Dale," I whispered. "We got to work fast."

We found Grandmother Miss Lacy dozing in a crank-up hospital bed. She looked fragile as a baby wren fallen from the nest. "Grandmother Miss Lacy?"

Her eyes fluttered open. "Mo," she said. "Oh. And Dale." She squeezed my hand. "Don't worry, I'll be good as new. What did the doctor say?"

"You're spending the night for more tests."

She yawned. "Don't worry, dear, doctors always over-

react so they can overcharge. Thank you for coming. Perhaps we could talk in the morning."

I kissed her face. "I love you," I said, nestling her navy pump by her side.

"Me too," Dale said. He leaned over her, his lips hovering over her face.

She laughed. "The kiss is optional," she told him, giving him a little push.

Dale gave her a shy smile. "Miss Thornton, emergency room sofas make you think. If I was you, I'd send out for pizzas every day before I'd spend fifty thousand dollars on a kitchen."

She sat bolt upright. "What did you say?"

Dale turned to me. "Has she gone deaf?" he whispered.

Take-out! Dale's brilliant, no matter how much evidence teachers stack up against him. "Dale's right," I said. "The café can cater the inn."

She beamed at Dale. "You're a genius."

"Thank you," he said, very modest.

She settled against her pillow as Miss Lana walked in. "Good news," Miss Lana said. "You'll go home tomorrow if the tests go well and you promise not to get stressed."

Grandmother Miss Lacy nodded. "And Lana, Dale's come up with a brilliant plan: The café can cater meals until the inn's on its feet. You don't need a kitchen."

Miss Lana tousled Dale's hair. "My little business-man," she said, and he blushed.

"As for *my* bad news . . ." Grandmother Miss Lacy took a deep breath. "I'm afraid you'll have to do the best you can until I get back."

"What bad news?" I asked. "You'll be fine."

She lay back on her pillow. "I'm broke, Mo. By now, the news is all over town."

Chapter 29
Harder Than if the Sky Lost Its Blue

Grandmother Miss Lacy nailed it: The next morning her financial disaster was the topic du jour. Nobody could remember Grandmother Miss Lacy not having money. People took it harder than if the sky lost its blue.

Even Miss Rose came to town seeking comfort. She sat at the counter, her back straight. "Hey Miss Rose," I said, sliding biscuits her way. Worry had lined her eyes. Grandmother Miss Lacy is her partner too. "Nice posture. I'm more of a slumpist myself. What can I get you?"

"The special, please," she said. "Has Miss Thornton called this morning?" She twisted her wedding band—a nervous habit. Old habits die hard, Miss Lana says, and Mr. Macon's a very old habit.

Miss Lana stopped beside me. "Not yet, but we're fine, Rose," she said in her "this-better-be-true" voice. She splashed coffee into Miss Rose's cup. "Pass the biscuits around, sugar," she told me. "Nothing comforts people like hot biscuits."

I darted through the crowd, delivering biscuits and taking in news. Grandmother Miss Lacy's woes had spread across town like ripples across a pond. She'd helped so many people, she owned a quiet slice of near every business in town.

Mayor Little, at the counter, poked a hole in his biscuit and filled it with molasses. "If Lacy Thornton goes under, Tupelo Landing goes under," he said, sending a tidal wave of worry cascading across the café. He stared longingly at the biscuits. "Are you offering seconds?"

I looked at his round belly. "I'd hate to see you lose your figure, but I'll see what I can do," I said as Miss Lana stepped to the counter and clapped her hands. Her Ava Gardner wig shimmered as the café clattered to silence.

"As most of you know, Miss Lacy's coming home today. As you may not know, she's worried about us," she said. Miss Rose and Sal's mother looked up. So did Skeeter's mom. And Hannah's father, who owns the service station at the edge of town. "She'll talk to each of us when she's ready. Until we have more details, I suggest we do what we've always done in difficult times: our best."

The café murmured like pigeons.

"If we lose the inn, we'll go out with style. I'm sure you all know what that means." She gave me a regal nod. "Mo?"

I stepped up on my Pepsi crate and waited for all eyes to find me. "Party," I said.

The café cheered.

"We'll throw the best bash ever," she said. "We'll set the scene. We'll laugh and dance and eat old-fashioned treats. Mo and I will don authentic 1938 costumes. . . ."

"What?" I cried, staggering.

Dale gasped. "Costumes?" He shoved Harm behind the jukebox and dove after him, out of the line of fire.

Attila stood up. "Costumes suit *Mo and Dale,*" she said, her eyes glinting. "But Mother and I draw the line at costuming. So will our friends."

I hate Attila Celeste Simpson.

Buddha Jackson put his fork down. "I'll MC the event," he offered.

Miss Lana blanched. I knew she was picturing him prancing across the stage like a tubby Mick Jagger. "Thank you," she said, glancing toward the kitchen. "But the Colonel has already volunteered."

A pan hit the kitchen floor. Poor Colonel.

I waited for the crowd to settle. "Plus I got a bonus announcement," I said. "We've signed the hottest musical group this side of Raleigh for The Bash."

"Excellent! Who?" the mayor asked, jumping to his feet.

Crud.

When Lavender showed up at Miss Rose's for his Mother-Son-Appliance Portrait, we'd been on the verge of choosing a name for Dale and Harm's group.

I grinned. That's it.

"On the Verge!" I cried. "Live at The Bash! A big round of applause!"

Sal's applause spattered lonely and uncertain in the silence. The mayor stared blankly, his jaw sagging.

Dale peeped over the jukebox. "Who?" Harm pulled him back down.

"On the Verge!" I shouted. "Don't miss it!"

I hopped down and wound my way through murmuring Tupelites. Dale beamed up at me from behind the jukebox. "On the Verge. It's us, isn't it?" he asked, his eyes glistening.

"It's you, Desperado," I said. "Break a leg."

"Figure of speech," Harm told him, and he nodded.

"We're going ahead with the party? Impossible," Lavender said later that morning as Miss Lana poured his coffee. "I can't get ready in time."

Miss Lana settled beside Lavender. Without the excitement of the café crowd to sustain her, she looked as tired and worried as Miss Rose had. "Everything takes as long as you've got, Lavender. We have two weeks. The show must go on, even if Rat Face rolls up the stage at the end of it."

I looked around the café. The crowd had bolted, chatting about party clothes and financial ruin. The Colonel had rumbled off in the Underbird to collect Grandmother Miss Lacy. Dale and Harm had caught a ride with Miss Rose. Only Thes sat at the counter, polishing off his special.

"I'm sorry," Lavender said, his voice firm. "I can't do it."

Miss Lana heaved her Report Card Sigh.

"What about the pavilion?" I asked. "We can have The Bash there."

"Outside?" Lavender said. He tilted his head, which means he's thinking, and opened his egg sandwich, which means he needs pepper. "In October?"

Good point. Autumn here's like the water in my flat: It runs hot and cold.

Thes spun on his stool. "My forecast *is* trending warmer," he said as I nudged the pepper to Lavender. "I'll check the specifics for you, Miss Lana." Like me, he'd taken a Personal Day from school.

"Thank you, Thes," she said. "With good weather, all we need's a dance floor and a stage. The river and the stars will do the rest."

Lavender peppered his sandwich. Three sharp shakes. "We've already got the pavilion shored up," he said. "That may be doable."

Lavender loves doable. He's like the Colonel that way.

He peeked at Thes and lowered his voice. "Miss Lana, I checked the electric lines after . . . what happened last night. The sparks, I mean. I can't find an explanation."

Miss Lana shrugged. "Apparently the contract's right. We're ghosty," she said, easy as if she'd said "we're toasty." Lavender choked. Miss Lana grew up in Charleston, where they take ghosts in stride. Lavender grew up at Miss Rose's place.

"C'est la vie," she added. "Live and let . . . whatever."

"Let whatever?" he said.

"So," she said. "Let's pick a theme for our dance."

My stomach lurched. "Dance? Do you mean with boys?"

She laughed a laugh full and sweet as a stolen pear. "A party then, sugar. People can dance or not."

"Great," I said. "Because Dale and me got a strict non-dance policy."

"Are you sure, Miss LoBeau?" Lavender asked, giving me a wicked grin. "Because all the Johnson men dance, including Dale. Mama sees to it. In fact, I'm hoping you'll do me the honor."

Me? Dance with Lavender?

I waited a beat for dramatic effect, like Miss Lana taught me. "You're on."

Chapter 30
The Horror Unfolds

As the week rolled on and Grandmother Miss Lacy slowly picked up strength, the horror of Miss Retzyl's academic scheme continued to unfold. "It's time to wrap up your interviews and get your rough drafts together," she said on Friday afternoon.

Attila raised her hand. "The full moon's Wednesday night," she said, turning to look at me. The Exums grinned and rubbed their hands together. Traitors.

"I'll expect to see everyone's rough draft a week from today, for Fishbowl Friday," Miss Retzyl continued.

"Fishbowl Friday?" Dale said, looking blank.

"On Fishbowl Friday, everyone's name goes in the bowl," she said with a normal smile. "I'll draw three lucky students to present oral reports."

Hannah raised her hand. "How can oral reports be lucky? In this universe, I mean." Hannah reads science fiction.

"Lucky because they receive extra credit," Miss Retzyl

replied, and the Exums whipped around to stare at each other.

"Excuse me, Miss Retzyl," I said, "but the entire town's trembling from financial stress. Oral reports could tip us over the edge, which could mean not only personal heartbreak, but a class action lawsuit. I'd hate to see you embroiled."

She smiled. I adore Miss Retzyl. "I'll risk it, Mo. Any questions about the assignment? Wonderful," she said as the bell rang. "Have a lovely evening."

"A lovely evening of homework," Harm droned as he headed for the door.

"Maybe not," I said. "I feel a plan coming on."

After two glasses of Miss Rose's iced tea and three Oreos, my plan pulled itself together. I looked up from my notebook. Dale, who'd slung his guitar over his shoulder, was practicing moonwalking across the room. Harm, who'd staked out the ladder-back chair, sat with his feet propped up on the bed.

The Colonel says being a leader means risking an occasional plunge in popularity. I strapped on my emotional parachute. "You know what Wednesday night is, don't you?"

"Full moon," Dale said, backing into his dresser and

setting a photo wobbling—the photo of him and his parents, from Miss Rose's piano. Interesting.

Harm looked up from his library book, *Moonshiners I Have Known*. He'd given up on interviewing Mr. Red and gone generic. "You guys don't really need me," he said.

"Yes we do," I said. "You're Ghost Bait."

"Isn't there a better way to say that?" he asked. "One where it sounds like I'm human and I survive?"

"The Exum boys are giving odds we don't show on the full moon," I announced, and waited for their outrage. Harm went back to his book. Dale moonwalked into his beanbag chair. "Sal told me," I added. "A reliable source."

Dale twirled. "We know," he said. "Harm bet against us. So did I."

"What?"

He shrugged. "If we cave on the full-moon interview, we'll use our winnings to go to a movie in Greenville. You like movies." He looked at me. "We might as well forget it, Mo. The Exums will try to scare us out to cover their bets. And if the Exums show, Nellie probably won't. She doesn't like strangers. So, no interview."

I tapped my pencil against my notebook. Newton rolled his warty head toward me and blinked. "Fine," I said. "We'll do the interview tonight."

"Tonight?"

"If we don't show on the full moon, you two collect on your bet, we go to the movies, and we *still* get our interview and pass history."

Harm looked up and grinned. "I'm glad you use your mind for good, Ghost Girl, because if you ever go bad, you'll be diabolical."

"Thank you," I said. "Dale, don't forget your questions. Harm, please wear a clean shirt. Nellie will like that. Queen Elizabeth, I hope you can make it. Your howls really help.

"You all bring flashlights and your notebooks. I got the tape recorder and the camera. And don't tell a soul. Especially not an Exum. I'll drop off a note for Nellie on the way home, advising her of our change in plans.

"Meet me at moonrise," I added, and headed for the door.

On my way home, I swung by the inn and dropped my note on the piano.

Nellie Blake, Ghost
The Tupelo Inn
Tupelo Landing, NC

Dear Nellie,
Emergency change in plans. Due to Exums,
Dale and me got to change our interview to
tonight at moonrise. We'll meet you near the

piano. Harm looks forward to seeing you and
will dress nice.

    Sincerely,

    Mo

That evening, I squinted at my glow-in-the-dark Elvis watch. 7:45 p.m. "Nellie's late," I said. "It's at least half past moonrise."

"She's not coming," Harm said. "Let's go home."

"And get laughed out of sixth grade? *And* flunk history? You're just nervous," I told him. "Relax, Nellie likes you."

He sighed. "That's what worries me."

I popped a tape into Miss Lana's old tape recorder. "We'll give her an hour," I told them. "Eternity could be in a different time zone."

The wind's bony fingers rattled the shutters as I leaned over the recorder. "Testing, one two three. Paranormal History Interview, Extra Credit Edition. Mo and Dale presiding. Harm Crenshaw, Ghost Bait."

"I wish you'd stop saying that," Harm muttered.

Dale propped his light against his pack, casting a soft glow across the old parlor. I looked past the old desk, beyond the piano to a tall window overlooking the river. Moonlight skated across the black water quick and bold. "You got your interview questions ready?" I asked, placing the camera in easy grabbing distance.

Dale tugged a crumpled paper from his pocket and placed it on the floor. Then he pulled four neatly wrapped slices of cake from his pack. "Angel food," he explained, placing the cake by my camera. "I hated to bring devil's food."

I hesitated. "Good social skills," I said, and he gave me a modest nod. "Now we just got to act polite when she gets here."

We waited. Nothing. Finally I shifted my legs. "My feet went dead asleep," I said, bumping my heels against the floor.

"Don't say dead," Dale whispered.

I sighed. "Okay, let's try the piano. I hoped she'd drift in on her own, but I'm not proud." Nobody moved. "Just one song," I said. "If she doesn't show, we'll take off."

Dale tiptoed to the piano. A graceful river of sound rolled through the silence. I listened for footsteps. Nothing. Crud.

"Come on, Harm," Dale said. Harm trudged to the piano. Suddenly it felt lonely on my side of the room. Very lonely. I grabbed my camera and casually sprinted to the piano as they sang: "Heart and soul . . ."

Queen Elizabeth sneezed and the temperature dropped like stepping off a cliff. Footsteps clattered along the upstairs hall as a pink glow swept down the stairs, hovered over our recorder and notebooks, and moved toward us.

"Say something polite," Dale whispered, his breath steaming in the frigid air.

"Hey Nellie," I said. "Thanks for dropping by."

The cloud slowed into a vaguely human form, a slender girl in pigtails and an old-fashioned dress. Dale elbowed me. "Grandmother Miss Lacy Thornton says hey," I lied. "She'd probably say more, but she's under the weather."

"Nerves," Dale explained, his voice pale. "We get on them."

A laugh soft as wind chimes flowed across the still room.

"I told you we'd take care of her," Harm added, his voice shaking.

She floated toward him. He backed up. She covered his hand. He pulled it away. Again, a laugh like wind chimes floated across the dark room.

"Nellie," I said, "we want to ask you some questions. For history. We're hoping we can help you too," I said, and Dale gave me a puzzled look. "Maybe you're tired of this lonely old inn. Maybe you want a different place to call home. We'll try to help you, only we don't know why you're still here."

Dale nodded. "A paranormal win-win," he explained.

Nellie almost looked at me. Then the swirls came faster and thicker, like cotton candy pulling itself into

being. She floated to the window and whispered against the glass.

The pane frosted over. I lifted my camera. *Click.*

"Why . . . why did she do that?" Dale stammered.

She started toward us. "Back up, Dale," Harm whispered.

Nellie's chill stung my face as she rolled by us, to the inn's old desk. One by one the desk drawers scraped open . . . all but the little one, at the top. The one Lavender couldn't open. *Click.*

She drifted back to Harm, lingered—and floated away.

"She's gone?" Dale said in the silence. "We risked our souls on a practically full moon for an icy window and a messy desk? What about our interview questions? What about my history grade?"

I crossed to the frosted windowpane—a patchwork of tiny snowflakes already melting in the warming room. "A clue," I said, staring at it.

"Clue?" Harm said, walking up beside me. "What's it mean?"

"I don't know yet. It's a clue," I said. "Not an answer."

"I'll tell you what it means," Dale said. "It means girls are a big fat mystery, dead or alive." He leaned closer to the frosty windowpane and tilted his head, squinting at the frost. His breath fogged the pane next to it. Harm and I saw it at the same time.

I grabbed Dale's jacket. "Dale," I said, yanking him back. "Watch out."

"What?" he asked, scrambling backward. "Is she here again?" He looked wild-eyed around the room. "Because I didn't mean anything bad by whatever I said. I think Nellie's sweet."

"Look," I said, pointing to the breath-fogged pane. On it, an unseen finger had traced a single number.

7.

"A definite clue," I said as water collected in the base of the 7 and picked a jagged path down the pane.

"But a clue about what?" Harm asked.

I turned to look at the oak desk, its drawers gaping open—all save one. I tugged the drawer. It didn't budge. "Locked," I said, tapping it.

Harm crouched in front of it, shining a flashlight on the tiny keyhole. "I can open it if I have the right tools." He straightened up. "We can come back tomorrow," he said.

Dale passed his cake around. "If Nellie has something to say, why doesn't she just *say* it?" he asked.

"Maybe she doesn't know how," Harm said, staring at the frosted window. "Or maybe she's saying it and we don't know how to hear her."

Dale wolfed his cake down and placed the last piece

on the piano. "Let's get out of here," he said. "I want to see people with skin on."

That night I woke up sharp as lightning. That ice on the window wasn't a snowflake. It was lace. *Lace*-y Thornton, Nellie's best friend. And the 7 . . .

I sprang out of bed and rummaged through the odd books on my bookshelf: *The Piggly Wiggly Chronicles, Karate for Beginners, Geometry.* "Here it is," I whispered, sliding out Mrs. Little's old pamphlet.

TUPELO SPRINGS CURE YOUR ILLS

SPRING 1. Cools fevers.

SPRING 2. Cures depression and illusions.

SPRING 3. Quickens faint hearts.

SPRING 4. Eases breathing.

SPRING 5. Invigorates the liver.

SPRING 6. Calms indigestion.

SPRING 7. Steadies the nerves.

"That's it," I said. "Spring Number Seven. For Grandmother Miss Lacy's nerves." I squinted at the clock: 4:00 a.m. I grabbed my phone and dialed.

Dale picked up on the second ring, mumbled, and

dropped his receiver. "Hello?" I said as it bounced against the floor. "Dale?"

Queen Elizabeth II growled into the phone—an unexpected development. "Dale," I called. "I'm down here with Liz!" Nothing. Queen Elizabeth's toenails scrabbled against the receiver as I whipped up a quick Plan B. "Liz," I hissed. "Squirrel!"

She yelped like a dog possessed.

"Hush, Liz!" Dale said. "You'll wake up Mama." He grabbed the phone.

"Dale, wake up. It's me. This is maybe life and death. Meet me at the inn. We ain't got a moment to spare."

A half hour later the three of us—me, Dale, and Queen Elizabeth—crept down the path to the springhouse. I wore jeans and a windbreaker, and carried a quart jar. Dale wore cowboy pajamas and red snow boots, and carried a hammer. I didn't ask why.

"Where's Harm?"

Dale shrugged. "Snuck out an hour before you called. Said he had business."

I skidded to a halt. "In the middle of the night?"

Dale nodded. "He went out the same way Lavender used to. Through the bedroom window. He said he'd be back by sunrise."

Lavender had a secret exit? I made a mental note.

"I'd have gone with him if I'd known you were going to drag me over here again," Dale said. "This better be good, Mo. Like A-plus good."

A breeze wafted across the river. "There's the springhouse," I whispered as we rounded a bend. Its pale walls and slate roof looked serene in the moon's flat light. The breeze shifted and I caught the scent of rosemary. Queen Elizabeth sneezed.

"And there *she* is," Dale said. "Nellie Blake, standing by the door." The pink mist slowed. Nellie looked at us, turned, and walked through the closed door.

"Show-off," Dale muttered. Like I said, Dale doesn't wake up good.

I marched to the springhouse, grabbed the door's chain, and gave the padlock a yank. "Stand back," Dale said. He lifted his hammer. *Crack.* The lock fell to the ground and the plank door creaked open.

Dale pulled a small flashlight from his left boot and clicked it on. Its beam crawled across the floor, across seven basins that marked the inn's springs.

Queen Elizabeth's hackles rose.

"It's okay, Liz," I said. "If Nellie wanted to hurt us, she'd have hurt us long ago."

"Where did those come from?" Dale whispered, spotlighting a single set of footprints in the middle of the red-clay floor.

"The question is, where are they going?"

The footprints marched across the clay floor. Dale's light beam shook as he followed them to a spring. "That's Spring Number Seven. I saw it on the blueprints," I told him. "She wants that water for Grandmother Miss Lacy."

The pink flared.

I knelt by the spring. Out of the corner of my eye I watched Nellie's footprints pad to the back of the spring-house—and through a door bricked shut seventy years ago.

Chapter 31
A Business Offer

"Grandmother Miss Lacy," I shouted later that morning, pounding up her steps. "We got your cure!"

"Over here, dear," she called from behind a potted fern. I skidded to a halt.

"Water," I announced, holding out the jar.

"From Spring Number Seven," Dale added, and she jumped like he'd pinched her.

The front door squeaked open. Harm Crenshaw? Here?

"There you are, dear," Grandmother Miss Lacy said like having him there was normal as permanent teeth. "Do you mind bringing four glasses? They're in the cupboard by the sink."

"What are *you* doing here?" I asked, staring at Harm. He smiled at me bleary-eyed, still wearing last night's clothes.

"He's cheering up an old woman," Grandmother Miss Lacy replied.

Harm leaned against the doorframe. "Actually I came

over with a business offer from Gramps, but she turned me down," he said. He looked at her. "You sure you won't change your mind?"

"Positive," she said. "That money is Red's. But he'd best move it if he wants it. Filch won't be as generous as Lana and I are."

"Think it over," he said. "If you change your mind, I'll bring the blueprints."

Red Baker's treasure map. Since when would Mr. Red part with *that?* And why would he give it to Harm?

"Excuse me if I'm accidentally not sensitive," I said, and Dale went tense beside me. "But Mr. Red's a hateful old miser, which thank heavens you only got part of his DNA, giving you a scientific shot at being nice. So how did you get those blueprints? He won't even let you in the house."

"Red and I had a heart-to-heart last night," he said, not quite meeting my eyes.

Not likely. For that to be true, Red Baker would have to have a heart.

"A fifty-fifty split makes sense, Miss Thornton," he said. "Red owns the map. You own the land."

Harm might be lying about Mr. Red, but his plan made sense. I looked at Grandmother Miss Lacy. "You need the money," I told her.

She patted her blue hair into place. "It's a wonderful offer, Harm. I'll call Red and thank him."

"No!" Harm said. "I mean, that would embarrass him. I'll tell him for you."

"Fine. Now if you would fetch those glasses . . ."

Moments later the door swung open, and Harm backed onto the porch awkwardly balancing four juice glasses on a small tray.

"Thank you," she said as he set them on a table. "Spring Number Seven. Mo, would you pour?"

I filled the glasses, and passed them around. She lifted hers. "To your health, my friends." She closed her eyes and sipped like she could taste her childhood. "Delicious."

"Glad you like it," I said, giving the swing a nudge and setting it rocking. "We can bring you water every day if you want. To steady your nerves."

"It's way better than you dying," Dale added, giving her a smile.

"*Dying?* I'm not dying," she said, reaching over to knock on the porch rail. Grandmother Miss Lacy's superstitious. "Who on earth told you I'm dying?"

Dale turned to me, his blue eyes accusing. "You said life or death. Me and Liz got up at *four o'clock* this morning."

"I said *maybe*. Besides, it felt like life or death at four o'clock."

"Many things feel like life or death at four a.m.," she said. "They generally look better in their day clothes."

Harm poured himself another glass of water. "No," Dale whispered. "You're supposed to fill their glasses first." Harm topped off our glasses.

"Yes, I'm fit as a fiddle," she said. "Just ashamed of letting everyone down."

My heart sank a little. "We're really going to lose the inn, then?"

"Probably," she said. "I'm sorry, Mo."

She closed her eyes. For a minute I thought she was praying. "My yard's an absolute mess," she said, sitting up straight. I scanned the yard, which stood ankle deep in red maple leaves and sweet gum balls. "I can't do yard work at the moment . . . Doctor's orders. What would you three charge me to do it?"

Harm hopped to his feet. "Nothing. Where do you keep the rakes?"

"In the garage," she said. "And certainly I'll pay you. I'm not that broke, but I *am* tired. Why don't you come back this afternoon," she said. "We'll have refreshments, and straighten this place out."

"Besides," I told Harm. "We got some work to do."

"At the inn," Dale prompted.

"Right," he said, and yawned. "Let's go."

∗∗*∗*

We soon dumped our bikes on the inn's lawn and headed for the steps. "Hold it, Harm," I said. "How'd you get those blueprints? Mr. Red would never give them to you. He probably wouldn't even let you see them."

"That's right," Dale said. "He pretty much hates your guts."

"Thanks for reminding me," Harm muttered, heading up the steps. "Give me time to settle things, okay? I'll tell you when I can."

I looked at Dale, who shrugged.

"Thanks," Harm said, opening the inn's door. "Let's get this done." It took less than a minute to pull out the open drawers and search them. Nothing.

Harm squinted at the lock on the last drawer and reached into his pocket. He pulled out Miss Rose's tiny screwdriver, the one she uses on her eyeglasses. Funny he thought to bring that, I thought, since he'd planned to be back at Dale's before morning.

He leaned over the desk, at eye level with the lock. He slid the tiny screwdriver into the keyhole and jiggled it. "Come on, baby," he whispered, sounding too much like Flick. "Got it!" he cried, and slid the drawer open.

Dale and I crowded close. "What's in there?" I asked.

"Nothing," Harm said, looking bewildered.

"Check the outsides then," I said. "Nellie wanted us to see *something*."

Dale pulled the drawer out and flipped it over. Nothing on the bottom, the sides, the back. He slid the drawer into place and opened it again. It snagged. I thought of my Salvation Army desk. "Let me try," I said. I grabbed the small brass knob, slid the drawer out, and slipped my arm all the way into the space.

"Good idea," Harm said as my fingers closed around a paper in the very back of the desk. I tugged the old paper free and smoothed it against the desk.

"A letter," I said, staring at the faded brown ink. "To Nellie."

Dale gulped. "I hope she doesn't mind us reading it." He nibbled his lip. "Aren't there laws about opening other people's mail?"

The cursive slanted tall and even across the paper. "It's from her father," I said.

Upstairs, a door slammed. We looked up as footsteps hurried along the hall and down the steps. Nellie clattered to a halt halfway down. I didn't blame her. I'd be too nervous to come closer too. I turned toward her and read:

"Darling Nellie, Forgive my greed, forgive my temper, forgive my ridiculous disagreement with Truman. How I wish he'd killed me and not you. I'd give my world to hear you laugh again. Father."

Nellie plunked down on the stairs. "I'd sit down too," I said softly.

"Looks like Truman Baker *did* tamper with Nellie's car," Dale whispered. The room went ice cold. Dale crossed his arms. "Please Nellie," he said. "I didn't bring a jacket."

"Truman Baker," Harm said. "That's Red's father. And my great-grandfather."

He took a deep breath. "I'm sorry, Nellie," he said, his voice going soft.

"We all are," Dale added.

From the stairs, the soft rustling of cloth. The sound of footsteps turning and plodding up the steps and down the hall. A heartbeat later a door closed and a key clicked a lock tight.

"I didn't know those doors had keys," Dale whispered.

"They don't," I told him. "Not anymore."

I folded Mr. Blake's letter and slipped it in my bag. "Maybe Truman Baker did tamper with that car," I said. "But there's no way to prove it. Not now."

"No way to prove what?" a voice behind us asked. I wheeled to the open door. There stood Detective Joe Starr, Red Baker by his side.

"Arrest her," Red Baker said, and pointed at me.

Chapter 32
True or False?

"Arrest *me*?" I cried. "For what?"

"Whatever it is, Mo didn't do it. Plus she has an alibi," Dale said.

I brain-scanned the last few days, searching for crimes.

Dale glared at Detective Starr. "Besides, you can't go around arresting kids."

"If Mo didn't do it, he did," Red Baker said, pointing at Harm. "One of these little bandits took my blueprints and I know it."

Harm went pale around the gills. So Harm *did* take those blueprints.

To my relief, Detective Starr turned on Red Baker. "Now you're saying *one of them* has your blueprints? A half hour ago you said you saw Mo running across your yard with them. Which is it?"

"And *what* blueprints?" Dale demanded. Smart move. Would Mr. Red actually accuse me of stealing his moonshine map in front of a lawman?

"You know what I'm talking about," Mr. Red shouted, flushing beneath his stubble. "My blueprints."

"Blueprints of what?" I said, innocent as rain. "You mean a map? A map from where to where?"

He clamped his mouth shut and I smiled.

Starr took out his notepad. "According to Mr. Baker's statement, someone slipped through his bedroom window last night, jimmied the lock on his dresser, and stole his blueprints." I glimpsed the desk out of the corner of my eye. Crud. Miss Rose's tiny screwdriver lay there bold as day. *That's* why Harm had it in his pocket. He broke in and jimmied that lock. I looked away.

"So?" Dale said. "What's that got to do with Mo?"

"I dusted Mr. Baker's dresser for fingerprints. Found a couple kid-size prints."

Fingerprints? I tried to remember what I'd touched. The blueprints, for sure . . .

"I'd like to check these prints against yours, if you don't mind," Starr said. "To eliminate you as suspects. That way I won't have to take you in."

"That's all you got?" Dale demanded. "Red Baker's no-good word?" He sounded angry, but his eyes had gone glassy with fear. Dale getting fingerprinted would break Miss Rose's heart.

Harm shoved his hands in his pockets. "You'll find my prints all over that house," he said. "I used to live there.

You'll find Mo's and Dale's too. I showed them around the first time they came, to make them feel welcome."

"It's a social skill," Dale explained.

"Dale's prints might be in Red's room, but I'll bet money you find Mo's. She picked up everything in sight. You know how she is," he said.

What was *that* supposed to mean? But like Miss Lana says: Any port in a storm. "Harm's right," I said. "Picking up things and setting them down is a habit I got."

"A bad habit," Dale said, his voice stern. "Very bad."

Starr wavered.

I took a chance. A big one. "The Desperados always cooperate with fellow law enforcement. Go ahead," I said, holding out my hands. "I been hoping to see your fingerprint kit. We're thinking of ordering one, aren't we, Dale?"

"Yes," Dale said, looking totally baffled. "I feel that could be true."

Starr squinted at me, and then at Mr. Red. "Mr. Baker, did Harm have access to your room? Did these two visit your home?"

Mr. Red scowled.

"I wish you'd told me earlier," Starr said, closing his notepad. "It would have saved me tracking these kids down."

"These scoundrels robbed me," Mr. Red snarled. "Do your job, confound you."

The pulse on Starr's forehead jumped. "Mr. Baker, these kids could worry the bark off a tree, but I don't appreciate you calling them names."

"Thank you," I said, very dignified.

"Do you kids have Mr. Baker's blueprints?" Starr demanded.

"No," we sang out like a choir of heavenly hosts.

"Search me," I offered, spreading my wings.

Starr ignored me. "Let's go back to your place, Mr. Baker," he said. "I'd like to take another look around."

I bet he would. Another look—for a still. Mr. Red seemed to have the same idea. "Forget it," he said, heading for the door. "I'll handle it myself."

"Fine. But stay away from these kids," Starr said.

Like I said, Starr secretly likes us.

Detective Starr stood by the window, watching Red Baker stomp across the yard. "Stay clear of him," he said, putting his notepad back in his shirt pocket. "You wouldn't know anything about his still, would you?" he asked.

"No," I said. Unfortunately it was true. I was beginning to wonder if we'd ever get another break on Harm's case.

"If you hear anything, let me know," he said. "I'm offering a reward."

"A . . . reward?" Harm said. "How much?"

Starr smiled the way Dale smiles when he hooks a fish. "Five hundred dollars for information leading to an arrest."

"Five hundred dollars? *American?*" I said, my heart pounding.

"Any thoughts you'd like to share?" Starr asked, clicking his pen.

"No sir," Harm said. Dale and me shook our heads.

Starr handed Harm his card. "Call if you think of anything." We trailed him to the porch and watched him climb into his dirt-colored Impala.

"That's a lot of money," Harm said as Starr pulled away. "Hope it's not enough to give you any ideas."

"I'm blank," Dale said.

"The Desperados never turn their back on a client," I told him. "Besides, he gave the card to you. Not us." Harm snorted and headed for his bike. "Hold it. Where's those blueprints?" I demanded.

He threw his leg across the seat, and studied us like he was balancing an equation. "I hid them in Miss Thornton's garage early this morning. Sorry I didn't make it back to your place by sunrise, Dale. Red surprised me and I had to hide."

"That's okay, I left Mama a note for both of us," Dale said.

"You better keep those blueprints hid or else get rid

of them, Harm Crenshaw," I said. "Starr won't give up as easy as he pretends he will."

"Neither will Red," he replied.

Early that afternoon we snuck around Grandmother Miss Lacy's house, past the Buick, to the old garage nestled in her juniper grove. Harm unfastened the door's clasp and it squawked open. "Shhhh," I whispered. "Grandmother Miss Lacy's napping."

My eyes adjusted to the dim light. We edged around a tarp-covered pile of machinery, slipped past some old luggage, and skirted a stack of empty buckets. Harm reached behind a stack of fertilizer bags and pulled out the blueprints.

"Over here," I said, motioning to the tarp. "Dale— your flashlight."

Harm and I spread the blueprints across the tarp. We leaned over the map, staring at the tiny fractions spattered across the page—some crossed out, some not. "Which cross-out looks newest?" I asked.

Harm squinted at the page. "This one, I think." *12/256 x 17/89.*

"The top numbers must be step-offs," I said. I nudged Dale. "We heard Mr. Red counting off steps in the forest. Remember?"

"Right," he said.

"But the numbers on the bottom," Harm said. "What the deuce . . ."

I tapped the page. "He got out of the truck here, and lined up with the roofline of the inn, here. And . . ." I hated to say it. "He looked over his shoulder, this way. I think he lined up with the cemetery," I said, and Dale gulped. "Then he started walking."

"The bottom numbers must be his which-way numbers," Dale said, and tilted the flashlight up into his own face. He looked like a freckle-faced ghoul. I tilted it back down. "They help him get his bearings, somehow."

Bearings. "That's it," I said so loud, they both jumped.

"The bottom numbers are compass bearings," I said, picturing the Colonel blazing a trail through the forest. "A compass is an old-timey GPS," I explained. "It's magnet-powered. You line the arrow up with north and then read the numbers around the compass rim. Those are your which-way numbers," I added, and Dale nodded.

"Right," Harm murmured. "Red keeps a compass lying around. These aren't fractions, they're locations. You step it off and dig."

Dale whistled. "Each number's a money jar? No wonder he called a lawman. Mr. Red's rich—if he can dig up his bank account."

He studied Harm. "Why'd you take it?" he asked. "For the money? I never figured you for a thief."

The word stretched between them flat and sad.

"*Thief?*" Harm said, his voice rising. The blueprints slipped, and I scooted them back in place, hoisting the edge of the tarp like the hem of a skirt.

Harm glared in the semi-dark. "True or false," he said. "If Flick and his rodent-faced girlfriend get their claws on his money, Red will never see another penny. Neither will Miss Lana or Miss Lacy."

"True," Dale said.

"True or false? Without his buried bank account, Red's broke."

"True," Dale said. "Most likely."

"True or false? If Red's broke, I'm never going home. If that's . . . really home, I mean," he added, his voice trailing away.

Dale didn't answer. "If you ain't taking the money, why take the blueprints?"

"I thought Miss Thornton could use some of the money and we'd keep the rest for Red. Besides, Red's the last person I'd figure to call the cops."

Dale frowned. I could practically see the wheels turning and smell the smoke. "You haven't been officially caught, which means you're still in a family-borrowing situation," he said. He looked at him, his blue eyes serious. "But you better give them back before you get caught, Harm. I mean it. Starr will take you in."

Harm gulped. "I'll put them in Red's truck," he said as the blueprints skidded.

"Dag this tarp," Dale griped, shoving the blueprints into place and dragging a handful of tarp with it. "What's under there, anyway? Lawnmowers?" Harm lifted the corner of the tarp and peeped underneath.

"Noooo way," Harm said. "Dale, give me a hand."

Dale grabbed a corner. Together they peeled the tarp back. A chrome bumper. A pale blue sculpted hood. An elegantly swooped fender. A whitewall tire yellowed by time. A running board, a cab, a handsome boot. "Ghost car," Dale announced, his eyes like saucers.

"*Ghost* car? That's a Duesenberg," Harm said.

Dale pressed his finger against the fender and looked at me. "It's 3-D," he said. "It's worth . . . I don't know. A lot."

Harm ran his hand along the sleek fender. "*Running,* it's worth a fortune. Broke down, I'm not so sure. Is the key in it?" Dale shone his light through the window, and whistled.

"Original leather, inlaid dash . . . She's a beauty."

"You're early," Grandmother Miss Lacy said, strolling through the door. I shoved the blueprints behind me. "I see you found Father's car."

"Does she run?" Dale asked.

"I doubt it," she said. "It's been here for years. It

reminded me so much of Father, I just couldn't part with it. The rakes are over here," she said, edging past me. I turned like a rotisserie chicken as she passed, keeping the blueprints hidden.

"Miss Thornton," Harm said. "This is a *Duesenberg*."

"I know, dear. A 1933 Model J. Father told me a thousand times."

"Do you know what it's worth?" he asked.

She turned to him, and I shoved the blueprints behind a cob-webby trunk. "Value's relative, dear. It's worth the world to me, because Father loved it. But in dollars? I'd have to pay somebody to haul it off, I imagine."

Harm's mouth fell open. So did Dale's. It wasn't a good look. "Miss Thornton, Duesenbergs sell for real money," Harm said.

"Tens of thousands of dollars, maybe," Dale added.

"Or more," Harm said. "Way more. Especially if they run."

"Do you think so?" she said, her hand fluttering to her throat.

"I know so," Dale said.

"Dale's people know cars," I added.

She sat down on the old trunk. "Thank you, Father," she whispered, and blinked back quick tears. "Perhaps we should have an expert look at it before we get too excited," she said.

"Lavender," I told her. "He'll know what to do."

Chapter 33
Jailhouse Interview

Lavender went to work on the Duesenberg that afternoon. "She hasn't budged since World War II," he warned. "The tires have dry-rotted and the seals need to be replaced, but if you can invest a little money in her, Sam and I will do the rest. No guarantees, but it *could* pay off big."

She gave him a crisp nod. "If it pays off, it pays off for all of us," she said. "Tell me what you need and I'll manage it somehow. Let's get started."

While Lavender and Sam set up in the garage, we raked leaves and watched for a chance to snag the blueprints from behind the trunk.

Our chance never came.

That evening, Dale and Harm practiced their performance pieces—again. "It's amazing what you can do with three chords and good harmony," Dale said, grinning at Harm. "I wish you could sing, Mo. If you could, you'd sound good."

274 • *The Ghosts of Tupelo Landing*

Miss Lana says Dale's compliments are an acquired taste.

He plopped into his beanbag chair as Harm grabbed his science book.

"We need to talk about Nellie," I said.

Harm turned a page in his book.

"I know. Murdered, or not murdered?" Dale replied. "I hate to ask her straight out," he continued. "It seems so . . . personal. Mama wouldn't like it."

While I digested that, he moved on. "Who's the hands-down expert on local crime? Not rhetorical," he prompted.

"Detective Joe Starr?"

He shook his head. "Daddy. And murder's the kind of story that gets passed down at family reunions."

"It is?" Harm and I said together.

"Tomorrow's Sunday," Dale continued. "Visiting Day. We could pay a visit and ask him, if you want."

I felt like magnetic north wobbled. "I didn't think you wanted to see your daddy—not after the way he treated you and Miss Rose."

Dale leaned over to tie his shoe. "It's always going to be *after* the way he treated us, Mo. You only get one daddy and he's the one I got." He looked up at me. "I got to talk to Macon again sometime. This is as good a time as any."

Hearing Dale call his daddy by his first name made me feel older than stone. "I'm with you, Desperado," I said.

"Me too," Harm said. "Didn't he do business with Red?"

"I ain't confessing him to anything," Dale said. "But you can ask him. Only thing is, Lavender won't leave the Duesenberg unless we got a 911 situation, and I can't ask Mama to take us."

"We'll ask the Colonel," I said.

The next afternoon, we climbed into the Underbird. "Used to be a Thunderbird, but the *T* and *h* fell off," I told Harm as he slammed the door.

A half hour later, the three of us sat across a lunchroom table from Mr. Macon. The Colonel and Queen Elizabeth waited outside.

Mr. Macon looked lean and tough as wire cable and his blue eyes glinted like glass. I remembered what Miss Lana had said just before we left: "Be positive, my intrepids. Remember: A caged bird warbles sweetest in sunshine."

"Why does she talk like that?" Dale had whispered as we headed for the Underbird.

"The Colonel says it's in her blood," I'd told him.

He'd nodded. "Maybe they'll find a cure."

Now, as I studied the stark room and the guard at the door, I thought I knew what she meant. I slapped on my sunniest smile. "Hey Mr. Macon," I said, taking out my clue pad. "Miss Lana says jumpsuits are making a comeback this season, but even if they don't, orange is a real good color for you."

"Shut up Mo," he growled.

I smiled like he didn't mean it. I've never been his favorite, and getting him thrown in the slammer hadn't honeyed him up. Still, if my Detective's Instinct was right, he secretly longed for conversation. I nudged Dale. Silence. I moved on to Harm. "Mr. Macon, this is Harm Crenshaw," I said. "Red Baker's grandson."

"Pleased to meet you, sir," Harm said, very smooth. "I understand you and my grandfather go back a ways."

Mr. Macon sliced a look at the guard. "We speak, that's about it." His ice-blue eyes found Dale's. "Hey, Dale. How are you, son?"

Dale looked up. "Hey Daddy," he said. "I'm good."

"How's fifth grade treating you?"

"Dale's in sixth," I said. "It's nosebleed difficult."

Dale nodded. "Very hard. Harm and me started a singing group. We're good."

Mr. Macon crossed his arms. "School's wasted on some folks. You're one of them."

Shock shot across Harm's face like lightning across

an unguarded sky. "Nothing's wasted on Dale," he said. "He's making B's. And we *are* good."

Mr. Macon leaned on the table. "How'd you get here?" he asked, darting a look toward the door. "Is Rose outside?"

A stupid question. Why would Miss Rose divorce him, and then come calling? "The Colonel brought us," I said. "He's outside with Queen Elizabeth."

"How's your mother, Dale?"

"Good. She got a dishwasher."

He leaned back and watched Dale through narrowed eyes. "Tell her I miss her. You hear me, son? Tell her I miss her."

Dale froze like a fox smelling metal. "We came because we got a question," he said. "For our history paper."

Good. A side-step.

I pulled the recorder out. "It's about Nellie Blake. You ever heard of her?"

Mr. Macon took a cigarette out of his chest pocket and tapped the filter end on the table. "Sure. My old man liked to talk. Nellie getting killed ripped the town apart. But that was lifetimes ago."

"Ripped apart how?" I asked.

He twirled the cigarette in his fingers. "Lacy Thornton's people claimed her death was an accident. But most folks blamed Truman Baker."

"Red's father? Why blame him?" Harm asked.

"Truman rigged the brakes." He said it flat and simple. The earth is round, the sky is blue, Truman rigged the brakes.

Harm flushed. I guess it's hard hearing you carry murder in your genes.

Mr. Macon smiled. "Don't take it so hard, kid. There's degrees of murder. First-degree, second-degree, manslaughter."

"Right," Harm said. "But there's only one degree of dead."

"Why would Truman Baker want to hurt Nellie or her father?" I asked as the guard started toward us.

"Ask Red Baker," he said as the guard stopped beside us. "He saw what happened. That's the way I hear it, anyway."

Red Baker? An eyewitness to murder?

"You got another visitor, Macon," the guard said, nodding toward the door. A slight man in a shiny suit stood tapping his foot. "Says he's your attorney."

"Send him away. I'm busy."

That's Mr. Macon for you. He bosses people around even when he's the one wearing orange. He stood up and slipped the cigarette back in his pocket. "I got to get back inside," he told us.

He reached over to tousle Dale's hair. Dale ducked.

"See you, Daddy," Dale said, a blush creeping up his neck.

I hate Mr. Macon.

"Tell your mama . . ."

"Tell her yourself," I said standing up. "Dale and me are busy."

"Hey Mo," Mr. Macon called as we reached the door, "tell the Colonel I'm grateful." I turned. He looked smaller standing there in Prison Issue, like a pocketknife folded to hide the cutting edge.

"Grateful for what?"

"He'll know," Mr. Macon said, and nodded at the guard, who led him away.

Chapter 34
A Perfect Match

The next day, Monday, I thumb-tacked a flyer to the school bulletin board:

ON THE VERGE!
Tupelo Landing's hottest musical duo!
Command Performance!
Where? The Tupelo Bash
When? October 22, 8 PM
For interviews and autographs, contact
Manager Mo LoBeau

Dale and I stepped back to admire my work. He'd been quiet since our jailhouse interview, but he was starting to come back around.

Hannah Greene skidded around the corner, her arms spilling over with library books. Hannah never studies. She doesn't need to. "Hey, where you been?" I asked.

"Dentist," she said. She tugged a note from her Ray Bradbury. "Mama and I stopped at the café. The Colonel sent this." I unfolded the note as she sped off.

Soldier. You have a UPS package from that weirdo Cousin

Gideon. It's by the jukebox. I'm going to Winston-Salem for a few days to pick up records from my old office. I'll call tonight, and I'll see you when I get back. Keep a low profile: Lana's plotting costumes. Love, the Colonel.

"Cool," Dale said. "UPS."

After school, we ripped into the box. "Wow," Dale exclaimed, pushing the packing away. "It's . . . one of those."

"Right." I lifted the black box onto a table. Dale squinted at its white gauge. I placed the electronic wand beside it. "A Geiger counter?" he guessed.

A letter fluttered to the floor.

Dearest Mo,

I borrowed this vintage do-flop from my ghost-hunting friend. It measures electromagnetic charge in the air. She says ghosts are made of it. Just place the wand in ghostly spots and the energy registers on the dial. Happy hunting!

Cousin Gideon

PS: Hope this gets you a footnote.

"This could get us more than a footnote," I told Dale. "This could get us hard evidence versus what we got so far—circumstantial and hearsay."

"We *are* pretty much eyewitnesses," Dale said. "Won't that count?"

I shook my head. "Miss Retzyl's sweet, but she'll

believe we saw a ghost like she'd believe we rowed George Washington across the Delaware," I told him. "We need proof."

"What on earth?" Miss Lana asked, rushing in from the kitchen in her parrot-colored fiesta outfit and Cher wig.

"Ghostometer," Dale replied. "From Cousin Gideon."

She smiled like a ghostometer's normal as a slip-cover—one of the things I like about her. "Mo, could you set out the chili bowls, please? And Dale, if you'd move the cactus out of the kitchen and string the lights?"

"*Sí*, ma'am," Dale replied.

"*Gracias*, honey," she said. "Oh, and Mo. You'll be glad to know I've found a gorgeous 1938 party dress on Skeeter-Bay—just my color and size."

Costuming? My heart sped up like Lavender's foot had hit the accelerator. "That's great, Miss Lana. I wanted to talk to you about clothes. For The Bash."

"Oh no," Dale said, veering toward the cactus.

"Costuming's the chili powder of life, sugar," she said. "Wait 'til you see what else I found. I had to guess the Colonel's size, of course, but I think he'll be pleased. And you're going to *love* what I found for you." The skin on my back tingled. "Don't thank me," she said as Dale dragged a potted cactus across the floor.

"Miss Lana, I think I might go regular," I said. "You know. As a sixth grader."

She put her hands on her hips, her bracelets clanking. She studied me, her gray eyes puzzled. "*Regular?* But why?" She sighed. "Perhaps you're rebelling."

"Yes," Dale said, squinting at me. "I think that could be it."

She shrugged and gave me a smile. "Well, we all know what Bill says."

Crud.

Miss Lana's on a pet-name basis with William Shakespeare.

I didn't have to ask what she meant. She's said it so often, I hear it in my sleep: "All the world's a stage, sugar, so hop on up there."

I tried not to imagine what she'd ordered for me. "Yes ma'am. I'll take the ghostometer to my flat."

The next day—Tuesday, a so-called teachers' workday—dawned bright and cool. I met Dale in the inn's polished parlor, after breakfast. "Harm says he has an errand," he reported.

"I hope that means he's putting the blueprints back," I said.

Dale shook his head. "He can't spring them from the garage. Lavender and Sam are working in there around the clock."

"Hey Desperados, what's *that?*" Lavender asked, elbowing his way through the inn's front door with an armload of boxes.

"Ghostometer," I said. "What are you doing here? I thought you'd moved in with the Duesenberg."

His eyes sparkled like Dale's when Queen Elizabeth learns a trick. "You know me going and coming," he said. "That car's a thing of absolute beauty. But I promised Miss Lana I'd work on the pavilion today. With The Bash just around the corner, she's on edge. So Sam's working on the car and I'm over here, trying not to be jealous."

Dale eyed Lavender's boxes. "You need help?"

Lavender tied a nail apron around his waist. "Now that you mention it, I could use some muscle and a woman's eye down at the pavilion for a few minutes."

A WOMAN'S EYE? MINE?

I grabbed my camera. "Mo LoBeau, at your service."

"I'll help," Dale said, and peered into a box. "Nice . . . plain old lightbulbs."

Lavender grinned. "Like me, they dress up good. Miss Lana splurged on paper lanterns for them. You two grab the boxes, and I'll get the ladder. How long since you've seen the pavilion?"

"A couple weeks, maybe."

"You're in for a surprise."

Surprise didn't come close. The trail sloped to the springhouse, turned, and headed down to the pavilion as always. But the weeds and washouts were gone, replaced by neat timbers and crunchy white gravel. Lavender stopped at the bottom of the trail. "We'll add a fancy archway here for folks to walk through. Miss Lana's idea."

Miss Lana loves to make an entrance.

"But for now, feast your eyes on Tupelo Landing's newest night spot," he said, with the flourish of a circus acrobat. "The Tupelo Pavilion—an outdoor paradise."

"It looks more like a huge platform with rails around the edges so we don't fall off," Dale said, worry skating across his face.

"You're a natural poet," Lavender teased. "It'll look better with the finishing touches. Note the stage for the talent," he said, setting his ladder by a tall corner post. "That would be you and Harm."

"I'm their manager," I said, like he didn't know. I picked up my camera and framed the small stage at the far end of the pavilion. *Click.*

Lavender scampered up the ladder. "Who are you guys coming with?"

Dale looked up at him. "What do you mean?"

"It's a social occasion," he said as I unraveled a string of lights. "You can come with somebody if you want to." He looked at Dale. "Like, a girl?"

"He's coming with Sal," I said. "He just doesn't know it yet."

Dale popped open a box of bulbs. "I am?"

Lavender shot his brother a grin. "Sal's sweet. Hand me that hammer, would you? How about you, Mo?"

"I'm available, if you're asking."

"Me? Go out with you?" He grinned like he always does when I ask him, which I've been asking ever since I turned six. He said what he always says: "You're a baby. Besides, I've already got a date."

I passed him the hammer. "Not the big-haired twins again. They're an environmental hazard," I said. "They use enough hairspray to shellac a lizard in its tracks. You need somebody ecological. Somebody like me."

He moved his ladder down. "How do these lights look, Mo?" he asked, holding the string of lights against the next post. "Does that seem about right?"

Everything seems about right when I'm talking to Lavender, but I backed up and unfocused my eyes, trying to get the feel of the lights against the river's soft lines. "They need to be looser," I said, and he let the line dip. "Like that. Miss Lana says everything about a party's got to flow."

An hour or so later I dusted my hands. "I'd love to

stay and enchant you further," I said. "But Dale and me got to wind up our investigation. We got rough drafts due Friday, with the possibility of oral reports hanging over us like guillotines."

"Oral reports. Ouch."

Dale gave Lavender a careful look. "I went to see Daddy," he said, very casual. "I didn't ask you because I knew you wouldn't want to go."

There's no love between Lavender and Mr. Macon. Not for a long time.

Lavender laid his hammer on top of the ladder. "How's he doing?"

Dale shrugged. "Same dog, same spots." Lavender's face went soft as Miss Rose's when she thinks I'm not looking.

"He means leopard," I explained. "A leopard doesn't . . ."

"I know what he means," Lavender said. "I'm sorry, Dale." He looked at Dale the way he looks at an engine when he's trying to figure out why it's running ragged. "Macon's broke inside. It's not our fault. It's just the way it is."

Dale nodded.

Lavender picked up his hammer. "If I thought you were the one that landed him in jail, little brother, I'd thank you for it," he said.

Dale jumped like he'd stepped on a live wire. "Thank me?"

"Sure. Mama's safe, you're safe. Macon's looking at hard time—which means he might find time to take a hard look at himself. It's tough knowing what's good and what's bad the first time you see things."

The river lapped against the pavilion, and the wind sent a shower of scarlet maple leaves cartwheeling to the water. Dale squared his shoulders. "That's what I was thinking too," he said. "More or less. Come on, Mo. Nellie's waiting."

Moments later, as we scampered up the inn's steps, I caught the glint of sun-on-chrome behind the cedars. I squinted. Detective Joe Starr's Impala! "What's Starr doing here?" I asked. Queen Elizabeth II, who'd been napping in the sun, lifted her head.

"Stalking Mr. Red's still, most likely," Dale said. "Which I wonder if he even has a still. Because if he's not out digging up money, seems like he's hanging around the house. Maybe he's retired," he said, reaching down to smooth Queen Elizabeth's ears.

I pushed the front door open. "Nellie? You home?"

Silence.

"Let's ghostometer the desk and piano," I said, veering to our equipment. I found a note stuck to the dial:

Meet me at the garage at high noon.
Lavender's away and Sam's going to the
café for lunch.
Harm

"He's moving Mr. Red's blueprints," I said. "Finally." I peeked at my Elvis watch. 11:25. "But that doesn't give us much time."

I clicked on the ghostometer. The needle on the dial quivered, and lay still. Dale ran the wand along the desk. Nothing.

I held the wand while Dale played a few chords on the piano and hummed.

Still nothing.

"I hope she's not depressed about her daddy's letter," Dale said, looking worried. "Depression kills. Of course, Nellie's already . . . you know."

"Maybe she's in the library," I said, turning the ghostometer off.

We trudged up the stairs, Queen Elizabeth bobbing behind. Dale eased the door open. "Nellie?"

I set up on the library table. "Maybe she's scared of the ghostometer," I said as Dale ran the wand along a shelf of books. "It *is* ugly," I added as his wand snagged on a book, toppling it to the floor. "I got it, Dale. You keep scanning."

The book, with its faded green cover, fit my hands. "*A*

Girl's Book of Poems," I read, and opened it. "It's Nellie's!" I ran my finger across a signature written in faded brown ink. "Look, she smudged this one too," I said. "Just like her geometry book. I guess clumsy is forever."

The room went ice cold and the ghostometer's needle shot across the dial. "She's here!" I cried. Queen Elizabeth sneezed.

Dale spun in a circle. "But where . . . She's gone," he said. "What happened?" Queen Elizabeth snuffled and he scratched her ears. "I think Liz is allergic to her."

"Liz is allergic to rosemary," I said, tapping the ghostometer to see if that might help. Nothing. I tapped it harder. Still nothing.

"What rosemary?" he asked.

What rosemary?

"Don't you smell it? It always smells like rosemary when Nellie's around."

Dale narrowed his eyes. "I never smell rosemary. You two got ghost noses," he said. "Like ghost eyes, only with nostrils." While I took that in, he ran the wand along the other bookshelves.

"She's gone," I said, slap-tuning the ghostometer. The needle didn't flinch. "Why was she even here?" I asked, trying not to picture Attila's sneer if we had to give an oral report without hard evidence.

"Maybe she liked your joke: 'Clumsy is forever,'" Dale said. The needle jumped.

"Why? It's not that funny," I said, staring at the dial. "Clumsy is forever."

Again, the needle jumped.

"What on earth?" Dale asked, padding to me.

"Or not on earth," I said. "Let's restage the scene. You knocked this book down, I picked it up . . ." I opened *A Girl's Book of Poems* with its ink smudge across the title page. I stared at the ink, every cell in my body tingling.

Of course. The ink.

"Dale, get Starr."

Dale let the wand swing to his side. "Why?"

"Because I know what Nellie wants. Are you ready to make an A in history and go Paranormal Famous? Because we got scientific ghost proof that will hold up in a court of law," I said, heading for the door.

"What scientific proof?" he demanded. "What court of law?"

"Give me time to go to the café and back. Find Starr and keep him here," I shouted, sprinting down the stairs. "You're practically Honor Roll!"

"I am? Why?" he shouted from the top of the stairs. "How did I do it?"

I jumped on my bike and sped away.

*٠*٠*٠*

"*Fingerprints?*" Detective Joe Starr said fifteen minutes later, staring at me like I'd sprouted wings—which, if I'd biked any faster, I would have. "You can't fingerprint a ghost."

"*We* can," I said. "This is foolproof, isn't it Dale?"

"I hope so," he said.

"We'd do it ourselves if our fingerprint kit had come in," I said.

Dale nodded. "It's been delayed by we didn't order it," he explained.

Joe Starr looked at his watch—a gift from Miss Retzyl. "I know you got a kit in your car," I said. "Normally I wouldn't ask, but this is a 911 history situation. It's for Miss Retzyl."

Starr tapped his foot. He keeps his shoes polished to a high sheen.

"Girls like guys who help kids," Dale added. "Miss Retzyl is a girl. Sort of."

Starr sighed. "She already likes me," he said, "but let's see what you got."

As Starr crossed the porch, Dale lunged and pinched my arm like an anxious crab. "Fingerprinting a ghost?" he said. "Have you lost your mind?"

"Trust me," I replied.

"Those words again," he muttered, but he followed

me to the window overlooking the river as Starr bustled back in with his kit.

"All right," Starr said. "Where's your print?"

I breathed heavy on the windowpane. Starr squinted.

7.

I pointed to the period. "Right there," I said.

Starr flitted a fine powder across the pane. A fingerprint stared back at us. We held our breath as Starr placed a wide piece of tape over the print and carefully peeled it from the glass.

"Looks like a good print," he said, holding it to the light. "But anybody could have put it here."

"But anybody didn't," I said. "That's Nellie Blake's print."

Starr snorted. "Not likely. She hasn't lived here in decades. And even if it *was* hers, you couldn't prove it. She wouldn't have a print in my data bank."

"It's in *our* data bank," I said, reaching into my messenger bag and pulling out Nellie's geometry book—the one we found our first day in the library. I opened it and handed it to Starr. He read the inscription:

"I hate math. N.B.—August 28, 1937."

Beneath her initials were Nellie's inky prints.

Starr frowned. "What the . . ." He held his tape over one print, the next . . . and stopped over her index finger. "This can't be right," he said.

I opened *A Girl's Book of Poems.* "Here's her signature, if you want to match the handwriting samples."

Starr shifted the captured fingerprint away from Nellie's print and back. "I'll have an expert take a look. But if you ask me, these prints are a perfect match."

Chapter 35
We Forgot About Harm!

"Harm!" Dale cried, smacking himself on the forehead as Detective Starr drove away. "We forgot about Harm!" He swung my arm up like I wasn't attached and stared at my Elvis watch. "It's already quarter past lunch," he said. "Hurry!"

A few minutes later, we dropped our bikes and rushed the garage door. Inside, tools littered the floor and the old Duesenberg's hood gaped open. Harm crouched over a workbench, his notebook open on Mr. Red's blueprints.

"Took you long enough," he said, shoving his hair from his eyes. "I've got Red's numbers down. I need you two to distract him while I put the blueprints in his truck."

"Distract who?" Grandmother Miss Lacy asked, strolling in with a lunch tray. "Oh. Hello dears, where's Sam?"

I stepped in front of Harm as he swept the blueprints to the ground. "Is that lunch?" I asked. "Because I'm starved."

"Me too," Dale said, lining up shoulder to shoulder beside me.

"Mo LoBeau, are you hiding something from me?" she asked, her voice playful. She leaned around me, and zeroed in on the blueprints. Her smile collapsed like last year's rusty lawn chair. "What have you got there, Harm?"

"Nothing," he mumbled.

"Wonderful. Because for a moment I thought those were Red Baker's purloined blueprints. The ones Detective Starr called me about. The ones I swore the three of you had nothing to do with."

If her voice got any colder, I'd need earmuffs. I lowered my eyes to the Duesenberg's disemboweled carburetor at my feet.

She slammed the tray on the workbench, grabbed the blueprints, and rolled them up. "I have never been so disappointed," she said. "I stood up for you, Harm Crenshaw. And for you two. What have you got to say for yourselves?"

Harm took a deep breath. "I'm sorry, Miss Thornton," he said. She didn't answer—the Waiting For Confession trick. It worked, as usual. "I haven't been completely honest with you. I hope you'll give me a chance to make things right."

"I'm not sure you can make this right," she said as

Dale slipped a sandwich off Sam's lunch tray. "But please come up on the porch and try."

A half hour later, she had the whole ugly story minus the ghosts: Red Baker in the forest, marking off steps. The blueprints with their mysterious code. Harm swiping the blueprints in the middle of the night.

"He was trying to protect Mr. Red and you from Flick and Rat Face," I said. "It's almost good in a Robin Hood way if you hold your head right."

"I don't believe my neck bends that way," she replied.

"No, ma'am," Dale whispered. "I expect not."

We needed a mega change of subject. I went for the ghost.

"We got good news too," I said. "We're close to naming the entity. We got proof that will hold up in a court of law—well, once Joe Starr brings it back to us: Nellie Blake's fingerprint." I watched Grandmother Miss Lacy's face, which went pale.

"Nellie Blake's fingerprint?" she said, rocking forward in her chair. "But how . . ."

"We got them off a windowpane she touched the other night. Joe Starr helped us," I said, and Harm whistled.

"Plus Nellie smells like rosemary," Dale added. "We have a witness to that—one that's not me or Mo."

I hesitated. That would make Queen Elizabeth our witness. I moved on.

"Rosemary?" Grandmother Miss Lacy said. "Are you sure?"

"Yes ma'am," I told her. "Sure on both counts."

Her old eyes filled with tears, and Dale's shoulders slumped. "I didn't know rosemary would make you cry," he said. "Girls," he muttered. "Even wrinkled they're a mystery."

"It's all right, dear," she said, pulling a handkerchief from her sweater pocket. "It's just that Nellie and I were good friends. And she did rinse her hair in rosemary water. There's no way you could have known that—I'd forgotten it myself. That's how we lose people . . . detail by detail, day by day, until they're pale, pale memories."

She blew her nose. "You three haven't been honest with me about the blueprints. But I'm afraid I haven't been very honest with you, either—about your ghost. I never dreamed she could be real."

"Nellie's real, all right," I said.

She dabbed the corner of her eye. "Come inside," she said. "I have something to show you." And she led us to her parlor. She crossed to her bookshelves and plucked down a small photo album. "Meet my best friend," she said. "Nellie Blake."

She opened the album, and a pretty, dark-haired girl

smiled at us. Nellie licking an ice-cream cone. Posing for a portrait with a one-eyed dog. Reading by the spring-house's shady back door. "We must have read a hundred books there," Grandmother Miss Lacy said. "Her father had that door bricked shut after Nellie died. He said he couldn't stand to see anyone use it ever again."

That explained why Nellie walked through that bricked-up door, I thought. I studied the next photo: two girls sitting at the piano in the inn. Nellie and Grand-mother Miss Lacy. "You're playing 'Heart and Soul,'" I said, and Dale gasped.

Grandmother Miss Lacy nodded. "Probably. We all played it. Me, Nellie, Red, Myrt...But it's Nellie I think of when I hear it now."

Harm looked from the photos to me. "You look like her," he said.

"A little, perhaps," Grandmother Miss Lacy agreed. "But my word, you act like her, Mo," she said, blinking away sudden tears. "Always thinking, always meddling." She reached over and patted Dale's hand. "Always get-ting friends in trouble. Such kindred spirits."

"And Nellie's dog?" Dale asked. Dale's a sucker for a dog story.

"Oh, that's Right-Turn Wilma," she said, laughing back tears. "Wilma had just one eye. She only turned right. That's the only way she could see to go, I suppose."

"You hid these photos from us," I said, trying not to sound hurt.

She brushed her fingertip across Nellie's photo like she could brush the messy hair from Nellie's face. "I did," she said. "Please forgive me, Mo."

"She does," Dale said, and I nodded.

She gave me a quick smile. "It never occurred to me the ghost rumors were true, and I certainly didn't want to breathe new life into Nellie's sad, sad story. You've discovered that story by now, I imagine."

"An automobile accident," I prompted, and the light slipped from her eyes.

"Yes, this time of year," she said, looking out the window. "Nellie was so excited. It was to be her first dance that night. Nellie and her father were speeding from the old store to the inn when their brakes gave way in a curve. We heard the crash at the store.

"Red Baker looked like a ghost, climbing into his daddy's Ford. I piled into the Duesenberg with Father and we flew along the Judas Trail, one behind the other."

"The ghost cars," Dale whispered.

"Red and his father arrived first," she said, looking at Harm. "Red found Mr. Blake hurt and dazed, but Nellie . . ." She sank to the settee. "Later, Red told me she said, 'Tell Lacy . . .'"

Harm sat beside her. "Tell you what?" he asked, his voice soft.

"That's all," she said, opening her hands and letting them fall. "She was gone." Her voice cracked. "She was my best friend," she said, her voice rising like a hurt child's. "I've wished a thousand times I had a chance to say good-bye."

Her eyes glittered with tears. "This goes back on my shelf," she said, closing the photo album. "Now that you've uncovered her story, I'll make you copies for your history paper—or for you to keep. You two are so much alike, Mo."

Usually I have a river of words flowing in me. Now my river ran dry.

"Maybe that's why Nellie likes us," Dale said.

Or because Grandmother Miss Lacy loves us, I thought.

"Thank you for the copies," I said. "We'll footnote you. We got something to show you too," I said, pulling Mr. Blake's letter from my bag.

She read the letter. "That poor man," she murmured, handing it back. "Was Nellie murdered? Mr. Blake certainly thought so, and other people did too. But Truman Baker swore he didn't touch their car. My parents believed him and tried to stop the gossip. Even with no

proof, the rumors swirled on day after day, keeping our pain so fresh, it felt like Nellie died day after day too. One day her parents had had enough. They packed up and left, and all I had of Nellie was gone." She closed her eyes and leaned into the curve of the settee.

"I'm sorry," I whispered. The moment felt rare and tender, delicate as a moth cupped in my hands. We rose and tiptoed toward the door.

Her eyes flew open.

"Not so fast," she snapped. "We still have those blueprints to deal with."

Crud.

She stared at Harm, her eyes icy sharp. "I've given you time to think, young man. What are your plans?" she demanded.

"Young man," Dale whispered. "That's not good."

"I'm . . . trying to come . . . to come up with a plan," Harm stammered.

She stood, snatched her navy blue purse from the secretary, and hooked it over her arm. "Fortunately for you I already have one," she said. "Get in the Buick, all three of you. We're paying Red Baker a call."

Chapter 36
The Ghost of the Boy He Used to Be

We rode in silence—past the school, over Fool's Bridge, past the old store. Harm sat in the front seat clutching the blueprints. Dale and me sat in back, Queen Elizabeth lounging between us. "She's getting a little pudgy," I whispered, poking her tummy. "Is she okay?"

"Ignore her, Liz," Dale said, and they both turned to stare out the window.

"Maybe we should rethink this," Harm said, his voice thin and brittle as old paper. "I thought I'd slip the blueprints in his truck, and let him think he's gone senile. Red has a temper."

"Who has a temper?" Grandmother Miss Lacy demanded.

"Gramps," he said as we bounced down the lane. "Gramps has a temper."

She slowed for a deep rut. "So did Nellie. I'd be surprised if either of them ever learned to count past ten."

I smiled. Something else me and Nellie have in common.

Mr. Red was crossing his dirt yard with a galvanized pail when we pulled in. He pushed into his dog pen, emptied the bucket into a trough, and headed for us, wiping his hands on a blue bandana. "Afternoon, Lacy," he said, opening her door.

"Hello, Red." She stepped out of the car, ignoring the pen's stench. "I'm sorry to disturb you, but these children have something to say."

Harm gulped.

"Act innocent," I whispered, climbing out of the Buick. "Hey, Mr. Red."

"I made a sweet potato pie, Lacy," he said like I hadn't spoken. "Come in and I'll cut you a piece."

Harm's mouth fell open. "I didn't know you could cook."

"Didn't need to with you here," Mr. Red told him without looking back.

Moments later we sat in a wreck of a kitchen. Towers of plates teetered by the sink. A pot lolled on its side on the stove. Mr. Red placed two saucers on the table: one in front of his chair; one in front of Grandmother Miss Lacy's. She didn't flinch.

"Thank you, but I don't believe I care for pie," she said. "We'd like to return something to you. And to show you something we think you'll want to see."

Harm dropped the blueprints on the table.

"I knew you three stole them," Mr. Red said, his eyes glinting.

"Not us three," Harm said. "Me. I took them."

"Red, I hope you'll hear him out," Grandmother Miss Lacy said. "We're probably going to lose the inn," she added. "Flick and his girlfriend will grab it up to get your savings. I'll lose every dollar I've sunk into the place—and so will you."

Mr. Red looked like she'd sent a flying sidekick to his head. "Flick double-crossed me?"

Harm nodded. "He can't find your money without the blueprints. I thought it would be better if we dug it up and shared with Miss Thornton, since . . ."

"We?" he said, his voice climbing.

Harm clamped his lips tight. Then: "I'm sorry I took the blueprints. I was trying to help. But I didn't dig up anything. Your money's still there."

Grandmother Miss Lacy nodded, giving me my cue. "We wanted to show you this letter," I said, taking it from my pocket. "We found it in the inn. It's from Nellie's father."

Mr. Red went pale behind his whiskers. "What's that got to do with me?"

Grandmother Miss Lacy reached for his hand. He pulled it away. "Red, I've been haunted by Nellie's death all my life," she said, her voice soft. "Can't you help me

lay that to rest? Won't you at least look at the letter?"

Smart, I thought. He'd do it for her before he'd do it for himself.

Mr. Red unfolded the letter and read it out loud, his voice rough as gravel in rain: *"Darling Nellie, Forgive my greed, forgive my temper, forgive my ridiculous disagreement with Truman. How I wish he'd killed me and not you. I'd give my world to hear you laugh again. Father."* Mr. Red's voice stumbled into silence.

"Red," Grandmother Miss Lacy said, "if you do know what happened that night, please tell me. Who could the truth hurt now?"

Mr. Red's eyes glistened. He dropped the letter to the table and stared at it so hard, I thought it might levitate. Behind me, tap water dripped into the sink. Plunk. Plunk. Plunk.

Mr. Red drew a shallow breath. "Papa was angry with Norton Blake that night," he said, his voice small and flat. "Papa's distillery helped put that inn on the map. You know it did." His voice gained strength. "But when Prohibition hit, Blake turned him out just like that." He snapped his fingers. "One day we were one of the finest families of Tupelo Landing. The next day—outlaws," he said, his voice bitter.

"Father told me," she said.

"When Prohibition ended, Papa thought Blake would take him back," he said. "He didn't. Without Blake we couldn't afford the rigmarole to go legal. Where did that leave Papa?" he demanded.

"It left him hurt, I imagine," she said. "And very angry."

He looked at her, his eyes blazing. "Did Papa and Blake argue that night? They did. Nellie and I heard every ugly word of it. Blake shoved Papa and stomped into the store, dragging Nellie behind him."

His face flushed. "You want to know the truth? I'll tell you. Papa cut Blake's brake line quick as cutting a man's throat. God help me, I stood in the shadows and didn't lift a hand to stop him. I've wished every day since I'd stopped Nellie from getting in that car. But I didn't. I stood in the shadows like a coward and watched Old Man Blake drive away."

He curled his hand into a soft, helpless fist. "So Nellie died. I'm sorry, Lacy," he added, his eyes brimming with tears. "I know you loved her."

"We both did. Thank you for telling me," she said, and her voice drifted away like a lost kite.

Dale propped his elbows on the table. It made him look smaller, somehow. "You were probably about twenty when that happened," he said, staring at Mr. Red.

I frowned. Twenty? Dale knew better than that.

"No," Mr. Red said, swiping his tears with the back of his hand. "I was about your age."

"Oh," Dale said. "The way you told that story, I thought you were way older. Because I can't go up against a grown man, especially one in a rage. I've tried."

Mr. Red looked at Dale like he was seeing him for the first time.

Grandmother Miss Lacy took Mr. Red's hand. This time he didn't pull away. "Dale's right," she said. "You were a child. I don't think for one minute you're responsible for Nellie's death. But you listen to me." She waited for him to look into her eyes. "I forgive you."

He gasped like something hard inside him cracked open. His life unwound across his old face, making him young, younger, until for a moment I sat face-to-face with the ghost of the boy he used to be.

"Nellie forgives you too, Gramps," Harm said. "I know she does because she's liked me ever since I walked through that inn door, the spitting image of you."

Mr. Red blinked and just like that, he was back: an old man in a dirty kitchen.

The stove clock ticked. A chicken clucked at the back door.

"You'd best clean up in here, Red Baker," Grandmother Miss Lacy said, picking up her pocketbook and looking around the room. "This is no way for a boy to live. Get in

the Buick, children," she said. "I have things to do."

Mr. Red stood up, walked down the hall, and closed the door.

Dear Upstream Mother,

Today, Mr. Red told the truth of Nellie's death. He's kept it secret all these years, guilt haunting his life like Spanish moss haunting a swamp.

Now that Red feels forgiven and Grandmother Miss Lacy knows who killed Nellie, do you think Nellie will move on?

I wish you could answer.

Miss Lana says telling a secret changes the heart of the teller and the listener, both. She could be right. Mr. Red called Harm after supper, and asked him to come home. Harm had already packed. He was back home before sundown.

Mo

PS: Skeeter's looking for a buyer for the Duesenberg, so keep your fingers crossed. And Fishbowl Friday's coming up fast. Without Nellie's fingerprint Dale and me got a C at best, and that's only if Miss Retzyl's in a good mood. If you're saving up to send me to Harvard, aim lower.

Chapter 37
Fishbowl Friday

Three days later—Fishbowl Friday—the sixth grade filed into class loaded down with notebooks, DVDs, and a sense of doom. Nellie still lurked in the inn—she moved Lavender's tape measure twice when he tried to measure a new threshold for the dining room. Cute, but not footnote-worthy.

I'd developed my last photos of Nellie with pitiful results: images so blurry and light-speckled, they could have been anything—including sloppy camerawork. Starr was still AWOL with our fingerprint. "We're doomed," I told Dale as the school door clunked shut behind us.

"Maybe Miss Retzyl won't call on us," Dale muttered, heading down the hall. "If we survive oral reports and get Nellie's fingerprint back, we got a shot at an A on the final paper. We're better off than Harm, anyway. He's only got three pages of notes."

Still, Harm swaggered down the hall like a World War

II pilot in an old movie. "Things must be working out good with Mr. Red," I said.

Attila sailed up to Harm. "Fishbowl Friday. I just know I'm going to flunk," she wailed, clutching his arm as we headed into the classroom. Harm looked at me and rolled his eyes.

"Good morning, class," Miss Retzyl chirped. "Please write your name on a slip of paper and place it on the corner of your desk. I'll take a quick look at your rough drafts and drop your name in the fishbowl."

"Tell us that deal again," Jake Exum said. He and Jimmy, who'd worn their brown Sunday suits, had combed their slicked-down hair clear to the scalp.

"Your name goes into the fishbowl," she said. "I'll draw names to see who presents an oral report. Feel free to use audiovisuals. We'll devote the afternoon to your presentations."

"That's for extra credit, right?" Jimmy asked, and she nodded. "Me and Jake volunteer. We got a talent for public speaking. Plus we brought exciting teaching tools."

"Wonderful," she said, her voice going tight. To me, she looked nervous. "I'll put you in the lineup."

Jimmy and Jake high-fived.

I leaned sideways in my seat and peeked at the Exums'

desks. Among the crumpled paper and bent books I could make out brown paper bags.

After lunch we slunk into the classroom, eyes down like Queen Elizabeth after a squirrel disaster. Miss Retzyl smiled. "Now for history."

I raised my hand. "Miss Retzyl, it's only one o'clock. We're facing two hours of history, which I feel is maybe criminal. I'd hate to see you get in trouble so close to your wedding. By the way, have you and Joe Starr announced a date yet? You'll want to reserve the café for your reception. Mr. Li comes back from vacation soon, and karate classes will start up again. It'd be a shame for your nuptials to get bumped by martial arts."

Sal whipped out her weekly planner.

"We haven't chosen a date, Mo. When we do, I'll let the class know," she said, and Sal put her planner away. Miss Retzyl looked at the Exums. Jimmy stood up and buttoned his suit coat. "We'll save the Exums for our finale," she said. Jimmy sat down and fist-bumped his brother. "The laptop's set up if anyone needs it for PowerPoint."

I pinched my nose to disguise my voice. "Anna Celeste volunteers." Attila's worth a good hour of mindless blather, more if her brain's left to graze on its own.

"Mo?" Miss Retzyl said. "Did you say something?"

"No ma'am," I said, and coughed.

"Hair ball," Dale explained.

Miss Retzyl dipped into the fishbowl. "Let's see what fate has in store." Dale stopped breathing as she pulled out a twist of paper. "Sal," she said, beaming. "You're up."

"Good luck," Dale whispered, and Sal blushed.

Sal took center stage. She inserted a flash drive into the computer, and shook her tight curls. I applauded. "Thank you, everyone," she said. "I interviewed my grandmother, whose mom was the finest seamstress this town's ever known. In fact," she said, walking over and tugging the window shades down, "if your ancestors looked good, it's because of mine. Hit the lights, Dale." Dale darted to the light switch. "PowerPoint," she told us, and I heard him stumble in the dark.

"Image one. Great-Grandmother Amanda heading to the Tupelo Inn to fit dresses for some la-de-da rich ladies. Photo courtesy of Miss Lacy Thornton.

"Image two," she said, perching on the corner of Miss Retzyl's desk and crossing her legs. "A dress designed by Great-Grand Amanda. Notice the mid-calf hemline and elegant sweep. Very classy.

"Image three. Great-Grand at her Singer sewing machine. Note the treadle. No wonder she had great legs." Sal rustled her paper. "Here's a quote from my aunt," she said. "'Tupelo Landing was a fashion mecca in its time, thanks to the Tupelo Inn and Great-Grand Amanda.'

"Lights," she said, and Dale slapped them back on.

Sal smiled. "I sew too. In my family we feel even accountants can dress good. Thank you for your time." She jettisoned off Miss Retzyl's desk and headed for her own, her expression a mix of pride and relief.

"Wonderful," Miss Retzyl said, dipping her fingertips into the bowl. We lucked out: "Anna Celeste."

Reprieve! Public speaking is to Attila as rotting banana is to fruit fly. We smiled, urging her on with our eyes. She didn't disappoint.

Attila's presentation hit me like Novocain between the eyes. Forty-five minutes into it, Miss Retzyl interrupted. "Thank you, Anna Celeste," she said. "I think I have the gist of your report on Miss Lacy Thornton."

"But I have decades to go," Attila said, looking shocked. "I'm only in the 1960s."

Dale's hand shot into the air. "I'd like to hear more."

"Me too," Thes said, lifting his head from his desk. The spiral pattern of his notebook's spine crisscrossed his face.

"Thank you, Anna," Miss Retzyl said. "Let's give someone else a chance before our finale." She reached for the bowl.

"Not another one," I begged. I hate it when I beg.

"Please not me," Hannah prayed, closing her eyes.

"Me neither," Dale prayed.

I closed my eyes, trying to sort the fishbowl entries with my personal chi, willing mine to the bottom of the bowl. "Not Mo not Mo not Mo," I whispered.

She reached in. "Mo," she said. "Mo and Dale. Who's giving the report?"

Dale moaned.

"Are our names in there?" I asked. "Because Dale's our spokesman and as his manager I'm saving his voice for The Bash. We can't let the town down. That would be wrong on a civic level and unless I'm mistaken, civic beats history."

She gave me the Surrender Glare. "Mo . . ."

"Yes ma'am," I said, my heart drooping like last week's roses. "Give me a minute to gather our massive trove of information." Dale rattled papers while I pawed through my desk. "While we do that, I'd like to remind everyone On the Verge performs live at The Bash, just one week from tomorrow. We're inviting you to cheer when Dale and Harm take the stage. This cheering's for sixth grade only. Seventh graders have asked and we've turned them down cold."

Out of the corner of my eye, I saw Jake Exum smile stiff as cardboard.

The Exums. It was a long shot, but I took it.

"It's going to take a few minutes to get my papers in order and I know the Exums put together a fantastic

presentation. Nobody wants to miss it, so I'm inviting them to leap-frog in. At this time, Dale and me yield the floor to Jimmy and Jake Exum! Put your hands together! Let's give the Exum boys a big welcome!"

Dale, Sal, Harm, and I clapped like maniacs, our applause drowning out Miss Retzyl's voice as the Exums jumped to their feet. Jake buttoned his coat and they marched to the front of the class, each clasping a crumpled brown paper bag.

"Good afternoon," Jimmy said, bowing stiffly to Miss Retzyl and then smiling at the class. "We're Jimmy and Jake Exum from the back row." He unfolded a paper from his pocket, and read. "Our report is on Miss Delilah's candy store, built in 1902. But when we went to interview her she had changed her mind, which is why we need extra credit. She gave us candy if we would go away," he said, nodding at Jake, who started down the first row, dropping a handful of candy on each kid's desk.

The class stirred as he dumped the leftovers on Miss Retzyl's blotter. "A bribe," Dale whispered. "Brilliant!"

Jimmy smiled. "Time was running out, so we went to our neighbor Hank. Hank fought in a war. He learned munitions."

Jimmy took two small jars from his bag. Miss Retzyl snapped to attention. "What's in those jars?" she demanded.

Jimmy looked at Jake. "I think Hank said mix these up," he said, opening the jars and tipping one over the other. "Or else he said not to."

"I know science," Thes screamed, tearing for the door. "Run!"

A pop. A flash. Black smoke billowed into Jimmy's face. "Everybody out!" Miss Retzyl shouted, covering her face. "Now!"

I slid my candy into my messenger bag and grabbed my camera. *Click.*

A half hour later I opened a lollipop and watched the volunteer firemen hose down our classroom. "There's Lavender. Hey, Lavender!" I shouted, rocking up on my toes. "That's a good look for you!" He tipped his fireman's hat. *Click.*

Mayor Little roared up in his Jeep. "Everybody stay calm," he shrieked. "We'll have this disaster in hand in no time."

The entire school had emptied out. Second graders milled around their teachers. First graders huddled together crying. "The Exums look wilted," Dale said.

Harm, who sat on a picnic table, nodded. "Probably seeing more homeschooling in their future."

"Mama says you should be kind in a disaster," Dale said. "Let's go say something nice."

We oozed over. "Hey Exums," I said. They looked

up from their polished shoes, their eyes guarded. "Your report really held my attention."

Dale nodded. "Good candy."

Harm unwrapped a Tootsie Roll and popped it in his mouth. "I wouldn't worry about those eyebrows," he told them, winking at me. "I hear they grow back fast."

Did Harm Crenshaw wink? At me?

The sixth grade swiveled as a dirt-colored Impala skidded onto the school grounds, blue dash light flashing. "Hey, Detective Starr! Dale and me are still waiting for our fingerprint report!" I called as Starr charged across the yard to Miss Retzyl.

"That's sweet," Attila said as Starr hugged Miss Retzyl.

"Gross," Harm and I replied in unison.

Attila smirked. "I don't think it's gross at all. Who are you going to The Bash with, Mo?" she asked, glancing at Harm. "Or can't you get a date?"

A date?

I looked at Dale. Sal moved a half step closer to him. Harm crossed his arms.

"Mo can go with anybody she wants to, except me," Dale said as Thes wandered by, staring at the clouds.

"Really?" Attila leered.

"That's right, Braces Breath," I said. "I didn't mention it earlier because I didn't want to break any hearts, but

I'm going with Thes," I said, giving him a Back Me Up Or I'll Kill You Look.

Harm turned and sauntered away.

The blood left Thes's freckled face. "Right, Thes?"

Thes worked his mouth like a fish tossed on the creek bank. "Yes, honey bunny," he croaked.

Miss Retzyl stormed toward us as water laced with candy wrappers surged out of the front door and swirled down the steps.

I stepped forward. "On behalf of the sixth grade, I'd like to say that was maybe the most memorable history class ever. Thank you, Miss Retzyl."

"Be quiet, Mo," she replied.

She stared at the Exums. Jake and Jimmy buttoned their suit coats and stepped forward, smiling like nervous jack-o'-lanterns. Her gaze lingered where their eyebrows used to be.

"Class dismissed until further notice," she said. "Your history reports are due October 24, regardless. Double-spaced and footnoted." She spun and walked away.

Perfect! Extra time to get our fingerprint report from Joe Starr.

The Exum twins unbuttoned their coats and high-fived.

"See you at The Bash," I shouted. "Remember: On the Verge, eight p.m.! Don't forget to cheer!"

Chapter 38
Good News

The day of The Bash started nice and exploded into perfection around 10:00 a.m. when Lavender walked through the café door. "Good news," he said, smiling at Miss Lana, the Colonel, and me. "Skeeter thinks she found a buyer for the Duesenberg. The town's problems are practically solved."

Miss Lana shrieked, threw her dishtowel in the air, and hurled herself into Lavender's arms. As Lavender laughed and spun her around, a tsunami of jealousy swept me under.

"Are you sure?" Miss Lana asked as he let her go.

"Almost," he said. "That old Duesenberg not only looks gorgeous, she purrs like she means it. Skeeter's still firming up the details and Sal's working on the math, but it looks like Miss Thornton's financial problems are in her rearview mirror and fading fast."

I looked at the Colonel. "So we can keep the inn?" I asked.

He untied his apron. "Maybe," he said. "Let's see what happens."

I smiled at Lavender. "I guess you'll be looking for a racecar soon," I told him.

"Already looking. When I find a good prospect, I want you and Dale to take a look. I always value the opinions of my official advisors."

An official advisor? Me?

"You're on," I said.

We closed the café and carted refreshments to the inn one carload at a time. Lavender's news put a snap in Grandmother Miss Lacy's step and a crack in her whip. Noon found her directing her troops around the pavilion like a blue-haired Napoleon.

"Set these tables for refreshments," she ordered, checking her clipboard. "And we'll want chairs and small tables around the dance floor. We'll set up the buffet here," she said, pointing. "White tablecloths, please. And candles. Everyone looks better in candlelight."

"It's good to have her back," Dale whispered, struggling by with a couple of folding chairs. "I just hope she doesn't work us to death."

She almost did.

Around four o'clock she put her clipboard down and beamed. "Excellent job," she told us. "As Lana would

say, we've set the stage. Go home. Rest. I look forward to seeing each of you tonight. Job well done!"

We scattered before she could find something else to decorate.

"Miss Lana says I got to move Cleo away from the inn's porch," Dale said. "You want to come?"

I shook my head. "I got to get ready," I said, grabbing my bike. "I want to look good for Miss Lana. And Dale, don't worry about tonight. You and Harm sound great."

Minutes later I charged through our front door. "Hey Colonel," I said, blasting into the living room. He sat on Miss Lana's Victorian sofa, his hands on his knees, his back stiff. "Is Miss Lana here? I want to ask her about a cure for stage fright, in case Harm needs one."

"Lana's in her suite, finger-curling Jean Harlow," he said, his voice dull. "I'm sure she'd be delighted to see you."

I stared at his scraggly bow tie. "Is that your Skeeter-Bay tux, sir?"

He sighed. "It is. Lana has many wonderful talents. Estimating isn't one of them." He stood up. His coat billowed on his lean frame. The trousers showed two inches of ankle.

The clock on the mantel ticked. "Sal's mama does alterations," I told him.

"Thank you, Soldier, but it's too late." He sighed again. The Colonel's spit and polish. He likes us to look good in a crowd.

Poor Colonel. Adjusting to memories of a lost life is hard. Adjusting in a bad-fitting tux seemed cruel and unusual. "At least you won't be alone, sir," I said. "I'm opting for a vintage costume too. It's hideous, but if anybody gives me grief, I got my karate skills to fall back on. Mary Janes can be formidable weapons on the right feet."

"That reminds me." He crossed to his duffel bag and slid out a shoe box. "I saw these in Winston-Salem, and thought you might like them."

I opened the box.

A pair of red-and-yellow plaid Mary Janes peeked out of orange tissue.

"They're perfect," I said, kicking off my plaid sneakers and slipping them on. I hugged him long and hard. He felt like angle iron, and smelled like somebody else's mothballs. "I just want to mention, sir, you look better in dress blues than anybody I ever seen. And since it turns out you never were actually in the military, your old uniform is costuming. Sort of." His brown eyes snapped to attention. "Excuse me, I got to get dressed," I said, and headed for my flat.

Miss Lana had laid the vintage outfit across my bed.

At least I have my signature plaid shoes, I thought. I picked up a note stilettoed to the jacket with Miss Lana's hat pin:

> *Never forget Bill's advice, sugar: "To thine own self be true." Wear what you like best. I'll love you in whatever you choose.*
>
> *Lana.*

To thine own self be true? That's the Shakespeare quote she meant?

I looked again. Suddenly the outfit didn't look so bad.

White polka dots on soft navy fabric. A skirt whose shirred waist somehow created the illusion of a waistline. A neat white blouse and ultra-cool navy bolero, something a matador might wear. Nellie would like these clothes, I thought.

I dressed, and knocked on Miss Lana's door. "Come in," she called, and turned to look at me. "You're as beautiful as I knew you'd be," she told me, her eyes glistening. She looked at my shoes and laughed. "One hundred percent Mo."

On my way out I detoured by my desk, snagged Volume 6, and dashed off a letter to leave on Nellie's piano.

Nellie Blake, Ghost
The Tupelo Inn
Tupelo Landing, NC

Dear Nellie,

Are you still here? If so, you are cordially invited to a dance tonight, at the Tupelo Inn pavilion. I'm going 1938 cool.

Dale and Harm will sing. Your friends Lacy Thornton and Red Baker will be there. So will Myrt Little—enough said.

The honor of your presence is requested.

Yours truly,

Miss Moses LoBeau, Esquire

PS: Sometimes you have to leave home to find home. I did.

"Wow, Mo," Dale said as I crossed the pavilion a couple hours later. "You look great." It was true: Even my hair had tamed down good.

"Thanks," I said. "You too." Dale's bash ensemble looked suspiciously like his funeral ensemble: black pants, black shirt, black tie. He'd styled his blond hair up in front, like Lavender. "What's that?" I asked, glancing at the suit bag slung over his shoulder.

"A surprise. We'll need about fifteen minutes before we go on," he said, hanging the bag on a corner post as Queen Elizabeth wandered by in a sequined collar.

"What surprise?" I demanded. "As your manager, I got to know."

"You'll see," he said, opening his guitar case and grabbing his guitar. Photos stared up at me from the bottom of the case. My old school photo, a snapshot of Queen Elizabeth, the family photo from Miss Rose's piano—him, Miss Rose, and Mr. Macon. Only he'd taped the photo of Lavender and the Colonel over Mr. Macon.

"I brought them for good luck," he explained, following my gaze. He placed his guitar in the case as Lavender walked up with a bag of ice. Lavender cleans up better than anybody I know. I grabbed my camera. *Click*.

"You two look great," he said. "Where's Mama?"

"She's not coming," Dale said.

Not coming? Lavender looked surprised as I felt. "Is she sick?"

"No. It's okay," he lied, adjusting Queen Elizabeth's collar. "She's heard us sing plenty at home." Dale don't lie good. "I think she wishes she had a date," he added.

Lavender winced. "Yeah, she probably does," he said, dropping the ice to loosen it up. I rushed to hold the cooler steady. "Thanks Mo. Mama's proud of you, Dale, whether she's here or not. I am too."

"I know," Dale said.

Lavender dumped the ice, and spanked the wet off his hands. "Listen Dale, I want you to dance with everybody you can tonight. Ask any girl old enough to walk, any lady who can get out on the floor without a walker, and every female in between—except Anna Celeste."

"But Sal and me are meeting up in a few minutes."

"Dance the first dance with Sal and dance with her most of the night. She'll understand if you explain it to her. Ladies love gentlemen, little brother. Trust me."

"Okay," Dale said, looking doubtful. "But if Sal kills me, it's on you."

"Deal," he said, and winked at me. "Don't forget our dance, Mo."

Forget our dance? Is he mad?

"I wore my dancing shoes," I said, and he hurried away.

The cars started grumbling up the inn's drive just after sunset. Tinks and Sam handled parking. Miss Lana, in her Jean Harlow wig and shimmering party dress, met the guests at the door while Dale and me kept the pavilion punch flowing. The Colonel strode up handsome and confident in his dress blues, his hat tucked smartly beneath his arm.

"My goodness," Mayor Little said, taking a cup of punch and smoothing his ruffled shirt. "I've never seen us looking so elegant. Did you bring your camera?" he asked, straightening his ice-blue bow tie. He held out his glass, turned his head, and fake laughed. *Click.*

He waggled his fingers at Attila's mom. "I'm sure the media will want copies," he said as she minced over in her beige dress.

"Good evening, Mr. Mayor," Mrs. Simpson said. Her gaze swept me head to toe, lingering on my plaid Mary Janes. "And Mo, don't you look . . . comfortable. Have you

seen Anna Celeste? She said she was coming with Sal."

I looked at the archway. There stood Attila—with Harm Crenshaw!

"No," Dale whispered. "Harm's gone over to the other side."

Mrs. Simpson's hand went to her pearls. "But isn't that . . . Red Baker's grandson?"

"Spittin' image," I said. *Click.*

Harm and Attila rolled toward us. Harm looked sharp in his usual black pants, plus Mr. Red's crisp white auction shirt and red bow tie. Attila looked frilly. "Mother," she said, "this is my friend Harmond Crenshaw. Harm? My mother, Betsy Simpson."

Harm grinned wide as Texas.

Mrs. Simpson stared a long, chilly moment. "Harm," she said. If her voice went any colder, the punch bowl would freeze solid. *Click.*

"There's Daddy," Attila said, leading Harm away.

I smiled at Mrs. Simpson. "They look nice together, don't they?" I said, cranking my film forward. "I hope they name their first child after me. Mo's a name that works for a boy or a girl. Refreshment?" I asked as Dale ladled a cup of punch.

Mrs. Simpson spun and walked away.

"How did that train wreck happen?" Dale muttered, staring after Harm and Attila.

"No clue," I said, unfocusing my eyes to scan the crowd. No sign of Nellie. Not yet.

The crowd seemed to breathe as townsfolk flowed in and out. "Wow," Dale whispered as Miss Retsyl walked up. "Why's she wasting time on us?" I could see his point. With her hair up and her long dress sparkling, she could have been going to the Country Music Awards.

"There's Myrt Little," I said, peering through a flock of preening Azalea Women.

Mrs. Little perched at the edge of the crowd like a vulture with a new perm. I unfocused my eyes and scanned. Still no Nellie.

Dale and me waved as Hannah Greene and her sister paused in the archway with the Exums. "Don't stare at the Exums' eyebrows," I added as the boys plowed toward us like a couple of tugboats in brown suits.

"Four cups of punch," Jake said. "We came with girls." I filled their cups, trying to ignore the wobbly black arcs sketched high on their foreheads.

"Nice face art," Dale said, very smooth. "Did you use Magic Markers?"

"Sharpies," Jimmy said.

Jake spun to look at Hannah. "The girls are getting away," he said, and they grabbed their punch and dove back into the crowd.

"Salamander's here," Dale said, dropping his ladle. I

waved at Sal, who'd gone Extreme Strategic Ruffles. She looked like a glittery bottle brush.

"Hey, Thes, your turn!" Dale shouted, pointing to the punch bowl. Thes, who stood at the pavilion's edge watching clouds drift across the moon, smoothed his orange hair and trotted toward me as Lavender walked by with a pretty auburn-haired woman. I did a double take. "Hey, that's not a big-haired twin."

"No," Thes said. "That's Miss Retzyl's little sister, from Winston-Salem."

My heart folded its wings and plunged into a screaming nosedive.

Imported competition? Is that fair?

As I struggled to regain my legendary poise, the evening's next Catastrophe Couple stepped into the archway. "Rat Face," I said as broad-shouldered Flick Crenshaw stepped up beside her. "What's she doing here?"

She scurried to the refreshment table.

"You again," Rat Face said, glaring at me. "Where's Lacy Thornton?"

The Colonel stepped from the crowd. If Rat Face had been a Chihuahua, she would have growled. "Thes," he said, "Skeeter's having trouble with the sound system. Could you give her a hand?" he asked, and Thes hurried away. "Miss Filch," he continued, his voice a velvet-draped dagger. "To what do we owe the . . . honor?"

"Where's Lacy?" she demanded, her beady eyes roving the crowd. Across the way, Harm and Lavender started toward us. "I want to make sure she hasn't forgotten our little agreement. And we want to admire our property."

"Admire it now because you'll never see it again," the Colonel said, tugging an envelope from his inside pocket. "A certified check for the inn's mortgage. Paid in full."

She stamped her foot. "What? But that's not possible."

He slipped the envelope in his pocket. "The possible shocks me every day, Miss Filch. We'll see you November first, as agreed," he said as Lavender and Harm stepped up beside him. "I believe that concludes our business."

Dale rocketed up. "What's going on?" he asked. "What's she doing here?"

"Still hanging with these losers, Harm?" Flick asked. "I'd move up if I were you."

Harm stared back steady and cool. "You never did have good taste in friends, Flick." Harm didn't look scared anymore. Or angry. In fact, he looked sure as the wind setting Miss Lana's lanterns swaying.

Flick grabbed Harm's shirt and dragged Harm toward him. "You little . . ."

"Leave Harm alone, Flick," I said, "or you got me and Dale to deal with."

"And me," Lavender said.

"And most of Tupelo Landing," the Colonel added, "including me."

Flick opened his hand finger by finger, and patted Harm's shirt back into place, a trace of sneer haunting his lips. "Good riddance, then." He turned to Lavender. "As for you, we'll settle things on the racetrack."

"I don't settle things on a racetrack," Lavender said. True. There's not a revenge bone in Lavender's body. Dale's neither. Fortunately I got enough for all of us.

"That's right, carrion breath," I said. "But Lavender will be back—soon. We'll blow you off the track. Dale and me are working honorary pit crew," I added. The last was more of a pre-truth than a lie. We've timed laps before.

Flick grabbed Rat Face's bony elbow. "Let's dump these low-lifes."

"One more thing," the Colonel said, his dark eyes glinting. "Miss Filch, you might like to know I've recommended you to your boss."

A recommendation? For her?

"Sir," I whispered, "is your amnesia back?"

He ignored me. "I'm sure your boss will be impressed with your creative use of bank records, Miss Filch, not to mention your stalking and badgering a customer." Her eyes flew wide. "I've never seen a bank employee so

skilled at taking property for her own," he said. "I'm sure your actions matched bank policy, didn't they?"

Dale frowned. "It sounds bad when you say it out loud, Colonel." He looked at Rat Face. "She could get fired."

She kept her eyes on the Colonel, quivering like a field mouse staring down a wolf. For a minute I almost felt sorry for her. Almost. I showed her my tongue.

She hissed, and burrowed into the night.

As Flick took off behind her, Lavender glanced at Harm. "Don't worry, you'll see him again," he said. "Life has a way of circling back around until things get finished."

"Spoken like a true racecar driver," the Colonel murmured.

Harm jammed his hands in his pockets and watched his brother walk away.

Moments later, Skeeter tapped the mic. "Testing, testing. Almost ready, Colonel."

"Nice move bringing that check, sir," I said. "Are you really back to being an attorney? I only ask because I hate change unless it's my idea. I need time to over-prepare."

"That wasn't a check, Soldier, it was our utility bill. I scribbled my opening remarks on it last night. But we'll have the check in time and yes, I'm back to being an attorney, of sorts."

He sighed. "I'd better get this show on the road. I don't know how I let Lana talk me into these things," he said, glancing her way.

Miss Lana stood in a group of friends, her head thrown back as she laughed. The lanterns' soft light played against her face. "She looks beautiful," I said. "Maybe it's the dress. Or the wig."

"No," he said, his eyes going soft. "It's one hundred percent Lana."

"Colonel," Skeeter called, putting her headset on. "It's time."

He nodded. "I'd hoped Miss Thornton would show up before I . . ." He chuckled. "Ah-ha!" he boomed, looking toward the trail.

The crowd turned to follow his gaze and fell silent. The frogs' song spiraled around us, and water lapped against the pilings. "What's wrong?" Dale said, looking around. "Are the police here already?"

Two figures made their way through the shadows at the pavilion's edge, to the archway. "It's Grandmother Miss Lacy," I said as she stepped into the light in a midnight-blue dress, dark blue sequins flowing across her shoulders like a stole of stars.

The figure behind her stepped into the light and the crowd gasped. The Colonel grinned. "And Red Baker. In a tux—one that fits."

Mr. Red adjusted his bow tie and held out his arm. Grandmother Miss Lacy hooked her hand in his elbow. An Azalea Woman dropped her cup.

"Red, you've managed to arrive with the most beautiful woman in town," the Colonel said. "Miss Thornton, will you join me onstage?"

Contrary to popular belief, the Colonel can be charming. And kind.

She smiled and shook her head. A small spotlight tracked the Colonel to the microphone. "Cut that light," he ordered, squinting. "You're blinding me."

"So much for Prince Charming," Thes said, taking his place at the punch bowl.

"Ladies and gentlemen," the Colonel said. "I welcome you to Tupelo Landing's 250th Anniversary Bash. And now, the man who promised to save my life by emceeing this event: Mayor Clayburn Little."

Mayor Little bounded onstage. "Hello, fellow citizens," he said. "Eat hearty, dance much, stay long. Before we get started, Reverend Thompson will offer a prayer."

"Brace yourself for the Shy Stampede," I whispered as he started his prayer.

"The what?" Thes whispered.

"Amen," Reverend Thompson said.

"Dance!" the mayor commanded, jumping onto the

dance floor as Skeeter revved up the sound system. As Mayor Little began his electric slide, every shy person within earshot charged the refreshments table, filling plates like they were filling lifeboats on a sinking ship.

Thes cleared his throat. "Want to dance?" he asked. "I'm not very good."

"Me either," I said as Dale and Sal spun by. "We need cover." After a few songs the dance floor filled, and we stepped onto its edge. Thes's hand felt like a feverish fish. "Here goes nothing," he mumbled.

We started out jerky, but when nobody laughed I relaxed. "We look good," Thes said, snigging my foot. "Get ready to twirl."

Before long, we all got good. Lavender looked like a movie star, dancing with Miss Retzyl's sister, and then with every woman and pre-woman there—including me. "You look beautiful, Mo," he said, holding out his hand. "Dance with me?"

Even the stars smiled.

Dale danced with everybody too, just like Lavender told him. Once he even struggled by with Mrs. Little. I was watching Sal wiggle past with Jake Exum when someone tapped my shoulder. Harm Crenshaw. "Oh. It's you," I said.

"Yeah, it's me." He held out his hand. "Dance?"

Me? Dance with Harm? I grinned. "Where's Attila?"

"Who knows? I didn't mean to come with her, really. It's just that you asked Thes, and Sal asked Dale. And I hated to be the only one coming alone. Attila asked me and I thought it would be fun to terrify her mom . . . Anyway, she's not with me now," he said as Grandmother Miss Lacy and Mr. Red tangoed past. "I thought Mrs. Simpson would cough up her pedicure when she saw me. So?" he said, jerking his head toward the dance floor. "How about it?"

Somebody shoved me from behind. "Hey!" I shouted, stumbling forward. Out of the corner of my eye I saw Grandmother Miss Lacy dance away, laughing. Harm grabbed my hand. "Come on, Ghost Girl. Give me a chance."

It's hard to dance and glare at Grandmother Miss Lacy at the same time, but it can be done. Not long, though. "Wow," I said as we skimmed along, "you're good."

"You're not bad yourself, once you escape Thes," he said. "Here's an analogy for you. Thes is to dance as fish is to ski."

I laughed as the song ended and Skeeter pulled the microphone close to her lips. "And now, our last number before special guest stars On the Verge."

Already?

Harm dropped my hand. His face went green. "Where's Dale?"

"Over there," I said, pointing to the stage. Dale grabbed his suit bag and shot out of sight. "Get ready. I'll introduce you slow. And Harm? You guys sound good," I said. "Really good."

Chapter 40
On the Verge

As the last strains of "Thriller" died away, I stepped up to the mic. Skeeter darted forward to lower it.

"Thanks, Skeeter," I said, stalling. "Great music selection. Let's hear it for Skeeter!" The crowd clapped. "Ladies and gentlemen," I said, "I know the sixth grade's excited about what's coming up next, and I feel sure the rest of you will be too."

"Pssssst," Sal said from the side of the stage. She put the tips of her fingers together and pulled her hands apart like pulling taffy. "Talk slow," she whispered.

I nodded as Skeeter set up a second mic. "I'm sure we're all dying to hear On the Verge."

"Don't say dying," Dale stage-whispered from somewhere behind me.

"But before they get out here, I'd like to congratulate Detective Joe Starr for landing Miss Retzyl. Where's Detective Starr?" I peered out over the crowd. Starr waved. He has dimples when embarrassed. Interesting. "Way to reel her in, Joe," I said. "The entire sixth grade

wishes you luck. Feel free to come to us for advice. And thanks for that fingerprint report. Dale and me appreciate it."

Sal waved her arms over her head. This time she gave me two thumbs-up.

I cued Buddha to spin the lights around the stage and went into my Prepared Remarks, spreading my voice out like a roller derby announcer. "Tonight's duo promises to shock and thrill. They got voices smooth as butter and moves sweet as Miss Lana's blackberry jam. Ladies and gentlemen, the pride of the sixth grade . . ." I pointed side stage. "ON . . . THE . . . VERGE!"

The sixth grade roared.

I backed into the shadows as Dale and Harm rushed onstage and skidded up to their mics, both of them sleek in tuck-wasted, broad-shouldered 1930s suits. They tilted their fedoras low over their eyes and the spotlight skinnied in on Harm as he stepped up to his mic. "Helloooo Tupelo Landing," he crooned.

"Wow," I told Sal. "Looks like he got over his nerves."

She beamed. "Mama's suits look just right on them."

"I'm Harm and he's Dale, and we're On the Verge of . . . well, something good, we hope. Our first number's our three-chord version of the 1938 hit 'Boogie Woogie.' If you can't dance to this, you won't ever dance. Everybody get up," he said, clapping his hands as Dale started

slapping out a boogie on his guitar. "That includes you, Gramps and Miss Thornton. Everybody dance."

The sixth grade careened onto the dance floor— dancing alone, dancing in pairs, dancing in clusters. The rest of Tupelo Landing swept around them, jostling and swinging. Thes hopped through the crowd like a berserk robot, twisting and turning nearly in time to the music. Hannah, whose sister had gone AWOL, danced with both Exums until Sal skidded onto the dance floor to take up the slack.

The Colonel and Miss Lana swayed by, the Colonel stiff and self-conscious, Miss Lana practically floating. Queen Elizabeth flew from dancer to dancer—a tornado of sequins and fur.

Dale and Harm sang and played and danced like the music had moved in and set up housekeeping in their souls, their voices clear and strong, their rhythm wild and true. They bridged into another song, and another, and another.

Twice I caught a glimpse of pink. The first turned out to be a scarf. The second, a sweater.

At the end of their set, Dale and Harm bowed and Tupelo Landing went nuts.

I rushed onstage. "On the Verge," I shouted above the hubbub.

"Encore," Miss Retzyl shouted, clapping her hands

over her head. "Encore!" The crowd took up the chant.

"Play an old-fashioned neon cha-cha," the mayor shouted, trying to herd the Azalea Women into a line. Dale grinned at Harm and stepped up to the microphone.

"Thank you all for clapping," Dale said, breathing heavy. "We were afraid you might not." He froze, his eyes on the archway. His first-grade smile broke across his flushed face. "Hey, Mama," he said, his voice soft. "You look wonderful."

We all turned.

Miss Rose stood in the archway, strong and elegant, and every inch herself. I ran to her as the crowd turned back to Dale. "Miss Rose," I said. "I'm glad you came."

She hugged me so strong, I almost didn't feel her tremble. "Thanks, Mo. It's never too late to make a better decision."

I took her hand. No ring.

Onstage, Dale looked at Harm. "This one's slower," he said, "so we can all catch our breath." He took a minute to tune his guitar while the crowd settled down. He hesitated. "I wrote this song for Nellie Blake. Nellie, I hope you like it," he said, looking into the night. He gave the rest of us a shy smile. "I hope you all like it too. Especially you, Mama. And you, Mr. Red. It's called 'Nellie's Waltz.'"

He played a sweet, simple intro and he and Harm stepped to their mics, their voices twining like wood smoke over the Colonel's campfire.

> *Waltz across lifetimes with me*
> *Spin through the stars in my arms*
> *When I look in your eyes*
> *I know love never dies*
> *Please waltz through these lifetimes with me.*

> *Drift down life's river with me*
> *Inhale the moon's secret charms*
> *We know love never dies*
> *as we say our good-byes*
> *Please waltz beyond heartbreak with me.*

The town whirled through "Nellie's Waltz," feet whispering, hearts floating until finally the night stood balanced on the last clear sound of Dale's voice. For a moment I heard only the slap of endless river and the sigh of wandering wind.

Then I smelled rosemary.

Queen Elizabeth sneezed.

Dale and Harm bowed, and the town burst into applause. "Bravo," Mayor Little called. "Bravo, boys!"

The crowd took up the chant, pressing close. I jumped onto the stage and grabbed the mic. "On the Verge," I

shouted, and Harm and Dale bowed. "Tupelo Landing's finest!"

They took another bow, and a woman screamed. Then another.

"Is it Nellie? Is she here?" Dale whispered.

The crowd flapped and scattered like terrified chickens as Dale's mule Cleo staggered onto the dance floor, flattened her ears, and trumpeted a ragged bray. She wobbled into a patch of grass at river's edge, sat on her haunches like a dog, and keeled over in the grass.

"Cleo!" Dale tore across the pavilion and leaped the rail. I sprinted after him.

"Is she dead?" I asked.

He looked at me, his face ashen. "Dead drunk. But how?"

Good question.

"Mr. Red's still," I whispered, and he nodded. "We got our chance to pay Harm back for being Ghost Bait. But we better find that still before Starr does."

I looked up. The entire town lined the pavilion's rail, staring. "Skeeter, can you get the music going?" Starr asked, leaping nimbly from the dance floor. "Everybody go back to your business."

"Don't sign anything, Dale," Skeeter called as Michael Jackson's "Thriller" hit the air again. "Let's see that moon-

walk, Mayor Little," she sang out over the sound system.

My plaid Mary Janes squished. How could we explain Cleo without tipping Starr off to Mr. Red's still? I stalled. "I accept full responsibility for Cleo's condition unless there's a penalty for contributing to the delinquency of a mule, in which case I had nothing to do with this," I said.

"Good," Dale whispered.

Starr clicked his pen. "Go ahead."

I took a moment. Miss Lana, who possesses world-class ad-lib skills, says the word *if* skirts the truth graceful as an ice skater skirts thin ice. I went for it. "*If* I recall, Anita Filch spiked the punch bowl early this evening."

"Really? When?" Dale asked. Dale ad-libs like a box turtle pole vaults.

"Also, *if* memory serves, I set the spiked punch aside and got a new bowl. It looks like Cleo got into the bad punch. I hope you'll go easy on her. We can get her into rehab *if* necessary. *If* I'm not mistaken, this is her first offense."

Dale nodded. "She's too sensitive to do time."

Starr jammed his pen in his pocket. "Keep her off the dance floor," he said. "I'll figure out how she got plastered myself—if I get over that load of *if*s you just served up."

Crud. He didn't buy it.

He climbed onto the dance floor and strode away.

I grabbed Dale's arm. "Dale, you moved Cleo today," I said, talking quiet and fast. "Where'd you put her?"

"In the meadow near Mr. Red's house."

The still must be close by. In the house? Ridiculous. The shed? No. The dog pen? Of course. "The brambles in the center of his stinking dog pen," I said. "His still was under our noses the whole time. Those dogs would keep anybody out."

I squinted across the pavilion, to Mr. Red's table. "We got to get to him before Starr figures it out."

Harm joined us as we threaded our way through the dancers. "We've found Mr. Red's still," I whispered. "But we got to hurry."

"You're busted, Mr. Red," Dale said, pulling a chair up beside Grandmother Miss Lacy. "A mule won't drink moonshine, but she'll eat corn mash dumped from a still. And you dumped yours in the meadow today, didn't you?" he asked, his voice accusing. "You were in too much of a hurry to haul it down to your pigs."

Mr. Red swallowed, bobbing his bow tie. "No idea what he's talking about, Lacy."

"We'll prove it," I said, pulling up a chair. "We'll follow Cleo's tracks to the mash, and your tracks to the still in your dog pen."

"The dog pen?" Harm said. "No wonder you didn't want me to mess with those dogs. Gramps, if Starr finds that still,

you're really busted. And where does that leave us?"

Mr. Red looked away from him. Not a good sign.

"Dale and me been thinking," I continued.

"I haven't," Dale said quickly, "unless what she says next sounds good."

I ignored him. "A faux still would be a good draw for the inn. A local history angle."

Grandmother Miss Lacy draped her arm across my shoulders. She smelled like powder and lemons. "A non-working still," she said, staring hat pins at Mr. Red. She placed a dollar on the table. "I'll buy that display, Red Baker, if it will keep you out of jail."

Red Baker looked at Harm, and then at the dollar bill. Then he locked eyes with Joe Starr. Starr sat watching us like a hawk watches a ditch bank at suppertime.

"Take the dollar," Harm said. I could almost feel the wind whistle through his heart.

"You can't pull the fur over Joe Starr's eyes," Dale warned.

"Wool," Harm and I said together as Detective Joe Starr headed for us.

"Mr. Baker," Starr said. "I'll start following Cleo's tracks tomorrow morning. If I find a still on your property, I'll turn you over to the Feds." He looked at Grandmother Miss Lacy. "I apologize in advance, Miss Thornton," he said, and walked away.

Chapter 41
We Say Our Good-byes

The party wound down hours later.

As the last guests straggled up the path with Mayor Little, Miss Lana yawned and surveyed the landslide of dirty cups and dishes. "Let's leave this happy mess for later," she said, hooking her arm in Miss Rose's. "Come on, Rose, I'll walk up with you."

"And I'll turn out the lights and walk with you," I told Grandmother Miss Lacy as Dale packed up his guitar.

Sal and Dale caught up with us halfway to the inn. "Did you dance with everybody?" Sal asked Dale, slipping her hand into his.

"Yes," he said, and then hesitated. "Well," he said, turning to look at the deserted pavilion. "Almost everybody. I'll catch up with you at the inn," he told her.

Sal shrugged. Dale handed me his guitar and trotted back down the path. "What on earth?" Grandmother Miss Lacy murmured.

"I think I know," I said. I led her to a bench in the crook of the path.

Harm stepped from the shadows. "Hey, Miss Thornton," he said. "Where's Gramps?"

"Red?" she asked, settling onto the bench. "Didn't he tell you?" Harm shook his head, his dark hair falling across his forehead. "He's helping the Colonel dismantle my new still," she replied, stifling a yawn.

"He went for it?"

"Hook, line, and sinker," she said. She looked at Harm. "You're the reason he agreed, Harm Crenshaw. Red could do the time, but he can't stand to think of you without a home."

"Son of a gun," Harm muttered.

Below us, Dale strolled to the center of the moonlit dance floor, bowed, and opened his arms. He tilted his head back and sang to the stars.

"Waltz across lifetimes with me.

Spin through the stars in my arms . . ."

"'Nellie's Waltz,'" Grandmother Miss Lacy said. "Nellie would have given the world to dance that dance with Red. Can you see her, Mo?"

"No," I said, my heart tumbling. "I'm sorry. I can't."

"There," Harm said, pointing. "Across the floor from Dale." He was right. A delicate pink mist floated up from the river, onto the dance floor.

"I still don't see her," Grandmother Miss Lacy said.

Harm smoothed his hair. "Maybe Lavender's right.

Maybe life does have a way of circling back around," he murmured. He drew a give-me-courage breath, and jogged down the path onto the dance floor. *Click*.

Dale stepped aside, still singing, as Harm looked at Nellie and opened his arms.

Maybe it was Harm's 1930s suit, or the moonlight, or the rhythm of the waltz. But time folded back on itself soft and easy as Miss Lana's silk scarf, and a dark-haired girl swept across the dance floor in his arms.

"I do see her," Grandmother Miss Lacy said, her voice full of tears.

Harm and Nellie danced until the music floated away on Dale's last crystal note. Harm bowed. Nellie smiled and looked up at us.

Grandmother Miss Lacy held out her hand and opened it, letting go. "Good-bye, dear friend," she whispered.

"I love you," Nellie mouthed, lowering her hand to her heart. Nellie's eyes met mine and she stood there, waiting.

I smiled. "That's what she wanted Mr. Red to tell you the night she died," I told Grandmother Miss Lacy. "I love you."

Nellie smiled like a blaze of sunshine, and she was gone. Truly gone.

I knew it to my bones.

Harm and Dale strolled from the pavilion, side by side. "Case closed," I whispered, and squeezed Grandmother Miss Lacy's hand.

> Dear Upstream Mother,
> Grandmother Miss Lacy's right. There's all kinds of ghosts in this world.
> There's Nellie Blake, who waited for her friends to understand and forgive, and say their good-byes. Ghosts of guilt and ghosts of sorrow.
> The ghost of romance between Miss Lana and the Colonel. The ghost of Dale's daddy fading away detail-by-detail—out of the living room, out of Dale's room, out of the house.
> Last but not least, there's a ghost of a chance. Which is exactly what Dale and me got of passing history if I can't get our history paper footnoted right for Monday morning.
> Wish me luck.
> Mo

Acknowledgments

So many people had a hand in the creation of this book!

Thank you, Rodney L. Beasley—my first reader and intrepid fellow traveler in life—for your love, your support and your unfailing sense of direction.

My gratitude goes to everyone who offered input on the early drafts of this book, especially Allison Turnage, Claire Pittman, Mamie Dixon, Eileen LaGreca, Miriam Taylor Bailey, and Patsy Baker O'Leary and her creative writing class.

Thank you, Eileen LaGreca, for the fantastic map!

Thanks to my agent, Melissa Jeglinski of The Knight Agency.

Thanks, Alisha Niehaus, for first welcoming Mo and Dale to Penguin. Thanks, Mary Jo Floyd, for everything. And thanks, Gilbert Ford, for the knock-out covers.

Hats off to the scores of wonderful people at Penguin Books for Young Readers who poured time and talent into this book. In particular, thank you, Lauri

Hornik, for your support. Thanks, Scottie Bowditch, Laura Antonocci, Sara Ortiz, Meg Beade, and Bridget Ryan for introducing Mo and Dale to libraries and schools around the country; and thanks to Doni Kay, Alex Genis, and their fellow sales reps for introducing Mo to booksellers from NC to CA. Thanks to designer Jasmin Rubero, copyeditor Regina Castillo, and publicist Marisa Russell. And thanks, Claire Evans, for always knowing what's going on and for keeping an eye on Mo and Dale when they're in New York.

Last but never least, thanks to my very talented editor and publisher, Kathy Dawson, of Kathy Dawson Books, whose clear-sightedness and wonderful feel for language helped make this a much better book—and a joy to write.

Tupelo Landing is a better place because of all of you.

Sheila Turnage grew up on a farm in eastern North Carolina. A graduate of East Carolina University, she now lives on a farm with her husband, a smart dog, a dozen chickens, and a flock of guineas. Sheila is the author of two nonfiction books—*Haunted Inns of the Southeast* and *Compass American Guide: North Carolina*—and one picture book, *Trout the Magnificent*, as well as the Newbery Honor–winning *Three Times Lucky*. *Three Times Lucky* is Sheila's first middle grade story and is also a *New York Times* bestseller, an Edgar Award finalist, an E. B. White Read-Aloud Honor Book, and was selected for many best of the year lists.

Visit **sheilaturnage.com** to learn more.

Tupelo Landing

to café

Lavender

Miss
Retzyl

Piggly
Wiggly

Miss
Lacy
Thornton

the
church

the
school

Westminster Public Library
3705 W. 112th Ave.
Westminster, CO 80031
www.westminsterlibrary.org